ALSO BY SUKI SCHORER

Balanchine Pointework

The Balanchine Essays
(videos with Merrill Ashley)

Suki Schorer on
Balanchine Technique

Suki Schorer on
Balanchine Technique

WITH *Russell Lee*

PHOTOGRAPHS BY CAROL ROSEGG

DANCE BOOKS · LONDON · 1999

PUBLISHED BY DANCE BOOKS LTD.

Copyright © 1999 by Suki Schorer
Photographs copyright © 1999 by Carol Rosegg

Dance Books
15 Cecil Court
London WC2N 4EZ

www.dancebooks.co.uk

Originally published in the United States by Alfred A. Knopf,
a division of Random House, Inc., New York.

Parts of the "Pointework and Related Relevé" chapter (and
significantly smaller parts of the "From the Studio to the
Stage" chapter) appeared, in different form, in "Balanchine
Pointework," an issue of *Studies in Dance History*, published in
the fall of 1995, copyright © 1995 by Suki Schorer.

ISBN 1 85273 071 4
A CIP catalogue record for this book is available
from the British Library.

Title-page photograph by Dick Darrell,
courtesy of Ballet Society

I dedicate this book foremost to George Balanchine, my teacher, and also to Lincoln Kirstein, the man who dedicated his life to making a place for Balanchine to do his work. Together, they founded and developed the School of American Ballet and the New York City Ballet, the institutions in which I have been privileged to work all my adult life.

I have no time to relax. I have only
a lifetime, a lifetime to force the most
exquisite use of the body.

—George Balanchine

Contents

Acknowledgments

My parents, Mark and Ruth Page Schorer, made my career possible by getting me to the best ballet lessons available in the crucial growing-up years. In addition, my father showed me what it takes to write and my mother has believed in me and loved me unconditionally all my life. My daughter, Nicole, and her father, George Macotsis, endured the intrusions on family life of my busy schedule that came to include writing a book, and Nicole has sacrificed some of her living space for the past two years as I turned her room into a part-time study.

I could not have done this book without the help of my special friend Russell Lee. He aided me in gathering and organizing my ideas and recollections, devised a format for presenting them, prepared a draft, and worked with me on the many revisions as I got the material on paper in the best way I could. He persisted even when I was very discouraged and doubtful I could finish.

Carol Rosegg photographed the technique demonstrations. She was ready with answers for every question and unhesitatingly cooperative with the models and me as she worked with crisp efficiency. Similarly, Anthea Lingeman of Knopf has presented an elegant solution for every problem I had visualizing the layout. Her designs have made the pictures alive on the page; in some cases, they even seem to dance.

Other people also helped. Conrad Ludlow, my friend, fellow dancer, and occasional partner at the San Francisco Ballet and New York City Ballet provided excellent ideas for the most difficult part of the book, on partnering. Observing Jock Soto's adagio classes at SAB helped me develop greater awareness of the smallest details of how the man partners and of the way those details are taught. Gloria Govrin, another friend from my NYCB years, who like me was a regular in Balanchine's classes, read the entire manuscript and contributed many useful suggestions. My dear friend Marjorie Bresler Thompson, also with me in NYCB, read much of the manuscript and asked me questions that prompted me to rethink the way I was presenting some of the material. Judith Deegan Anthony, who was trained at the Washington School of Ballet, read the entire manuscript with the knowledge of a professional dancer, but one who knows Balanchine's work only as an occasional member of the audience. Her suggestions and questions have made the technical material more useful to qualified professionals who are new to Balanchine. Peter Martins, Kay Mazzo, and Nathalie Gleboff of SAB have been most cooperative about the periodic details that have come up, and I thank them for that. Barbara Horgan of the Balanchine Trust gave her permission to me to present an authorized statement on his technique and teaching. Without her support and cooperation, this book could not exist.

Finally, a big thank you to my patient editor, Robert Gottlieb. He has stood by me in every way and has believed in this book for more than a decade. Without his confidence, I would not have had the courage to start.

PHOTOGRAPHIC MODELS

Seven members of the New York City Ballet generously made themselves available to demonstrate the technique for the camera. I am very grateful for their ready cooperation and for the enthusiasm they showed for this project.

Peter Boal

Deanna McBrearty

Basic Technique Models

Dana Hanson

Partnering Models

Darci Kistler and Nikolaj Hübbe

Wendy Whelan and Jock Soto

Preface

When I became a member of the corps of the New York City Ballet in 1959, I was already a professional dancer. I had joined the San Francisco Ballet in 1956 and had performed with them in the Bay Area and on foreign and U.S. tours. I had danced in many ballets by Lew Christensen (the director of the company and a former dancer with Balanchine who was his first American Apollo). Although still a corps dancer, I had begun to do small solos, but the ballets I danced that meant the most to me at that time were *Concerto Barocco* and *Serenade,* two masterpieces by George Balanchine.

After only a few weeks in Balanchine's daily company class, I was ready to let go of my past dancing ideas to reach for the "here and now" implicit in his teaching. I did not want to hold on to what I knew, which had brought me some success, and miss what Mr. B was teaching. My little solos with the San Francisco Ballet did not mean very much to me now. I was astonished at the way the New York City Ballet danced. I wanted to dance that way. I wanted to move that quickly, that slowly, that grandly, that clearly, and especially, that beautifully. Mr. B's classes were joyous, inspirational occasions, privileged moments exploring the beauty of classical movement. Years later, Balanchine told me that he was amazed at how totally I had changed the way I moved. He hadn't thought it possible, but it was possible for me because, although the work was hard, it was never drudgery.

I loved his ballets. I loved performing them, because in his ballets, the corps really danced. The choreography for the corps was often as demanding as that for the soloist dancing in front. And it fit the music perfectly, as if Balanchine and the composer had worked together on every ballet. There was very little parading around and hardly any of the "three steps and pose" typically seen in traditional ballets. Costuming was minimal, so the dancer could really be seen. And the patterns were extremely varied, often composed of unusual numbers of dancers.

Everything Balanchine had to say was fascinating. He seemed to know so many things, certainly everything needed for the work. I admired his way with people. He was patient, good-humored, never flustered or frustrated. He always seemed to have time for each dancer in the company. In the evening I would think back over what had happened during the day and try to apply it not only to my dancing, but also to my life. I felt he knew not just how to dance, but also how to live.

I believed in Balanchine. Seeing and then dancing in his ballets made me believe in his aesthetic. Sharing the life of his company and school made me believe in his approach to work and to life in general. In my teaching, in my lectures, in my writing, and in videos on the technique, I have tried to convey not only his aesthetic, but also his beliefs about how to work, how to deal with each other, and how to live.

At Balanchine's instigation I began to teach in the early 1960s while still a member of the corps de ballet. During the company's seasonal layoffs, he arranged for me to teach intermediate and children's classes at the School of American Ballet, which is the official school of the New York City Ballet. One day, as I was adjusting a tendu front in a class of nine-year-olds, Balanchine walked into the studio with Lincoln Kirstein, the school's longtime president. As they left, I heard Mr. B say to Lincoln, "I knew she would get down on the floor and fix feet."

In the 1960s, with the support of the Ford Foundation, Mr. Balanchine was given a national role in developing dance talent and in upgrading the teaching of ballet. I was one of the small group of dancers he chose to serve as talent scouts, traveling around the country and holding auditions to identify gifted students. He also asked me to serve as his assistant in several of the training seminars for teachers that he gave, also under the auspices of the Ford Foundation.

Mr. B often had morning appointments that delayed him briefly, so he appointed me to start class if he was more than about five minutes late. Once he had arrived and had taken over the class, he often told dancers needing repeated correction or extra explanation, "Ask Suki how to do. Ask Jacques [d'Amboise]." When the company grew to seventy and eighty dancers in the late 1960s, he formed a "newcomers' class," which I taught two or three mornings a week. In this class I concentrated on the special refinements of ballet technique developed by Mr. B. I helped newcomers to understand what to work on in company class to develop the special finesse and skill necessary to move as he wanted. Not all of this could be taught at the school at that time, so it was my job to help prepare young company members for his demanding class and, more importantly, for his choreography.

In 1972, when I retired from performing with the New York City Ballet, Mr. B asked me to take on two assignments. First, he invited me to become a full-time teacher at the School of American Ballet. He created a position for me by selecting the most talented girls from the advanced and professional classes (then known as C and D, respectively) and setting up the class known until the fall of 1998 as C2. I was the primary teacher of this class, and it was my job to prepare its students for him. Second, he made me responsible for the NYCB lecture demonstration program that takes ballet to schools and asked me to expand and develop it. For the next twenty-three years I designed the programs, determined what was danced, wrote the scripts, selected the casts, rehearsed the ballets, and prepared the SAB dancers to present the material and handle the public.

Balanchine was thoroughly trained in the technique and choreography of Petipa, the longtime director of St. Petersburg's Imperial Ballet, whom he revered as the true master of classical ballet. Those years gave him his credo: "What I believe is what I learned myself, in St. Petersburg, in what was probably the most elaborate and refined school." He was also familiar with the new directions fostered by Fokine and other twentieth-century innovators. As his works reveal, Balanchine used this knowledge from the beginning as the basis for continuous exploration of ballet style, expression, and vocabulary. As a teacher he said, "We teach not for teaching's sake, but to prepare dancers to entertain the public, to appear onstage. That is the purpose . . . If you have that in mind you use everything that looks very nice when you need it. Somebody can do better and faster, you allow for that. You become very personal. That's the beauty of it. We cannot stick to the rules. The rules are for us to break." As a choreographer, he reexamined every detail of classical technique, developing the refinements that allowed him to make ballets with a new look. A new look, but a classical look. He said, "We are talking about the principles [of classical ballet]. A dancer does it almost right. It looks nice. You can adapt yourself to certain things, if you don't spoil the quality or the meaning of the gesture."

My purpose in writing this book is to record what I learned from him about ballet dancing and teaching ballet, insofar as that is possible on paper. I often cite examples from the Balanchine repertory to illustrate the application of technical points in finished choreography. Readers who cannot see the ballets danced live may be able to locate videotapes or films of performances. Under the auspices of the Balanchine Foundation I also have prepared (in collaboration with Merrill Ashley) a set of videotapes (*The Balanchine Essays: Analysis and Aspects of Balanchine Technique*) that give another kind of documentation of the technique and show how it is used in the ballets. Especially for teachers and advanced dancers, the fullest understanding will come from seeing the ballets, reading this book, and looking at the videos. By helping others deepen their understanding of Balanchine's art, I hope to contribute in a small way to the preservation of his unique and extraordinary legacy.

Except when a point applies exclusively to men, the pronoun "she" is used for women and for men. The context or subject matter (e.g., pointe technique) will show when "she" refers only to women.

I have not tried to say all there is to say about an exercise, nor have I written about every classical step or movement. This is not a general syllabus for teaching ballet. Rather, I have focused mainly on what was distinctive in Mr. Balanchine's approach, how he wanted certain movements done, and any special considerations for music, accent, phrasing, and so on. In most cases I have tried to offer the corrections that I find I have to make most often and insist on most strongly to get the desired result.

Suki Schorer on
Balanchine Technique

Introduction

Mr. Balanchine used to say that he had only 1 percent of the ballet world and that anyone who didn't like his 1 percent had all the rest from which to choose. Once I arrived in Mr. B's part of the ballet world, the idea of going anywhere else never occurred to me. There was a special atmosphere that emanated from him. It had drawn and retained a collection of quite remarkable people around the New York City Ballet. This book is about Balanchine's classical ballet technique, but there was much more to Mr. B than steps. His people are a sure sign of that.

The general director, Lincoln Kirstein, was the man who brought Balanchine to America. I did not know about Lincoln Kirstein when I arrived in New York, but I came to realize that he was a brilliant, insightful intellectual. He was tall, generously proportioned, but not fat, with a large head and a wide face—in short, a big man. He was thus doubly equipped to be a dominating presence, but the paradox is that he went about his work without creating a stir. Far from dominating us, he was so silent we could forget he was there. And then, quiet as a mouse, he suddenly appeared from nowhere, maybe stayed awhile to watch what was happening, and as quietly left. He had done crucially significant work in poetry and modern art, he was an important man before Balanchine came, and yet he devoted himself completely to letting Mr. B do his work. He was so selfless in his devotion, he put his name only on his books, he did not call attention to himself, and I think we took him for granted. Only now, when I watch company and school directors around the country trying to cope with everything, do I begin to appreciate fully what he gave us.

Conversation with Lincoln could take disconcerting turns. He was a profoundly serious man, and the social niceties did not suit him. When greeted in the usual way—hello, how are you, and so on—he could answer with a scowl, "Peculiar," and walk on by without pausing. When I was nursing my two-week-old daughter and trying to resume work, he saw me teaching class. I had not fed her for several hours and he told me that I was the only woman he knew who had gotten larger after childbirth, rather than smaller. Well, due to complications in delivery, I had had a difficult time and lost thirty pounds! I wasn't bigger, I just had swollen breasts from the milk. In later years, we exchanged little missives on the subject of cats, an interest we shared. I can't say I miss him acutely or actively, because he was not a regular part of my life, but I do miss him and I know there won't be anyone like him again.

There were Balanchine's wonderful ballerinas to learn from by observation and example. When I danced in the corps in the "Snow" scene of thirty consecutive performances of *The Nutcracker*, I needed to find a way to keep each performance fresh and alive. To prevent boredom and to avoid slipping into a routine, I went on some nights with the idea of emulating the personal qualities that one of the ballerinas showed in her dancing. I was not trying to be someone else or playing at being a ballerina; I just wanted to see if I could capture the way of dancing that made each of them different from all the others. I tried emphasizing an expansive, beautiful port de bras and open, lifted chest like Jillana's, or a delicate but definitely nuanced attack and phrasing like Violette Verdy's, or the tall and elegant, long, slightly cool and remote presence of Diana Adams, or the vulnerable, inward, doll-like presence of Allegra Kent, or the light-up-the-stage incandescence of Melissa Hayden, or the dazzling speed and technique of Pat Wilde. It never occurred to me to try to emulate the powerful, dominating presence of Maria Tallchief, but I surely tried to incorporate her many useful suggestions—for example, on how to walk and run when onstage. I learned a lot of stagecraft just watching Jacques d'Amboise, Arthur Mitchell, Edward Villella, and Nicholas Magallanes. Later, after being promoted, I had the opportunity to dance with each of them and learned even more. There were extremely capable ballet mistresses and a ballet master to rehearse the repertory they knew in every detail: Janet Reed, Vida Brown, Una Kai, Francia Russell, and John Taras.

Robert Irving had come from Britain's Royal Ballet to be the music director and principal conductor; he and Mr. B almost invariably agreed on musical matters. Irving was a masterful pianist and conductor who was always sensitive to the flow of the dance. In fact, he was so accomplished, he could come onstage to play one of the two piano parts accompanying *Liebeslieder* and then be in the pit after the intermission to conduct the next ballet. Gordon Boelzner was a remarkable pianist whose flexible, responsive playing enhanced the class exercises. Igor Stravinsky was usually present for some rehearsals of new ballets to his music and on some other occasions. He and Mr. B consulted in Russian

at the piano or sitting together watching us dance. Stravinsky was not directly a presence for the dancers, but we could certainly see Balanchine's respect and consideration for him, long before the Stravinsky Festivals, long before the famous toast Mr. B and Lincoln drank to him posthumously before the curtain.

Betty Cage, the general manager, was a smart, perceptive lady with a great sense for business. She could also read tarot cards, and she practiced Tai Chi when necessary. Traveling by train on tour, we sometimes had an hour or two layover in a station. Dancers got out to stroll or stretch, and there would be Betty doing "Step Back and Repulse Monkey." At Thanksgiving she cooked dinner for longtime friends and some members of the company who had no other place to go. It was a very thoughtful welcome for me and others in my generation of young dancers away from home for the first time. There were many other interesting, bright, and able people in the office. One was Barbara Horgan, an assistant manager and my dear friend. She helped me in many ways. One of the most important was to encourage me to overcome the natural hesitancy of a very young dancer and approach Mr. B with my questions. Fortunately, I did and I began to use the opportunity I had to find out everything I could from him about dancing, performing, teaching, and living. Another was Edward Bigelow, also an assistant manager, who was always around and available and seemed able to take care of any problem. The knowledgeable, helpful production staff included Karinska, whose superb, magical theatrical craftsmanship was built on very long tradition.

With all due respect to the other people he had gathered, it was still Mr. B's spirit that pervaded the New York City Ballet. The 1 percent he had was completely his.

The atmosphere that Balanchine created gave us a unity of purpose, a reason for being that we all shared. The dancers all made the maximum effort to please him as much as we could, every time we danced. The young dancers I teach today have only the slightest idea, I think, of the amount of energy we put out, of how hard we tried. It's not that they don't work hard and very seriously to learn to dance, because they do. But Mr. B somehow got that little bit extra, the "more" that raises everything to a higher level. Things were clearer, life was simpler, even if more demanding, because there was only one answer: to please Mr. B.

We were not all the same, of course. We did not all work in the same way. Some did not always come to his classes, which were very demanding. And it was different for the men, because Mr. B was more interested in the women. He is the one who said that "ballet is a female thing; it is woman." He made some wonderful roles for men in *Apollo*, *Prodigal Son*, *Who Cares?*, and *Harlequinade*, among others. However, his aesthetic did not allow for some of the showy steps that men usually enjoy doing just because they generally get a reaction from the public and because they are fun to do. When Mr. B told a very famous male star from Russia that he was welcome to come around when he had finished being a "prince," we all understood. We all wanted to be cast, to get roles, to dance his ballets as he wanted them danced. Mr. B did not want (and, as the passage of time has shown, did not need) a collection of stars pulling out the same bag of tricks they used everywhere else. We knew he was not complacent, that he did not believe that what he had done so far exhausted the possibilities in himself or in the art he served. We knew we should not be complacent either, even though we had the best lives dancers could have.

Mr. B died in 1983, but I am still living in his 1 percent of the ballet world. Much has changed, as it inevitably must, as he would want it to, because he was always ready to use what was new to extend himself and his craft. Because of what I got from him, I continue to live in his 1 percent, because he did not make it only out of steps. He set an example out of deep moral conviction that I still try to emulate, even though, or maybe especially because he is not here to guide me in person anymore. He is also not here to be an example.

I hope that would please him, because he cer-tainly believed that dancers learn by imitation, and I think he believed that people in general learn best that way, too. He did not preach to us or lecture us; he was not a moralist. Instead, he simply lived, and in living, he set a good example.

His good example began with a small and trivial habit. He was always careful to appear for work neatly dressed and groomed. He had a few colorful touches he enjoyed, notably his "Western" dress, but he always presented himself nicely turned out, without any pretension or stuffiness, or concern about being in fashion. In a subtle way he let us know that his preference was for the essentials, for simplicity, for clarity. He also underlined his inter-est in making an *American* (not European or Rus-sian, and not just New York either) ballet company. And yet, for Balanchine, its name was always the *New York* City Ballet, even if he drew on the cul-ture of the entire country for his work. New York City was the place that mattered most to him in all the world, not just the United States; he lived on its energy, its excitement, its cultural institutions. I am still not accepting of today's abbreviated name, "City Ballet," because I never heard him use it.

He always enjoyed fine food and wine. Poking at his waist, he once told me, "I'm getting a little out of shape, I need to exercise." So even though he did not enjoy exercise, he would get himself to a Pilates studio. He realized that since he was in front of us every day in class and rehearsal, we would natu-rally be very aware of the way he looked after him-self. Of course, ballet dancers need a trim figure, but he knew there is a place in life for enjoying other things, and sometimes he shared that with us, inviting or joining various ones of us for a drink or a meal or both.

The teachers Balanchine had invited to join him at the School of American Ballet also set a good ex-ample of the refinement appropriate to ballet dancers. I recall seeing the Russians who had been trained, as had Mr. B, at the Marinsky (Pierre Vladimiroff, who had been at SAB from the begin-ning, Anatole Oboukhov, Felia Dubrovska, and Alexandra Danilova); Muriel Stuart, who had trained and performed with Pavlova; and Elise Reiman, one of the first students at SAB and a Balanchine dancer who created roles in the major ballets *Serenade* and *The Four Temperaments* (she was Terpsichore when *Apollo* was first danced in America). They each had a certain perfume, a certain elegant presence. On occasion he would call attention to that, not by telling us to be like them, but by saying, for example, "Look how Madame Dubrovska enters the studio, how she looks, how she presents herself." They also tried, as he did, to pass along their sense of how to live as a dancer, how to dress, how to speak, how to carry yourself. When I joined the faculty, for example, Madame Dubrovska counseled me, "Always iron your skirt before teaching."

Jacques d'Amboise took class from Pierre Vladimiroff (a principal with Diaghilev and Pavlova's last partner) from the time he was a boy and he tells of his early awareness of the difference in being a dancer through Vladimiroff's example and stories. According to Vladimiroff, a man who dances goes to the theater like anyone else going to work, but when he opens the stage door, he becomes a *dancer*. Entering this special place, he no longer walks like an ordinary man. He stands taller, his chest lifted, his head carried proudly; he "walks on air," lightly, with the weight on the balls of the feet. As he prepares for the performance, making up, warming up, dressing, he maintains an aristocratic bearing. At the end of the evening, when he has given everything he had to the work, he bids everyone a good night and closes the stage door. Only when again on the street does he relax his bearing, put his full foot on the ground, and make his way home like an ordinary man.

Madame Danilova joined the faculty of the school in the early 1960s, when I was still in the corps of NYCB. On company layoffs, or when my schedule was less busy, I took her variations class. This was a class about dancing the classics, but it was a lot more than learning the steps. As she gave us each of those jewels of the Imperial Russian repertory, she not only passed on Petipa's choreog-

raphy but also tried to teach us how to give each dance its particular nuance, its particular fragrance. She firmly believed that a dancer who could learn to dance the classics that well was prepared technically to learn to dance anything. Her conviction is widely shared in the ballet world, and the school continues to employ a Petipa teacher. However, in her classes, the variations were not museum pieces to be taken out very carefully once in a while to be adored. They were as fresh as if they had been made yesterday.

Learning and dancing the variations from Fokine's *Les Sylphides* with Madame Danilova was a particular joy. She made me cover so much space! I felt I was flying through the air like a real sylph. One of the first workshops was being planned at that time, and Madame Danilova went to Balanchine to discuss the casting. She suggested that I should be in *Les Sylphides,* but Mr. B decided that the workshop should present only SAB students, and so it has remained. It is much better that way, but I'm still sorry I never prepared a role with her.

When I joined the faculty of SAB, Madame Danilova and I got to know each other as colleagues and in the teachers' dressing room. This was a ballerina to the nth degree. She arrived for work every day impeccably dressed down to her underwear, the most beautiful I have ever seen. One day I admired a wool scarf she wore that has a subtle weave in muted tones. The next day, she gave it to me and I still have it. It's a little too scratchy to be completely comfortable; maybe there's a lesson there in the depth of her sense of the responsibility of a ballerina to her public. Certainly they responded, from the great to just folks. One of the former, General George C. Marshall, saw her dance in Washington, D.C., and invited her to lunch the next day at the Pentagon. Danilova replied, "I would like to meet you, but, *mon Général,* I don't know where that restaurant, Le Pentagon, is." She told me that story years later as if it were the most ordinary thing. Only Danilova! A person totally of the theater.

People always noticed that she seemed to see

everything that was performed in New York, right down to the end of her life. It was true; she saw more than anybody else I know. Once in the theater, she also saw more. She saw a new production of *Coppélia* danced by the American Ballet Theater a month before she died. ABT ballet master David Richardson met her right after the performance and asked how she liked it. She said she had enjoyed it, but she had some notes. She proceeded to give him some useful suggestions for the corps de ballet. As she always said, dance was her business. It was her profession at all times. The last note I got from her arrived a couple of weeks before she died and was to compliment me on my staging of *Divertimento No. 15* for the 1997 SAB workshop.

Elise Reiman and I also became friends after I joined the faculty full-time. As much as I appreciated the Russians, I always knew that they were a more distant example. They had grown up so differently, I could never have much of what they had. Elise, in contrast, was truly American, loyal to the end of her life to Terre Haute, Indiana, where she grew up and where much of her family still lived. There was something very direct, very down-to-earth about her; she never lost the Midwestern twang in her speech.

There was, of course, more to her than that. She came to Balanchine because she read about the new ballet school in New York City in her favorite magazine, *Vogue* (not *Dance*), and decided that his school was where she should be. So she picked up and left San Francisco, where she was working, and came to New York to study. As a teacher, she was very straightforward and clear with the children she taught, but also warm and caring, good-humored and witty. One day, a girl was dancing below her usual level in class, and so Elise asked matter-of-factly if she had her period. No euphemism, no beating around the bush. The class tittered, the girl blushed. Elise settled them down and the class went on as does life, period or no.

I enjoyed her sense of humor, too, and also her way of being sophisticated and chic with a very basic wardrobe. From the time we became friends, I only bought evening clothes when she could be present with her all-knowing eyes. Her exquisite taste and judgment ruled my decisions. Once, she told me to meet her that day at a certain shop. I should buy a beautiful long black dress, because it was just right for a dinner in Washington. I had no invitation to Washington, but I bought the dress. She was a genuinely elegant woman, but on a rainy night, when we were trying to get home from a performance or a party somewhere, she could hail a cab better than anyone.

That generation of teachers has all died. The classical technique and its teaching have evolved, and the children we teach have been raised in a new world. However, I miss the teachers I met when I came to New York who are no longer with us, and I keep the example they set in mind as I do my work. I try to set as good an example for those I teach as the old-time teachers set for me.

Being our director and choreographer was a way of life, a calling. It was not just a job, a paycheck for Mr. B (in fact, at the time of the Ford Foundation grants, he wasn't even drawing a salary, a situation Ford insisted had to be changed). The stage, the studios, and the theater were like church to him.

This was even more true when, in 1964, the company moved to the New York State Theater, which had been designed mostly according to Mr. B's conception. When dancers sat out front (in the auditorium) to watch stage rehearsals, Mr. B let it be known that sprawling and slumping in the seats, putting our feet up figuratively, and very often even literally, was not appropriate. He wanted us to sit properly and treat our new home with respect.

His feeling for the building extended to what was in it. Pianos, for example, were beautiful instruments. They were not furniture to store dance bags, substitute barres, or places to park ashtrays, coffee cups, and soda cans. Costumes were put on just before we were due to go on, according to Mr. B and his formidable Russian wardrobe mistress, Madame Pourmel, who seemed to have a relationship with each costume equal to Dr. Coppélius's relationships to his dolls. They did not want to see us lounging around eating and drinking or even just sitting in them. The ladies had to learn not to rest their hands on their hips, which causes the fabric to become dingy and dirty. Instead, we held our hands palms up, backs of hands down, just above the tutu or skirt. And even though money is never plentiful around a ballet company, the message we got was respect for everything used in the theater, rather than a small-minded worry about the budget. At one point many of the women began to wear brand-new pointe shoes in class. To save time, some of them cut slits in the pointe shoes, so they could just pass the ribbons through and avoid sewing them on in the time-honored way. This horrified the Russian teachers in the school, and I think their disapproval helped put an end to the practice.

The one time I recall Mr. B being truly angry came when he discovered a stage hand casually dropping ashes from his cigar on the freshly mopped stage just before a performance. "Don't you know where you are? You're not in the street! This is not a gutter!" he yelled. "This is the theater, a place where people *dance!*" I can recall no tantrums, no displays of the posturing *artiste*. Even though he was, as Diana Adams and some senior company dancers half-jokingly called him, "The Boss," and we all certainly knew it, he was invariably direct, matter-of-fact, and very cordial with us. Through his example, by the way he treated every one of us dancers, and the other people in the theater as well, he made life in the theater very much a calling for everyone who worked there.

His sense that his work was more than just a job meant that he was involved in every aspect of the performance, not just the choreography and the dancing. And he was involved all the way through the process, not just at the end and not just to complain about something he did not like when it might be too late—music, costumes, makeup, hair, props, lighting, bows, everything. He was in the theater from early in the day through the performance, looking with a knowing eye at each one of us, at every aspect of our work.

He was very proud of all of us. I remember hearing that he told the press, when New York City went wild over the Bolshoi in 1959, that he had the most beautiful dancers in the world. His pride in us and his careful attentiveness to the details of how we looked helped us to become aware of how to "feel beautiful within," a state of mind he thought essential for looking beautiful onstage. He suggested ways each one of us could enhance our stage appearance.

For example, my hair was quite blond, and Mr. B liked blond hair, which caused him to observe, playing with the blondes-have-more-fun saying, "Now, dear, blond is fun and fine on the street, but not so good onstage." I also have a high forehead. Since there was very little contrast between my skin and hair, my face and hair blended together. Soon after I joined the company, he talked to a beautician about me. He then suggested to me that I make my hairline visible by darkening it with a washable light-brown dye, which he brought for me to use.

But his observing and thinking were constant, not just a one-shot look-over for newly hired dancers. When I joined in the late 1950s, the ladies often used a "classical" hairstyle that covered the ears and had a bun that sat low on the head, at the top of the neck. By the mid-1960s we wore high, flat buns and, eventually, a French twist; both pulled our hair back and up, uncovering the face, ears, and the top of the neck. This change revealed more fully the facial features and length of neck of his beautiful dancers. Both styles, high buns and twists, are still seen today.

Later, when I was first cast as the Dew Drop Fairy, I added many rhinestone sprays, extra jewels, and sparkles to the headpiece to give it more brilliance. Mr. B didn't like the result at all: "Too much, dear," he said, "looks like shiny skullcap. Less is better." He sometimes worked with us on our headpieces to get exactly the effect he wanted, which was to finish the look appropriate to the ballet yet flattering to us. He generally did not like large, elaborate ornaments that overpowered the features of the dancer, and he preferred that headpieces sit back from the face so they could be seen. And he wanted nothing so large that we looked top-heavy.

Mr. B admired Karinska and trusted her craftsmanship. He was often present for first fittings of new costumes, but he did much more than just check to make sure we could move in them. Theirs was a true collaboration, and his ideas were a necessary part of developing the design. When he thought it necessary, he would suggest changes in the colors or in any other details. My costume for *La Source* was a tutu in dark purple. When he saw it, he said the color was for an old woman and suggested we try light blue. Over the years he tried light blue, blue with black lace trim, and pink lavender for that tutu. He was always thinking how the costumes could be better.

The original cast for *Raymonda Variations* included me, the smallest girl in the company, and Gloria Govrin, the tallest, who is about seven inches taller than I am. Madame Karinska, as well as Mr. Balanchine, knew about the range in heights, because at the fitting, each girl's skirt was cut proportionately to her height. Mine was short and very small, while Gloria's was longer and larger. This meant that each dancer's legs could be seen. To Mr. B, a good costume was one that showed the dancer wearing it to her best advantage. The most beautiful garment imaginable was not generally interesting to him if his dancer could not be seen as fully as possible and looking as beautiful as she could.

There were exceptions, of course. Ballets such as *Prodigal Son, The Nutcracker, Firebird, La Sonnambula, A Midsummer Night's Dream, Union Jack, Harlequinade,* and the waltz ballets *Liebeslieder Walzer* and *Vienna Waltzes* all use elaborate, enveloping costumes. But in each of these ballets the dancers are portraying characters in a story or types drawn from a very specific historical era. That is unusual in his repertory.

Unlike most dancers and choreographers, Balanchine was a musician. He studied scores on his own and came to rehearsal with very detailed, clear, and firm ideas about how the music should be played. He never had to ask a company pianist to play a few bars to remind him of the music, so he could think what to do next. And, when necessary, he could get very exclusive, very special help. Sometimes Mr. B would come into rehearsal and announce with a smile that he had spoken to Tchaikovsky the night before. Tchaikovsky had told him the right tempos for a passage in the music or had agreed that a repeat of the *Tema Russo* in *Serenade* would be just fine. In one case the strategy did not work: Balanchine had choreographed a solo for Mimi Paul in the "Emeralds" section of *Jewels,* but in this very unusual case Irving never conducted the music as slowly as Mr. B had expected it would be when he made the dance. After Mimi left the company, I danced this variation, and still he was not satisfied with the way the dance looked when performed to the faster tempo. Eventually he gave up on telling Irving what tempo he wanted. Although he did not rechoreograph the variation for me, he did so several years later, when Karin von Aroldingen first danced the part.

Mr. Balanchine had time to talk to everyone in the theater who approached him; he did not just "speak" to dead composers. And live ones. This was so even though he never affected an American informality. He was universally addressed as *Mr. Balanchine* or *Mr. B.* No dancer would have called him George in front of the company.

Before performances, he was almost always backstage. He was available to us as he walked around chatting with dancers, checking their costumes, makeup, and hair. During the performance he was usually in the first wing watching the ballet. At intermission he often stayed backstage, but not necessarily to give us corrections or compliments on our performance. He was there for us as people, and it was natural for any of us, even the most junior members of the corps, to talk with him about anything at all. As a result, he knew his dancers very well as people: interests and problems, a lot about the families and what the parents did for a living, where the family came from in the United States or elsewhere, and where it had come from originally.

In class, Mr. B once asked a young dancer why he had taken her into the company. "Because you like me," she said. "Yes, dear, I like you," he replied, "I like everyone I take. No, it's because you can jump. . . . So, JUMP!"

One time of the year when he was not a constant presence was Russian Orthodox Holy (Easter) Week; during that week, we knew if we did not see him that he was probably at home preparing his famous Easter dinner.

His easy, approachable way was one source of the family-like atmosphere he fostered. Even though he was our "boss," he was someone we could talk to like an older, wiser, more sophisticated friend. Another source might have been his remarkable patience, because unlike the impatient, he could often take a longer view and wait for things to develop. He had responsibility for the whole company and for a performance every night, and yet in the situations when we needed a little more time, he made us feel he could wait for us.

His classes were very demanding, because they were not just a rote recital of the standard steps and combinations. In class he was trying to help us to dance better than we knew we could. He was also trying to extend the technique, making it richer in expressive resources. Sometimes, after correcting a dancer several times, he saw that the step was still not quite right. He would ask, "How old are you?" The dancer would say something like twenty or twenty-two and he would answer, "Oh, there's still time." That did not mean that we could relax and take it easy. It did mean that we needed to change, and we knew he would be there to work with us and wait for us to develop. Even so, Mr. B could show some slight frustration when we didn't change. Or wouldn't change. He would say, "I should have been a dentist! This is harder than pulling teeth." Or he would tell us, "I must sound like a broken record. Every day I have to say the same thing!"

Not only could he avoid being pointlessly impatient with us, he also could calm our own exaggerated haste. Soon after joining the New York City Ballet, I learned that a recent chronic weakness in my right shoulder was the result of a mild case of polio. I was naturally very alarmed. Damage from polio is not reversible. So I went to Mr. B to talk to him about my problem. He was very calm, very reassuring. He said, "You know, it is like the carrot. You plant the seed in the ground. You can't see anything happening, but after a while, you pull out a carrot. That will happen to you. Other muscles will gradually compensate and one day your arm will be fine."

Waiting for the healing process to run its course is also the most practical thing to do, to be sure. And whether the problem was a large one like my polio or a small one like the usual run of transient aches and pains, Mr. B did not want us to do class or perform if we would aggravate an injury. On occasion he substituted a step with equivalent musical value to work around a problem. A big développé followed by tombé could, for example, be put in for a grand jeté, if the dancer had a bad knee. If necessary, he would eliminate a repeat, cut a variation, or even pull a ballet from the program and replace it with another, when no other solution was available.

While we were on tour in the Soviet Union, I hurt my foot. Balanchine came by while I was warming up for performance; I was already in my makeup, determined to try to go onstage in *La Sonnambula*. He insisted that my part (the Pas Mauresque) be cut for that performance. He assured me that no one would notice.

When Balanchine was choreographing a ballet, he generally preferred not to call understudies for the principal roles. At such times Balanchine often must have felt that if he couldn't have the original person, he would rather substitute a different work rather than call another dancer. He almost postponed the premiere of *Movements*, which he had just finished, but after seeing some rehearsals with Suzanne Farrell replacing the suddenly unavailable (due to pregnancy) Diana Adams, he put it on. Several years later, Dulcinea in the new *Don Quixote* was exclusively Suzanne's; the ballet was not to go on unless she could dance. But when she left the company, Sara Leland and Kay Mazzo learned and performed the role.

When a ballet has been around for a couple of seasons, the complications of scheduling, interest in seeing a different dancer in a part, resignations from the company, injuries, and the normal succession of generations of dancers produce changes in principal and solo casting. Putting on someone new in place of the dancer on whom the work was made is the way ballets are kept in the programs. Sometimes, however, the original performer had a special facility with a step or movement that one or more successors lacked. On such occasions Balanchine would substitute a step with equivalent musical values and probably a similar look so that the newly cast dancer would feel more comfortable and therefore look as good as she could. An effective performance by the dancer going on tonight was more important to Mr. B than keeping his choreography untouched. Again, he was not some self-important *artiste* who saw himself and his works as more important than presenting the best possible performance every time the curtain went up.

No one should assume that the dancers performing, and consequently the look of a ballet as seen at the premiere, are necessarily representative of what Mr. B originally had in mind. The dancer on whom a part was begun or even entirely made has to be replaced for the premiere oftener than most realize, especially in a company with as busy a schedule as that of the New York City Ballet. But even when the original dancer went on at the premiere, she might not have done all the steps Balanchine originally set. When he was making the dances for the second soloist in *La Source* on me, he originally choreographed échappé relevé, plié, entrechat six, repeated several times. When we found after several days of work that those steps required more wind than I had at that moment, he substituted échappé relevé, attitude relevée, which is what I did at the premiere. Other dancers have written and spoken of similar experiences.

Adjustments could even be made to long-established ballets to make a single evening's per-

formance go better. For example, Edward Villella was sometimes cast in a hard ballet followed by the lead in the third movement of *Symphony in C*, a killer. So Mr. B would cut the repeat of the principal dancers' first entrance, which had many flying jumps done in a circle. Knowing that, I thought there would be no problem when I was cast in *Tarantella*, a very taxing pas de deux, with the lead in the third movement of *Symphony in C* to follow, in this case without an intermission. I asked Mr. B if he would cut the repeat. "No," he said, "the man is soaring in the air. No one sees the girl." So in other cases, adjustments could not be made. We did the ballet as Mr. B wanted, and the performance went fine.

That focus on getting the show on in the best possible way in the circumstances of the moment was the basis of much of Balanchine's practicality. He did not let anything get in the way of productive effort; he adapted to the situation at hand and accomplished whatever he could. I had not yet come to New York when *The Nutcracker*, by far the biggest production the company had until then undertaken, premiered. Dancers still remembered that the costumes were not completely finished a couple of hours before curtain. Mr. B's response was to ask quietly for needle and thread and sit down and sew on decorations.

Serenade carries evidence of this attitude in the unusual numbers of dancers who are often onstage. When he was making the ballet, different combinations of dancers showed up for each day's work, and that is how the ballet is still performed. He even used a real-life late arrival for a bit of the choreography of the ballet. He also worked within the dimensions of the different stages the company used as it moved to City Center and then on to the New York State Theater. *The Four Temperaments* was made for a high-school stage that was really more a speaker's platform, very shallow. When he mounted it at City Center, Mr. B reset it to fill the full depth of the stage. Later, when it was taped for television, he reset the finale so the groups would be more visible and then adapted that ending for the still larger stage of the State Theater. In other cases (*Swan Lake, Symphony in C*), he increased the number of girls in the corps to fill the stage of the State Theater.

Ultimately, the most crucial part of Mr. B's practicality resided in his awareness that for his audience, ballet is an entertainment. He knew that the audience would only come and, more importantly, come back, if what we did onstage was beautiful, musical, and interesting. Mr. B understood that he had to first capture the interest and arouse the enthusiasm of the public who came to his theater. Then they would want to come back, and he could show them something new and start to educate them further. He needed the initial interest and enthusiasm to show them they could learn to enjoy pieces that were not readily accessible, that did not disclose their qualities on first exposure.

The music for the repertory was carefully chosen to maintain a balance among familiar classical music, such as that for ballets such as *The Nutcracker, Swan Lake,* and *Firebird;* lighter fare such as *Tchaikovsky Pas de Deux, Western Symphony,* and *Stars and Stripes;* and works that challenged his audience, such as *Agon, Concerto Barocco,* and *The Four Temperaments.* Programs were often arranged to include a work of each type—for example, *Swan Lake, Agon,* and *Western Symphony.*

Morton Baum of the City Center of Music and Drama suggested that NYCB needed a ham-and-eggs program like the one the touring Ballets Russes always had available, because they needed one sure sellout. He suggested a very effective and popular matinee made up of *Swan Lake,* Jerome Robbins's *Afternoon of a Faun, Firebird,* and *Western Symphony*—ham and eggs and a sweet roll, but no broccoli! Mr. B knew when to attract new customers and when to challenge the ones he already had. Of course, the ultimate ham-and-eggs ballet when I joined was *The Nutcracker,* and over the years since Mr. B revived it, the ballet has become the ham and eggs of companies all across the country.

Sometimes people left during the second inter-mission if they did not like the last ballet or were not sure about it. Lincoln Kirstein would say to Mr. B, "Look how many people are leaving!" Balanchine would calmly reply, "Yes, but look how many stay." However, he could see that simply ensuring that each kind of ballet was represented in a performance was not in itself enough to win an audience for more challenging works. His tactic for exposing his audience to work they might tend to reject was to arrange the program with the "hard" piece in the middle. No ballet needed this treatment more than *Liebeslieder Walzer.* Mr. B made it to two song cycles by Brahms that are less well known, even to the lieder public. When it was new in the repertory, *Liebeslieder* was last on the program, and some people who thought they would not like it for one reason or another left after the second ballet. Others even left *during Liebeslieder.* So Mr. B moved it to second on the program, people stayed to see the last ballet, and over time they got to like *Liebeslieder,* too.

Mr. Balanchine was at all times a cavalier, a real gentleman. He was unfailingly considerate, which made everyone feel special. In the most casual moments around the theater, he was able to acknowledge each person's presence, his or her existence. He knew how to offer his hand to a lady or take her arm when walking. And if he saw one of his female dancers outside, he would assume a gentlemanly, protective posture. Patty McBride remembers how he always took her arm and carried her dance bag when he saw her walking in his direction from the theater. One night after a performance, they were walking arm-in-arm as he saw her to the subway. It was snowy and slushy, so as they came to a corner with a flooded crosswalk, she looked to see where to cross. Instantly, Mr. B picked her up and carried her across the street. Although a bit extravagant, his gesture was wholly in character.

Mr. Balanchine's graciousness was inbred. It never had the feel of something learned after his character was formed. Although he applied it to almost everyone, it took on a special niceness for the women in the company. It had a friendliness, an openness, a spontaneity that was maybe a little American. For the public who sees his ballets, there is a residue of this special quality in the way he made dances for couples and even trios. He showed that a partner could be fully a cavalier yet dispense with the grand manner, and I think that was easier for him, because that is the way he lived.

Mr. Balanchine showed his sense of how to treat us in another way, this one closely related to his position as the head of the company, the head of our family. He knew of the private difficulties many of us faced in running our lives, because he was around and easy to talk to. So he did what he could to make things run a little more smoothly for us. He would help people locate a place to stay or an apartment to share, a doctor to see, and so on.

When I married a man who later moved to Boston, I thought I was not going to be able to stay on with the company. But Mr. B made this possible for me by giving me special consideration for months, even though at that time he was not generally very accepting of marriage for his dancers. First, although he usually determined each principal dancer's repertory without consulting us, he asked me to let him know what roles I wanted to learn for the next season. I gave him a list of ten, and he picked three. During the rehearsal period, he allowed me to come to New York for just a few days to learn the new ones, leaving it to me to practice them on my own in Boston. I only had to be in New York for the last week of rehearsals before the opening, so I could get final corrections and run through the ballets with everyone else. Once the performances began, my schedule was Tuesday through Friday in New York and Saturday through Monday (our day off) in Boston, "so you can be home for the weekend." This meant I was unavailable for half the performances, because we did two shows each on Saturdays and Sundays. Without his special attention to me, my dancing career could have taken a very different form or even ended prematurely.

Mr. B came to live and work in New York, in the United States, and his whole life here showed how much he liked what he found. But he avoided picking up some of our bad habits, such as the frenetic New York pace and workaholic intensity on the job. He remained very much a man of the world in his general outlook on work and on life. Even though the theater was his calling, he knew how to relax and have a good time after work and even while working. He enjoyed doing his work, he loved his dancers, and he always brought moments of lightness and humor, even at the hardest times. He did not work compulsively; instead, he worked to maximum effect when it was time to work. Mr. B understood and exemplified the idea of really working when you are working, but then stopping at the right time to do something else.

He could even apply that idea within a class or rehearsal. Sometimes, while we were working very hard, a dancer might relax or try to take it easy as she did some movement. Mr. B would usually challenge that. "Why relax? Why take it easy?" he would ask. "What are you saving yourself for? Do! Now is the time! Relax is for the grave, dear."

On the other hand, when we did very strenuous exercises at the barre, Mr. B on occasion would say, as we turned to the other side, "If you need a breather, now is the time!" and let his shoulders droop, his chest collapse, and his stomach relax for a moment. Not that he welcomed an undisciplined look; it was rather that he wanted us fully "on" for the exercise itself, the way he was. Just as he saw no value in elaborately choreographed arms for each barre exercise, so he saw no value in choreographed turns to the other side or transitions to the next exercise, because both took attention away from what we should be getting from the exercise itself.

Some of the dancers would get to class tired from hard performances or rehearsals. If he gave a strenuous exercise, such as sixteen grand battements at the barre or thirty-two slow changements in the center, he would say, for those who were tired, that it is better to do fewer with maximum effort and awareness and then stop. He did not want us to slavishly do all sixteen or thirty-two, with many of them done with only partial effort, meaning they would probably also be done wrong in some way. Partial effort or less than full awareness were, of course, "bad," even if there was no visible fault. "I give you a smorgasbord, but you don't have to take it all!" he would remind us. Holding on to some useless idea of finishing the exercise, we would have practiced a mistake several times. Clapping his hands to stop the music for our tendus to the front, he would say, "Look how you closed your fifth! Heel, then toe. You did it wrong the last three times. You are memorizing the wrong movement." Teasingly, he added, "Don't practice bad habits!"

One of his sayings was to the effect that he only had a literary approach to literature. That meant that he needed no external (to the music) reason for a dance, but it did not mean that he was not interested in literature for itself. In fact, he loved poetry and even read a critical study of William Blake by my late father, Mark Schorer, who was a professor at the University of California at Berkeley. It's a hard book. I haven't even read it yet myself! Mr. B was not inclined to theorize and analyze, and he was skeptical about dance writing. However, based on his reading of the Blake study and their talks, he approved the idea my father had for a study comparing the creative processes in literature and dance. But perhaps he had second thoughts, because when my father died before doing the book, Mr. B said to me, "Maybe the book was never meant to be."

Mr. B had a cultivated interest in the other arts as well. For example, I was reminded in a funny way that he really knew what was in the Metropolitan Museum of Art. When I was preparing to dance one of the Muses in *Apollo* for the first time, Mr. B suggested I go to the Met Museum to study the flat profile figures in the early black and red terra-cotta vases. He mentioned that parts of the finale of the ballet were meant to look two-dimensional. I dutifully followed his advice, went to the museum, and studied the vases. Years later, when I had stopped dancing and was married, we were talking about

my years onstage. I mentioned my visit to the Met to him and said, "Look what good it did me."

Mr. B said, "But you married a Greek, didn't you?"

Yes, I had married a Greek. I had also been reminded that the dance does not exist with music in isolation from the other arts. Conversation and work with Mr. B showed that he was widely acquainted with the great tradition in all the arts. I think it informed his work in many ways.

My parents were very interested in painting and sculpture, and many of their friends were artists. So when I came to New York, they gave me a membership in the Museum of Modern Art. When special exhibitions were presented, I received an invitation to the black-tie preview for the patrons of the museum. Because Pavel Tchelitchev had designed several ballets for Balanchine (*The Four Temperaments* is still in the repertory, although not with his designs), I invited Mr. B to come with me. As we walked around the show and through some of the galleries in which related works were hung, I realized that he had known almost every artist.

His wide culture certainly made Balanchine more effective talking to us. Even though he never lost his accent, he always came up with an expressive word or phrase or a little story, or he would make a pun. These came from sources as different from one another as traditional Russian folk culture and American pop culture and everything in between. Some of his best words were not "right" in the conventional sense, but they were precise as he used them and very memorable. When members of the "old gang" get together, when talk turns to Mr. B, we all have vivid memories of him that are based in part on his turns of phrase, his special words. Examples are scattered all through this book; I hope they convey something of my experience with him aside from steps and exercises.

As a teacher today, I work very hard to help my students develop a technique and a musicality that meet today's standards. But when I think of how much Mr. B knew aside from the classical technique and music, and how easily he could draw on it, I wonder how our young people will ever pick any of that up.

Mr. B was also a very worldly man in the way he counseled dancers with a problem in getting along with people. His approach was not at all clinical. He did not delve into the history or psychological causes of some problem. Instead, he came up with a suggestion based on his keen observation of what people do and say.

Dancers, like other performers, generally prefer being onstage to a night off. Even when a dancer is scheduled for many rehearsals and performances, there is a great temptation to accept or even ask for more. Mr. B was usually the first to know when a dancer was at the limit. Once he told a principal dancer much in demand at NYCB and for guest appearances all over, "To survive, you will have to learn to say 'No.'" It was the kind of wise counsel he was uniquely able to give.

The New York City Ballet has long been notable for the number of siblings employed simultaneously in the company. Sometimes one would not be comfortable about the faster progress of the other. Mr. B would say, "That dancer needs to change her name."

Once, at about 2:00 a.m., Mr. B went into the coffee shop near the theater and noticed the gloomy husband of one of the dancers sitting there alone, disconsolately smoking a cigarette. Balanchine joined the young man, who said, "She left me, she moved out."

"Oh, I'm sorry," Mr. B said, "but if you want her back, send her two dozen long-stemmed roses with a letter telling her how much you love her and how much you want her back."

The next day the dancer told Mr. B that her husband had sent two dozen long-stemmed roses and a note to tell her how much he loved her, so she was moving back.

Mr. Balanchine's generosity went far beyond his time and these kinds of attention to us in the company. He never treated his ways of teaching as some special mystery only he could know and understand. He did not like "guru" teachers, and he

certainly was not one himself. In fact, he gave the "secrets" of his teaching yearly in the Ford Foundation seminars to all the teachers who came. He and I and the others who assisted worked very hard to make every movement clear and simple to understand, even if not always very easy to do. We tried to remove the mystery, because Mr. B wanted the teachers to take back something that would raise the level of the work in their own schools, rather than trying to hold some kind of exclusive franchise at SAB or in the company. He also gave his ballets far more freely than other choreographers, and often without a fee, especially to former company dancers who were starting to direct companies of their own. So the public could see his work in many places, not just in New York or the few cities we visited on tour.

He also gave his "secrets" daily to his dancers in class. He often set the combinations and gave corrections so we would understand the reasons and purposes of each movement in each exercise, rather than simply doing as we were told. One sign of his openness to his dancers is the number of them who have gone on to have companies of their own and/or to teach across the United States and abroad.

Mr. Balanchine lent his name to the publication of one earlier attempt to set out on paper something of classical ballet technique. That was the book written by Muriel Stuart—an English dancer with a Cecchetti background—and illustrated magnificently by Carlos Dyer. It was a very basic, general statement of the traditional technique. As Mr. B says in his preface, it is largely what he learned in his youth. By the time I began to work for him, he had been making dances, listening to new music, living in new places, and developing dancers for his ballets for more than thirty years. He had moved beyond the world he grew up in, but he did not reject it. Throughout his career he gave homage especially to Petipa. But what he taught and what he put in his ballets constantly changed. In the late 1950s and thereafter, he was no longer working exactly as portrayed in the Stuart/Dyer book.

There is another plausible explanation for the difference. In his preface, Mr. B writes (I actually think it is Lincoln Kirstein writing for him) that the book is meant to serve as a reminder of good practice in places where there are not good teachers. In those days, such places would have seen good professional dancing only on very rare occasions. And he says that the book may serve as a reference in schools in larger centers. I think it is important to remember that the Stuart/Dyer book was published in 1952, long before Mr. B's Ford Foundation seminars for teachers, long before there was much ballet on TV (and, of course, no videos), and long before the regional dance movement that has brought many professionals together for workshops. I think Mr. B hoped to correct some of the most egregious misconceptions on the basis of which technique was being taught by teachers working very far from the professional theater.

My book is based mostly on his teaching while I was a member of the New York City Ballet (1959–1972) and in part on his seminars (at which I assisted him) for teachers under the auspices of the Ford Foundation in the 1960s and 1970s. It is also based on his comments about my teaching of NYCB from the early 1960s through the 1970s and of advanced students at SAB until 1982, when his final illness began. Thus the material in this book is appropriate for *use* mostly by experienced teachers, professional dancers, and those students who are very advanced and who show some real promise for professional careers. It is not a teaching manual or syllabus for the general run of classes. For other readers, it is to let them know how we worked and why.

Mr. B concentrated in his own teaching on advanced students and young professional dancers. He was interested more in helping them than in starting the training. This is not to say that he was uninterested in the training of young children. He developed a curriculum for the early years, but he had little personal interest in teaching that level himself. On the other hand, he did watch SAB teachers work in class with young students and always had valuable observations. Based on his experience, he introduced a number of ideas for teaching children beginning their studies.

He agreed that first-year children (generally eight years old at SAB) should begin their studies facing the barre or standing behind the barre (between the barre and the wall). This helps them learn the directions (front, side, and back) and makes them more aware of maintaining a straight back and keeping their hips and shoulders square. More recently, many schools have used portable barres in the center, so each student can see herself in the mirror. While she is learning to feel the correct form in her body, she will be able to see for herself when she is not properly aligned. The mirror also seems to help her pay better attention to the lesson, perhaps because the mirror provides more visual stimulation than the wall. Children, like nearly everyone else, are fascinated with themselves, after all. Only as young students become aware of the directions (front, side, and back, all very specifically defined by Mr. B) and the principles of good ballet posture, and have the strength to begin to apply them, should they stand in the traditional position perpendicular to the barre for selected exercises.

He asked that the first-year children concentrate and maximize progress on a few basic skills, rather than trying to start learning many different ones. As they learned to stand at the barre, he wanted teachers to use first, second, and, after a few weeks, fifth position. They were to give mainly plié, battement tendu, battement dégagé, grand battement, and going to sur le cou-de-pied. In the center, he wanted the beginners to learn the basic ports de bras linking first, second, fifth high, and fifth low. As the year went on, exercises were added, so that at the end they could do frappé to piqué, rond de jambe par terre, and sauté in first and second and changements, at the barre.

In the center they practiced sauté in first and second and changements. They learned emboîté and practiced it on the diagonal, and they learned to dance the polka.

At every level of instruction, Mr. B placed great emphasis on how to take the foot off the floor when brushing, as in battement tendu, and when lifting, as in going to sur le cou-de-pied. Most teachers know how to analyze a whole step, such as glissade or temps lié, and some routinely give them to beginning children. For Balanchine, these complete steps required far too much for a beginning child to handle all at once. Mr. B wanted the children to be taught much smaller elements, believing that children are more likely to learn to do them correctly that way. Therefore, like all his older dancers, the children did countless battements tendus. Mr. B also devised a moment-by-moment analysis of how to go to sur le cou-de-pied, which he wanted used. Glissade, temps lié, and other complete steps were not given until some skill had been developed in doing the individual movements that make them up. His very detailed approach to dance technique began to give SAB children, from the beginning of their studies, an extra awareness of how it is developed and maintained.

Mr. B was also concerned that the children start to learn a specific modification of the traditional general shaping of the hands. He wanted the thumb curved up, around, and in to touch the side of the last joint of the index finger, which curved in toward the thumb. Each joint in both fingers was to be used to achieve the curve. The middle and ring fingers were curved alongside the index finger, and the pinkie was held gently curved and separated outward from the ring finger (see page 57). This is not what he wanted as an end result from his company and older students, but it set the very young ones on the right path from the first days.

He asked for more musical variety in class than is generally provided in the early years. Again, he wanted to start laying the groundwork right from the start. Since his choreography is often made on more complex music, he wanted the children to start learning early how to find the counts in any music. In addition to the conventional tunes in 2/4 and 6/8, he wanted his teachers to ask for waltzes, polkas, polonaises, and mazurkas. He also wanted

beginning students to use the same accents and phrasing they would use later. Tendu battement, for example, was done with one count to point, then stay two, three, four; and close in one count, then hold two, three, four. They did not take four counts to point the foot and four counts to close the foot.

The early training in a syllabus like his can be very tedious. Serious, disciplined study begins at an age when most children are used to being entertained as they are being taught. That is probably truer today than it was when Mr. B developed his ideas. But he never forgot that his own first inspiration to take his studies seriously came from performing. Maybe that is one reason why he used children in many ballets: *The Nutcracker*, *Harlequinade*, *A Midsummer Night's Dream*, *Coppélia*, the "Costermonger" section from *Union Jack*, "Garland Dance" from *Sleeping Beauty*, *Mozartiana*. The opportunity to perform and everything it involves give an extra incentive to come to class regularly and to pay attention and work hard once you are there.

He believed that very young students should have a limited number of classes; that only at about age eleven or so should they start daily lessons. SAB still works on that premise. The class schedule for the younger children allows for attendance at regular schools and full participation in family life until the child is old enough that the faculty can see that she has real professional potential. By about fourteen or fifteen, children with professional potential should expect to be in a special academic school with a flexible schedule that allows for their many dance classes, rehearsals, and performances.

Many of the advanced students at SAB and most of the members of the New York City Ballet began their studies elsewhere. Mr. B's experience and that of the school since his death is that a dancer can learn his technique, even coming to SAB as late as sixteen or even seventeen, if the dancer is sufficiently advanced for her age. The range of places at which former NYCB principal dancers received their early and even their professional-level training is very wide. They came from all across the

United States and from companies in Europe, especially the Royal Danish and the Paris Opéra. The dancer new to Balanchine must show the potential and the desire to change so she can learn to move in a new way. Also important is that any dancer learning his technique be musical.

Talking in the seminars about teaching children, Mr. B would say, when someone asked a detailed question about the "best" way to help them learn some specific element of the technique, "Use what works, what gets the result. You just teach them, but in the end (meaning when the step is done by an advanced student or a professional), this is what it should look like." So children and even professionals could have learned a variety of ways to do a step, but if they had really learned that way at their level, had full control of the technique offered to them, he could teach them how to dance his way, if they wanted to learn. That is the key question: Do they want to learn to dance his way?

Mr. B's interest was in how ballet looked in his 1 percent of the ballet world. He was always the first to acknowledge that there are many other ways to dance ballet and that each of them can be "right" for other choreographers and for other company directors and teachers. He just wanted us to dance his way so his ballets looked the way he wanted.

In his preface to the Stuart/Dyer book, Mr. B said it would be useless to try to learn to dance sitting at home reading. That goes for this book, too, but I will go beyond his statement, because it is a lesson I take from my own experience with him and from watching many dancers pass through the company since I joined it in 1959. The most important factor is that the dancer be willing, if necessary, to let go of her prior schooling to absorb Mr. B's way. The more advanced the dancer, the scarier that can be. Absorbing his way can mean losing confidence, a certain security, and even some steps an advanced dancer has had for a while. She might

have been able to do a double or triple pirouette from fourth, as long as the fourth was the small one with two bent knees that is generally taught. Trying to pirouette Mr. B's way, from his large, lunging fourth with a straight back leg, facing the corner, yet spotting front, might mean she has trouble getting to pointe, finding her balance, and/or difficulty finding her spot.

Some dancers he tried to teach could not let go of what they had in order to learn something new, and we still see that today. Somehow they could not take the temporary two steps back that are sometimes necessary to get the next *jeté* forward. Because of his experience trying to get dancers to change, he loved the folk saying "You can lead a horse to water, but you can't make him drink." Finally, it is always up to the dancer; or, "Teacher suggests, but dancer must do."

Mr. B's way to dance is much more demanding than any other I know, but for any dancer who wholeheartedly embraces it, there is an incomparable reward. The Balanchine dancer moves with far greater freedom as she devours space. The expanded range of motion and the contrasts in direction and accent give her an enhanced clarity in motion. The ways she shapes and energizes every part of her body make her far more radiant. She can absorb the impulse to move in a much wider variety of music, including pieces at much faster and much slower tempos. She is quite simply more beautiful.

When I joined Mr. B's company, I was not a bad dancer. But I remember how good I felt as, little by little, I changed and came to look more and more as he wanted us to look. Nothing in my career pleased me more, before or since.

For any dancer who learns to dance Mr. B's way there is the chance to move like a Balanchine dancer and thus to join those of us who live and have lived in his 1 percent of the ballet world. This makes us a family, his family.

From the Studio to the Stage

No teacher can succeed by simply copying what another teacher does in class, but we can all benefit by understanding and thinking about the ideas behind another teacher's corrections and methods. This is even more true when we encounter an especially effective teacher. Balanchine's approach to class was unorthodox, but I liked the way his dancers moved, and I learned from his example. I do not teach exactly as he did, but I generally know what his purpose was, and I try to find my way to help the students achieve a result in keeping with his aesthetic.

In a perfect world, one with limitless time and tireless dancers, Balanchine's "ideal" class (not that "ideal" was a word he would use) would include many variants of each step. Jumping steps would be done in their basic form and then, when possible, with beats; exercises at the barre on flat would then be done, when possible, on demi-pointe by men and on full pointe by women; steps in place would, when possible, then be done traveling to the front, back, and sides. Any exercise that could be reversed would be done that way. And every exercise would be done to a wide range of tempos. But Balanchine was completely practical, believing in working without reservation with the time, the dancers, the music, the space—in short, with whatever he had. He did not trouble himself because ideal conditions could not be. He worked in each day's company class with steady concentration, usually on a few related technical elements, leaving many others to be dealt with on another day.

It is not uncommon for a company teacher to have a fairly set routine for class that is in effect a full-body warm-up at the barre, followed by a variety of center exercises such as adagio; tendus; pirouettes; small, medium, and large jumps; and a beating step. Another teacher may have a warm-up routine that varies the barre and center exercises by the day of the week. In contrast, Mr. B's class had as its impetus a specific artistic idea: that we dance better and better, that we move more beautifully and interestingly onstage. Because everything we did in class was done to make us better onstage, what he saw in performance was often the reason for including certain of the exercises the next day in class. He noticed details onstage that he thought we could do better or that were becoming unclear. The next day in class we would do exercises focusing on those details.

It is also often useful for a company teacher to be ready with combinations that are specially apt for ballets about to be rehearsed and/or performed. Because Mr. B was an active choreographer who also taught his company, the combinations he set for us in class very often turned up in some form in the next hours or days in rehearsals of new works.

Mr. B did not write anything out in advance for

the class. Instead, he looked at the way each exercise was done and decided what we needed to do next. In other words, even though what he saw in the performance gave him some preliminary ideas for class, he kept adjusting based on what he saw in the way each exercise was done. New teachers typically try to set most of a class in advance. I did that in the beginning, and Mr. B had to persuade me instead to use my eyes to determine what to give as the class went along. "After the first step at the barre, you will know what they need. Maybe even do the first step again," he said.

A good class from Balanchine's point of view was one that began to get a result, that got us to start to develop or change. He wanted us to make progress toward what he was teaching or at least to know what the goal was. He tried to persuade us that a good class from our point of view was one in which we recognized what he was teaching and put maximum effort into achieving it.

On occasion he asked some company members, "How was class at SAB today?" They typically replied, "It was a good class." To most dancers, most of the time, that means they were pleased because the class made the dancer feel good, the barre was neither too short nor too taxing, and the combinations were fun to do—jumps for jumpers, turns for turners—and no pressure, no real insistence that mistakes be corrected, that they do better. This annoyed him and he would try again, asking how they, the dancers, did. "How did *you* do?" he would ask. His point was to get each of us to focus on how well we had done in the class: on how well we had understood what the teacher taught, on how well and how hard we had worked, not on how much we enjoyed the exercises the teacher gave.

The dancer does not go to class expecting to feel safe and comfortable. A good class should make the dancer reach for the best she can do technically and then a little beyond that. The little beyond her best should make her feel a little at risk, a little uncertain of the immediate outcome. Meanwhile, the teacher provides direction, technical support, and encour-

agement as the dancer tries to progress. To do her best, the dancer must focus completely on the dancing. That focus will help foster her emotional commitment, enthusiasm, and *joie* in dancing. The teacher helps keep these strong by recognizing progress as it comes and maintaining confidence when it seems not to. The stimulus of working with spirit will help give each person's dancing the special life that to Mr. B was an essential complement to the technique.

Because dancers are entertainers, they need an active sense of offering something to the public. They need to "sell themselves"—that is, their true selves, not a mask they compose for effect. Mr. B wanted us to show or model ourselves. He talked of our "showing," "presenting," and "serving" when indicating the way to do our steps. Mere proficiency was not enough; for him, four pirouettes, ten pirouettes were meaningless if there was no beauty in what the dancer was doing. This point of view is built up from the first barre exercise, from the smallest details of every exercise in class.

Balanchine had a concise definition of dance. He said it is movement of the human body, in a limited space, in relation to time. The neat brevity of that definition is typical of his economical way of speaking without pretension or affectation. As a ballet dancer, teacher, and choreographer, he practiced one form of dance. He was confident in his aesthetic, which was rooted in classical ballet. He knew what his work was, and he set about doing it. His work, ballet dancing, began with the first exercises at the barre and was guided by a consistent view of what should be seen in performance.

To obtain the kind of performance he wanted, he required Balanchine dancers. The commonly accepted notion of the Balanchine dancer makes physical type—long and thin—central. However, there was a wide variety of shapes and sizes when I was a member of the New York City Ballet, which shows that the commonly accepted notion is more true for others than it was for him. Mr. B looked for pleasing proportions, whatever the overall size, but he generally insisted on the potential to achieve certain qualities of movement. To me, the key characteristics of the Balanchine dancer are achieved through working in his technique, starting in class, at the barre. There is no other way to develop quickness; speed; energy; legibility of gesture; full articulation of every step; a sensitive response in movement to any part of the music; a natural, open face; and an individual nuance within the overall dance design. "Make it interesting."

Dancers working in the Balanchine aesthetic still need these qualities. Because standards steadily rise and because there is tough competition for every job, dancers also need a very strong technique. In Balanchine ballets the corps usually dances as much as the leads, often the same steps. However, their dancing cannot just be a display of technique; it needs to demonstrate the key Balanchine characteristics.

There will always be some students who become professional dancers if they move well, even if they lack some element of the technique. In most cases they will prevail because they have the qualities of movement required in a certain aesthetic, such as those I offer as the keys to Mr. B's. And they will prevail because the way they move shows enthusiasm and joy in being a dancer. However, their commitment should keep them working to strengthen and improve their technique. This work should continue even after they become professionals.

Even some soloists and principals lack an exceptionally strong technique, but this is not new. Certain dancers in every generation have had remarkable individual qualities that grew naturally as they studied and were cultivated or brought out as they worked. In Balanchine's day these dancers originated more roles—or even stimulated him to modify existing roles—to take advantage of what they had. Through his casting, choreographing, and rehearsing, Mr. B actively worked to enhance the special gifts of those dancers in each generation who had an extra dimension beyond technique. Anyone who regularly saw his companies from the 1920s to the 1980s will have favorite dancers. Some of the most celebrated of his principals had specific steps they could not do or did not look good doing, but they all *danced*. For Mr. B the desired result was that the audience see the dance and the dancer.

It is the teacher who must find a way to obtain maximum effort and constant striving to master every aspect of the technique while allowing the dancer's individual gifts to develop. Yes, Mr. B wanted a tall, slender body, a long foot, good turnout, high extension, extreme quickness, mastery of every step in the vocabulary, refined musicality, and on and on . . . and yet, it was the dancing *person* who finally engaged his attention. Even though they must constantly insist on the best possible execution of the entire technique, teachers need to remember where it is to be used. They must remember that they are not drilling soldiers or training circus performers and that very few ballets call for dolls or robots.

Mr. B taught clarity, musicality, purity of form, and simplicity. Any overt display of personality was superfluous; there was no place for any play-acting or hard sell. "Don't pretend to dance," he would say. He wanted the dance to speak for itself, guided by the music. The result could be romantic, chic, passionate, sad, elegant, sensual, mysterious, flirtatious, witty, etc. When the choreography called for the dancer to go onstage and take a pose before starting, Mr. B wanted us to walk quickly or run to place and set ourselves immediately to dance—no slow processional to place in the grand ballerina manner. "Run like a sandpiper," he said, meaning fast legs and feet and no noise. When the dancer had finished, he wanted a brief, modest bow and then quickly off. We were not to stand out there and woo the house for more applause.

Mr. Balanchine's classes had only one purpose: to prepare us to dance his ballets better and more in keeping with his aesthetic. Balanchine was the one who said, "I don't teach health." Class was not a generalized warm-up or conditioning, not even the barre. The company schedule allowed no time for that, even had he been willing. We were expected to start class ready to work full-out on the technique of classical ballet, meaning that some of us had to warm up before class began. The purpose of class-work was to give our movement the qualities required for a beautiful and interesting performance. The goals were refinement, control, articulation, and the highest possible levels of skill and finesse, all aimed at making real, if only briefly, the idealized beauty of the human body.

We worked on perfecting the movements specific to ballet. Balanchine thought of classical technique as a language with its own vocabulary, rules of grammar, capitalization, punctuation: A stop in fifth was like a period, dance phrases were separated by implied commas and connected with pliés, and so on. Whatever the specific aspect we were trying to develop, he made sure we never lost sight of its function in the overall scheme.

It's as if the dancer speaks with her legs and feet. To Mr. B, the clarity of steps, all steps, was equivalent to good enunciation. Just as a person speaking has to say each word clearly for the complete meaning to be conveyed, so too Mr. Balanchine made us understand that each gesture, each step had to be clearly legible for the audience to see and appreciate the beauty of the movement as a whole. Even when we were working most intensely to extend ourselves in one way or another, to do a certain step as we had never done it before, we could not throw away what came before, nor what followed. Participating fully in the present moment really meant participating fully in each of the many moments.

Mr. B would remind us that the Greek orator Demosthenes had to put pebbles in his mouth and practice speaking aloud to learn to enunciate clearly. Otherwise, how could he address the Athenian assembly? In the same way, we needed to learn to clearly and beautifully articulate our movements; otherwise, how were they to be seen across the orchestra pit and to the back of the house, to the top of the house? So we repeated them over and over in a variety of combinations and at the widest possible range of tempos.

Mr. B often used very simple combinations to remind us what classical form entails—for example, échappé sauté, jump to second and jump back to fifth. He could start by correcting anyone whose starting fifth position was not exact (feet crossed and glued together, no toes sticking out, legs properly turned out). Next, he would watch to see if we made a good plié and then, when we pushed off the floor, that we took ourselves into the air with the chest lifted and the hips up, and then he would look to see if our legs had opened—POW!—to second position (an immediate, precise second; no splitting way out and pulling back into second), and if our feet had pointed instantly, as we made a beautiful picture in the air. Finally, he would see if we landed on the tips of our toes and came down through our feet in second position, bringing our heels forward (with the same precise spacing between them) and knees side, with the weight over the balls of the feet. "No noise! Like bird landing on eggs," he would say, "catch yourself and descend." Jumping from second back to fifth would be looked at with the same care. And, of course, the upper body and the timing all through. If the details in the dancing are not precise in class, there is a great risk that the steps will lose their distinctive character when the dancer is onstage.

As with any other language, classical ballet fluency is built up through regular drill in the smallest elements. By working in class to perfect the smallest details and then integrating them into combinations, he expected that onstage the bigger movements and longer dance phrases would be clearer. Once, I was in the wings watching the performance, and one of the soloists onstage, while executing a series of en dedans pirouettes, was carelessly slapping her foot to the floor, letting her heel go back and her leg rotate in as she stepped into plié, rather than placing her toes to the floor, bringing her heel forward, and maintaining the turnout in her whole leg. Under my breath I muttered, "Place your foot, heel forward, all the time, every time." I was startled to hear Mr. B answer, "Oh, *yes, that's* right, Suki!"

In some traditional classes you might hear the teacher say, in giving tendus at the barre, "Now, point your foot on one and flex it on two." We didn't practice flexing. Balanchine believed that anyone can flex, but that what is hard to achieve is the beautiful, refined pointe. Or some places, the teacher might say, "Tendu, turn in the leg, now rotate it out, and close." We never practiced turning in. "We are born with our feet and legs parallel," Mr. B would say. What's hard to achieve is the ninety-degree rotation outward from the hip.

I know that is true, but on rare occasions, when I see that a few of my intermediate or advanced students have forgotten some aspect of shaping the foot or of turning out, I might refresh their memories by giving one of these "special exercises." So I look heavenward and ask Mr. B's indulgence and then I set the combination. If, for example, they are not pointing the ends of their toes sufficiently, I will give a combination with pointing, then flexing, and pointing again. Or I may see that my students are not using their turnout to the maximum. So I give battement tendu, rotate the leg in and then rotate it fully and completely out. Such exercises can sometimes help the students better understand how to fully point the foot, how to turn out completely and from what part of the body. Perhaps Mr. B's greater consistency was a sign that in his view, professionals, unlike students, should no longer need that occasional brief reminder.

Mr. B worked consistently in class for maximum turnout. He knew that only a very few were completely turned out, so he conceived his exercises at the barre to help us develop our best possible turnout in both legs, but with a priority on the working leg. It was essential to show the working leg and foot fully turned out, because that was the one that was actively moving and thus the one the audience saw most clearly. "Do your maximum," as Mr. B put it. The maximum possible turnout in the working leg also enhances the viewer's sense that the foot is being presented or served and by implication that the dancer is offering or serving something—a glass of champagne, perhaps—to the public. Meanwhile, the supporting leg had to be in a knee-over-toes alignment, even if that meant there had to be some accommodation in the amount of

turnout on it. It is important that in each exercise the dancer works on achieving her best possible turnout: leg rotated out and heel forward.

Recognizing that each one of us was different, he sometimes gave a dancer specific, individual suggestions on what detail to consider in order to enhance the look of her turnout. Sometimes he would take the working leg in the air and turn it out for us, thus instilling in us the look our leg and foot should have.

Balanchine did not like to theorize, even about something as central to ballet aesthetics as the turnout. If pushed in an interview, he would simply say we turn out because it is beautiful. But when I was preparing to take over the New York City Ballet lecture demonstration program, I felt I needed something more to tell the public, so I went to him and asked if he could explain to me why ballet dancers turn out. Mr. B got up and, putting his feet in a tight little "V" and mimicking a bulky woman tilting forward, said, "In the old days, dancers wore long dresses with bustles, they had big hips and breasts, and they hardly moved, maybe just a minuet with a little bit of turnout." Widening his "V" and mimicking a fashionable lady closer to our time, wearing a romantic-era tutu, he said, "Then the dresses got shorter and we turned out more and we danced more." Opening his feet to a correct first and standing up as straight as he wanted us to be, he said, "We really move. Now we dance in leotard and tights, we are thin, and people see the whole body." He thought for a moment and said, "We turn out for the same reason poets write beautiful poetry." I thought, writing poetry is harder than writing prose. Poetry is stripped down to the essentials, and it is beautiful. We strive for the same effect dancing in leotard and tights.

This is not to say that Mr. Balanchine did not use the "natural" flexed foot and "natural" parallel feet in his choreography. In the First Theme of *The Four Temperaments,* for example, the dancers flex their feet and then point them to show even more beautifully the stretched foot. They also turn their legs in and then out to show the contrasting lines.

On the stage, in his ballets, Mr. B used what was needed to obtain the desired effect, but in class he developed our classical technique.

Balanchine learned to dance at the Marinsky in the tradition of the Russian Imperial Ballet. He took the classes everyone took, but he must have watched what was going on with supernormal insight. He even looked at what he wasn't supposed to see, as when he watched through a keyhole while the ballerinas rehearsed. He noted some technical details that day, such as how they rose to pointe and came down. He must have watched some part of the work in that way every day. He knew and never lost interest in all the intricacies and expressive potential of the Petipa classicism in which he grew up, even though he extended it. He could always be somewhat amused when he saw that he had made a combination that focused on a particular kind of step or movement in a way he could not recall having seen. For example, he once gave a combination at the barre with all kinds of rond de jambe: rond de jambe par terre, grand rond de jambe jeté, battement dégagé front and passé extend to the back, brush to the front with plié and demi-rond to the side straightening the supporting leg, rond de jambe en l'air in à la seconde and passé followed by a grand rond de jambe en l'air closing fifth back; then reversing with a développé back, grand rond de jambe en l'air to the front, close fifth front, passé développé front with plié and a standard fouetté turn (which incorporates a demi-rond) ending in passé, développé front with plié in order to relevé, turning the supporting leg and body to the other side as the working leg remains where it is (another kind of fouetté). This makes arabesque. Close fifth back plié and recover to fill out the music. At such times he might express his delight by exclaiming, "Never been done before!"

Balanchine said, "I never 'became a teacher'; no, I am a person who teaches. Bad dancers 'become teachers.'" He knew the look he wanted onstage, and it was a new, American look, even though the technique was rooted in the classical tradition. This American look was about energy, because Americans are energetic. It was to be expansive, because Americans occupied a whole continent. It was to be open to diverse influences, because America incorporated elements from around the world. It was to be about the future, about becoming, because America was a new society still being formed.

Mr. B taught because he needed dancers with his new look to make his new kinds of dances. He taught dancers how to be classical, but bold, even brash. Careful, picture-perfect dancers in cautious, mistake-free performances were dull. "Don't be polite!" he would sometimes say, referring to small, contained, proper dancing. "No polite dancing. Polite is boring. We don't need that." In America there was no settled tradition of style, repertory, and technique. Classical ballet could be, had to be, made new, because the old kind, imported from Europe, had no settled homes like those that had already been built for the symphony or the opera.

Balanchine was not content simply to pass on what he had learned. He must have sensed very early that what he learned was merely the latest stage in a long evolution. He must have realized that the classical technique he learned incomparably well was both a basis for performance now and the platform on which further developments could be grounded. One of the immediately recognizable characteristics of what is called the neoclassical in ballet is the use of poses and alignments of the body that are outside the strict limits of the classicism taught in imperial Russia. However, Mr. B carried the basic idea of breaking out of Petipa classicism well beyond what anyone else knew how to do and still remain within the ballet aesthetic. To make their dancers as free as Mr. B made his, other people generally had to work in jazz or modern dance or some other idiom. In contrast, he could simply incorporate in the language of classical ballet what he found useful in these other idioms.

To achieve the adaptability he needed so that we could dance *all* his ballets, Mr. B gave us exercises in class in which we practiced exaggerated forms as well as exercises in which we stayed within the standard ballet tradition. The exercises in which we practiced exaggeration showed any one of several characteristics or a combination of them. In a port de bras, the hands might cross the center line of the body, might even seem to be doing something, like taking off a sweater or painting the air. The body might be balanced for a moment off the vertical alignment. In a relevé step the legs and arms might swing, or seem to swing, echoing a jazzy strut or the Charleston. In addition to the difference in shape, there was often an extreme of tempo, fast or slow. Often the unfamiliar look achieved additional impact through sudden change in direction, by a stretching out over time, or by being done very fast. Exaggerated forms shown in surprising, unexpected ways added interest to the dance design.

Vida Brown, ballet mistress of the New York City Ballet for several years when I was dancing, routinely told the dancers during rehearsals and in the wings, as they were about to go onstage, to "smile, bend, and count." That succinct advice took care of a lot, because it reminded us of three important values for Mr. B: having a pleasant, alert (not fixed) expression, dancing with our whole bodies, and staying very precisely on time. In many, probably most, ballet companies of the time, she would have been wasting her breath. In those repertories, dancers mostly didn't bend, instead affecting a formal-looking stiffness. The conductor often followed the dancers, so counting was less critical. As for smiling, the star system generally provided many chances to play to the house, so dancers learned quickly how to mug, a practice Mr. B very strongly opposed.

Mr. B taught because he choreographed. He taught because dancers who could only do the traditional steps in the traditional way were not prepared to dance in his ballets. His dancers needed to be able to do the extended and larger, or smaller and faster movements he used in his ballets. They also had to be able to execute the steps and other movements of the traditional vocabulary with far greater finesse. He required beauty in the smallest details—placing the foot on the floor, for example.

Mere efficiency was not enough. Had he been content to make dances using only the established classical vocabulary he learned in Russia, his teaching would not have been necessary. Company class could have been given by any of a number of Russian émigré teachers active in New York.

He was dedicated to his teaching, because he wanted his dancers to move in his aesthetic. His dancers needed his presence and all-seeing eye to develop. He felt only he could obtain the effort and energy necessary to get the look he wanted when we danced his ballets. He said, "You cannot just tell them what to do, you must demand, you must insist." He did both.

One day he went up to a girl who was not making much effort while doing frappés at the barre. He asked her if she wanted to dance; distractedly, she said yes. He asked her again and she lackadaisically said yes. This went on quite a while, he asking and she yes-ing until she lost her patience and answered loudly and emphatically, YES! He said, "Oh, now I believe you. Then *show me*."

Some dancers had a habit of chewing gum in class, even though it was not permitted. Balanchine wanted all our energy and awareness focused on what he was teaching, so those who wanted to chew needed to try to hide it from him. With his little smile, he would say as he walked around, "No gum allowed, too much effort not to chew."

Balanchine had several very specific ways of fostering a productive working atmosphere in class. The chewing gum story demonstrates a way he had with people that kept a positive, good-humored, pleasant tone. The frappé anecdote demonstrates another: his insistence on seeing a result. He did not trivialize his work by trying to make class "fun," but he also avoided an atmosphere of drudgery, even though the effort required was very intense. His amusing stories and his wordplay, including his puns, also kept the mood interesting and light, while often delivering a subtle, often profound lesson about life. I cannot do what he did in class to get a result. But I try to be guided by my memories of his example and the lessons I draw from them. I share these characteristic and significant memories to try to convey a sense of the way he approached his teaching.

For several reasons he generally did not like to have visitors in company class. The presence of distinguished visitors might, for example, turn the class into a pseudoperformance. Class was a private time when he could work with us to help maintain or try to improve our technique. That always requires criticism, and he did not want to correct or criticize us with outsiders present. Improvement, especially, required that we each feel free to risk, to attempt to do movements about which we were not yet completely secure. In the attempt, a dancer might look silly or at least nothing like her safest best. Our class was the time and the place to try to push ourselves beyond what we knew how to do, with him to guide us.

Mr. B liked to observe that a baby starts to learn to walk by taking very short steps while firmly holding on. A bigger step without support usually means a fall. But in a very short time, after quite a few falls, the baby is walking all over the house. As adults we would be embarrassed by our "falls," but Mr. B wanted us to be free to "fall." In private, he encouraged us to try our next "big steps."

It is fair to say that he viewed company class as more private than stage rehearsals even of new works, when he principally was on the line. He said, "You do a lousy ballet, so what? Sometimes I know it's lousy. It's not a tragedy." There was something very reassuring in the way he shielded us but left himself open to whatever came. He also let us know that his development, like ours, was a long-term affair. Our individual success was not a matter only of this or that step, just as his success did not depend on that "lousy" ballet.

(The School of American Ballet exists primarily to train professional dancers, and in doing that it also shows how ballet dancers are taught and what conditions are necessary for their development. Qualified observers are therefore welcome in the more advanced classes when appropriate arrangements have been made.)

The first days back at work after a layoff, nearly every member of the company would be in class. People would be trying to get off to a good start, to be selected for a new part, to turn over a new leaf, etc. After a week or so the class would dwindle to those of the dancers who were interested in absorbing his lessons so we could dance better. Sometimes he would count and find only about half the company there. "I have thirty dancers here. Where are the other thirty?" he would ask. Everyone else would have drifted off to some place that was less taxing, and perhaps some found a relaxing warm-up and/or a stretch class.

Since his classes worked specifically to improve our skills, he was very aware of the effect on us of taking class with other teachers. He noticed details in the way we worked that could not have come from him. He would tell us, "Maybe I should make you pay and then you will come and remember. Instead, I give you this class for nothing." Sometimes Mr. B would give us a correction in class in a stage whisper. Holding his index finger before his mouth with a mock conspiratorial air, he would say, "Don't tell anyone over at Ballet Theater, not even Lucia Chase!" He thought that by making a "secret" of his correction, we would pay closer attention and value more what he said. He was right; it nearly always worked.

Although I took class from time to time from other teachers in New York when Mr. B wasn't teaching, I only missed his class when I was too sick to take it. Company class was the center of Mr. B's 1 percent of the ballet world. Having had the good luck to land there, I was not about to let any opportunity to learn from him pass me by.

Even though he seemed to ask where the rest of his dancers were, he certainly knew the answer. Some of the older, more established dancers in any company will have reached their peak and will prefer a more comfortable class that is more traditional, with a predictable routine. They can seem afraid (some with good reason, due to past injuries) to put their bodies in an unknowable situation. They will be the ones who don't come even on the first day back, because they have the ballets they usually dance and they are not looking for anything more. Even so, they still can be highly skilled, know a lot of repertory, and have years of experience, so they still are valuable members. But usually they were not the ones Mr. B wanted to teach, so I think there was a tacit understanding about their not coming to his class.

Some younger dancers also don't want to put out the kind of effort that Balanchine wanted to see in class, and they may in general just not want to work so hard. So they may sleep a little later, they may find an easier or a later class, they may warm themselves up with their own routine and show up just when called for rehearsal and when on for the performance. Even in the ballet world, there are people with varying levels of ambition and commitment, despite the fact that it takes more ambition and commitment than most people will give to get there at all.

Balanchine even taught during some of our layoffs, and in the late 1960s he offered a class on our day off; we called it the "Monday class." Only a few came to those classes, because there were no rehearsals and no performances to prepare for. We came because we wanted everything he could teach us. I came, and I think the others came, because we wanted to learn and to change the way we danced, and we were ready to put out the effort. He seemed pleased to work with this enthusiastic quarter of his 1 percent of the ballet world.

Among the non-NYCB professional dancers who came to SAB in the 1970s to take class were Rudolf Nureyev and Mikhail Baryshnikov; like many other professionals, they were attracted to Stanley Williams's Advanced Men's class. Sometimes the class would applaud the stars' execution of a particularly showy or difficult combination. When Mr. B heard about the applause, he was not pleased. He did not want applause in class for anyone. It sets the wrong tone. Class is not a performance; each person is there to improve from the level already attained. That included Nureyev and Baryshnikov. In that sense, everyone was "equal,"

even if some could do this or that step better than the others.

Similarly, Mr. B did not accept the traditional round of applause at the end of class when he taught the company. He usually ended class by saying "That's enough for today" as he nodded to us and walked toward the pianist to say thank you. Despite this, we sometimes began to applaud, causing him to say, "No applause, please!" We stopped, and that was that—for that day, anyway. He was there to work with us and with the classical technique. We were there to try to dance better, which is not easy. He was there to help us, and in doing so to see what worked best in getting us to change, which is also not easy.

We needed his technical and his human insight as much as we needed his presence. All three were necessary if we were to be Balanchine dancers. They were even more necessary if we were to improve our dancing and if the technique was to develop. He adapted to himself the old saw dancers use about being away from class. He would have to go away for a few days and left us taking class and working in rehearsal with his ballet masters. When he came back and taught his first class, he would tell us, "After one or two days away, I know; after a week, other dancers will know; and, after a month, everyone knows."

Every day he came to class with something to give us that required our full attention and maximum effort to make progress. "If you want to take it easy, go sit on a porch in Saratoga and rock," he would say jokingly, referring to the many elderly residents and spa visitors we saw there during the early years of our annual summer residency. Since he was there ready to work, that was not a choice.

He took complete responsibility for watching, for seeing exactly what we were doing and how we were doing it. It was his job to explain how to do the steps better, as well as to demand the additional effort needed to accomplish that. Seeing us fixated on our images in the mirror, he would say, "Don't look! Show! I'm here to look." He was very clear that it was our job in class to do and his to watch. "Don't think, dear. Do!" he would tell us.

Even worse than staring in the mirror was a dancer touching her body to remind herself of what she was doing or to reassure herself that she was doing as she should. "Is my hip down?" a dancer might wonder, and the wayward hand would check and invariably the hand looked out of place. And it was out of place! So even if the hip line was perfect, the hand touching the body ruined the overall appearance. In addition, a dancer can't use her hand to check herself onstage. Why get in the habit of using it in class, rather than memorizing the feel of the line, to know if her position is correct? We had to know where each part of our body was without looking in the mirror or down at ourselves, and above all, without touching ourselves. In other words, we had to feel the line, not feel ourselves.

Mr. B liked to tell us that a snake, no matter how long, no matter how many curves in its body, always knows where its head and tail are. The head might be far away, but it knows what the tail is doing. He wanted his dancers to be like that, to be aware of every part of the body from the tips of the fingers to the tips of the toes.

As often as he said not to think, Mr. B still wanted intelligent, thoughtful dancers and believed in the mind working together with the body. At one time the New York City Ballet included a young woman with a perfectly exquisite body who was a real beauty. At the same time, we had a brilliant young man who compensated for his not ideal body by using his unusually quick and thoughtful mind. By conscientious and intelligent daily practice, he was able to continually change, develop, and improve. He eventually became a principal dancer. Talking about them one day, Mr. B said, "If those two were one person, we would have the most wonderful dancer—her body and his brain." He was not really interested in dancers who don't think; he just did not want dancers who calculate their effects. He simply expected us to think at the right times and on the right subjects. Seeing per-

formances from out front was a good time to think.

Because of the injury I had while we were on tour in Russia in 1962, I couldn't dance for six weeks. So every night I was out front watching the performance. I could see how certain dancers, even some in the corps, moved beautifully, interestingly, each with her own individual perfume or flavor. They had not fallen into predictable routines of perfectly proficient, but dull and matter-of-fact dancing. By the time the *Nutcracker* season opened in New York, I was back onstage. After my first performance, Mr. B came to me and said, "Good! You look good. What happened? You've changed, you're different."

I said, "I've been out front, seeing the performance every night. I try to figure out why my eye goes to the same people night after night. I think I understand better what is really important." What I did not say to him, because I did not need to, is that I wanted him, and the public, to look at *me*.

Using our brains at the right time meant using them on the important aspects of the lessons. He was no ballet pedant. In class he could ask us, "What flavor of plié shall we do today? Chocolate or vanilla?" (meaning, for example, music in two or three, or a combination with demis or just grand, and so on). Or, while showing, "What arabesque is this? Number twenty-five?" Learning names of steps, especially the more elaborate and arbitrary aspects, such as the numbers of arabesques, was less important than knowing how to do them. He wanted us to know the basic terms for the movements and poses. Then he wanted us to really show each movement clearly and understand how the step should look, the aesthetic.

Of course, Mr. Balanchine knew the traditional names for all the steps and poses and orientations and so on. He considered alternatives that would be more specific, more precise, especially to Americans. What we could understand was colorful language with lots of colloquial expressions. Many of his most effective personal expressions were drawn from some part of American pop culture, and they showed he had a very sensitive ear for language and meaning. These were often used as a way of being very direct, very succinct. Although he never lost his accent, he expressed himself extremely well. He knew exactly what he wanted to say and found a way to say it with just the desired effect.

On the other hand, Mr. B did not use colloquialisms that served no expressive purpose, such as "okay" instead of yes. In fact, he even encouraged new teachers at SAB in the use of correct English, because he wanted us all to be good examples in every way to the students. Younger dancers identify not only with company dancers but also with teachers, and they imitate them as much as they can. He also did not use foul language and did not appreciate it from others. It was one of his ways of showing reverence for the place we were in and for the work we were doing. All the dancers, the professionals and the students alike, were to acknowledge that we were very privileged to work in such a special place, and he wished us to behave accordingly.

Mr. B often suggested that a dancer might need two little black books, the usual one for addresses and telephone numbers and the second one for notes from class with corrections on how to do the steps. The act of writing this material down helps the dancer remember what to do, why to do, and how to do, and helps clarify the focus of each exercise. He sought to have us understand corrections not simply as remedies for the problems with particular steps, but also for general knowledge of the principles of movement. Once a dancer understood the underlying reasons for a correction, there was greater likelihood that she could work effectively on her own. "The disaster," he said, "is not knowing you are wrong. First, you must know you're wrong, then you must know where you are going, what the step should look like. When you can do correctly, then you may break the rule. You have a choice. But first you must be able to do correctly."

He believed that as professional dancers we should be able to practice and work alone, although that is not generally a good idea in earlier training. In fact, he often suggested to a dancer that she take one step and work on it alone every day for a month. In class he could help us learn what we needed to do to obtain the desired improvement, but he would not usually be able to spend enough time on it in class to get the desired result from every one of us. Remember, "The teacher suggests, the dancer must do"; he could have said that the dancer must do and do and do and do until she has it. The first week we could do several daily sets of sixteen battements tendus, for example, at a moderate-to-slow tempo. Our aim would be to perfect the action of the leg and foot. The second week, our sets of sixteen could be a little faster, the third week faster still, and the fourth week as fast as we could do them. "By the end of the month, you'll be surprised what will happen," he would assure us. He knew we would somehow get better, but because we were all different, at different rates, so he did not tell us what would happen or when it would happen. He looked forward with the same anticipation we had to see what the change would be.

A dancer might tell him she could not find time to practice. Jokingly, he might ask her if she cooked at home. If she said yes, he would suggest that, while stirring the soup, she practice her ronds de jambe, which is also a round, continuous motion. Or he would suggest working on shaping the hands while waiting for the bus or talking on the phone, or perhaps do stretches during TV commercials.

Mr. B disapproved of older or out of shape teachers who demonstrate movements "full out," in tempo, and to the right and the left. It can be a temptation, since most of us are retired performers. "But who wants to see?" he would ask. Most important to Mr. B is to remember that the class time is the students' time. Mr. B usually gestured or marked the steps we were to do, setting the tempo and adding a very few, very apt words as he went. However, his movements were clear and expressive of the music and dance qualities he wanted. We usually knew exactly what was required moment by moment in timing, shape, accent, energy. If our execution showed we did not know, it was his job to stop us, correct us, and do whatever else was necessary to get his meaning across. We could not always achieve his objective right away, but it was imperative that we know what it was.

Preparing his dancers for the stage meant making us better dancers so we would move more beautifully, more freely. Nothing was done in class just to make our muscles feel good, make us feel good. Balanchine said, "Nothing in ballet class is for your health, nothing is for the stretch in it. It's for the beautiful movements that we can learn to make. Then we take those movements and put them into the ballets." He said, "If you want to stretch and feel good, go to the health club, do Pilates, get a massage—that's fine!"

Sometimes when you go to a conventional ballet class, the teacher gives a port de bras forward, saying, "Now reach and stretch way out, lengthen out, now put your hands on the floor and put your nose to your knee and s-t-r-e-e-e-t-c-h on coming up, reach away, reach, reach!" Those dancers now have an exercise about lengthening the spine and keeping it straight like a board, about stretching the backs of their legs or some other anatomical or physiological idea.

Instead, Balanchine took the key ring out of his pocket and said, "Pretend it's a flower." He then put it on the floor in front of a dancer and said, "Take a breath, look down and see that flower, now you bend forward to pick it up and, then, as you come up, continue to look at it." By setting a little scene, he gave us a reason drawn from life to bend over and stand up again. He also gave us an approach to that movement that suggested the quality it should have. The whole gesture could look beautiful, because it was not just a stretch. No dancer in his class was just bouncing her nose on her knee. He wanted a complete integrated movement with all the parts of the body coordinated so we were as beautiful as we could be.

Very often in his ballets, Mr. B gave the corps and soloists, and even the principals, relatively straightforward ports de bras or basic movements such as battement tendu. It could even be repeated several times or done en masse. Because our focus was always on beauty, even in the most basic exercises in class, he could be confident that very simple material would look beautiful onstage. What is simpler than battement tendu, the step he gives the dancers arranged in a "U" open to the audience in the finale of *Symphony in C*? Another personal favorite of mine is the port de bras forward and back in a lunging fourth, which he gave Patricia McBride as Columbine in Act II of *Harlequinade*. There are many more examples of the most basic classroom exercises being taken intact into the ballets. It was natural for him, because in class his constant focus was on beautiful movement.

Balanchine often noted that the human body is very limited. We have only two arms, two legs, two feet. The dancer needs to be aware of every part of her body and the possibilities of each part for expressive movement. In each exercise we had to give form and life not only to the parts primarily involved but to all the rest as well.

He liked to compare the possibilities of the dancer with those of the centipede. He pointed out that the centipede, with one hundred legs, could ignore three or four of them and still come up with something interesting to see. We dancers have only two legs, so he wanted us to use both of them. "We must take charge of them and know what they are doing at all times," he would say. Probably the most important application of this concept was that a foot lifted from the floor had to be properly placed onto it again. It should not be allowed to return to the floor any old way through gravity or inertia, the dancer unaware of where and how it lands. "Place each foot, all two of them," he said.

Mr. B wanted us to be in control of all our movements. When dancers do grand battement, they often throw the leg up to the extended line, and then gravity takes hold and the leg falls down to the floor by its own weight—BANG! But Mr. B wanted the dancer to defy gravity. He wanted us to throw the leg up with speed and energy and then bring it down quickly, placing the foot precisely and silently into fifth position to fit the music, to be on time. The leg was started down faster than gravity would cause and yet the slower, soundless placement of the foot shows the dancer is still in control. He said, "When you *bring* the leg down, that can also be a beautiful movement."

It's only by being in control that we can appear out of control. The greater the control of the technique, the greater the look of freedom and abandon. This principle applied especially to dancing off-balance. Sometimes he wanted us to fall off pointe incorporating a backbend, looking like we would fall over and yet still be in control. In general he wanted us to push ourselves just beyond the safe plane and take a risk. This extends the dancer's technique and lends excitement and variety to each performance.

Suzanne Farrell had an unprecedented facility for dancing "off-balance." She could fall out of turns in a very interesting way. Patricia McBride covered space effortlessly, beautifully. Gloria Govrin had a huge, high, open jump, especially for a woman, and a slow, soft, catlike landing controlled with a very deep plié. Pat Neary showed Mr. B fluent multiple turns, and another dancer had brilliant, fast turns. I had fast, clean beats and I could hop on pointe; Allegra Kent produced an elastic, pliant quality in adagios and had very high extension. Few, if any, could phrase with more nuance than Violette Verdy.

No one of us had it all, of course. When Mr. B noticed that someone could do a certain kind of movement better than he had seen it done before, he would think about how to develop a comparable power or finesse in the rest. Then he would set combinations using that special quality, and he might ask the dancer best suited to demonstrate for us. For example, he would ask a very fast "natural" turner to do piqué turns from the corner as fast as she could; then the rest of us would try to do them that quickly. Sometimes he would ask a second dancer, who was less adept at that step, to show it, too. He would work with her, giving her corrections and suggestions from which we were all expected to benefit—remember the second little black book! Whatever the exercise, whatever one dancer

could do "naturally," every one of us was expected to work toward that level of proficiency.

On some days Mr. B would decide to do a familiar step in a different way just to explore the possibilities of movement. The different way was not at all a substitute for the familiar, standard form, and it would not be a way to get around some technical difficulty. Instead, it was an experiment intended to explore the possibility of adding something new to his choreographic choices. These ideas also often came from watching us individually.

"Now we're going to do different," he would say. We might have landed from very quick changements the day before with straight knees and no plié and today we would be doing them extremely slowly with a very big plié. Instead of doing grand rond de jambe jeté with attitude he might ask for grand rond de jambe jeté with a straight leg. Once we could do the traditional form of the step and his new form equally well, he could use one or the other or both. In some cases he concluded that his new way was better: very fast rond de jambe par terre without accents, and relevés rolling up and down through the foot, for example. In others he would see he liked them both, and each would turn up regularly in choreography: pas de bourrée with the working knee bent and the working foot lifted to coupé or passé, and pas de bourrée with straight knees.

Mr. B often set exercises that aimed to take us beyond where we thought we could go, beyond what we thought was our maximum. He took each dancer and pushed her to her limit, and when she had reached it, he then asked her for more. It often seemed that he knew each one of us better than we knew ourselves. This approach helped keep each class fresh and interesting as it strengthened our individual classical technique, meanwhile extending the technique as a whole.

Asking always for a little more than we were comfortable doing also helped ensure that our performances were more committed, more energetic, more exciting. A dancer accustomed in class and in rehearsal to working at her maximum—and to working to extend her maximum—gives a fuller, more complete look to each movement onstage. She has nothing left to use on premeditated, calculated effects, nor on fussy, "polite" dancing.

Sometimes when a visitor came into company class, I used to wonder, "What can this person be thinking?" At the barre we could look like we were just shaking our legs as we did very, very fast frappés. Or the company might hardly be able to stand up as we practiced landing with a very slow and very deep plié on one leg from a soaring grand jeté. However, it didn't always matter how something looked at the moment. It was the principle behind the movement—the energy, the attack that mattered. It was our approach to the movement that had to change. Balanchine understood that class was not a performance—and he did not want it to become one—so each exercise could be designed to push the dancer a little past her limit in order to obtain the maximum improvement.

When the commercial was running on the radio, Mr. B liked to underline his incessant demand for more by singing us its jingle, "More Park sausages, Mom." He usually had a nice way to prevent an atmosphere of stress and strain in his classes and in his rehearsals, despite his insatiable quest for higher levels of achievement, for more finesse, for more beauty. A little story drawn from "just folks" life or a banal little jingle could each do the trick. The trick was to make unimaginable an atmosphere of drudgery, even if we were working harder than hard. He could get his point across with a light touch, often with humor. Some of the dancers wanted to come to class as much for the amusing stories and clever puns as for the work itself.

Mr. B was always right there, working with us, encouraging us; if a dancer "got it" now, fine. If a dancer didn't get it, he would persist in a very positive, very encouraging way, "No, I want to see more, you can do more." To dancers who seemed not to be making the maximum effort, he could appear tough; "I don't see *nuttin'!*" he would say. If the dancer still did not achieve what he wanted,

even after trying very hard, he would say, "There's still time."

By setting his standard in class well above the minimum needed just to get by in performance, Mr. B made it more possible to give each of us time to come up to reach it. There were usually some who could do what he wanted with a particular movement, not that their success would allow them to think there was nothing more to do: He would soon enough suggest a different approach to the step that posed a subtly different challenge or find another step that needed improvement. Anyone who needed more time was encouraged to work in an orderly, directed way to master the technique. This prevented a frantic atmosphere.

Mr. B was very definite about the way each step or movement should look. We reached for a higher extension; a deeper plié; better control at extremes of speed, fast *and* slow; a longer, lower line in lunges; more turnout; and so on. He noted what each one of us looked good doing and then cast us appropriately or used our established capabilities in new ballets. Or else he cast us in ballets that were a big challenge to stimulate us to work in a new way. He also noted which ones of us had changed, developed, or improved in class and then often gave us recognition and encouragement by casting us in better roles.

He knew how hard it is to achieve change, especially continuous improvement, and so he liked to tell a story about a Russian peasant trying to get his donkey to go up a hill. Partway up, the donkey stops and won't move. The peasant tries pushing, pulling, kicking, hitting; the donkey won't move. Then the peasant stops and thinks for a minute and says, "Oh, good idea!" He gathers dry grass, twigs, sticks, and arranges them under the donkey. Then, by rubbing two sticks together, he finally starts a fire under the donkey's belly. Success! The donkey moves! It takes two steps and then stops. Mr. B indirectly compared us to the donkey, because he had to work so hard for every little change.

He wanted each dancer to learn, through working at her limit, her complete range of possibilities.

If she knew how fast she could turn, if really pushed, then in music that was fast but not extreme, she would have a stronger sense of being in control, of using just the right amount, because she would have done more. "It's like money," Mr. B told us. "If you have only a dime, that's all you can spend and you get very little. If you have one hundred dollars, you have a choice. You can get a lot or you can get a little." For each movement, he wanted us to be able to choose to do a lot or a little, depending on the choreography and the music.

As I have noted, and it cannot be repeated too often, Balanchine's classes were not intended to be warm-ups or general conditioning sessions. He did not want us to depend on him for that. In working to make us better dancers, he often gave a class or part of a class with a theme based on a detail: movement of the leg and foot in and out of fifth in tendus, a change of épaulement with specific attention just to the line of the neck, correct placement of the foot when stepping onto pointe, taking the foot off the floor through sur le cou de pied, doing a movement with unusual counts, placing the foot on the floor, etc. He worked to develop in us ever higher levels of skill, ever more finesse.

In such a thematic class, we could spend fifteen or twenty minutes on a small detail, on a technical fragment so brief it flashes by in normal performance before anyone in the house is aware of it. Since the dancer's technique can for many reasons become less exact onstage (and even in rehearsal), class is a time when there can be an extreme emphasis on precision. Later in that class or the next day, he often gave an exercise incorporating in a larger combination the detail we had just practiced by itself. He wanted to see our new finesse and skill integrated into the flow of that movement.

Even his larger combinations were often very sharply focused. It's commonly thought that most centerwork for advanced dancers involves lengthy combinations with lots of steps that are almost choreography. In contrast, Mr. B often gave an exercise based on as few as two steps that were repeated eight or sixteen times. For example, he could give passé relevé on "and," plié with the working foot closing front on count one, entrechat six landing on count two. The repetition of such a brief combination in sets of eight permits effective work on refining every detail of the execution.

No one should doubt, however, that helping us build our stamina seemed to be one of Mr. B's aims in class. Usually there were several combinations in each class that left us thoroughly winded. And he often ended with a combination of sixteen slow entrechats six or with one of his personal favorites, thirty-two emboîtés front and thirty-two back. "Just like jogging in Central Park," he liked to say of emboîté back. Very often you can see end-of-class jumping combinations reduced to drills just for stamina. They become a kind of wind sprint for dancers: the whole class dancing, the emphasis on repetition, little or no correction. Classical form can then largely be lost, and the dancers are still in class. What will happen onstage? In contrast, Mr. Balanchine maintained his focus on classical form from the first to the last exercise.

Similarly, no one should doubt that Mr. B's goal in class was to create the most interesting and beautiful flow of movement on stage. The primary way to help us achieve it lay in very detailed, very specific, very fundamental exercises. In rehearsal and in performance we applied to the choreography what we had learned and practiced in class to his longer *enchaînements*. At the NYCB this requires that *everyone* really dance. SAB students focus on technique in class and then apply it in variations classes every week and in a limited number of carefully chosen performances, culminating in the Workshop each June.

When I was new in the company, I worked very hard in class on every technical detail and on an energetic attack. When time allowed, I also took Madame Dubrovska's class at SAB. She noticed my perhaps overdeveloped work ethic and intense concentration and counseled that the stage is different. "When you are onstage, just *dance* and don't worry about the technique," she said. I tell my students every time I stage a ballet that they should enjoy "the dance," because that is what we work for in class. The dancer must work all through every class so her technique becomes second nature to her, so it is always there for her, even when technique is farthest from her mind. Then the difference in the level of technique between the studio and the stage will be small, almost nonexistent.

The thematic approach gave Mr. B other ways to organize his class. On different days or for different exercises, he could emphasize an exaggerated shape or movement, or extreme speed, or slowness, or unusual timing, or some other facet, or any combination of facets. In part he wanted to avoid our slipping into a routine we could follow without paying attention. He wanted each movement in each class to count for us as if it were the last time we could do it and we would be remembered by that last time.

Showing the movement exactly as he had put it on the music is a critical requirement in Balanchine ballets. Fulfilling it is generally straightforward because his steps fit the music so perfectly and follow one another with such clear dance logic. However, there is a special challenge because of the wide variety of music he used and because of the musical sophistication with which he used it. Therefore, although basic musical precision was always a quality he looked for, a more refined musicality was a theme of many classes and exercises. We could do almost any movement in unusual rhythmic patterns, not simply at slower or faster than normal speeds. For example, we might do three fast changements in two counts, two normal changements in two counts, three more fast changements in two counts, and a changement with a count in the air and a count to land. Or he might set a combination in five and ask for music in three or four.

Classwork of the quality expected by Mr. B requires that the dancer begin to prepare for class well before it starts. For many of us, that meant arriving early. I came to the studio at least a half hour before class so I could do a warm-up consisting of a complete barre and some stretches. That was my way of being sure that I was ready physically and mentally—because that personal warm-up helps clear the mind as well as loosens up the body—for whatever would come up in class. Other dancers might do Pilates exercises or a floor barre or go for a swim and some water exercises.

If a dancer was doing the exercises with a preoccupied air, Mr. B would stop and ask, "What are you thinking about? Meeting your boyfriend? You are here now!" He wanted us totally "here now," not just our bodies. Sometimes he might notice a dancer who was doing the exercises absentmindedly, daydreaming, not making the necessary effort. He would come and stand next to the dancer at the barre as if he were giving a private class. By his presence alone, or by making suggestions and giving corrections, he could get the person to put out the needed effort. "Oh, now I see it," he would eventually say, and move on.

DRESS FOR CLASS

Another aspect of the preparation for class is being properly dressed. For Mr. B this was partly a matter of respect for the work we do, the place we do it, and the class. It is also functionally necessary, because the teacher must be able to see the dancer's body. Women were expected to take class in a simple leotard and pink tights; a short skirt was optional. Men were expected to take class in a fitted white shirt and short white socks with black tights. No dancer should take class in anything that hides the body, that is loose or bulky or tattered.

Once in the 1960s, when rubber sweatpants were much in vogue among dancers, Mr. B came to class dressed top and bottom in a rubber sweat suit. We all laughed when he came in and giggled some more as he showed the first exercises—probably with some exaggeration for comic effect—and then asked us if we understood the exercises. Typically, rather than taking a disciplinary tack, he made a little joke we all could enjoy, but he got his point across anyway. The crucial work of a real class cannot be done if the teacher cannot see the dancer.

I never hid in the shapeless rubberized sweat

clothes or in long bulky sweaters, but I did tend to wear black wool tights, since they provided a little coverage from his all-seeing eye, as well as being a little warmer. One day I wore just the pink tights and leotard with a short skirt, and when Mr. B came in he went around poking at various bulky outfits, asking, "What's this? What's this? What are you hiding for?" Then he got to me and said, "I want to see you. Everyone should dress like Suki." Well, I didn't deserve that much credit, because even after that day I usually wore the wool tights. But I knew what he wanted.

Everyone in class was expected to wear neat, serviceable shoes. For men, these were black or white, canvas or kid ballet slippers with elastics; no holes, no tape holding them together, and even if not clean, certainly not unnecessarily grubby. Women took all classes in pointe shoes.

Balanchine wanted his female dancers ready to work on pointe at all times. He expected them to take his entire class, from the barre through the closing big jumps, in pointe shoes. Occasionally, and only partly in jest, he even suggested that the men experiment in class with pointe shoes, so they would get a feel for this way of dancing. Men could benefit from working in pointe shoes, he said, not only because it develops stronger, more flexible feet, but also because it would help them become better partners and increase their understanding of how to teach women and how to make dances for them.

Thus, for Balanchine's women, ballet class was synonymous with pointe class. The pointe shoe was part of the "uniform," and all the classical steps were practiced wearing them. Sometimes this specially made shoe forced the dancer to work a little harder than if she were wearing soft slippers. At other times the extra support provided by the shoe made it a little easier to execute certain steps, including those that did not involve the use of full pointe.

Balanchine expected all the women to wear pointe shoes for the whole of company class, shoes in which we could relevé to pointe and pirouette on pointe. He ruled out the old, battered pointe shoes with the shanks removed that were used in class by the few dancers in other companies who wore pointe shoes at all. These battered shoes were nearly as pliable and soft as the ballet slippers that most women were accustomed to wearing in class. He explained that he not only wanted his dancers to be able to work full-out and completely on pointe in class, he also wanted them to learn to work with this special shoe even when they were not actually on pointe. Simple tendu battements at the barre in serviceable pointe shoes require much more skill than is the case with ballet slippers, and the dancer also builds much more strength and stamina in the feet and legs. By the late 1950s Balanchine also made it a policy at his School of American Ballet that female pupils in the advanced levels work in pointe shoes at all times.

MUSIC IN CLASS

In his choreography, Balanchine was guided by the composer, but in the classroom, the music plays a supporting role; it is not the show. Often, pianists arrive with stacks of music. They come to give a performance, show off, or practice their technique with cascades of notes, trills, crashing chords. Mr. B warned beginning teachers to guard against this, saying, "Watch the pianists, they always want to take over. Pianist should play simply, with exact tempi." Pianists can also be in the habit of "following" the dancers. It is essential that the teacher prevent the pianist from doing this. "Don't watch the dancers, play the tempo," Mr. B used to say.

In class, just the right musical presence is needed, and sometimes this is the minimum. Music is played mainly to mark the tempo the teacher has set for the dancers in the preparation. The music shouldn't hinder or get in the way of the movement, and the music shouldn't try to do the step for the dancer. For example, you often hear the music for grand plié being played in a 2/4, which is too suggestive of a "natural" or "comfortable" division for the dancers. Because the music is evenly divided, the plié, which should be a continuous movement, tends to get divided into demi-plié and grand plié, both going down and coming up, with little pauses at the quarter and halfway marks. In this case the music is interfering with what Mr. B wanted the dancer to be doing. When Mr. B gave a grand plié exercise, he usually asked for an arpeggio or a held chord, or a tune in three. None of these has definite musical divisions that suggest to the dancer that the pliés should be divided in halves or quarters.

When I give a grand battement exercise, I don't necessarily allow the pianist to play a loud, strongly accented march, which most will routinely choose. There is a lot of energy that the dancers hear and therefore feel in that kind of strong beat, but they may not be expending much energy themselves. They may not be exploding out of fifth, and they probably won't be bringing the foot and leg back down sharply to be placed quietly into fifth. In this case the music takes over and the dancers do less. When I ask the pianist for much softer music, the dancers have to put their own effort and physical energy into the step, and they'll know exactly what they are doing. If they put no energy out, nothing will be happening, and there will be no musical camouflage to cover for them.

Frappé is another exercise for which the teacher may want only one chord per measure, in this case not held. To start, Mr. B typically asked the dancers for four frappés per measure. The sound of our toes striking the floor let him and everyone in the class know how musically precise we were. It will also be apparent if the dancers are striking the floor with enough energy. Next, he would ask the dancers for eight frappés per measure and tell the pianist to slow the tempo a little. If the pianist is allowed to play more than just a chord, what will usually come is a lot more notes or louder or both. This demonstrates the tendency of many pianists to "play the step." Dancers can really believe they are moving rapidly and with energy, because they are hearing a lot of sound. Meanwhile, it is harder for the teacher to hear if the frappés are still musically precise and have the right attack. Once again, when the dancers are supposed to be doing more, it is often better to have the pianist do less.

For many exercises in the center, really lively, "dancey" music is, of course, what is needed. However, for certain center exercises, the use of slower music with fewer notes can still be helpful. For example, adagios are often set with four or even eight beats for each développé. But Mr. B would sometimes ask the pianist to play a very slow tempo and ask the dancers to développé in one or two counts. The speed of the développé is the same, or faster, but the change in the tempo fosters a calmer, stretched-out feeling in the music and in the dancer.

Mr. Balanchine did not want pianists to casually choose to play excerpts from the great classics (Tchaikovsky symphonies, Verdi operas, Beethoven concertos, etc.) in class. He believed that great music would not be played in a way that presented it with due care and respect. Some class pianists will not play well enough to accomplish that under favorable conditions. With the many nonmusical priorities of the ballet class (exact tempos, not too much sound, not too much feeling, just the right number of bars, etc.), conditions are quite unfavorable. He often suggested music by composers like Minkus or Glinka, show tunes (*Tea for Two* and the folk-style waltz *Edelweiss* were favorites), and really light fare like *Mairzy Doats*.

The essential idea is that the teacher needs to set the tempo and the movement for each exercise with a clear purpose in mind. Classwork should cultivate a subtle and flexible musical response as well as skill and finesse in the technique. She needs to be sure that the music played supports the work of the class. When Mr. B was unable to persuade a pianist "in love with his own playing" to play as he wanted, he sometimes said, "No music!" He accompanied the exercise himself by counting out loud, or snapping his fingers in tempo. Any teacher with a similar problem might consider such a solution. No music is better than the wrong music.

Balanchine objected to the dancer anticipating

the beginning of a combination by starting before the music. Dancers can get nervous about being late in fast combinations, so they start early or they do the steps faster than the tempo requires. Dancers sometimes also anticipate the end by slowing the final movements, easing into the finish while blurring the steps rather than keeping the tempo. Alternatively, a dancer may resist making maximum effort and putting out maximum energy and therefore move a little lethargically. Or she may involuntarily hang back from a step she finds difficult, almost as if she were hoping it would just go away. It was very important to Mr. B that we start and end on time, fitting our dancing precisely to the tempo.

"The most important thing is to be on time, then it's how you look on time," Mr. B said to us. However, he did not want us to depend entirely on being able to hear the music or on seeing the conductor. In the theater the music from the pit can be drowned out by applause. Instead, Balanchine wanted the timing of the steps to come partly from within the dancer. For example, when I danced *Tarantella* with Eddie Villella, the cue for my entrance was always drowned out by the applause for his variation. So I had to pick up the tempo before the applause and keep it in my body without hearing the orchestra for several bars. The music in class must help the dancer cultivate the musical awareness required to keep the beat accurately, whether or not she can hear anything being played. Frappés and other exercises done to just a chord are excellent training for developing this kind of awareness.

PHRASING

"The audience hates to see something indifferent. They are mesmerized, hypnotized. They go to sleep. When a leg or arm moves too slowly, it is like invisible process. It only annoys people."

Mr. B believed that the dancing in his ballets should not be uninflected, like sand going through an hourglass. Most people think, when they hear the word "hourglass," that he was referring mainly

to slower movements, but he was referring to movement at any speed. He therefore gave every step in class a specific timing and phrasing that the dancer must show in addition to staying on the music. Generally, this would be characteristic of the step as it is generally used, but sometimes he gave something a little different to help cultivate a more sophisticated musicality in us. Dancing the steps with appropriate timing and phrasing gives each movement a clear beginning and destination and makes it more legible and interesting. Thus the dancer works in class to learn each step or movement so she can execute it with the proper timing and phrasing so it has the required look. In addition, she learns to execute it at a range of tempos.

Mr. B asked for special attention to beginnings and endings. If a dancer seemed to creep into the beginning of the movement, he would say, "They're going to fall asleep, dear." By the same token, we had to show that the step had ended: "You have to tell them it's over." He would joke that since most of the audience forgets the middle, we have to be sure to give them the beginning and the end or they go away with nothing. In the way he showed and in his corrections, in his insistence that the exercise be done full out, with maximum energy and focus, he developed this awareness from the beginning of the barre through to the end of class. It is an important part of making the dancer offer or present herself to the public.

The general principle for phrasing is applicable both to the hands and arms and the feet and legs. At moderate and slower tempos the dancer starts quickly, slows slightly, and then moves more quickly before slowing to arrive in the final position or extended line. When the movement is faster, the dancer starts quickly and continues rapidly until just before the end of the movement, when she slows down to reveal the extended line or other final destination, such as placement of the foot in fifth position or the finishing "extra" turnout of a développé.

Mr. B wanted an energetic, on-top-of-the-music attack, so he often said we should throw the leg or swing an arm, but that referred only to the impetus at the start. He did not want to see any uncontrolled endings. Depending on the movement, the dancer resists, turns out, places to give the desired aesthetic effect to the finish. The foot is never banged or slammed to the floor in fifth or any other position. Knees do not snap as the leg extends, leaving the foot and leg to jiggle or rebound from the force. The hand is not flipped out to the side in a careless, throwaway fashion.

Much of the finesse that is required of the Balanchine dancer is in the mastery of his phrasing within the overall requirement that she be on time. It usually develops gradually and without any obvious breakthroughs. Acquiring this finesse brings a subtle, qualitative improvement in the aesthetic pleasure of the dancing that the teacher will need to recognize.

VERTICAL DIVISION OF THE BODY, PLACEMENT

Most people, most of the time, think of the body as divided into horizontal zones. For example, different items of clothing are related to the feet, the legs, the lower torso, the upper torso, and the head, and they all have old, traditional names. In our time, a garment was developed that covered the legs and the torso, and a new name, unitard, had to be invented for it. Dancers and dance teachers also work much of the time with the attention directed to a zone of the body that is defined horizontally. "Point your toes. Place your feet. Stretch your knees. Square your hips. Pull in your stomach." This way of thinking is habitual, and probably necessary, for most of life.

Mr. Balanchine found, however, that the traditional horizontal division of the body interferes in a way with achieving the artistic result he wanted. So even though he generally worked, as other teachers and choreographers do, by setting feet and legs with coordination of the upper parts of the body,

he shifted his frame of reference when defining the dancer's center and front, back, and side. He divided the body vertically, recognizing that what we see from the front or the back is made up of two symmetrical halves. He then brought the halves together and defined center as the line on which they join. Front and back are on that line, and side is on the line perpendicular to it at the center of the dancer's body. One can think of the front-to-back line running from twelve to six on a clock face, and the side-to-side line running from nine to three, with the center of the dancer's body and the intersection of the lines right at the center of the dial.

Balanchine's definition of front, back, and side makes very precise the point at which the dancer aims her foot when she points it. To be front, the toes, the pointe, of her working foot must be right on the center line, in front of her breastbone or navel, rather than almost anywhere vaguely before her. To be back, the toes of her working foot must be right on the center line, in back of her spine. To be side, the toes of her working foot must be right on the line perpendicular to the front-to-back line, directly opposite the supporting heel, rather than anywhere from a little behind to a little in front of it. These directions are applicable from the floor to the highest extension.

Awareness of the vertical symmetry of the body, and of the directions precisely defined based on it, is cultivated all through the class. This begins at the barre, which serves as a straight line reference: The dancer stands at right angles to the barre or facing toward it or facing away from it. In Mr. Balanchine's classes we very rarely stood facing diagonally to or diagonally away from the barre. Maintaining this squared-off relationship provides an assured and constant line of reference that clarifies the location of precisely correct directions and helps recognition of incorrect ones. It also helps to maintain correct alignment of the hips and shoulders. In the center, some exercises were set by Mr. B to have us directly facing the front or the side of the studio; this helped reinforce the awareness of precise directions he started developing at the barre.

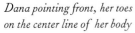

Dana pointing front, her toes on the center line of her body

Dana pointing back, her toes on the center line of her body

Peter pointing side, his toes opposite his supporting heel, on line with his shoulder

The traditional horizontal division of the body tends to foster a major emphasis on maintaining a square alignment of the hips and shoulders, often with the weight distributed over the whole foot. This emphasis can produce dancers who look better in static poses than they do moving around the stage, because "perfect" placement is most apparent when the dancer is not moving. It often leads to smaller, more careful movements, to "polite" dancing. The movement is less plastic, because the finishing and even some transitional poses or positions take priority over the movements or gestures that link them.

A visiting teacher at one of the Ford Foundation seminars in the 1960s noticed that some of the company members doing the class were not "placed" according to traditional standards. "Look at that one," she said to Mr. B, "she's not placed at all."

Without ever looking at us, Mr. B said with a little smile, "What is 'placed'? To me, a dancer is placed when she can stand on one foot without falling over." Mr. B was teasing that teacher, but his underlying point was, as always, that some sort of carbon copy of a "perfect" pose, or of a "perfectly placed" position, was less important to him than that the dancer be ready and able to move in a beautiful way with energy, creating interest in the move-

ment. Perfection, as in "perfectly placed," implies arrival, completion—at that point, there is nothing more to come.

We did work on keeping our hips and shoulders square, especially when the working leg was extended front. Even though he liked high extensions, Balanchine often said that he would rather have a more correct position (leg and foot turned out, hips and torso aligned, even if it meant a slightly lower leg) than hike a hip up or distort the whole body. But his primary goal was that his dancers move with great energy and full commitment to the step, often lending a welcome unpredictability to the dancing and making it harder for the audience to sense what is next. If the dancer is not moving that way, then not much is happening, and to Balanchine that was definitely not good.

THE FOOT, POSITIONS OF THE FEET

Balanchine preferred a long, flexible foot, although, as with his other physical preferences, this was not an absolute requirement. Many schools try to select girls with an extreme arch, but Mr. B did not strongly emphasize this. When the dancer is in relevé, especially on pointe, a very high arch actually shortens the line of the foot and therefore the look of the supporting leg. What mattered most to him was that his dancers used their feet with great finesse, starting with precise positions.

Balanchine was interested in only four of the five long-established, turned-out positions of the feet. He did not set exercises using third position, because it lacks the rigor of fifth, and therefore it did not merit attention in class. He said, "Cecchetti let the back toe show. He was a very nice man, but that was for court dancers. We are ballet dancers. We hide the back foot." The attempts in our times to add parallel positions to the standard five did not interest him, since they are part of everyone's capability; he joked, "Maybe there are six, but I couldn't find the sixth." Just as he did not want to use precious class time for general stretching and warming up, so he did not want to use it to practice skills everyone already has. The parallel positions and third position were, however, occasionally used onstage.

In all positions, Balanchine wanted to see the turnout develop from the hip down. The legs are rotated out from the hips, with the inner thighs, calves, and heels brought forward. Some dancers were more naturally turned out than others, and achieved this full turnout more readily. Balanchine worked with all of us to achieve the desired aesthetic effect, and he expected us to work consistently to apply his suggestions.

Dancers who have less flexibility in the hips may have more flexibility in the knees and ankles. They can use this to supplement to some degree the turnout from the hips. Every dancer needs to master a fully crossed, tight, "glued together" fifth position (as well as comparable qualities in the other three positions). For all dancers, but especially for those who are less naturally turned out in the hips, it is the consistent effort to maintain their maximum turnout that creates the look Mr. B wanted: that the foot is being presented or served or placed.

The positions of the feet apply to all dancers,

when on flat or full foot. The terms "flat" and "full foot" refer to the stance the dancer is in when her entire foot is on the floor. Unfortunately, both terms also convey mental images that are not useful, but there are no better ones. For a discussion of the positions of the feet on pointe and demi-pointe, see page 232.

In first position the backs of the heels are touching, the toes pointing directly to the side. The knees are also directly to the side, so that in plié the knees go out over the toes. Mr. B called it "a flat position." When standing on two feet, the weight is mostly over the balls of the feet, not settled into the heels, as the thighs lengthen up into the hips, which are over the feet. Side, as we have seen, was defined by Balanchine to mean directly side, not toward the front and not toward the back; a straight line should run along the center line of the feet. Sometimes dancers have a little more flex in the knee and ankle and will make a small adjustment to achieve the required turnout. If necessary due to the shape of the leg (e.g., hyperextended knees), some dancers will need to release the knees slightly, while still pulling up their legs, to bring the heels together.

It is important for the dancer to learn first position as a clear indicator of where side is: straight out from the supporting heel, the toes pointing di-

Peter and Dana in first position

rectly away from the hip and shoulder and ear (when the dancer's head is facing front). Already in first position, the dancer begins to center her weight over two places, not four: It is mostly over the balls of her feet, rather than evenly distributed over the balls and heels. First position is rarely used as the starting or finishing position for exercises in the center. It is mostly a position through which some steps pass—for example, rond de jambe par terre, balançoire, pas de basque, grand jeté.

In second position the dancer's heels are separated by the length of her foot—not more, not less. To find her true second position, the dancer does battement tendu directly to the side while keeping her weight over the ball of the supporting foot and then, while leaving the toes where they are, lowers the working foot to the floor. She does not adjust or move either foot into a wider stance. The knees and the toes face to the side, pointing to three and nine of the clock with a line running through the center line of the feet, as in first position.

Many schools teach or accept a wider second position, some a very wide second, but Balanchine wanted us to memorize the smaller "true" second. In a very wide second, it is harder for the dancer to move, and she has less power. A grand plié in a wide second position is useful for many dancers as a stretch, but Mr. B left that to each dancer to do on her own.

In second position the dancer's weight is again centered over the balls of her feet (remember, not on four points, ball, heel, heel, ball). In grand plié she should try to keep the heels on the floor, but if this is impossible, it is better that they release slightly so her knees can fully bend, than that the dancer widen the position or settle for a shallow grand plié. This difference from traditional teaching will come up at a number of points in this book. For now, let me simply note that Mr. B's priority was movement rather than static, stationary poses and positions, so he wanted the dancer ready to go at all times. When

rigid insistence on keeping the heel on the floor, or any other detail, interfered with the dancer's readiness or ability to move, he was prepared to rethink the traditional teaching.

Fifth position must have had an almost mystical significance for Mr. Balanchine. In the hospital, during the last weeks of his life, he received a visit from one of his principal dancers. As the dancer and Mr. B talked about dance, Balanchine, by then confined to his bed, made fifth position with his hands and rotated his arms to the right and to the left. He said, "This is where it all is." Even close to death, he was still pondering it. He saw fifth position as the dancer's home base, because the great majority of steps start and end in it. It is the most adaptable, because the dancer can move in any di-

Peter and Dana in second position

rection more easily from fifth than from any other position. It is the most concentrated, because it brings the feet together on the center line of the body.

In fifth position the feet are fully crossed with no toes and no heels hanging over at either end. The inside thighs are rotated front, and the knees and toes point directly side. The feet are held tightly together for their entire length, "like glued together," Mr. B liked to say. In fifth position, "there is no compromise. Middle of the road is no good." If necessary (which it is for many dancers), the front knee is released slightly when standing, or when closing the working foot into fifth position, to enable the feet to touch. However, when this is done, the muscles in the front leg are still active and maintain the turnout. The correct position of the feet in fifth position was most important to Mr. B, and in this case the legs have to accommodate the feet. Unless the dancer's legs are perfectly straight, she can't make fifth without releasing the knee. As he did about many technical details, Balanchine looked at each dancer individually and made the adjustments so she would look her best.

To Mr. B, the importance of fifth included the dancer's heightened awareness in that position of the center line of the body. A dancer in a good tight fifth position had the center line of the body passing through at the crossing of the knees. The weight is centered over the balls of the feet.

Fourth position to Balanchine was essentially an extended fifth, in that the feet are just as fully crossed and the legs are just as fully turned out.

Rather than being "glued" together, the front foot and back foot are separated by just about the length of the dancer's foot. The dancer's weight is evenly distributed between the feet and centered over the balls. The hips are square. Mr. B rarely gave grand pliés in fourth, saying, "We don't need this."

As I have indicated, Balanchine wanted most of the weight concentrated over the balls of the feet in each position: "Right before you start, you have to be there." This did not mean that the rest of the foot was not in contact with the floor. It did mean that when the dancer started to move, no shift of weight, or at most only a slight shift toward the ball of the supporting foot, was necessary. When the teacher notices that a dancer's weight is settled back in the heels and that she must make a consequential shift before she can move, the teacher needs to be ready with a correction that will help the dancer achieve the needed distribution of her weight.

Peter and Dana in fourth position

Peter and Dana in fifth position

What the teacher says will depend on the step being done, the tempo, and the body of the dancer. The result the teacher works for is that the dancer is always ready to move instantly. I always think of Mr. B's cat Mourka, ready to pounce.

POINTING THE FOOT

Because of the construction of the pointe shoe, the simple matter of pointing the foot as in battement tendu or battement jeté is not, in fact, so simple. As Balanchine would say, dancers need to do extra work to keep the feet pointed. When standing on pointe, the weight of the body is so concentrated as to help shape the pointe of the supporting foot. With no weight on the foot, this concentration does not exist, so the dancer has to work more actively at keeping the pointe alive and strong. The toes are not straight in the pointe shoe; instead, the dancer needs to bend the sole of the shoe by actively pressing her toes against it with extra force in order to shape the shank and the stiffened box into a curved pointe. See page 230 for further discussion of pointing the foot in pointe shoes.

For the male dancer wearing kid (which are preferred) or canvas ballet slippers, the technique for pointing the foot is actually the same as it is for a woman, but less strength is required, because there is no hard, stiff sole in the shoe for him to bend. As noted, one probable benefit of working occasionally in pointe shoes for any male dancer is stronger toes and stronger, more flexible feet.

In general, Balanchine was not in favor of the practice sometimes known as "winging," in which the upward curve of the foot at the end of an arabesque or other pose is intentionally exaggerated, to highlight the upswept line and extended thrust of the lifted leg. To do this, the ankle is slightly beveled, giving a "finishing" curl to the end of the foot. Balanchine, in contrast, insisted on the foot being fully pointed but still with the heel forward and the toes back. He often treated it as an integral part of the working leg. Rather than isolating the foot, changing or adjusting its position as the working leg extended in arabesque, he wanted us to concentrate on working the whole leg in a fully turned-out manner, sometimes opening the hip itself, as in arabesque. In arabesque the working leg

1. Incorrect pointes: straight toes in tights. The foot on the extreme right has the highest arch; that on the extreme left, the lowest.

2. Correct pointes: bent toes in tights

3. Incorrect pointes: straight toes in pointe shoes

4. Correct pointes: toes pressed against the soles of the pointe shoes. Note the well-shaped look of the pointe compared to the shape of the pointe when the toes are straight.

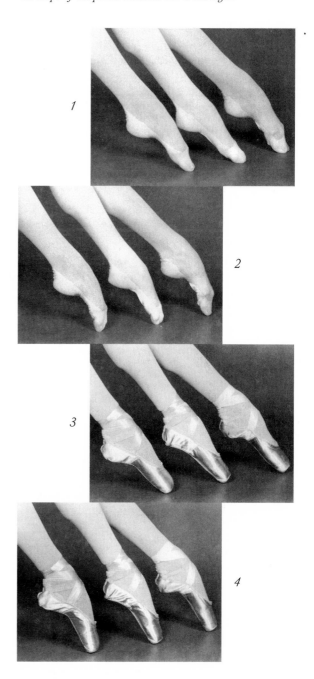

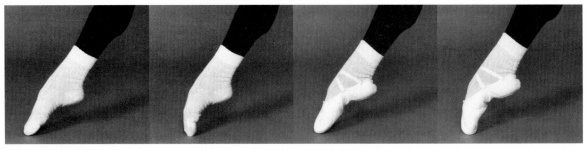

Incorrect man's pointe; straight toes in tights   *Correct man's pointe; bent toes in tights*   *Incorrect man's pointe; straight toes in ballet slipper*   *Correct man's pointe; bent toes in ballet slipper*

and foot present a stretched, turned-out line, with the foot beautifully shaped and fully pointed.

Every part of a stretched, straight leg lifted off the floor contributed to making the look he wanted the audience to see: turned out; stretched knee; a strong and well-shaped pointe. At times when he was working to achieve this, Balanchine would question the accuracy of one of ballet's most familiar terms. "To point your toes," he would say, "is not exactly right. It's more like bending or curling them against the sole of the shoe." He also questioned the accuracy of another familiar term. "What does it mean to stretch your knees? It means," he would explain, "to straighten and stretch your leg." Balanchine wanted to see that stretch from the top of the hip to the tips of the toes.

RELEVÉ

There are two ways to rise onto pointe or demi-pointe: the press relevé, in which the dancer rolls up through the foot; and, the spring relevé, in which the dancer executes a small jump.

Balanchine often preferred that his dancers practice rolling through the foot rather than springing to and from pointe and demi-pointe, because rolling demands greater strength and control, thus enabling the dancer to get on and off pointe or demi-pointe at any speed. In adagios, a slow roll-up relevé can complement the music and clarify the gesture. For example, near the beginning of the second movement of *Concerto Barocco*, the balle-

rina rolls up to pointe as she unfolds her leg in a développé, then falls in tombé over the extended legs of the ensemble. When a dancer has to move very quickly, it is easier to keep in tempo by rolling up, using very little plié, than by springing, which often requires pulling the toes under the center, and more plié. For example, in Balanchine's *Swan Lake*, in Odette's fast entrechat quatre passé section, the ballerina rolls up to relevé. Another advantage of the roll-up relevé with its minimal plié is that it almost always ensures a straight knee when arriving on pointe or demi-pointe, which is not the case with the spring relevé.

The press relevé can be done from any position of the feet or when standing on one foot. I do not, however, recall Mr. B giving consecutive roll-up relevés in fifth or fourth positions, perhaps because, in both cases, the dancer would be on pointe in an open (i.e., incorrect) position. The dancer needs to think first of using the floor, of pressing or going into it as she lifts her torso and pulls up out of her hips and legs. This pressing along with the pulling up is what makes the relevé happen. When she arrives on pointe, she is not relaxed, sitting into her hips and legs; it is especially important that she is not settled down into her pointe shoes. Instead, she lifts her weight up and out of her feet by using the muscles of her legs and hips as well as the muscles of her feet. Her torso complements this lifting by pulling up out of the hips (although the shoulders remain, as always, pressed down).

In a relevé from two feet, the action usually begins with the dancer moving into demi-plié and, when the tempo is slow, then continuing with a slight straightening of the knees. The heels then release, and the knees continue to straighten as the dancer maintains her maximum turnout. On pointe (or demi-pointe) the heels cannot be quite as far forward as they are when the dancer is on the full foot or in plié. As the heels continue to release, the dancer rolls up to pointe or demi-pointe through the feet. She arrives on pointe (or demi-pointe) as the knees are fully stretched, with most of her weight over the first two toes (or on demi-pointe, over the ball of the foot). When the tempo is moderate or faster, the knees and heels can almost seem to begin together from the demi-plié, and the dancer arrives on pointe or demi-pointe, as usual, with straight knees. The faster the tempo, the less the dancer pliés. It is very important to arrive on pointe or demi-pointe with the knees fully stretched. The same technique is used for the roll-up relevé on one foot.

When standing on demi-pointe, the men used a high relevé. In class, Mr. Balanchine did not define and set exercises for various gradations of relevé, one quarter, one half, three quarters. Some steps onstage were done at lower than full relevé. Chaîné turns is an example of this. Women might find it difficult to do a high demi-pointe relevé in new pointe shoes because of the higher, tighter vamp and stiffer shank.

We also practiced spring relevé in class. A common exercise at the barre was demi-plié in fifth and then spring to pointe or demi-pointe as the working leg made a dégagé of about forty-five degrees to the front, side, or back. Mr. B wanted to see us arrive "POW!" with the working leg extended by the time we were on pointe. He also gave spring relevés in the center when he wanted to see the "picture": dancers arriving on pointe with their working legs simultaneously arriving in the designated line. See page 249 for a discussion of some steps using the spring relevé.

When the men are on demi-pointe, the weight is centered over the ball of the foot, with most of the weight concentrated at the base of the big toe and

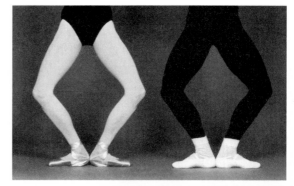

Dana and Peter in first position demi-plié

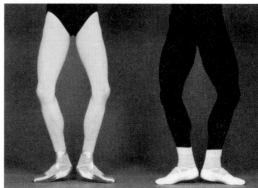

Dana and Peter in first position, legs straightening and heels releasing

Dana and Peter in first position, legs straightening and rolling up through the feet

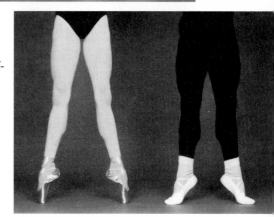

Dana on pointe and Peter on demi-pointe in first position. See page 232 for further discussion of the positions of the feet on pointe or demi-pointe

the toe next to it, but the dancer again pulls up and off the foot. However, the foot should not be rolled in, and it is certainly not sickled to the outside. The stance on pointe is comparable and is discussed in detail on page 232.

Many exercises at the barre were set to be done both on flat and in relevé (on demi-pointe by men and on pointe by women). In addition, Mr. B gave exercises on pointe and demi-pointe at the barre and in the center. Examples at the barre are covered on pages 237–238.

SPACE AND TIME FOR CLASS

Mr. Balanchine had no fixed allocation of time between the barre and the center. When there were no rehearsals or very few, we had a lot of time for class, and it could last two or two and a half hours. Then the class occasionally began with a very long barre, perhaps as long as forty-five minutes or even an hour, because he wanted to clean up a lot of fundamental technique. Or he might want to see if he could develop a refinement of some basic detail best practiced at the barre. He generally had a lot of steps he wanted to work on in the center, so during the season, when the class was usually only one hour, and in rehearsal periods he often limited the barre to about twenty minutes, to have time for them. He saw no useful purpose in automatically doing the traditional last set to the side of exercises given en croix, so we sometimes did front, side, and back, and then he stopped the music, saying, "Why should side get twice as much as front or back?" This saved him some time. He also typically omitted some exercises at the barre, usually different ones each day. And later in the center he often included exercises he had omitted at the barre.

Until the New York City Ballet moved to Lincoln Center, insufficient space was a serious problem. I think many people today would find the space Mr. B had at City Center and at SAB when it was on upper Broadway a critical limitation. But Balanchine calmly went on with the work. On some days the class could be so full that most teachers would have let the dancers stand at the barres any old way. But Mr. B wanted each dancer standing square to the barre. Sometimes he divided the class into two groups so we could be properly placed at the barre. "It is better to sacrifice time and make them stand separately." Or he simply deleted some exercises and modified others so he did not need to make two groups, which gave each dancer the space she needed at the barre. For example, large, extended movements usually done front, side, and back, such as grands battements, développés, and enveloppés, might be done only à la seconde, omitting front and back. Or to include front, he had us put our backs squarely to the barre, and to include back, he had us squarely face the barre.

When people look at classes they often concentrate exclusively on details of the technique being taught, or they take lots of notes on combinations, especially the big ones. Some try, even secretly, to take pictures. But I learned from Mr. B that the basic effectiveness of ballet class is partly, but crucially, determined by some of the aspects I have just described. It is worth noticing what Mr. B was very insistent about: appropriate dress for everyone, pointe shoes for women, the right music, just the exercises needed to achieve the aesthetic result (not a general warm-up or conditioning), space for each dancer to work correctly, and so on. It is equally worth noticing how he adapted to the conditions at hand and adjusted when necessary.

CONCLUSION

Company class was one way for Mr. Balanchine, our choreographer and teacher, to get ideas for his new dances. He knew how to use class as a laboratory for trying out ideas that extend the technique beyond its limits in any given area at any particular time. By watching his dancers he could learn what new possibilities for movement might be worth exploring. Contrary to much that has been written and said, there really was no such thing as a Balanchine dancer in terms of body type, temperament, or even in terms of prior training. Mr. B liked to say, "My company is like a garden. A garden with only roses is boring. I like variety." The diversity of our responses to the opportunities presented by his classes and choreography pleased him and gave him much to think about. The results are visible in his ballets.

Mr. B's classes often conveyed lessons in living as a dancer that were implicit in his way of working and asking us to work. He might be asking us to do frappés so fast that our working leg could barely straighten and our foot barely point, or to plié so deeply and slowly in landing from a jump that we would be fighting for control. His point at such a moment would be a lesson to us in what it felt like to push ourselves to our maximum, rather than routine classical correctness. He was also asking us to gamble, to take a chance on something we were not quite sure of. In class he liked to see us surprise ourselves and him with what we could dare to attempt and could sometimes achieve.

Precision was also important to him. Certain aspects of our dancing had to be very exact. They required more basic awareness than advanced professional skill: The toes front and back were right on the center line of the body, as were the fingertips of a hand stretched front in first arabesque, the feet were precisely crossed in fourth and fifth position, and so on. However, he did not want to limit himself to basic movement qualities that can be drilled to produce the precision of soldiers or marching band performers or Rockettes.

Instead, he wanted every dancer, not just the soloists and principals, to be working at the outer limits of the technique. His demand was that each dancer do what she could to approach that ideal— for example, going through the foot in landings from the biggest jumps, rolling up through the foot to pointe in a slow relevé passé. Since each person is different, progress is not uniform, so the essential is that each person do her maximum. "Try, and try, and try." He knew that our effort and energy would make us more interesting, more exciting.

The company class was primarily our time with him, a time when Mr. B gave himself fully to us and the time when we gave ourselves fully to him. It was up to each of us to get the largest possible benefit from his teaching. If we succeeded, then we had more to give him in rehearsal, more to give the public onstage. Unlike many other teachers of that time, he did not sit down, smoke, sip coffee, eat, chew gum, or look out the window while he was in class. He was always asking us to be ready to work with full attention, minds cleared of other matters. He expected our full participation, and he gave us his full attention. Again, a little lesson about life and work: work full out when it is time to work, and then be free to relax when the work is done—play a little poker, have a little dinner with a good red wine, go for a drink. He was very proud to be our "dance supplier," as he called himself, and he wanted us to be proud of him as our teacher.

His manner was pleasant and cheerful, yet serious. He enjoyed little moments of humor, often based on wordplay. Many of his little stories had an immediately light or funny aspect, but, when remembered, a more serious underlying message. And he sometimes showed us what not to do, often with comical effect, as when he demonstrated flailing arms, a zombielike lifeless face, or feet landing haphazardly and noisily on the floor. He wanted to see that dedicated yet pleasant atmosphere reflected in our faces. He did not want us to relax, in the sense of taking it easy, but he did want a relaxed, open, good-humored, agreeable, and gracious air about us, just as it was about him. It is not easy to look beautiful with a frown, a furrowed brow, or the tongue stuck in the cheek, after all.

He enjoyed the life and work in his 1 percent of the ballet world, and he wanted us to do so as well. I know I did . . . and I still do!

Barre Work

Barre work develops the fundamental skills on which classical technique is based; barre work is the foundation on which classical technique is built. The barre is the place where ballet dancing begins. Balanchine compared doing barre work to brushing one's teeth: Each must be done *very well* at least once a day.

The purpose of barre work, according to Balanchine, is primarily to develop the dancer's skill and finesse in the use of the feet and legs. This does not mean that nothing else mattered to him at the barre. It does mean that he directed the major part of his comments and corrections at the barre to those aspects of the technique involving the feet and legs so we could focus maximum attention, energy, and awareness on them.

Nonetheless, he still wanted us to look like ballet dancers, and that requires a certain bearing. His ideas on posture were strict: an erect carriage with the weight over the balls of the feet, the stomach pulled in, the chest up "like Thanksgiving turkey on the platter," fanny "like Rock of Gibraltar," shoulders down, the neck lengthened, the eyes alert and projecting out (the energy does not die in front of your face, I remind the dancers). As he walked around the studio, he would see details he did not like, and he let us know with good-humored but direct comments. "What did you have for breakfast? Well, that's nice, but I can still see it! Now take your stomach in!" Or actions, such as poking soft backsides to get us to tighten them up.

Even though he was a great choreographer, Balanchine did not believe in choreography at the barre. We did very simple, elementary exercises many, many times, until the movement was not only exact but even "automatic." When you dance a ballet, you can't think, "Am I pointing my toe, maintaining my turnout, making fifth position, passing my foot through first, picking my foot off the floor properly, etc., etc.?" All that and so much more have to come together and be part of the dancer's technique so she is free just to dance, to respond to the music.

There are ironies and paradoxes in this. There is nothing "automatic" about good technique. Barre work must be done diligently every day to maintain good technique. Next, making the elements of good technique "automatic" in us made it hard for us to dance any other way. Mr. B's barre trained us to use the feet and the legs as he wanted, but freed our bodies and minds so we could move like people who are ballet dancers and not like machines or people who are soldiers. An irony is that dancers who come from schools that place great value on complicated, intricate barre exercises, on mastery of numerous, detailed, constantly repeated changes of arms and head or choreographed turns to change sides at the barre, are generally *less* able to move freely once they are in the center and, what is worse, are not as well prepared to move freely onstage. In the occasional instances when Mr. B did have us make several arm and head movements at the barre, we really had to *dance* them, rather than just repeat them mechanically. For example, in adagios at the barre (see page 123) meant to reinforce our sense of front and side, we might développé to the side with the arm to the side, then passé with the arm to fifth low, and then attitude in effacé back (but remaining square to the barre) with the arm through first to fifth high and the head slanted toward the center of the room. Another exercise might be développé to the back with arm to the side, then arm down to fifth low and up to fifth high, then extend the arm to second arabesque; from this point we might do penché or some relevés in second arabesque. All arm movements had to be done with the qualities discussed on pages 146–160. These are dance qualities. Because the ports de bras we did at the barre were not part of a daily routine repeated by rote, without a particular purpose, they had not grown stale from too-frequent and unaware repetition. They were made part of certain exercises for very specific reasons, and we did them with awareness of the skill to be developed.

PLACEMENT AT THE BARRE, RELATION TO THE BARRE

I touched briefly on both these subjects, but want to cover them more fully, because their importance is so often overlooked. Making the technique automatic included precise muscle memory not only of movements but also of the directions front, side, and back. The dancer must be able to move her arm or her leg or herself in the desired direction without hesitation. Balanchine took special care to ensure that we had regular practice designed to cultivate that memory. This included many more sets of battements tendus, battements jetés, and

battements frappés, each done front, side, and back, than would be given in most other classes.

Mr. B was always concerned that we practice correctly, rather than just warm up or work out. Learning the directions is greatly helped if the dancers are placed square (shoulders and hips perpendicular) to the barre. When class is allowed to become just exercise, there is a temptation, especially in limited space, to cram people on to the barre at various angles. He did not agree: "Turn somewhere to allow somebody a little more room, you have no front any more. Unconsciously, you avoid correctness." Mr. B might give some exercises side only, so there was no need for dancers to turn at odd angles. For exercises with the leg higher than forty-five degrees (and thus likely to hit the adjacent dancer) that he wanted to give in all three directions, his preference was to form two groups. He thought it was better, if necessary, to do fewer exercises, being sure each dancer had space to do them correctly. It is not ideal to have to take turns at the barre, but it need not be seen as a complete loss. Professional and advanced dancers, and even dedicated younger ones, can learn from watching class and paying attention to what is said to others. When SAB students are unable to take class because of an injury but are able to get around, we encourage them to come and watch for this reason.

When the dancer stands square to the barre, her working leg feels parallel to the barre when she does, for example, battement tendu front or back. And it *is* essentially parallel to the barre when the toes are on the center line of the body. The barre should help the dancer sense correct alignment of the working leg. If the pointe was not on the center line and he still needed to correct us, Mr. B would tell us it was still not front (or back) and put it into line so we would feel the crossing of the thighs that was similar to what we felt in fifth position. Front is an extension of fifth.

The leg moves straight out from fifth, and the foot accommodates the action of the leg by pulling the toes into the center line. If the dancer points slightly to the side, for example, in front of the sup-

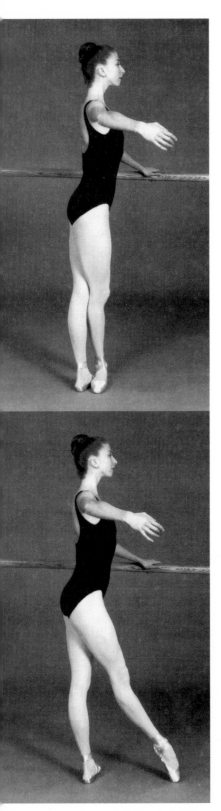

Dana in fifth position at right angles to the barre

Dana in tendu front at the barre; her hips and shoulders are square to the barre and her working leg feels parallel to the barre.

porting heel or working hip, front is no longer an extension of fifth, the thighs are no longer crossed, and she is actually making the leg accommodate the toes. Back is also an extension of fifth position and the principles that apply to the front apply to the back as well.

When the dancer moves her leg to the front, her hips and shoulders remain (with rare exceptions) square to the barre. However, when she moves her leg to the back, she opens the working hip, but only as much as needed, to reveal a fully turned-out leg. The shoulders remain (with rare exceptions) square to the barre, and the supporting hip stays aligned over the supporting leg and foot.

There are several reasons why the dancer moves the legs directly front or back. One is the aesthetic—it looks better. In some schools they say to point your toes in front or in back of your standing heel or opposite the working hip and move your arms in front of your shoulders. If a dancer walks straight toward you with her feet directly in line with her hips, she will look like a toddler wearing diapers. But if she walks with her feet on one line directly in front of her center, you will see an elegant, chic young lady.

The other reasons feel more geometric and scientific. From fifth position, which is the classical dancer's home base, it is faster to move the working leg straight front or back, foot on the center line. To move the leg from fifth diagonally forward to a place in front of the working hip (or diagonally back to a place in back of it) seems farther away, and thus seems to take more time until the toes are pointed. The other reason is balance. If a dancer transfers her weight forward or back onto pointe or demi-pointe and her foot goes straight front, toes right on her center line, and her body comes right over on top of her pointe, she is on balance. If she puts her toes in front or in back of her working hip, it is a little to the side. In addition to transferring her weight front and back, she now has to adjust her weight laterally in order to be on balance. As Mr. B said, "You now have a move to correct it. So it is two for one. You lose speed."

There is only one line directly side, one second position, one à la seconde: It is directly opposite the heel of the supporting foot, the shoulder, the ear. The toes, or pointe, of the working foot go to the same spot from fifth front or fifth back, a straight line to that point; there is no rond de jambe action. From fifth front the leg and foot move ever so slightly back on the diagonal, and from fifth back they move slightly front on a diagonal to the same spot. In some places, teachers say don't adjust your hip line at all to make second. However, if the dancer is not totally turned out, the leg can only get so far to the side without adjusting the hip line. Mr. B was aware that many teachers disagreed with him on this point, but his ideas came from long reflection; in this case it was more important that the dancer know and show clearly the difference between front and side than that the line of the hip remain "perfectly" placed.

When I teach, I sometimes see that a few of my students can use some help in feeling the working leg rotated out when it is side, rather than feeling it is being simply pushed back. I suggest that the working pointe may be *very* slightly in front of the supporting heel when it is tendu side. I let them point it opposite fifth front, so to speak, an inch or so in front of second. This very slight accommodation depends, of course, on the individual dancer's body.

When the dancer remains square to the barre, she will sense movements to the side as perpendicular or at a right angle, as straight out from the barre. Thus the barre serves in much the same way as a straight line reference as it does in movements front and back.

Mr. B liked to tell the story of the only dancer he ever knew who was naturally completely turned out. She could show all five positions perfectly with straight knees, and she could take either leg front, side, and back completely turned out with the hips perfectly square. There was only one problem: "Couldn't dance!" The moral was that it is more important to be able to move, to link steps and poses in beautiful phrases, to *dance*, than

to have perfect turnout and perfect placement.

When the directions from the body are not understood as Balanchine taught them, there is a big risk that front is not front, that back is not back, and that second and à la seconde are just somewhere generally to the side. He gave dancers a front that is directly in front, a back that is directly in back, and a side that is directly to the side. The result is a much fuller range of movement for the dancer to do, for the choreographer to use, and for the public to see.

STANCE AT THE BARRE

"Stand up straight, like you swallowed a yardstick," Mr. B would say as he looked around the room. He might then bend forward stiffly from his

"Walk like this, you'll dance like this."

"Walk like this, you'll dance like this."

releases a foot, as in tendu or développé, a very slight, very minimal shift of weight is all that is needed. In many cases it will be possible to slip a sheet of paper under the dancer's heels when she is in demi-plié. The dancer must be able to keep her weight over the balls of her feet. This part of the technique should be automatic.

Balanchine made "not settling" into a moral principle. "Don't just settle," he would say, "you must know what you want." Maybe that was a lesson he drew from the story of his own life. He had barely started to perform when he began to make ballets, and he kept on making ballets in each place he went until he finally had his own place to make them season after season. It took about twenty-five years, and along the way there were many interruptions, detours, and disappointments, but he never settled in until he reached a place where he could do his work. And he didn't settle in to rest, he settled in to work.

waist to a forty-five-degree angle or so, sticking an arm out in front next to his ear. Saying, "Walk like this, you'll dance like this," he took a few halting steps. Then he stood straight with his chest lifted and his head held high and repeated, "Walk like this, you'll dance like this," and stepped gracefully forward on the balls of his feet. As I watched him, I always felt myself pull up a little taller and straighter, subtly reminded as well to keep my weight forward.

Standing on two feet, the dancer's weight should be centered, over two points, over the ball of each foot, rather than distributed over four points, the balls and the heels. In this way she is almost always ready to move. When a dancer in fifth position

Standing with the weight settled down and back into the heels, it is very easy to relax, to feel comfortable. There is a feeling of arrival. One can settle in. "You can go to sleep that way," he said. I have no doubt that this was contrary to Balanchine's sense of the dancer as alert, always prepared, always ready to move. That is the essence of the energetic, on-top-of-the-music attack he wanted in performance. Remember Mr. B's cat Mourka, ready to pounce.

To me, this is an important example of a lesson about dancing being applicable also as a lesson about how to live. It is important because it is so clear and basic; it can be understood by students who have not been dancing very long at all. And it is important because it conveys an idea that applies very broadly to life in general, and yet it has its roots in a very small technical detail.

UPPER BODY, ARMS, AND HANDS

For nearly the entire barre, Mr. Balanchine wanted us to stand straight, with the shoulders square to the barre, held down and open. The chest was proudly lifted, "Like a woman showing off a diamond necklace," Madame Danilova would say. How typical of them both! Speaking of the chest, Choura thought of diamond necklaces and how they are worn, of great ladies and grand entrances. Mr. B thought of turkey breast on a platter and a wonderful meal and how it is presented to the guests.

Mr. B saw no point to the repeated tipping forward and back, turning the head, and the changes of épaulement that are very commonly given as each barre exercise is set, since for him the barre was mainly the time to work on the feet and legs. Any exception had a very specific reason—for example, as an integral part of exercises such as ports de bras forward and back or arabesque penchée.

There are detailed descriptions of the arm positions and of the way the arms and hands move from one position to another in the next chapter. Mr. B did not devote a lot of attention to the arms at the barre, although he did correct obvious problems. However, some readers may find it helpful to look at pages 146–150, Basic Arm Positions, and pages 150–160, Movement of the Arms.

We typically began exercises square to the barre, with the arm next to the barre placed lightly on it below shoulder height, just forward of the dancer's body but not reaching out to a point on the barre

1. Dana in fifth position, free hand just in front of the thigh and a couple of inches in from the outside edge of the thigh
2. Dana in fifth position, free arm in first position
3. Dana in fifth position, free arm in second position, complementing the arm at the barre (but not matching its slope)

way in front of her. The elbow was slightly bent, being supported from the back in a gentle curve. The shoulders were down but the elbow was not pulled down, nor did the dancer let it droop. All this meant that we were farther from the barre than is often the case. The free arm was down in preparatory position—that is, lengthened, but also curved, with the hand just in front of the outer part of the thigh, palm facing in. Mr. B did not want to see our hand hanging low and between our legs.

Mr. B gave a two-count introduction, counting and often snapping his fingers, before the music started. It was in the tempo for the exercise to follow; we lifted the free arm to first on count one and opened to second on count two. In second, the free arm was supported from the back, sloping very slightly from the shoulder to the supported elbow, and continuing to the wrist and hand, palm facing front. The slope should be gentle, so the hand is just a little below the elbow. The elbows should be very slightly in front of the back, with the forearms continuing the curve. In this position, looking front, the dancer should see in her peripheral vision the fingertips of the hand in the air and the hand on the barre; her arms and hands should match. This is the position she would assume with arms in second position in the center, so no habit reinforced at the barre had to be unlearned in the center (of course, the arms will also match in height in the center). As always, the final detailed adjustments were those that made each dancer look her best.

In the course of the exercises Mr. B generally used first, second, and fifth low and fifth high for the free arm and hand. Most of the detailed work on the arms (aside from the second position just described) was done in the center.

We began most exercises with the hand lightly on the barre, and it usually remained that way. We did not, for example, do many balances or turns at the barre. For a few of his exercises we faced the barre (or put the back to it) and rested both hands lightly on it. Sometimes we used both hands to grasp it quite firmly or to press down on it to support some of our weight. Mr. B adjusted standard

practice as needed in order to proceed as directly as possible toward the specific result he wanted in each exercise.

The quality and shape of the free hand was another story altogether, a clear exception to his overall emphasis on feet and legs at the barre. It was at the barre that he taught the basic hand position he wanted to see, and he made sure we memorized it. I am not referring to *his* hand position as *basic* without good reason. He refined the presentation of the hand, and he wanted us to think of it as basic in the same way that his precise fifth position is basic for the feet. He paid attention not only to the hand as a whole, but also to its parts, the back of the hand, and the palm of the hand, the thumb and fingers individually. Balanchine admired Spanish dancing for the eloquence of the dancers' hands, and he wanted our hands to be articulate and expressive, too.

Some teachers say the four fingers separated are not very pretty, so they put the fingers together, and they say the thumb is ugly, so let's hide it by putting it down and close to the palm and then turn the wrist so the palm faces down. Perhaps aware of this practice, Mr. B used to say, "Hands should not become a handicap! We have them, so we should use them, and they should help us. If dancers hide what they have, what do you see? Not much! God gave us four fingers and a thumb, and I want to see them all." Like every other part of the dancer's body, the hands could be beautiful to Mr. B.

One of the most distinctive formal elements of Balanchine's rethinking of the hand is the thumb. Often treated almost as an embarrassment and buried somehow, it was for Mr. B the counterpart to the other four fingers. He wanted the thumb to come out from the palm in the first joint, then curve in toward the tip of the middle finger in its second joint. Held this way, the thumb was visible most of the time.

All of the fingers are rounded and curved. It is the differing amount of bend in each finger, as well as the slight spaces between, that separate them. The middle finger is curved in the most, the little finger is straightest and is held out most. The ring

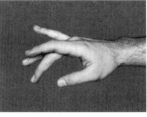

Dana's hand and Peter's hand in profile; the fingers on each hand are curved and separated.

finger is slightly less curved than the middle finger. The index finger, which Mr. B liked to call the "pointer" finger, will tend to separate without specific attention; Mr. B wanted it to curve in slightly, but less than the middle and ring fingers. Seen from the side, the little finger is out the most, then the index finger, then the ring finger; the middle finger is curved in the most.

Balanchine wanted his dancers' hands to look round and soft but not to be soft. The inside (the palm) and the back are held curved, rather than being held stiffly flat or being allowed to hang relaxed and straight. They are held by muscles that maintain the shape he wanted. The soft, relaxed hand hangs lifeless from the wrist, almost certainly with a drooping elbow. Mr. Balanchine called this look "dead chicken wing." His carefully shaped

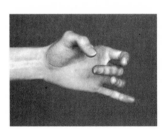

Palm of Dana's hand; there is an inner curve to match the outer curve of the back of the hand.

hand with its balanced inner and outer curves and separated fingers can be viewed as a flower, with its petals opening and looking up to the sun, with energy, trying to reach that sun. The droopy hand is the wilted flower ready for the compost heap.

In the early 1960s, Balanchine was so concerned about our hands that, at the barre, he suggested that we each hold a rubber ball that was a little smaller than a tennis ball but larger than a Ping-Pong ball. A ball of this size fit comfortably in the palm, enabling the inner surface of the palm to gently mold itself to surround the ball in the center of the palm,

forming a shallow "pocket" for the ball. The thumb wrapped the top of the ball; the index and middle fingers closed around the center of the ball; and the little finger was held out. The ring finger might be on the ball or could be held rounded, but just off the ball. This teaching device helped us with our hands in two key ways. First, it made us aware that we had a hand to which we had to give life and energy. If a dancer working at the barre forgot she had a hand and relaxed it, the ball would drop. At first, to be sure, there were balls bouncing everywhere. But after about three weeks of holding the balls, we could remember that we had hands and that we needed to hold them and to keep them alive. The balls stopped dropping. Second, it gave us a reliable, consistent, round shape for the muscles of our hands to memorize while we learned to make and maintain a gentle curve in the palm, back of the hand, thumb, and middle finger. We did not have to guess about what was right.

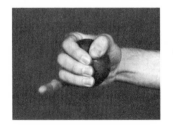

Peter's hand holding a ball, forming a shallow round "pocket"

Using a ball to keep the hand alive while doing barre exercises also helps to make the dancer aware of holding the arm from the back and maintaining support for the elbows.

When Mr. B observed that we were beginning to have the look he wanted in our hands, he would tell us to practice during otherwise lost time. For example, while waiting for the bus, waiting for the water to boil, or during the TV commercials, a dancer could say to herself "Hands!" and look to see if hers instantly assumed the correct shape without the ball. If not, she needed more practice.

Sometimes I see a student with a limp hand and hanging fingers, or a hand that looks stiff and flat. I start by suggesting that she hold her thumb gently on the top side of the last joint of her index finger with the little finger held out, which is the way Mr. B wanted the children to start learning the correct hand shape. If this does not seem to help her to form the required roundness, I suggest that she get a ball to hold at the barre, and after a while her hands look better. Recently I heard that a nearby store was having a sale on balls of a suitable size, so I gave a student ten dollars to buy as many as possible. She came back with twenty-five, and at the next class we passed them out to "needy" straight-fingered students. Dancers should practice without and, if necessary, with the ball until the correct shape is automatic and immediate.

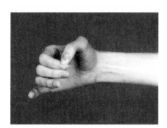

Dana's hand in the position generally used in the younger children's classes at SAB

BALANCHINE'S BARRE

On most days during the season, the barre exercises were comparatively brief, but then class as a whole was comparatively short, about an hour. There were generally too many other demands on Balanchine's time and on ours (and on studio space) to allow for a conventional ninety-minute class. And it must not be forgotten that Mr. B left each dancer responsible to work on her own to further polish and refine her technique and for her own preperformance warm-up. He did not come each day to "give class" in some generic sense. He came really to teach us, so he gave us just what we needed to ac-

complish his purpose for that day. Since his specific purpose was different each day, he didn't have a standard class in the ordinary sense.

There was, however, a virtually unvarying core to his class:

1) two grand pliés in first, second, fifth front, and fifth back at a moderately brisk tempo;

2) one set of eight battements tendus front, side, and back at a moderate to bright tempo, or sixteen to the front and then turn to do the other side, sixteen to the side and then turn to do the other side, and sixteen to the back and then turn to do the other side;

3) at a faster tempo, thirty-two battements tendus side closing alternatively fifth front/fifth back, or sixteen side closing front followed by 16 side closing back, or some variation of this;

4) one set of two fast battements tendus and three quick battements jetés front, side, and back, and then repeat on the other side or sixteen jetés front, side, and back, and then repeat on the other side;

5) at a very fast tempo, thirty-two battements jetés side closing alternatively fifth front/fifth back, or sixteen side closing front followed by sixteen side closing back, or some variation of this; and

6) simple ronds de jambe par terre at various tempos.

Any reader of this book who has heard the stories about the numbers of tendus we did will see some confirmation. In addition, there were typically three or four more exercises that usually came from among the following: battement tendu with plié, rond de jambe par terre with a big plié or with passé relevé and unfold the leg to tendu front/back; port de bras; fondu; frappé; rond de jambe en l'air; grand battement; an adagio; and petits battements. The daily "treat" we hoped for, and only sometimes got, was battement tendu with plié. On the days when I started class for Mr. B, the company always pleaded with me to get it in before he came. At the end of the barre, if there was time or when he felt we really needed them, he added relevé combinations facing the barre, such as those discussed on pages 237–238.

On layoffs and on Mondays (the day off for the New York City Ballet), he taught a class that was not bound by scheduling considerations. Those classes could last two hours or more, and the barre could even be an hour. We might do every exercise listed above and more.

The exercises that follow do not therefore constitute the barre exercises for a Balanchine class. I selected them to convey the essence of how we worked at the barre, and they include the ones he gave more often. They are not necessarily in normal class sequence for Balanchine or anyone else. Instead, I have arranged them for easiest understanding by readers.

At the end of the discussion of most of the exercises and at some other places, there is a box like the one that follows. The contents of the boxes serve in part as a recapitulation of some key points in the discussion of a technical matter, a group of exercises, or an exercise. They also serve to let the

---

DETAILS I OFTEN INSIST ON DURING
THE BARRE EXERCISES:
  1) weight over the ball(s) of the supporting foot (feet)
  2) no rolling in with straight legs or in plié
  3) hips pulled up and over the legs
  4) stretched supporting leg or legs
  5) stomach pulled in
  6) chest lifted; don't lean back
  7) lengthen the waist between the hips and the rib cage
  8) neck lengthened
  9) head up, chin lifted (not tilted back)
  10) face alive, eyes alert, focused
  11) arms held, elbows not hanging down, palm facing front
  12) hand properly shaped, not flat with the fingers straight and held together

---

reader know the corrections or suggestions I most often make. They sometimes overlap and repeat, but I do not see that as a problem. As a ballet teacher, I find that insistence has two aspects: first, I have to bring up the same details over and over and over; and second, I have to stay with whatever I am talking about until I see a change.

THE BARRE EXERCISES
Plié

Plié is probably the most important movement in ballet. It joins or links each movement to the next. "You don't do plié to warm yourself up. It is a special step that has to be developed. *Everything* comes from it." Plié is to dance as breathing is to life: It never stops. The moment it stops, the movement dies, the dance is finished.

Both demi-plié and grand plié are continuous, uninterrupted movements. There is often a sense that the demi-plié is separated from the grand. On the contrary, the plié should be continuous. There is no stop or change in speed at the moment when the heels release. When they do release, the dancer should keep them as close to the floor as possible as she continues down. On the return she should bring them back to the floor as soon as she can without any pause or hesitation as she moves through demi-plié.

The central purpose of plié is to collect energy. "The knee and the ankle bend together. It is not just one bend, it is two. Double force like double engine with two pieces working for you." This collection of energy is enhanced by bending with resistance. To ensure that we were really using our muscles and not relaxing into the plié, Balanchine would sometimes provide resistance by holding us up at the waist as we pushed down against his resistance. The descent in plié should store energy, especially in the thighs, in the same way as compressing a spring. Dancers must learn to have this feeling of resistance as they plié by themselves.

Resistance coming up as well as going down builds additional control and strength, so Balanchine sometimes created resistance on the ascent by putting his hands on our shoulders and pushing down as we came up. Developing extra strength, especially in the thighs, in both the descent and the ascent allows the dancer to control the speed of the movement and enables her to plié to fit any tempo.

Plié is not like an elevator: straight down, stop or bounce, and straight up. It does not run on a straight track up and down; instead it has a slight elliptical feeling because of the use of turnout and phrasing, along with resistance.

Turnout is an integral part of plié. As the dancer starts to descend, she turns out from the hips, bringing the inside of her thighs front so her knees are bending over her toes. As she ascends, she feels as if she turns her legs out even more—to the maximum. When moving into grand plié, the weight is in the middle of the balls of the feet. As the heels release and come ever so slightly forward, the dancer keeps the weight in the middle of the balls of the feet, not rolled in, but also not rolled to the outside. This helps to maintain the turnout and keep the heels front. At the bottom of grand plié in fifth position the back heel should maintain contact with the front heel.

Correct placement of the feet was important in all positions, but Mr. Balanchine was specially watchful of the correct spacing of the feet in second. Many teachers allow a wide second so that everyone can keep the heels on the floor in a deep grand plié, but Balanchine did not favor this. He preferred to allow the heels to release, if necessary, because it is more important for the dancer to learn where the correct second position is. The correct second is also a stronger position from which to move. Finally, a wide second is a useful stretch, but, as I have noted, pliés were done with active resistance, and stretching was not the purpose of plié.

Plié is the only barre exercise Mr. B regularly gave that required us to change our feet from first position to second position to fifth position before turning to the other side. In going from one position to another, the dancer may find she has moved too far away from or too close to the barre. There is then a tendency for a vague shuffling of both feet to take over as she uses a trial-and-error approach to restoring the correct distance from the barre and getting into a correct position. In contrast, Mr. B wanted the dancer to execute a battement tendu (see the next exercise) correctly and establish the new position. If she then determines that an adjustment in her distance from the barre is necessary, she can place her feet as needed. This should require no more than two crisp movements of the feet.

The plié takes the same time to go down as to come up, but within this equality there is variation, there is phrasing. After the clearly articulated, relatively quick start, the plié slows as the dancer continues down, gathering energy. The plié also starts back up quickly, but slows as the knees straighten. Because the dancer turns out even more at this point, there is a braking action that slows the end of the ascent and thus reveals or announces the end of the movement.

The plié starts down without delay, beginning exactly on the first beat of the music, helping to show the beginning of the movement. Often dancers delay the beginning of the plié. It seems that they are not yet fully alert, completely ready for class, so they don't start down right on the one of the music. Instead, they start late and creep into the movement. When this happened, Mr. B would clap his hands to stop the music and tell us, "You're already late!" We had barely begun the first exercise at the barre, and already we were behind. So we would start again. His insistence on musical precision from the first moment of class made clear how important musicality was to him. It also reminded us that the plié in class was neither a casual warm-up nor a throwaway stretch, but an essential part of the work we needed to be ready to do.

As I mentioned before, it is very important that the music not suggest unwanted divisions in the plié. Mr. B often asked for something in triple meter, such as a slow three, which we danced one count down, one count up, and one count to open

Dana in fifth position, arm in fifth low

Dana pliéing, opening her arm side

Dana in grand plié, arm fully extended

Dana reverses the arm as she starts to ascend.

Dana continues up as her arm closes.

Dana's knees are almost stretched as her arm approaches fifth low.

the arm to second. An alternative was a slow four: We went down on count one, came up on count two, opened our arms on count three, and held count four. Other good alternatives are a chord with the pedal held to mark each descent, or an arpeggio. It is also important that the music not be sentimental, because the dancer should not indulge in sentimentality in class. Pliés with the qualities I have described (resistance, turnout, phrasing, etc.) demand full awareness. The dancer should not melt into the floor full of feeling or to search for her soul. Although he was specially interested in our mastering very slow, controlled pliés while jumping, Mr. B gave the first pliés at the barre at a faster tempo than is the practice in most other schools. The grand pliés at the barre usually took about two seconds down and two seconds up.

During plié we mostly held the body upright, with the head straight front in a regal and proud position, slightly lifted, eyes directed out and front. Aside from slight adjustments in head level, very little changed; above all, we did not do the detailed bending and tilting favored by many teachers. "The head should not be involuntarily involved."

For demi-plié Mr. B often wanted the working arm in fifth low. The dancer took a breath and pulled up as she descended, the working arm opening directly toward the side, leading with the back of the wrist and finishing about two to three inches off the thigh and also slightly in front of it. As the dancer straightened the legs, the working arm, leading with the under side of the wrist, returned to fifth low. For grand plié he might also want the arm to start in fifth low, and it moved as it did in demi-

Dana in fifth position, arm in second

Dana takes a preparatory breath.

Dana descending in plié

Dana continues to descend in plié.

Dana ready to come up from grand plié

Dana coming up from grand plié

DETAILS I OFTEN INSIST ON IN PLIÉ:
1) back straight (shoulders over hips, hips over feet), especially in grand plié; maintaining the turnout; hips pulled up and knees in line or over the toes
2) lift up to go down; no tilting forward, back, or to the side
3) continuous movement throughout the plié, without a pause or stop at the demi-plié or at the bottom of the full plié
4) use muscles; resist
5) heels touching in first, correct second position, back heel forward in grand plié in fifth
6) stay in tempo, starting on the first beat of the music and finishing on time

plié, directly to the side, finishing two or three inches off the knee. More often he wanted the working arm in grand plié to start in second. Now the dancer took a breath and lifted or pulled up before starting, giving the arm impetus to rise slightly as the wrist and palm turn to face the floor and then the knees start to bend. The descent of the arm is timed so the hand reaches a point just outside the knee as the dancer approaches the bottom. As the dancer straightens her knees, the hand comes up to first with the fingertips on the center line of the body. If Mr. B saw the arm and hand hanging inside the knee or thigh at the bottom of grand plié, he might tell us, "Looks like monkey. Delay your arm." Just as the knees straighten, the arm opens to second.

I noted that this book is intended primarily for advanced and professional dancers, because some technical details vary at that level. One example is the faster tempo of the plié. Another is the heel in demi-plié. In early training it is important that the children learn to keep the heels down in demi-plié. At that age they are learning the most basic ballet technique, so they need to attain the control of the release of the heels. And we want them to stretch their tendons so that they have the deepest possible demi-plié. However, advanced dancers have that control and may, if necessary, release the heels in demi-plié. They may need to release due to the tempo of the step, the depth of the plié, or the shortness of their Achilles tendons. It is more important to have a full, juicy, dynamic demi-plié than to keep the heels glued to the floor.

A rigid emphasis by the teacher on the heels being down in the advanced or professional dancer will tend to produce a much less mobile dancer, because demi-plié is about bending the knees to collect energy for the next step, not about keeping the heels on the floor. Plié is not done in the Achilles tendon, and the dancer's awareness should not be directed there; plié is a bending of the knees controlled in the thighs. The heels should be kept down as long as possible, but they often release when a deeper demi-plié is needed to make the next step what it should be. The more crossed the position (i.e., fourth and fifth), the more difficult it is to achieve a deep demi-plié with the heels down. Therefore, in these positions dancers with shorter tendons often need to release the heels slightly to accommodate the

Dana almost up from grand plié   *Dana with stretched legs, arm in first*   *Dana in fifth position, arm in second again*

fuller demi-plié. Whether or not the heels are kept on the floor in demi-plié, it is vital to the movement that the weight remain over the balls of the feet and that the plié never stop.

We usually began the barre with two grand pliés in each position: first, second, fifth front, and fifth back. This took care of our grand pliés. There was no need to turn to the other side, because first and second are the same, and we had done both fifths. Mr. B almost never gave grand plié in fourth position, because it puts unnecessary stress on the knees, is rarely used when performing, and because pliés in fifth build the same strength in the legs.

Battement Tendu

Tendus were done daily and in large numbers, because for Mr. B and his company, the saying was, the more tendus, the better. We usually did sixteen, or perhaps thirty-two, front, side, and back at a moderate tempo, but often with this difference: We did one leg to the front and then turned to do the other leg front. Then we did the same thing side and side, and then back and back. By working this way, Mr. B helped to ensure that we did each set with a relatively fresh leg and therefore more correctly. It is interesting to note that when Balanchine had us do front, side, and back without changing

sides, he did not need to have us finish with a final set to the side. He often said to us, "We don't need side again. Front and back only got sixteen. Why should second get an extra set?" The conventional practice—front, side, back, side (usually called "en croix")—is based on musical structure, not on the logic of the directions. After the tendus at moderate tempo, we often did eight front, side, back, and, perhaps, side at a faster tempo, followed perhaps by thirty-two side only, but at an even faster tempo.

The action of the foot correctly moving out from and returning to fifth is one of the most elementary skills and a basic foundation of Balanchine's more articulate footwork. (Another way in and out of fifth of comparable importance is the action of taking the foot off the floor discussed in Sur le Cou-de-Pied.) Certain qualities essential to the way he wanted us to dance could only be developed through mastery of this seemingly simple exercise. These included maintaining the fullest possible turnout of the working leg and foot throughout the movement as well as the fullest possible turnout of the supporting leg, maintaining the weight over the ball of the standing foot (not evenly distributed over the whole foot or settled in the heel), a light caressing touch of the toes on the floor with the metatarsals lifted, a careful and gentle placement of the foot back to fifth, a fully pointed and stretched working foot at any speed, and the facility to start

Peter in fifth position front

Peter leading forward with his heel, toes lightly caressing the floor (no demi-pointe!)

Peter in tendu front, toes just touching on the center line

and stop quickly. All of this was so fundamental, so critical, that he often advised us to practice tendus on our own, alone, every day, to achieve the correct motion and to develop muscle memory.

In many schools the dancers are taught to go through demi-pointe as they point and again on the return to fifth. Their focus thus becomes dropping down on the metatarsals, and therefore going through the demi-pointe on the way to pointing the toes and returning. Balanchine, in contrast, observed that dancers do not actually go into a full demi-pointe when jumping or on the way to plié when landing. He therefore taught us to think of tendu as done in the ankle, rather than thinking of it as done by going down through the demi-pointe.

In addition to the daily tendus from fifth, we also occasionally did them from first. Tendu side from first is the simplest way to learn the correct location of side, directly opposite the supporting heel. Tendu front or back from first requires moving the entire leg on the diagonal so that the toes reach the center line of the body, which consequently brings greater awareness of its location. The common error in tendu front from first is to let the toes finish opposite the working hip or the supporting heel rather than on the center line; this is poor preparation for the rest of the technique. The reason is that in dancing, fifth position is the dancer's home base, the place to which she most often returns and from which she leaves for the next step. When she goes forward or back from fifth, her working foot must be on the center line of her body. The details of foot and ankle action are the same for tendus from first as they are for tendus from fifth.

From fifth front, going to the front, the heel leads and the toes follow. As the heel leads the entire inside of the leg forward, the heel releases off the floor while the tips of the toes lightly caress the floor. They point in, on the center line of the body, when the working leg is fully extended. The foot is fully stretched, with the arch up and the toes pressed against the sole. The foot is pointed down in line with the leg, but with the heel up, neither sickled nor winged. When the dancer's weight is

Dana pointing directly front, crossing her thighs, "squeezing her legs," and holding the money

Oops! Dana doesn't point directly front, releasing her legs, and she drops the money.

over the ball of the supporting foot and her tendu front is in the correct position with her head held straight front, the toes are in front of her nose, which was pretext enough for Balanchine to pun, "Your nose knows." At other times he would take a ten-dollar bill from his money clip and place it

Dana in fifth position front

Dana in tendu side, toes opposite the supporting heel

Dana extending side, toes back and heel forward, lightly caressing the floor (no demi-pointe!)

between a dancer's thighs while she stood in fifth. Mr. B would tell her that if she could hold it there while doing her tendus front, she could keep the money, for her pointe was on her center line, her thighs were properly crossed with the muscles of the inside thighs rotated front and firmly held together, and her hips were pulled up. Needless to say, he never offered the bet to dancers who knew and did a correctly crossed tendu front.

From fifth front or fifth back going to the side, the toes start back, leading the leg to the side, the heel comes forward as it releases off the floor and as the ankle begins to stretch. The toes again have a very light touch on the floor and are aligned in tendu side with the heel of the supporting foot and opposite the shoulder. To reach this position from

fifth front requires that the foot travel on a very slight diagonal back; to reach this position from fifth back requires that the foot travel on a slight diagonal front. The diagonal is a straight line—there is no curve, no "rond de jambe" quality. Maximum turnout is maintained. From fifth back going to the back, the toes lead to the back and point in on the center line right behind the dancer's spine. As the leg goes back, it rotates out, showing the inside of the leg from thigh to heel. This is possible only if the hip line opens.

The feeling of the working leg is the same in all three directions and so is the look. This is because the dancer maintains maximum turnout as she presents the inside of the entire working leg and foot. To achieve this look when the leg is to the back, the

Peter leading back with his toes, lightly caressing the floor (no demi-pointe!)

Peter in fifth position back

Peter in tendu back, toes on the center line

working hip must be released, which is contrary to more traditional teaching. But for Mr. B, it was more important to have the leg turned out—that is, the inside of the leg from thigh to heel showing from underneath—than to have square and level hips. Also, keeping the hips down and squared when moving the leg to the back gives the dancer a locked-in feeling and a contained look. When the working leg is back and its hip is released and opened, the dancer feels free to move, her line is extended, and her dancing, when that comes, is expanded. Meanwhile, at the barre the dancer is freed to point directly back, toes on the center line while maintaining her turnout. Therefore each dancer releases her working hip, but only as much as needed to present the look Mr. B desired. It is, however, very important that she stand straight "like you swallowed a yardstick." The supporting hip does not tilt back. The upper body is also held straight; it does not tip forward.

While doing a series of tendus back, the working hip is maintained in the opened or released position. It is returned to the normal position, level and square, only when the dancer changes direction or ends the exercise.

The idea of the release of the working hip when the leg is back is introduced in tendu exercises at the barre. It is the basis of the look Mr. B wanted when the leg is to the back in almost all poses and movements (e.g., the arabesques). The same pattern applies to other differences I have cited so far between the traditional approach and his teaching (e.g., plié with resistance, and continuous; no demi-pointe in tendu; pointing on the center line of the body in tendu). To become a Balanchine dancer it is necessary to begin to understand these details from the time they come up at the barre and to work persistently, yet patiently, to acquire the skill to apply them in each movement. Nothing less is required technically and also nothing more, although many other factors do come into play to make a successful dancer.

Returning to fifth from each direction precisely reverses the order of the foot action, but certain details are essential to note. The action is back to fifth, not down into the floor, mostly because the dancers do not drop to demi-pointe; the metatarsals stay lifted, and only the tips of the toes contact the floor (lightly!) until the foot is placed gently in fifth. Only when the working foot has reached a fully crossed fifth position do the dancers put the heel down on the floor, but with very light contact. Also, the weight is still held over the ball of the supporting foot. From tendu front the toes lead back as the heel stays forward and the entire leg and foot return to fifth. From tendu side, the heel comes forward as the toes move back and the leg and foot move into fifth position. Closing to fifth front, the dancer can feel as if she is covering the supporting foot with the working foot. From the back the working heel leads and should reach the little toe of the standing foot just before or at the same time as the big toe of the working foot touches the standing heel to establish fifth. Closing to fifth back, the dancer can feel as if she is hiding the working foot behind the supporting foot.

Sometimes Mr. B saw that he needed to help us understand how deeply the dancer needs to cross into fifth when closing from the side. Standing behind one of us, he placed his foot at a right angle to the dancer's supporting toe. As she brought the working leg and foot into fifth, she and he both needed to feel her working heel make contact with his foot (see page 66).

The working foot, including the heel, is placed into fifth position very lightly. It looks as if the dancer is standing with equal weight on each foot, but her weight remains over the supporting foot when she does a series of tendu battements with the same leg. She transfers her weight only to work the former supporting leg; she divides her weight equally on the balls of both feet only at the end of the exercise.

As I noted at the beginning of this chapter, Mr. B was very concerned with fifth position. Fifth position is made by turning out both legs, crossing the thighs, and crossing the feet. The feet in fifth are not only fully crossed, with heel to toe; they are

Dana fully closed from the side, making contact with Peter's foot

also "glued together," as he liked to call it. This is usually impossible with both knees locked straight, because of the shape of most dancers' legs. Some try to accommodate the closing of the working leg to the front by pulling the hips back, but the hips should remain pulled up, square, and level. Therefore, most dancers need to release the working knee slightly to close properly into fifth front. When closing to fifth front, the dancer begins with her working knee stretched and then releases it as much as necessary to continue to close into a tight, crossed fifth. Also, most dancers need to release the supporting knee slightly to close properly into fifth back. When closing to fifth back, the dancer keeps her supporting knee straight until she needs to release it to allow the working leg to close into a tight, crossed fifth. As the supporting knee releases, the thigh must maintain its turnout; the knee should not twist to the front. Standing in fifth position, there should be no space between the legs or between the feet.

Mr. Balanchine valued consistent correct execution and maximum effort above many qualities. When I write "maximum turnout" or "maximum energy," it is because I remember the times when he tried especially hard to get us to sustain that level. He wanted the maximum even in the smallest details, rather than only in the big, showy steps. There are two good examples applicable to tendu. Returning to fifth or first from tendu side, dancers can momentarily lose the maximum turnout in the working foot and allow the heel to slip back. Sensing the loss of precision as they approach fifth, they adjust the foot to achieve a tight position. Mr. B called the resulting movement "snaking." Similarly, closing from front, dancers may lead with the heel and let the toes lag, closing by "whacking" the toes in at the end to achieve a tight fifth position. Closing from back, the toes might lead, so the heel has to be "whacked" in. He would say, "If you are doing your maximum, there is no room for correction; you are already correct."

To achieve the levels of consistency and effort Mr. B's aesthetic demands requires unwavering concentration. Dancers who lose their concentration will be less precise. For example, tendu front and back are extensions of fifth position. From fifth front or back, the working leg moves directly front or back, the thighs remain crossed, and the foot accommodates the action of the leg by pointing into the center line. But dancers can lose their concentration and let the thighs uncross, which then requires correction to achieve the desired tendu position. Seeing that, Mr. B would ask, "What are you thinking about, what you'll have for lunch?" We needed to be in class with our entire beings.

The toes make minimum contact with the floor during the tendu. There is almost no friction and no weight. "Don't polish the floor," Balanchine would say, and then he would tell us how the marble floors were cleaned in Russia. The cleaning women trapped a rag under each foot and, shuffling their feet with pressure, polished the floor. He did not want our energy and effort directed into the floor, as if we were cleaning women. Instead, he wanted

us to have very little friction with the floor. His approach gave a lightness and a fleetness to the movement.

Similarly, once the working foot has reached the tendu position, there should be no weight on the toes. "Don't dig into the floor." It should almost be possible to slip a piece of onionskin paper under them. The energy of the toes is applied to stretching, pressing, or curling them against the sole of the shoe, not pressing the toes into the floor. The dancer must be especially aware of this in tendu back, because there is a tendency to push the big toe into the floor and "wing" the foot. The resulting stretch of the instep can feel good and is probably useful to some as a warm-up. But in class and onstage, a properly pointed foot was one with the arch fully stretched, the heel forward, and the toes back and bent down, pressed down against the sole.

We did the majority of our tendus at an even, moderate tempo, with the foot pointing on the "and" and closing into fifth on the beat. Mr. B compared battement tendu to the even tick-tock of the clock. But within the even tempo, the tendu is phrased. It starts out rapidly, then slows slightly to reveal the full point. It starts in sharply and then slows as the foot is placed in fifth. At a slow or moderate tempo we stop in fifth, our home base, the place we always return to.

In moderately faster tendus the foot starts rapidly out of fifth and points, then is brought in sharply, but is still placed (never banged or

---

DETAILS I OFTEN INSIST ON IN BATTEMENT TENDU:

1) precise pointing of the working toes in front and in back (on the center line of the body); to the side, point them directly side, never back of side
2) maximum turnout at all times
3) a light touch on the floor
4) fully pointed working foot with the toes pressing against the sole of the shoe in tendu
5) not working through demi-pointe; keeping the metatarsals lifted
6) the clean stop in fifth, except when the tempo is too fast to do so
7) when the leg is back: working hip line open —"leg is part of hip"; supporting hip line straight; shoulders square; back straight; and stomach pulled in

slammed) into fifth. When the tempo is very, *very* fast there may not be enough time to get all the way back into fifth, and there is certainly not enough time to stop and put the heel down. Then the foot is brought in toward fifth as much as possible and then returns to point. The emphasis is on making the foot point fully when the music is too fast to allow for a tight, or, when closing from the side, a crossed fifth position. However, the dancer must stop in fifth, or at least try to, before changing direction; this stop, or pause, "announces" the change. Sometimes, to clearly enunciate the new direction, we held on to the fifth, delaying the start of the next tendu to show that position, but speeding up to catch the beat on "and."

Careful attention to a clean stop in fifth position before starting the foot out of fifth again, rather than rebounding out of fifth, develops speed in the foot and leg. From nothing, "WHAM!" as we moved the foot and leg sharply out of fifth. Sometimes Balanchine would call for a tempo so fast that we could barely do the tendu movement at all, but by attempting it, we got the sense of always reaching for more—in this case, more speed. By pushing to this extreme, a slightly slower but still very fast tempo seemed more feasible.

Careful attention to precise fifth and first positions; to exact directions front, side, and back in tendu; to light contact with the floor; to avoiding dropping to demi-pointe; and a fully pointed foot develop precision and articulation.

Battement Tendu with Plié

Tendu close fifth *and* demi-plié is a frequently given step that everyone understands; it combines a normal tendu and a normal demi-plié. We sometimes practiced this step as part of the barre exercises, using Mr. B's technique for each part. The combination went tendu out on "and," close fifth on count one, plié on "and," straighten the legs on count two.

In many schools tendu *with* plié is done rather haphazardly. From the tendu position, both knees start to bend as the working leg starts to close, ending in a demi-plié, with the heels down and weight settled on them. As the dancer moves her working leg out of fifth, both knees remain bent too long or straighten immediately, which is too soon. Mr. B realized that this is not exactly what we do when we dance. He therefore worked on a tendu *with* demi-plié that is based on the technique used when dancing, and we did this at the barre as well.

From the tendu position, when the dancer closes to fifth, she starts the toes and the entire leg back in toward fifth with straight knees for two or three inches, and then she begins to bend both knees. In other words, the tendu begins to close before the plié begins. Then, as she begins to bend her knees, she resists the plié in both legs to build strength and collect energy. However, until she closes, the weight is centered over the ball of the standing foot, and the working foot has only light contact with the floor. As she reaches the deepest point in the demi-plié, her weight is over the balls of her feet, and the heels may release if needed. It is important that the plié is continuous and deep enough to gather energy. The dancer never sits in plié and the hips do not fall back. There is energy in both legs and the toes almost seem to hold on to or grasp the floor. The foot does not relax and flatten down on the floor.

Turnout is strictly maintained in both legs throughout the entire movement, and especially in the plié. The knees are aligned over the toes as they are in a standard plié.

Coming out of plié, the dancer begins to straighten both knees slightly before starting the working leg out to tendu. Both legs usually straighten together.

The timing of this step is the same as for tendu straight. The "and" is the tendu, and the count is the fifth-position demi-plié. However, this step has a distinctive phrasing that keeps the plié continuous. From the extended line, the leg and the foot start in sharply. It's almost as if the body lifts up to go down. The dancer goes into the plié slowly, rela-

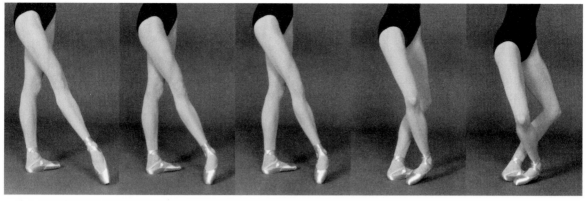

Dana in tendu front *Dana starting the foot in, toes pulling back, both legs remaining stretched* *Dana starting to bend the supporting knee as the working knee starts to bend* *Dana closing to fifth position as she pliés* *Dana in fifth front, with the weight over the balls of her feet*

DETAILS I OFTEN INSIST ON IN
BATTEMENT TENDU WITH PLIÉ:

1) point the working toes precisely front, side, and back; no weight on pointe
2) maximum turnout at all times, knees over toes in plié, hips pulled up
3) light touch on the floor
4) fully pointed foot with toes pressed against the sole of the shoe in tendu
5) not working through demi-pointe; not dropping down to demi-pointe
6) continuous plié
7) start back to fifth before plié begins; start up from plié before leg and foot move out of fifth

tive to the overall timing, and with resistance; there is a stop in fifth but no stop in plié.

Mr. B's active and continuous plié differed, as did much else, from what many other teachers taught. We were often made emphatically aware of this when we did class with other teachers. The company took the train on tour to Los Angeles one year, stopping in Chicago for a five-hour layover. With a couple more days on the train ahead of us, Gloria Govrin and I found a professional class, and we went off to take it. The teacher started barre as usual. By the second combination, tendu with demi-plié, the teacher noticed my continuous movement, and he came over and stopped me. He pointed out that I was not doing what he had showed and told me I must stop in demi-plié and "sit there like a dead person." I couldn't believe what I was hearing. I went back to the train and re-counted the story to Balanchine. He loved it so much that sometimes, with a private wink to me, he would later tell dancers in class, "You know, you are sitting in plié like dead person."

Battement Tendu Jeté

Battement tendu jeté is the traditional name for an exercise I call jeté battement or battement dégagé. Often, Mr. B indicated he wanted this exercise by slapping his thigh a few times, or he did a few, saying, "Sixteen front, back, and side" or "Thirty-two side."

Jeté battement uses the same action as tendu but brushes off the floor. At moderate tempos the toes are two and a half to three inches in the air, at slower tempos a little higher (four inches or so), and at faster tempos lower. Jeté battement develops strength and speed in the leg and foot and the skill needed to rapidly point the foot, particularly the ends of the toes.

The refinements Balanchine developed for tendu carried over to jeté battement, in particular the action of the working leg and foot as they moved into and out of fifth. He did not want us to go down through demi-pointe and emphasized that there should be a very light touch on the floor. This was necessary to develop the fast, articulate movement he wanted in the instep and toes.

Coming to a clear stop in fifth helps develop speed and strength in the leg and foot and the ability of the dancer to move instantly. At any speed the dancer should make each jeté battement happen; she should not bounce out of fifth or ricochet off the supporting heel in first. At very fast tempos there is no time to stop in fifth and often it is not even possible to close to fifth (or first). So the toes are brought back to the floor, aiming for first or fifth and moving in as far as the tempo allows. Then, staying on time, the dancer brushes the foot out, and the toes point again on the center line of the body or precisely to the side.

Characteristically, Mr. B wanted a little more of these qualities. He gave us jeté battements at a range of tempos, but especially at very fast ones.

We might do eight, sixteen, or thirty-two front, side, and back at moderately fast tempos and then repeat the exercise at an even faster tempo. At the fastest tempos the working leg seemed to be just shaking and the toes barely pointing. Still, we had to maintain the turnout, point exactly front, side, or back and perfect the movement of the ankle. One other benefit was that normal fast tempos seemed easy by comparison.

In my classes at SAB, I sometimes give a jeté battement exercise at a moderately fast tempo in which the dancer just brushes the foot out, points, and pulls it partway back aiming for fifth, brushes it out, points, and pulls it back, and so on. This gives the students a chance to practice and perfect the movement needed in the ankle and the toes before working at maximum speed.

The emphasis in jeté battement is on pointing the foot and on ensuring that the pointed foot is exactly front, side, or back. But it is essential to maintain maximum turnout of the leg and foot and to aim for the fifth or first position even when the tempos are very fast. Correct form in closing as explained for tendu had to be observed: Mr. B especially wanted at slower tempos to see the foot placed properly into fifth, including putting the heel down onto the

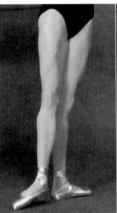    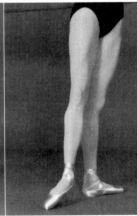

Dana brushing out moderately fast to the side, toes actively pressing the sole of her shoe (no demi-pointe)

Dana continuing to brush out moderately fast, toes in light contact with the floor

Dana's leg extended side; her foot shows a fully stretched instep and toes pointed. At very fast tempos, her foot would be just off the floor.

Dana's leg coming in from the side, heel starting front and toes back (no demi-pointe)

Dana's leg coming in from the side, heel continuing front and toes back (no demi-pointe) as the foot aims for fifth

floor only when the feet were fully crossed. He was also vigilant to see that we did not "snake" the working foot in from the side.

People like to talk about "hands-on" teaching, but Balanchine also employed "foot-on" methods. Here is another example. When he saw that a dancer had trouble closing to fifth from the side, letting the working toes slip forward when closing front or letting the heel slip back when closing back, he went over to that dancer. Placing his foot parallel to her supporting foot and leaving enough space for her to slide her very turned-out (heel forward, toe back) foot in without snaking, he asked her to demonstrate the correct technique. Any contact let them both know she still did not have it.

When doing jeté battement Mr. B generally had us point on the "and" and in fifth on the beat. Dancers must develop the skill to get instantly out of fifth; the effect should be explosive. "It's like the cobra," Mr. B said, "the 'and' is stronger than the one." This is a necessity, no matter what the tempo of the music. Mr. B used words from the funnies or cartoons, such as "BANG!" or "POW!" or "WHAM!" to get the idea across.

To develop greater musical awareness, speed, and control, Mr. B sometimes asked us to brush out like a lightning flash on the one. We stopped at about forty-five degrees and held the leg; he varied the count for bringing the foot in—sometimes on two, sometimes on four. It came in toward fifth, very rapidly, but was carefully *placed* in fifth in the usual way.

Dana aiming for fifth position back

She made it and Peter didn't feel a thing.

Dana's foot aiming for fifth front just before brushing out again. She does not drop down on her full foot; her heel remains forward and her toes back. Her foot will not reach fifth.

DETAILS I OFTEN INSIST ON IN BATTEMENT TENDU JETÉ:

1) exact directions front, side, and back—no "rond de jambe" action to the side
2) maximum turnout of the working foot at all times—no snaking foot
3) maximum effort to achieve a pointed foot and a stretched instep
4) maximum turnout to the back, open hip
5) straight, stretched knee to the back
6) closing from the side at faster tempos, try to make a good crossed fifth, not just a third position
7) the hips and torso remain pulled up and the torso is calm

Another means of developing musical awareness is to have the pianist play chords for fast jetés. The dancers do four or eight evenly spaced jetés per chord. In this way the dancers learn to hold the count internally. Mr. B also liked to ask for chords, because it neutralizes the temptation many pianists feel to overplay for this kind of exercise, distracting the dancers with more music than they need. When pianists play lots of notes with great energy, the dancers can feel they are working very hard, when they are really coasting on the energy in the music. Instead, the dancers should be making the maximum effort, and the music should be minimal, serving only to mark the beat. Peter Martins often gets the same result by asking for an adagio melody.

At any tempo, Mr. B wanted the dancer at least to try to clearly announce each change in direction. This is done by very slightly holding the last fifth position before the new direction, by "borrowing" a bit from the next beat. The dancer catches up by accelerating her next movement, so she is on the music by the "and." In exercises set squarely on the music (e.g., to music in four, four front, side, back, and side, or eight front, side, and back), dancers held the fourth or the eighth fifth positions. At faster tempos dancers must make an extra effort to try to announce each change in direction. A musically more challenging exercise for the dancers uses a movement pattern of three and five set over music in four or eight. Such exercises are an important part of class because they teach

the dancers to count the music accurately rather than simply to listen. This skill is essential for dancers who want to dance certain Balanchine repertory.

Mr. B wanted us to focus most of our attention at the barre on our legs and feet, and therefore we usually held the arm in second or fifth low. But on occasion, when we did fast jeté battements, he would give a port de bras to make sure we could maintain energy and speed in the legs and feet while moving the arm, hand, and head in a fluid and gracious manner. Meanwhile, the body is kept pulled up but quiet, the dancer seeming to ride "serenely" on top of the legs.

One day I was concentrating extra hard at the barre on a series of very fast jeté battements, my effort making me stiff and tense. Mr. B noticed the cords standing taut in my neck and came over and began to chat. He said, "Pretend we are at a cocktail party. White wine or red?" He wanted an easy manner even when we made a very big effort and concentrated very hard on the movement.

Jeté battement is important because its mastery enables the dancer to do very fast glissades, jetés, or assemblés—any movement requiring the dancer to brush her leg quickly out of fifth and point her feet instantly and then bring her leg back into fifth. It also helps to develop the facility needed for fast batterie.

Battement tendu jeté is also given with plié. The principles applicable to tendu with plié apply also to this exercise.

Battement Tendu Piqué

Mr. B often supplemented his usual jeté battements and other exercises with precisely focused movements intended to develop in us some aspect of the look and facility needed to dance his ballets. An example is battement tendu piqué.

This exercise starts in fifth position. At moderate tempos the dancer does a normal battement tendu jeté and stops her leg in the air, holding it there for a moment. Then, instead of returning the foot to fifth, she maintains her leg fully stretched and turned out and her foot fully pointed as she brings the toes sharply to the floor for a very light tap—like a pinprick. The leg and foot instantly are lifted back to the position in the air, which is held as long as the tempo allows. When the prescribed number of taps have been done, the foot is returned to fifth in the way described in battement tendu jeté.

The most important characteristic of this exercise is that the accent of the working leg and foot is UP! from the floor. The up accent had to come entirely from the dancer—she had to be in control, there was to be no passive bounce or ricochet from the floor. In fact, to get his idea across to us and to have us make the right action, he occasionally had us execute the step without actually touching the floor—"and UP, and UP, and UP." Each time we stopped in the UP position. On the descent the foot must be brought sharply down, rather than being allowed to fall by gravity. A free fall is not as quick,

is out of control, and thus often results in a ricochet from the floor.

Even though the point of the exercise is the clarity, lightness, and quickness with which the dancer rapidly brings her working leg and pointe to the floor in order to instantly lift it off, she cannot let other technical elements go. In the air and at floor level, the foot must be fully pointed and the toes actively pressed against the sole of the shoe; the working foot must be presented exactly front, side, or back; turnout must be maintained in the working and in the supporting leg. There should be little or no sound. The teacher might hear a light tapping sound from new toe shoes, but no solid knocks and no dull thuds.

At moderate tempos the dancers stop each time in the up position, about four inches off the floor. At faster tempos the leg stops with the pointe of the working foot closer to the floor (one to two inches); at even faster tempos there is no time to stop at all, but the accent is still up. Whatever the tempo, the interval between taps is controlled and constant; the leg does not simply twitch, as in a spasm.

This exercise builds the skill and strength necessary to start the leg up and down very quickly and to stop the extended leg in the air. This is especially important preparation for glissades in all directions and for cabrioles and grands jetés. Tendu piqué also helps in developing the speed needed for beats. The pulling-down action develops the instantaneous response in the inner thighs that helps achieve the scissoring action required.

DETAILS I OFTEN INSIST ON IN BATTEMENT TENDU PIQUÉ:

1) no bouncing or rebounding from the floor
2) each movement up ends with a stop, when the tempo allows
3) precise directions front, side, and back

Grand Battement

The action of grand battement is essentially the same as the one for battement tendu and for battement tendu jeté, except that the leg and foot are thrown higher into air, while maintaining proper alignment of the body. The height depends on the dancer's strength and flexibility and the available musical time. If the studio was crowded, Mr. Balanchine had a couple of ways of getting this exercise in without sacrificing our having a specific alignment to the barre. On some occasions he divided the class into two groups so we could stand, as is usual, perpendicular to the barre. Another solution was to give grand battement front, with the dancers standing back to the barre and grand battement back, with the dancers facing the barre. Or he might omit grand battement back and front at the barre but include it in the center. We never did them (or any other exercise) arranged haphazardly at the barre.

Mr. B's insistence that the dancer always be in control gave her more freedom of movement in the end. "Dancers must defy gravity," he said. In grand battement he wanted to see that the dancer defied gravity by the speed and energy with which she threw her leg into the air and, just as important, by the speed and energy with which the foot returned to the floor—faster than it would get there in a simple fall. Both movements should happen because the dancer makes them happen. Finally, once the foot has reached the floor, the dancer places it into fifth, as she would from battement tendu or battement tendu jeté. The foot does not slam into the floor or whack the supporting foot.

To start grand battement, the dancer initiates the action from the toes and foot of the working leg. There is no preliminary heave of the torso, nor does the dancer anticipate the movement by tilting her body. It's as if the foot and toes are trying to point, but the floor is in the way, so they push down and out as they brush and point immediately off the floor. She does not just lift the leg from the thigh and then point the foot. The "throw" happens in both the working foot and the leg. The thrusting foot adds energy and speed to the movement, which give it a quality of lightness. Maximum turnout, a stretched leg, and a fully energized and shaped foot are required throughout.

Mr. B wanted us to stand very straight in grand battement, which is different from what many teachers want. There is no bending or tilting away from the working leg; if anything, the upper torso should feel as if it meets the working leg as it reaches its full extension; in fact, the torso should not move in grand battement front and side. The temptation to tilt away from the working leg is strongest when the dancer is doing grand battement to the back. "Don't move your hand," he would say when he noticed a dancer moving her hand forward on the barre so her torso could more easily tilt to accommodate the action of the leg to the back. On occasion Balanchine would put his hand an inch or two in front of the neck of a dancer as a good reminder to stand as straight as possible. Throughout the entire movement, proper alignment of the hips, back, and shoulders is maintained, and so are exact directions: front, side, and back.

The essential quality that grand battement must have is the explosive burst of the working foot out of fifth and the throw into the air at maximum speed and energy. From stillness to maximum force in an instant. This is true for all tempos; grand battement is always a throw, never a lift. "Grand battement is *not* like a rocket launching," he would say, noting that rockets usually seem to struggle off the

---

DETAILS I OFTEN INSIST ON IN GRAND BATTEMENT:

1) instant speed from fifth
2) place the toes to the floor, don't let the foot slam down
3) make a clear stop in fifth, when the tempo allows
4) show exact directions to the front, side, back
5) the grand battement is not initiated in the torso; there is no movement before the leg moves
6) stand straight/stay straight

pad. If the tempo was moderate, the extra time was used to close, placing the foot into fifth position and stopping there.

Balanchine encouraged us in several ways to try for maximum speed. He often put his hand out at about the eye level of the dancer or a little higher and then he asked her to hit it hard (see photo page 48). If her working foot did not move with enough energy and speed, he would then say, "Harder! I barely felt a thing. It's not a love tap, and it shouldn't feel like one!" If that didn't get a result, he would say, "Get angry!" One way or another, he was going to get that explosive start.

As soon as the working foot reaches full extension, the dancer immediately starts the leg down, but under her control, not by gravity. Mr. B said, "Use your own force to put your leg down. Don't wait until the leg starts falling. Only people who control gravity are dancers. We force gravity." She begins quickly, then slows a bit to fit the tempo as she places the toes on the floor. The working foot is placed in fifth, as it is in battement tendu jeté. When the tempo allows, the dancer comes to a complete stop in fifth position. But even when the exercise calls for fast, continuous grand battements and there is no time for a stop, the foot does not rebound from the supporting foot or the floor.

The timing of grand battement calls for the dancer to be in the extended line on "and" and in fifth position on the count.

The speed and control developed in grand battement are especially important for grand jeté, cabriole, and other steps that require the working leg to brush explosively off the floor.

Other Forms of Grand Battement

Mr. Balanchine liked to give a variant of grand battement that called for the dancer to throw the straight leg and foot with speed just short of her maximum height and stop it there. Rather than bringing the foot down to fifth, as she would in a regular grand battement, after the stop, she immediately tries to lift it slightly. "Stop, lift!" he would say. Correctly done, this technique enables the dancer to stop her leg in the extended line without its shaking. Throwing the foot to the maximum extension and trying to freeze it there usually cause it to drop slightly and bounce or jiggle. This exercise built strength and muscle memory for "make a picture" jumps and a more dynamic grand jeté.

Other variants of grand battement include frappé with grand battement (see page 106), développé battement (see page 94), and enveloppé battement (see page 97).

Battement Dégagé

Battement dégagé is another exercise that typically is done from fifth and incorporates the action of battement tendu. The working leg continues in the same path as grand battement on the way up and down. However, unlike grand battement, which is always fast and in which the working leg is thrown, battement dégagé is often done slowly and with the working leg being lifted.

The lift comes from the entire working leg, from the tips of the toes to the top of the leg. The inside thigh muscles can be used only if the turnout is strictly maintained. The working leg pauses or stops, depending on the tempo, in the extended line. At ninety degrees or higher to the front, the dancer should be able to hold a glass of water on the heel of her working foot. My first director, Lew Christensen, ballet master of the San Francisco Ballet, used to say, "Pretend you're holding a glass of nitroglycerin. If it drops, you know what will happen." Balanchine, in his elegant, worldly way, used to say, "Balance a glass of champagne on your heel." To the side at ninety degrees or higher, this amount of turnout is basically impossible to achieve, but the inside of the leg and foot should be presented. To the back, the dancer releases or opens the working hip to achieve the required turned-out line.

Battement dégagé can be done at all tempos and

to a range of heights. Mr. Balanchine specified differing combinations of tempo and height to which he wanted us to lift the working leg. Practicing them enhanced our control and musicality.

When battement dégagé is done at moderate to slow tempos, the dancer shows the quick (but not explosive!) start out of fifth, then, in keeping with the tempo, slows the working leg a little as it lifts. It pauses or stops at the designated height. Holding as long as the tempo allows, she starts down with accent to show the beginning of the closing. She then lowers the leg more slowly and carefully places her toes and foot into fifth.

When battement dégagé is done at faster tempos, it can resemble other exercises. High (ninety degrees or more) battement dégagé is almost grand battement with a hold in the extended line; low (usually forty-five degrees) battement dégagé is almost jeté battement.

The torso is held very erect in battement dégagé. As in grand battement, the feeling is that the working leg meets the torso, front or back.

When battement dégagé is done correctly, it builds strength in the entire body: legs, abdomen, back.

DETAILS I OFTEN INSIST ON IN
BATTEMENT DÉGAGÉ:
1) maintain maximum turnout
2) exact directions front, side, and back
3) stand straight, no tilting

Sur le Cou-de-Pied

There are two ways to get the foot out of fifth. The first way is the brushing motion (glisser) discussed in battement tendu. The second way is picking it up off the floor, as in sur le cou-de-pied. The technique practiced in taking the foot from fifth to sur le cou-de-pied develops the quality of movement Mr.

B also wanted in taking the foot from fifth to coupé, passé, and so on.

Sur le cou-de-pied is often overlooked, although it is not so difficult to achieve. The technique for reaching it from fifth position requires awareness, concentration, and effort. The details of the position and of the technique for getting to it should be mastered in early training. Getting to sur le cou-de-pied and returning to fifth correctly was an essential base for moving Balanchine's way. Also, the more open and turned-out look Mr. B wanted us to have was enhanced if we could show the position correctly. So Mr. B had us practice going to sur le cou-de-pied and returning to fifth as an exercise in itself. He wanted these movements to become second nature to us.

Mr. B redefined the technique for picking the foot off the floor in ways intended to give the movement subtlety and nuance and to help each dancer give her foot the most beautiful possible shape. His insistence on consistent attention to the details (e.g., heels forward, toes back) trained our feet in ways that helped us avoid sickling, the "bent spoon" look. He also worked to make the action articulate and delicate and to maximize the turnout throughout the movement. The refinement he worked for is crucial to his aesthetic, because it trains the feet in the correct action. Even when the dancer does not go through sur le cou-de-pied, she still takes her foot off the floor, with the toes going back and the heel coming forward. The awareness and the energy for the fully wrapped position have to be there. When, for example, Mr. B had us do steps that required us to plié on the supporting leg as we picked the working foot up off the floor, we did not wrap the working foot in sur le cou-de-pied. However, the foot releases from the floor in the same toes back/heel front way used in going to sur le cou-de-pied, but moves to or through coupé front or back (see Coupé, page 80, for a discussion of this). In fact, when the dancer is jumping, the feet should release off the floor with almost the same feeling, the heels coming forward and the toes going back and down.

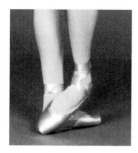

Dana coming out of fifth, heel forward, toes back, as the knee bends and pulls back

Mr. B was insistent that in early, intermediate, and, often, advanced training, dancers practice the movements to sur le cou-de-pied whenever the foot is picked up off the floor from fifth flat. It is important to practice this movement to help the dancer memorize how to pick the foot off the floor and how to shape and point it. Once this was accomplished, it was no longer necessary always to move through sur le cou-de-pied. The way the foot released was important. The toes-back-and-heel-forward motion was the way to arrive at a fully pointed and stretched foot. We never lifted the heel up, making demi-pointe on the floor, before pointing the toes. His aim was to have dancers whose feet were as pliable as an elephant's trunk when it picks up a peanut, yet very strong (also true of the elephant's trunk).

From fifth position front, the movement starts when the toes curl back just grazing the floor and the heel releases from the floor and stays forward. The toes immediately wrap around the smallest part of the supporting ankle, the heel finishes in front of the ankle, and the toes in back just off the

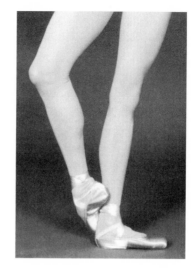

Dana in sur le cou-de-pied front, her foot hugging her ankle and her knee side

floor. The dancer may feel that her working foot grasps, or hugs, the supporting ankle. Sometimes in class Mr. B would see that we were not in the correct position, and he would stop. Indicating his neck, he would say, "Cou! The neck! You know, the neck of the foot." The foot is not fully pointed—straight up and down, with the toes aiming directly to the floor; it is angled or slanted back, in a beveled position. This happens as the working knee pulls back to the side, maintaining maximum turnout, while the hips remain pulled up and square.

From fifth back, the toes of the working foot move and curl back (no demi-pointe) as the heel releases to come forward. It is essential that the heel not initiate this action by lifting up and off the floor. In moving to the sur le cou-de-pied position,

Dana in fifth position back

Dana leading back with the toes (no demi-pointe)

Dana releasing the heel forward as the toes continue to lead back and the knee bends side

Dana arriving in sur le cou-de-pied back

the foot does not make demi-pointe. As the toes begin to move toward the back and the heel forward, it is necessary to bend the working knee and take it clearly to the side; if the dancer does not do this, the working foot will be overcrossed and not attached at the back of the supporting ankle. The heel attaches to the back at the supporting ankle so that the toes are just off the floor. Again, the foot is beveled. The working knee maintains maximum turnout by pulling back to the side, while the hips remain square. The action of the working foot and knee is the same as from fifth front.

In sur le cou-de-pied back we naturally don't have an ankle to wrap the foot around, and yet, because the action is the same, the foot should have the same shape in sur le cou-de-pied back that it has in sur le cou-de-pied front. Sometimes, to make his

point clear, Mr. B would stand very close behind a dancer and place his foot so his leg was right behind hers. As she made sur le cou-de-pied back, she simultaneously wrapped his ankle in sur le cou-de-pied front. He would say that if we had a third leg, we would wrap it.

Balanchine also redefined how to put the foot on the floor, especially from sur le cou-de-pied back. Like his redefinition of the details we saw in tendu and related steps, his concern grew from his insistence that the dancer be aware and in control of *all* her movements *all* the time.

When placing the foot onto the floor from sur le cou-de-pied front, the working leg begins to straighten and the toes, still held back, slide down the supporting ankle, making contact with the floor next to the supporting heel. The working heel comes forward, aiming for the floor in front of the big toe of the supporting foot as the working foot slides into fifth position without passing through demi-pointe. As the working heel moves into a crossed fifth position, the working thigh rotates out even more. The dancer pulls up on the supporting hip to make room for the working leg. Placing the foot to the floor from sur le cou-de-pied back requires maximum awareness of and attention to Balanchine's refinement of the traditional technique. The action is especially important to learn, because it is also used when closing to the back from coupé, passé, enveloppé, etc. The working foot is maintained in its beveled position as it lowers, which places the toes on the floor away from (not against or next to) the back of the supporting heel. As the working knee continues to straighten, the foot adjusts slightly as the heel is lowered toward the floor and is pulled in to the lit-

Dana in sur le cou-de-pied back, wrapping the "third leg" supplied by Peter

tle toe of the supporting foot. The toes of the working foot are held back as long as possible as the foot is brought into fifth position. This avoids sickling the foot or the snaking described in Battement Tendu. Again, the working foot does not make demi-pointe on the way to fifth.

When closing into fifth back, the supporting knee may have to release slightly to allow the dancer to make a tight fifth position. A correct closing motion is easier to achieve from the front, because the supporting foot is there. The working toes aim just in front of the supporting heel, and the working heel is forced to remain forward. If it slips back, it will come down on the toes of the supporting foot.

Sur le cou-de-pied offers an excellent example of the teacher adjusting the combinations at the barre as the class goes along. When Mr. Balanchine saw that dancers could not pick their feet up properly doing passé or développé, for example, he might give an exercise comprising only picking the foot up, going to sur le cou-de-pied, and then putting the foot back to the floor, or he might have us go

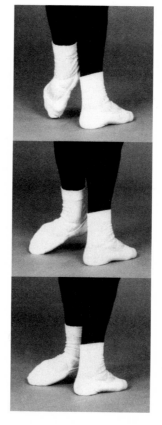

Peter places his toes to the floor away from the supporting heel.

Peter holding the working toes back (no demi-pointe) as he moves his heel toward fifth position back and slightly releases the supporting knee

Peter closing to fifth position back (no demi-pointe); his supporting knee is slightly released to allow his working foot to close tightly.

DETAILS I OFTEN INSIST ON
IN SUR LE COU-DE-PIED:

1) from fifth to sur le cou-de-pied—the toes start back, the heel releases forward; no demi-pointe

2) in sur le cou-de-pied in back position— the foot is "wrapped" (beveled, not a full pointe); the toes are curled, not flexed; the shape of the working foot is the same, front or back; the foot is at the same level, front and back; the toes are just off the floor, front and back

3) closing from sur le cou-de-pied in back to fifth, the toes aim away from the supporting heel, and the working heel leads into fifth before the toes (no sickling)

4) no demi-pointe closing front or back

---

from sur le cou-de-pied to passé and then return the foot to the floor. Another alternative was to give us pas de cheval. In each class he gave us what he thought we needed, not only in the center, but, perhaps more importantly, also at the barre.

Sur le Cou-de-Pied (Relevé)

The sur le cou-de-pied position is basically the same on demi-pointe and on full pointe as it is on flat. In sur le cou-de-pied front in relevé, there is slightly less space between the supporting heel and ankle. Therefore, depending on her proportions, the dancer may have to adjust the working foot slightly. She does this by sliding the working heel a little more forward, to the front of the supporting ankle, or, if necessary, she may lift it very slightly higher. It is important that the toes continue to wrap around the neck of the supporting ankle, fin-

Dana on pointe in sur le cou-de-pied front, toes wrapped behind the heel

Peter on demi-pointe in sur le cou-de-pied front, toes wrapped behind the heel

ishing behind the heel. The foot may have to bevel a slight bit more to maintain the wrapped position with the toes behind the heel.

Sur le cou-de-pied back in relevé is much easier to do because there is nothing to wrap, and the supporting heel is not in the way. The working foot is basically in the same shape and at the same height in the back and in the front. Therefore the foot does not change shape or height when going from front to back.

Coupé

Going from fifth to coupé and returning to fifth was not practiced as an exercise in itself, unlike going from fifth to sur le cou-de-pied and returning to the floor. At the barre, coupé was most frequently practiced passing through while doing passé or exercises incorporating passé. Coupé was also practiced in exercises in which the dancer is in plié on the supporting leg (e.g., fondu).

Mr. Balanchine emphasized the importance of mastering the action of picking the foot off the floor and bringing it to sur le cou-de-pied. The facility developed in that practice helped us achieve the heel forward/toe back action of the working foot that he also wanted in coupé, that he in fact wanted whenever the foot is picked off the floor. Also, he never wanted to see the foot go through a full demi-pointe as we picked the foot off the floor and returned it to the floor, whether or not we were

going through sur le cou-de-pied. It was also essential in coupé that we show the foot exactly on the center line of the supporting leg, not open and not overcrossed.

When a dancer goes to coupé from fifth front standing on full foot, and the supporting leg is to remain straight, she often moves through sur le cou-de-pied front. From sur le cou-de-pied the dancer lifts the working knee so the arch can fully stretch as the toes are drawn in front of the ankle and as the foot fully points. The working knee continues to lift straight up and out so the pointe is on the center line of the supporting ankle or a few inches higher on the supporting leg. The pointe touches very lightly; it is not at all pressed into the supporting leg, and the working heel remains forward. The working knee is held strongly to the side throughout the movement.

When the dancer starts in fifth position and moves to coupé front with plié, she does not go through sur le cou-de-pied. To have the toes wrap around the ankle when the supporting leg is moving into plié requires an ungainly, exaggerated beveling of the working foot. (This applies to intermediate and advanced dancers; children who are still learning to articulate their feet do use sur le cou-de-pied when in plié on

Peter in a low coupé front, toes on the center line of the supporting leg

Peter in a low coupé front, heel forward, toes back

1. Peter in fifth position front 2. Peter releasing the foot from fifth position front, heel forward, toes back 3. Peter lifting the knee up and out to the side as he begins to plié 4. Peter in coupé front, lowering into plié (and making a baseball diamond)

the supporting leg.) From fifth position on straight legs, she takes a little breath as she releases the working foot from the floor, using the toes back/heel forward technique but no sur le cou-de-pied and no demi-pointe. Instead, she lifts the working knee up and out to the side as she starts to plié, bringing her heel forward and her toes under her center line as she fully points her foot and draws the little toe to the center line of the supporting leg at the ankle or a bit higher. Once again, the foot does not go through demi-pointe on the way to coupé. The working foot is not crossed over the ankle and is not open. When I'm teaching, I often check to see that the legs form a baseball diamond when the dancer is in coupé in plié, as a sign that the dancer is in a large "juicy" plié and that the turnout is being maintained in both legs.

The dancer can also go from fifth position to coupé without passing through

sur le cou-de-pied while maintaining a straight supporting leg. She starts by lifting the heel forward and up as the toes pull back (to the center of the supporting foot) and point under. Again, there is no demi-pointe. This is basically the same action for the working foot that is used when the supporting leg bends. Her working knee starts to lift up and to the side, drawing the pointe to the center of the supporting foot (also the center line of the body). Continuing to lift, her working knee draws the pointe up past the anklebone on the center line of the supporting leg to the designated height. This is

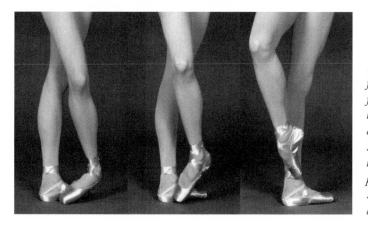

1. Dana releasing her foot from fifth position front, heel forward and toes back (again, no demi-pointe)
2. Dana maintaining the heel forward and pointing the toes under
3. Dana arriving in coupé front

1. Peter releasing his foot from fifth position back (again, no demi-pointe) 2. Peter attaches his ankle-bone to his supporting leg as he pliés; his toes are just off the floor. 3. Peter in coupé back in plié

working foot is not crossed over the ankle and is not open.

In all coupés back, the dancer must pay extra attention to holding the working knee back and keeping the hips aligned and square.

Coupé with demi-plié is used in steps such as fondu, as well as in a variety of jumps, such as emboîté, jeté, or temps levé in coupé. It is essential to memorize the proper placement of the working foot in coupé so it doesn't bounce or scratch up and down in allegro movements. It needs to freeze.

the technique used for passé, développé, pas de cheval, etc., when not going through sur le cou-de-pied, so the pointe can continue as high as it will go, depending on the exercise.

When a dancer goes to coupé from fifth back, and the supporting leg is to remain straight, she always moves through sur le cou-de-pied back. From sur le cou-de-pied back, the working knee lifts out and up at least enough so the foot can fully point with the toes back and just off the floor; it may lift enough that the toes are a few inches off the floor. The depression between the anklebone and the inner edge of the heel of the working foot lightly touches the midline of the supporting leg.

When the dancer starts in fifth back and moves to coupé back with plié, she again passes through sur le cou-de-pied back and fully points her foot in coupé. She releases the working foot from the floor using the toes back/heel forward technique described in Sur le Cou-de-Pied and starts to plié. She draws the working foot into full point with the anklebone on the center line of the supporting leg and the toes one or two inches off the floor as she continues to plié. The foot does not go through demi-pointe on the way to coupé. The

We did a variety of exercises that moved through coupé and closed to fifth position (e.g., passé and enveloppé), so it was important to know precisely how to get into fifth from coupé. As noted, the action from coupé back is the same as the action from sur le cou-de-pied back. The working foot lowers from coupé back to sur le cou-de-pied and into fifth. When the dancer starts in coupé front, her foot is not wrapped, so the working toes can simply aim for the floor just in front of the supporting heel and then the foot continues to close as it would from sur le cou-de-pied front.

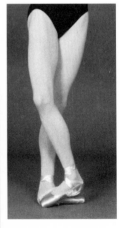

1. Dana aims for the floor near the supporting heel. 2. Dana starting to lower her heel to the floor to make fifth position front 3. Dana lowering to fifth position front, no full demi-pointe

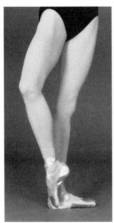
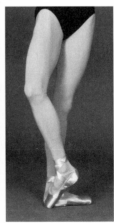

DETAILS I OFTEN INSIST ON IN COUPÉ:

Moving into coupé with a straight
supporting leg:
  1) move the heel forward and maintain it
     as the toes pull back to point
  2) keep the working knee out to the side
  3) no overcrossing in back

Moving into coupé with plié:
  1) lift up to go down
  2) no sickled feet
  3) show the exact position—not too high
  4) maintain maximum turnout in both
     legs
  5) maintain the weight over the ball of
     the foot in plié

Passé

Passé is an exercise that incorporates sur le cou-de-pied and coupé, so the technique for picking the foot off the floor and moving up to coupé, as well as the technique for placing the foot to the floor, should be used when working on passé.

Passé was practiced as a movement of the leg and foot from fifth front to fifth back or vice versa. Mr. Balanchine watched carefully to see that we picked the foot off the floor and put it back on the floor correctly. His other special concerns were maintaining maximum turnout throughout the movement by keeping the working knee back and to the side, and a refined and controlled action in passing the working foot, which was achieved by focusing on the lift of the working knee rather than on the foot. He also wanted the toes of the working foot precisely on the center line of the supporting leg as the working foot traveled up and down. If the toes are overcrossed, the working foot seems to, and sometimes does, slap or kick the supporting knee.

In some schools passé exercises are given from fifth or even first, in which the working pointe comes up the side of the supporting leg. For Mr. B this movement could not be a passé, because the pointe starts on the side of the supporting leg and goes up and down in the same track. It therefore does not "pass" from the front to the back or vice versa.

Starting from fifth front, the dancer brings her foot into and through sur le cou-de-pied front in the way I described. From sur le cou-de-pied the working knee is lifted to the side, the dancer maintaining the heel forward as the toes come to the front of the ankle, and the foot stretches strongly to make a full point as it moves to and through coupé. The working knee continues up and out to the side, maintaining the turnout and drawing the toes of the working foot up the center line of the supporting leg (the middle of the shinbone), neither overcrossed nor on the inside of the supporting leg. Mr. B told us to think of a puppet with a string attached to the knee, not the foot. He also said, "It's the knee that takes the foot" in going from fifth front to fifth back. Thinking of the movement in this way helps avoid an uncontrolled foot slapping or hitting the supporting knee; it also helps to maintain an open and symmetrical look. When the toes reach the front of the supporting knee, the dancer lifts her working knee a bit higher to the side and then pulls it around to the back in a kind of "rond de knee." Sometimes the dancer mistakenly takes a shortcut by lifting the working foot to the back of the supporting leg too soon, forgetting to lift the knee high to the side. The working foot can consequently go higher than the working knee, giving Mr. B cause to say, "It looks like you are spanking yourself. Why do that?" The working foot does not beat in the front and the back; it feels as if the toes of the working foot almost surround the supporting knee. Thus the working foot reaches its highest position while at the side of the supporting leg. As the pointe passes from the front to the back, the working knee can lift so high that the toes often are an inch or so off the supporting knee. The toes describe an arc as they follow to the back of the supporting knee. So it is really the working knee

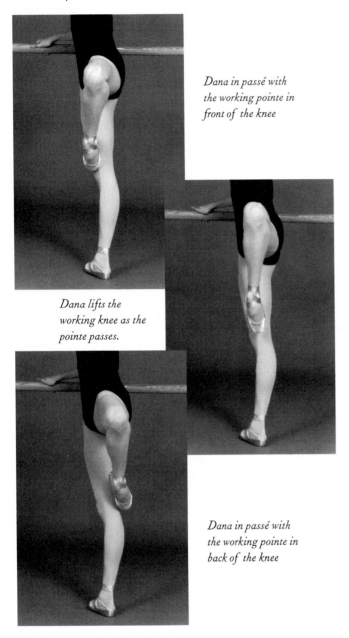

Dana in passé with the working pointe in front of the knee

Dana lifts the working knee as the pointe passes.

Dana in passé with the working pointe in back of the knee

foot into sur le cou-de-pied back. She lifts the knee up and to the side, drawing the toes of the working foot into full point, and through coupé back while maintaining the heel front. Because of the position of the foot (heel forward, toes back), the inside edge of the heel moves along the center line on the back of the supporting leg. The feeling is working hip and heel forward, working toes and knee back. It is particularly important when doing passé at a moderate tempo that the dancer avoid taking a shortcut by coming to the front of the supporting leg before the toes reach the back of the knee. The working knee continues lifting, drawing the heel up the center line of the back of the supporting leg. When the foot reaches the top of the calf in back, the dancer lifts her working knee a bit higher to the side, drawing the tip of the pointe to the back of the supporting knee. From the back of the supporting knee, the heel of the working foot takes over, leading up, over, and forward, enabling the toes to pass while the working knee is held back, thus maintaining maximum turnout. The pointe describes an arc as it is drawn up and around the side and to the front of the supporting leg. Again, the working foot reaches its highest position while at the side of the supporting leg. With the heel of the working foot maintained forward, the toes go diagonally down the front of the supporting knee and down the center line of the supporting leg until they reach the ankle. Just as the toes of the well-shaped working foot are about to reach the floor, they aim for fifth, not the sur le cou-de-pied position. The working foot lowers into fifth going through the foot, but without dropping down to a full demi-pointe on the close. The action is the one used when closing to fifth front from coupé front.

Passé can also be done without passing through sur le cou-de-pied. However, the dancer must be sure to pick the foot off the floor in the heel forward/toe back way as it is brought to coupé and to maintain the heel forward and toes back as the foot is drawn up the center line of the supporting leg.

In passé from front to back, it is the working knee passing the hip that makes the action; in passé

that passes the hip and draws the toes around and past the supporting knee. The working foot, with the heel forward and the toes back, then moves down the center line, with the inside of the heel making light contact with the back of the supporting leg. The foot continues through coupé and sur le cou-de-pied back and closes into fifth in the way I described.

Starting from fifth back, the dancer brings her

from back to front, it is the heel of the working foot passing the supporting knee that makes the action, but the dancer must maintain the turnout by keeping the hips pulled up and square, avoiding hiking the working hip up and pulling it back as the knee lifts. She also keeps the working knee back and to the side.

During the passé movement, the working toes barely—in fact, sometimes don't even—touch the supporting leg. This is especially true at the highest point of passé, when the pointe passes around the supporting knee. When the foot goes up and down the front of the leg, the pointe makes very light contact. When the foot goes up and down the back of the leg, the inside edge of the heel has very light contact. The working foot should never be pressed against the supporting leg to help maintain the turnout. Balanchine wanted to see both legs actively working on turning out; he did not want to see the working pointe passively jammed into the supporting leg.

When I was a young dancer, marley floors were not available. We still danced on wood floors, often very old, worn wood floors, and most dancers used rosin in class. When we did a lot of exercises using sur le cou-de-pied—passé, pas de cheval, frappé, etc.—my tights got quite dirty at the ankles from the wrapping. I had really learned to "hug my cou."

Passé refers both to a pose and to a movement. This exercise helped teach us the movement and gave us muscle memory of the pose. In the pose passé front at the barre, the dancer has the pointe or little toe of the working foot on the center line of the supporting leg, at or just below the knee. The

little toe touches the supporting leg very lightly; if Mr. B saw a dancer resting the working pointe on the supporting leg, he would suggest that it be held a millimeter off the leg, just enough to slip a piece of paper between the toe and the leg. The working knee is held to the side and pulls back against the squarely held working hip. In the pose passé back at the barre, the heel is forward and the toes are back; the big toe of the working foot is on the center line of the supporting leg at or just below the back of the knee. Again, the working toe barely touches the supporting leg. The dancer must be careful that the working foot is neither overcrossed nor open or to the side of the supporting leg. The working knee is held to the side and pulls back against the working hip.

The precise definition of the passé pose at the barre is important for building awareness of where the working foot is. However, when the dancer assumes passé in the center, the precision of the working pointe is less important than the overall look of energy, the turnout, maintaining the knee lifted and pulled to the side, the way the dancer moves as she does the combination. The tip of the pointe might, for example, be held away from the supporting leg by the lift of the working knee, or in passé back it might slightly overcross.

When passé is done at moderate tempos, it is important to show the beginning by picking the foot up quickly through sur le cou-de-pied, then slowing to show the height of the movement, and to show the start of the descent of the working foot by starting it quickly and slowing as it is placed into fifth. Passé is also given at fast tempos that do not allow time for the dancer to achieve the wrapping

DETAILS I OFTEN INSIST ON IN PASSÉ:
1) from front to back, keep the knee lifting up and around to take the foot over the top to the back
2) keep the hips square and stay pulled up as the knee lifts up and over
3) maintain the shape of the foot with the heel forward at the height of the passé—no sickling
4) make the movement continuous or establish the pose, but no beating as the foot passes
5) no jamming the working pointe into the supporting leg

of the working foot in sur le cou-de-pied and
sometimes, especially when actually dancing, so
fast that the working pointe does not reach the
knee. But it is still necessary that the foot be taken
off the floor in the toes back/heel forward shape
and that the knee lift the foot as high as possible
toward the supporting knee so the movement retains its characteristic look and energy.

Sometimes, for passé, Mr. B gave a simple port
de bras in which the hand lowered from second to
fifth low, as if it were reaching down to take the
"string" attached to the working knee and coordinated its rise to fifth high, as if it were pulling the
knee up. The head and eyes followed the hand,
helping to announce to the audience the taking of
the foot from the floor and the energy of the passé.
This is an example of his giving new life to a standard port de bras often done by rote. He got the
participation of the whole dancer.

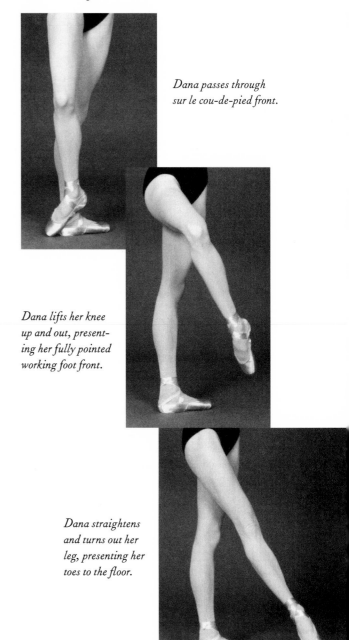

*Dana passes through
sur le cou-de-pied front.*

*Dana lifts her knee
up and out, present-
ing her fully pointed
working foot front.*

*Dana straightens
and turns out her
leg, presenting her
toes to the floor.*

Pas de Cheval

Pas de cheval is another exercise that incorporates
sur le cou-de-pied, so it is beneficial to understand
sur le cou-de-pied when working on it.

Mr. Balanchine wanted his dancers to present or
show themselves to the audience. A number of details of the technique have this underlying sense.
His pas de cheval is a good case in point, because its
motion is up, out, and then down, with extra
turnout. The dancer seems more to be presenting
the working leg and foot to the floor (and to the audience), rather than just pawing the ground.

Passing through sur le cou-de-pied front and
going to the front at a moderate tempo, the knee
lifts slightly up, out, and side, the heel leads forward as the foot makes full point, presenting the inside thigh, calf, and heel forward. As the knee
continues to lift up and out, the lower leg begins to
unfold and then the thigh is brought down cleanly
toward the floor with the toes on the center line of
the body as the straightening leg turns out even
more for the final presentation. This is a circular ac-

tion. At moderate tempos there can be a pause to
show the extended (tendu) line. This movement,
from sur le cou-de-pied to the floor and pause, can
be called a low développé to the floor. The foot
then closes into fifth, using the technique discussed
in battement tendu, where at moderate tempos it

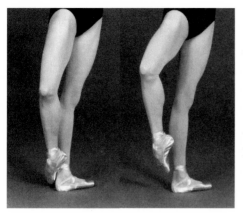

1. Dana in sur le cou-de-pied front 2. Dana lifting her knee up and out as her foot fully points 3. Dana continues to lift her knee up and out, presenting her heel forward. 4. Dana's leg straightens and turns out as the foot is presented on top of the floor.

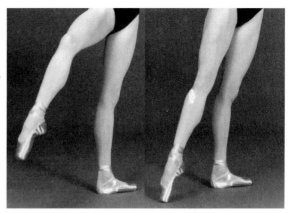

usually pauses again. The contact with the floor is very light; only a muffled brushing sound is heard as the tips of the toes caress the floor, pulling back to fifth.

Going to the side at a moderate tempo moving through sur le cou-de-pied, the principles are the same. The key difference is that the pointe is exactly side, rather than front.

Going to the back at a moderate tempo passing through sur le cou-de-pied back, the knee lifts up and side as the foot makes full pointe; then the thigh lifts slightly up and back and turns out to reveal the underside of the leg, causing the working hip to release; then the lower leg unfolds as the pointe is brought toward the floor. The remainder of the action is again based on the same principles as for pas de cheval front.

The basic look of the movement is the same in all three directions, because each is based on a circular action made up of the lift of the knee and the extension and lowering of the leg and foot. By maintaining maximum turnout and a fully stretched and pointed foot as it leaves sur le cou-de-pied, the look of the working leg remains the same.

Pas de cheval at moderate tempos (développé to the floor) is done to show the extended line, with the toes pointed on the floor, and the fifth position. The pas de cheval movement is phrased, starting quickly and ending with a slowing to present the foot to the floor. Two or three inches before the leg is fully straightened, the dancer tries to turn out even more, and this works as a brake that slows the

movement and announces the placement of the foot. Pas de cheval is also done at somewhat faster tempos without the pause in fifth, but still passing through sur le cou-de-pied. At even faster tempos the circular motion is constant; there is no pause at all. Also, it may not be practical and may even be impossible to reach the wrapped position in sur le cou-de-pied, in which case the working foot should still be taken off the floor with the heel forward and the toes back. The working foot is brought up the midline of the supporting leg before lifting to go up and out to the front, side, or back. Mr. B also gave pas de cheval at very fast tempos when we did not attempt to pause in fifth or move through sur le cou-de-pied before lifting the knee and extending the lower leg again; this exercise develops speed and very articulate feet.

As the name tells us, there is some similarity with the motion of a horse pawing the ground in this exercise, particularly as the tempo picks up. The horse lifts his "knee," and the action is circular. However, Mr. B's dancers do not imitate horses in two crucial respects. First, no one ever saw a turned-out horse, and the dancer maintains her turnout throughout the movement. Second, a horse often paws the ground with real force, sometimes dislodging the dirt, little stones, or the turf, but the dancer's foot makes only light, skimming contact that leaves everything in place. In some cases, knowing what the ballet terms mean in French is very helpful in knowing the quality of movement required, but in this case the French only broadly

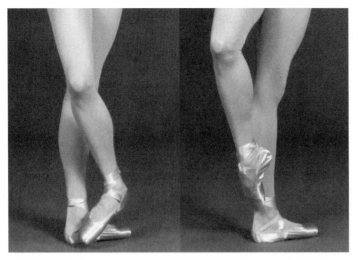

*Dana demonstrating the action of the foot and ankle in the beginning of a
fast pas de cheval, when there is no time to make sur le cou-de-pied*

suggests the action, conveying little of its desired
qualities.

The rounded lift, unfolding, and placement to
the floor of pas de cheval is an essential preparation
for stepping onto demi-pointe or pointe, which is
the start of many steps and combinations—for example, piqué arabesque. It is also often used when
stepping onto the whole foot—for example, pas de
cheval and then tombé, pas de bourrée. When pas
de cheval is used in this way, it is often called a small
développé. Whatever it is called, Mr. B was only
concerned with our showing a certain look, doing

DETAILS I OFTEN INSIST ON IN PAS
DE CHEVAL:
1) proper sur le cou-de-pied when there is
   time; if not, heel forward, toes back
2) this is a circular motion; lift the knee, do
   not kick the foot up into the air
3) maintain maximum turnout of the legs
   and feet
4) lift and open the working thigh when the
   leg is moving to the back

the step in keeping with his aesthetic.
The movement must be mastered so the
dancer can effectively present or announce the beginnings of whole variations as well as phrases within them.

Pas de Cheval with Plié

We also practiced pas de cheval moving
into plié. The strength this built in our
thighs was useful for doing slow, controlled relevés and jumps.

The plié began as the working leg
made the circular movement toward the
floor. This was usually done at a relatively slow tempo, so we could move
into a deep plié, often so low that Balanchine might advise us to release the heel at least
enough to slide a piece of paper under it, but at
most an inch or so. He would often look at us as we
pliéd and say, "Lower . . . lower . . . lawyer!" For a
knowing few of us, this was a little joke about
Karinska's trouble saying "lower." At costume fittings Mr. B would tell her the bodice on a costume
should be lower and she would say, "Yes, yes, a little lawyer."

Even though Mr. B wanted a very deep plié in
this exercise, he naturally wanted us to maintain
correct form in other aspects of the movement. The
dancer centers her weight over the ball of the supporting foot, while she maintains maximum turnout of the supporting leg, being careful not to let
her knee roll in. She holds her back straight with
the hips aligned; she does not tilt back or forward.

The same phrasing is used as in the basic pas de
cheval. The movement starts quickly, but then
slows as the dancer pliés, turns out the working leg
even more, and presents the foot to the floor. The
plié begins when the working leg starts downward
toward the floor; the coordination of the two legs is
very important.

I have indicated the importance Mr. B placed on
the dancer achieving a lift or an "up" feeling in the

action of the working leg in pas de cheval, even though the foot is placed to the floor. A variant form of pas de cheval that he gave with plié called for the dancer to lift the knee high enough to bring the working foot almost or even to passé and then to raise the knee a little higher when starting the unfolding and the circular movement presenting the foot to the floor. With the higher lift of the knee, the plié begins as usual as the working leg starts downward to the floor.

DETAILS I OFTEN INSIST ON IN PAS DE CHEVAL WITH PLIÉ:

1) a low plié, weight over the ball of the foot
2) supporting knee aligned over the foot; no rolling in
3) hips aligned over the supporting foot
4) working leg turned out to the back

Pas de Cheval with Relevé

We occasionally practiced pas de cheval with a relevé without plié and lowered onto a straight supporting leg as the working leg straightened and the foot pointed on the floor.

The working foot begins the action of going through sur le cou-de-pied (without plié) as the dancer rises to demi-pointe (or pointe). It does not push into the floor to assist in the relevé. Using only the supporting foot to relevé strengthens the feet,

---

DETAILS I OFTEN INSIST ON IN PAS DE CHEVAL WITH RELEVÉ:

1) turnout in both legs and feet when lowering to the floor
2) no use of the working foot to help initiate the relevé
3) pull up as you lower down

---

which helps to control relevés and landings from jumps. The relevé continues as the working leg is lifting, and the descent from relevé begins as the working leg is extending and lowering toward the floor. As the dancer lowers her supporting heel lightly to the floor and the working leg extends to tendu, she works on turning out both legs. This requires extra effort to turn out the supporting leg, because there is no plié. Then the dancer closes into fifth position, where she might pause momentarily or she might move through the fifth position into the next pas de cheval action.

We also did pas de cheval with relevé moving into plié. This incorporates the two actions I have discussed. The dancer can also plié in fifth position to initiate the relevé action (see page 243).

Développé

Mr. Balanchine gave développé exercises in many forms. We did développé on flat and in relevé, presenting the foot from floor level (pas de cheval) to above our head and with the working leg ending in attitude as well as straight.

Certain material should be understood before working on développé. The technique for picking the foot off the floor is described in Sur le Cou-de-Pied and Coupé. When développé is done at hip level or higher, the foot goes up through passé and then, after the working knee has lifted even higher, extends. The foot usually returns to fifth in the way described in Battement Tendu.

The dancer's precise awareness of the directions was also important in doing développé Mr. Balanchine's way. Whether the working foot was in the air or on the floor, the toes had to be exactly front, side, or back. Mr. B also wanted the dancer to feel she was presenting or "serving" the working foot to the audience, no matter how high the développé, no matter which direction. As usual, maximum turnout was the norm throughout the movement, but in développé, as the working leg finished unfolding to the desired height, the dancer turned out even more, which might cause the leg to lower slightly, giving a slight roundness that softens the movement (remember the elephant's trunk). The finishing gesture articulates the sense that the working foot is being presented or served. "The end becomes important." Concentrating on the final, extra turnout ruled out any uncontrolled throwing or kicking of the leg and foot into the air, which some dancers do because they are unaware of the correct form and others do just to maximize the extension. Balanchine also wanted the working foot brought back to the floor in control, rather than being allowed to drop, which often means it bangs down or slams into fifth position.

A more conventional idea seems to have the dancer lift the working knee very high and then extend the lower leg without the final turning out. This often makes the leg look like it is: divided into two parts at the knee. The last upward movement is often the knee snapping into line as the foot kicks up and out. Then, if the développé is badly done, the leg often jiggles in its slightly turned-in line before dropping or lowering haphazardly to the floor. In contrast, after the dancer has lifted the working knee as high and as close to the body as she can, the unfolding of the leg with the extra turning out at the end of the développé can make the leg look almost jointless, can seem to present or serve the foot, can stabilize the leg in the extended line, and can help the dancer stabilize the leg as she holds the extended line, as well as maintain control of the return of the foot to the floor.

When Mr. Balanchine gave développé, the height of the presented foot was usually clearly specified, and he expected us to observe that carefully as we did the movement. "You must know where your foot is going," he might say, adding, "without looking at it." For example, in développé to forty-five degrees from fifth flat, the dancer starts through sur le cou-de-pied, then lifts the working knee up and to the side as the foot points fully. The toes are drawn into and up the center of the supporting leg until they are about halfway up the lower leg. If the développé is front or side, she

holds the working knee back, but lifts it slightly as the heel leads forward, ending by "serving" the foot directly front or to the side. The stretched leg makes a forty-five-degree angle. If the développé is back, she lifts the knee up and back, which opens the thigh as she extends the lower leg, ending with the foot placed directly to the back and the stretched leg at a forty-five-degree angle.

It is essential that the mechanism for "serving" the working foot be fully understood. In each direction and at any height, the dancer unfolds the lower part of the leg until the toes are about two inches short of full extension. Then, as she stretches her working knee, she turns out even more. The knee seems to, and may actually, lower very slightly as she presents the whole inside of the leg from thigh to heel, which means that, on the unfolding, the knee may lift a little higher than its finishing level. Whether the leg stretches front, side, or back, or was high or low, the same technique applies to those last two inches. The purpose is to show the end of the movement and clearly reveal the line of the turned-out leg. It is as if she is offering, presenting, or serving her foot to the audience; she could be placing her foot on a table or shelf. The additional turnout also works as a brake to slow down the movement so the working leg does not kick up, and it helps prevent the knee from snapping as it straightens.

Développé front can start with the working foot in fifth back, as well as in fifth front, and vice versa. When the working foot has to "pass" the supporting leg to do développé, it does so at the level where the working leg begins to extend. It does not pass near the ankle and anticipate the direction of the développé.

Balanchine wanted to be sure we knew the difference between a straight leg to the back in développé and an arabesque pose. In développé with the leg to the back, the supporting hip and the back must be absolutely straight. "Développé never starts with preparing the body [meaning tilting forward]. It starts with the leg going up," he said. It is important to know what being straight inal muscles to support and lengthen her back) to raise her working leg, but it should always feel as if her leg is lifting to meet her back. She does not want to lean backward into her lifting leg. The arm usually moves to second or fifth high (see pages 150–160). Arabesque (or attitude) may include a slight adjustment to the hips and back and involves a variety of arm and head positions.

When développé is done from sous-sus (demi-pointe or full pointe), the working foot is already correctly shaped (heel forward; fully stretched arch.) There is no purpose to reshape it by wrapping it in sur le cou-de-pied. The only adjustment needed is by dancers on demi-pointe, since they have to point the ends of their toes. The technique for taking the foot off the floor from fifth flat detailed in Sur le Cou-de-Pied is im-

1. Peter in passé back
2. Peter lifting his thigh and knee to the back
3. Peter in développé back

looks and feels like, even at the cost of a lower leg in back. Some dancers can raise the leg to the back only to forty-five degrees, some perhaps not even that high, some perhaps only a little higher. The height of the leg to the back depends on the dancer's body: her turnout, her flexibility. Once the dancer has learned what it feels like to be straight, a variety of adjustments is permissible. She can adjust her supporting hip and back (using her abdom-

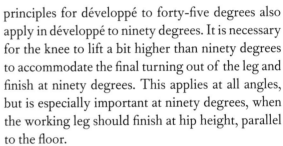

1. *Peter and Dana in sous-sus*
2. *Peter and Dana have picked the working foot off the floor, maintaining its fully pointed shape.*
3. *Peter and Dana lifting the knee to the side, bringing the pointe of the working foot up the center line of the supporting leg toward passé*

portant because it trains the whole foot how to come off the floor (toes back, heel forward) and how to achieve the correct shape (not sickled!). As I have noted, this technique must become almost automatic, so it is part of the dancer's vocabulary, even when she is not actively thinking about it.

In développé to ninety degrees, the dancer goes through passé. There is no stop, not even a pause, in passé; instead, the dancer "passes through." The

principles for développé to forty-five degrees also apply in développé to ninety degrees. It is necessary for the knee to lift a bit higher than ninety degrees to accommodate the final turning out of the leg and finish at ninety degrees. This applies at all angles, but is especially important at ninety degrees, when the working leg should finish at hip height, parallel to the floor.

High développés finish with the working foot at

1. *Peter in passé front* 2. *Peter lifting his knee, leading with his heel* 3. *Peter showing the final turned-out line*

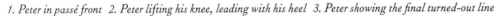

1. Dana in passé front 2. Dana lifting her knee close to her body, toward her "armpit" 3. Dana in développé side

shoulder height or above. Although Mr. B certainly wanted "more" in extensions, just as he did in most aspects of the technique, it had to be achieved without losing the essential quality of the movement. The dancer starts a high développé front by coming to passé from fifth front or back. She lifts her knee as high and as close to her body as she can. Then the working heel takes charge, leading the lower leg up and out so the heel is presented up with the additional turnout and the pointe is on the center line of the body. Développé side can start from fifth front or fifth back and continues to passé front or back. When the dancer has lifted her working knee to its maximum height and as close to her body as she can, she extends her lower leg so the foot is "served" exactly side. I usually say, "Lift your knee to your armpit," but Balanchine offered a more elegant way to visualize it: "Lift your knee out of your décolleté evening dress." Développé back starts from fifth front or fifth back and continues to passé back or front. The dancer lifts her knee up and back, opening her thigh, while keeping her supporting hip as straight as possible and her back as upright as possible. Keeping her shoulders

square, she releases the working hip as necessary to reveal a fully turned-out thigh as she unfolds her lower leg so the toes are on the center line of her body (see photos, page 91).

Whatever the height and direction of the développé, the working foot must be brought down under control, rather than being allowed to fall from its extended line. It starts down quickly for approximately the first three inches to show the beginning of the downward movement, then slows to fit the tempo, and is placed in fifth using the technique discussed in tendu. Even from the highest développé, and with the fastest tempo, the toes of the working foot never bang the floor.

Développé was given at moderate tempos to ensure that we mastered the basic form. Mr. B also gave it at very slow tempos to build strength. This challenged the dancers to maintain energy and awareness—and life!—in the whole body. He gave it at very fast tempos to build speed and the control to quickly show the final extension and the final turning out. At any tempo he might ask us to present the foot at a given height, low to high, hold it there for one or more, even for many counts, and then start it smartly down to fifth.

Most développés start relatively quickly to show the beginning of the movement, slow a little based on the tempo, then accelerate until the last straightening of the knee, when the leg slows for the final presentation. This phrasing is one of the elements necessary to keep développé interesting and alive.

Mr. Balanchine paid particular attention to the alignment of the body in développé, because there is great temptation to "cheat" to achieve a higher extension. He did not want us to sacrifice a correct position for a higher leg. The back must remain straight in développé front and side, neither tilting back nor tipping to the side. The hips remain level and square to the barre in développé front, and as level and square as possible in développé to the side. In développé to the back, the working hip releases as necessary to allow the dancer to continue to raise the turned-out working leg, but the dancer stands as straight as possible over her supporting hip. As her leg rises and her hip opens, there is some necessary adjustment in the torso, but she does not prepare for développé back with a tilt forward. She uses her strong abdominal muscles to help her to remain as straight as possible with an open, lifted chest and outward projection of the face and eyes. Balanchine kept us square to the barre (rather than have us turn at an angle), in part to help us remain aware of front, back, and side and in part to help us be aware of the placement of our hips and torso. Weight was maintained over the ball of the supporting foot.

Although we usually did développé with simple arms, Mr. B sometimes gave us a variety of head positions and arm movements in développé, but more often in arabesques and attitudes. However, even in effacé, croisé, and écarté, we rarely turned diagonal to the barre and we rarely used the inside leg as the working leg. Instead we remained square to the barre and used the various head and arm positions for each line. As usual, the movements had to be done with full energy, awareness, and control.

Mastery of slow développés and of holding the working leg in the extended position were especially important for the women because supported développés with promenades are much used in pas de deux work. Mastery of faster développés is necessary as preparation for fondu relevé.

Grand battement with développé uses the same path as a high développé, and almost all the same principles, but the leg is, of course, thrown up and out rather than being lifted. Because of the speed of the movement, the foot usually bypasses sur le cou-de-pied, and the leg does not stop in the extended line. The usual timing is développé battement on the "and" and close to fifth on the count.

DETAILS I OFTEN INSIST ON IN DÉVELOPPÉ:

1) turning out a little more just as the knee straightens to present a fully stretched foot and leg; hold and show the extended line

2) start on time, stay in time, finish on time

3) in high développés to the front and side, lift the knee as high and as close to the body as possible before beginning to extend the lower leg; to the back, lifting the thigh

4) in développés to the front, hips square and straight supporting leg

5) exact directions, especially to the side, where there is a tendency to let the leg wander toward the front; and to the back, where there is a tendency to let the leg open slightly side

6) in développés to the back, supporting hip aligned, back straight, fully stretched, straight working leg

7) in all directions, stay pulled up, with the torso and chest lifted; do not sink into the hips or lean back

Enveloppé

Enveloppé is the reverse of développé. One point of the exercise is to work on the turnout and maximize its effect while returning the leg and foot from an extended line back to the supporting leg and to fifth position.

Mr. Balanchine wanted to see that, from the extended line, as the dancer draws the foot toward the supporting leg, her working knee lifts and turns out. This lifting and sideways opening of the knee, which gives the movement an "up" feeling and on occasion a slightly circular look, fully reveals the turnout and makes the dancer more aware of maximizing it. As the working foot goes down the supporting leg to the floor, the dancer is again more aware of maintaining the turnout, of the way her toes meet the floor, and of the placement of the heel forward as she moves into a fully crossed fifth position.

Enveloppé begins with battement dégagé from fifth position and includes elements of passé or coupé as the foot is returned, so those exercises should be understood.

When enveloppé is executed with a low (forty-five degrees or less) leg, the tempos are usually faster. The dancer dégagés from fifth to the front, side, or back and can pause, but more usually the dancer continues with enveloppé immediately, lifting the working knee slightly as she starts to bend it. From the front, the knee not only pulls back against the working hip but also to the side, drawing the foot back toward coupé. The hips remain square, and the weight is aligned over the ball of the supporting foot. The toes of the working foot move down the midline of the supporting leg, and when they are in front of the supporting ankle, they aim for fifth. The working heel is placed forward into a crossed fifth in the usual way. The tips of the toes are placed to the floor first, and then the dancer goes through her foot, but she does not drop down to a full demi-pointe. At brisk but not too fast tempos the working foot could stop in fifth, but as the tempo picks up, the movement becomes continuous.

From dégagé side, as the working knee lifts slightly and bends, the dancer tries to bring the lower part of the leg forward a little so the heel is in front of the working knee and thigh. As the working knee continues to bend and stay out and back, the dancer tries to maintain this maximum turnout, which fully reveals the inner thigh. If she closes to fifth front from the side, the working foot aims for coupé front and closes in the usual manner. If she closes to fifth back, the working foot aims for coupé back and moves through sur le cou-de-pied back and closes in the usual way.

From dégagé back, the working knee lifts slightly up and to the side as it bends. It is especially important that the dancer not only stay straight on her supporting hip but that she also bring her working hip forward and into proper alignment. It almost feels as if the working hip brings the working heel into coupé back, while the working knee stays back and out. The working foot should not rise much higher than midcalf if the dégagé is to forty-five degrees. The working foot closes into fifth position from coupé back through sur le cou-de-pied back in the usual way. Naturally, the shoulder line is square throughout the movement.

When enveloppé is executed with a high leg (ninety degrees or more), the tempos are usually slow to moderate. The dancer dégagés from fifth and may pause for a moment or stop in the extended line, if the tempo allows. While the hips stay square, for dégagé front the working knee then lifts slightly as it bends and pulls back against the working hip, drawing the foot in to the highest passé possible. The working pointe does not press on or jam into the supporting leg at any time. Depending on the tempo and the exercise, the dancer may pause to show this pose. The working foot then closes to fifth as it usually does from passé. Depending on the tempo, the dancer may pause to show the fifth position. We usually did.

From dégagé side at ninety degrees or higher,

1. Dana in high dégagé side
2. Dana lifting her knee as she brings her pointe with her heel forward toward passé
3. Dana continuing to lift her knee as her toes aim for passé
4. Dana arriving in passé front

the working knee lifts as it bends. It should not look as if it drops down to passé. On high extensions, as the knee bends, Mr. B gestured to his armpit, reminding us to "lift the knee." The dancer tries to keep the working foot (think heel) in front of the knee and turned-out thigh as the leg makes a high passé line. Again, the working pointe does not press on or jam into the supporting leg at any time; in fact, in high passé it may not touch it at all. Coming in from high extensions, there may be as much as an inch or two between the working toes and the supporting knee. The working foot then closes to fifth, as it usually does from passé. Depending on the tempo, the dancer may pause to show passé and/or the fifth position.

From dégagé back at ninety degrees or higher, the knee of the working leg lifts up and out as it bends. Again, it is important that the knee remain lifted and that the foot not be higher than the knee. The working hip seems to bring the heel into passé back. The dancer arrives in passé back with proper alignment: straight back, hips level, and square to the barre. The working foot closes to fifth as it usually does from passé.

In any dégagé, the leg should be lifted fully turned out by using the inner thigh muscles, rather than being lifted slightly turned in and mostly with the muscles on the top of the thigh. By maintaining maximum turnout during the movement, the dancer avoids arriving in a turned-in passé that has to be corrected and adjusted by pulling back the knee. "If you do your maximum during the movement, there will be nothing left over to correct," Mr. B again reminded us.

DETAILS I OFTEN INSIST ON IN DÉGAGÉ WITH ENVELOPPÉ:

1) maintaining maximum turnout during the entire movement, but especially when the leg and foot begin to move toward coupé or passé
2) exact directions and full turnout in extended lines
3) no jamming toes into the supporting leg in passé position
4) heel forward as the tips of the toes are placed to the floor in fifth
5) body held straight for enveloppé front and side; as straight as possible for enveloppé back
6) do not sit into the hips; pull up out of the supporting leg and hips, especially when closing into fifth
7) strong abdominal muscles to support the back and help keep the torso still

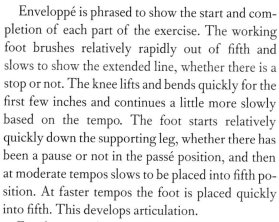

Enveloppé is phrased to show the start and completion of each part of the exercise. The working foot brushes relatively rapidly out of fifth and slows to show the extended line, whether there is a stop or not. The knee lifts and bends quickly for the first few inches and continues a little more slowly based on the tempo. The foot starts relatively quickly down the supporting leg, whether there has been a pause or not in the passé position, and then at moderate tempos slows to be placed into fifth position. At faster tempos the foot is placed quickly into fifth. This develops articulation.

Enveloppé is also practiced at very slow tempos to build the strength to hold the leg out and sustain it in a high pose.

Grand Battement with Enveloppé

Grand battement with enveloppé uses the same path for the working leg and foot as dégagé with enveloppé. However, instead of lifting the working leg, the dancer throws it, and the enveloppé is executed very quickly. It is necessary that grand battement and enveloppé be understood before beginning this exercise.

Even though the enveloppé is done quickly, the dancer must demonstrate finesse and control in the

1. Dana's leg is extended to the back.
2. Dana lifting her thigh and bending her knee as she brings her working hip and heel toward passé
3. Dana in passé back

way it is done. Mr. B was specially concerned that the working knee be held out to the side, that the turnout was constantly maintained, and that the tips of the toes touched the floor first.

Starting from fifth position, the dancer does a normal grand battement front. From the extended line, which for most dancers will be higher than the extended line in dégagé, she draws the working knee back and to the side, even trying to lift it as she aims for her highest passé. She maintains a lifting feeling as the working foot reaches passé, avoiding jabbing the working toes into the supporting leg or resting by pressing the toes against it. The foot closes to fifth front from passé in the usual way.

After the dancer does grand battement to the side, she does the enveloppé, in which the feeling is that the knee lifts as the lower part of the leg maintains the turnout and the foot moves into a very

DETAILS I OFTEN INSIST ON IN
GRAND BATTEMENT WITH
ENVELOPPÉ:

1) maximum turnout throughout the
   exercise, but especially when the working
   leg moves from the extended line to passé
2) in all directions maintain the effort to lift
   the working knee as the foot aims for the
   supporting leg
3) don't jab the supporting leg or jam the
   toes into it in passé
4) when closing, the tips of the toes aim for
   fifth and are placed on the floor first

high passé. In reality, the thigh hardly lifts because it is already so high, but her effort prevents the movement to passé from looking like an uncontrolled drop down. The working foot closes from passé to fifth front or fifth back in the usual way.

After the dancer does grand battement back, she lifts her working thigh as the knee lifts and moves to the side and the foot comes under the thigh, thereby maintaining the turnout in the entire working leg. As this happens, the hips come square and aligned, almost seeming to bring the working foot to passé. The working foot closes in the usual way from passé back.

Depending on the tempo and the way the exercise is set, the dancer may pause in passé, or she may close immediately to fifth position.

We usually did the grand battement on "and," then closed fifth on one. If we showed passé, we could pause there on one and closed to fifth on two.

Fondu

In fondu the dancer starts to integrate elements of technique refined in other barre exercises to produce larger movements very like the ones used onstage. It incorporates demi-plié, coupé, développé,

and, often, relevé so these exercises must be understood before addressing fondu.

Mr. Balanchine went beyond the traditional technique for fondu in three important ways. First, he wanted us to present the working leg to the audience more fully. Traditionally, dancers simply straightened and stretched the working knee, taking the working foot straight from coupé to the extended line. He taught us instead that, from coupé, we should lift the knee, drawing the foot up the supporting leg before extending it, and then we should turn out the working leg that extra amount, presenting it to the audience. To the front and to the side, this reveals the inside surface of the fully turned-out leg. Its circular motion is similar to the action of pas de cheval and développé. Second, when the extended line was at ninety degrees or higher, the working foot and leg did not take the same path up and back. He wanted the working leg brought down from the higher extended lines with a straight knee, as it would be when returning from battement dégagé, to about forty-five degrees. Then he wanted both knees to bend and the working knee to move to the side, bringing the foot to coupé. Third, Mr. B modified the coordination of the working and supporting knees in fondu; traditionally this called for the knees to straighten together, no matter what tempo, no matter how high the extended line. The result, particularly at slow tempos or to high extended lines, was a movement that looked heavy and labored. He wanted us instead to move up and out of plié relatively quickly in order to be on a straight supporting knee sooner. The look, also helped by the lift of the working knee and turnout of the working leg, was light and strong. The final presentation of the working leg and foot was coordinated with the tempo and could take more time, but the supporting knee always straightened comparatively quickly. In other words, we did not creep up out of plié, even at slower tempos. Consequently, when doing fondu relevé, the supporting knee was straight as we arrived on demi-pointe or on full pointe. The coordination of the straightening of the knees was therefore basically the same whether going to flat or doing fondu relevé to demi-pointe or full pointe. However, the interval between the straightening of the supporting knee and the full extension of the working leg varied according to the tempo. At very slow tempos the supporting knee straightened much sooner and the interval could be long; at fast tempos the supporting knee straightens or seems to straighten just before or at the same time the working leg was fully extended.

Mr. B usually began fondu exercises from fifth position rather than from tendu side. The dancer moves the working foot into coupé as she goes into demi-plié on the supporting leg. As noted in the discussion of coupé with plié (see page 80), the supporting knee is aligned and also extends over the toes of the supporting foot, which keeps the weight over the ball. This enables the dancer to move into a continuous demi-plié, even slightly releasing the supporting heel, if necessary for a deeper plié and if the tempo allows. Of course, there should be no rolling in at any point in the exercise.

In fondu to a low (from toes on the floor to about forty-five degrees) extended line or to any level at faster tempos, the dancer can feel and should feel as if she straightens both knees together. The braking action of the final turnout prevents a jerky arrival and also slightly slows down the final presentation of the working leg. Fondus to a low line include presenting the toes on the floor and a millimeter off and, at these levels, the action of the working leg is more similar to that in pas de cheval, except that the foot does not go through sur le cou-de-pied. From the extended low line, the dancer slightly lifts herself and the working leg up (taking herself up to go down as she reacts to the breath). She then bends the supporting knee in plié as she bends the working knee and brings it to the side to draw the working foot to coupé, maintaining a fully pointed foot. The plié should be continuous, but in the extended line there is a pause (or stop, if the tempo allows) to show the completion of the movement. The bending and straightening of the knees should be precisely timed.

In fondus to a higher extended line (ninety degrees and above), the développé technique is used. However, when the tempo is moderate to slow, the coordination of the supporting and working knee is changed, because the dancer does not at all feel as if the knees straighten together, as she did in the faster fondus. Instead, the supporting knee is straight, while the working foot continues to extend at higher levels. The supporting knee is usually fully stretched as the working foot moves through

---

DETAILS I OFTEN INSIST ON IN FONDU:

1) correct timing of getting up and out of plié and of the straightening of the legs
2) lift of the working foot along the center line of the supporting leg, almost to passé if the final line is ninety degrees; lift of the knee as high and as close to the body as possible, if the final line is much higher than ninety degrees
3) extra turnout of the working leg as it is straightened and presented, and held, if time allows
4) from ninety degrees or higher, bring the working leg straight down to about forty-five degrees before bending the knee to return the foot to coupé
5) maintain the turnout of the supporting leg (no rolling in), knee extending over the ball of the foot to make the fullest demi-plié
6) no stopping in plié
7) exact coupé position, not overcrossed
8) exact height without looking (know where your foot is going)
9) exact directions front, side, and back

Dana in plié coupé front

Dana lifting toward passé as she begins to straighten her supporting knee

Dana on a straight supporting leg and in a high passé front, ready to lift her knee to extend front

Dana lifting her knee and presenting her heel forward as she extends front

passé. The working foot and leg do not pause or stop in passé, but continue as in développé to the designated line. In the high extended line, after a pause (or stop, depending on the tempo), the straight working leg starts down relatively quickly for the first few inches to show the beginning of the movement and then slows to fit the tempo as it is brought to about forty-five degrees. This is similar to the lowering used in dégagé battement. At this level the working knee bends and moves to the side, bringing the working foot to coupé while the supporting knee bends in plié. The lowering of the working leg from higher extensions at slower tempos is phrased, but the movement is continuous.

The height of the extended line in fondu ranges from the floor to above the head. Mr. B liked to give us a fondu exercise including to the floor, to a millimeter off it, to 45 degrees, to 90 degrees, and very high, and he expected the first four heights to be exact. With a twinkle in the eye he might ask for the last one to be to 180, meaning to reach for your maximum, because we couldn't all be like Allegra Kent.

When moving into coupé with plié from fifth position or from a low extended line, there is a slight breath that gives a little lift when the working foot is released or brought down. The dancer starts the plié a little faster to show the beginning of the movement, but then slows to fit the tempo, to keep the plié continuous by controlling its speed. Above all, the dancer must start on time, not creep into the beginning of the plié, nor stop or sit at the bottom of the plié.

The start up and out of plié is also more rapid. The supporting leg continues to straighten at about the same speed, until it slows slightly as the knee fully stretches to avoid jamming and snapping the supporting leg straight. The working leg starts quickly, adjusts to fit the tempo, and then slows slightly at the end of the movement because of the extra turnout, which works as a brake to slow the leg and show the final line. Here the dancer pauses or stops for a moment. If the tempo is fast, the

Dana with the final turn-out in the extended line, "serving a glass of champagne" on her heel

Dana has lowered her straight working leg to about 45 degrees.

Dana lowering toward coupé front as she begins to plié

Dana arriving in coupé front in plié. The end of each fondu is the beginning of the next (see first photo in this series).

knees seem to straighten at the same time; this is true at any height. In other words, when the tempo is fast, the working leg moves more rapidly than the supporting leg so that both legs are fully stretched at, or almost at, the same time, no matter how high the extended line. The final turning out (braking) is especially important in the working leg.

If the tempo is moderate to very slow, which is somewhat more common when the height is ninety degrees or higher, the supporting leg straightens when the working leg is at or a little beyond passé, and sometimes almost passing through attitude, and then the working leg continues to unfold and extend at whatever speed is called for. Again, the first part of the fondu is more rapid than the final unfolding.

A straight posture is maintained throughout fondu; the torso does not tilt as the leg is presented to the front or side, even in high lines. In fondu back, some slight adjustment is necessary, but the dancer does not tilt back or tilt forward in anticipation and keeps the feeling that the working leg is lifting to meet her back. A simple port de bras was the norm for Mr. B: from second to low fifth as the dancer pliés, through first to second as the leg extends, unless it is to a very high line, when fifth high may be used. On occasion he used other ports de bras, but they all had to be done with full awareness and vitality.

Mr. B often gave fondu relevé. The principles are the same as for regular fondus on flat, but now the timing and continuity of some of the coordination are even more important. In fondu relevé the action of the supporting knee and ankle must be coordinated so the dancer has straightened her supporting knee just as or slightly before arriving on demi-pointe or full pointe. She presents her working leg and foot at faster tempos as she completes the relevé; at moderate or slower tempos the presentation is delayed, in keeping with the music. At ninety degrees and higher and at a slow tempo, she continues drawing her foot up the supporting leg, presenting the working leg and foot in keeping with the music.

*Dana in plié
in coupé front*

*Dana rolling up to
pointe as she lifts her
knee side*

*Dana on pointe in a
high passé front*

*Dana lifting her
knee side, up, and
close to her body*

*Dana in the high extended
line to the side*

*Dana on a straight supporting
leg with the working leg
lowered almost to 45 degrees*

*Dana starts to plié as she
bends her working knee.*

*Dana in demi-plié in
coupé front. She continues
into plié to start the next
fondu, as shown in the first
photo of this series.*

On the return she starts off demi-pointe or full pointe as she begins the plié.

Another variant he gave called for the dancer to start in fifth position and move into demi-plié on both feet. Just before the dancer starts to rise from the bottom of the demi-plié, she releases the working foot so it does not participate in the action of the relevé. As she continues to move up and out of plié, she brings the working foot through coupé, and using the same technique as fondu, lifts and presents it at the exact height and in the direction required (see page 243).

Battement Frappé

The basic idea of frappé is that the dancer shoots the foot rapidly out from sur le cou-de-pied to hit the floor lightly and continue out and up, finishing with a straight knee and the foot several inches off the floor. On the return, the working knee maintains maximum turnout as the foot returns to sur le cou-de-pied.

Mr. Balanchine wanted a correct sur le cou-de-pied in frappé exercises. He did not want to see the working foot in full pointe or somewhat relaxed

directly front, with the upper thighs crossed. The foot stays out for as long as the tempo allows, and then the working knee draws quickly back toward the side as the foot comes in with the toes aiming to clasp the ankle in sur le cou-de-pied front. If frappé to the front is done in a series, the dancer tries to pull the knee back toward the side between each frappé in order to maintain the turnout. Her torso and hips remain quiet.

Mr. B wanted some very specific qualities in the strike on the floor that apply with one minor variation in all directions. These qualities might make it easier to execute frappé Balanchine's way in pointe shoes than in the soft ballet slipper. The working

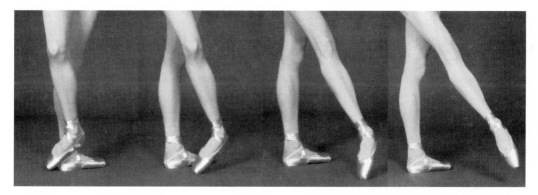

1. Dana just leaving sur le cou-de-pied front
2. Dana's toes strike the floor in frappé front.
3. Dana's pointe about to leave the floor in frappé front
4. Dana's foot pointed front after striking, about three inches off the floor

with the toes flexed, whether in front of or in back of the ankle. Mr. B wanted frappé to look as if the dancer's foot went not only out but also down to come up. This requires a slight lift of the thigh as the working knee straightens. The toes finish higher off the floor than they typically will when dancers are taught frappé in the traditional way, which does not involve the slight lift of the thigh. The down-to-come-up look is enhanced by the use of a light, grazing strike of the floor, rather than a heavy, into-the-floor blow.

In frappé front, the working heel shoots forward from sur le cou-de-pied, while the knee is held back. As the toes strike the floor directly front, the heel is lifted up and forward as the foot points and rapidly brings the straightening knee into the center line of the body. The pointe finishes in the air

Peter striking the floor in frappé front

foot is beveled in sur le cou-de-pied and contacts the floor between the tip and the first joint of the big toe. In frappé front the contact is very near the tip of the big toe, between the side and the bottom. In frappé side the contact is not so close to the tip of the big toe but is still between the side and the

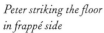

Peter striking the floor
in frappé side

Peter's foot pointed
in frappé side

doesn't like that idea, I tell her to imagine a cockroach down there. However it's done, each dancer must find her way to hit the floor with conviction. It should certainly not be a caress.

Mr. B wanted frappé to have an "up" look and feel, so the energy of the complete movement was down and out and away to come up. This is achieved by letting the energy from the action of the frappé take the foot and the lower leg up, causing the thigh to slightly lift. There is a slight resistance as she straightens the leg to establish the line, which avoids a jerky, jarring snap of the knee. At moderate tempos the foot is about four inches off the floor. As the tempo picks up, the foot ends lower, until at very fast tempos the foot barely leaves the floor and the movement is almost continuous.

A way of visualizing the quality Balanchine wanted in frappé is to think of the motion when a person is whittling a piece of wood. The stroke is often away from the worker and into the wood, but then a little up and out at the end as the sliver or chip is separated from the block or stick. The motion can be smooth, steady, and rapid with a good worker, and frappé can be the same.

There were many steps and jumps in which Mr. B wanted us to stop or freeze a movement to make a picture. This helped us understand getting quickly to a prescribed pose, holding it for a moment to show it to the audience, and then continu-

bottom. In frappé back the contact is more on the side of the big toe and not on the bottom. Because the foot is not fully pointed as it strikes the floor, the dancer does not "flick" the tip of the pointe, which is seen in some schools. Also, the dancer does not drop down to demi-pointe in frappé. The foot is beveled, and the toes are bent down and back. The strike is a real hit on the floor, one that can be clearly heard, not a true brush, as in scrubbing or polishing, and certainly not a gesture in the air in the interest of avoiding stubbed toes or for some other reason. Consistent quality of the strike is more likely "when the dancer knows where the floor is," Mr. B observed, insisting on precise sur le cou-de-pied. However, it is a glancing hit that moves out and up and away from the supporting leg, rather than a heavy blow directed down and into the surface.

Frappé is about getting rapidly, energetically out from sur le cou-de-pied. When a dancer's strike of the floor seemed to lack energy or conviction, Mr. B would say to her, "Show me how angry you can get!" In my classes I tell my students to think of someone they strongly dislike and imagine that person's face on the floor at the point of the strike. If a student

Peter in sur le
cou-de-pied back

Peter striking the floor
in frappé back

Peter extending his leg in frappé
back, his knee about to stretch, his
foot about to point fully

ing. I will use this idea often in this book, and a barre exercise to which it applies very well is frappé. The "picture" the dancer makes in frappé shows the leg extended out and the foot fully pointed. The accent of frappé is out, and the movement is very fast. The extended line is held as long as the tempo allows before the quick return, and the next shooting out is equally fast. However, even though the return is quick, it is not accented—the contrast between the accented movement out and the quick "in" to go out must be maintained. When Mr. B was urging us to maximum effort, he would say, "And OUT! And OUT! And OUT!" If we forgot the contrast, that probably helped us to remember. Mr. B also gave exercises with double and triple frappés.

There is a tendency to allow the foot to creep up the supporting leg, especially to the back. As with petit battement (see page 108), it is important to ensure that the working foot returns to the "cou"— that is, to the smallest part of the ankle, very close to the floor front and back.

In frappé side from sur le cou-de-pied front or back, the knee is held back and the heel is forward as the lower leg extends, shooting the working foot out in a straight line—no "rond" going out or coming in. The toes strike the floor, then the leg stretches and lifts slightly as the foot points fully. Again, the extended line is held as long as possible. Then, as the foot comes in to sur le cou-de-pied with the heel forward and the toes back, the working knee continues to pull back against the hip.

In frappé back from sur le cou-de-pied back, the toes strike the floor, aiming for the center line of the body and bringing the working knee into the center as it straightens. The working hip must release slightly to permit the dancer to reveal the fully turned-out working leg. The fully pointed foot finishes with a slight lift in the air directly back. After showing the "picture," the dancer returns to sur le cou-de-pied by bringing the working hip and heel forward while maintaining maximum turnout by holding the knee back and out to the side. When doing a series of frappés back, the working hip re-mains very slightly open. It is only when the dancer changes direction or ends the exercise that the hip squares off again.

Frappé is also given on demi-pointe and on pointe. The action of the working leg is the same in each direction as it is on flat, but there is no strike on the floor. Nevertheless, there should be the same energy down and out as if actually striking the floor and the same energy in the slight lift as the knee straightens and the foot points. When frappé is done on demi-pointe or full pointe, the dancer must still make full effort to return to sur le cou-de-pied.

In frappé the foot reaches the extended line on the count and returns to sur le cou-de-pied on the "and." Mr. B often asked the pianist to play just a chord as we did a series of frappés and listened to our feet striking the floor to see if anyone was early or late. We most often did sets of eight en croix, but he also gave us other counts: three front and five side over eight, or seven and hold one, or some number of frappés, with the last one held for a specified number of beats. In double and triple frappés the principle is the same, so all the beats have to be completed on the "and." To further cultivate our musicality and the articulation of our legs and feet, he gave us combinations of singles, doubles, and triples.

At moderate tempos the "picture" is held longer than at fast tempos. Even at faster tempos the "picture" is held a split second for it to register with the audience. As the tempo was increased, some dancers (I was one) became nervous about keeping up and anticipated the count. Mr. B would come around and say, "No panic, dear, stay calm, there's time." Or he would see someone with a strained and harried look and come over and engage the person in a little chat. He wanted to see a pleasant and relaxed demeanor even as we made maximum effort. At very fast tempos it is impossible to hold the extended line to show the picture, and the dancer gives the "whittler" look—continuous motion, but with the accent out. Because the emphasis in frappé is on the OUT!—strike and point—at very fast tempos, the foot cannot return all the way

DETAILS I OFTEN INSIST ON IN
BATTEMENT FRAPPÉ:
1) exact directions front, side, and back
2) at all speeds, when coming to sur le cou-de-pied or aiming for it, toes pressed against the sole of the shoe, not flexed up
3) fully pointed foot in the extended line (no clubfoot)
4) end with a slight lift and stay out as long as possible
5) fully stretched knee to the back
6) maintain turnout when coming in
7) when doing double or triple frappés, really try to show the beat front and back within the available time; do not just scratch the side of the leg

to sur le cou-de-pied. "Actual distance is shorter." It aims for the position, but shoots out again to make the pointe on the count and to stay in tempo.

At the superfast tempos Mr. B sometimes called for, it was almost as if our legs were just shaking, but still we tried to show the accent out. He said, "Very, very fast, it is like a movie. Every picture is there."

Frappé builds the speed and control and the look necessary for jeté and other steps requiring that the leg shoot out quickly to a specific place. Because the return to sur le cou-de-pied is quick and rapid, the exercise also develops the responsiveness required in the inner thigh muscles for good beats.

A variant of frappé that Mr. B also gave was a frappé and an immediate continuation to grand battement from the extended frappé line—that is, the foot strikes the floor in the usual way and the knee straightens as in frappé, but the leg continues as it does for grand battement. Instead of shooting off the floor to stop at frappé level, the working leg explodes off the floor into the throw to the high grand battement line. The return, however, was to sur le cou-de-pied.

Battement Frappé Piqué

Battement frappé piqué is a valuable exercise because it brings together a few elements of the technique especially important to Mr. B.

In battement frappé piqué, from sur le cou-de-pied, at slow to moderate tempos, the working thigh and knee lift very slightly in a sort of développé action; then the knee straightens to place the toes lightly—delicately, even—onto the floor in the tendu position. The feeling should be that the foot is being placed on top of the floor and presented.

At faster tempos there is no time to lift the knee or thigh. The toes travel in the most direct way to the tendu line and are placed *lightly* onto the floor. Even without the little lift the dancer must present the foot and place the toes onto the floor with delicacy.

Exact directions must be observed, maximum turnout must be maintained, and there is no tilting at any tempo and to any direction.

We often did this exercise with demi-plié and relevé. Usually we started tendu side and, with a demi-plié on the supporting leg, did a relevé on the

DETAILS I OFTEN INSIST ON IN
BATTEMENT FRAPPÉ PIQUÉ:
1) on flat or in relevé, a fully wrapped foot in sur le cou-de-pied front; not too high and the same beveled shape in the back
2) maintain the weight over the ball of the supporting foot when in plié; therefore there is no weight on the working foot as it is presented to the floor
3) maintain the turnout of the supporting leg throughout, but especially when going through the foot into plié
4) presentation of the working leg and foot, usually with a slight développé action

supporting foot as the working foot came to sur le cou-de-pied. Then we moved into plié, placing the toes on the floor with the slight développé action. At moderate tempos we could give the slight lift to the thigh, but at faster tempos the toes were placed directly but *lightly* on the floor. The weight remained over the ball of the supporting foot as we went through the foot and into plié.

Both forms of this exercise (on flat and with relevé) were done with a single beat, but usually with double beats.

Battement frappé piqué with relevé not only builds strength and control in the supporting leg and foot, it also enables dancers to practice presenting the foot in all directions with energy and a very light touch.

Ballonné Battu

Ballonné battu is in one respect the opposite of frappé: In frappé the accent is out, but in ballonné the accent is in.

I had never done ballonné battu as a barre exercise until I began taking Mr. B's class, although I had taken class with a variety of teachers, including some émigré Russians. Because the action of the leg is in the thigh and is much larger than petit battement, I think ballonné battu is preferable for building the strength and responsiveness required for beats.

In theory, ballonné battu can be done to the front and back as well as to the side, but Mr. B gave it most often to the side. From sur le cou-de-pied front or back, the dancer throws her working leg energetically side to a little higher than forty-five degrees. The dancer thinks of throwing the foot out fully pointed. It does not come up the supporting leg at all, nor does it brush on the floor; instead it goes in a straight line from sur le cou-de-pied to the designated height. This involves a slight diagonal lift of the knee and thigh. The torso remains still, properly aligned over the hips. The working foot is directly side. The leg and foot are instantly pulled down and in to sur le cou-de-pied, using the inside thigh muscles. There is a pause in sur le cou-de-pied, and then the leg is thrown again to the side to be brought down again to sur le cou-de-pied.

When going front, it is important to throw the working foot (the dancer thinks "heel") forward on the center line of the body to about forty-five degrees while keeping the thigh as fully turned out as possible; the working leg does not swing forward turned in, as does a kicker's. On the return the

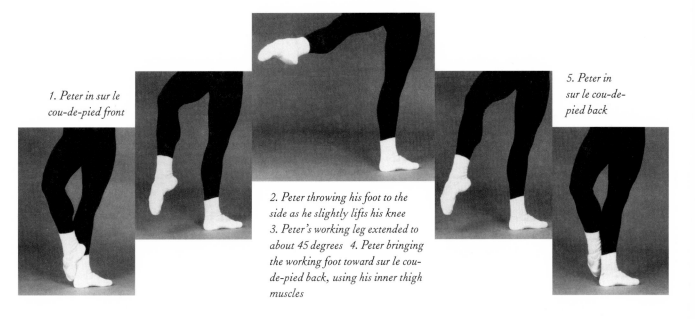

1. Peter in sur le cou-de-pied front

5. Peter in sur le cou-de-pied back

*2. Peter throwing his foot to the side as he slightly lifts his knee
3. Peter's working leg extended to about 45 degrees   4. Peter bringing the working foot toward sur le cou-de-pied back, using his inner thigh muscles*

dancer pulls the working knee back and to the side, aiming the toes to sur le cou-de-pied, where the foot wraps. When going back, the thigh is opened and the working foot is thrown to the center line of the body; on the return, the working hip comes down and squares off as the knee opens to the side and the heel is rapidly brought into sur le cou-de-pied back.

Ballonné battu is usually done at moderate to brisk tempos. The dancer is in the extended line on the "and" and in sur le cou-de-pied on the beat. The accent is sharply in. On occasion Balanchine asked to hear the sound of the foot arriving at sur le cou-de-pied, not so much for the sound itself as for the evidence it gave of energy, effort, and speed.

Ballonné battu can also be done with double beats in sur le cou-de-pied.

DETAILS I OFTEN INSIST ON IN BALLONNÉ BATTU:
1) throw the foot out with a slight lift of the thigh
2) bring the foot in and pull the leg down forcefully with speed, energy, and effort
3) the accent is sharply in
4) maintain knee back and to the side

Petit Battement

Petit battement is an exercise that helps develop the speed and precision needed for batterie. Mr. Balanchine gave it, and I must say it was one of my least favorite exercises at the barre. Perhaps in part for this reason, I often omit petit battement. In its place I sometimes give an exercise I learned from Patricia Wilde, a Balanchine dancer we all admired for her wonderful technique, featuring speed and excellent beats. Mr. B would not have given it, because it uses a flexed foot, but remembering his admiration for Patty, I figure this little exception is all right with him. I have my students face the barre and do the entrechat six action with a flexed working foot,

starting and ending tendu side. The advantage of Patty's exercise, as I see it, is that the dancers practice deeply crossing the working leg, which develops the scissoring action needed for good beats. Another useful substitute for petit battement is ballonné battu. But here is Mr. B's approach to petit battement that is done in sur le cou-de-pied.

Many schools teach that the working foot should be fully pointed, especially in petit battement to the back, or flexed, or else that the toes alone should be flexed. Mr. Balanchine wanted the working foot in the beveled shape used in sur le cou-de-pied front and back (see page 76). Also, he wanted the working foot held low enough that the toes were just off the floor in sur le cou-de-pied back as well as in sur le cou-de-pied front. No creeping up in back!

We typically began petit battement with a three-count preparation. Starting in fifth position with the arm in fifth low: arm to first on count one; arm to second and working foot tendu side on count two; arm down to fifth low as the foot moves to sur le cou-de-pied on count three. With the working thigh held to the side and very still, the lower leg opens to the side to allow the foot to pass from front to back or vice versa. Each beat must be clear and distinct, showing the working foot front and back. The exercise should not look as if the dancer is scratching her ankle or twitching uncontrollably.

There are three qualities the exercise must have that require particular attention from the dancer. When the working foot is in sur le cou-de-pied front, it must be properly wrapped at the ankle, and when it is in back it must be correctly shaped and attached low on the ankle so the toes are just off the floor. When the working foot passes from front to back, there is a tendency for the knee to come forward and for the foot to lift up; the knee must be held firmly back and to the side, and the foot stays down. The action is in the lower leg, which moves in and out, making a shallow "U"; the thigh does not move. Finally, the beveled shape of the foot must be maintained throughout the exercise: no full point, no flexed foot.

Petit battement was also given with a double

beat, with the foot returning to the starting position on the count. The dancer holds that position as long as possible, pausing or stopping there momentarily, and makes the back-to-front movement as quickly as possible. Mr. B would emphasize the timing by saying, "and FRONT!, and FRONT!, and FRONT!," or "and STAY!, and STAY!, and STAY!" Then we could do the reverse and he would say, "and BACK!, and BACK!, and BACK!" Now the accent was on the movement in, on the second beat.

Mr. B sometimes had us do continuous petit battement to a medium-fast tempo and then often repeated it faster and faster, pushing us for maximum speed. Another exercise he often gave us was eight counts of double beats with accent front followed by eight counts of very fast continuous (unaccented) beats and then eight counts of double beats with accent back followed by another eight counts of very fast continuous (unaccented) beats. On occasion he would ask for the riding rhythm in the *William Tell* Overture just after the bugle call ("Lone Ranger" music). Its incisiveness fostered clean, sharp beats and musical clarity. He also used various combinations of beats and holds, occasionally with unusual counts such as threes and fives.

Often we simply held the arm in fifth low to better concentrate on perfecting the movement, but we could do a circular port de bras involving the head.

Petit battement was also given on relevé. As in petit battement on flat, the dancer maintains the working foot in the beveled (sur le cou-de-pied) shape throughout the exercise. The action of the working foot and leg is the same.

DETAILS I OFTEN INSIST ON IN
PETIT BATTEMENT:
1) working knee held back and side, especially as the foot goes back
2) foot in sur le cou-de-pied low—at the ankle—in front and in back
3) clean beats in correct counts

Dana in position to tap under the instep in battement serré front

Battement Serré (Battu)

In her classes at SAB and for the New York City Ballet, Madame Dubrovska called this exercise "ex–*Swan Lake*" because Mr. Balanchine had omitted the step from his version of the lakeside pas de deux. But we did the exercise in class nonetheless!

Traditionally, the working foot tapped the supporting foot with the toes at the anklebone. It could be done on flat or on relevé. Mr. Balanchine always gave the exercise on relevé, and he wanted the toes of the fully pointed working foot to tap under the instep of the supporting foot when done front. We almost never did this exercise to the back.

The dancer's preparation for battement serré front often began with tendu side or in effacé front in plié; then she rolls up to pointe (demi-pointe for men) as she draws the fully pointed working foot to the supporting foot, turning her body square to the barre. The ball of the working foot is lightly touching the supporting instep, and the toes are pointed under it. The working knee is held strongly back and to the side. The working lower leg opens slightly and closes.

The preparation for battement serré back could

Dana in position for battement serré back

begin with tendu side or in effacé back in demi-plié, then relevé on the supporting foot. However, the fully pointed working foot is drawn to the back of the supporting ankle. The working knee is held strongly back and to the side. The lower leg opens and closes in a back and forward action, bringing the anklebone of the working foot to tap low on the back of the supporting ankle.

The working foot is maintained in full point in battement serré front and back. The working thigh is still; the dancer uses the inner thigh muscles to do the movement of the lower leg when in front.

Mr. B sometimes gave us specific counts for the taps in combination with tendu in plié. The count was usually down. For example, plié tendu effacé front on count one, relevé and do two quick taps in front on "and-uh," followed by a slight développé action of the working leg ending plié tendu effacé front on count two. We could do this eight times. Mr. B often wanted to hear the sound of the working foot lightly hitting the instep. The sound he listened for was produced by our energy, effort, and control; the taps should be rapid and evenly spaced. He did not want to see or hear any nervous twitch or spasm of the working leg and foot. To underline the point, Mr. B sometimes asked the pianist to play only chords. He then listened to hear that our feet were tapping out the counts he had asked for. These might be unusual ones—five, for example. So we stayed up in relevé, the pianist played a chord every eight beats, holding the pedal down, and we did five fast taps and held three counts, repeating this pattern several times.

We could stand very straight and square to the barre as we beat, but typically ended each set of taps in plié tendu side or on a diagonal away from the barre in effacé front. An alternative Mr. B preferred had us facing the barre, holding it with both hands, and doing the same exercise. We faced the barre squarely on the taps and diagonally in effacé in tendu with plié. We used the barre for support to help build the strength necessary to do a controlled roll-up relevé and descent.

Battement serré front is important to practice be-

> DETAILS I OFTEN INSIST ON IN BATTEMENT SERRÉ:
> 1) correct placement of the working foot
> 2) working thigh turned out and quiet
> 3) fast, yet controlled tapping

cause it builds responsiveness in the inner thigh and develops the dancer's finesse in combinations such as those often used onstage. I do not believe battement serré back provides any particular benefit to the muscles, and the movement is not used onstage, so, like Mr. B, I very rarely give it.

The free arm can be held in fifth high while beating front and opened to the side when the dancer is in tendu effacé.

Rond de Jambe par Terre

When talking about rond de jambe par terre, Mr. B sometimes suggested we practice the movement when we were at home cooking. As we stirred our pot of soup with a long wooden ladle, so could we "stir" our leg as we traced circles on the floor with our toes. Maybe this was a subtle way to remind us that the shape commonly taught to beginners was a pie half traced with stops, at least in the front and back. It is not used by advanced dancers. The actual shape of rond de jambe par terre at moderate to slow tempos is less than a pie half. The diameter is curtailed because the toes reach the circumference outside the center line. However, the dancer's feeling should always be that she is drawing a circle, and, as the tempo picks up, that is what she does.

Stirring our soup, or at least thinking about it, helped keep us aware that *rond* is a French word for circle, and Mr. B wanted a continuous circular movement on the side of the body with the working leg. There was no stop or even a pause to mark front, side, or back, for as Mr. B reminded us, a circle has no beginning and no ending; it is continuous. The dancer should feel that the entire working leg is rotating as a unit in the hip socket. It is the "jambe" that makes the "rond." If he saw someone who was overcrossing or moving the leg in front-to-back fashion, Mr. B often stopped the music and asked her to do some ronds with her working foot flexed. Working this way, the circular action of the leg is easier to do and is more clearly felt. Or he might demonstrate himself. Looking down then at his circling leg with its flexed foot, he might interject, "Oh! We must point the foot, because we have one," and look around at us with a little smile. We "stirred" with the whole leg, passing each time through first as we made the circle. The dancer should feel as if her big toe is drawing a circle on the floor. The circle is entirely to the side of the body. The dancer does not cross over in the front or back until she changes direction or stops doing rond de jambe par terre. Then the dancer will stop in normal tendu front or back (toes on the center line of the body), or in fifth, in order to end or reverse the exercise or to do an entirely different movement, such as a port de bras.

We could start rond de jambe par terre with a standard preparation: tendu front with plié on count one, demi-rond to tendu side as the supporting leg straightens on count two; or in fifth; or in tendu (back for en dehors, front for en dedans). At a moderate tempo, going en dehors, as the working leg and foot pass first (or leave fifth) position, the inside thigh and heel of the working leg lead it almost straight forward until the foot points where the toes are. The toes do not point on the dancer's center line; this would be "overcrossed" with reference to first position. The toes do not pull in toward the center line of the body, as they do in tendu battement. Instead, as the foot points, the arch and ankle stretch toward the toes, making a slight arc outside the line of the working hip (from fifth, the working leg is naturally a little less open). The energy of this stretch gives a slight impetus and accent that helps start the leg around and the toes tracing the curve of the circle. The working leg continues to circle in the hip socket until the toes are a little more than three quarters of the way around

Peter in first position

Peter tracing the curve to the front as he fully points his foot

Peter almost at the back limit of the curve

Peter going en dehors from first, his foot pointing out on the curve, not on the center line

Peter's foot à la seconde

Peter bringing his heel forward toward first position

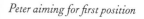
Peter aiming for first position

to the back. As the toes and foot complete tracing the arc in the back, the dancer continues to maintain the turnout, and the working heel leads the foot to first position. It is by continuously turning out the working leg that the circle is formed. The leg is not haphazardly swung around.

Going en dedans at a moderate tempo, as the working leg and foot pass through first position, the toes of the working foot start back, leading the leg until the foot points, making an arc outside the line of the working hip. Again, as the foot points, bringing the heel under and forward, the arch and ankle stretch toward the toes; the toes do not pull in toward the center line of the body. The energy of this stretch again gives a slight impetus that accents the start of the leg around and the toes tracing the curve of the circle. It is by turning out the working leg that it continues to circle in the hip socket until the toes are a little more than three quarters of the way around. Then, the toes of the working foot pull back, leading the foot to first position and completion of the circle.

There is often a tendency to cross over the center line in front and back or to cut the circle short as the dancer starts to bring the working foot toward first position. This stingy circle is seen in the back in en dehors ronds de jambe and, less often, in front in en dedans ronds de jambe. It is important that at moderate tempos the dancer feel the working leg rotate in the hip socket and stretch to make a full three fourths of the arc before the working foot starts in to first. It will feel as if the working leg goes a little

more to the back in en dehors and a little more to the front in en dedans. The rond should be as full as the tempo allows without overcrossing.

In both directions, the heel of the working foot touches the heel of the supporting foot as it passes through first position. If the working leg has come around to the correct point on the circle, no adjustment will be necessary for the working foot to pass through first with the heels touching. If the dancer overcrosses to the front or back or both, the working leg and foot are no longer making a circle. She will have to adjust the step by weaving back to first.

Maximum turnout is maintained through the entire rond with special awareness of the way the working foot goes through first position. Doing en dehors, the dancer tries to make the heel pass just ahead of the toes; doing en dedans, she tries to make the toes pull back and pass just ahead of the heel. This doesn't actually happen, but the result of this maximum effort is that the working leg and foot go through first as completely turned out as possible. In both directions the dancer must be careful that she does not allow the working foot to roll in while it goes through first.

When the dancer points as she moves away from first or closes in toward first position, she does not drop down onto demi-pointe. Instead she uses the same technique as in tendu battement. As the working foot passes through first position at slow to moderate tempos, the dancer may allow the toes to slightly release, putting the ball and the heel of the foot down lightly to the floor, going through the

---

DETAILS I OFTEN INSIST ON IN ROND DE JAMBE PAR TERRE:

1) no overcrossing
2) maintain maximum turnout of the working leg and foot throughout the circle as well as when passing through first position
3) no rolling in when passing through first position
4) the working foot passes first precisely on the count and continues around
5) at faster tempos, make circles more to the side; the circles are smaller
6) the body is held very straight (no tilting forward or back) and the hips are square, with the supporting hip remaining quietly aligned over the ball of the supporting foot

foot a little more, and not stopping. At faster tempos she passes first position with the foot lightly skimming the floor, but there is not enough time to put the foot fully down.

When I first took his class, Mr. B gave rond de jambe par terre to a waltz. We went from first through the pointing of the foot and a little around on one, and with an accent to match the accented one in the music. On two and three we took the working leg around as we slowed to complete the circle. Later he began to say, "What will we do with the 'three' of the one, two, three but make a mistake [stop]?" He switched to 2/4 and had us go through first and start around the circle on the one. It was a continuous movement. It can be done with an accent around or more evenly when faster.

At slower tempos the dancer concentrates on making the largest possible circle without overcrossing. When rond de jambe par terre is done to faster tempos the circle is naturally smaller and even more to the side because there is less time to move toward the front and toward the back. However, the dancer tries to point her foot fully at least by the time she arrives à la seconde. It is sometimes done to very fast tempos; in this case the dancer makes very small circles at the side. She must always think, "around, around" and never "front, back; front, back," especially at faster tempos.

It is very important to hold the supporting hip aligned straight, with the weight over the ball of the supporting foot and the hips square to the barre. No "rond de hip"—that is, letting the action of the working leg pull the dancer's weight back and forth, and onto the heel of the supporting foot, or pull her hips back. The dancer's torso remains quiet as the working leg makes the rond.

Rond de Jambe par Terre with Plié

Rond de jambe par terre was sometimes done with a very deep plié—so deep that the supporting heel released. This develops greater strength in the sup-

porting thigh than is possible when the supporting heel is kept on the floor. The deeper plié also enables the working leg and foot to make a larger circle. This fuller movement of the leg develops a longer reach, which is useful, for example, in having a more dynamic and bigger pas de basque; the strength of the supporting thigh is especially important for controlling the plié in one-legged relevés and slow landings from jumps.

In one kind of rond de jambe par terre with plié, the supporting leg begins to make plié (and the working knee bends) as it passes through first and starts around. The deepest point in the plié is usually reached just as the foot points fully. The dancer begins to straighten the supporting leg after the working leg makes the first part of the curve, starting around toward à la seconde. The supporting leg is straight before the working leg arrives at the three-quarter point. The plié is continuous; it does not stop. The other kind of rond de jambe par terre with plié calls for the dancer to plié only when she can do so without bending the working knee. The supporting knee is therefore straight in first position and makes plié as the working leg extends toward the front or back. The plié is deepened as the toes trace the first part of the arc, and then the supporting leg begins to straighten as the working leg approaches second position. The supporting leg is again straight before the working leg arrives at the three-quarter point in the circle. Again, the plié is deep and continuous; the dancer feels that she goes down to come up. In all cases, it is important that the supporting hip is pulled up and that the weight remains over the ball of the foot.

There are closely related supplemental exercises that are not really rond de jambe exercises, because the working leg does not make a circle; it only makes a large arc. One is usually done to a slow waltz or a slow 2/4. The dancer does a deep plié on the supporting leg as she makes tendu front, sweeps the working leg around to the back, and then returns it to the front. After the two sweeps she usually straightens the supporting leg and does a port de bras with the working foot in tendu front or

---

DETAILS I OFTEN INSIST ON IN ROND DE JAMBE PAR TERRE WITH PLIÉ:

1) in the plié, no rolling in on the supporting foot and leg; hips up and supporting knee extending over the toes
2) maintain the weight over the ball of the supporting foot
3) plié so deeply that the supporting heel will have to release slightly
4) pull up and stand straight on the supporting hip, especially when the working leg goes to the back

---

closes fifth. One alternative after closing fifth front is to move through passé and extend the working leg to tendu back with plié on the supporting leg and repeat the exercise in reverse. To a polonaise, Mr. B might give développé front lowering to tendu front in a deep plié on count one (this is in effect a large pas de cheval with plié), sweep around to the back on count two, still staying in plié, and sweep back to tendu front on count three; this is the first phrase of the music. Repeat the step to the back by straightening the supporting leg as the working leg goes from tendu front through passé and then extending the working leg to tendu back, as the supporting knee bends in a deep plié on count one. And then we reversed the sweeps.

In these exercises the dancer stays *down* in plié while the working leg "swishes" back and forth. However, it does not feel as if the plié has stopped; the dancer does not sit in plié. The thigh muscles are actively working to maintain this deep, low plié. Her supporting hip is aligned over the ball of the supporting foot, and her knee extends well over the toes. She does not tip forward or back, but holds the body very straight, except that on occasion she might bend toward and away from the barre. As the working leg moves to tendu front, the torso bends away from the barre with the arm moving through first to second, and as the leg sweeps around to the back, the torso bends over toward the barre, with the arm rising from second to fifth high; then as the working leg sweeps around to the front, the torso bends away from the barre as the arm opens out to the side.

The action is a sweep of the working leg through an arc that is a little more than half of a circle—the working foot comes to the center line of the body front and back but does not pass through first position. Especially in these exercises, Mr. B might tell us to plié so deeply that he could slip a matchbook under the heel.

In giving a variety of this kind of exercise, Mr. B might simply say, "We need a big, 'lawyer' [lower] plié," indicating that he wanted a very deep plié. Sometimes he would tell us he should be able to slip a sheet of paper under the supporting heel, indicating that the plié should be only so deep that the heel will just release. I sometimes say, "not the whole Sunday *New York Times*, just the front page," to get the necessary result. When I want to see a slightly lower plié I tell my students I want to be able to slip the "Arts and Leisure" section under the heel. This variety of images makes the idea of different depths of plié clear. Generally, when doing plié on one foot at the barre, the dancer should not allow her supporting heel to come more than a quarter inch off the floor. As the pliés get deeper, the dancers have to work with greater intensity and expend much more energy. Of course, each dancer has to apply the idea to her own body, using the actual depth of plié that is right for her. That means she has to know her body and its capabilities and limitations, and have control over it.

Grand Rond de Jambe Jeté

In this exercise the working leg is thrown, rather than lifted into the air to trace a large circle to the side of the body. It further extends the turnout and develops flexibility in the hip joint. It is important

Dana's leg has made the first part of the arc and is being thrown toward à la seconde.

Dana's leg continues the circle and is passing behind à la seconde.

Dana's leg continues the circle through the part in which it is most difficult to maintain the full roundness and turnout.

to understand grand battement and rond de jambe par terre to get the full benefit of this exercise.

Balanchine restudied grand rond de jambe jeté to help dancers avoid making errors commonly seen when it is done in a perhaps more traditional way. Grand rond de jambe jeté has usually been done with the working knee bent in a low attitude when the leg is front or back and straightened as the working leg is thrown around to the side, the knee being fully stretched just before the working leg passes through à la seconde. Mr. B generally had us practice this exercise with a straight leg to avoid three tendencies: to pause in attitude front and back (breaking the rond in two); to overcross in attitude front and back; and, to turn in, dropping the knee in attitude back.

Grand rond de jambe jeté usually starts in first

position or tendu back (for en dehors) or tendu front (for en dedans). It is also given with other exercises, such as rond de jambe par terre.

Doing grand rond de jambe jeté en dehors, the working foot starts in or passes through first position and continues front, as it does in rond de jambe par terre. Coming forward, the foot stretches toward the toes, and the instep pushes the foot up and out as the toes point. As the dancer brushes through first, she gathers force to throw the working leg as a unit out and up and around so it makes a circular arc to à la seconde. Because of the force applied to the throw, the first part of the rond is usually faster than the second. From à la seconde, the leg continues in a circular arc toward the back and down. This is the most difficult part of the movement: from à la seconde through écarté back and around, while remaining as straight as possible, with the weight over the ball of the supporting foot. The dancer must be aware of maintaining the turnout and the circular—not flattened—quality of the arc. The toes touch the floor about where the three-quarter point is reached in rond de jambe par terre. From this point the heel of the working foot leads the leg and foot to first position.

Grand rond de jambe jeté en dedans starts with the working foot in or passing first position and continuing back as it would in rond de jambe par terre. As the foot points back, the instep pushes out as the toes point and the dancer throws the working leg around in a circular arc through à la seconde. It is important that the dancer avoid the tendency to overcross in the back and that she maintain the turnout as the foot leaves the floor and the leg continues on its circular path. The toes touch the floor about three quarters of the way around, and then the toes pull back and lead the foot into first position.

Mr. B usually set a series of ronds de jambe jetés, so in practice the working foot passes, is almost thrown, through first position into the next rond, or else passes through first position to tendu front or back in order to change directions.

In both directions the dancer should feel that the working leg is circling in the hip socket as it does in rond de jambe par terre, the difference being that in this case the pointe is in the air. Because of this circling, the big toe traces a large circular (or oval) arc in the air, from first position up and around to the highest point at à la seconde and continuing on around. However, to achieve this it is usually helpful for the dancer to aim to make the highest point just behind à la seconde in both directions, but especially doing en dehors. It is better to have a slightly lower leg and a fuller circle than to do a movement that looks something like grand battement side. The entire movement is executed to the side of the body—there is no overcrossing. The working foot comes to the center line only to change directions or to stop.

The dancer must maintain her weight over the ball of the supporting foot. The abdominal muscles are held firmly in to help hold the torso still and the back as straight as possible, which helps the dancer to move only the working leg. There is no tipping back and front and no pulling away from or leaning into the barre.

The working leg usually reaches at least shoulder height in à la seconde. The arm is therefore best held in fifth high to ensure that the foot can pass easily. If the arm was held to the side in second position, Mr. B would have us lift it slightly to give room for the leg to pass. As soon as the leg had passed, we gracefully lowered the arm to a standard second position. We could repeat the rond

---

DETAILS I OFTEN INSIST ON IN GRAND ROND DE JAMBE JETÉ:

1) no overcrossing front or back until the finish or a change of direction
2) the working leg is thrown from first, not lifted; the rond happens in one movement, not two
3) make the fullest possible circle in the air to the side of the body, with the highest point in or just past à la seconde
4) don't skimp on the arc in the back
5) the working leg and foot must be turned out passing through first and throughout the circle, especially just behind à la seconde in en dehors and when leaving the floor and starting the circle en dedans
6) maintain a firm midsection, so only the working leg moves
7) minimal adjustment of the torso, forward or back; no pulling off or leaning in to the barre

and the port de bras several times before reversing the step.

This exercise was usually done in 2/4 time with the working foot passing first and moving around on one and in one movement. Peter Martins often gives this exercise from fifth front to fifth back in one count, with one count to hold in fifth back and then reverse it so the entire grand rond jeté returning to fifth front is also done in one count followed by one count to hold. He sometimes repeats the step on pointe (or demi-pointe), returning to sous-sus.

Battement Dégagé, Passé, Développé

Although not a rond de jambe, this exercise is similar in that it develops more flexibility in the hip joint as well as further strengthening the turnout. Dancers will benefit more from this exercise when the material on battement dégagé, développé, and passé is understood.

Mr. B wanted to see the working leg continue to lift and turn out as it moved through passé and stretched into the extended line. The dancer must avoid the tendency to let the working leg lose energy, turn in, or drop down as it comes through passé. Also, he emphasized that there is no stopping or even pausing in passé. "Passer" means to pass, not stop, he reminded us. The working leg and knee move continuously until they are fully stretched in the extended line.

From fifth position front, the dancer does a brisk battement dégagé front to about hip level and can pause there. The working knee then pulls back and

1. Peter's leg extended in battement dégagé front
2. Peter lifting his knee side, bringing his foot toward passé
3. Peter continues to lift his knee and opens his thigh as he releases his working hip.
4. Peter's leg extended back, where it reaches its maximum height

Peter in plié in battement dégagé back with no tilt

side, lifting strongly, and the working foot passes the supporting leg. The knee continues to lift and the thigh opens as the working hip releases to allow the leg to extend to the back, where it reaches its maximum height as it stretches. The back is square to the barre, and the upper body and the supporting hip remain very straight, with the weight centered over the ball of the supporting foot.

This exercise is often combined with rond de jambe par terre. In this case it is important that the dancer remember that when battement dégagé passes through first, the pointe aims for the center line of the body, rather than in front of the working hip. When Mr. Balanchine gave battement dégagé, passé, développé, he usually set it to be done by itself and in series. Then the working leg was brought down from the extended line and it

brushed through first position, aiming for the dancer's center line.

We could also dégagé to forty-five degrees. In this case the knee pulled back and to the side as before, but lifted only enough to enable the toes of the working foot to pass the supporting leg near mid-calf. The leg extended to the back at forty-five degrees or a bit higher. Another variant had us pull the working knee back just before the leg fully established the line to the front; we did not pause or show the front position. The aim was to arrive to the back as quickly as possible. However, we always showed the end, the extended line back.

The toes of the working foot barely graze and might not even touch the supporting leg as the foot passes. They may be an inch or so away when the battement dégagé is to hip level and the knee is lifting to its maximum.

Battement dégagé, passé, développé may be done on a straight supporting leg or with demi-plié. When it is done with plié, the descent is completed by the time the working leg is extended in the battement. It is important that the plié remain continuous; the dancer does not sit in the plié and stop the action of either leg when doing the battement. As the working knee lifts up and pulls back, the supporting leg starts to straighten and is stretched again at about the time the working foot moves through passé.

When battement dégagé, passé, développé is reversed, it is very important that the supporting hip and torso remain as straight as possible as the dancer does the battement dégagé back. Again, the abdominal muscles support the lower back; there is minimal adjustment of the supporting hip and torso. The working knee lifts up and out as the foot comes under to move through passé. As the working foot continues through passé it leads heel forward as the leg stretches to the extended line.

We usually began the exercise at a moderate tempo—battement on count one, slight pause; passé without stopping on count two, extend on count three; hold count four. With this timing we usually did the exercise four times, the fourth time

DETAILS I OFTEN INSIST ON IN BATTEMENT DÉGAGÉ, PASSÉ, DÉVELOPPÉ:

1) no unnecessary tilting at any time, front or back; minimum possible adjustment of the torso and supporting hip when the dancer's leg is extended high to the back

2) the shoulder line remains square to the barre; when the arms are à la seconde they are in front of the back

3) the working foot does not hit the supporting leg, it passes to the side; also, it does not stop as it passes the supporting leg

4) the working leg lifts to the final line

5) the final straightening of the leg in the extended line requires the extra turnout (acts as a brake)

6) pass through first turned out

7) if done with plié, the plié is continuous

finishing tendu front on four and then reversing. Then we might do battement on count one with a slight pause, passé and extend on count two, and hold counts three and four; or battement on "and," then without pause, passé and extend instantly, arriving to the back on count one. Mr. B sometimes combined fast and slow timings in the same set. The same timings were used when we did the exercise with plié, but now the dancer did not freeze the battement and, as usual, the plié did not stop.

Many schools teach a variety of tilts and often include an arabesque in this exercise. Some schools allow the dancers to stand on various diagonals to the barre. Mr. Balanchine wanted the dancers as straight as possible and square to the barre at all times in this exercise, so this is one for which he was especially likely to divide the class.

The dancer usually lifted the arm to first position on the battement and then opened it to second as the leg extended back or front. When the leg extends to the back, there is a tendency to let the upper torso twist, letting the side near the barre come forward and the other side pull back. Again, Mr. B wanted the dancer's back and shoulder line to remain square to the barre.

Battement dégagé, passé, développé is useful for teaching control of the working leg for steps like renversé and fouetté. The dancer learns to brush the working leg slightly lower than or only to the level of the final line, rather than throwing it up too high and letting it drop down or needing to lower it to complete the step. This allows continual lifting of the working knee and leg throughout the movement. She also learns to maintain the turnout.

Rond de Jambe en l'Air

The name of this exercise is slightly misleading, because it is not the whole jambe, but only the lower leg that "circles" in the air. Also, in reality the lower leg causes the toes to trace an elliptical rather than a circular shape. But even though an ellipse is flatter than a circle, Mr. Balanchine still wanted to see that the toes traced a curving shape in the air, an "egg-shape," rather than simply moving in and out on a straight line, as in ballonné. He therefore expected to see a clear difference between en dehors and en dedans ronds.

Rond de jambe en l'air is like rond de jambe par terre in that it is done to the dancer's side. The working foot does not cross in front of or behind the supporting leg. The tip of the pointe passes (except in high ronds) on the side of the supporting leg between midcalf and just beneath the knee.

In some schools this exercise is given only in its standard form, with the thigh parallel to the floor (at about ninety degrees), the working foot describing a comfortable shape, with minimum curve at moderate tempos. In contrast, Mr. B regularly gave

*1. Dana's working leg à la
seconde at 90 degrees
2. Dana tracing the curve to the
back
3. Dana grazing the bump on
the side of her supporting knee
4. Dana tracing the larger curve
to the front*

it at a variety of heights and speeds, which meant in a variety of sizes, and usually with an accent at the straightening of the working knee on completion of each rond. Also, he wanted it done exactly to the side of the body with a fully turned-out working leg; the dancer must take care to keep the working knee pulled clearly to the side, rather than letting it drift toward the front, and she must not let the thigh turn in as the lower leg makes the back part of the rond. It should almost feel as if the entire rond is done in front of her turned-out and pulled-back thigh.

Rond de jambe en l'air in its more traditional form starts with the working leg à la seconde at ninety degrees, with the knee straight. Doing en dehors from à la seconde, the working knee bends as the lower part of the leg starts back, making the toes of the fully pointed working foot trace an elliptical shape, curving ever so slightly back and in toward the supporting knee. The pointe of the working foot lightly grazes the side of the supporting leg just below the "bump" on the inside of the leg just beneath the knee as it continues to trace the second and larger part of the ellipse. The lower part of the working leg then starts curving forward as the knee straightens, completing the elliptical shape with a slight accent and a pause (or stop, if time allows) in à la seconde. The en dedans exercise precisely reverses this sequence, with the lower leg starting forward as the knee bends, and so on. When the working knee straightens at the end of the en dedans rond de jambe, it is important that the leg turn out fully. When doing a series of ronds de jambe with the working thigh at ninety degrees, it can almost feel as if the dancer lifts her knee when it starts to bend and very slightly lowers her thigh as she straightens and turns out her leg.

This basic rond de jambe en l'air at ninety degrees was initially done at moderate to moderately fast tempos. At faster tempos the dancer does not have time to touch the supporting leg, but the working knee still straightens fully to present the foot à la seconde. At very fast tempos the dancer may also be unable to fully straighten the working knee, but she comes as close as she can, still presenting the foot à la seconde as much as possible. Alternatively at very fast tempos, Mr. B might have us trace two or more small, more circular ronds that were like a stirring action, without fully stretching the knee until the last one.

There are two tendencies the dancer must especially guard against as the tempo picks up. No matter how fast the tempo, the dancer must not turn the exercise into a kind of ballonné, simply bending and stretching the knee, waving the working foot in and out on a straight line. Also, she must avoid letting the entire rond be done close to her supporting leg. This sometimes can look as if the working foot is spastically jabbing the supporting leg. She keeps the rond somewhat away from her by emphasizing the straightening of the working knee, which, because of the fast tempo, limits the bending that brings the toes back toward the supporting leg (or body at greater heights). Each tendency is avoided by maintaining full awareness of the working lower leg and foot.

We also did another traditional rond de jambe en l'air with the working leg at forty-five degrees. The action of the lower leg is the same, except that the

Dana's working leg extended above shoulder height

Dana's thigh does not lower as she traces the curve of the rond de jambe. Her knee straightens as her lower leg comes forward and turns out to the line shown in the first photograph.

toes graze the inside of the supporting leg at mid-calf. As the tempo picks up, the ellipse again shortens, as it does at ninety degrees, but still the direction of the rond is revealed at all speeds.

In many schools, a "high" rond de jambe en l'air exercise is done in which the actual ronds are done somewhere at or even below hip height, after which the working leg and foot are thrown or kicked high into the air. Rond de jambe en l'air with the ronds done at shoulder height or slightly above was, in contrast, very important to Mr. B. By practicing the following exercise, we developed the strength, control, and muscle memory to ensure that the working leg arrived at least at ninety degrees before we started the rond when we did the step onstage. At the barre the dancer does dégagé (or développé) at least to shoulder height; pauses, if the tempo allows; and makes one or more small ronds high and away from the body, stretching the knee after each rond, if the tempo allows. The thigh does not lower and lift during these high ronds; the dancer holds it in the high line and circles with the lower leg. As she completes the last one, she fully stretches the working knee with a little accent and turns the leg out to present the foot and show the extended line. An alternative technique for which the previous exercise develops the strength required for control, calls for the dancer to dégagé to about ninety degrees; from this height she bends the working knee and starts the lower leg on its rond. Then, as she begins to straighten the working knee, she lifts the thigh to the designated height, stretching the knee and turning out the leg to present the foot as before. This step is done with a double rond by Odette in *Swan Lake*.

Double, triple, or continuous ronds de jambe en l'air are done at each height, with the same principles applying. As the tempo picks up, each rond is done slightly farther away from the supporting leg or, if high, the torso, but is made as large as the tempo will allow, with the curved shape maintained. If the leg is at ninety degrees or lower and if there is time for the toes to come in and touch the side of the supporting leg and for the knee to

straighten fully, the dancer can do quick singles. At very fast tempos there is not time for the toes to come in and touch the supporting leg, nor for the knee to stretch fully. The ronds (or rond) before the final one are quite small, and the knee does not really straighten at all. However, the effort to make the ronds as full and as large as possible gives the step life. The ronds are continuous until the last one, when the knee stretches with a little accent and pauses in à la seconde.

Certain qualities should be maintained in all ronds de jambe en l'air. The entire "circling" action is in the lower leg. The working thigh remains turned out all through the rond; it is held firmly and quietly à la seconde. The working knee has a "fixed place." The lower leg works as a unit; the dancer must guard against "rond de pied"—a circling of the foot. The foot must be fully pointed (heel forward/toes back) at all times. Each rond should be as full as the tempo allows, in both length and width. The toe "retraces" the same ellipse in each rond. Neglecting the curving action makes the step a kind of ballonné; neglecting the length, especially the straightening of the knee, robs it of dynamism. Finally, each rond—single, double, or triple—should finish with the working foot presented for a moment à la seconde. But the exception proves the rule, or as Mr. B liked to say, anything is possible.

He liked to give one variant of rond de jambe en l'air in which the working foot begins and ends in fifth without a pause in à la seconde. In this exercise the dancer brushes to the side from fifth position. As soon as the toes leave the floor, the knee bends and the rond starts. The dancer continues to lift the thigh until it reaches the desired height as the working leg circles. The thigh remains at that level until the final rond. Then, just before the working foot has reached à la seconde, the thigh lowers as the leg stretches and continues down into fifth. We usually did this exercise low, at about forty-five degrees, to a very fast tempo. We generally did only one rond, going from fifth front to fifth back, holding there for a count, and then reversing, but we could also

DETAILS I OFTEN INSIST ON IN ROND DE JAMBE EN L'AIR:
1) the working thigh does not turn in, allowing the knee to come forward as it bends
2) the working leg turns out fully as the knee stretches
3) circle with the lower leg; really show the direction
4) maintain a fully pointed foot—no "rond de pied"
5) usually done with the accent out at the straightening of the knee

do doubles or a series of continuous ronds before closing in fifth.

In rond de jambe en l'air the accent is usually on the straightening of the knee or away from the body. We generally did it to two measures of a 2/4, sometimes brushing out on count one and sometimes earlier, making a rond on the "and" before count one. The actual ronds often took one beat, with the knee straightening on the count. As usual, Mr. B often set unusual combinations of ronds and holds to develop our musicality. For example, to a 2/4 he might have us brush out on count one, do a rond finishing on count two, then two fast, but full-sized, ronds finishing the first one on the "and" and the second one on count three, and then close on count four. To two measures in three, such as a polonaise, he might tell us to brush out on count one, do one rond finishing on count two, close in fifth on count three, and then reverse. The exercise continues with brushing out on count one, doing ronds on counts two and three, closing on count four, holding counts five and six, and then doing it in reverse.

Mr. Balanchine sometimes gave an exercise for rond de jambe en l'air at ninety degrees in which the entire combination, from start to finish, was done with the working leg moving continuously, without stops or accents. Starting in fifth position, the dancer brushes side on count two of the preparation, ronds on count one, ronds on count two, bends her working knee as in a rond to bring her foot to passé, continuing on to développé through the front on count three, carries the leg side (a demi-rond) on count four, and immediately begins the combination again. The entire combination can be done three times; after the second rond de jambe of the fourth set, the dancer closes to fifth back and reverses the combination. The dancer builds awareness of maintaining the working leg and foot in the same plane at ninety degrees and of maintaining the turnout as the working leg moves from the rond de jambe to passé and through the front and the demi-rond back to the side; this is important for Mr. B's approach to fouetté turns (see page 277). She also practices circling the leg maintaining an even, constant movement. This exercise can also be done pausing after each rond de jambe as well as in front (or back) and à la seconde. The pauses make it look entirely different; it feels different and it is different.

Rond de jambe en l'air is important not only for relevé and sauté with rond de jambe but also for piqué with rond de jambe and gargouillade. It should regularly be given in all forms with relevé. On page 24, I describe a "never been done before" exercise that includes many different kinds of rond de jambe.

General Considerations on Adagio

Balanchine had a well-known reputation for developing dancers who could move with great speed, clarity, and sharpness and for making ballets that used those qualities. Less well known is that he developed dancers who could move more slowly than most thought possible, and do it exquisitely. Adagio exercises were therefore an important part of his classes. When a movement is done slowly, there is more time to work on perfecting the form and shape; the dancer has time to correct and refine the line. Adagios also build the strength and stamina needed to sustain various shapes and slow, extended movements.

He taught his dancers to move beautifully, both slowly and quickly. However, beautiful movement is of great importance in adagio work, because the moment lasts a long time. A dancer starting and stopping, losing the sense of flow, of continuity, or moving slowly in a disjointed, uncoordinated way is not pleasing to watch.

To achieve the most interesting and beautiful movement he wanted to see the dancer's whole body participating—face and head, arms and chest, the entire torso, and so on. The energy of the movement should take over the dancer's whole being so that even her breathing is part of it. This is true of slow and fast movement, but the absence of this quality can be more noticeable in adagio. When Mr. B saw one of us staring into space in a dazed, fixated manner, he might gently tap us on the head and ask, "Is anybody home? Are you there?"

We usually stood square to the barre for adagio, rather than on the diagonal, because Mr. B wanted us to continue to have the barre as reference for front, side, and back. When an exercise called for an effacé or écarté line, this was accomplished by changing the position of the free arm, the direction in which the head was turned and slanted, its level, etc. We changed the level of the head and the focus of the eyes, in coordination with the movement of our arms and legs, to bring attention to our foot on the floor, to announce movement from it, and to reveal the final line. We looked down as our free hand lowered, then the arm and hand and head raised, announcing that the working foot was being picked up off the floor. As we extended the working leg, and as our arm opened side or elsewhere, we looked proud with our chest up, head erect, eyes alive and projecting out.

In the next chapter I discuss Mr. B's teaching for épaulement, body directions, and ports de bras in detail. In this section of the barre exercises, I am sketching just enough to indicate the general look of the movements, omitting most of the details addressed later. This parallels his emphasis in setting and correcting the exercises: at the barre somewhat more attention to legs, feet, etc.; in the center port de bras exercises, somewhat more attention to the upper body. Even so, the adagio exercises had to be done observing his basic ideas of correct form for the whole body for them to have the specific qualities he wanted. So Balanchine certainly corrected more than just feet and legs when he felt it necessary. Teachers and dancers not trained in Balanchine's way of working may want to read pages 146–160 and 179–188 before trying to work in detail with the material that follows for the barre. In the interest of readability I have not given specific page references for terms and technique not already covered, but it is all found therein.

Adagio exercises were nearly always done with phrasing and accents to show the beginning and the end of the movement. But the movement was usually continuous until we reached the extended line; the phrasing and accents did not indicate points at which the dancer would stop or hold. When a dancer does développé, there is no letting the toes of the working foot rest on the floor to help her find her balance when she has picked her foot up out of fifth, nor is there jamming the toes into the supporting leg in passé, for example. The working leg does not settle in or down or relax in any way while executing a développé. Once the dancer reached the extended line, she "grew" in the held position so it did not look static and lifeless. Each movement must maintain a vibrant energy throughout.

At the barre, the adagio or at least some part of it would often be on pointe for ladies and on demi-pointe for men. I think this is important because in most ballets the adagio work is done on pointe by the woman, partnered by the man. Adagio on pointe or demi-pointe also makes the dancer more aware of pulling up out of the supporting leg and hip and helps to develop balance and proper stance as well as strength in the supporting leg and foot.

Mr. B gave simple adagio exercises that very often were focused on one or two movements—

développé (see page 89), dégagé (see page 75), or enveloppé (see page 95). They should be understood in their basic form at the barre and used in these adagios. He generally did not give long, involved, complicated enchaînements, including a wide variety of steps, poses, and body directions. Such exercises demand great effort to memorize the combination, preventing maximum attention to perfecting execution of the step. Instead, he might have us do the same movement to the three directions (front, side, and back), at a variety of tempos and phrasings. For example, one développé, done slowly in four counts: announcing the foot off the floor on count one, the arrival of the leg on count two, holding and showing the extended line on count three, and then the closing to fifth on count four. And then a very fast développé—développé and extend the leg on count one, hold count two, close to fifth on count three, hold in fifth on count four, in each direction. We would do this kind of combination in each direction using développé, enveloppé, or dégagé.

Mr. B gave a variety of simple ports de bras for these basic adagio exercises. The free arm was opened to second in the preparation, and usually passed through fifth low and first as it returned to second or moved to fifth high. In exercises based solely on développé, enveloppé, and dégagé, he generally did not use any of the arabesque lines with the arm reaching front when the working leg is extended to the back. He wanted us to develop clear muscle memory of the position with the torso lifted and the back as straight as possible and square to the barre so we had a basis for comparison with the extended lines of arabesque.

We often did exercises in which we moved the working leg from one position to another, such as développé front, carry side, close fifth. As the working leg is carried side, the dancer must maintain the turnout in it as well as in the supporting leg. Also, the working leg must remain in the same plane or, even better, lift slightly, alive and growing, as it reaches à la seconde. The back is held square to the barre; it does not rotate toward the working leg. But it is held with the chest lifted up and the weight maintained over the ball of the supporting foot. Then we might développé side, carry back, and close. As the working leg is carried to the back, the turnout in the working leg is maintained and the back remains square to the barre and as straight as possible. As the working leg moves toward the back, the working hip is released and opened to enable the leg to maintain the turnout and extend the line. It is better to have a beautifully turned-out working leg, even if it is necessary to slightly adjust the turnout of the supporting leg and foot, than to maintain a full turnout on the supporting side and allow the working leg to drop down and turn in. It should look as if the working leg lifts and grows as it extends, coming to a climax when it arrives directly back.

We also practiced this exercise en dedans: développé back, carry side, close back; développé side, carry front, close front. The working leg moves from the back to the side because of turnout. The dancer does not bring the leg side and then flip it out; rather, the energy and effort involved in maintaining the turnout carry the leg side as she brings the hips into proper alignment. This applies as well when the working leg is brought front. Once the working leg is front, the turnout is maintained with the muscles of the inner thigh, not those of the top of the thigh, and the hips are square. The working leg and well-pointed foot remain in the same plane or lift slightly (again, the leg "grows" as it moves) as the leg is carried around from the back to the side and from the side to the front. We might repeat this entire exercise on pointe.

Mr. Balanchine usually gave simple ports de bras that complemented the rest of the movement in the exercise. On the développé to the front carry side, the dancer could move the arm from fifth low through first to fifth high as the leg extended front, then open the arm to second as the leg is carried side. On the développé to the side carry back, the dancer moved the arm from fifth low through first (working foot to passé), then raised it to fifth high as the leg extended to the side, and opened it to second as the leg is carried back. When the dancer does développé back carry side, she can move the arm from fifth low through first (working foot to passé) to fifth high as the leg extends, then open to second as the leg is carried side.

As noted above, relatively more emphasis in setting the exercise and in correcting it is given to the feet and legs in the work at the barre. And yet, when Mr. B saw an uncoordinated port de bras or a dull or lifeless look about the upper body, he would remind us that the life displayed by "growing" legs was the same life displayed by a lifted chest, a proud head, supported elbows, and so on, by a dancer happy to be there. The teacher must find the right balance in emphasis as she works with each class.

Adagio: Arabesque

Arabesque is a pose that involves a variety of specific head and arm positions and is therefore different from leg to the back (see Développé, page 89).

DETAILS I OFTEN INSIST ON IN ARABESQUE:
1) working leg directly behind the center, and the arm and hand, if in front, directly front
2) working leg fully turned out to partially reveal the underside of the thigh and heel, knee fully stretched, foot well shaped and fully pointed
3) stand as straight as possible on the supporting hip, back straight, torso lifted, chest up, and face forward

However, as in leg to the back, the dancer releases and opens the working hip while standing as straight as possible on the supporting hip and leg.

"I do not want to see an ironing board," Balanchine would say as he gave an arabesque exercise. He meant that he wanted the torso up, the chest lifted, the back as vertical or as straight as possible, and the working leg lifting to meet it at a right angle. He did not want to see us tilt forward and flatten out like a board. He wanted to see the effort of the leg meeting the back in its upright position as we stood aligned over the supporting hip.

A typical arabesque exercise could combine leg to the back with an arabesque. For example, the dancer does a développé back as she moves her arm to the side, keeping the shoulders square to the barre—she might pause in this basic leg to the back position. Sometimes, to convey the idea of remaining as straight as possible in our upper bodies when our arms were held to the side and the leg was to the back, Mr. B said it was like "Christ on the Cross." The exercise continues with a breath and a lift in the chest and

Peter with his back straight and leg extended back, arm in second, "Christ on the Cross"

1. Peter in second arabesque 2. Peter making a "juicy" plié, holding his back up 3. Peter relevés maintaining the same line.

arm and then the dancer does a port de bras through fifth low, her head and eyes looking down to follow her hand; next, she moves her arm forward to second arabesque as her head lifts and slants, her eyes focus out over her hand, and the shoulder line lengthens. The back stays as straight as possible as the working leg continues to lift against it; there could be a slight, subtle adjustment in the supporting hip and the back to lift the leg higher, but there is no visible tilt forward. This is not a static, settled position—there should be a feeling of life; a sense that the dancer is growing, extending, reaching.

While maintaining this arabesque pose, the dancer can do plié relevé several times. As she goes into plié on her supporting leg, she lifts her working leg even higher while maintaining her back straight and her chest up, helping to give vitality to the movement. There should be no tipping or rocking forward in the plié as the knee bends and extends over the ball of the supporting foot and no heaving back in the relevé. Her arm, which is directly in front of her (hand on the center line of her body), at the same time does not look stiff. As she pliés, the elbow softens with a slight bend and the wrist and fingers gently resist the air, and, as she relevés, the arm lengthens and the back of the wrist leads up. She then returns the arm to second as she assumes the "Christ on the Cross" position.

Adagio: Arabesque Penchée

"No penché!" was a common correction from Mr. B whenever we lifted the leg to the back. What he meant was that we should not relax the back and let it tilt forward in order to raise the leg, maybe even to raise it a little higher. But we certainly practiced penché as Balanchine wanted it done.

For Mr. B it was the leg lifting against the back that takes the body down, rather than the body bending forward and down followed by the rising leg. It most certainly was not a stretch! Once the dancer has mastered the "Christ on the Cross" feeling—body straight, leg lifted—she can maintain this relationship of the working leg to the back as the upward thrust of the working leg takes her upper body forward. To come up, she lifts the back against the leg, maintaining the relationship of her back to her leg or even sharpening the angle a bit. Her weight is over the ball of the supporting foot during the whole movement—no pulling back in the hips and letting the weight settle on the heel.

Mr. B did not give penché at the barre very often, but when he did give it, we usually did it on flat. A typical exercise began with développé back, with the arm doing a port de bras from fifth low through first to second position—that is, "Christ on the

closing her leg to fifth position and moving her arm to fifth low.

I sometimes give arabesque penchée in first arabesque with the working leg the one next to the barre; this is the most stable. However, when the inside leg is supporting and the outside leg is working, several ports de bras, aside from the effacé back, can be used, such as the standard second arabesque; or arm in second to fifth low and then to fifth high as the dancer makes penché, ending with the dancer

Peter in arabesque penchée in effacé back

Dana in arabesque penchée looking under her arm in fifth high

Cross"—and then, while maintaining the line of the back and leg, a port de bras down through fifth low, and up to second arabesque. Penché begins with a little lift, a breath that slightly raises the chest, arm, and head, and even the leg, to highlight the downward movement that follows. Raising the working leg against the back (which the dancer keeps arched), the torso goes forward and down as the arm sweeps down and back. The dancer turns her head and follows the hand, finishing looking up and back at it in a kind of effacé back. After a hold, she lifts her back to come up straight as her arm and leg return to second arabesque. She then opens her arm to second position while continuing to hold her leg up against her back. She finishes by

1) maintain the relationship of the leg to the back throughout the movement—do not flatten out: no ironing board!

2) maintain the weight over the ball of the supporting foot; do not pull back in the hips

3) maintain the body in proper alignment—working leg in back of the center line of the body, no tilting off the supporting leg

looking under the arm when she is all the way down. In any such port de bras, the elbow, wrist, and hands should convey the sense of an energized softness and life.

I also occasionally give penché on pointe. The dancers can be at a slight diagonal to the barre, with the inside leg the working (lifted) leg. Working on pointe in this way allows the dancer to practice maintaining her weight over the pointe with the stability provided by the barre. It helps prepare her for supported adagio and certain variations. Penché on demi-pointe is generally not done by the men.

Adagio: Attitude

Attitude, like arabesque, is a pose and also includes specific head directions and arm positions.

In attitude back, like arabesque, the back and the supporting hip are as straight as possible. Also, the working thigh is directly behind the working hip and is lifted strongly against the back to form a ninety-degree angle. The working hip is open to allow the working thigh the freedom to lift and turn out. The working knee is level with the foot; it is on the same plane. The angle of the lower leg to the thigh is also ninety degrees. We rarely practiced attitude allongée, which is a more open attitude, and we never practiced an attitude with the knee tipped down and the foot lifted up.

We often practiced moving to attitude from passé. The dancer lifts her thigh up and back, which requires her to release the working hip to allow the thigh to open to the ninety-degree angle.

We also practiced moving to attitude from second position through arabesque as well as directly from arabesque. When going from arabesque to attitude, the thigh must remain directly back; it must not wander out to the side. The working foot reaches for the opposite shoulder; the dancer's feeling is that her leg tries to wrap around her body from the back.

In attitude front the turned-out thigh is in front of the working hip, with the knee bent a little less

Dana in arabesque penchée on pointe at the barre

This is not arabesque penchée. Peter's ready to do his ironing.

Dana on pointe in attitude effacée back, with her back square to the barre

Dana on pointe in attitude croisée back, with her back square to the barre

Dana on pointe in attitude front, hips and back square to the barre

than ninety degrees and the heel lifted as high as possible. To the front the foot cannot and should not be on the same level as the knee.

We almost always practiced front and back attitude at the barre with a head and arm position; we very rarely if ever held the head straight front. Nevertheless, we usually stood square to the barre and almost never turned our body on the diagonal toward or away from the barre to make effacé or croisé. Instead, we practiced attitude effacée back by looking out toward the center of the room, away from the barre. When the working foot reaches passé, the dancer's head is straight front and the arm is in first position. As the working thigh lifts the leg to attitude back or as the working foot leads the leg to attitude front, the arm moves from first to fifth high and the head slants out to make attitude.

For attitude croisée back the head turns toward the barre and slants as the arm moves from first to fifth high, finishing with the tips of the fingers over the center of the head while the working leg moves to attitude back.

A typical exercise incorporating these poses is développé à la seconde, with the arm moving through fifth low and first to second, passé as the arm moves down through fifth low and then continues through first to fifth high as the leg lifts to make attitude effacée back (body still square to the barre, but head and arm in the proper effacé position); then, as the leg extends to arabesque, the arm moves to second arabesque. We could also reverse this exercise. From attitude front, we extended the leg front as the arm moved from fifth high to the same line as in second arabesque, the hand almost seeming to brush (or paint) the working leg as it did. This exercise could be done on flat or on pointe, or with one or more relevés.

Many dynamic steps (sissonne to attitude on pointe, sissonne jumping to attitude, sauté in attitude, grand jeté in attitude, renversé) used frequently by Mr. B were done in attitude or moving to attitude, so it was very important that this pose be learned well in adagio. Attitudes are also common in various kinds of turns and in supported adagio.

Développé Écarté

On rare occasions we did stand on the diagonal to the barre and do développé écarté front or back, but most often we stood square to the barre; again for this exercise, Balanchine wanted us to have the barre available as ready reference in sensing side. In one exercise Balanchine gave, the dancer begins with développé side, the arm moving à la seconde. After a pause she might port de bras to fifth low as she lowers her head and gaze to follow her hand. Then, without stopping, she could raise her arm through first to fifth high, turning her head toward the center of the room, lifting her gaze slightly, and looking just behind the forearm— this makes écarté front. To make

> DETAILS I OFTEN INSIST ON IN DÉVELOPPÉ ÉCARTÉ:
> 1) working leg fully turned out and precisely side
> 2) don't lean back; keep the chest lifted and the back long
> 3) in écarté front, direct the gaze behind the arm
> 4) in écarté back, keep the fingertips over the center line of the head

écarté back from développé side, she can do a port de bras to fifth low and then to fifth high, turning her head to the barre, lowering her gaze, and slightly inclining her torso toward the barre as her

Dana in développé écarté front, square to the barre

Dana in développé écarté back, square to the barre

arm establishes fifth high. By standing square to the barre the dancer is aware that her working leg is directly side, whether in écarté front or back.

This exercise could be done on pointe starting from sous-sus or with a plié as the arm is brought to fifth low and a relevé as the arm lifts to fifth high.

Adagio: Grand Rond de Jambe en l'Air

Balanchine wanted us to know and show the difference between développé front and carry the leg around to the back, and grand rond de jambe. In grand rond de jambe en dehors, which can begin with a dégagé or développé, the foot and leg carve a circular shape in the front; the dancer does not establish a leg to the front position. Starting with dégagé from fifth front, the heel leads forward, the toes are drawn in, similar to tendu battement front, but now slightly cross the center line. As the toes leave the floor, the pointe starts a curving arc around and up through à la seconde at about shoulder height and continues around to the back. It is important to maintain the lift and the turnout of the leg as it passes second and continues around—the leg should not drop down and fall in. The back position, whether arabesque or attitude, should be

DETAILS I OFTEN INSIST ON IN GRAND ROND DE JAMBE EN L'AIR:

1) maintain the turnout throughout the movement

2) stand as straight as possible on the supporting hip and leg when going back; stand with the hips square when bringing the leg from à la seconde to the front

3) the leg should only lift, ending the movement on the highest, most extended line

4) the working leg should try to meet the torso; in other words, don't tilt or lean away from the working leg

the climax of the movement. This is achieved by maintaining maximum energy and standing as straight as possible on the supporting leg while the constant upward thrust of the strongly raised leg meets the back of the erect and lifted torso.

In grand rond de jambe en dehors that begins with a développé, the working pointe aims to slightly overcross as it leaves passé, and it does cross the center line of the body. However, the working knee does not stretch in to establish an overcrossed front position. Instead, before the knee reaches the center line, it straightens to draw the pointe of the working foot into a rising arc passing across the center line of the body and around. From here the pointe continues to trace a rising arc up and out, passing through second position and around to the back.

In grand rond de jambe en dedans the same action and energy are used; we do not establish the back position. It is the maintenance of maximum turnout in the working leg that brings it around and to the front.

The dancer starts grand rond de jambe with an accent to show the beginning of the rond, as the leg moves continuously throughout until the final line is established. This continuity is important in showing the difference from développé front, carry side, in which the dancer pauses to establish the développé line in front and sometimes to the side and back as well. Mr. B usually gave a simple port de bras.

Mastery of grand rond de jambe is essential preparation for many supported adagios as well as renversé and other movements.

An Adagio Exercise

Mr. Balanchine made many combinations combining the positions and poses we have just discussed. Here is one example. Starting fifth position flat with the arm in second, the dancer lowers her arm to fifth low on the "and" before count one, then starts a développé à la seconde on count one, arriving in à la seconde on count two as she lifts her arm up through first position and opens it to the side. She coordinates the movement of her head and arm from fifth low to first with the working knee and opens her arm to second as the working leg extends to the side. She demi-pliés on "and" as the arm goes to fifth low and she directs her gaze down. Without stopping the plié, she continues by lifting her arm to fifth high on count three as she relevés, her head and gaze following her hand; she usually holds this position with the leg à la seconde for count four. She starts turning to face the barre squarely on count five, taking it with both hands on count six as she makes arabesque by leaving the working leg where it is, at right angles to the barre, but lifting it to maintain maximum extension and turnout. Then she completes the movement by bending the working leg into a sharp attitude back on count seven as she lifts the opposite arm to fifth high (but—rare exception—no slant of the head). After showing this pose on count eight, she switches arms as she extends the working leg back through arabesque on count one. Leaving the working leg at right angles to the barre, she again turns it out and lifts it to maintain or increase the extension on count two as she returns her body to its original position with her working leg à la seconde on count three, one arm on the barre and the other to the side. She holds à la seconde on count four. She closes to sous-sus on count five and does a half-soutenu turn to face the other side on count six. On count seven she demi-pliés as she lowers her arm to fifth low, then straightens her legs on count eight as her arm opens through first to second position. In this exercise the working leg does not stop or even pause in either of the arabesques. It moves through the initial arabesque to establish attitude, which the dancer holds. Then she straightens her working leg, moving through the next arabesque as she continues by turning front, where she establishes and holds second position. This exercise is valuable because it takes effort to maintain maximum turnout and extension (no dropping the leg down and in). It builds more control and strength to move the leg from attitude through arabesque to à la seconde than it does to move the leg from attitude through passé to à la seconde, which is often given. Mr. Balanchine generally tried to refine the traditional exercises in ways that made them most efficient in obtaining the result desired.

Port de Bras Forward and Back

In many classes a port de bras forward and back is given as a stretch, as a moment of relaxation, or as part of getting flexible and warmed up. Class time was far too precious to Balanchine for any of that. We were responsible for being ready to work throughout the class, and we stretched on our own. His exercises were designed to explore the classical technique and to help us refine and perfect our execution of it. They were not intended to make us feel good or to relax us.

When Mr. Balanchine gave port de bras forward and back, he wanted us to perfect a beautifully coordinated and integrated movement. He wanted a continuous flow from beginning to end: from straight, all the way forward through all the way back, and, finally, to straight again.

Standing in fifth with the arm à la seconde, the dancer starts with a breath, making a slight arc with the arm as the back of the wrist lifts while the palm turns to face the floor. The arm starts down, followed by the head and torso—the wrist, hand, and arm lead the body down, rather than the head going first, followed by the arm. The direction of the hand and arm is down, rather than forward; the hand, leading with the inside of the wrist, aims for the floor about three inches in front of the feet on the center line of the body. The head generally stays straight (rather than tilting to the side) as the hand continues down. The hand comes into the peripheral vision almost immediately, when the body is about a quarter of the way down. When the body is about three quarters of the way down and the hand is fairly near the floor, the eyes focus on the hand.

*Dana takes a
preparatory breath,
lifting her wrist.*

*Dana bending forward to pick
up the flower. Her hand is
in front of her face and body.*

Dana picks up the flower.

*Dana coming up
through her back,
looking at the flower*

Sometimes Mr. B would feel that he needed to make this expressive movement more vivid. He would take his keys out of his pocket and put them on the floor three or four inches in front of a dancer's feet. "Pretend it's a flower. Reach down with your hand to pick it up. Look at what you are picking up," he would say. After all, when picking something up from the floor, the hand is brought down to it in the most direct path, the arm and hand starting before the head. The chin does not lead the way; the head tilts slightly forward, and the eyes focus on what is being picked up. In most ports de bras it is the wrist that takes the hand into the movement. In this case it is the inside of the wrist that brings the hand down to the "flower."

The back does not remain straight; instead, the spine can gently round near the bottom of the bend forward, which can also be viewed as the beginning of coming up. He did not want us to touch the leg with the nose or grasp the ankle with the hand, or place the palm on the floor, any of which might help some people to stretch but none of which makes for a unified, aesthetically pleasing gesture or is attractive to see. The dancer does not start up by lifting the head and/or arm away from the legs while maintaining a straight back. Coming up, she starts by gently rolling through the spine, with the arm following, raising her head and eyes to watch her hand, or that "flower." The elbow bends as the arm is lifted to fifth high, and her neck is also not rigid and straight.

The port de bras back continues in an uninterrupted movement from the upright position—there is no stop in the movement followed by a little preparatory bend forward before continuing back. The dancer lifts her head up and over to lead into the bend back. The arch is mostly in the upper back as the chest opens and extends. She avoids the tendency to thrust the pelvis forward and let the knees bend. In many schools the head may be turned or inclined to the side, but Mr. B most often wanted the head straight as it leads up and over and back. The neck is not stiffly held. The arm is usually in fifth high, slightly in front of the face. She watches her flower as she lengthens up to "paint" the ceiling with the back of her hand and continues back. The dancer starts up again with her torso, followed by her neck and head as the arm moves side, remaining slightly ahead of her face and back.

For the port de bras back it is especially important that the dancer does not thrust her pelvis for-

ward and sit into her lower back; instead, she stands as straight as possible and lengthens her back from the base of her spine to the top of her head. As her head leads up and over to the back, she opens her chest, and bends and arches her upper back. She holds the knees stretched and maintains the turnout, keeping a tight fifth position, without rolling in.

Mr. B often gave port de bras as a separate exercise, rather than incorporate it with grand plié or rond de jambe par terre. He also liked to give it from tendu front with plié. The dancer, in tendu front on a straight supporting leg, starts with the familiar breath and a lift in the arm with the palm turning down and then does demi-plié as she starts her arm down, leading with the inside of the

Dana straightening up as her elbow bends and her arm lifts

Dana starting to "paint the ceiling," still looking at the flower

Dana reaching up and back, still looking at the flower (head not turned)

DETAILS I OFTEN INSIST ON IN PORT
DE BRAS FORWARD AND BACK:
1) don't reach away
2) keep the arm in front of the body on the
   way forward and down; not body and
   head first, then arm
3) keep the head straight forward, rather
   than turned to the side
4) don't touch the leg with the hand or head
5) come up through the back
6) do not allow the feet to roll in when
   bending back
7) do not let the arm drift behind the back

wrist, completing the plié when the torso is about halfway down. The hand aims roughly for the ankle of the pointed foot, and the eyes focus on the hand and follow it as it picks up the "flower"; the nose is not brought to the knee. The dancer starts to come up through the back as the supporting leg straightens, coming straight and bringing the hand to fifth high as before. When she does port de bras to the back, she uses the same technique described above. When he gave port de bras in tendu back it was often with a deep, lunging plié. In each case there was little or no weight on the tendu foot.

Although the movement in port de bras is usually continuous, without any pauses or stops from start to finish, it is not done entirely at the same speed. The dancer must show the beginning with a quicker start, then slow as she continues smoothly down. She does not completely stop when she is down and certainly does not grab her ankle or sweep her hand over the floor. Coming up, the same principle applies: She starts up quickly and then slows, she starts back quickly and then slows, and so on. To prevent his dancers from creeping down, or relaxing into the movement, or getting sentimental about it, Balanchine advised us, "Faster down, slower up."

The Lesson Without an Exercise

We did not typically do nearly as many exercises at the barre as I have described. However, anyone who has ever danced at the intermediate level or beyond will know that a taxing, difficult barre is not necessarily a matter of length in time or in the number of exercises. A strenuous barre is a matter of what exercises are given and, more importantly, how the exercises are set (including the required details of execution, tempo, and number of repetitions); how they are corrected; and what, if anything, the teacher does to obtain the desired result. Looked at with these criteria in mind, intermediate and advanced dancers will recognize the exercises I described as the kind that make up a hard barre. (The student, of course, has to decide how much effort she is going to put in to those demanding exercises, but more on that later.)

When I think back to Balanchine's class and its barre, what comes immediately to mind is not that it was hard. It was hard, but what I remember is how much I learned. There was something for me and for every other dancer to work on and think about in each exercise. His barre could last fifteen minutes or fifty minutes or longer, but whatever its length, Balanchine gave us something precious every day. In my years of classes with Mr. B, I gradually built a whole new foundation for my new technique. It was a new foundation for a new technique because I had joined NYCB as a young professional.

I, of course, needed the new technique to learn to dance Balanchine's way. But Balanchine had the whole company to take care of, new ballets to make, repertory to rehearse, and so on. If I was going to succeed in learning to dance his way, I was going to have to do a lot of developing and changing on my own time. With the perspective now of my own dancing years and of more than twenty years since then teaching and watching hundreds of other dancers, I see that the details of the technique were also the means for Balanchine to teach us an even more important lesson. That lesson is how to learn to learn to dance. I doubt that the teacher can give her students lessons expressly designed for them in how to learn to learn to dance. I think she has to stick to teaching dancing, but dancing can be taught so that students are prepared to learn and develop and get everything possible out of class.

Balanchine observed that a teacher does not have to be (or to have been) a better dancer than her students, but that the teacher must know more. Knowing more enables the good teacher to see more. I think that is a very important distinction. She sees what needs to change and why; she knows how to help dancers change. To teach talented dancers how to learn, the teacher must know how the technique works. She must be able to break the bigger movements down into the smallest possible parts and show her students how to do each small part better and better. At the same time, she needs to keep them aware of how each small part of the technique contributes to the quality of the whole.

The whole toward which the student and the teacher are working is beautiful movement. Some beautiful movement is based on hard, or very difficult, or "impossible" steps, but learning how to learn is not about these challenging steps. It's about learning how to find and work on the critical fundamentals that are as necessary to all beautiful movement as they are to doing the challenging steps beautifully. No dancer has all the challenging steps, if for no other reason than because some hard steps are either for women or for men. Even some very good dancers have only certain challenging steps or certain kinds of them. But all students with ability can begin to learn to dance beautifully, can learn to move beautifully, at a certain level, if they learn the fundamentals they are capable of learning. Moreover, challenging steps, no matter how spectacularly done, become tricks when they are not seen in the setting of beautiful movement, when they are not done beautifully themselves. That's the way "impossible" steps are presented at

the circus, and at the circus they are called tricks, not at all as a put-down. The teacher must know more about how to learn the fundamentals than her students, because the fundamentals are the basis of beautiful movement, including doing the most challenging steps beautifully. To be done beautifully (rather than just astoundingly) the challenging steps must be done with skill, finesse, articulation, clarity, phrasing, and musicality.

Some quite wonderful ballets have, by the way, no really difficult, much less any "impossible" steps at all. *Serenade* is my favorite example. It can be danced by most advanced students and, excluding the solos, by many intermediate students.

Students learn how to work on technical problems all through the class. At least they should. Advanced and professional students should gather from most exercises insights on what they can practice on their own to improve (e.g., simple tendu battements, controlled relevés at the barre, épaulement and port de bras in the center, and correct timing and phrasing of every kind and size of movement). The barre exercises are the ones that should convey the most fundamental insights. The most basic know-how of the classical dancer all comes from the barre. In practicing the fundamentals at the barre, the classical dancer learns how to perfect the basic gestures that are essential when she begins to really move, to dance.

The teacher needs to exhibit patience. Learning to dance takes time. It cannot be speeded up. Each dancer has a rate at which she can progress, and she needs to learn to work effectively within it. Balanchine taught patience by the calm way he said to those of us having trouble with an exercise, "There's still time. I can wait." He also reminded us to do everything we could by the way he said to us, "Do it now. Now is the time."

There are no shortcuts. TV dinners were still a new idea when I came to New York. For Mr. B, who was a wonderful cook, they were an amazing idea and probably not at all welcome. He frequently drew comparisons between cooking and dancing. He must have believed there is no good way to prepare a meal except by starting at the beginning. His analogies between cooking and dancing make that clear. Likewise, learning to dance always has to start with the basics. It is not instantaneous; it takes years. Furthermore, the basics don't automatically stay learned. They have to be practiced and reviewed every day as long as one is dancing. No matter how advanced a dancer is, daily, conscientious practice of selected basic movements is the inescapable necessity to maintaining and polishing a complete technique. The wise dancer selects what she does *not* do best for the daily extra work. Similarly, the teacher constantly reviews the basics in the way she teaches, especially what she finds hard to teach. "You have to force yourself," he said to dancers. It applies to all of us.

Probably the most overlooked aspect of the right way to teach is insistence. I chose that word quite intentionally as the key for the summary boxes at the end of the exercises. There are many teachers who know what is required to achieve good classical technique. They know what to say when they give class, and they even say it. There appear to be not nearly as many who *insist* on seeing a result. I often note that some way of doing a movement that Mr. B did not accept is characteristic of what is taught in other schools: at the barre, dividing or stopping the plié, overcrossing in rond de jambe par terre, dropping the foot to the floor in grand battement, etc.; in the center, lack of épaulement, stiff arms and hands, doing assemblé without bringing the feet together in the air, etc. Teachers sometimes protest that what I see their students do is not what they teach. In many cases I do not doubt the truth of what they say. What I do know, however, from the way students change every year at SAB, is that too often correct execution is not insisted on. As Mr. B said, "There comes a point when even the teachers get relaxed." Or, perhaps, too many students do not respond with the extra effort necessary to continue to improve. This can sometimes be a particular problem for the very talented student who is clearly the best in her school, who has no model, no example of someone

who is more accomplished than she is in her classes.

Insistence on seeing a result (correct execution now, more effort bringing the student closer to correct execution, or, at a minimum, evidence of an understanding of what the dancer needs to learn to do) brings benefits to students and teachers alike. Students obviously progress more rapidly. But the teacher also progresses. When a correction is given, but the execution doesn't change, or changes less than it might, something more must be done. The teacher must find a way to get something to happen. She needs to think about what she sees, change the words she uses to ask for what she wants to see, concoct a metaphor, change the exercise, devise a special exercise to work on a crucial detail, change the tempo. . . . She needs to think about the results she does or does not get and keep working at it. This is the most important way she reviews the technique. As her students see how she helps them identify and solve problems, they learn how to learn. This obviously requires that every student pay careful attention to each and every correction. Only students hungry to learn will sustain such consistent focus.

Learning to dance takes hard work, real effort, dedication, etc. Everybody knows it, everybody says it. We say it or hear it so often, I wonder how much attention is paid. Not every teacher shows that *teaching dance*, in particular teaching the talented students who have the potential to do well the kind of work described in this book, also takes hard work, dedication, etc. Insisting on a result is much harder than just letting little problems go. It's not easy to keep up with everything that is happening in the dancing and in the class and to react to it in a way that will help the students. If they see the teacher working "full out" for better dancing and for their progress, I think they will respond with more and better work of their own. Certainly we never doubted that Mr. B was totally absorbed in us for the entire class, and we never doubted that he put as much into it as he asked of us. By his example, he showed us how to be a dancer; the memory of his commitment to teaching us is the model many of us carry now of how to be a teacher.

Mr. B asked for total commitment to the work, to the here and now, to the step of the moment. I think we continue to ask for it at SAB. When we get it, when any teacher gets it, when we see dancers putting out maximum effort, energy, and concentration, I think we are in part seeing the students' response to the same way of working in us. Mr. B once saw that one of his good dancers had begun to take it a little easy in his class. She still came, but he didn't see the effort, energy, and concentration he was used to from this dancer. So he went up to her one day and said, "Well, dear, you know, you are married now, so why don't you just go home and take care of your husband." She came to class the next day still furious at being dismissed so casually and determined to show him how much she still wanted to dance. A couple of months later, he stopped in front of her at the barre and said so everyone could hear, "Good, dear! Very good!" Turning to us, he added, "She's happily married and she can dance, *too*." Her renewed dedication was partly a response to his constant dedication. It

was also an example of teaching *that* dancer how to learn. Today she is one of the most highly valued of those who teach and stage his work.

Teachers and dancers work so hard for so many years to achieve, on a routine basis, a level of performance that is anything but routine. One night, at the end of a performance, I introduced my guest to the ballerina, and she said she hoped he had liked the show. He said that he enjoyed it, "it was nice." The ballerina exploded, "NICE?! Nice is nothing!" Nice was not good enough for her, and it was not good enough for Mr. B. Ballet dancers are young and slender and go onstage in costumes and makeup under lights and with music. Nice is almost guaranteed. Mr. B wanted us to know how to "wake up" the audience and make them really take notice. He provided the dances and he taught the technique. Performing his dances with his technique, consistent with his aesthetic, *will* make the audience wake up and look. The good dancer must believe that is true, that there is no other way. She will then also believe that she needs to learn how to learn the technique. She will understand that nice is never good enough.

The Upper Body

Mr. Balanchine usually began the center work using very basic elements of classical technique. Typically he started with combinations that fully explored the body directions and ports de bras: a temps lié, a series of tendus with changes in épaulement and linking ports de bras, or other exercises of this kind.

When he did not like the way we moved our arms, or hands, or heads, or when we did not clearly show the intended direction or position, he could make a simplified, yet interesting, even challenging, combination to work on even the smallest detail that needed improvement. Just as he had no set routine at the barre, he also had none for the center. A good teacher should give what she sees is needed. For Mr. B this often began with what he saw onstage the night before; for any good teacher, it is also based on the way the last exercise was done. Having seen details that needed work, Mr. B could spend five, ten, fifteen minutes—even longer, if necessary—to get closer to the look he wanted and to draw our attention to what we should find time to practice.

At the barre Mr. Balanchine largely eliminated épaulement and elaborate ports de bras so we could concentrate better on the lower part of the body: plié, turnout, extension, refining the shape of the foot and its use, and so on. Nonetheless, he did have very definite ideas about posture and centering the

weight (see page 52), and he taught a basic technique for the arm and hand (see page 54). Exercises that in a similar way helped us to concentrate on the movement of the upper torso, neck and head, arms and hands were thus part of our center work. In some center exercises he gave us only very simple movements for our feet and legs, or none at all, so we could work more effectively on the upper body: head, arms, hands, and épaulement. Even so, he still expected good form in the feet and legs: precise positions and directions, maximum turnout, weight maintained over the ball of the foot, correct timing and accents, well-shaped feet, and so on.

For Mr. B the entire human body was beautiful. He wanted to see all of its expressive dance possibilities used in class, not just the legs and feet: all five fingers, articulation of all the joints of the arms and hands, etc. In this chapter I intend to present his ideas on port de bras and épaulement as he worked on them in class. I also describe some of the exercises he gave when he worked in detail on specific parts of the upper body, because his attention to them was unusual. We worked very thoroughly so we could make each pose, position, and direction of the body fully legible. It was equally or perhaps even more important to him that we move from one position to another smoothly, clearly, interestingly, and, above all, beautifully. This demanded that every part of the body be energized and that we maintain full awareness.

Energy and awareness are qualities I often mention as part of the look Mr. Balanchine wanted when we danced. They are the outward signs of an inner discipline or state of mind, an approach to dance, that the dancer will cultivate in herself with the help of the teacher's suggestions, reminders, and encouragement. He wanted us, for example, to be aware of the shape of our hands and to hold the fingers in a particular way, just as much as he wanted us to point our toes and sense the way in which they almost grasp the floor as we land. Mr. B often wanted us to dance very big or to dance very fast or both. But dancing big or small, fast or slow, he also wanted us to dance musically, and skillfully, with precision, finesse, and delicacy. And beautifully. These qualities are dependent in part on energy and awareness in every part of the dancer's body. Because of this energy and awareness the dancer will feel different and look different.

HEAD AND NECK: HAIR, EYES, FACE, EXPRESSION

An example of the difference concerns the hair. Mr. Balanchine said that even the hair should feel alive. We all know that this is not literally possible, and he certainly knew that, too. He probably was referring to the entire back lengthening and reaching up through the neck and head and even through the last extremity, the hair. And yet, when following his usual standards for hair, his dancer should be less aware of it while dancing than many might be. He generally did not want any large or overpowering coiffures or headpieces. With either one, the dancer will be more "aware" of her head and hair because of weight or bulk, but the awareness will be from the outside rather than from within herself. It may even distract her, make her look and feel a little top-heavy, and perhaps cause her to move a little differently.

If there was a headpiece, it was usually small and relatively light, something to complement the dancer and her costume. More often, he wanted the hair pulled back and off the face to help reveal its features. The hair could be secured in a flat, high twist or bun that did not distort the shape or exaggerate the size of the head. Its arrangement should not obscure or shorten the line of the neck but should usually give the illusion of lengthening it. For performance he wanted a result that enhanced the dancer's appearance, while for class he wanted the hair out of the way and not a distraction.

As usual, there are almost no absolute rules. He did make a few elaborately costumed roles for which the dancer wore a large headpiece. More to the point of awareness are the "hair down" roles in ballets like *Walpurgisnacht, Serenade,* or *Chaconne.* In these roles, dancers with heightened awareness will feel the difference with extra effect when the hair is taken down. In *Walpurgisnacht* they will dance with greater abandon; in *Serenade* or *Chaconne* they will feel more windswept, more feminine, more romantic, because their hair moves freely.

The men were expected to keep their hair fairly short and nicely trimmed and, of course, no mustaches, no beards. A regular part of company life was the appearance at the end of each layoff of a collection of somewhat shaggy characters. I guess they needed to display that little spark of boyish rebellion. By the last days of rehearsal before opening night, the partners we knew emerged from their disguises.

Unlike the hair, the eyes can be controlled actively by the dancer, both where and how they look. But Mr. B taught us that the look of the eyes grows out of a presence that begins in the upper torso and includes the entire head and the face. If the dancer does not cultivate this presence she can seem to be staring or look glassy-eyed.

In fact, if she gets into the habit of looking at herself in the mirror, she can get hooked into her image and end up actually staring. The focus of her eyes will shorten to a very shallow field, the presence in her upper body will diminish as she is attentive to following herself in the glass rather than modeling herself for the audience and, as a result, the outward projection will stop. Trying to dissuade us from using the mirror, Mr. B would joke that since the image was reversed, it was wrong anyway. Furthermore, it is flat and one-dimensional. When we got totally involved looking, he would say, "Zombies! You look like zombies."

"I want to see your eyes," Balanchine would sometimes say. This suggests another reason for avoiding regular use of the mirror. The eyes tend to lose projection and open a little less widely when they are trying to focus at shorter ranges; they look dead or glassy to the audience. In class, the dancer should start to develop the ability to focus outward, on a point beyond the mirror or the walls of the studio, so that onstage her features are fully revealed to the very back of the house.

The dancer's general demeanor in class and onstage should be pleasant and aware. This is another quality likely to be lost in the dancer who is constantly following herself in the mirror, because most dancers are concerned about how they look, and this focus and concentration will show. She should look alive, should radiate life, and yet not be overtly lively or animated or put on a face. This again is playacting, and it takes attention and energy away from the movement to music that Mr. B wanted us, as dancers, to embrace as our specialty. Among the most frequently seen put-on faces is a fixed, unchanging smile. This can have a surface charm to it, but after a few seconds it, too, looks lifeless.

The eyes and face of the dancer often help to direct the attention of the audience. Mr. B set exercises in the center designed to teach us how to draw attention to a particular place or to a movement. For example, as the dancer picks her foot off the floor, she might look down, announcing that it is leaving the floor. Or she might look diagonally toward the foot as it points side, or diagonally over and past the knee as the foot moves into passé, thus

Dana looking down to draw attention to her foot before lifting it

Dana looking down, announcing she is picking her foot off the floor

Dana begins to lift her foot, knee, arms, and head.

Dana moving through passé

Dana in a high développé side as she projects out and beyond

Dana looking down at her foot, saying "Look at my foot"

"Hello, Dana!" "Hi, Deanna!"

Dana bending toward her knee in passé, saying "Look at my knee"

leading the eyes of the audience there. The change in the head and eyes was simultaneous, as in directing the gaze down as a plié begins before a quick relevé, or up and out as the dancer développés side or does sauté in arabesque. Often the eyes and head are coordinated with and lead or follow the movement of the arm and hand.

Mr. B wanted his dancers to let the music, chore-ography, and dancing speak for themselves, so his dancers did not play to the house with their eyes or face, flirt, act a part that was not there in the music, indulge in cliché poses, or try to win the public with calculated or consciously displayed personal charm. In certain ballets there are very specific directions for the eyes and face, but these were given as part of the rehearsals for those ballets rather than as part of class. Very often they called for looking at or reacting to other dancers onstage. "Say hello to your friend," Mr. B might say in rehearsal, encouraging us to make the gestural greeting legible. In part that came through real eye contact, seeing the other dancer, acknowledging her and relating to her. When a greeting was called for, it had to be so credible that the audience might imagine they had heard our voices and yet be danced in keeping with the music, rather than acted.

Incorrect carriage: Peter leaning back, holding himself up by the neck and head, Dana tucking her chin

Peter and Dana demonstrating correct carriage of the head

None of the characteristics of the parts of the head I have discussed is going to have its desired effect unless the head itself is presented properly. And the pleasant demeanor in the face will be undermined if there is tension in the neck. Generally, the most important factor is to avoid leaning back; the shoulders should not be behind the hips. This leads to trying to hold oneself up with the neck and head, so to speak. Also, the upper torso and head must not be pulled back with the chin tucked in or tipped back like a military cadet's. In either case, the cords in the neck stand out, a problem I had—and had to solve. The shoulders must be held down and open—that is, not slouching forward; the breastbone should be lifted and the chest expanded. Mr. B was also specially vigilant and quick to correct when he saw a dancer with the shoulders hiked up, or a closed chest or hunched back. With the neck lengthening up and out of the back, the head slightly lifted up and forward (the face and chin almost come forward), the shoulders aligned over the hips, and the chest open, the neck separates clearly from the torso, and the head is visible above the neck.

HANDS

"Some people don't know what to do with the hands. Maybe cut them off. I need them. The hands give you strength, force. They give direction." On pages 55–57, I discuss in detail Mr. Balanchine's ideas about the basic hand position when dancers are working at the barre, and I describe the ball exercise he gave to help us cultivate the look he wanted. In this chapter I will discuss his ideas about the ways in which the hand should move through the air, because it should change shape as it does so. However, the basic shaping of the hand practiced at the barre is essential to what follows, because the hand returns to that shape often. It serves the same purpose as does fifth position for the feet.

Mr. B often used imagery to make his ideas more graphic, more concrete, so we would apply them with more awareness. For example, when we were practicing grand plié in the center, he wanted us to think of the plié as a movement down in order to collect energy to come up, rather than as a feat of balance during which we might concentrate on our feet and ankles and knees and consequently wobble around. "Your hand is like a parachute," he would say as we pliéd, asking us to think of the parachute holding the air after it has opened and to hold the air the same way with our hands. As the body starts down, the arms follow with a slight delay, just as the parachute opens after the jump.

Dana "holding the air" as she descends in plié

The details of the action of the hands vary as the dancer moves from position to position and as the hand goes in different directions, but some important characteristics are consistent. When the dancer moves her hand, the wrist and the finger joints always react. Balanchine reminded us that the space through which we move is not empty; the air is not a vacuum. We should therefore move the hands with a kind of resistance. I sometimes compare this resistance to the branches of a weeping willow tree moving in a gentle breeze or to the arms and hands moving through water.

Sometimes Balanchine likened the action of the hand and fingers to the bristles of a paintbrush. Depending on the direction the arm is moving as the brush is pulled along, the bristles are drawn along behind, held back by the resistance of the surface being painted and the paint. We were to cultivate fuller awareness of the hand, fingers, or wrist, or of one side or the other of them, depending on which part is leading and which is following.

No matter what the movement of our arms and hands, Mr. B wanted to see every part of the hand as we went along: all five fingers, including the thumb, the back, the palm. For him, the separation of each of the four fingers and thumb gave a pleasure akin to that of seeing the individual petals of a flower or each of the features of the face.

Articulation of the wrist and the fingers gives life to the hands and helps the dancer execute the steps and phrase the movement to the music. It is the articulation of the wrist that makes the hand and fingers more visible. It can give the illusion of softness, although the dancer's hands are firmly, yet gently, shaped. As the articulation changes at different speeds and with varying resistance and intensity, the movement gains further depth and interest. The sense conveyed by a movement can be altered completely by using or not using the articulation available to us. For example, at the very beginning of *Serenade,* most people believe they see the dancers simply drop the hand from the flexed wrist position, but Mr. B taught us to lift the wrist, which is a sign of life and energy, as the palm faces down and the hand extends. If the hand just drops, it risks looking lifeless. This apathetic look is actually desired in the Phlegmatic variation of *The Four Temperaments,* when the dancer does drop the hand, the first sign of the crumpling and pulling in that shrivels the whole body.

Certain of his dancers let their hands flap quite a bit, sometimes displaying a "broken wrist" line. He seemed not to mind, even though he did not specifically teach that look in class. Although he was very exacting about certain details, such as the shape of the hand or fifth position for the feet, there was room for individual dancers to be themselves and to adapt his ideas, provided he found the result aesthetically pleasing.

There is a solution to the apparent contradiction. Ballet is an art performed by living beings; it is not geometry or mechanical engineering. Mr. B had a point of view that emphasized life, movement, and energy and a vision of how beautiful we could look. In class he explored the limits of what we could do to try to make that vision live. When he liked what he saw, he kept it, and used it in class and in choreography. He always wanted each dancer to look her best, and he was willing to adapt certain of his ideas and the classical steps to achieve that. "Teach each dancer the way she was born," is how he put it. So, it is important to apply his ideas with a certain flexibility, trying to keep in mind the underlying principles, which include being faithful to a vision of good form, staying precisely in time with the music, and putting forth maximum effort to achieve the best possible result.

BASIC ARM POSITIONS

In discussing the look of the eyes and face, I explain that the life radiating from the dancer grows out of a total presence: an awareness in the upper torso, especially the chest, that spreads up through the neck and head. That same awareness also helps the dancer to stand fully erect with the back straight and the shoulders open but over the hips, the weight forward so it is centered over the balls of the feet, with the breastbone lifted front—this is *not* a military "attention" with the weight tilted back, the lower ribs jutting out, and the chin tucked in.

Balanchine would say to take the shoulders down, but he did not stress moving the arms from the back. He probably assumed that if we had the rest of the stance correct (e.g., with our arms in second position, shoulders down, chest up and forward, elbows lifted, and palms facing front), we would support the arms from the back and use those muscles to move them as well. Standing with the arms in second, the dancer is aware that the arms are held by the muscles at the sides of her body and by those going around toward her shoulder blades. It almost feels as if she has placed her arms on a shelf, because those muscles are held so strongly. The muscles in the center of her upper back, between her shoulder blades, are held as if gently coming together. This helps the upper chest to come forward, lift, and open; the dancer avoids the tendency to thrust the lower ribs out and forward. The impetus for movement of the arms is initiated in the center of the body, then the movement flows from the center through the arms, the hands, the fingers; the arms do not move just from the shoulders in the way a policeman directs traffic. When I teach, I remind the dancers to hold the arms from the back and to move them from there.

Keeping the shoulders down is a near universal rule for classical dance. But when Mr. B had a dancer with a very long neck, it seemed that he minded less if the shoulders were momentarily a bit up in the course of a movement, provided he liked the resulting look. As with his acceptance of the "broken wrist" line on some dancers, this shows us that he looked at each of us as an individual and could accept differences in certain details. The key was that the energy and thrust of the dancer's movement had to fit the music and complement the desired look of the dance as well as enhance the look of the particular dancer.

As every ballet teacher knows, there have been several attempts, a couple of them quite elaborate, to codify the basic arm positions in a way analogous to the five positions of the feet. No attempt so far has won the widespread acceptance needed to become a universal standard. Mr. B spoofed the confused state of things by asking us, on occasion, as he showed an arabesque, "What number is this?" The answer, which he didn't care about at all and usually didn't wait to hear, depended on which book was consulted or what system had been memorized—if, indeed, any. When a detailed, graded syllabus is being taught, when dancers are being prepared to pass an exam, or when they expect to work in an aesthetic that seems to emphasize precise reproduction of held poses, such information is probably a very useful shorthand.

In contrast, Mr. Balanchine's dancers were helping him explore possibilities for extending the technique and using it in new dances, rather than documenting the existing vocabulary. More important to him than written definitions and specific names was knowing how to get dancers to move with the qualities characteristic of the step being practiced. It was finally how the dancer looked in motion and in time—that is, with the music—that mattered most.

His response was to teach very clear positions for the arms, and especially the way he wanted us to move from one position to another. He did ask for some positions by name or number, but more important for our understanding were what he showed and his explanations, followed by the corrections he gave after we had done the port de bras exercise. This approach developed in us the ability to do whatever was needed in a specific exercise or ballet while avoiding the memorization of a lot of terminology.

To achieve the look required for his ballets, he had us practice a port de bras technique that included, for example, crossing the wrists and more flexibility in them, as well as more bending in the elbows. The arms of his dancers may simply seem to be freer in their movements. In fact they are also more fully energized, because the muscles are frequently being used to articulate all the joints: "God gave us elbows, wrists, fingers that bend and move. Use them!" was the way Mr. B put it. Energy, dynamics, and controlled abandon were more important to him than having every dancer's arm in the same line, because that approach generally demands more constrained, more carefully calculated movement. Remember, "No polite dancing!"

The six arm positions that follow are the ones that Mr. B most commonly used in class, with the numbers he most often used for each one. However, since he communicated his wishes more by showing than by telling, it would be a mistake to think of this as a "system" to be memorized that everyone will recognize. He showed to convey the quality he wanted in each movement and the look of each position or pose; his demonstrations were beautiful and elegant, mini-lessons in classical form. It is most important to understand each of the positions and how to move from one to another.

In first position, the arms are held rounded in front of the body, with the elbows slightly below the shoulder line. The hands, which continue the line of the forearms, are approximately at the level of the bottom of the breastbone. The fingertips may be separated as much as an inch or so. The feeling is, as Mr. B said, that of hugging a tree trunk. The arms and the hands make a circle, the elbows bending, the palms facing in to the dancer. The energy is gathered in by the dancer rather than being thrown out by outstretched arms with straight elbows and with the palms open and facing up. The arms are, as usual, supported from the back, with the shoulders down and open and with the elbows rotated and lifted up, just below shoul-

First position of the arms; Peter's are more traditional, Dana's are overlapped.

der height. There is a feeling of the arms being placed on top of a shelf while the "tree trunk" is hugged. Mr. B might give some exercises using this traditional position, but in the center and in his ballets, he more often wanted a first with the hands overlapping. Depending on the tempo and the look desired, this overlap might involve only the hands, but it more often went as far as the wrists. In some ports de bras, when the dancer passes through first without a stop or pause, she can occasionally feel that her arms are crossing as far as her elbows, although it is probably not more than her forearms. See page 156 for a port de bras using an overlapped first position.

In second position, the arms are held to the side in a gentle curve only slightly forward of the body. The curve is suggestive of an arc from a much larger circle than the one shown in first position. The elbows are supported just below the level of the shoulders, and the hands are held just below the level of the elbows, with the palms facing forward. The arm should not look as if it is just stuck out to the side like the arm of a scarecrow or hung like the laundry. With the arms supported from the sides of the back and with the chest lifted, the dancer's feeling is once again that they have been placed on top of a shelf. Because the shoulders are back and down with the elbows rotated up and held just below shoulder height, while the forearms and palms face forward, the dancer can, when learning this position, feel that her upper arm is in a vise, while her lower arm is being gently rotated into place. However, as this shaping of the arms becomes habitual, it also begins to feel "normal." There is a slight bend in the elbow and a roundness in the palm of the hands. Partially, but not entirely, as a joke, one dancer shaded the inside of her elbows to make them look bent in case she kept them straight, forgetting to bend them. She was so conscious of what Mr. B wanted, she probably bent her arm as needed—I doubt the trick would have worked by itself. When the dancer is seen en face, the entire arm should look held, but pliable, with a gentle curve and smooth contours. The rotations of the upper arm and the forearm should prevent the elbow from hanging down and breaking the line. The hands and fingers are shaped. The elbows are only slightly forward of the back. The alignment of the elbows with the back helps to achieve a full openness of the chest and the largest possible circle.

The position fifth low, which is often called "preparatory," was generally known to us as "arms down," because the arms are lengthened down with the chest open. They should feel almost heavy, as if the wrists are slightly weighted down. However, the elbows are supported in a gentle curve, held out to the side with the shoulders remaining open. The forearms and hands curve gently toward the center line of the body; the fingers and palms face each other. The hands are slightly in front of the thighs.

Mr. B did not want the hands hanging down inside the legs. When the dancer is standing in fifth position (of the feet), the fingertips of each hand are approximately three inches in from the outside edge of the thighs, about four inches apart. When the dancer is standing in first position, the fingertips are again approximately three inches in from the outside edge of the thighs, about six inches apart from each other. When the dancer is in second position, the hands are still just about three inches in from the outside edge of the thigh and even farther apart from each other. In addition to the more traditional arms down, which could begin or end a combination, Mr. B also used a hands-crossed variant, but the dancer always passes through it without a stop or even a pause. In many ports de bras from fifth low with a "going away to return" (see page 152) or passing through it, Mr. B wanted the dancer to cross her hands in front of the center line of her body as she lifted her arms to an overlapped first on her way to another position.

In fifth high the arms are lengthened but curved over the head with the shoulders down. The elbows bend so there is space between the head and the arms. The tips of the fingers of the two hands are

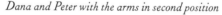

Dana and Peter with the arms in second position

Peter with his arms in fifth low standing in fifth, first, and second position

about two inches apart or less, equally distant from the center line of the head. The palms are facing down and the elbows open out to the side, rather than coming forward. The arms frame the head; they are not pulled behind it, but instead are held just in front of it. When the head is held straight front and level and the eyes are directed up, the little finger on each hand should be visible.

Third position combines one arm raised as in fifth high and the other to the side as in second posi-

Peter and Dana with the arms in fifth high

tion. However, the tip of the middle finger of the raised hand should now be on the center line of the head; the dancer must bend her elbow a bit more to achieve this position.

Fourth position combines one arm raised as in fifth high and the other rounded as in first. The tips of the fingers of both hands in fourth should reach the center line of the body. The dancer must bend both elbows enough to achieve this.

In these positions of the arms, the hand is generally seen as an extension of the arm, complementing the curving line of the arm. The wrist is bent somewhat more, which complements Mr. B's more rounded shape for the hand. As the arms change position or move within a position or pose (e.g., during a series of relevés in first arabesque in the center), the hands are seen even more distinctly through articulation of the elbows, wrists, and fingers.

MOVEMENT OF THE ARMS

In the very basic ports de bras that follow, the dancer is assumed to be en face, with no change of épaulement and in general no head movement other than lifting straight up and down while facing front. The technique described includes some that is quite traditional, some that Mr. B modified in certain details, and some that represent his extension of the traditional technique. The usually related movement of the torso, neck, and head will be treated in sections dealing with épaulement and the orientation of the body to the front (see pages 169–179). However, for the sake of clarity, I am not including it here.

The dancer takes a breath that gives impetus to many ports de bras, and this breath also initiates movements of the chest, neck, and head. The feeling should be that the impetus arising from inhaling gives energy to move and that this energy flows from the center through the body and all the way out to the fingertips. This flow is integral to the port de bras as it is done, rather than being indicated by any extra flapping or waving. Mr. Balanchine was very sensitive to all the extremities and also did not want to see the energy and awareness flag. Stiffly immobile hands with straight and rigid fingers or slack hands with limp fingers were no more acceptable than feet that were not properly pointed and placed correctly to the floor.

The important point to understand about breathing is that the timing and depth are intuitive rather than calculated and depend on the movements being done, the tempo, and the phrasing. For example, the dancer will generally inhale when starting and when raising or opening the arms, and exhale when lowering the arms and at the finish. However, a single breath might last only while the arms move from one position to the next, or it can last while they pass through several positions. Mr. B said little about breathing, generally leaving it to us to see what he wanted by the way he showed. I will indicate some points when a breath is usually taken, but the dancer must finally evaluate each situation for herself.

In many schools, dancers are taught to move the arm somewhat as a unit, with little or no bending of the elbow and wrist. Sometimes the elbow bends and not the wrist or vice versa. Mr. B, in contrast, wanted his dancers to use both elbow and wrist in most movements and avoid any hint of stiffness. For ports de bras that utilize his crossed-hands technique, the elbows will bend even more. In general he wanted the movement of the arm initiated by the muscles of the back, then by the upper arm, which brings the elbow, which brings the forearm, which brings the wrist, and so on down to the fingers.

To enhance the legibility of arm movements, it is often helpful to begin by moving slightly away from the intended direction or destination—usually in the opposite direction. When Mr. B said, "Take a breath," he also meant that the breath should stimulate movement through the arms and hands, involving all the joints. I think of it as a kind of "going away in order to return," an idea he also used in larger movements (see page 189). If the dancer does not do this, often the audience can think nothing much has happened—the change is less noticeable. Preliminary movement away will be indicated in many of the exercises. However, like breathing, "going away" needs to become almost automatic and to a considerable degree will depend on the dancer's intuitive understanding. This understanding is cultivated through practice as she breathes and articulates her arms, wrists, and hands in a variety of movements large and small, done at a range of tempos.

Another aid to legibility of arm movements is to phrase them. Each of the ports de bras that follow is phrased, but the details vary based on the step being done and the tempo. However, this general principle nearly always applied: At the beginning and at each change in direction, there was likely to be a little extra energy or accent followed by a smooth slowing. The movements away were not as fully phrased and yet they would not be effective if the dancer did not also do them with some energy. Mr. B wanted us to *show* each of the beginnings; he did not want us to creep into them with slow, careful, almost imperceptible starts. Intermediate positions are identified, but the dancer does not relax and linger in them, although some exercises were set with specific pauses or even full stops to help show the positions and make the dancers more aware of them.

FIFTH LOW (OR ARMS DOWN) TO FIRST

First position is generally transitional, a position the arms and hands pass through; Mr. B did not set exercises beginning or ending in it.

The first method is traditional for classroom preparations. It is used for the free arm at the barre (see page 54) and for both arms in the center. Starting in fifth low, the dancer lifts the upper arms and the elbows, leading the forearms, wrists, and hands up to first, the "hug the tree" position, where they arrive on one. As they rise, the elbows bend a little more than they do in some traditional methods, bringing the fingertips in to the center line of the body. As the elbows bend, they lift the forearms, and the forearms lift the wrists, allowing the hands to trail slightly, with the palms facing the body. There's just enough softening that the movement is not abrupt, that the arms do not look like sticks, like they belong to a robot or a doll. The fingertips now almost touch on the center line of the body. Since many exercises start with the arms in second, the dancer will normally open her arms to second on two (see page 153). Alternatively, she may raise one or both arms on two to fifth high (see page 155) or assume any other position.

In the second method the dancer brings the hands from standard fifth low into a slightly overlapped fifth low before bringing the arms smoothly to an overlapped first. Thus, with the arms in fifth low, the wrists rotate so the palms of the hands are facing the dancer. The inside edges of the wrists lead toward the center line of the body, the elbows slightly straightening, lengthening the arms down. The hands, and even the wrists, cross at the center line of the body as the upper arms begin to lift, drawing the elbows, which bend more and lead the forearms, wrists, hands, and fingers directly up to an overlapped first. This method was rarely used as a preparation in the center and not at all at the barre. It is often used as part of a port de

Having opened to the side with her preparatory breath, Deanna now closes her arms, inside edges of wrists leading.

Deanna lifting her arms up with crossed wrists, leading with the upper arms and elbows

Deanna about to arrive in first position, inside edges of her wrists leading

Deanna in an overlapped first position of the arms, about to move on

bras within a combination in class and in the ballets.

Either method can include a "going away to return." To make that part of the port de bras, the dancer allows her intake of breath to give impetus to her arms. Starting in fifth low, they open slightly

DETAILS I OFTEN INSIST ON IN PORT
DE BRAS FROM FIFTH LOW TO FIRST:
1) do not let the hands and arms reach away from the body when moving to first— hug the tree trunk
2) be sure the hands get up to first (about level with the bottom of the breastbone)
3) bring the hands in to the center line
4) chest open, elbows supported

about the look of the hands in all the exercises. I've left it out of the boxes to avoid a broken-record effect, but in most classes new to the Balanchine aesthetic, the teacher will have to bring it up all the time.

FIRST TO SECOND

This is count two of the port de bras used in the standard preparation. Starting in first, the dancer moves her arms to the side as she expands and opens her chest. The arms do not extend front or reach forward. Instead, the upper arms bring the elbows out to the side, and then the elbows bring the forearms, and the forearms move the backs of the wrists and the hands to the side. To help us to visualize the swelling chest and the sideward path the arms should take, Mr. B might inhale deeply, ex-

to the side, leading with the backs of the wrists and with the elbows slightly straightening. To return her arms to fifth low she can lead straight in with the insides of her wrists, or to move through fifth low she can rotate her wrists (as in the first photo) so the palms face her body and the inside (thumb side) edges of the wrists lead toward the center line of the body. The movement may also be done so the hands and even the wrists cross at the center line. From fifth low the upper arms and elbows (with the elbows bending) lead the forearms, tops of the wrists, thumb sides of hands, and fingers up to first. The hands will be overlapped if the dancer crossed them in fifth low. "Going away to return" was rarely, if ever, used as a part of the standard preparation at the barre. It is more often used for preparations in the center and is quite often used as part of a port de bras within a combination in class and also in Mr. Balanchine's ballets.

In the ports de bras just described and in those that follow, the hands start and finish in Mr. B's standard shape for the hand (see page 55) and they also return to it during ports de bras especially when they are not moving through the air. It is very difficult for most dancers to be consistent about this because they are usually accustomed to much stiffer, straighter fingers (flat hands) or they have not been made aware of their hands when dancing and just let them hang in a relaxed, unshaped state. Remember, "Dead chicken wings." Most dancers have not heard constant correction of their hands. The teacher must therefore be especially insistent

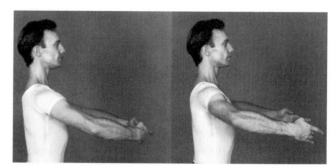

Peter with his arms in first position

Peter starting to open his arms from first to second, opening to the side, not reaching front

Peter continuing to open his arms to the side, really "parting the curtains"

Peter arriving in second, chest expanding, arms extending

panding his chest as he moved his arms to the side and, his eyes lighting up, say, "Ahhh! It's like parting the curtains on the Mediterranean Sea." Watching Mr. B, we felt it was a sunny morning in Monte Carlo. The port de bras should show a slight resistance: the weight of the "curtains" being pushed to the side.

DETAILS I OFTEN INSIST ON IN PORT DE BRAS FROM FIRST TO SECOND:
1) open side ending with palms facing out toward the front; do not reach forward with straight elbows and the palms turned up
2) support the elbows, do not let them drop down as the upper arms move side or at the finish
3) hands finish just slightly (three or four inches or so) below the shoulders

---

SECOND TO FIFTH LOW

Starting with the arms in second, the dancer rotates and slightly lifts the upper arms and elbows, making a gentle, upward curving arc with the backs of the wrists and hands (going away in order to return), as the forearms and hands rotate to a palms-down position. The dancer lifts the backs of the wrists up as the palms turn to face down and the

---

DETAILS I OFTEN INSIST ON IN PORT DE BRAS FROM SECOND TO FIFTH LOW:
1) do not move the arms and hands as a unit—bend elbows gently; flex wrists; fingers react to the air (slightly trail)
2) lead with the insides of the wrists
3) lengthen the arm during the movement but do not lock the elbows

---

Peter in second position

Peter at the top of the arc, with palms turned down

Peter softens his elbows as they bring the insides of the wrists down.

Peter's wrists have taken over the lead as his arms lengthen out.

arms gently lengthen. The elbows soften slightly and begin to lead the arms down with gently flexed wrists; the hands and fingers trail, and the fingers slightly straighten and extend as they resist the air. The arms continue down, now led by the insides of the wrists, followed by the hands and fingers as the elbows straighten and the arms extend. When the upper arms are lowered into the position they will have in fifth low, the elbows bend enough to allow the forearms to assume the fifth low position with the hands just in front of the thighs.

SECOND TO FIRST

With the arms in second, the dancer gently extends the elbows, wrists, and hands to the sides as the wrist rotates the hand into the palm-down position. This little straightening brings her to an extended second position. Then the thumb sides of the hands and wrists (inside edge) followed by the trailing fingers (think of the paintbrush) lead the lengthened arms, with the hands turned palms down in front of the body to first. The elbows bend as the upper arms arrive in first position, ending with a rotation of wrists and hands to establish the rounded "hug the tree" feeling, with the palms facing in toward the dancer. Note that she lengthens the line of her arms before she brings them in front of her. She goes away to return.

FIRST TO FIFTH HIGH

In the more traditional method, which we occasionally used, the dancer raises her upper arms from first while ensuring that the shoulders remain down and that the elbows remain to the side. The elbows bend a little more in Mr. B's technique than they do in some traditional methods. As the elbows are lifted, they bring the forearms and the gently trailing rounded hands up; the arms do not move as a single unit. It is the muscles at the sides of the back that bring the upper arm up and make this movement happen. When the elbows have arrived at about the level of the face, the sides and then the backs of the wrists lead the arms to fifth high as the face lifts gently up. The movement of the face is coordinated with the movement of the hands. The elbows slightly extend to establish the final line. The fingertips are on either side of the center line of the head, about one inch apart. Since the palms begin in first facing in to the dancer and remain that way during the movement, there is no separate turning over or rotation of the forearms or wrists when arriving in fifth high. They are automatically facing down as they arrive in fifth high.

DETAILS I OFTEN INSIST ON IN PORT DE BRAS FROM SECOND TO FIRST:
1) don't move the arms as a unit
2) lengthen the arms before the upper arms start in (go away to arrive); maintain the length until the elbows bend to make first
3) lead the arms in with the inside edges of the wrists as the palms face down
4) the hands turn over to end palms facing in; the fingertips finish on the center line or overlapping as requested—hug the tree
5) the fingers (and hands, if overlapping) do not touch

DETAILS I OFTEN INSIST ON IN PORT DE BRAS FROM FIRST TO FIFTH HIGH:
1) keep the elbows out to the side, not collapsed forward; arms and hands are not pulled behind the head
2) the elbows bend to lift the forearm; the arm is not in one piece
3) keep the hands close together so the fingertips finish only one or two inches apart
4) head should change levels (up) as the arms are moved to fifth high

Dana's hands crossing near fifth low

Dana's wrists overlapping as her hands go to the opposite sides

Dana lifting her elbows, drawing her hands up her sides

Dana "washing" her face

Dana ready to extend her forearms to fifth high

FIFTH LOW TO FIFTH HIGH THROUGH OVERLAPPED FIRST POSITION

In the traditional technique, the dancer can go from fifth low to fifth high simply by starting as described for fifth low to first and having the elbows continue to lead the forearms up through first to fifth high, as described in the preceding port de bras. Although Mr. B used this at the barre and occasionally in the center, he was more interested in alternatives that required the dancer to bend her elbows more and to overlap the hands or arms. He usually had us go from fifth low to a first with the wrists or hands crossed. From the overlapped first, the elbows, by lifting up and out and bending a bit more, lead the forearms and hands up to fifth high. The hands remain crossed until they have passed the face, and then the backs of the wrists take over the lead as the elbows extend; the hands uncross to make fifth high. He also used a port de bras from fifth low to fifth high that required maximum bending of the elbows. From fifth low the dancer gently rotates the wrists to face her body as the edges of the wrists

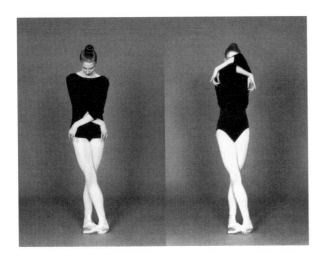

Dana shows that she really can take her sweater off with this port de bras.

lead the hands from fifth low down lower and then across to the opposite side of the body. The forearms must cross a lot so the tips of the middle fingers can trace a line along each side of the torso as the elbows bring them up. Balanchine would say to us, "It's like taking off your sweater." When the hands are at shoulder height, the elbows are in front of the face and the elbows continue to lead up until the upper arms are nearly in the position they will reach in fifth high. Balanchine often compared the moment when the forearms pass the face to washing your face, but no one washes her face this way, so I concluded he must have been thinking of his cat Mourka, or perhaps, more likely, of a swan. At this point the backs of the wrists take over, bringing the forearms up as the elbows continue to move out to their respective sides in fifth high.

This port de bras feels very uncomfortable to dancers when they first do it, because most have not bent their elbows in this way. But the bending must become part of the dancer's technique, so I give the port de bras periodically, alone and in very simple combinations. I give it when I have been seeing a lot of stiff elbows, and then I repeat it within the same class or in the next few days to help my students remember it.

DETAILS I OFTEN INSIST ON IN PORT DE BRAS FROM FIFTH LOW TO FIFTH HIGH THROUGH OVERLAPPED FIRST POSITIONS:
1) keep the shoulders down
2) the elbows and then the backs of the wrists lead the arms up to fifth high

---

FIFTH HIGH TO FIRST

In the more traditional method, as taught and sometimes used by Mr. B, the dancer brings the arms down from fifth high almost as a unit, but with softened elbows so the look is not stiff, as if she were a robot. She leads just slightly with the elbows, with the wrists and the hands slightly and gently trailing. This softens the movement through the gentle flex in the elbows and wrists and ends with a little roundness to the finish as the elbows go slightly to the side, the forearms level, and the wrists bring the hands into place. Mr. B typically used this port de bras at the barre and in more stationary exercises in the center, when only one arm was coming down from fifth high—for example, to meet the other arm in first, or when the other arm was in second. When we started to transfer weight, to travel, or to bend and incline our bodies, he used the technique for crossing the hands described below in the first part of Fifth High to Fifth Low Crossing the Arms.

FIRST TO FIFTH LOW

In the more traditional method the dancer brings the arms down from first almost, but, again, not quite in one piece. She gently softens the movement by letting the elbows bend slightly in order to draw the forearms and then the little finger edges of the wrists down to the level of fifth low. The elbows go slightly to the side, drawing the forearms and hands into place. See the next port de bras for a description of the crossing technique Mr. B usually preferred in the center and used more often.

FIFTH HIGH TO FIFTH LOW CROSSING THE ARMS

Traditionally, the port de bras from fifth high to fifth low can be done by simply combining the last two movements. More often, Balanchine modified the traditional port de bras so the hands and wrists crossed as they came down from fifth high. The dancer achieves this by drawing the elbows just a slight bit toward the center line of the body as they start down from fifth high, causing the hands and wrists to cross. The upper arms and then the elbows lead almost all the way down; then, near the end of the movement, the backs of the wrists take over and lead the hands, forearms, and upper arms into fifth low. When only one arm was coming down from fifth high (e.g., in temps lié from croisé to écarté), the same action (but in moderation) could be used to bring the hand somewhat across the center line of the body. This made a larger movement and gave a look of freedom, although our knowledge of the traditional technique with the fingertips on or near to the center line means that for the dancer it was freedom within an aesthetic.

An alternative version that Mr. B sometimes used in his ballets was occasionally given in class. It requires much more bending in the elbows, allowing a full crossing of the arms. The backs of the upper arms and the elbows draw each hand toward its opposite side so that they pass the face with the forearms crossed. This requires that the elbows bend and come in toward the center line of the body as the upper arms bring them down. When

> DETAILS I OFTEN INSIST ON IN PORT DE BRAS FROM FIFTH HIGH TO FIFTH LOW CROSSING THE ARMS:
> 1) bend the elbows close to the body
> 2) the head participates in the port de bras

the hands reach shoulder level, the fingertips on each hand are approximately at the sides of the upper arms. Then the elbows take over and continue to bring the forearms down. When the upper arms have reached their position in fifth low, the elbows straighten gently as the backs of the wrists bring the hands into fifth low. The path the fingertips take is similar to the one for fifth low to fifth high through overlapped first position (take off your sweater), but in this case the fingertips do not reach the side of the torso.

Like the port de bras from fifth low to fifth high with crossed arms, this will feel quite awkward to dancers new to Balanchine. It, too, should be given alone and in simple combinations until they are comfortable with it.

Deanna begins to lower her arms from fifth high, drawing her hands in.

Deanna lowers her elbows, drawing her hands to cross in front of her face.

Deanna continues the movement down.

Deanna lowers her elbows and hands further.

Deanna brings her hands to fifth low, leading with the backs of the wrists.

Peter extending his arms down and out toward the side

Peter extending his arms side, a little below second, his wrists taking over

Peter passes through second, lengthening his arms.

Peter continuing to lead with the backs of his wrists

Peter turning his wrists to make fifth high

Peter checking his hands in fifth high

FIFTH LOW TO FIFTH HIGH MOVING THROUGH SECOND

From fifth low, the dancer gently stretches her elbows, lengthening the arms down and out, with the hands and fingers trailing. The backs of the wrists take over the lead, continuing the movement of the arms out and up without pause. The dancer often takes a breath, expanding the chest and adding impetus to the entire port de bras. When the upper arms are in a very gentle slope down from the shoulders, the elbows continue to extend, bringing the backs of the wrists up. The backs of the wrists

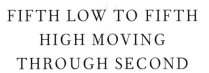

DETAILS I OFTEN INSIST ON IN PORT DE BRAS FROM FIFTH LOW TO FIFTH HIGH MOVING THROUGH SECOND:
1) lead with the backs of the wrists; do not lead with the fingertips
2) the level of the head must first lower, then rise in coordination with the hands

continue to lead, maintaining the hands in the palms-down position, with the fingers trailing. The focus of the dancer's awareness is the backs of the wrists, but she ensures that her shoulders stay down. The arms can stop anywhere en route to fifth high, depending on the line needed in the exercise given. If the final position is fifth high, the upper arms stop at the appropriate level and the elbows bend and are held out as the forearms, wrists, and hands rotate to finish in the fifth high position. The last movement is the turning over of the wrists, which brings the hands and fingers into the final fifth high position. The dancer does not lead to fifth high with the fingertips. Think of the paintbrush. Because the initial movement of the hands is down, the dancer's head and gaze will at first lower, before lifting in coordination with the arms and hands.

FIFTH HIGH TO SECOND

The traditional practice when opening the arms from fifth high to second is to move them as a unit, turning the arms during the movement to end palms front or down in second position. Mr. B did not want to see this, and we did not use it. He preferred that we lead with the backs of the wrists and the elbows, saving about half of the rotation to bring the palms to face front until the very end. He wanted the dancer to start to open her arms to the side by extending them slightly up and out from fifth high as she inhaled, giving the movement more life at the start. Growing up and out for a moment before going down to the side gives another kind of "going away to return." The backs of the elbows and wrists then lead down, the upper arms rotating slightly as they near second. The upper arms finish rotating the elbows back and up in a little arc, drawing the forearms and hands so the palms face front; at the same time, the elbows straighten a bit as the dancer thinks "long arms." This completes second position. If the exercise called for port de bras from fifth high to

Peter's arms, having passed through second, are just starting the arc back and up.

Peter beginning to lift on the back curve of the arc

Peter at the height of the arc, wrists facing down, ready to lower through second position to fifth low

DETAILS I OFTEN INSIST ON IN PORT DE BRAS FROM FIFTH HIGH TO SECOND:
1) do not move the arms and hands as a unit
2) the head participates in the movement

fifth low without a stop, the dancer would rotate the arms so the palms face down, rather than front, making a slightly larger arc, or even a very small semicircle, as she passed slightly below the level of second position and then lifted slightly above second position before continuing as described for going from second to fifth low (see page 154).

PORT DE BRAS EXERCISES

The foregoing descriptions of the way Mr. B wanted us to move from one arm position to another are meant to convey the details of the technique he taught and something of the quality of the movement, but no one should think that we drilled on this material only in this form, standing throughout the exercise en face. Most of our exercises included at least one change of épaulement, and many included several. Also, what is described here is symmetrical, both arms doing the same thing at the same time, but more of our exercises had parts when each arm had its own movement, usually simultaneous, but sometimes not. And there is an emphasis on more traditional form (e.g., fingertips moving on or near the center line of the body), although in his ballets and in most class exercises, Mr. B stretched and extended that form to include movements with the hands at least overlapping and, more typically, with the wrists crossing.

Balanchine wanted us to know and be able to do the traditional form of almost every movement. Then, when he asked for an extended version that gave the look he wanted, we could use our knowledge of the traditional form as a point of reference. Our ability to sense the difference meant that we could vary from the more traditional as much as he asked and we could look much more free, yet we could still dance with control. To ensure that we could do a more traditional port de bras, he occasionally gave exercises in which we stood in fifth

position en face and did a port de bras among a few positions, using the traditional form. Sometimes Mr. B thought we needed to pay more attention, to be more aware of our arms, wrists, and hands. He included just two or three or four positions, varied the tempos and the counts, and reversed the exercise but gave no épaulement, no turning or slanting of the head. This approach allowed us to fully focus on a few key details. For dancers new to his way of moving, I find that exercises like the next two are often a good way to start to learn his ports de bras and then to refine and perfect them.

The dancer starts the first exercise standing in fifth position en face, arms in fifth low. She executes the following sequence at a steady tempo, but takes care at the start and at each change of direction to begin relatively quickly, with a little extra energy and then to slow as she approaches the next position or change of direction, when she will again begin the same way. For dancers new to this technique, it is often good to give this kind of exercise at a slow tempo, with an actual stop at each position. As the dancers begin to have some control of the many details, the tempo can be picked up. Then the dancers can be asked to accelerate and then smoothly slow at each change of direction but never entirely stop. The effect is to create the illusion the dancer has stopped, even though she has not. But she must still show each start and the finish; the acceleration shows the beginning, and the slowing announces the end. From fifth low, on count one she raises her arms to first; on count two she opens them to second; on count three she raises them to the side to fifth high; on count four she opens her arms to the

---

DETAILS I OFTEN INSIST ON IN THE FIRST PORT DE BRAS EXERCISE:
1) move the arms using the muscles in the back and at the sides of the back
2) keep the shoulders down
3) be aware of the wrists, hands, and fingers; shape the hands and fingers properly
4) be aware of which specific part of the arm or wrists leads at various moments in the port de bras
5) raise and lower the head and direct the gaze in coordination with the movement of the hands and arms

side to second; on count five she raises her left arm as she would to fifth high, taking care to bring her fingertips to the center line of her head, thus making third position; on count six she raises her right arm as she would to fifth high (again taking care to bring her fingertips to the center line of her head) as her left arm opens side to second (thus maintaining third position, although with a switch of arms); on count seven she lowers her right arm side to second position (thus changing from third to second position); on count eight she lowers her arms to fifth low, being sure to start simultaneously with the lift and arc with both arms as she rotates her palms down. The dancer must be sure that the arms move together as they go from second to fifth low.

For the second exercise the dancer is again standing in fifth position en face, this time with the arms in second. It is done at a steady, moderately slow tempo, but with phrasing to make the positions visible. After a preparatory breath she lowers her arms to fifth low on the "and" before count one, and, without pausing, raises them, passing through an overlapped first using the arms-crossed technique. She arrives on count one in fifth high. On the "and" before count two, she lowers her arms through first and fifth low, using a crossed-arms technique. She continues through fifth low, opening to the side without pausing and lifts her arms, arriving in second on count two. On the "and" before count three she raises her left arm as she would to fifth high (again taking care to lead with the back of the wrist before ending with her fingertips over the center line of her head) and brings her right arm in to first, leading with the inside edge of the wrist (making fourth position), arriving in the position on count three. On the "and" before count four she lowers her left arm from fifth high to first, where the fingers can meet on the center line or the hands overlap, and both arms open together to second on four. Then repeat on the other side.

The degree of the crossing of her arms in this kind of exercise is controlled to suit the tempo and give the desired look. The dancer can bend the el-

bows slightly and show only the fingers or hands overlapping, or bend the elbows a bit more and show the wrists just crossing, or she can bend the elbows until she shows the "take off your sweater" look, with the entire forearm overlapped and each hand on the opposite side of the body. It is beneficial for the teacher to vary the tempos and the movements so the dancers can practice many different ways of moving their arms. Usually the degree of crossing shown when the arms are going up to fifth high is matched when the dancer brings the arms down to fifth low and vice versa.

DETAILS I OFTEN INSIST ON IN THE SECOND PORT DE BRAS EXERCISE:
1) be aware of your elbows, wrists, hands, and fingers and of which part leads the movement; shape the hands and fingers
2) the head and eyes participate, coordinating with the arm and hand movement

---

THE LOOK IN PERFORMANCE

The effect on the dancer of learning ports de bras Mr. B's way as well as the more traditional ways is to give her arms a look of greater energy and amplitude. This can be visible in *all* her dancing, even in a very brief, almost stationary movement.

A very common introduction to a combination will serve as an example. At the beginning of a variation onstage or a combination that moves across the floor on the diagonal in class, the dancer often steps back through fourth position plié, ending in tendu front (as in temps lié back). Her port de bras could typically take her arms from second up and over to fifth high, her hands coming down in front of her chest through first to fifth low and then opening out to an extended second. If she has been

Dana moving her arms from second to fifth high

Dana's arms arriving in fifth high

Dana lowering her rounded arms to first as she starts to transfer her weight to the back leg

Dana lowering her rounded arms past first toward fifth low as she bends forward and continues transferring her weight to the back leg

Dana straightens her supporting leg as she opens her arms, leading with the elbows and the backs of the wrists.

Dana finishes on a straight supporting leg in tendu front with her arms in an extended line.

Dana, leading with the backs of her wrists, approaching fifth high

Dana turning over her hands as she passes through fifth high to cross her wrists

Dana's elbows lead, drawing her hands down as she begins to transfer her weight to the back leg.

Dana's elbows continue to draw her hands down as she bends forward and transfers her weight to the back leg.

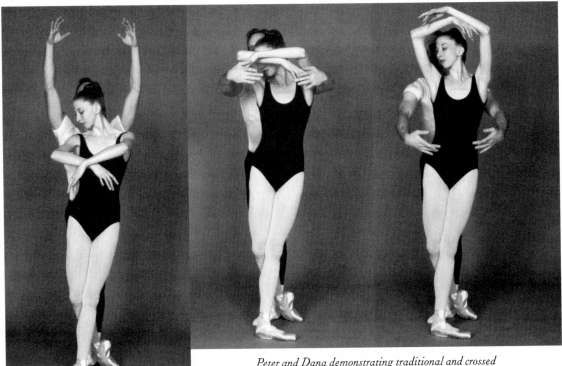

Peter and Dana demonstrating traditional and crossed arms ports de bras used together

taught and has practiced only the traditional ports de bras, her fingertips will "naturally" come down from fifth high to fifth low several inches apart, each on its own side of her body. Her arms will move more as round units as she goes from fifth high to fifth low. If she has also been taught and has practiced Mr. B's more dynamic, more fully articulated technique, she will just as "naturally" bend her elbows and wrists more, and her hands will cross her center line and overlap. Her sense of how to use her arms will have been shifted, and the result will be greater movement. This difference will also be visible at times when only one arm is moving (see page 216).

When a person who prefers a very traditional look sees the arms used as Mr. B wanted, the result is often characterized as unschooled, unclassical, and the like. In fact, it is another schooling, a new classicism for his 1 percent of the ballet world.

In his choreography, Balanchine could combine the traditional approach with his extension of it and in some cases used them simultaneously. In the example on the bottom of the opposite page, the man is going from fifth high to fifth low, enveloping the woman who is going from fifth low to fifth high, crossing her arms.

Dana passing through fifth low; she will open her arms and extend them as she did in the more traditional port de bras (see page 163).

"SMALL ARMS" PORTS DE BRAS

Among the traits for which Balanchine choreography is noted are quickness and speed. Achieving those qualities entails some adaptations of the tech-nique. At very fast tempos the arms move closer to the body and the elbows bend more to stay on the music without looking like they are frantically trying to keep up. Also, when practicing small footwork and legwork at very fast tempos, there can be some standard arm positions and ports de bras that are not very suitable. Balanchine dealt with this not only by having us move our arms closer to the body but also by exploring what we called "small arms." But this technique for "small arms" can also be useful and beautiful at a variety of tempos. "Convenient" was Mr. B's word, perhaps reflecting his liking, at times, for using just the amount needed to give the look desired and his satisfaction when he saw that it was also comfortable and practicable for the dancers. "No emotion at all. Just arms, hands, and wrists." Remember his little bit of wordplay: "Hands should not be a handicap."

One way in which we practiced "small arms" ports de bras was standing en face in fifth position, using our arms and hands coordinated with our heads, which moved up and down without slanting or turning. The dancer typically started in fifth low. She can begin with a small preparation, taking a breath to give impetus to the chest and head to lift gently and to the arms to move slightly side, gently extending the elbows and leading with the backs of the wrists. The wrists rotate the palms in toward her body and aim for fifth low, leading with the inside edges of the wrists and the sides of the hands (she has gone away to return). As the hands come in to fifth low, the head lowers, following them. She begins the "small arms" port de bras as the hands pass through fifth low and arrive in front of the center line of the body, very close together, the inside edges of her wrists could almost touch. The elbows rise to the sides and away from the body, lifting the hands *very close* to her body, with the palms remaining facing her, wrists and hands trailing. When the hands reach a point a little below the waist, the dancer turns the palms face up, makes a small rising arc with the wrists, and extends the arms very slightly forward, as if she is offering or

Dana has taken a preliminary breath and opened her arms to the side.

Dana closing her arms, inside edges of her wrists leading in

Dana lifting her elbows up as her palms turn to face her

Dana turning her hands over to offer something

Dana opening front and offering

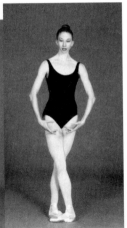

Dana three quarters of the way side and still offering

Dana raising her arms with a little arc up and back to turn the palms over

Dana closing her arms leading with the inside edges of her wrists

Dana about to cross her wrists to continue or . . .

. . . rotate her wrists to end in fifth low

serving something with her hands. She raises her head to follow the movement of her hands, looking directly front as her arms extend. The dancer then moves the hands toward the sides with the elbows slightly bent, being careful to maintain the correct shape of the hands. The tendency, which is not desirable, is to straighten the elbows, reaching too far forward with the arms and/or to flatten the hands and fingers, eliminating the curve in the palm and putting the pinkie, ring, and middle fingers together while sticking out the index finger and thumb. It is also important that she maintain the elbows away from the body as the forearms move toward the low second, rather than allowing them to drop in to the waist. The arms and hands do not reach all the way to the side; instead, when they are about three quarters of the way from front to side, they pause and then close to fifth low. The port de bras is done in front of the dancer. In closing, the upper arms and elbows slightly lift as the wrists make a slight arc and the backs of the wrists lift up and the palms turn over. The hands do not come above the waist. Then the inside edges of the wrists lead the arms down to fifth low, and the forearms rotate so the palms face her body as her head lowers. We might repeat this exercise four or eight times, ending in standard fifth low.

Another "small arms" port de bras to which Mr. B gave some attention had a similar general look, but because of a few crucial details, a quite different flavor. It was a finishing movement that had the message, "I've done it, I've finished, I present myself to you." We did not practice it in class, but he used it in the choreography of some of the ballets. It is similar to the other "small arms" ports de bras in its small scale of movement, but it ends with the arms somewhat outstretched and the palms up about halfway between front and side. The arms are brought into fifth low to start the movement. From fifth low, they are brought close to the body and kept near or slightly across the center line as they lift. Then the elbows straighten somewhat, extending the forearms partway toward the audience as the hands are rotated up and toward the audience showing the palm side, but the hand is still properly shaped—that is, rounded with curved and separated fingers—not flattened and together.

DETAILS I OFTEN INSIST ON IN "SMALL ARMS" PORTS DE BRAS:
1) remember to keep the shape of the hands
2) do not permit the elbows to drop in to the waist
3) do not permit the arms to fly up toward shoulder level—remember, this is a "small arms" exercise
4) the entire port de bras is done in front of the body; the arms do not reach second position or à la seconde

The forearms now open to the side in a gentle curve out and away. The feeling is that the dancer is presenting herself. The gesture is gracious and almost modest. It is light in tone and fits well into the flow of movement. "We dancers were slaves. Always we serve, obliging all the time, so we serve everyone. We bow, we have to be grateful." This has nothing in common with the big, self-congratulatory finishing poses (arms extended, elbows stretched, fingers stiffly pointing) that are often seen.

PUSH

Another kind of arm movement we explored in class was the "push." Like "small arms," the "push" is a refinement of the traditional technique but is also an extension of it. Mr. B used the "push" in many ballets, and he included it in combinations he gave in class. For example, standing in croisé or en face in fifth position, the dancer raises her arms from second as if she is bringing them to fifth high. When her arms are at about the level at which the forearms would have started to rotate the hands into fifth high, she begins to bend her elbows and to lower her upper arms, bringing the hands toward the center line of her body as she turns the palms front. The wrists cross when they are approximately at forehead level, and the upper arms continue to lower the hands close to the body until the elbows are at about shoulder level. Then they straighten gently, extending the forearms and the hands at about chest level. The palms face front with flexed, crossed wrists, fingers extending, pushing the air. This is the "push" part of the port de bras. From the "push" the dancer might begin to move her arms to second by gently raising and bending the elbows, bringing the forearms slightly in as the hands rotate over to a kind of overlapped first with the palms facing the dancer. Continuing without a pause, she pulls her elbows down and away, drawing her hands to the sides, leading with the backs of her wrists, on a line below second position. She then raises her elbows, rotating her upper arms so the palms face down and the elbows and hands make a little arc up and back to a line slightly above second position. She finishes by gently softening and straightening her elbows as she lowers into second position. Mr. B would at times use this port de bras with bourrée suivie (see page 281) forward and back; traveling front, the arms move from second position to the "push," and traveling back, they return to second position. In his usual way he could also give this port de bras reversed: bourrée forward when opening the arms to the side, and then bourrée back pushing forward. He could further amuse himself and us by giving it two or three more ways. For example, the dancer can bourrée forward

Deanna bringing her arms from second toward fifth high, leading with the backs of the wrists

Deanna lowers her elbows, drawing her hands to the center, palms facing down.

Deanna's hands at face level, ready to push forward

Deanna pushing front, leading with palms and separated fingers

Deanna extending front

moving the arms from second through fifth low to fifth high on counts one-two-three, plié in coupé back on count four, and then bring them down to push forward during the bourrée back on counts five-six-seven, plié in coupé front on count eight,

then open the arms from first to second during the bourrée forward on counts one-two-three and finish with plié in fifth on count four, échappé to pointe with arms to fifth high on count five, close fifth with plié changing feet as the arms open side on count six, sous-sus with the arms in à la seconde on count seven, and plié in coupé front on count eight. Repeat to the other side.

Alternative looks for the "push" include to the side or into first arabesque, rather than front. From second position the dancer closes her arms past first, bending her elbows to cross her forearms at the wrists. She rotates her palms to face out and opens her arms forward and to the sides, stretching her elbows and pushing the air with the palms of her hands. This port de bras is done by the corps de ballet near the beginning of *Serenade* and is seen moving to first arabesque in the carry lifts in the second movement of *Symphony in C* and in the "Sanguinic" section of *The Four Temperaments.*

The men did not do exercises based on bourrée-ing. However, the port de bras itself is one that men

---

DETAILS I OFTEN INSIST ON IN PUSH PORT DE BRAS:

1) keep the shoulders down
2) show the five fingers; pretty hands!

also use in some ballets, so they usually practiced it.

There are two aspects of Balanchine's work with the arms that are especially well illustrated by the "push" port de bras. First, although I have given indications of when certain movements occur and where the arms or hands are, this port de bras, more than most, was adjusted for the step being done, the look desired, and the individual dancer. Second, even though this is not a standard port de bras—that is, it is not a movement from one position with a number to another—the principles Mr. B applied to the standard ports de bras apply to this one (and to any other nonstandard port de bras): awareness and use of all the joints, reaction or resistance to the air, go away to arrive.

Mr. B constantly gave us a rich variety of arm movements as he set center combinations. We typically started in croisé with the arms in fifth low or, after a two-count preparation, in second and moved among the positions as well as through arabesque or attitude, generally with épaulement or change of direction, and finished, again most likely in croisé with the arms in fifth low, which is where we started. Basic classical steps typically included tendu battement, grand battement, fondu, and fondu relevé, or he could give an adagio or any kind of jump. He also incorporated a variety of tempos and phrasings, different looks, and so on. But along the way, these ports de bras would be used, passing smoothly through some positions and pausing, stopping, or even freezing in others to make a clear picture. When moving from second position to croisé, effacé, and écarté, we almost always used both arms ("all two arms," Mr. B would say), passing both arms through fifth low to first and then one arm lifting to fifth high and the other opening to second. The finishing position was usually a standard one; on the rare occasions when it was not, the technique was adapted to achieve a harmonious movement.

These ports de bras represent Mr. B's ideas about practicing with maximum awareness and control and about working in the extremes. Once these qualities were established in exercises in which the arms were the focus, he might have us do less, or permit us to do less. The dancer must master the correct form in class, and be able to extend or exaggerate it as directed, because onstage she will tend to do less. These ports de bras must be as much a part of the dancer as any technique for the feet and legs if she is to dance his ballets in his style and to achieve the look he wanted. As always, the idea is to use what is needed to achieve the best artistic effect. Mastery frees the dancer when onstage to respond to the choreography and the music and the moment instead of worrying about her technique, trying to be perfect.

ORIENTATION OF THE BODY TO THE FRONT

The point of changing the orientation of the dancer's body to the front—that is, to the audience—is, of course, to multiply the available looks, making the dancer and the dancing more interesting and more beautiful. The audience sees her straight on, front and back, in profile, and at angles in between. Balanchine worked to enhance this effect by ensuring that each dancer knew the location of her own front, side, and back (referred to as her directions). Since these refer to her own body and remain the same no matter how she is oriented in the room or to the public, each orientation of her body in the room has its own very distinctive look (i.e., each change in the direction she faces produces a change in the way she looks). And Mr. B set our exercises with very specific orientations (épaulement) of the body and positions of the head, arms, legs, and feet to help us acquire muscle memory. We became more aware of the differences among the positions and orientations so we could show each of them clearly in class and, more importantly, make them all legible onstage.

There are systems for numbering the corners

and sides of the stage (and the corresponding points in the studio or classroom), but Mr. B never used them, preferring instead simply to show what he wanted. What he wanted most importantly is that each dancer be precise with reference to herself. If she did tendu front standing en face, her pointe was on her center line, extended directly in front of her. If she did tendu front standing in croisé, her pointe was still on her center line, directly in front of her, because her own directions are the same no matter where she is. Her pointe in croisé might aim precisely for the corner, but it might not. That depended on her exact location in the room or onstage (and the room or the stage being perfectly square). In either case Mr. B wanted her pointe directly in front of her own center. The dancer needs to carry that awareness of her directions within herself and then apply it. Perhaps that is why he did not emphasize memorizing any of the numbering systems based on the space (studio or stage), rather than on herself.

Much of what is described in words in this book is much more easily shown by a teacher in class. That is why technique books are hard to read. Sometimes the words almost get in the way, and this topic is one of those times. In the discussions that follow I am using "direction" to refer to front, side, and back with reference to the dancer. I am using "orientation (to the front)" to refer to en face, croisé, effacé, and écarté.

Dancers have agreed on the names of the orientations, so the terms and their meanings are familiar. Mr. B used them and he also demonstrated. However, in addition to asking us to remain precise about our own directions, he refined certain details to sharpen the contrast, to make the pictures more vivid, and to intensify the aesthetic effect.

EN FACE

Balanchine observed that when en face, "dancers try to hide themselves, they move as if a little embarrassed."

En face is the purest orientation because the dancer is most fully revealed. It is also the simplest. Young children begin learning center port de bras standing en face. There is no camouflage: no épaulement, no curve of the neck, no slant of the head. Everything shows, making the dancer more vulnerable. And yet she must still look beautiful as she moves.

To look beautiful and feel beautiful so fully revealed is very difficult. Mr. Balanchine compared dancing en face to cooking a veal roast with salt and pepper and no garlic and having it come out tasting delicious. The dancer can and does change the level of her head and therefore her gaze in coordination with the movement; the head may lift up and lower, but that is all. Since she cannot call on the "spicing" of épaulement while dancing en face, she must maximize her energy and awareness, her radiance. She resists the sense that since this is somehow easier, because less technical (no tilting the head, no curving the neck, no turning the body), she can let up. Dancing en face means the dancer is parallel to the front of the room or stage, so her front (face, shoulders, hips, and feet) is facing the public, her back is directly away, and her sides are straight to the wings. In tendu front or back (pointe on the center line; thighs crossed!), her working leg feels parallel to the sides, perpendicular to the front (and the reverse in tendu side, but pointe opposite heel). Any wandering off the precise directions is immediately apparent.

Mr. B did not make a lot of use of en face when we really moved or in his ballets. However, he gave us a variety of mostly stationary exercises en face to practice positions and ports de bras in which the dancer will be especially aware if she is not correct, such as opening from first to second ("parting the curtains") and closing to first ("hugging the tree"), painting the ceiling, the "offering" small arms, etc. He also gave us smaller movements, such as piqué walks and tendus, and a few bigger ones, such as grand battement and développé, for which precise knowledge of front, side, and back were particularly important.

Deanna, Peter, and Dana en face with the arms in fifth high

right foot and right shoulder are front). "Perfect" alignment of the pointe in tendu to one corner and of the shoulders to the adjacent corners is possible only when the dancer is standing at the center of a square stage (or studio), where the two diagonals cross. This illustrates Balanchine's reason for wanting each dancer to cultivate her own sense that she is standing alone at the center of her own square space; she makes croisé with reference to herself and her space no matter where she is placed onstage or in the studio. Dancers taught in schools that emphasize orientation to the corner in croisé (and effacé and écarté, discussed in detail in the next two sections) have a tendency to adjust the position of the working foot so it is "correct" with respect to the corner, rather than keeping the relationship with the body constant. For Balanchine the relative positions of the legs and feet must remain consistently constant, just as at the barre. In the center, and later onstage, front and back continue to refer to the center line of the body, and side remains directly to the side. Doing tendu, jeté, grand battement, frappé, fondu, développé, etc., the action and position of the feet and legs are the same whether the dancer is en face or in croisé.

Mr. B taught a technique for the neck and head in croisé that added greatly to the aesthetic beauty and distinctiveness of the orientation. In his croisé the dancer's head and gaze are directed as is usual to the

CROISÉ

The basic idea of croisé is familiar from Renaissance painting and sculpture. The dancer is seen between profile and facing, the shoulders and hips generally facing one diagonal, with the shoulders aligned generally on the other diagonal. The crossing of the legs seen by the public gives the name. The feet and legs are in exactly the same relation as they are en face; they look different only because the entire body has been rotated (e.g., the downstage shoulder, generally toward the corner. The dancer can see herself in the mirror. However, the neck curves and the top of the head slants toward the downstage shoulder, thereby bringing the ear toward it. The head is usually level or very slightly tilted up; the chin is not thrown back, nor is it tucked. The effect is to bring the cheek forward, presenting it to the audience. "Ask for a kiss," Mr. B would say. This technique produces in the dancer the feeling of a gracious curve from the top of the head along the neck and down into the upper chest. A common tendency is to turn the head toward the downstage corner without slanting it, which is not nearly as warm or aesthetically pleasing. Another is to

Deanna, Peter, and Dana in croisé; Deanna and Dana are showing standard croisé arms while Peter's arms are in fifth high.

turn the head and slant it back without bringing the cheek forward, which tends to present the neck and chin while losing the face, or to tuck the chin in and down, losing the neck. When I see a dancer tucking her chin down and apparently trying to bury her head in her collarbone, I tell her, "Be long like the swan" or "The turtle should not go home." What I work to develop in each of the girls is a personal presence, perhaps a sense of glamor, that is beyond the details of ear and neck and slant, the presence Mr. B evoked so well in telling us to "ask for a kiss."

This placement of the head is deceptive in its simplicity. Achieving the skill and flexibility to move smoothly in and out of the line Mr. B wanted takes regular practice, sometimes only moving the

head and neck. To help us memorize this turned and slanted head position with a curved neck, Mr. B might ask us to stand in fifth in croisé, arms down. On one, we straightened the head and neck and looked toward the corner. On two, we slanted the head as we brought the cheek forward by curving the neck. We could repeat this four or eight times at a moderately slow tempo to ensure that we perfected the form.

There can be something almost feminine about the line of the head and neck in Mr. B's croisé, but only when shown by women: Think of Botticelli's *Venus*. When men do this movement there is a different projection, in part because of the difference in male and female proportions in the head

Dana, offering her cheek, asks for . . .   *. . . and gets a kiss from Peter.*

and shoulders and in part because of the musculature of the male neck. Again, think of Renaissance painting and sculpture—for example, Michelangelo's *David*. Encouraging the men, Mr. B would say, "Contraposto!" His images intended to help us sense the look of the head and neck in croisé also included "lean on a cloud," which is a little ethereal, or, with a different projection, a little godly, and "put your head on a pillow." Although much of what he said was directed at his women, he wanted his men to display the same aesthetic, but with manly projection.

Slanting the head takes its center line off the center line of the body, so the arm and hand must ac-

commodate the head to keep the fingertips over the head, on the center line. The elbow bends more than it does when the head is straight, which, once again, takes more effort and awareness from the dancer.

This is the croisé that Balanchine used most often in choreography and that we practiced most frequently in class: body straight, working leg directly front or back, neck curved, head slanted, upstage arm in a fifth, framing the face (meaning the hand is toward the front of the head, rather than pulled to the back) so the fingertips are over the center line of the head.

In many schools, when the working leg is front

Deanna's arm frames her head and face; her fingertips remain over the center line of her head.

Deanna, Peter, and Dana, heads turned but not slanted, not croisé . . .

. . . Deanna, Peter, and Dana, here with heads turned and slanted, giving the gracious curve needed in croisé

Dana in the more traditional croisé back, looking up "at the moon"

Deanna in an alternative croisé front

The downstage arm is in fifth high, with the fingertips over the center line of the head, which is slanted to the upstage shoulder; the upstage arm is in second. The dancer's face is more lifted, so she looks out from under the forearm, as if peering up at the moon. In his usual way Mr. B wanted his dancers to look as if they were really seeing something—in this case, the moon in the night sky.

For some steps (e.g., battement tendu, jeté battement, low fondu front and back, and frappé front and back) Mr. B on occasion used another traditional alternative croisé with a really different look. In croisé front the upstage arm is in first or even slightly lower. Therefore the head slants to the upstage shoulder and is tilted gently down to look up and over the forearm of the upstage arm. The position of the head and arms could be reversed when we went to the back, and the dancer directed her gaze over and past her downstage arm. Perhaps recalling the grander architecture of places she had worked, such as Paris

the torso is tilted back in croisé, and when the working leg is back the torso is tilted way forward. Mr. B's standard exercises for croisé called for the torso to remain erect, just as it does in barre exercises such as tendu, dégagé, and so on. Depending on the look required, the torso could bend somewhat to the side in some steps to enhance the croisé line—for example, croisé attitude back and développé croisé to the front. This was especially true when we were really dancing, moving across the floor. At times he also used a cambré back in choreography, usually just as the dancer finishes a développé front as she tombés forward over and off pointe or off demi-pointe. She pushes her hips forward as she lifts her torso up to extend it and bend slightly back. However, the dancer needs first to master Mr. B's standard croisé, which he used much more frequently—in fact, almost exclusively—to have a clear point of reference from which to bend or incline the torso.

On occasion Mr. Balanchine also used the traditional croisé back or an alternative croisé front.

Dana in croisé back, "looking over a balustrade"

or Monte Carlo, Maria Tallchief compared the head position and direction of the gaze to "looking over a balustrade."

DETAILS I OFTEN INSIST ON IN CROISÉ:

1) the legs remain in the same relation to one another no matter the direction in which the body is turned (i.e., working leg directly front or back, toes on the center line of the body)

2) a correct curve of the neck and slant of the head

3) fingertips over the center line of the head, framing the face, not pulled back, away from the face; the arm in second is not pulled behind the torso

4) torso straight, not inclined, unless the exercise is specifically set that way

5) in the croisé variant, the head is slanted away from the upraised downstage arm and toward the upstage shoulder

---

EFFACÉ

In effacé the dancer is seen in the same orientation found in croisé—that is, with her body rotated from en face, the hips and shoulders generally facing one diagonal, and the shoulders generally aligned on the other diagonal (e.g., right foot front, left shoulder front). To the audience, the legs in effacé appear to be open rather than crossed, but for the dancer, the pointe in tendu is still directly front (or back) of her center. Her thighs are still crossed. Once again, the relation of one leg to the other remains unchanged no matter how the dancer is turned. The chest is very open and lifted and projects up and out. Remember the upper back muscles drawing together between the shoulder blades; this helps to establish the correct feeling and the correct line. The shoulders are also fully opened, and as

usual are lowered; the dancer senses them as pulled down and back, almost as if they are draped to the back.

The underlying principles for the use of the neck and the placement of the head that are used in standard croisé also apply to standard effacé. The head is again turned in the direction of the downstage shoulder and it is slanted, bringing the ear toward that shoulder. The neck is again curved, bringing the cheek forward. In effacé the head is usually lifted gently up.

The lift of the head is very slight in standard effacé. The face is raised just enough to direct the gaze up and out to the front, past and in front of the upper arm or elbow of the downstage arm, which is raised in fifth high. If the working leg is lifted close to ninety degrees or higher, the face can be raised a little more, so the gaze is directed past and in front of the forearm. The fingertips of the raised hand are over the center line of the head.

Deanna, Peter, and Dana in effacé; Deanna and Dana are showing standard effacé arms while Peter's arms are in fifth high.

Dana in effacé front, "looking over a balustrade"

Deanna, Peter, and Dana in effacé; Deanna and Dana are showing variant effacé arms while Peter's arms are in fifth high.

The body remains straight in Mr. B's standard effacé front and back; just as in his standard croisé, the body is not tilted forward and back. However, he also could use a slight cambré back in effacé, when that gave the look required; it is often seen when the dancer tombés over and off pointe or off demi-pointe.

Mr. B did give a variant of his standard effacé with the upstage arm in fifth high and the downstage arm in second position, but keeping the head in the same line. We rarely practiced effacé back or front with the top of the head tilting toward the upstage shoulder, looking under the downstage arm.

We more often practiced a traditional alternative effacé with the downstage arm in first or slightly lower than first. That was the port de bras often

---

DETAILS I OFTEN INSIST ON IN EFFACÉ:
1) the toes of the working foot are on the center line of the body when front or back
2) the hips are level and square to the dancer's torso when the leg is in front
3) the chest is open; the neck is curved and the head is slanted, with the cheek brought forward. The head is not pulled away from the audience—"offer the cheek"
4) the fingertips are over the center line of the head, framing the face, not pulled back, away from the face
5) the arm in second position is not pulled behind the torso
6) in standard effacé maintain a straight, pulled-up body; do not tilt back or forward

used for brisé front, and it was also used in other steps when the working foot was near the ground. As with the similar low arms in croisé, the dancer looked out over the forearm of the arm in first.

ÉCARTÉ

Although dancers and teachers have traditionally defined écarté largely in reference to the corners, Mr. B liked to say, "Écarté is a position, not a place on the floor or in the corner; it can be done in any direction." And indeed, at the barre he usually, as I noted in describing adagio at the barre (see page 131), set an exercise calling for "écarté devant" with his dancers square to the barre. We practiced this adapted écarté to help ensure that the leg went directly side. The head was turned and tilted up so the gaze was *behind* the forearm of the free arm, which was raised in fifth high. For a dancer with a secure and constant sense of her own directions, of her place at the midpoint of her own square space, her own little box, this is very logical and clear. In the center we could conceivably have done a promenade in écarté devant or derrière, although I do not recall his ever giving it. What he did give still extended the meaning of the term.

In traditional écarté, which Mr. B often used in the center, the dancer is on a diagonal once again and is seen with her hips and shoulders facing a diagonal, the orientation that is familiar from croisé and effacé. However, the feeling is quite different. In croisé and effacé the working leg is front or back, and the upper body shows curves. Both characteristics give it depth; they give a three-dimensional look. But in écarté the working leg is directly side and very turned out and, except for the lifted chest, the dancer feels almost two-dimensional. She should feel as she would if she were standing with her legs

and hips pressed against a wall. Mr. B made it clear by walking to the front and assuming écarté tendu flat against the mirror: "Écarté is a very flat position."

The working leg in écarté is in the same relationship to the torso as it is when en face with the leg à la seconde. Mr. B wanted the dancer to be aware of maintaining maximum turnout, even though she was turned on the diagonal, and to stand very tall and straight, with the chest lifted.

For traditional écarté devant the working foot is on the downstage side. The torso is very erect, the downstage arm is raised in fifth high, and the upstage arm is opened to second. The head is turned far enough to the side and is tilted so the gaze is upward, *behind* the forearm of the downstage arm. If she could see herself in the mirror, Balanchine told her, "You are already wrong!" because her head was not in the correct line. For traditional écarté derrière the upstage foot becomes the working foot, and the arms are reversed. However, the gaze remains generally downstage, on the diagonal—that is, over the downstage arm and hand, which are ex-

Peter in tendu écarté devant

Dana in développé écarté devant

Peter in tendu écarté
derrière

*Dana in développé écarté
derrière*

DETAILS I OFTEN INSIST ON IN
ÉCARTÉ:

1) if the dancer looks at herself in the mirror
   in écarté devant, she is already wrong;
   her head is lifted and turned so her gaze is
   directed behind her arm and upward
2) maintain a well turned-out, almost
   extreme, à la seconde (feel the thigh,
   knee, and foot behind the arm and in line
   with or behind, not in front of, the
   shoulder)
3) in écarté the chest is lifted up and open,
   the look is regal
4) the fingertips of the hand in fifth high are
   over the center line of the head

tended in second. In écarté derrière the dancer
may incline her torso gently away from the working leg, especially when the working leg was raised
to ninety degrees or higher. The shoulders and
head are tilted away from the raised
working leg in écarté derrière, so the
dancer's head is also slightly slanted
and the gaze is along the line of the
arm in second. The fingertips of the
hand raised in fifth high are over the
center line of the head.

In class, dancers always display a
proud, upright bearing, but this quality
is especially important for écarté. Mr.
B called écarté regal; I tell my classes to
picture a queen with her chest lifted
and open, holding her head up, as if
wearing a high ruff on her neck.

Mr. B's approach to these four very
familiar terms—en face, croisé, effacé,
and écarté—is an example of the
kind of thinking he wanted from his
dancers. "Dancers must be intelligent,"
he said. He also said, "Don't think,
dance." This mostly meant: In performance, don't
calculate your effects, don't be cutesy, don't play a
part, don't be pretentious, just do the steps on time,
just dance! But the dancer must be prepared to take
risks, to go all out, while still keeping the time. How
to do this? Generally in class, and especially in the
more technical exercises, he did want us to think
about what we were doing. He wanted us to be
aware of every detail and to take nothing for
granted, even, or maybe especially, when it was a
matter of something we all "knew," such as how to
stand en face or in croisé. His use of these four
terms and the tendu exercise on page 195 show how
he made us think, for example, about positions and
directions and orientation to the front. He probably
changed the way most of us looked at ballet technique. I know that moments such as these certainly
changed me. Also, he expected us to work on some
of our detailed, individual problems on our own—

executing a proper tendu battement, placing the foot to the floor, holding the hand or making a certain port de bras look right, or presenting the head in croisé. This was not possible unless the dancer thoroughly understood the technique. This required a cultivated dance intelligence that came in part through thought.

Almost always in performance, generally in rehearsal, and often in exercises in the center, Mr. B wanted us just to dance, to appear to move with abandon while we still maintained control. A cultivated dance intelligence helps the dancer to know when and where and to what degree that enthusiasm and that daring can be used. Good work in class and lots of practice, both done with effective thinking about the technical details, build muscle memory so the dancer remembers in her

Peter's a helpful guy, but it's probably better to think for yourself.

body and does not still need to think when she wants just to dance. There is much more to beautiful dancing than pure technique; technique is only the first ingredient. "Good dancers develop a strong technique with an individual, personal style," Mr. B said.

I recall a rehearsal of *Raymonda Variations*. During the coda, a pair of dancers "fly" downstage doing sauté, step, glissade, traveling assemblé en avant. Mr. B stopped rehearsal and said to one of the dancers, "No! Not big enough, does not travel enough, feet come together too slowly in assemblé. Do again." The entrance was repeated, and the dancer put more effort and energy into the steps. Mr. B said, "Better, but not good enough." The dancer went back upstage, determined to give it everything. Putting every ounce of energy she had into each step as she came downstage, she came flying through the air in a big assemblé with her feet together . . . and landed on her bottom, right in front of Mr. B. "That's right," he said with a smile, "now I see something." Of course, he did not really want her to crash-land that way in performance. But he knew she had the right approach, and he trusted her to make it work.

THE TRADITIONAL POSES: ARABESQUE AND ATTITUDE

For anyone who completely accepts Mr. Balanchine's aesthetic, the word "pose" presents a problem. It carries with it some "flavors" that are not what he liked, and yet there is no good substitute.

Balanchine was always more interested in exploring and refining the qualities of the dancer's movement in class than he was in trying to "perfect" the moments of stillness that punctuate it. Posing, pose, to pose—all of these words fit more comfortably in an aesthetic that focuses more than he did on the stillnesses, on carefully calculated, fixed images that are brief tableaux vivants. As I have shown and will show in the rest of this book, he wanted precise positions of the feet and legs, of the arms and hands; he wanted precise directions in relation to the body; in short, he wanted each element of the technique to display its distinctive quality. But all this had to be achieved through correct and energetic movement. When dancers are taught to work more for the "perfect" line when they are *not* moving than for the best possible movement, they move with less energy and commitment; they don't take the necessary risks; they hold something back; and, ultimately, they begin to pose, because the pose is more important than the movement to it. The dance becomes tame, polite, calculated, it loses the interest and excitement and the fresh beauty that Balanchine wanted. His priority is clear in his definition of dance: *movement* of the body in relation to time.

As with flexed and parallel feet, the absence of work on posing in class did not mean that he did not use poses in the ballets. Memorable examples to me include the three Muses leaning on Apollo, each Muse with her working leg raised at a different angle and, in *Serenade*, the opening tableau of the corps with upraised arms and, later in the ballet, the "Dark Angel" covering the man's eyes.

I will thus use "pose" to refer to arabesque and attitude, those two traditional poses, and I use it at other times when it is the most suitable choice. But this usage is not to suggest that the dancer ever poses in class; always, she moves, and occasionally she moves into a pose where she may momentarily remain.

ARABESQUE

Balanchine made arabesque longer and stronger for his dancers than it is for dancers trained in other ways. It is longer because he opened the hip line and lengthened the shoulder line. It is stronger because he expected the dancer to stand with the supporting hip as straight as possible over the supporting leg, with the torso and back held up to meet the lifted leg.

By allowing the dancer to open her hip in arabesque, he freed her to lift her leg high in a turned-out and extended line while keeping her working pointe behind her center, qualities that every advanced or professional dancer can work to cultivate. Even if a dancer is not perfectly turned out, she can learn to enhance her arabesque line by releasing the working hip as she lifts her leg while maintaining her placement of the supporting hip, and her torso upright. She can demonstrate life and vitality through the way she lifts her leg and extends the line as the raised leg tries to meet her back. And instead of settling down onto her supporting leg and becoming fixed in the pose, she can seem to grow as she pulls her body up and opens her chest, expanding and extending the line of her arms as she keeps an active gaze out over the wrist and hand.

In almost all arabesques the dancer stands as straight as possible on her supporting hip and leg, with the pointe of the working foot directly behind her spine (see page 126). As usual when the working leg was back, Balanchine wanted it turned out. The dancer must therefore open the working hip to the degree necessary to achieve the desired turned-out line. The working leg is stretched, with the knee straightened and the foot fully pointed. The torso is not inclined forward or tilted to the side; instead, the back is as straight as possible, and the chest is lifted up. The dancer needs to use her abdominal muscles to help support her lower back and upper body. The neck is lengthened and the head is up (the chin is not tucked or thrown back).

The arms are stretched long, but the elbows are not locked or hyperextended; instead, they are very slightly lifted, which softens, lengthens, and enlivens the line. The hands are held palms down, and the fingers of both hands are slightly separated and extended with energy, but they are also not stiff. The index and ring fingers complement and extend the line of the arm, the middle finger is slightly lower, and the little finger is a little higher. The thumb is below the palm and just under it, complementing the line of the middle finger.

Balanchine used four basic arabesques and a couple of variants, but he generally indicated what he wanted mostly by showing, supplemented with a few descriptive words or an illustrative figure of speech. However, what he showed did not always conform to the standard versions I describe here. It is important that the dancer know the standard versions, in part so they serve as a point of reference. Then she can quickly adjust when the line of an arm or leg should be higher or lower, etc. As arabesque is used with different steps and at different tempos; it is adapted to give the required look and to permit the dancer to do the step in the time available.

After a performance of *The Nutcracker*, Mr. B spoke to the Dewdrop who had led "The Waltz of the Flowers." She had a wonderful jump, and she usually danced with great freedom of movement, but that day he said to her, "How do you feel? Are you all right?" She told him she felt fine. "But what happened? You're dancing differently. Nothing is happening. It's dull, *borrring*. It looks, uh . . . calculated, dear." Disappointed, she replied that she had been trying very hard to stretch her legs in all the arabesques and grands jetés en tournant and to place her arms correctly. Perhaps because of her disappointment, she had not noticed that his comment was not about her technique. "No!" he replied. "Don't think, dance." He preferred to see an explosive attack and an energetic, lively approach in keeping with the music of the performance rather than a proper, precise, and contained dance. With "perfect" arabesques.

FIRST ARABESQUE

In first arabesque, with the dancer in profile, the upstage arm is extended to the front, and the downstage leg is extended to the back. The front hand is on the center line of the body, usually only slightly higher than the shoulder line. The other arm is extended diagonally back, about midway between side and back. It harmonizes with or complements the line of the working leg, generally appearing aligned with it. The line of the arms runs from the tips of the fingers of one hand to those of the other.

The fingertips-to-fingertips line is made smooth and continuous by lengthening the shoulder line

Peter in first arabesque

DETAILS I OFTEN INSIST ON IN FIRST ARABESQUE:
1) stand straight on the supporting leg and over the ball of the foot; do not let the hips pull back
2) keep the back as straight as possible, with the chest lifted
3) do not allow a sideways lean off the supporting leg
4) the working foot is directly behind the center line of the body
5) the working hip is open; the working leg is fully turned out and stretched; and the working foot is fully pointed (not sickled down and not winged up)
6) the leading hand is on the center line
7) the back shoulder is down and released; the back arm is not too far to the back
8) the head is erect and lifted slightly up and forward; the chin is not tucked; the eyes are looking out over the wrist and past the middle finger of the leading hand

Peter looking over his wrist and through his hand in first arabesque

somewhat and holding the shoulders down. The dancer must be careful not to pull the trailing arm too far back, nor to lengthen and open her shoulder line so much that it looks like second position. When a dancer combined exaggerated arms pulling the shoulders far out of line with a working hip opened and lifted up more than necessary, we jokingly called the result "à la sebesque."

The head is held erect and the face is directed over and past the wrist and hand, the dancer's eyes looking out a few inches above and beyond the middle finger. "The dancer's head and arm are one piece," Mr. B said to help us understand. The dancer must look as if she really sees something she wants, reaching toward it with her face and gaze as well as with the fingertips of her front hand. Balanchine encouraged us to "look like you are trying to pull yourself forward. You have to follow your hand."

Mr. B often gave us exercises with first arabesque in profile, rather than on the diagonal. That made the dancers more aware of keeping the front hand in front of the nose and the working pointe behind the spine, because the leading arm and the working leg should reach directly toward the sides and feel parallel to the mirror. This "muscle memory" helped keep our pose precise when we practiced on the diagonal and in other directions, or did promenades. For example, if he gave consecutive relevés in first arabesque to make one rotation, he watched to see that we modeled the pose from all angles.

SECOND ARABESQUE

In second arabesque, with the dancer seen in profile, the downstage leg remains extended back as it is in first arabesque, but the rest of the pose is changed.

The downstage arm is extended front, with the hand on the center line of the body, only a bit higher than shoulder level. The upstage arm is angled back, not quite midway between side and back.

The upstage shoulder and the foot extended back should feel related, connected. The chest is lifted and projected up and forward, while the back is held as straight as possible and the upper back is slightly arched.

The head slants gently to the downstage side, and the gaze is directed over and beyond the hand. An alternative look can be achieved by slanting the head more strongly and turning the head so the gaze is directed over the arm and out to the side.

Peter in second arabesque

DETAILS I OFTEN INSIST ON IN SECOND ARABESQUE:
1) the first six points applicable to first arabesque also apply
2) feel the relationship of the working foot to the opposite shoulder
3) slant the head to the side of the leading arm

Dana in third arabesque

THIRD ARABESQUE

In third arabesque the dancer is in virtually the same pose as in second arabesque, but it looks completely different for three reasons. She has turned from full profile to a diagonal line, approximately a three-quarters view. By making her upstage leg the working leg, she has changed from the open line to a crossed line. The only real difference in her pose is that the head is now held straight and the dancer looks out over her wrist and past her front hand.

The dancer's chest and shoulders are fully visible in the croisé line. The chest should be open, and the dancer should make a long and smooth line through the arms and shoulders. However, the downstage arm is only slightly behind second position.

DETAILS I OFTEN INSIST ON IN
THIRD ARABESQUE:
1) points 1–8 for first arabesque and point 2 for second arabesque all apply
2) downstage arm only slightly behind

DETAILS I OFTEN INSIST ON IN
FOURTH ARABESQUE:
1) points 1–6 for first arabesque
2) an extended shoulder line to show the back
3) the head slanted over the front arm and shoulder

FOURTH ARABESQUE

In fourth arabesque the dancer is in the same croisé that is used in third arabesque, but again the pose looks entirely different. The downstage arm is front; the upstage arm is back; and the torso is rotated, yet still held up.

The front (downstage) arm is lifted slightly above the shoulder line, and the back arm is slightly below. The shoulder line is now very long and extended, with the shoulders down. The dancer tries to show her back to the audience, giving the impression of a continuous line from the fingertips of the front hand through the shoulders to the fingertips of the back hand. But she should not let the lengthening of her shoulder line through her back cause her to lean sideways, off the supporting leg, or cause her back shoulder to creep up.

The head slants gracefully but strongly to the side of the forward arm and toward that shoulder and turns just slightly to that side, directing the gaze out a bit to the side and toward the audience.

Dana in fourth arabesque

ARABESQUE VARIANTS

In many ballets Mr. Balanchine used a first arabesque line with effacé arms. It is often seen in sauté as well as with piqué. We also practiced this line in class, both on the diagonal in effacé and facing side (in profile to the audience). The dancer, when seen in profile, is standing on her upstage leg, with the downstage leg extended in arabesque. Her downstage arm is raised in fifth high, and her upstage arm is in second position; her head is tilted back as her cheek is brought forward, and her gaze is directed in front of and past her arm—in short, a standard effacé back for the head and arms. Another more traditional variant called for the dancer to extend the arm in fifth high, stretching the elbow, wrist, and fingers and turning the forearm so the hand finishes palm down. The head is in basically the same standard effacé line, but now the gaze is directed up, over and beyond the back of the hand. The arm in second also extends, the forearm turning the hand palm down. The feeling and the look are that the arm is slightly behind second. The chest is open and expanded and there is an even stronger connection between the upstage shoulder and the pointe of the working foot. The resulting pose could be called "arabesque effacée allongée," although, as I have noted, Mr. B generally indicated what he wanted more by showing and gesturing than by naming.

The arabesque effacée allongée pose is commonly seen in Russian schools, but with some dif-

Dana in arabesque effacée allongée on the diagonal

Dana in arabesque effacée on the diagonal

ferences. In those schools the head and upper torso tend to tilt forward, but Mr. B wanted the head to retain the effacé back line and the torso to be held as fully erect as possible.

In these variants, as in all the standard arabesques, the dancer must be careful to observe certain details. The working leg is fully stretched, even though the arms are in effacé; the common tendency is to want to make attitude. The chest is lifted and projected forward, and the back is held upright; the dancer must resist the tendency to tilt forward. She must also maintain her weight over the ball of the supporting foot; her hips must not pull back toward the heel, nor can she allow herself to twist her shoulder line and lean to the side. The tendency is to let the upstage shoulder and its arm in second come forward, away from the lifted leg.

ARABESQUE PENCHÉE

The technique for arabesque penchée presented on page 127 was used, with some additional emphasis, for the more numerous penché exercises in the center. The dancer must be careful to maintain the relationship of the working leg to the back; that relationship is based on the feeling that the working leg is reaching to meet the back, so the angle between them should remain the same or get smaller as the dancer penchés. The working foot must remain on the center line of the body as it is raised. The weight remains centered over the ball of the foot, rather than settled back toward the heel, and the hip is aligned over the supporting leg; also, the dancer does not lean off to one side or the other. It

is probably best for the dancer to think of penché as a movement down to come up, rather than as a slow-moving balancing act.

If the arms are in first arabesque, the front arm must remain on the center line of the body, and the

---

DETAILS I OFTEN INSIST ON IN
ARABESQUE PENCHÉE:
1) don't pull back in the hips, and don't let the weight settle on the heel
2) lift the leg to the back and keep the connection (no ironing board)
3) don't lean sideways off the supporting leg
4) the hand of the front arm and the working foot are on the center line of the body

---

Peter and Dana in arabesque penchée

back arm must complement the line of the working leg as the leg is raised. Both arms should have life and use a little flex in the elbows and a bit more in the wrists as the dancer moves down to penché and then back up to arabesque.

ARABESQUES IN PLIÉ

Mr. B gave us many exercises in arabesque using deep, low pliés. They help build strength, as other deep one-legged pliés do, but they also let the dancer practice maintaining energy and vitality. This is important, because so many combinations incorporate landings in arabesque. In many schools

Peter in first arabesque on a straight supporting leg and in plié

the dancer tips the body forward and lifts the working leg higher as she does a shallow, timid plié. Mr. B wanted the reverse: a deep, juicy plié, at times so low that the heel released, done in the knee and ankle, with an actively used thigh. Balanchine often asked for more, especially plié. "Americans know what more is!" The torso is held, lifted up as much as when the supporting knee is stretched. The entire shape is unchanged as the dancer pliés and straightens; the angle of the back and the working leg remain the same. The dancer should, if anything, feel that this angle becomes smaller, because of her constant effort to lift her leg against her strongly held back as she pliés. The weight remains over the ball of the supporting foot; the hips are not pulled back.

On occasion we did exercises including promenade in first arabesque in plié. This is quite difficult, but it certainly builds strength in the thighs.

DETAILS I OFTEN INSIST ON IN ARABESQUES IN PLIÉ:
1) no tipping forward; weight over the ball of the foot (not back on the heel)
2) the supporting knee makes the plié
3) plié as deeply as time allows

ATTITUDE

The principles of front and back attitude discussed on page 129 apply to the center as well. Working without the barre, the dancer will need to be careful to maintain certain elements of good form especially important to Balanchine. We almost always practiced attitude in croisé or effacé or doing a promenade; we never practiced it en face with the head and gaze straight front, nor did we practice attitude back with the knee "dropped" and the foot raised, as in some versions of attitude effacée alongée.

In attitude back the dancer must stand as straight

DETAILS I OFTEN INSIST ON IN ATTITUDE:
1) body as straight as possible; don't lean sideways
2) in attitude croisée and effacée, curve neck and slant head; fingertips of the upraised hand over the center line of the head
3) in attitude effacée back, knee bent to form a ninety-degree angle and thigh raised to hip level

Peter in attitude effacée back

Deanna in attitude croisée front

Deanna in attitude croisée back

de jambe ending in attitude) in which the dancer really does bend the torso.

In attitude front, the basic position of the legs is the same as it is at the barre: supporting leg straight,

Peter in attitude effacée front

as possible on the supporting hip, releasing the working hip only as much as necessary to allow her to raise the working thigh to about ninety degrees, with the knee lifted up and behind her center. By strongly using her abdominal muscles, she supports her back, helping her torso to remain straight, tipping neither forward nor back, nor leaning to either side; the shoulders are level and square. The dancer must establish this standard form because it is frequently used, as well as being important as a point of reference in certain steps (e.g., renversé, grand rond working thigh in front of the working hip, knee bent a little less than ninety degrees, with the lower leg and heel lifted up. The hips and shoulders are square, and the back is straight.

PRACTICING PORT DE BRAS, ÉPAULEMENT, DIRECTIONS, ARABESQUE, AND ATTITUDE

Classes with Mr. Balanchine often included some center exercises done mostly in place, integrating port de bras, épaulement, directions, arabesque, and attitude. It was equally possible that we would not work on this material at all; it depended entirely on what he had seen, on what he thought we needed the most, and on how much time we had.

The purpose of these exercises was to cultivate the quality of movement needed for the ballets. Balanchine worked to make this part of the technique "automatic" in us so it was there when we went on in class to pointe work, to jumps, to turns, when we did combinations that moved across the floor, and in rehearsal. It should then be completely ours when we really danced in performance. Remember, "Don't think, dance!" He had no interest in our memorization of terms and numbering schemes or in seeing us in perfect poses and static positions. And he did not use his class time to give us a stretch, or incorporate little "breaks" in the form of easy exercises. When he felt we needed a break, he amused us with a story, one that made a point relevant to the exercise of the moment and often to life in general.

To achieve the result Mr. B wanted, we sometimes had to practice with exaggeration. That does not mean distorting or completely losing the form, but it does mean working with maximum awareness and energy to perform each movement at the extremes of the possible. For example, the dancer has an elbow, a wrist, and fingers that move. So when she moves her arms, practicing to the maximum, she must bend her elbows a lot, as much as they will bend, flex her wrists, curve and stretch her fingers. She must make her elbows, wrists, hands, and fingers come alive. Once a dancer knows where her maximum is, she can always cut back to less, even to the minimum. And if she is used to working at her maximum in class, a moderate amount, when needed in performance, will seem easy.

The valse lente exercise on page 216 is an example of practicing with exaggeration. An exercise of this kind is designed to let the dancer explore her limits in several ways—in this case, her strength, range of movement, flexibility, and musicality, among others. However, Mr. B would not have accepted the result, even if it was in some ways wonderful, if, let us say, she forgot, or seemed to forget, how to place her foot on the floor or crept into a movement or let her leg turn in. The teacher must help each dancer find her ways to be beautiful, but within the aesthetic that guides them both.

Mr. B also wanted us to work in class for maximum clarity and precision, and this also demands maximum energy and awareness. Most of the movements I have discussed in this chapter lose their specific quality if the dancer does not adhere consistently to certain details. Generally these involve being on time, precise knowledge of the directions of the dancer's body and of her orientation to the front. So when the hand or foot or fingertips are supposed to be on the center line of the body, they should be there. Clean fifth positions of the feet at the barre, clear croisé in the center.

The tendu exercises with which I begin, because tendus were such a major part of our work with Mr. B, are an example of practicing to achieve maximum clarity and precision. They allow the dancer to confirm her precise muscle memory of how to move and where she is supposed to arrive, as well as her ability to coordinate her arms with the rest of the movement, and the entire movement with the music. And yet Mr. B would not have been pleased with the most "perfect" fifths and tendus anyone had ever seen if we were working like robots, without an evident sense of life and pleasure in what we were doing. The teacher must keep alive the ideal of beauty, no matter how close to a drill an exercise might need to be.

Mr. Balanchine therefore watched to see that, in exercises such as the ones that follow, we were clear and precise when that was needed and that we tried for the more exaggerated or extreme form when he wanted to see, and wanted us to feel, how much we could do. I remember feeling like a "Pushmi-Pullyu," yo-yoing back and forth between trying to push myself to dance beyond my limits, dancing in the extremes of bigger, faster, lower, smaller, higher, slower, and trying to pull myself back to ideal clarity, precision, elegance, articulation; always in time. Where to strike the balance? How to do both at the same time? The effort alone changes the dancing. The dancer has a wider range of articulate movement from which to choose. In any given ballet, or part of a ballet, the choreography may call for a little more "pull" and a little less "push." Or the reverse. Sort of like salt and pepper, rosemary and basil. In performance the dancer must know how to give the right amount of each "flavor." She has the choice. Remember, "Dancer must be intelligent." But in class she goes for the appropriate maximum in each exercise. "More, I want to see more! Nothing is happening!" was one of Mr. B's most frequent reactions as we did an exercise. And just when a dancer thought she had it, Mr. B asked again for more.

Mr. B used to say that dancers were the only people who could "have their cake and eat it, too." His remark was obscure to me then, but now I think he meant that dancers are people who can learn to do it all, and enjoy it. And then, do more, still enjoying it. If they can, then they certainly should.

In discussing the barre exercises, I often note that Mr. B wanted the dancers to present or serve the working foot to the audience. Even in those most basic movements, he wanted us to cultivate an

Peter trying to serve a cup of coffee from his heel as he presents his foot

awareness that the end result is performance, even though class is not itself a performance. When we practiced port de bras, épaulement, directions, arabesque, and attitude, he wanted that awareness to continue. The dancer sometimes presents herself: *Me voici!* Sometimes bringing a little surprise: *Et voilà!* "We are entertainers."

One means by which the dancer enhances the sense she is presenting or serving a movement is to "go away to arrive." If the dancer starts, for example, in croisé in fifth position, right foot front, and (as in temps lié) steps directly forward into croisé ending in tendu back, only moving the arms in a somewhat traditional way directly from fifth low to the croisé line, not moving or changing her upper body, there is a pretty, contained, "polite," little movement for the audience to see. But if the dancer, starting in the same position, opens her arms gently to the side with a preparatory breath, and then switches her head to the opposite side (slant), and inclines her torso to the left, meanwhile bringing her arms through fifth low to an over-crossed first; steps forward into croisé tendu back, the movement is much fuller, much more interesting visually for the audience. If, in addition, the music allows her time to take a really "juicy" plié and a really big step forward, the effect will be even greater.

Dancers are generally taught to make some use of this idea, but Mr. Balanchine was very consistent, very systematic, in making it part of movement from one direction or place or pose to another. He also wanted the movement *away* to be generally as large in scale as the movement *to*. A halfhearted "mini" gesture away would not do. In discussing specific elements of the technique, and in the exercises that follow, I have indicated many points at which the dancer should make a movement away to enhance the legibility of the next movement. When trying to do a movement not specifically described here in his way, it is generally better to use a little more "going away to arrive" rather than less.

The dancer also achieves the sense that something has been presented to the audience, that something has happened, by putting the movement in time. This is done partly by staying on the music overall, but, just as important, it is done by phrasing throughout a combination. Many indications of phrasing are included in the discussions of the individual steps and movements, but it is most important to understand Mr. B's underlying idea on this and to apply it. Each segment (i.e., the start and each change in direction) in an exercise in class

must have a clear beginning, generally announced by starting with a little extra energy or accent that gives a smooth but quick start. This is followed by a slight slowing on arriving in the next position. Through her phrasing the dancer should distinctly feel each beginning and ending in her own body and, if she feels them, it is more likely the audience will see them, and thus see each of the steps.

I think Mr. B valued good beginnings and good endings in large scale and small. It was an important part of making a ballet; of choreographing a dance; and, as his emphasis on phrasing shows, of dancing each phrase. He even told us half seriously that the audience sees only the beginning and the end. What happens in the middle, they may somehow forget. He applied the idea down to the smallest scale.

At very fast tempos and when doing very small movements, achieving instantaneous yet smooth starts and stops and gauging the correct amount of slowing take a great deal of practice, patience, and passion for this work. So the dancer must work at it very regularly all through class. Very small movements require practice at a wide range of tempos. The required quality of arm and hand movement is important and not easy to achieve; in this way it is like proper placement of the foot to the floor and into fifth position (no banging or slapping, etc.).

Peter going away from fifth position croisé to arrive in tendu back croisé

Also, correct phrasing is, like maximum movement and maximum precision, more difficult to maintain as part of a step or combination, so the dancer needs to try to perfect it and make it her own in these relatively stationary exercises. Finally, the dancer must remember that in class Mr. B never liked to see a dancer creep into a movement. So, when in doubt, the dancer makes extra sure she shows a clear start, and she phrases very fully; once the skill is mastered, she can always do less.

In the exercises that follow I assume that the reader is familiar in detail with the technique discussed in Barre Work and to this point in this chapter, so there are no more page references to material already covered. However, achievement of the quality of movement Mr. B wanted is not possible unless that material is thoroughly understood. The essentials are not in the larger combinations; they are in the details taught at the barre and in the smaller center exercises described earlier in this chapter. The dancer's aim must be to incorporate the details in the way she dances the bigger, traveling movements and combinations. The truth of this statement is shown, among other ways, by the frequency with which Mr. B gave very fundamental exercises in company class and by the care with which he corrected them.

Sometimes we did an exercise and didn't remember, or were not yet skillful enough, to apply all of Mr. B's suggestions or corrections. He then typically came up with an exercise that concentrated on a particular detail. The exercise I described for the head and neck ("ask for a kiss," see page 172) is an example of that approach and might very well be given if we did not show him the correct line of the head and neck, my first detail to insist on. The correction and/or the supplemental exercise might have revealed details the dancer needed to help herself remember, so she could work on them effectively outside of class. This was the reason he suggested we carry that little black book, to make our own personal notes of the general corrections he gave, and above all, when he gave one of us an individual correction.

My intermediate and advanced training was at the school of the San Francisco Ballet, where I began to dance professionally. When I joined the New York City Ballet I began daily company class with Balanchine. I felt that I had to make up for all I had missed by not going through his School of American Ballet, so my black book got very full. Of course, I wrote down my own personal corrections. I also wrote down the corrections he gave other dancers. And I even wrote down Mr. B's statements on steps and exercises and dance in general and anything else I could get in my book. Mr. Balanchine said, "You must be hungry." I was.

TENDU BATTEMENT

(Four typical exercises with various head and arm positions and orientations)

Tendu battement was often Mr. B's choice of movement to use with basic ports de bras, because tendu is the most important path in and out of fifth position and needs constant honing. More skill is required to do tendu in the center than at the barre, partly because the dancer no longer has it for support and partly because she must correctly coordinate her arms and her head with her feet and her legs. As I will indicate, these sequences can also be used quite well with other movements.

First Tendu Battement Exercise

This exercise is tendu to the front in croisé, en face, and in effacé with linking ports de bras. The dancer starts in fifth position croisé with the arms in fifth low. On count one of the preparation, she slants her head and gently inclines her body away, slightly lowering her gaze to look toward her hands, which have arrived in first (this is a third method for moving the arms from fifth low to first). On count two of the preparation, she returns her head and body to the standard croisé line as she establishes croisé with her arms. This preparation uses "going away to arrive" in the torso, head, and arms. The tempo is set by the teacher in the timing of the "one-two" of the preparation. Already standing in fifth position, the dancer is now actively alert: chest lifted, body pulled up, weight over the balls of her feet, fully energized. The two-count preparation gets her set to move in time and to start on time: out on the "and," in on the count.

The dancer does two tendu battments to the front in standard croisé; two tendu battements to the front in croisé looking under her downstage arm; two tendu battements front en face with the arms in fifth high and two more with the arms in second; two tendu battements front in standard effacé; two tendu battements front in the effacé variant with reversed arms; and four tendus to the side with the same leg, with the body remaining on the diagonal and with the arms in second, ending with the working foot closing fifth back, the head and body inclining away from the front, and the arms ending in fifth low. The dancer is now ready to repeat the exercise on the other side.

After the first set of two tendus in each orientation, there is a port de bras and a new line for the neck and head; after the second set of two tendus, there is a new orientation to the front. The dancer must phrase each tendu so she coordinates it with the rest of the movement, her arms and head arriving in the new line on the "and" as she points her foot the first time in each set. The effect is that she changes her orientation at the beginning of the tendu, not on the closing of the previous one. This principle also applies when she changes arms while keeping the same direction. Mr. B said, "It's the hands and arms that give force and strength and indicate direction."

As I noted in describing the uses of the head, eyes, and face, they also participate as the dancer moves. The head, eyes, and face will follow the moving hand (or precede it) or change level to complement the port de bras and announce the new position. Or they may look away from the final line to make the change more legible, a small "going away to arrive." For example, in this exercise, after the dancer has completed the first tendu battements in the standard croisé line, she lowers the downstage arm from second position to fifth low as her head gently lowers, her eyes looking toward the back of her hand. The overhead (upstage) arm moves to second simultaneously. As she lifts the arm from fifth low to fifth high, she raises her head, in coordination with her hand to look under the arm. After two tendus in this croisé variant she lowers the upstage arm from second to fifth low, and again her head and eyes lower slightly in coordination with that arm. As the dancer lifts the arm to fifth high, she raises her head, following her hand with her eyes; as it matches the other one in fifth high, the dancer raises her head a little higher than level to complement her arms in fifth high. The dancer changes from croisé to en face on the beginning of the tendu front, not on the closing of the last tendu in croisé. After two tendu battements en face with the arms in fifth high, the arms move up and out to open to second position. As the arms start to open to second, the dancer takes a breath, and the head lifts gently up to complement the arm movement, then lowers almost to level while the arms make second. After two tendus en face with the arms in second, both arms come down to fifth low; the head and eyes lower to follow the hands. The arms, head, and upper torso move to the standard effacé line at the start of the first tendu in effacé front (on the "and") and remain there for the two tendus in effacé, the head and gaze lifting as the arm is raised to fifth high. Then the dancer switches the arms to the effacé front variant. As the downstage arm that was in fifth high opens to second, the upstage arm that was in second moves to fifth low, and the head and eyes also lower slightly. As this arm then moves to fifth high, the head resumes the effacé line for the two tendu battements. As the upstage arm opens up and out, the head gently rises and then levels, looking toward the downstage arm as the upstage arm arrives in second on the "and" for the four tendus to the side. As the working foot closes to fifth from the last tendu to the side, the dancer looks away and down as she closes her arms to fifth low. She is now ready to begin the other side.

In describing the barre exercises I identify the specific details of leg and foot action Mr. B wanted, and in this chapter I identify comparable details for head and arm movement. To achieve the result he wanted it is necessary to incorporate them as fully as possible. For example, movements up of the arms and head are sometimes preceded and accompanied by taking a little breath; when the arms change position, there is usually articulation of the elbow and wrist as the hands move through the air; the fingers, resisting the air, generally straighten slightly or become more curved before returning to their more standard shape as they stop; the head and eyes nearly always move together; and, the complete action should look coordinated, calm, and pleasant. Generally, the faster the exercise, the closer the arms move to the body (and the more the elbows bend), and the movements of the head sometimes become somewhat subtler. The reverse also applies: When the tempo and the movements become slower, the head and arms move bigger. At any speed Mr. B wanted maximum, but appropriate, participation of the whole body in the dance, not just wonderful feet and legs.

These principles apply to almost all port de bras exercises. Although I am not writing them out so fully in all the exercises that follow, the teacher must keep them in mind as she sets each exercise and, more importantly, apply them as she corrects. When in doubt, she should ask for a little more— use of the elbow, slanting the head, and so on—and see what happens, rather than settle right away for less. If the dancers do too much, the teacher can always ask for less, once she has made them aware of how much more their maximum is. In that way the teacher will be closer to the spirit of what Balanchine did.

It is generally good practice to reverse combinations whenever possible. On occasion Mr. B carried this idea one step farther. Without warning he could say, "Let's see it to the back!" And we would do the whole sequence to the back without his having worked it out for us or given us time to work it out for ourselves. That would probably not be a good idea in earlier stages of training. For advanced and professional dancers it is one way to keep their minds alert. It also forces them to dance without calculation. "Don't think, dear, do."

It is typical of Mr. B that this exercise is based on only a few elements of the technique. This allows

---

DETAILS I OFTEN INSIST ON IN TENDU BATTEMENT WITH PORT DE BRAS:

1) the head is properly slanted in croisé and effacé; the arms arrive quickly and on time
2) the fingertips of the hand in fifth high are over the center line of the head
3) show precise directions from the dancer's own body
4) be aware of the arm in second position and keep it alive; don't let it wander back or forward
5) bend the elbows when moving the arms, especially when lifting them up
6) keep the timing and accents of the tendu battements clear and precise; as at the barre, be sure to show each fifth, placing the foot into fifth and to the floor when the tempo permits
7) maintain the weight over the ball of the supporting foot
8) no weight on the working foot when pointed in tendu
9) no shift of weight to the working foot in tendu or when the foot is placed to the floor in fifth position, unless changing to the other leg to start the other side (or for some other reason)
10) show fully crossed, tight fifth positions
11) change from croisé to en face, en face to effacé, etc., at the beginning of the tendu, not on the closing of the last one

the dancer to concentrate on perfecting just those. Its simplicity helps to reinforce her sense of croisé, en face, and effacé. It makes concrete the idea that the relationship of one leg to the other is the same in these three orientations of the body.

Second Tendu Battement Exercise

This exercise is tendu front and back in croisé, en face, and in effacé, with weight changes and linking ports de bras. The dancer again begins in fifth position croisé with the arms in fifth low. After the same preparation, the dancer does two tendu battements in croisé front with the standard croisé arms; two tendu battements in croisé back in the croisé variant looking under her arm; two tendu battements front en face with the arms in fifth high; two tendu battements back en face with the arms in second; two tendu battements in effacé front with effacé arms; two tendu battements in effacé back with the variant arms for effacé; and four tendus to the side, keeping her body on the diagonal and the arms in second, again finishing back with the head inclined away and the arms in fifth low. The dancer is now ready to do the other side.

This exercise is very close in kind to the first one, differing mainly in that it changes the weight from one leg to the other. The dancer must ensure that she transfers weight only when the working leg becomes the supporting leg and that she does so cleanly and inconspicuously, centering her weight over the ball of the supporting foot. The details I insist on for the first exercise are therefore applicable to this one and to the next.

Third Tendu Battement Exercise

This exercise is two tendus in all directions, the working leg moving around the circle like the hands on a clock. The dancer is again in fifth position croisé, with the arms in fifth low. After the same preparation, the dancer does two tendu batte-

ments front in standard croisé; two tendu battements front en face with the arms in fifth high; two tendu battements front in effacé with standard arms; two tendu battements in écarté front; two tendu battements side en face with arms in second; two tendu battements in écarté back; two tendu battements back in effacé; two tendu battements back en face with arms in fifth high; and two tendu battements back in croisé.

This exercise takes eighteen counts. The common response is to tack on the fourteen counts of movement required to complete the phrase, but this risks introducing unrelated material or pointlessly extending the exercise. Particularly when working with dancers new to Balanchine's aesthetic, it may be preferable to employ one of his tactics, stop the music at this point, and start again on the other side. It is better to do a shorter exercise very well than a longer one with mistakes, he thought. An alternative is to eliminate the last two tendus to croisé back and start croisé front on the other side. This is what Madame Antonina Tumkovsky, my colleague at SAB, does. She gives two tendus front in croisé; two to the front en face; two front in effacé; two in écarté front; two to the side; two in écarté back; two in effacé back; and two to the back en face. The dancers now do the other side and then repeat the combination starting to the back.

The teacher might wish to fill out the original exercise in a way that recalls Mr. B's approach and uses thirty-two counts. In this case the expanded sequence could go like this. The dancer is once again in fifth position croisé, with the arms in fifth low. After the preparation in which the dancer moves her arms to first on count one and to croisé on count two, she does two tendu battements front in standard croisé; two more tendu battements front in the croisé variant looking under the arm; two tendu battements front en face with the arms in fifth high; two more tendus front en face with the arms in second; two tendu battements effacé front with standard arms; two more tendus front in the effacé variant with opposite arms; two tendu battements in écarté front; two tendu battements side en face with arms in second; two tendu battements in écarté back; two tendu battements back in effacé; two more tendu battements back in the effacé with variant arms; two tendu battements back en face with arms in fifth high; two more tendu battements back en face with the arms in second; two tendu battements back in standard croisé; and two more tendu battements back in the croisé variant looking under the arm. This makes a total of thirty counts, which will leave two counts in which the dancer can move the arm in fifth high to join the other in second position on the first and then port de bras to fifth low on the second. Now she is set for the other side, her arms moving to croisé as she tendus out on the "and" before count one.

These sequences work equally well with jeté battement or grand battement and should be given with both of them. And there are many other variations on these sequences using tendu battement, jeté battement, and grand battement alone and in combination. Teachers should think of them (and, for that matter, of all the exercises in this book) as starting points for further exploration. Just remember: not too long, not needlessly complicated; focus on only a few elements of the technique at a time.

Fourth Tendu Battement Exercise

This exercise is tendu battements turning to face each side of the room. The dancer is in fifth position croisé and does a two-count preparation, bringing the head and arms to standard croisé, and does two tendu battements to the front and two to the back in croisé; two tendu battements to the front and two to the back en face; and two tendu battements to the front and two to the back in effacé. See page 192 for changes in épaulement and the ports de bras during this exercise.

At this point the dancer is in effacé when seen from the original front, but she is also in croisé when seen from the adjacent sidewall, if she slants her head to the opposite side and switches the arm in fifth high. Mr. Balanchine reinforced his lesson

about the relatedness of croisé and effacé by having us repeat the same sequence using the sidewall as front, which brings the dancer to face the back of the room. We then repeated it twice more, bringing us once again to face front.

This combination should be repeated on the other side, but the wrong foot is front. The teacher can stop the music in the middle of the phrase, have the dancers switch feet and change épaulement, or she may want to add a simple step that will change feet and also fill out the musical phrase.

TENDU BATTEMENT WITH "SMALL ARMS" PORT DE BRAS

Mr. B liked to give exercises that included using the "small arms" port de bras—for example, four tendu battements front in croisé, four front en face, and four front in effacé, finishing with "tombé," pas de bourrée traveling forward on the diagonal (see page 202) concerning placement of the foot to the floor when traveling; also see page 241 and page 283 concerning the "tombé" pas de bourrée). The tendus are done as usual with the working foot pointing on the "and," then closing to fifth on the beat or count. During each set of four tendu battements the dancer completes a "small arms" port de bras.

The dancer begins in fifth position croisé with the arms down. On the two-count preparation, which, as I have said, establishes the tempo, the dancer can open her arms slightly to the side on count one and close on count two, or she can do a small arms preparation closing on two. In either case, on count two of the preparation her wrists turn her palms in to her body as her hands close to fifth low and as her head starts to turn away and she looks down. On the "and" before count one, as her working foot points, her hands, which have come together on the center line of the body, are drawn up, with her palms facing her body as her elbows lift gently to the side. On count one, as she closes the working foot to fifth, her hands and arms continue to lift a little more as her head slightly lifts. On the "and" before count two the palms turn up (forward) and start to move front as her head starts to turn and slant toward croisé. On the two and the "and" her hands continue opening toward the side. On count three her arms are open almost side but are still in front of her with the palms up; her head is in croisé. On the "and" before count four the backs of the wrists lift slightly to make a small arc to turn the palms over in order to close; her head lifts slightly before lowering. On count four the dancer turns her head away and looks down again as her hands reach fifth low. Although the foot stops in fifth position after each tendu battement, the movement of the arms is continuous. In other words, she does one small arms port de bras for each set of four tendu battements. On the "and" before the next count one, as the foot points, the dancer turns en face and does the port de bras and head movements as described in the basic small arms exercise, but while doing the four tendu battements. On the tendu front of the third set the dancer turns to effacé; the gaze is directed down, and the head is slanted toward the downstage shoulder—the dancer does not "look away in order to arrive" in effacé as she does in croisé. As she does the first three tendus in effacé, her arms lift and open toward second and her head moves in to effacé. On the "and" before count four (tendu out to point) her head lifts slightly up, then on count four she closes the working foot to fifth as she makes demi-plié and lowers her hands to fifth low with her head and eyes following. On the "and" before count one she does a small développé in effacé front as the supporting leg quickly stretches; the

head starts to move up to assume the standard effacé front line; and the hands, which have closed to the center, lift up to start one more small arms port de bras. Continuing without pause, the dancer quickly pliés on the supporting leg and lowers the développé leg to the floor to transfer her weight to it in effacé on count one, as the arms open forward and toward the side. The plié and transfer are referred to colloquially as "tombé," although it is not a true tombé (see page 241). On the "and" before count two the dancer does pas de bourrée forward (see page 283), finishing in sous-sus (see page 234) as the wrists lift to rotate the palms down. On count two the dancer does demi-plié as her hands close to fifth low and her head turns away, the gaze lowering to follow the hands. On count three the dancer straightens her legs, and her head returns to the croisé line as her arms open to small second. On count four her hands close toward fifth low, and her head lowers. She is now ready for the other side. Mr. B also gave this exercise in reverse.

This exercise was usually given first at a moderate tempo and perhaps repeated at a slightly brisker one. It is also very good at an even faster tempo, substituting jeté battement for tendu battement. Mr. B also liked to give small arms with quick allegro jumping steps and small, fast pointe steps. This port de bras with detailed use of wrists and hands led Mr. B to say, "Like Spanish dancer. Spanish people are fantastic dancers, because they have beautiful hands." When the tempo is faster the timing of the pas de bourrée could be développé on count one, tombé on count two, pas de bourrée ending in sous-sus on count three, plié on count four. In fast combinations of this kind, small arms ports de bras are very useful. As Mr. B would have said, they're "handy" hands.

DETAILS I OFTEN INSIST ON IN TENDU BATTEMENT WITH "SMALL ARMS":

1) when the tempo allows, make a clear stop in fifth after each tendu battement

2) maintain continuous movement of the arms (see also page 165)

GRAND BATTEMENT

(With crossed wrists to the front)

We often practiced grand battement in the center. When working without the support of the barre, more strength and control are required from the dancer to remain on the supporting leg as the working leg is energetically thrown up and brought down and placed into fifth. We did a variety of grand battement exercises, but I particularly liked this kind. Doing an exercise in class with the arms extended to the front and with crossed wrists, a position used in ballets but not usually practiced in class, really intrigued me.

The dancer again starts in croisé, with the arms in fifth low, and prepares by moving her head and arms to standard croisé. She does one grand battement croisé front with standard croisé arms; one grand battement croisé front with third arabesque arms; and one grand battement croisé front, crossing the wrists in front. She does this by bringing the back arm up and over to meet the arm in front. In each case the arms arrive in position on the "and" as the working foot is thrown up in the extended line.

If the music is in four, the teacher can give another grand battement croisé front, this time with the arms in fifth high, and perhaps a pas de basque ending in tendu back, close fifth, and repeat on the other side. If the music is in three, the teacher can follow the three grands battements with a passé on count one, bringing the working foot to fourth back on counts two-three, two pirouettes en dehors (see page 269), finishing in fourth back on count two, hold count three, then tendu back on count one, close to fifth on count two and arms to croisé on count three, and start the step to the other side. Balanchine regularly gave the same step to different music or to the same music, but at a different tempo, to help us develop mental agility and physical skill as well as musical awareness, and I try to follow his example in this.

GRAND BATTEMENT ENDING WITH PLIÉ

Mr. B also liked to give grand battement exercises that ended with the working leg extended in the air and the supporting leg in a deep plié.

First exercise: The dancer starts in fifth position croisé with the arms in fifth low. She does a two-count preparation, bringing the head and arms to standard croisé, and does two grand battements croisé front. As she does the next grand battement, she changes to en face, lowering her upraised arm to second as her working foot reaches the extended line and does a second grand battement en face. As she does the next grand battement, she changes to effacé (using "all two arms") and then does a second grand battement in effacé. Next she does a third grand battement in effacé, this time brushing through first position to third arabesque and ending in a deep plié, BAM! The arms do a port de bras from effacé to third arabesque line and arrive there as the working leg extends in arabesque. This happens on count seven; she holds count eight. On the next two counts she slowly straightens her supporting leg as she assumes attitude croisée back; then she promenades en dedans a quarter circle for two counts to attitude effacée back. On count five she makes a deep plié as she extends her leg into arabesque effacée allongée while continuing to hold her back up. On the "and" before count six she does pas de bourrée with one extra step (see page 283) to end with the other foot front and moves her arms to second, finishing on count six. On count seven she makes demi-plié in fifth position croisé, moving her arms to fifth low, and turning her head away and lowering her gaze to follow her hands. On count eight she straightens her legs as she brings her arms and head into the standard croisé line. The combination of the explosive throw of the working leg up from the floor to the front and its equally rapid brush through first to third arabesque in a deep plié make this step an ex-

DETAILS I OFTEN INSIST ON IN
GRAND BATTEMENT ENDING WITH
PLIÉ:

1) the deep plié is in the knee and controlled
by an active thigh; don't tilt the body
forward or lean back or throw the head
back

2) arrive instantly—"BANG!"—in the third
arabesque

3) the hips stay up and over the ball of the
supporting foot in arabesque; don't let the
hips pull back

4) maintain the turnout in the supporting leg
and foot while moving rapidly into plié

5) the front hand and working foot are both
on the center line of the body in
arabesque

6) the eyes focus out, over, and beyond the
front hand

7) the leg is thrown up on the "and"; the
dancer arrives in arabesque pliée (or fifth
position) on the count

cellent exercise to build strength and control. The
dancer needs to hold the arabesque without letting
the working leg bounce or jiggle when it stops,
without letting the supporting leg and foot wobble
or turn in.

Second exercise: The dancer starts in fifth position en face with the arms in fifth low and does a
two-count preparation, opening the arms to second. She does four grand battements side, closing
fifth back to change legs each time. After the fifth
grand battement side she brushes directly through
first to end in arabesque pliée on the diagonal as
the arms move from second position to third
arabesque. Everything happens "BANG!" After
establishing the pose on count five, she holds count
six. She straightens the supporting leg on count
seven and the working leg can remain in arabesque
or can lower to tendu back. On count eight she

closes the working foot to fifth position and comes
en face as she moves her arms to second. She is now
ready for the other side.

This exercise is even more difficult to control because it is harder to throw the leg to arabesque from
à la seconde than it is from the front, but Mr. B
watched us in both of them to see there was no loss
of good form as the dancers ended the movement
quickly and cleanly in a deep, low plié.

GRAND PORT DE BRAS

This is an especially good example of an exercise
that can easily turn into the "health" Mr. B said he
did not teach. Grand port de bras was not therapy, a
stretch to relax the muscles and destress the mind.
He made sure it remained artistic by insisting it be
truly *grand* and beautiful and that we did it on the
music with appropriate phrasing.

The dancer starts with the right foot in tendu
croisé back with standard croisé arms. She begins
with a breath and a little lift in the upper body and
in the arms. She very slightly rotates her torso
toward the left downstage corner, pliés on her front
(left) leg, and bends her back leg as she begins to
bend and reach toward the corner (midway between forward and side). The turn of her upper
body to the downstage corner means that her bend
is not straight forward and down but also to the
side. She leads with the elbow of the upraised
(right) arm, bringing her hand across the center
line of her body, back and side of the wrist and
hand leading, fingers slightly trailing, as she pliés
on the supporting leg and continues to bend forward. The left arm remains in second. She then
continues the reach and bend forward and still
toward the downstage left corner by slightly extending the elbow, wrist, and fingers, presenting
this hand to the audience. Her head and gaze follow
the movement of her right hand. As she starts to
bend more forward than side, she leads with the
back of the right elbow, wrist and hand out, front,
and across the center line of her body, meanwhile

starting her other arm down from second, out and across, leading with the inside (the side nearest the thumb) of the wrist and hand, fingers trailing, palm down, showing the movement of this hand to the audience. It is important that she reach gracefully from the center of her body. She should not be stiffly flailing her stretched arms. There is almost a feeling that the first hand now draws the second into the movement. Her gaze shifts to the second hand as it comes down to pass the center line of the body, and this arm now takes over, leading out and across, as she begins to transfer her weight to the back leg in plié. She bends, reaching out toward the other (right) downstage corner, continuing to transfer her weight as the upstage (first) arm opens à la seconde and slightly beyond and as the torso continues to bend to that side. The downstage (left) arm and hand must extend to the opposite side before the dancer starts to bend back; the elbow leads, bringing the back of the wrist. She completes the transfer of weight to her back foot, bending side and around toward the back, continuing to reach as far out as she can from her center. She is now on a straight supporting (back) leg, with the working foot in tendu front. She continues the movement, now keeping it as circular as possible by bending around through straight back, reaching out and bringing her left hand over (really more directly back of) the center line of her head. Her left hand and arm draw her torso toward the side, and as the left arm begins to

1. Dana starts in tendu back croisé.
2. Dana begins to plié and bend, reaching toward the downstage corner. 3. Dana continues to plié and bend. 4. Dana continues the circular movement, bending forward as her front hand moves past the center line of her body. 5. Dana's left arm and hand are drawn into and take over the movement as she continues around. 6. Dana bending side as she transfers her weight to her right foot, her left arm leading side and then around to the back 7. Dana's weight is transferred to her right leg as she bends back. 8. Dana about to finish the circular movement 9. Dana arriving in tendu croisé front

extend to the side, it leads her torso to continue the circular motion, and she extends that arm into second position. As she gracefully brings her torso up, continuing the circular motion, she raises the upstage (right) arm around toward fifth high, leading with the back of the wrist. The feeling is now that the left hand is drawing the right up into croisé line. She transfers her weight through plié to her front leg as she completes her port de bras, and ends as she began, in croisé tendu back.

This kind of port de bras is, in some schools, often practiced with flattened curves, more shallowly elliptical than circular, because the dancer has been taught or is allowed to bend straight forward, around, and back in a comfortable range of movement. In contrast, Mr. B wanted the biggest, roundest shape we could make, as nearly circular as possible. Sometimes, to get this idea across, Mr. B would slowly walk around a dancer, holding out his hand and saying, "Reach here . . . reach here . . . reach here . . ." as he went. It made me think of Bottom going for the grass Titania is holding in *Midsummer Night's Dream.* The dancer should bend and stretch the sides of her torso to reach out to every point in the circle, as if there is something she truly wants that is just beyond her grasp.

The larger range of movement, when done with the phrasing Mr. B wanted to see, gives the sense that first one hand and then the other initiates the action: "The hands give direction." The simpler port de bras that is executed mostly forward and back, usually without accent, can look less dynamic, slightly dull, somehow uninteresting. It did not interest Mr. B, and he did not give it. As the raised arm begins the port de bras, starting to lead across the body, there is a clearly accented start, followed by a slower continuation. When the other hand and arm start from second, there is another such start and slower continuation and another acceleration when that hand and arm start up, around, and back. Finally, the first arm announces its return to croisé in the same way. This port de bras is continuous; there are no holds or stops. However, the energized starts, the slowings and the accelerations

---

DETAILS I OFTEN INSIST ON IN GRAND PORT DE BRAS:
1) make the movement as circular and as continuous as possible
2) the whole body participates, including the face and eyes
3) do not creep into the movement; remember to phrase

---

can give the dancer a slight feeling of a controlled swing and can look that way to the audience.

"Port de bras like you bow, not like butter melting," Mr. B liked to say. In this simple comparison he reminded us of tendencies to be avoided. The dancer should not melt downward nor flow evenly, sluggishly, through the movement. The dancer should use phrasing as she projects energy outward, downward, and upward. The dancer models herself as she participates with her entire body in the movement.

Grand port de bras includes a lot of movement that is not part of the standard vocabulary for going from one numbered position to another. However, the underlying principles for hand and arm movement are applied. Also, the head and eyes participate, the gaze usually following the hand that is leading.

TEMPS LIÉ

The temps lié exercises that Mr. Balanchine gave in advanced classes are really not the same exercises that are given in earlier stages of training, when basic skills are being developed.

The dancer starts in fifth position croisé, arms in fifth low. She begins with the basic two-count preparation, lifting her chest, gently inclining her torso, and slanting her head away, as she lifts her arms to first on count one, then, expanding her chest, opening her arms to second and bringing her torso and head to the croisé line on count two. She starts to plié on both legs and then releases the front foot (toe back, heel forward!) to move through coupé front as she again slants her head and inclines her torso away, closing her arms to fifth low. As she lifts her knee to make a circular développé front to the floor, she starts to straighten her torso and brings her arms to first. She pushes strongly off from the supporting foot, stretches the well-turned-out working leg toward the floor, and steps on to a straight and stretched leg. She catches her weight on the tips of her toes and lowers herself by going through the foot to flat (maintaining her weight over the ball of the foot) as she establishes the croisé line in her torso, head, and arms. The entire movement from the initial plié, through the release of the front foot, développé, and step is continuous, as is the movement of the body "away to arrive" and the movement of her arms. The dancer typically holds croisé tendu back to show the line. Lowering the upraised arm to first, she closes to fifth plié and then releases the front foot (this has a slight coupé feeling) and gently rotates her body to the other corner as she starts a low développé side, toward the upstage corner, her arms opening toward à la seconde. She transfers her weight as before, again leaving her downstage foot in tendu, this time to the side in écarté. Her arms having arrived in second or in an extended à la seconde (élongé), with palms turned down, her head is slanted as in écarté, and her torso is very gently inclined toward the working leg. After holding to show this line, she closes to fifth in plié, slants her head and inclines her torso away, and brings the arms to fifth low. She is now ready to do the other side.

Three aspects of this step are important to note, aside from the port de bras and the bending of the body. The step applies Balanchine's teaching on

picking the foot up off the floor and presenting it. The dancer lifts the working knee up and out to the side, pulling the toes back and under and bringing the heel forward, which maintains maximum turnout. She then unfolds her leg in a low développé. The plié, which is always continuous

Dana releasing her foot, starting to plié, inclining her torso and head away

Dana having done a low développé to the front

Having stepped way out, Dana transfers her weight to the front foot.

Dana in tendu croisé back

and as deep as time allows, is used to move the dancer smoothly in the direction of the développé, so she places the working foot beyond the place it would land if allowed to drop by simple gravity. If the tempo was moderate or slow, we did a bigger plié and traveled a little more. Finally, the dancer transfers her weight as she steps cleanly on to an extremely straight leg, placing her toes to the floor, lowering herself to full foot. The dancer does not jump or fall onto the working foot or heel. She places her foot toes first to the floor and lowers through the foot, bringing the heel forward, maintaining a fully turned-out leg. When she transfers her weight forward, she takes her hips and back with her over her supporting leg, and her arms move to croisé to frame her face (they are slightly in front of her). This more dynamic transfer of weight must be mastered, because it is the method Mr. B normally prescribed in class and it is used frequently in the ballets. It is almost always used when stepping onto demi-pointe or full pointe (see page 254).

Temps lié is the first step I have discussed in detail in which the dancer places her foot to the floor while traveling. It is therefore important to clarify once again the meaning of maximum turnout, full turnout, and other such terms. Mr.

Balanchine did not expect every dancer to match the look of the few who were the most naturally turned out. He defined, for example, the fifth position he wanted to see, but he recognized that not everyone could achieve it solely from the hips, so he helped each of us find our way to the best fifth we could make and often showed us how to make the subtle adjustments necessary to achieve the tight, "feet glued together" look. Once a dancer knew how to get her best fifth, he expected to see it all the time, rather than a lazy approximation. As always, her awareness, effort, and energy would give her dancing the vitality in movement that was his real goal.

It is very similar for placing the foot to the floor. Mr. B knew that not everyone was completely turned out, and he did not need to have the dancer put her foot to the floor 100 percent turned out and maintain it. He did need each dancer to place her fully pointed toes to the floor on the right spot, at the right time, with minimal noise. He wanted her to lower her weight going through the foot under control, rather than falling onto the full foot or the heel. As she lowered, she maintained the turn-out of her leg and brought the heel somewhat forward, maintaining the weight over the ball of the foot (but not rolling in). Depending on a number

---

DETAILS I OFTEN INSIST ON IN TEMPS LIÉ:

1) coordinate the arms and the head with the legs and the torso
2) use, move, and bend the torso
3) don't leave the arms behind when moving forward
4) finish in correct croisé and effacé lines with the head slanted and the fingertips of the raised hand over the center line
5) a beautiful, small développé action is needed—pick up and hold the knee back and present the leg and foot; maintain a fully turned-out thigh when going back
6) straighten the leg before stepping onto the working foot (toes to the floor first) and go through the foot when lowering to flat or step correctly to pointe (see page 254)
7) do not let the weight settle back on the heel or heels
8) do a full, continuous plié, and use it to step way out and to project the body in the direction of the développé
9) step in the exact directions from the body—front, side, and back

of factors, each dancer might be somewhat more or less turned out, but no dancer's foot would be turned in or have the weight settled back on the heel. Each dancer was showing him (and the audience) *her* full turnout, *her* maximum but *usable* turnout.

Another typical temps lié exercise incorporates more changes of épaulement (orientation). Using the same preparation and low (but circular) développé, the dancer steps to croisé and closes in plié, steps en face and closes into plié, steps to effacé and closes into plié, and steps diagonally back to écarté and closes fifth front into plié, leaving her ready to do the other side.

After giving these combinations to the front, Balanchine regularly gave them to the back. He also gave them with the dancer stepping onto pointe (demi-pointe for men) and relatively quickly bringing in the original supporting foot to place it into an exact sous-sus (see page 234). As we became more skillful, he typically began to make exercises combining temps lié with another step, such as tendu battement, grand battement, échappé, passé, pirouettes, pas de bourrée, etc.

I give temps lié regularly in my classes because it is the beginning of really moving and transferring weight and because it requires the dancer to coordinate her legs and feet with the movement of her torso, head, and arms. It is often the first exercise I give off the barre, because I like to remind the students, as soon as possible after the stationary time at the barre, that dance is movement, that the reason for all the detailed work on their feet and legs is to move better and more beautifully. For me, a stationary adagio or port de bras or a tendu exercise that will barely move—for a variety of reasons, none of those work as well for that purpose. I give temps lié alone and in combination with other movements and steps because I want them to transfer weight while traveling, to bend—in short, to feel that they are dancers, that they are dancing. A favorite is to combine a couple of temps lié with a large, sweeping pas de basque, ending in fourth arabesque in plié.

PROMENADE

The most basic idea of promenade is that the dancer assumes a pose or position and slowly turns it, modeling herself in the same pose or position as she turns, and thus presenting it from every angle. In a sense she is like a figure on a lazy Susan, turning to face every point on the circle. Promenades in class (and most onstage) are usually done in arabesque, attitude, or with the working leg à la seconde, although I sometimes give promenade in passé.

Promenades are usually done on the full foot and most often rotate en dedans; promenades on pointe with a partner are naturally more varied. The dancer centers her weight on the ball of the supporting foot and, maintaining the turnout in the supporting leg and foot, turns herself by just releasing her heel from the floor and moving the heel forward in small increments. Since her weight is over the ball of the foot, she is able to move herself smoothly by continually turning out, staying on top of the supporting leg and hip.

In Balanchine's promenade exercises the dancer's head is almost always held without change, even turning en dedans in croisé attitude back. On occasion, however, he allowed this exception: If the dancer is starting a promenade en dedans in croisé attitude back, she slowly can change her head from the slant in croisé to that in effacé as she leaves croisé and passes through en face to effacé. As she continues the promenade, she gradually returns her head to the croisé line if she is finishing in croisé. If she is finishing in effacé she could leave her head in the effacé line for the remainder of the promenade.

Although the dancer turns herself without changing the pose or position (except for the head in attitude), she must maintain life and energy throughout her body at all times. She should feel as if she is performing in a theater in the round, because she must present herself to each segment of the audience and look her best from all sides. "Dance with your back," Mr. B reminded me as I turned my back to the audience while completing a circular pattern.

ADAGIO EXERCISES

Adagio is an Italian word that in its origins means at ease. Musicians use it to indicate a moderate slowness; they have other words (*lento*, *molto lento*) to tell them to play really slowly, but for many dancers and teachers, it means simply slow. Balanchine used the word, just as others do, but for him it held a different meaning. Adagio movement in his classes reflected his background as a musician and also an aspect of his refinement of the traditional technique.

1. *Peter in attitude croisée back*
2. *Peter in attitude effacée back, having changed his head to the effacé line as he completed a quarter of the promenade*
3, 4, 5. *Peter continues the promenade, modeling attitude effacée back for the entire rotation.*
6. *Peter finishes the promenade in attitude effacée back.*

In more traditional classes music for adagios is full of deep feeling, in effect inviting the dancer to become sentimental or dramatic. "No Chopin. Too depressing. Always wrote in a minor key," Mr. B said. Of course, that's not true of everything Chopin wrote, but it is true of one aspect of the music pianists often choose for adagio exercises, so it can serve as shorthand for what he did not want. In his usual way he made a little joke as he tried to encourage the pianists to select different music. Compared to the music played for many other teachers, the music for Mr. B's adagios was brighter in feeling, even when slow, and sometimes it was only moderately slow or even moderate in tempo.

Many teachers also let the pianist fill the studio with music, playing lots of notes even if the tempo is very slow. As with other kinds of steps, this can delude the dancer into thinking she is doing a lot (she thinks she must have held this pose a long time because she has heard a lot of music go by).

Because of the way the exercises are set and corrected, slow tempos can foster tendencies in the dancer that Mr. B did not want. She might indulge in a leisurely, boring creep to the extended line. She might pause or even stop during a movement. In développé, for example, she might pick her foot off the floor and interrupt the movement to rest the working toes on the floor, steadying herself before being able to balance on one foot, or she might jam her toes into her supporting leg in passé, then start to slowly unfold her lower leg and suddenly kick it up to the extended line before letting her leg drop to the floor. Balanchine generally preferred that the dancer move faster and arrive sooner in the extended line; one advantage is that the dancer does not linger where she might make a mistake.

"Dance is not a static pose," Mr. B liked to say, and it is especially important to remember this when doing adagio. Contrary to the origins of the word, the dancer is not "at ease." She does not settle or relax, but rather extends the lines. She "grows" as her entire body participates. She assumes an extended line or a pose, holds it, showing and modeling herself, maintaining the life and energy even though she is not moving or is moving very little. Creating interest in adagio is more difficult than it is in allegro, because whatever movement there is takes more time, and consequently less seems to happen. In addition to timing and phrasing, she must use the head and face, the arms and hands, and changes in épaulement.

"Don't put the audience to sleep!" Mr. B would tell us. He did not want the movement itself to be prolonged, no matter how slow the tempo. He wanted us to phrase, to make the movement breathe, because movement to slow tempos without phrasing can be monotonous. He wanted, for example, a relatively quick start in développé to announce the beginning, continuing with a slower stretch of the working leg, and a longer, maybe a very long, hold in the extended line. In fact, to help us build strength and stamina, he often had us hold for several counts. He had no set pattern of counts for movement and holds. The same movement could be given in one, two, three, or more counts, with correspondingly longer or shorter holds.

When the tempo was slower, the movement might be completed in fewer beats (e.g., a développé in one count), in a sense faster; when the

tempo was faster, the movement might be completed in more beats (e.g., a développé in two or three counts), in a sense slower. He cultivated in us the ability to move musically at any pace, sometimes independently of what we might be hearing in the music, and yet still come out on the time that was set. This is analogous to having an instrument or group of instruments play a separate line.

Balanchine's adagio exercises were not long and complex; they were generally short and simple but usually included a change of épaulement. By paring them down to the essential elements he let the dancers concentrate on how the movement should look, rather than on memorizing the sequence of the combination. The exercises were often designed to work on lifting the turned-out working leg high to the front, side, and/or back and presenting the beautifully shaped and pointed working foot. Also, he liked to give such combinations, including slow demi-pliés on the supporting leg, because he wanted us to develop the strength we needed in the thighs for slow relevés and for controlled landings from jumps.

In many schools adagio exercises are often designed to practice balances on pointe or demi-pointe and grand pirouettes. Mr. B had little interest in long balances because he did not want to see his dancers teetering and tottering on pointe or demi-pointe just to balance. Furthermore, he very rarely used long balances in his ballets. Grand pirouettes were usually done in other combinations in which they were the main focus.

DÉVELOPPÉ

Mr. B gave développé exercises to help us perfect the action of taking the foot off the floor, lifting the knee high and to the side, unfolding the leg, and presenting the well-pointed foot, all while maintaining proper alignment. He wanted us to develop high extensions with fully turned-out legs and well-shaped feet while we practiced the various directions and ports de bras. As usual, he wanted these simple movements to be both beautiful and interesting.

The quick start needed in développé requires that the dancer remain always ready to take the working foot cleanly off the floor. This means that her weight must be over the ball of her supporting foot, that she must stay well pulled up on her supporting hip and that she must have the strength to sustain the degree of turnout she uses in the supporting leg and foot. If a dancer is not perfectly turned out—and very few are—it is better to be slightly less turned out on the supporting leg and more turned out with the active working leg. As Mr. B reminded us, the working leg is what the audience sees. With the weight controlled over the ball of the supporting foot and the maximum, but appropriate, turnout of the supporting leg and foot, it should never be necessary to rest the toes of the working foot on the floor while locating balance, usually by turning the supporting foot in.

First Développé Exercise

This exercise is développé front in croisé, en face and in effacé, développé à la seconde closing fifth back, thus finishing in croisé on the other diagonal, and repeat on the other side, with linking ports de bras. It is the counterpart to the first tendu exercise (see page 191). The dancer is in fifth position croisé, arms down and head in the croisé line. She does a standard preparation as I have discussed, bringing the arms to first on one and to second on two.

The dancer could take a breath as she lifts the backs of her wrists to the side in a small arc and perhaps exhales as she lowers the arms to fifth low on the "and" before count one while the head turns away and down, eyes following the hands. The dancer begins the développé on count one as she raises the arms to a slightly overlapped first, the arms arriving as the toes of the working foot pass the supporting knee; at the same time, she turns her head to her front as she brings it level. The dancer continues to lift the knee and unfolds the leg to croisé front as the arms, head, and upper torso assume the standard croisé line. After holding one or more counts, she closes through tendu front to fifth in croisé, lowering her upraised arm to second on the tendu and both arms to fifth low as she closes into fifth. Then, before count one (usually on four), as she closes into fifth, her head turns away and tilts down as her gaze follows her hands. The port de bras is coordinated throughout so that the hands, arms, head, and eyes participate with the working leg in the développé, which is continuous but phrased. Next, when she picks the foot up off the floor to begin the développé on count one, she rotates en face as the leg makes the développé front and the arms complete the port de bras from fifth low through first to fifth high. It is very important that the dancer change her orientation to the front as she begins the développé, rather than as she closes into fifth position. The port de bras and the head are coordinated in the same way: The hands start in fifth low with the head and gaze directed down; the head and eyes slightly precede the hands as the arms are raised through a slightly overlapped first, the head and eyes follow the hands to fifth high; the hands are in first with the head and gaze front as the working toes pass through knee level; the arms are in fifth high and the head and gaze are slightly up as the working leg extends (the head and arms often precede the leg by an instant). After holding one or more counts, she closes through tendu to fifth, remaining en face as she coordinates the lowering of her arms through second to fifth low. Again, before count one (usually on four), as she closes fifth and brings her arms to fifth low, she lowers her head. On count one, as she picks up the working foot off the floor for the développé effacé, she starts the rotation to the other corner. The rotation is smooth and is done as she développés, so that as the leg extends front, the body has arrived in effacé. Again, there is the same coordination of the head and arms with the working leg and foot. She holds one or more counts, and closes in fifth, lowering her upraised arm through second. On count four, as she closes into fifth, she brings both arms to fifth low, turning her head to her front, and lowering her gaze. Finally, she développés à la seconde as she opens her arms through the slightly overlapped first to second, raising her head and then turning and slanting it toward the downstage arm. She is still on the diagonal. She then closes fifth back as she turns her head away and lowers it, closing her arms to fifth low on count four. She is now ready to repeat to the other side. This exercise would also be done in reverse.

The timing of the head and arms in coordination with the working leg is critical to the look of the movement. "The hands lead the way" was often Mr. B's idea about picking the foot off the floor. To help us visualize the look he wanted, he could tell us that the working knee is being pulled up by a

---

DETAILS I OFTEN INSIST ON IN THE FIRST DÉVELOPPÉ EXERCISE:

1) the head, arms, and working leg are coordinated

2) the head and gaze change level in coordination with the port de bras and the extension of the working leg

3) lift the working knee as high and as close to the body as possible before extending the lower leg

4) the rotation to the next orientation is done at the beginning and during the développé, not on the closing to fifth

5) turn out the working leg a little more just as it straightens, which can make the leg almost seem to lower as it straightens to enhance the presentation of the foot and leg

6) show correct croisé and effacé line of the legs, head, and arms

7) the working foot in développé is drawn up the center line of the supporting leg, no matter the direction in which it finishes

---

string in the hand as the toe comes up the supporting leg as high as possible. Then, as the leg extends, he wanted a sense that the arms and working leg are opening in the air together with the arms arriving just ahead. Even though the movement is described in stages, there is no stop, not even a pause, except for the designated holds in the extended line and in fifth position. The entire développé should give the illusion of a smooth, continuous emergence rather than an unfolding joint by joint, like a robot or a puppet. "We say, not like a stick, bent and straight. We want the leg to develop, *développer*, not open in two parts," according to Mr. B. The coordination of the tilt of the dancer's head and the focus of her eyes serves to unify the movement. Again, the dancer's head and eyes usually precede, but in some cases follow the hands, depending on the movement. "The nose knows," Mr. B would say when he wanted the head and eyes (and nose) to lead the way. The whole body participates harmoniously, and all the elements combine to make the final picture. The details are not written out so fully in the exercises that follow, but if the teacher keeps these principles in mind in setting and, more importantly, in correcting the exercises she gives, a good result should come.

Mr. B usually set an exercise like this in four counts at a moderately slow tempo for the first time through—pick up the foot on one, développé (extend and arrive) on two, hold three, lower and close to fifth on four. We could then repeat it with the music played at the same tempo, but with a faster développé in which we did the whole movement in one count, then held on two, lower to tendu front with the arms going to second on three, close to fifth position with the arms lowering to fifth low on four; or développé on one, hold two and three, close four. Mr. B could also ask for very slow music and then tell us to développé in one or two counts, stay for one or two, and close on four, or, on rare occasions, développé in four counts, hold on five and six, lower to tendu on seven, and close on eight. This exercise can and should also be reversed.

Dana in développé croisé front

Dana in fourth arabesque

Dana bending her knee and about to take it back, drawing her foot toward passé

Dana takes her knee back as her foot passes the supporting knee.

Second Développé Exercise

This exercise is développé croisé front, lift the knee and pass it through to fourth arabesque, close back, with ports de bras; and repeat to the other side. The dancer is in fifth position croisé, arms down and head in the croisé line. She does a standard preparation as I have discussed and follows with the same développé croisé used in the first exercise. After a hold of one or more counts in the extended line, the working knee lifts and pulls back and to the side, drawing the working toe through a high passé as the body starts to rotate toward the other down-

---

DETAILS I OFTEN INSIST ON IN THE SECOND DÉVELOPPÉ EXERCISE:
1) show a beautiful croisé line to the front
2) lift the knee up to pass through to arabesque
3) show the back in fourth arabesque
4) show both arms extending and reaching
5) the head is slanted over the front arm in fourth arabesque
6) hold the back up against the lift of the arabesque leg

stage corner. As the knee pulls back, up, and around the supporting leg, the elbow of the raised arm comes slightly toward the center and gently bends, leading the arm to the dancer's front. The wrist, followed by the hand and fingers of the leading arm, takes over, bringing the wrist to the center line of the body. The arm in second moves toward the back, starting with a small downward arc of the elbow that leads, followed by the wrist and hand and fingers, which take over and stretch gently toward the back corner. The head shifts from croisé front to the other side as the body moves into fourth arabesque. The shoulder line extends, exposing the dancer's back and revealing the long line from the leading fingertips through the arms and shoulders to the trailing fingertips. The fully stretched and turned-out working leg extends to arabesque as the arms open, the thigh being strongly lifted up toward the back. The dancer is now in fourth arabesque. After a hold of one or more counts, the dancer closes to fifth back as she does port de bras to bring her arms to second and her head to croisé. She is now ready for the other side and begins again by closing her arms to fifth low as she turns her head away and down and picks up her foot.

In this exercise it is important to lift the working knee and thigh as they pass to the back so the working leg only gets higher (or at least gives that illusion) as it moves from front to back. Then, as the knee passes the hip, the dancer must release the working hip to continue to lift and to turn out the thigh to achieve a high, long, fourth arabesque line.

Mr. B typically set an exercise like this to be done in four counts to a slow tempo or in eight counts at moderate tempo. At the moderate tempo, after the preparation, the dancer lowers her arms from second to fifth low on the "and" before count one, picks her foot off the floor and moves her arms through an overlapped first on count one, raises her arms to croisé as she completes the développé on count two, and holds counts three and four. On count five she starts to pull the knee up and around,

arriving in arabesque on count six. She holds count seven and closes to fifth on count eight. Or, to a slower tempo, he might give a slight variation on the step with an alternative timing: Pick up the foot on "and" and arrive développé croisé front on count one, hold count two, take the knee back through passé and extend to arrive in fourth arabesque on count three, hold on count four, switch arms to third arabesque on count five, hold on count six, lower the leg to tendu back on count seven, close on count eight. The tempo is slower but the movement is slightly faster. Of course, it is necessary that each part of the exercise be phrased.

DÉVELOPPÉ FOLLOWED BY DEMI-ROND DE JAMBE EN L'AIR

This is an exercise that shows two aspects of Mr. B's teaching. Given en face it helps the dancer develop her sense of front, side, and back, so we did it more often that way. It starts with a développé front or back and then after a pause continues by moving the leg to the side (a demi-rond de jambe en l'air) so it should not look like the first half of a grand rond de jambe. To help us recognize the difference he sometimes followed this sort of exercise with another one incorporating grand rond de jambe. Or he might combine the two in one longer exercise. He wanted us to show and feel the difference between développé with the working foot presented and held front or back before moving on, and grand rond de jambe with the pointe of the working foot carving a circular shape without stopping in the front or back and continuing without pause to go on around to reach the extended line.

The dancer starts in fifth position en face with the arms down and does the standard two-count preparation, raising the arms to first and opening them to second. On the "and" she lowers her arms to fifth low, raising them on count one to first or fifth high (as usual, with her head and torso partici-

DETAILS I OFTEN INSIST ON IN
DÉVELOPPÉ FOLLOWED BY DEMI-
ROND DE JAMBE EN L'AIR:
1) stop after the développé with the leg
   front, side, or back, and then make the
   demi-rond
2) maintain turnout, especially when doing
   the demi-rond from back to the side (do
   not lose turnout and then rotate the leg
   when it is à la seconde)
3) don't let the working leg drop when
   going from à la seconde to the back or
   from the back to à la seconde
4) the body "grows" throughout the
   exercise; the feeling of lift is especially
   strong when going from one extended
   line to the next; don't sit into the hips, and
   don't let the chest sink—it stays lifted up

pating) in coordination with the développé (also executed in one count). The music is slow, but the développé in one count is brisk; it certainly doesn't put the audience to sleep. Mr. B would generally call for the arms to first if the développé front was set at ninety degrees or less and for fifth high if the développé was set at more than ninety degrees. The dancer establishes and shows the front position. On count two, the movement grows as she carries the leg side, lifting it as it goes. The dancer coordinates the opening of her arms to second with the demi-rond of the working leg; when the leg is à la seconde, it is behind the arms. The dancer holds count three, then closes fifth back on count four as she lowers her arms to fifth low. She now repeats to the other side. The exercise could continue with a développé à la seconde on count one as the arms move to fifth high. On count two the dancer does a demi-rond to the back as the arms open out to second position. She holds count three, then closes fifth back on count four as the arms lower to fifth low. Now she repeats on the other side. This exercise was also done in reverse.

This exercise makes the dancer very aware of her directions when done en face. It also builds the strength necessary to sustain the extended line and the turnout. Mr. B would watch to see if we could hold that glass of water on the heel in front, and he might suggest that we try to keep it there without spilling as we carried the leg to second. This was, of course, impossible for all of us, but he liked the energized look of the leg when we were trying. Also, the working leg should at least stay at the same level and usually lifts as it extends and moves to the final line. It was given at a slow tempo with holds as I have indicated to show the extended line. However, as I noted in other développé exercises, he would change the number of counts for the développé and the holds, or change the tempo, or even give the exercise in three to develop our musical awareness. For example, at a moderate (not so slow, but not at all fast) tempo, the combination could be set starting with développé on count one, arrive on count two, hold on counts three and four, start to carry side on count five, arrive à la seconde on count six, hold on count seven, close on count eight. An example of a slow three is développé on count one, carry side on count two, lower and close to fifth on count three.

ARABESQUE PENCHÉE

I first saw this exercise in class with Balanchine, who gave quite a variety of penché exercises in the center. For me, arabesque penchée had been an exercise done in profile or on the diagonal, usually in first arabesque, and not as difficult. But setting the dancer en face was an approach Mr. B sometimes preferred. It gives another opportunity to reinforce awareness of the directions from the dancer's body while helping to clarify technical details. Being en face with her arms to the sides, the dancer will more likely sense whether her working foot is on the center line of the body and avoid leaning off her supporting leg. In the same way, she will feel more clearly the connection between her back and her lifting working leg when she is in arabesque and throughout the penché.

The dancer starts in fifth position en face, right foot front; sometimes Mr. B set a combination with développé front and brush through first position to arabesque and then proceed with the penché. Or he might simply have the dancer développé back and proceed with the penché. I'll take that approach and include a typical novel challenge: The dancer releases her head toward the end of the penché, making a beautiful swooping movement, but also making it difficult to maintain her balance and the contact between her back and the working leg. The dancer does the standard two-count preparation, raising the arms to first and opening them to second. On "and" she lowers her arms to fifth low, raising them with the crossed-hands technique

Deanna looking into the "pool"

through first to second as she lifts her knee, drawing the pointe of the right (working) foot up the front of the supporting leg to passé, passing the working pointe around the supporting leg in the usual way, and continuing by lifting her thigh to développé straight back on count one. She arrives with her leg to the back and her arms in second on count two, giving the "Christ on the Cross" look. On the "and" before count three, she takes a breath, slightly lifting her working leg, upper torso, and arms (going up to go down). On counts three-four she penchés straight forward, arriving on count

four, "looking into the pool like Narcissus," rather than holding her face to the front. The arms stay out to the side and are gently pulled to the back, a little behind à la seconde, almost until the dancer is all the way down; then they come together and cross at the bottom of the penché. As the hands come together on the "and" before count five, the dancer releases her head, allowing it to lower a slight bit more. On counts five and six the dancer comes up to arabesque, raising her arms to fifth high, again with the crossed-hands technique, but this time more crossed—almost "wash your face." She holds on count seven. On count eight she closes back, opening her arms to the side to second position, ready to do the other side.

Here is an example of penché in which a développé front is included with an interesting port de bras. As the working leg extends to the front in développé, the arms open from first to second position. Then, as the working leg brushes through first to the back, the arms lower to fifth low and then go to fifth high, using the crossed-hands technique. As the dancer starts to penché, her arms start to come down with the crossed-arms technique in front, and continue to fifth low and then lift around through second to fifth high and down again across her center through fifth low to end out to the side and slightly behind her body as she arrives all the way down in penché. I sometimes call this "loop-dee-loop" because of the circles the arms and hands trace in the air. As the dancer comes up to arabesque, the arms are raised again from second through overcrossed fifth low and up through "wash the face" to fifth high.

It may come as a surprise to learn that Mr. B even gave the "Giselle" penché. We started in fifth position croisé and could step or développé into first ara-

Dana in the Giselle arabesque penchée

besque in profile on counts one-two. Or the dancer can développé à la seconde on counts one-two and turn to first arabesque in profile on counts three-four; it really doesn't matter how she gets there. The counts will vary depending on how the exercise is set. The front arm then opens to second, making "Christ on the Cross" on counts five-six. She penchés down, holding her back and head up on counts seven-eight as she crosses her arms in front of her chest and perhaps holds the penché on counts one-two. She comes back up to first arabesque on counts three-four, pliés in first arabesque on count five, does pas de bourrée ending in sous-sus on count six, pliés in fifth in croisé on count seven, and does one slow entrechat six (see page 307), landing and straightening her legs on count eight. She can now repeat on the other side.

Since Mr. B was more interested in the movement and in the dancer maintaining the relationship of the working leg to the back than in seeing how long we could hold a balance, which can often turn into a static pose, the timing for penchés was typically not extremely slow.

DETAILS I OFTEN INSIST ON IN ARABESQUE PENCHÉE EXERCISES:

1) maintain contact between the back and the working leg
2) keep the hips over the ball of the supporting foot
3) the toes of the working foot are on the center line of the body in développé front, in arabesque, and in penché
4) do not lean to the side, off the center line of the body
5) maintain life, energy, and softness in the arms
6) the head and eyes participate in the movement
7) think of arabesque penchée as a movement of the working leg with the back held up, not as a feat of balance

GRAND ROND DE JAMBE EN L'AIR

Grand rond de jambe en l'air almost always began and finished in croisé and includes a change in direction, unlike the développé with demi-rond de jambe exercise usually done en face. And since it is a grand rond de jambe, the working leg and foot do not stop in front before going around to the side. It can begin with développé or dégagé; both will be described. This too is phrased, starting faster and slowing through écarté and revealing the line in back.

The dancer starts in fifth position croisé with the arms down and does the standard two-count preparation. On "and" she lowers her arms to fifth low (head and gaze down toward the hands and away from the front), raising them to first as the working knee lifts the foot to passé (head lifts). The working foot takes over, aiming *across* the center line and leading the leg forward with the heel front as the arms and head assume the croisé variant line (looking under the downstage arm) on count one. The leg does not straighten and hold in croisé; instead, it traces an arc through croisé as the working knee becomes fully stretched and the foot passes the center line of the body. As her leg stretches, the dancer starts to open her arm and to rotate her body to the other diagonal and shifts her head, and the leg continues through a kind of effacé. As she continues to lift and turn out her leg, it circles through second and on around to arabesque on counts three-four. She releases the working hip to the degree necessary to maintain the turnout as the leg passes to the back. As the working leg passes à la seconde, the dancer continues to open her upraised arm and then begins to lower it to the back to make the line of fourth arabesque, while the arm that was in second lowers and then lifts to the front, softening very slightly in the elbow, and leading with the back of the wrist as it rises to assume a long line in fourth arabesque.

If he began with dégagé, Mr. B could give a different port de bras. For example, as the working leg

Peter began with a dégagé
and is about to pass
through a low croisé front
and move on.

Peter has lifted his leg
past effacé front and is
moving it to à la seconde.

Peter is lifting his leg
through écarté derrière.

Peter maintains
the lift of his
back and the
turnout and lift
of his leg
as it moves to
the back.

Peter
passing
through
arabesque

Peter finishing in attitude
croisée back in plié

DETAILS I OFTEN
INSIST ON IN GRAND
ROND DE JAMBE:
1) no stop or pause as the
   working leg goes around
2) maintain maximum
   turnout in both legs and
   a continuous lift of the
   working leg, especially
   as it passes from à la
   seconde to the back
3) make sure the whole
   body participates, that it
   grows through the
   exercise

dégagés, the arms are lifted from fifth low through first to fifth high—think of that "string," the link between the hands and the working foot. As the dégagé starts, the foot passes through a low but over-crossed croisé and continues to lift through a kind of effacé front as the body slowly changes to effacé. The leg continues to lift without pause around past à la seconde to the arabesque line. The arms grow up and can open to fourth arabesque, or they can open to the side, usually ending with the palms up. The body also can bend in this croisé line.

Either version of this exercise can use various ports de bras and end in attitude or arabesque. The exercise could finish in fifth or continue in many ways. Also, Mr. B sometimes wanted us to end the grand rond de jambe with plié in arabesque or attitude, usually with a bend of the body, which feels very much related to renversé.

DÉVELOPPÉ À LA SECONDE AND TURN TO ARABESQUE

Balanchine very rarely gave the quite common grand fouetté en tournant with relevé in class and he never explained why, although he did use it in several ballets. We did practice développé à la seconde and then a turn to arabesque, which is basically the second part of grand fouetté; maybe Mr. B preferred this approach because it isolates the harder part of grand fouetté en tournant. This exercise starts en face and turns to profile, helping with awareness of the directions. It complements the demi-rond de jambe en l'air from à la seconde to the back, but now the dancer turns her body instead of moving her leg. She must still maintain the turnout and the strong lift in her working leg as she turns to arabesque, staying pulled up on the supporting hip and holding up her back to achieve a beautiful line.

The dancer starts in fifth position en face with her arms in fifth low and does the standard preparation, raising her arms to first on count one and opening them to second on count two. On the "and" she lowers her arms to fifth low, on count one raising them to first with the crossed-hands technique as the working toe comes to passé or just a bit higher. Continuing as usual without pause, she arrives in développé à la seconde with her arms in fifth high on count two. Maintaining life and energy, she holds counts three-four, then with a breath and gentle lift through the torso, head, arms, and leg, turns to first arabesque on count five, arriving on count six, and holds on counts seven-eight. It is essential that her supporting leg turn out as she turns to arabesque and that she remain as straight as possible on it, with her weight over the ball of the foot. The working leg remains in place as the body turns. It should feel as if the working leg lifts up and turns out as she lifts her torso and chest up to change to arabesque. The pointe of the extended foot should not swing down and up or diagonally back. Instead, the dancer sustains its line, and the pointe rotates in the same spot. The dancer in arabesque should appear big and beautiful. From

Peter in a high développé à la seconde

Peter lifting his leg and extending his arms as he is about to arrive in first arabesque

first arabesque she can continue in a variety of ways—for example, open the arms à la seconde and then penché à la Giselle or a promenade in first arabesque, plié, pas de bourrée, battement tendu the back leg to the side, close fifth front. She is now ready for the other side.

Peter growing upward as he starts to turn to arabesque

DETAILS I OFTEN INSIST ON WHEN MOVING FROM DÉVELOPPÉ À LA SECONDE TO FIRST ARABESQUE:

1) the working leg should lift and turn out even more, not drop down and turn in
2) lift the torso up and maintain the back as straight as possible; stay alive
3) stay up over the supporting leg; do not pull back in the hips
4) do not lean to the side
5) in arabesque, the hand in front is on the center line of the body
6) bring the back shoulder and back arm around to make a correct arabesque (avoid "à la sebesque")

An alternate approach starts in almost the same way, bringing the dancer to développé à la seconde with the arms in second on count one, hold count two. On the "and" before count three, she pliés and lowers her arms to fifth low, looking down, while still maintaining the lift in her working leg and upper torso; then on count three she raises her arms to fifth high with crossed wrists and lifts her head and upper torso as she relevés. On the "and" before count four she lifts and opens her arms as she turns to first arabesque, remaining on pointe (demi-pointe for men), meanwhile also lifting her working leg. Again, it is essential to maintain the turnout in the supporting leg and good placement on it; she must resist the tendency to allow her torso to tip forward or to let her hips pull back. On count four she descends into plié and continues, perhaps as given above, perhaps in another way.

In this relevé combination the dancer must ensure that she shows two pictures on pointe (demi-pointe for men): the first one with the working leg à la seconde and with the arms in fifth high, and the second one in first arabesque. She should seem to grow from à la seconde to first arabesque. The arabesque, not the à la seconde, is the main climax.

A VALSE LENTE

The barre exercises and some in the center are very repetitive, deceptively simple and stationary. I looked forward to exercises like this one because it travels, the body bends a lot, it is done to a waltz—in short, it feels more like a dance. I think Mr. B liked it for some of the same reasons, but he also worked in the use of some very deep pliés on one leg to help us build strength and control.

The dancer starts in croisé with her left foot tendu front and her arms in an extended second with palms down. We could have a two-bar introduction in which we held the first and began dancing on the second: step front (on the diagonal) "on two" (to musicians on count one of the second measure), going through the foot and bringing the

heel forward as the knee bends into plié with active muscles in the toes and foot, calf, and thigh. Again, "heel forward" does not indicate that it is jammed out and down; it means that the turnout is maintained as the dancer goes through the foot. The arms soften a bit as the dancer steps front, then level in second position at the start of the glissade. On "and," start glissade lente (see page 342), traveling to the right side, using a lot of plié, staying low to the floor, and reaching out with and stretching the working (right) leg in order to make a very long, extended glissade. Then, as the first (right) foot of the glissade reaches the floor, the dancer continues a port de bras in which she brings the front (right) arm up and around toward fifth high.

On count one of the first measure of the phrase, the dancer finishes her glissade lente by bringing the second leg of the glissade (her left leg) across to a large, overcrossed fourth and transferring her weight onto it, ending in a very juicy plié on her left foot. As she brought her left leg across for the "failli," the dancer continued the port de bras by moving her arm through fifth high and reaching to the other side (back to the left, or in the opposite direction from the way the dancer is traveling), bending her body and looking back in that direction. The other arm maintains its line in second position. Staying in a deep plié, she begins to move her back (right) leg forward in a low développé, close to the floor, as the backward-reaching (right) arm comes down through fifth low and starts to move toward the first arabesque line, her head and gaze coordinated with the movement in the usual way. She continues with the low développé of the right leg close to the floor. On "two" (to musicians on count one of the second measure), the dancer pushes off the supporting (left) leg and steps far in front of herself onto the right leg, traveling directly side, into arabesque pliée, assuming first arabesque line with her arms and head, etc. She is now in profile—indeed, this combination to this point has traveled directly side. She holds her arabesque in the deep, low plié for the next (third) measure, then could straighten her supporting leg on the fourth measure. This is

Deanna in tendu croisé front

Deanna transfers her weight to her left foot and starts into a plié as her arms lower.

Deanna staying down in plié, extending her right leg front as she starts to bend back in the opposite direction

Deanna has brought her second (left) leg across ("failli") to an overcrossed fourth, placing her toes to the floor and transferring her weight.

Deanna's weight is on her left leg and she pliés into a near kneel as she reaches back.

Deanna is transferring her weight onto her right leg while staying in plié.

Deanna in a deep plié in first arabesque

the basic part of Mr. B's exercise. I sometimes continue it for twelve more measures (for a total of sixteen), but for some classes the teacher may not want to make it so long. In that case she can have the dancers hold in arabesque (or do a promenade) for the fifth and sixth measures, step across in front with the left foot, step back with the right foot with a little pas de basque, ending with the right foot front in croisé tendu front (seventh and eighth measures).

In the longer form, the exercise continues for the next four measures (five through eight), with the dancer doing promenade remaining in first arabesque without change to the pose. Sometimes Mr. B asked for this promenade in plié, in which case the dancer remains in plié after stepping into arabesque. She arrives back in profile at the end of the phrase.

During the first measure of the second phrase (dancers say "on one"), the working (left) leg bends, trying to wrap around through attitude back and on through passé to développé to effacé front as the dancer begins to rotate en dedans to make effacé (facing the other diagonal). The arms, which

DETAILS I OFTEN INSIST ON IN
VALSE LENTE:

1) *travel* and *bend* the body on the glissade
2) maintain maximum plié on the supporting leg when stepping out into arabesque pliée; the head remains level, no rise and fall
3) as the plié from the overcrossed fourth "failli" is used to project the dancer well forward, the dancer needs to catch herself on her toes and to move her weight onto and over the ball of the supporting foot in the arabesque
4) the arabesque pose remains unchanged in the promenade
5) model yourself to all sides during the promenade (like theater in the round)
6) the "holds" are not settled and static— keep the life, make the "holds" grow

start to close as the working leg bends, move through the crossed first position as the working foot moves through passé. The dancer completes her rotation to the adjacent corner and extends her working leg to développé effacé front; during the second measure her arms also move to effacé. She holds the third measure, then places her working foot to the floor and does a "tombé" (see page 241) on count one of the fourth measure. She does pas de bourrée forward (on the diagonal), ending with her right foot front in sous-sus on five (count one of the fifth measure) as she opens the upraised arm to join the other in second position. On count one of the sixth measure (dancers say "on six") the dancer steps forward on the diagonal on her right foot into plié, with the back foot in coupé back and her arms extended to the front, crossed at the wrist at about waist level as she bends away. On count one of the seventh measure she steps back on her left foot through fourth position plié, stretching her right leg in croisé tendu front, and slowly returns her arms to the starting position for the exercise. The dancer is now set to repeat to the other side; on the final (eighth) measure of the phrase the dancer steps onto her front foot to begin.

The primary purpose of this exercise is for students to begin to push themselves to move at the extremes—for example, long-lasting, continuous, and very low pliés; very long, reaching steps; and large, sweeping bends of the torso. The musical indications are generally limited to where she should be at the beginning of the measure.

Declaring his independence from plots and characters, Mr. B said, "Our business is to show that movement is important in itself. The first requirement is that it is satisfying, usually in connection with the music." Exercises like this are a good start.

ATTITUDE EXPLORATION

I have described tendu and développé exercises that thoroughly explored those elements of the most basic technique along with the directions. Mr. B often gave such simple but very concentrated combinations, and yet we always felt and tried to look like dancers dancing. The following combination explores attitude and épaulement (the orientations). The dancer assumes attitude in one orientation and then promenades and assumes it in another, but the only change is the slant of the head. He wanted us to understand that, to think about that. Perhaps to help make the idea memorable, he liked to joke that he should build a theater in which the audience moved, swung around from one place to another, while the dancer remained in the center and needed only to change the line of the head.

Well, this reverses the lazy Susan idea: the dancer as the figure rotating on the pedestal at the center of the table. A theater with an audience that revolves around the dancers also reverses the normal relationship between the performers and the public. Mr. B liked to say that a choreographer is a person who sees, implying that most of us don't, really. Maybe I would add that a choreographer is also a person who enjoys playing, as he evidently did, with the images of dancers seen from every angle, doing every step at every tempo . . . and never getting turned around or confused.

The dancer starts in fifth position croisé, arms down. She does the standard preparation, moving her arms to first on count one and to second position on count two. On the "and" she lowers her arms to fifth low. On count one she développés to attitude croisée front as she raises her arms and head to standard croisé. She holds count two. On count three she promenades one quarter of a circle, passing the front (en dehors) to end in attitude effacée front. She only needs to change the slant of her head to make this pose, which she holds, on count four. On count five she extends her working leg in a développé to effacé front as she lowers her upraised arm to the front and extends it, complementing her leg; then on count six brushes the working leg through first to the back as she changes her arms to assume third arabesque pliée (the arm in front moves up through fifth high and on to the back; the arm in second lowers to fifth low and extends forward). The dancer straightens the supporting leg on count seven as she makes attitude croisée back with her head, arms, and torso, then holds count eight. On count one she promenades one quarter of a circle, passing through front (en dedans) in attitude, changing her head to standard effacé line, then holds attitude effacée back on count two. She has now shown attitude front and back in croisé and effacé.

This exercise can be completed in many ways, but here is one typical of Mr. B, because it adds a turn in attitude and thus an opportunity to explore the pose in another way. On count three the dancer pliés as she extends her leg to arabesque effacée allongée, then on count four does pas de bourrée "tombé" (see page 241) to fourth with a straight back leg, attitude turn en dedans on count five (see page 271), plié arabesque allongée on count six, and pas de bourrée to fifth plié on count seven, closing the arms to fifth low and slanting the head away. On count eight she straightens her legs as she moves her arms up through first to second position. She is now ready to repeat to the other side.

This simple exercise makes clear that in both attitude front and back, only the head changes as the dancer moves between croisé and effacé. Also, the dancer does not actively bend her body, but she does actively slant the head first one way and then another as the direction changes. However, if the head slants as it should in both directions and if the fingertips of the raised hand are maintained on the center line of the head, the illusion of a bend in the torso will be created for the audience. When done with the right approach, a simple, balanced exercise like this one will be beautiful for the dancers to do in class and will develop a sense of the beauty they need to display onstage.

DETAILS I OFTEN INSIST ON IN ATTITUDE COMBINATIONS:
1) the fingertips of the raised hand are over the center line of the head
2) really use the head and neck to show the change in slant, really show épaulement
3) in attitude back, keep the thigh and knee lifted, the knee tightly bent and aiming directly back (no "doggy at the hydrant")

AN "AMERICAN" PORT DE BRAS

Some of our exercises in class did not immediately seem traditionally classical at all. They seemed new, fresh, American, which is not a surprise, because Mr. Balanchine admired and adapted to his work much that he found here. For example, here is a little port de bras exercise showing that aspect of his teaching. The music is typically a 4/4 in moderate tempo.

The dancer starts in fifth position croisé with the arms down and does the usual two-count preparation, raising the arms to first and opening them to

1. Deanna in tendu croisé front
2. Deanna placing her left foot to the floor and transferring her weight onto it as her arms start to move toward first 3. Deanna with her arms in an overlapped first as her right leg starts up and is about to pass the supporting leg
4. Deanna lifting her right leg forward, presenting her heel front

5. Deanna in tendu effacé front
6. Deanna transferring her weight onto her right leg as her arms are starting to move toward first 7. Deanna with her arms passing through first as her left foot passes her supporting leg 8. Deanna returns to tendu croisé front.

second. On "and" she lowers her arms to fifth low (her head and gaze lowering in coordination) and with the front leg does a low développé, ending on count one in pointe tendue front in croisé, meanwhile raising her arms through the overlapped first to standard croisé. The upstage arm lifts to fifth high, leading up with the elbow and then the wrist relatively close to her body and at the same time the other arm opens to second; the movement of her head and arms is coordinated so that they arrive in croisé just before or as the foot arrives in tendu croisé front. Then on the "and" she places her foot to the floor moving through fourth position plié as she lowers her upraised arm in front of her (her head and gaze can also lower as she moves the arm in second through fifth low), then raises it to meet the other in an overlapped first. On count two she straightens and does a low développé to pointe tendue front in effacé as she raises the arm to fifth high, leading up with the elbow and then the wrist and lifting her head up to effacé, at the same time opening the other arm to second. Then on the "and" she

places her foot to the floor again moving through fourth plié as she lowers her upraised arm in front of her with her head and gaze again lowering as she brings the arm in second down through fifth low, then raises it to meet the other in an overlapped first. As she moves into plié, her head and gaze lower, as do her arms; as she comes out of plié, her head moves up to croisé or effacé as her arms move energetically up, almost swinging, into the designated line. She continues this way as directed, changing feet as she struts diagonally forward, with the result that she is alternately in croisé and effacé as she comes forward, and yet the exercise does not feel like typical "proper" classical dancing. Instead it feels like an informal, arm-swinging walk with a little strut.

In this exercise, the legs and feet do a low développé and not just a kick. The foot is presented to the floor on the center line, not just thrown out. The arms look energetic but not stiff, because of the articulation of the elbows and wrists. Even for this not traditionally classical exercise, there is a consistent approach that bit by bit brings a result in harmony with the rest of the technique. The underlying principles are the same and are the bases for a new classicism that allows the incorporation of movement styles that are America's own—jazz, in this example. It's not surprising that Mr. B was able to use this look in a ballet, *Who Cares?*, made to some of George Gershwin's Broadway musical numbers. But it is also seen in the opening of *Theme and Variations,* a most classical ballet made to Tchaikovsky, when the male and the female principals begin with a very similar walking step.

The teacher can make a port de bras exercise in two measures based on this walk. The dancer can start by doing four strutting steps on the diagonal, ending in tendu effacé front. Then she pliés on the supporting leg on "and" and does a quarter rond de jambe with the tendu leg to effacé back as she pivots to face the other downstage corner ending on a stretched supporting leg on count five. On "and" she transfers her weight through fourth position demi-plié to her back foot. On count six she straightens her back leg, pointing her front foot and opening her arms to the side. On "and" she transfers her weight in the same way again to the front foot. On count seven she stretches her front leg, pointing her back foot and moving her arms through fifth low and an overcrossed first to fifth high. On count eight she transfers her weight again through fourth position demi-plié to her back foot, opening her arms to the side. She can repeat the combination on the other side, stepping forward on the diagonal on "and" and arriving in tendu croisé front on count one.

KEEPING THE SPIRIT, FEELING THE JOIE

Ballet dancing is very hard work. Learning to be a ballet dancer requires many years and many hours of detailed, repetitive effort. That effort continues in largely the same ways even when one is a professional. Most of us persevered in the study of ballet and persevered as professional dancers because dancing did not feel like hard work. Even though we worked very hard, dancing brought us great pleasure. One of the challenges that any teacher faces is helping her dancers achieve the results needed while making it possible to experience the pleasure and joy in dancing and especially in dancing well. This is not exactly the same thing as having fun, as people generally use the expression. Like the fun of other very accomplished people, part of the dancer's fun comes from the satisfaction of doing well what she has prepared long and hard to be able to do. Another part of her fun is her enjoyment and delight in the process of learning to dance to her potential.

There are other pleasures a student can have from ballet lessons: getting better at something very hard to do; learning to soar through the air; being stronger; having better balance, more flexibility, improved posture, or a more elegant presence; or, maybe just looking better in general. But the student who is likely to become a good dancer in the Balanchine aesthetic will also get a very particular pleasure. It will come more from her enjoyment of beautiful movement in harmony with the music than from an ability to pull off tricks calculated to dazzle, or prolonged balances meant to astonish. She will also not be satisfied with the kind of static beauty best captured in a posed photograph. Movement that is beautiful partly because the dancer is musically sensitive and responsive to the nuances of individual performances will be especially pleasing to her. Everything Mr. B taught in class had such movement as the ultimate goal. Movement. Movement to music. Beautiful movement to music. I can go on adding qualities that he wanted, and each addition will improve our understanding of his goal, but the core, what is primary, remains the same. MOVEMENT!

With movement in mind as the goal, I have to acknowledge that the explanations of technique, the descriptions of exercises, and the correction details might have the unintended effect of inhibiting movement. The materials covered so far, and even much of what follows, sound very prescriptive, rigid, stiff, full of do's and don't's. Teachers and dancers could be afraid to do anything for fear of doing something less than correct, or actually wrong. But it's acceptable and at times even encouraged for the dancer who is making maximum effort to get the movement right, to be wrong, to make mistakes, to struggle, to fall, to look ridiculous. The teacher is there to direct her effort in the most useful way. Every year, part of my time is spent persuading some of the students that maximum energy, awareness, and focus, leading to maximum possible movement given the step and the tempo, are the most essential qualities. Without them there is no learning to dance in the Balanchine way, no matter what the talent. With them, the result becomes, according to Balanchine himself, 10 percent a matter of talent and 90 percent a matter of hard work and enduring commitment to the art.

Balanchine felt that way about teaching the New York City Ballet when I was in the company. Classes were often full of many simple but difficult steps and combinations, and he often gave many suggestions and corrections. He asked for a lot, and we tried very hard. On occasion Mr. B might pause and, as he mimed jamming food down the throat of an unwilling goose, say to us, "In France they force the food, they stuff the goose. So goose hates to eat, almost dies from being stuffed. And here I stuff you full of steps and corrections. Who knows what the result will be?" Our little breather over, we would dance some more.

Effort alone is naturally not enough. The dancer must have the ability to absorb the material, make it her own, and move on. There are certain essential qualities that Mr. B insisted on without exception: best possible fifth position of the feet; maximum turnout possible; precise and elegant placement of the feet to the floor; adherence to front, side, and back; being on time, which is not necessarily always the same as dancing exactly on the music; and energy in every part of the body. The teacher of advanced or professional dancers must set exercises that practice the entire technique. Her observations of where they need improvement help her to orga-

nize the classes so her dancers develop as well as they can. She must also challenge her dancers to explore the limits of what they can do. She must insist on the essentials at all times in her corrections. With respect to other important but not essential qualities (e.g., phrasing is important, being on time is essential) she must give corrections individually, and to the class, ask to see again, and insist on the beginning of improvement or, at least, on awareness of the need to improve and of what to improve. And then she must move on, because it can't all be done in one day or one week, because sometimes it gets done and then is lost and has to be redone. To change is very hard for the dancer; to bring about change, the teacher also must work very hard.

One day Mr. B watched a class, and when it was over he asked the teacher why she had not corrected the arms in glissade. The teacher explained that she had corrected the arms in glissade on Monday, Tuesday, Wednesday . . . and now it was Friday, and she didn't want to sound boring, like a broken record. Balanchine said, "Oh, I have to say the same things every day to my company. But it can't be boring. Tell a story." And it will not be boring to those students who enjoy and delight in the *process* of learning to dance to their potential. One lives the process, not the outcome.

The teacher needs to keep alive her own delight in beautiful movement and in dancers. When her students do well or even just begin to make progress, she must be delighted in them, not because it validates her effort, but for them and for the work. Precisely because it is she who must insist on the standard—after all, no one else can—she must let them know that good dancing is a joy to her, and she must celebrate them when their good dancing brings joy. Certainly we were never in doubt of that with Mr. B. And the person who knows she brings joy is usually more joyful herself.

Balanchine liked to tell the life story of the butterfly. It starts as a caterpillar, munching and munching, saying to itself all the while, "I want to be a butterfly." On it goes munching, munching, saying, "I want to be a butterfly." In time, the caterpillar spins a cocoon, still saying, "I want to be a butterfly." Then, one day, it comes out and flies around and says, "I am a butterfly, I am so happy, I am free." And then, BANG!! The butterfly is dead. But while it was flying around, it did not worry about what would happen. It enjoyed every minute of freedom, it celebrated its butterfly self. To Mr. B, we were like butterflies. We work so long to become professional dancers and then most of us perform fewer years than we spend preparing. So while we dance, let us dance totally, full out, completely involved in the now, every moment, every step; let us dance as beautifully as we can. Let us not worry about the next pirouette, the next role, the next new ballet. Not in class, not onstage, not at all.

For Mr. B, dancing beautifully normally included using more of the possible range of motion than was called for in the tradition as he learned it. For the dancer, the effect is to extend the movement, to open it up, to make it happen more quickly, to make it last longer, to make it fill more space, to use more energy. For the audience, one effect is that the dancer looks freer. And as the dancer becomes more technically accomplished, she actually does become freer. But the dancer is never completely free, because she is governed by the music and disciplined by classical ballet technique, which is the source of a dancer's consistent sense of good form (the essential qualities). Mr. B made use of his more expansive technique even in his 1951 setting of Act II of *Swan Lake* (the first lakeside scene), probably the most universally recognized traditional classical choreography. He kept most of Ivanov's structure, but increased the amount of movement for the dancers through his extension of the traditional forms. Each dancer bends her torso, moves her arms, and covers space much more than in Ivanov's original choreography. The tempos in the NYCB performances of *Swan Lake* (and other ballets) are also faster than those generally used.

In the 1960s Maria Tallchief returned to the company after an absence of several years and was cast again as Odette in Balanchine's *Swan Lake*. During the final orchestral rehearsal she abruptly stopped dancing and clapped her hands loudly to stop the conductor. The orchestra came to a halt. We corps dancers had never seen anything like it! "George!" she called out—we had never heard him called George—"it was never that fast!" she exclaimed. Balanchine looked at her calmly and said, "Things have changed since you left, dear. Now, it's like this." And he began to sing and conduct to show her the brisk tempo and incisive phrasing he wanted.

I recall another occasion when the female corps was being rehearsed by an assistant for its first entrance in Mr. B's *Swan Lake*. Like many ballet masters, this assistant placed great emphasis in performance on uniformity of line throughout the corps de ballet. Such ballet masters expend tremendous energy and endless rehearsal time achieving this uniformity, along with perfect spacing, perfect lines, perfect circles, etc. We worked and worked until every line was straight, until every arm was raised at exactly the same angle, until we were in perfect unison. Balanchine appeared, and the ballet master proudly showed him what he had accomplished. When we had danced the passage, Mr. B paused, sniffed, and said, "Mechanical ducks! I don't want to see mechanical ducks." For Mr. B, the energy, the life, the awareness, and the beauty *each* of his dancers displayed were always more important; it was how you got to your place and arrived at a position that mattered more. This is not the same as saying that the other qualities did not matter at all; they mattered, but less.

That ballet master had lost the balance between drilling for "perfection," which can't be achieved because it doesn't exist, and working for the essential qualities while keeping alive the spontaneity, the risk-taking, the spirit, the joie. Teachers also need to keep that balance.

Pointework and Related Relevé

More than any other figure in twentieth-century ballet, George Balanchine concentrated on the development and use of pointework. The proof of its importance to him is in the ballets he made and in the consistent interest he displayed in his classes for the dancers of the New York City Ballet and elsewhere—for example, the Ford Foundation seminars.

Balanchine certainly did not object to teaching men—on the contrary, he wanted the men of the company to come to class. He taught everyone who came to his class, but his special effort, attention, and insight was directed mostly at his women. His classes were made up of material that every ballet dancer must work on and also included some material generally more suitable for the men (but some women would do it), along with a lot of material that was specifically for the women, such as pointework. The men were left to some degree to fend for themselves. The "girls" (as Balanchine called us) could be practicing échappé to pointe with his corrections and variations in tempo or counts, for example. He might then make a similar combination for the men—say, simple échappé jumping and then with beats. Many of us then did that step as well.

It often happened that a pointework exercise clearly for women only—say, bourrée suivie—would be done in several ways, and he could work on it with us for five or ten minutes. Finally some

man would cough loudly, reminding Mr. B that men were in the class, too. Occasionally, Mr. B told the men to practice the step along with us, or he might then give the men something entirely different to do—men's steps such as turns à la seconde or slow cabrioles from the corner. But, again, some of the ladies would do the men's steps anyway. The more a dancer could do, the better. He wanted his dancers to be hungry to dance, and we were.

In the years we worked together, Mr. B and I had conversations on many aspects of pointe technique and aesthetics. More than once I heard him talk about how the pointe lengthened the dancer's leg and enhanced its beauty and how a longer foot magnified the effect. He often recalled that his early fascination with the pointe led to his interest in choreography. We discussed different ways to approach various aspects of every pointe step: for example, how to get onto pointe, how to come off pointe, how to dance without letting the heels "bang" to the floor. There were conversations about the way different dancers looked on pointe and on the effect of having different proportions in the legs and feet. Women were required to take class in pointe shoes for several reasons, but we can believe that one reason was that he liked the look.

In his ballets Balanchine used pointework for every expressive purpose imaginable. It did not trouble him that dancing on pointe was a matter of convention, that it had been invented purely for theatrical effect. The theater itself is an invention, as is ballet. What mattered to him was having dancers who could do the steps he set with technical finesse and musical sensitivity so that the dances expressed what he found in the music. Usually that was a mood, the atmosphere of a relationship, or some other quality that is often very elusive in words. Because he used a very wide variety of music, his dancers had to be able to do pointework with a very wide variety of nuance.

Throughout his career, but especially in the process of building the New York City Ballet, Balanchine worked to achieve a high degree of technical expertise in the use of pointework. Moreover, he demanded this from the entire female ensemble. In his company, advanced and articulate pointework was less and less the province of a very limited number of leading female dancers. By the early 1960s it was required of all the women. Since the late 1960s, and even more in recent years, most of the women taken into the company have successfully performed a principal or solo role in the annual SAB workshop. The dances for soloists and principals usually include more technically intricate and musically complex combinations, but every season's casting shows that many in the corps can learn and dance them.

Mr. B built on the pointe technique in use when he was a student at the Imperial Theatrical School and a new member of the former Maryinsky company in the early 1920s. He developed and then stressed in class a full articulation of the foot in the relevé to pointe and the return to full foot (see page 44). In many steps he wanted a "roll-up" or "press" relevé in which the dancer rises to pointe or descends from pointe by rolling up or down through the metatarsal and toe joints of the foot. In class he largely abandoned the "spring" relevé he saw as a youth, in which the dancer moves onto pointe by means of a small spring or jump that pulls the supporting toes under her supporting hip, approximately to where the middle of her foot had been on full foot. Dancers in those days also

came off pointe with a small spring. It was often completed by falling freely onto the full foot, meaning in practice that the weight settled over the heel. At that time, when rising to pointe and descending, the foot was treated as a jointless appendage. The toe shoe had a very heavy, stiff shank perfectly suited to that way of working. Mr. B changed all that.

He did not ignore stepping to pointe or the spring and jump to pointe in his extension of the technique. He gave us practice in all of these in class and used them all in his ballets. He wanted the dancer to cover more ground, to place the working pointe on the floor, or to spring or jump onto it, at a much larger distance from where she started. It made steps like sissonne or even a simple piqué much more dynamic than they had been. In some ways it is easier to do these stepping, springing, and jumping movements than it is to do his roll-up relevé, which requires more strength. Moreover, when the dancer comes off pointe she has to roll down or, after a slight spring off pointe, she catches herself; no matter which way she started down, she continues through the foot. The full articulation of the foot makes it seem more alive, sensitive, and sensual, affecting many other steps and for all these reasons it is the more important innovation.

As important as the roll-up relevé is for achieving the highest levels of technique on pointe, it should not be seen as separate from the rest of Balanchine's technique. In learning to do relevé as he wanted, we also learned that the leg and foot have more to offer as a means of expression than we had suspected. He showed us how to present the leg and foot before stepping, whether to pointe or flat. We learned to put our feet on the floor in a very specific way in any step, on pointe or not. He taught us how to refine the step to pointe—piqué—by placing our toes—that is, the edge of the box—to the floor in a very specific way. As we learned to use each part of the foot and to make it articulate, the corrections we heard each day—place the toes to the floor, control the descent, "present" the heel, maintain the turnout—took on new meaning. "You have only two feet," Mr. B would say with a twinkle in his eye. "You must know what you do with all two of them. Show me this one, then show me that one." Mastery of pointe made our feet more a part of us; we were proud of them and we wanted to show them off, to model them.

Awareness of the foot's individual joints—the toes, the base of the toes, the ball of the foot, and so on—carried over to the rest of the body. "Your arm is not a stick!" Balanchine would say. "God gave us an elbow, a wrist, and five fingers that move. We must use what we have." He applied this point of view to the whole body and to the whole performance, and even to life. Nothing was to be taken for granted; every moment had to count.

The spring relevé is, as noted, akin to piqué in that it does not require the control and strength needed for the roll-up method. Higher and higher levels of achievement among his dancers, notably including general mastery of rolling up and down through the foot, made possible a new look in Balanchine's choreography, a look we see realized more and more fully in each succeeding period of his work. Thus the pointework in his *Serenade*, originally choreographed in 1934 for the earliest students of the School of American Ballet, is based largely on piqué and spring- or jump-to-pointe steps. By the time he made *Concerto Barocco* in 1941, the dancers were much stronger. In the pointework for this ballet, especially as it has been danced since the 1960s, the roll-up technique is utilized throughout, both for the two soloists and for the eight women in the ensemble.

By 1957 Balanchine was making ballets like *Square Dance*, in which the corps and the soloists perform many of the same, very difficult steps, and *Agon*, which demanded a much more sophisticated musicality to match its quirky syncopations. In the 1960s he could give five of the solos in *Raymonda Variations* to members of the corps. And in the 1970s and 1980s he could produce large-scale festivals (Stravinsky 1972 and 1982, Ravel 1976, Tchaikovsky 1981) that demanded from the entire company an unprecedented ability to master new

material, in some cases material created during the festivals themselves.

Balanchine's fascination with pointework and the exhaustive use of the technique in his choreography give his works a look of sparkling virtuosity and glowing simplicity. Because all his women worked on pointe with skill and polish, Balanchine made the artificial technique seem natural. What can elsewhere seem extraordinary, and thereby a trick, becomes commonplace. His pointework is not isolated or highlighted, as if in quotation marks; it is, rather, a given for every woman on the stage, an integral part of her expressive being. Thus, for all her characteristically formidable virtuosity, his ballerina is never a stunt artist. In Balanchine's ballets, more than in those by other choreographers, she is typically part of an ensemble in which all the women dance basically the same steps. This can already be seen in two of the earliest of his ballets made in America, *Serenade* and *Concerto Barocco*, both of which are still in repertory at the New York City Ballet and many other companies. In the finales of large ballets like *Piano Concerto No. 2*, *Western Symphony*, and *Theme and Variations*, the women dance almost all the same steps; there are many more examples in his ballets.

The ballerina stands a bit apart because in one or more ways she reveals to a heightened degree qualities that all ballet dancers share. She has greater strength and stamina; she is more responsive to music, which allows her to shape her dancing in a more personal way while staying in time; she moves on a grander scale, with greater amplitude (i.e., dances "bigger") and greater clarity of shape; she can sustain slower phrases and longer poses or move faster in allegro. And in some ballets, even Balanchine ballets, her exceptional emotional or dramatic expressiveness enables her to fill out a role.

Balanchine stressed pointework in the studio as well as onstage. His technical advances (presenting the leg and foot, the detailed refinement of stepping to point and coming off, and the important roll-up relevé and roll-down from pointe) and his careful work on them in class produced dancers able to move onstage smoothly at any speed and with a wide variety of textures or feelings to the movement—sharp, soft, forceful, gentle, sensual, and so on. With such dancers he could weave pointe steps into the fabric of classical dancing set to any music he chose. Dancing on pointe had a new adaptability. It was no longer necessary to restrict the use of pointe to designated virtuoso roles, as Fokine and many others had done. Balanchine's dancers could dance as freely on pointe as other ballet dancers do in soft slippers.

In 1964 the New York City Ballet opened the New York State Theater at Lincoln Center. Every woman in the corps de ballet who came to the new theater with Balanchine lived her artistic life through pointework.

POINTE SHOES

We wore pointe shoes for all classes because Balanchine wanted us to be able to do everything naturally in the pointe shoe—to walk, run, jump, turn, execute grand plié—in short, to *dance*. We even practiced grand adagios standing on one foot, a kind of movement he rarely used onstage. "Perhaps one day you will do *Giselle*," he would joke, watching us practice arabesque penchée standing on the full foot. We must have learned that step, because he eventually used it in several of his ballets—for example, for the second soloist in the "Rubies" section of *Jewels* and in *Harlequinade* for Columbine, the Bonne Fée, and even for eight birds.

Balanchine was very much aware of the expense to the company caused by the need for so many pairs of pointe shoes. He therefore did not object to our wearing old shoes for class, as long as they were not so old that they failed to give us the support we needed to dance full-out on pointe. Also, for me and for some of the other women, it was easier to start class in softer shoes. We had better articulation of the foot and pointed our toes more easily,

so we wore older but serviceable pointe shoes for the barre exercises. Then, as the center work began, we changed into newer, slightly harder shoes.

Before I was promoted to soloist, I tended to wear my newer, stronger shoes in class in order to work better on Balanchine's center combinations, rather than saving them for performances with less demanding work. So I went through a period of keeping my older shoes for, say, *Swan Lake*, while saving the newer ones for class. And for the half-hour warm-up I gave myself before class, I would use my very oldest shoes. I never wore brand-new shoes in class. I broke them in for the next day after class or during my warm-up for the performance. Each dancer needs to manage her shoes so she is able to work full-out in class as well as have the right shoes for performance.

Once a dancer has become accustomed to working in pointe shoes, it is hard to go back to ballet slippers. Soft slippers give much less support, and, although in jumps you have to point your feet extra hard against the end of the pointe shoe in order to bend the shank and box, the shoe actually helps the dancer when landing: The box provides resistance, which helps control the foot as it makes contact with the floor. Because it is soft, the slipper offers no such resistance, which makes it more likely that the dancer will land on the ball of the foot and go immediately onto her whole foot, rather than landing on the tips of the toes and easing down through the toe joints and then through the rest of the foot.

Balanchine preferred the look of fresh, shiny pointe shoes in performance. Many dancers like to apply pancake to their shoes to dull the surface to match the matte finish of their pink tights, but he did not approve of this. When the pointe shoes became dirty, which happened much more easily in the days of wood floors, dancers removed the surface dirt when necessary with some cleaning fluid.

How the pointe shoe fits the foot is of utmost importance to the look of the foot when pointing, walking, running, or doing ballet steps on pointe— in other words, when dancing. Balanchine was naturally very much interested in the look of the pointe—that is, the look of the shoe with the foot inside shaping it. In the 1950s and 1960s many dancers wore shoes too small for their feet. He noticed that when standing on flat, their heels rested on two or more inches of satin. So he suggested to such dancers that they try a slightly larger shoe with a longer sole. Another effect of wearing a shoe that is too short or with a box that is too narrow is that the dancer must jam her toes in, creating an effect a little like having the toes bound. I developed soft corns from wearing too tight a box until I learned better—or maybe I got tired of visits to the chiropodist.

Mr. B wanted us to be in control of the shoe, rather than allowing our feet to be passively controlled by the shoe. In fact, once our feet had developed sufficient strength and we needed to rely less on the rigidity of the shoe to relevé, many of us began to order lighter shoes and often would use only about three quarters of the shank, the leather stiffener running along the inside of the sole of the shoe. Also, many of us ordered shoes with a flatter—that is, lower—box, which gave a more tapered line to the pointe. Balanchine's observations led to useful improvements in the design of the pointe shoe. In time, ballet shoemakers developed new models based on his suggestions. Manufacturers also became used to accommodating individual needs, including tailoring the pointe shoe for individual dancers. Such shoes are known as "special order" shoes and are used by many dancers in professional companies.

In the 1990s many dancers seem to have made comfort a very important criterion, choosing shoes that are too wide and/or too long. The shoes may be comfortable, allowing the toes to spread out, but they begin to look like tugboats. Some shoes in the 1990s are so hard and stiff, they look like they are made of wood. They may seem in some ways easier to work in, but they surely prevent full articulation of the foot. Other shoes apparently designed to last a lifetime are made out of an unyielding synthetic material; they look like they have been made

for dancing in outer space. There may be some short-term savings, but the advanced student who is serious about a career needs to work with the kind of shoes she will be using as a professional. This means shoes with a firm but not binding fit and made of material her feet can control.

Even though Mr. B preferred fresh, shiny pointe shoes, he also wanted us to dance soundlessly. He did not want to hear pointe shoes banging on the floor or hear the squeaking caused by the rosin that dancers rub their shoes in to keep from slipping. "I don't want to hear squeak," he would say. "If I hear squeak . . ." At one point, he actually had the rosin box removed from backstage. Squeaking shoes interfere with the music and detract from the atmosphere of the performance. He even said that he would rather see a dancer slip than hear her shoes squeak while she danced. To do without the rosin, we learned to roughen the soles of our shoes with a rasp or score them with a razor to get a more secure grip on the floor.

Although Balanchine was able to reduce the squeaking by limiting the amount of rosin available in the wings, he did not tell us which pair of shoes to wear in order to eliminate the banging and clunking of stiff, new boxes. To run without noise in pointe shoes the shoe must be relatively soft. So, when we prepared to dance *Serenade*, a ballet that is full of running but fairly elementary in its use of pointework, he would stress the importance of wearing older shoes. Sometimes he threatened to take a ballet off pointe altogether if we could not control the noise of our shoes. He never did this with *Serenade*, but he did carry out his threat with the dances for the Butterflies in *A Midsummer Night's Dream*, when the clunking of the ensemble destroyed the light, flitting atmosphere of the choreography. So he put the Butterflies in ballet slippers, and they danced on demi-pointe. This left only me, the solo Butterfly, in pointe shoes. The ballet was performed in this way until several years after Balanchine's death, when the Butterflies went back on pointe. I prepared my shoes by banging the boxes on a cement floor or tapping them with a hammer. This helped me to dance quietly but did not make the shoes too soft.

There were times, however, when he did want to hear our feet striking the floor. In a frappé exercise at the barre, for instance, he might ask the pianist to hold a chord for eight counts, while our feet struck the floor on each of the eight beats. Typically he did this to make us hold or maintain the tempo without picking up speed or slowing down. He wanted us to keep the tempo as precisely as a metronome.

POINTING THE FOOT IN POINTE SHOES

In my early training in San Francisco I was taught to keep my toes straight in the pointe shoe, whether standing on pointe or pointing in the air. As I explained (see page 43), Mr. B wanted the toes firmly pressed against the sole of the shoe to give the curved shape he wanted when pointing the foot. Developing the strength and stamina to achieve and sustain the required look is one of the basic goals of a female dancer's training. He compared the resulting quality to an elephant's trunk. The dancer's foot should have the same pliability and flexibility, she should be able to use it with great delicacy, and yet her foot must be strong and untiring. These qualities depend mostly on correct execution of the necessary exercises in class.

Advanced and professional dancers will also need to reserve time to supplement class with their own practice of standard barre exercises that develop "elephant's trunk" qualities in the feet and toes. These include battements tendus for practice shaping the foot and to build strength

in the toes to point the tips, relevés to build strength all through the foot and ankle, and sur le cou-de-pied for practice shaping the foot and using it with delicacy. Here are two additional barre exercises that are beneficial for stretching the instep and bending the tips of the toes when wearing pointe shoes.

In the first supplemental pointe exercise, the dancer stands on pointe in first position facing the barre; she pliés on pointe. As she demi-pliés, she goes over on pointe, bending the tips of the toes and the end of the pointe shoe as well as stretching the instep. She maintains her weight over the big toe and the toe next to it and brings her heels forward. When she straightens her knees and pulls up and out of her legs and feet, she holds the insteps out and keeps her heels forward and her legs turned out. This exercise is also helpful to men because, al-

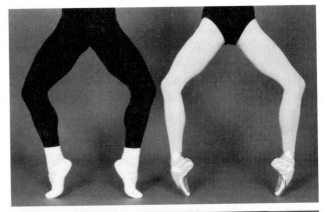

Peter and Dana plié on demi-pointe and pointe, stretching their insteps.

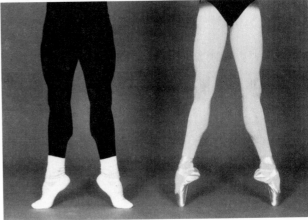

Peter and Dana have stretched their knees while trying to maintain the shape of the foot.

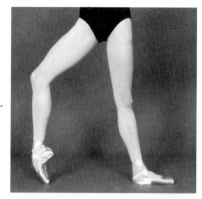

Dana pushes over on her pointe to stretch her instep and bend the tip of the box.

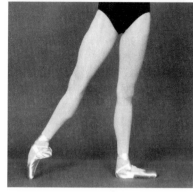

Dana straightens her knee while keeping her instep lifted and toes bent, and while trying to keep the entire tip of the box on the floor.

kles; it works equally well in pointe shoes and ballet slippers, so I give it to boys and girls. The dancer starts in fifth position at the barre and does tendu side. When the working leg is fully stretched and the foot pointed, the dancer lowers slowly to demi-pointe with resistance and quickly points, then lowers slowly to full foot with resistance and quickly points, and finally lowers slowly to demi-plié and then quickly points. In this exercise the dancer does tendu on "and," demi-pointe on one, pointe on "and," full foot on two, pointe on "and," demi-plié in second on three, pointe on "and," and close fifth on four. This kind of exercise, done with resistance in the toes, feet, and ankles helps the dancer build the required strength.

Pilates exercises (matwork, reformer, the "Cadillac," or bed, and spring chair) have also long been seen as useful to build strength in the body as a whole, and certain ones are especially good for the feet and ankles. In the 1990s the Theraband, a newer device useful for developing strength in the toes, feet, and ankles, also became generally available as a supplement to the barre exercises.

though not on pointe, they can plié in the same way on demi-pointe and stretch their insteps.

In the second supplemental pointe exercise, the dancer stands in fifth position at the barre and tendus side in the usual way. When her working leg is fully extended, she bends the working knee and shifts some of her weight over onto the foot, stretching the instep and bending the end of the toe shoe. She slowly straightens her working leg, trying to hold her foot fully pointed, with the tip of the box (not just the bottom edge) of the toe shoe on the floor, with the heel forward.

Although the men require less strength to achieve a beautifully pointed foot in a ballet slipper, maintaining the shape of the point requires equal awareness. And they have their own reasons for needing to develop very strong feet. When they land from jumps, they catch their weight at the toes and grasp the floor with the toes as they lower into plié by going through their feet. I give this supplemental barre exercise because it is beneficial for building strength in the toes, metatarsals, and an-

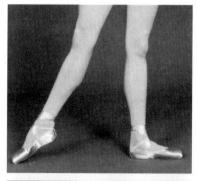

Dana, resisting the floor with the toes, lowers toward demi-pointe.

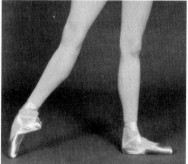

Dana rapidly points her foot again.

TOE STANCE

When the dancer is standing on pointe, most of her weight should be borne by the big toe and the toe next to it. The toes are usually not straight to the floor, which would place the dancer on the tips of her toes. Instead, they are slightly bent under. This is achieved by placing the weight above the top of the supporting foot and by stretching the top of the foot. The dancer does not intentionally bend the toes; rather, the placement of her weight and the flexibility of her instep determine their shape and position in the shoe. The dancer pulls up off her feet and out of her shoes; she does not relax and sit into them (see page 44).

How much the toes are bent depends on the dancer's foot and the shape of her leg. The dancer with a higher arch will usually have straighter toes; the dancer with a lower arch will usually bend the

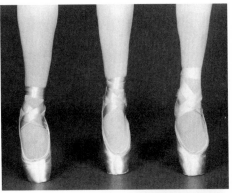

Correct toe stance viewed en face

Correct toe stance viewed from the side. The higher the arch (extreme right), the straighter the toes; the lower the arch (extreme left), the more they are curved or bent, bringing the foot forward over the box of the shoe.

toes more. These rules of thumb are useful, but only as a guide. Balanchine considered each dancer individually and would adjust, as necessary, some of the finer details to enhance the look of a particular foot. Ultimately the dancer must make her toe stance her own. Her toe stance cannot be precarious to her; she must feel comfortable and secure. At the same time, she works to achieve her optimal look.

POSITIONS OF THE FEET ON POINTE (AND DEMI-POINTE)

Positions on pointe correspond to four of the standard five positions of the feet. They apply both to women on pointe and to men on demi-pointe. The four main positions (as I noted, there was never any thought of third position in Balanchine's class, on pointe or off) were practiced with an awareness of what was to be achieved: The step was designed for a particular aesthetic effect, or it was designed to build strength, or both. On pointe or demi-pointe, the legs and feet cannot be as fully turned out as they are in plié.

The standard first position on pointe was rarely used by Balanchine in his choreography. However, it was a position Mr. B used in class to build strength in the feet and toes and to perfect the action of the knees and ankles in relevés. We rolled up onto pointe from first position, a movement that left the toes where they had started and resulted in a wider stance. More often, however, we used what Balanchine called "small first," a position on pointe in which the heels almost touched. This was the position we often moved through when executing quick pas de bourrées on pointe (see page 283).

Second position on pointe was more interesting to Balanchine choreographically. It was the position assumed in one kind of échappé, and Balanchine included it in many exercises to help his dancers learn it precisely. Traditionally, when standing in second position on flat, the space between the heels should equal

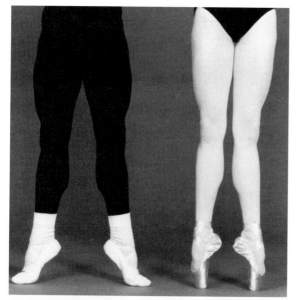

Peter in standard first position on demi-pointe; Dana in small first position on pointe

Deanna (on left) in standard first position on pointe; Dana (on right) in small first position on pointe

rolled down from second on pointe to second flat, which would not be possible if the pointes had been drawn toward the center. Consequently our échappé to second on pointe resulted in a distance a little wider than two times the length of the dancer's foot. This is a rule of thumb meant to help dancers avoid the tendency for the position to be too small; Mr. B did not go around measuring, and neither do I. If dancers begin to open too wide, it is relatively easy to have them cut back. We did practice consecutive relevés in second (and also first) to build strength and coordination in the feet, ankles, calves, and thighs and to help us reinforce muscle memory of the position. When the tempo was fast, the échappé became smaller in class as well as in ballets such as *Square Dance*.

In fourth position on pointe, we could have the two feet separated, as usual, by the length of our foot or a little more. It was essential that the thighs be crossed and that both pointes be aligned on the center line of the body to define the dancer's center;

Peter in second position on demi-pointe; Dana in second position on pointe

the length of the dancer's foot. When we rolled up from second to pointe (demi-pointe for men), our feet were not only opposite one another, but also the space between them was wider than if the pointe position had been attained by spring relevé, during which the dancer draws the pointes under and in toward her center as she rises. Some teachers want to see the pointes directly under the outer edge of the hipbones. But Balanchine wanted the distance between the heels to be the same when we

she should look as if she were standing on a tightrope. This meant that in fourth position on pointe (as on flat) the relationship of the legs had to remain constant. This could not be achieved by merely rolling up out of fourth position. If we were making a pose in fourth position on pointe at the barre in an adagio, we rolled up on the back foot as we brought the front foot over to achieve the "tightrope" alignment. Usually some spring action was necessary. When we moved from fifth position plié to fourth position on pointe (échappé to fourth), the tips of the toes on pointe had to be brought into this same alignment. This was a matter not only of spacing but also of centering, of crossing the legs until the toes reached the center line on the floor. Seen from the front, Balanchine's fourth position on pointe is a close relative of his fifth on pointe: toes precisely aligned on the center line of the body, heels showing on either side.

When fourth position on pointe was part of a combination in the center, the length of the stance became more flexible. If there was time in the music, Balanchine preferred a slightly wider position. It was more dynamic to see the legs shooting out to a big fourth or second position, and it made the choreography more interesting because the steps became more differentiated and thus clearer. He often said, "I want to see the difference between this and that." We learned to enunciate with our feet and legs, thus making the movement more legible, even to those farthest from the stage.

Like fourth position on pointe, fifth position on pointe required a spring or an adjustment of the front foot. Balanchine never gave consecutive roll-up relevés that required an adjustment of the front foot to arrive in fifth position on pointe. He preferred instead the action indicated by the now generalized term "sous-sus."

To Balanchine, sous-sus meant both fifth position on pointe and the springing action to get there. In sous-sus the little toe of the front foot is held

Peter in fourth position on demi-pointe; Dana in fourth position on pointe, en face

Fourth position croisé; Peter on demi-pointe, Dana on pointe

against the big toe of the back foot with the heels showing equally on either side; the illusion from the front is that of a single pointe on the floor. However, sous-sus should not be thought of only in terms of the position of the feet. From the upper thighs down, the fully turned-out legs should be clearly crossed and held together, one in front of the other, with the pointes touching, if necessary slightly releasing the front knee.

The spring comes out of the demi-plié in fifth. He wanted to see both the feet and legs participate. This meant that from the bottom of the plié, the dancer had to spring slightly off the floor so as to pull both pointes under her. The toes of each foot moved in equally to her center, landing simultaneously. At the same time, the legs turned out, bring-

Peter in fifth position on demi-pointe; Dana in fifth position on pointe, en face

ing the heels forward as the insides of the thighs came together and the legs stretched, thus revealing sous-sus.

In executing sous-sus in adagio, the dancer may need to adjust subtly to soften the usual sharpness. She uses just the minimum spring, the tips of her pointes almost skimming the floor; once on pointe, she continues to grow into her fullest stretch. In the adagio in *Symphony in C*, for example, some ballerinas use this approach. In recent years, others have rolled up to pointe on the back foot and brought the front foot into fifth; this can be even more in keeping with the lyrical feeling of the slow legato melody.

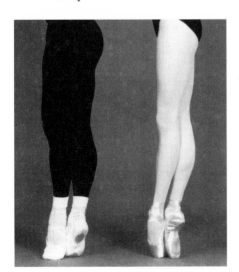

Peter in fifth position on demi-pointe; Dana in fifth position on pointe, side view

We generally used one of three ways of coming off pointe from sous-sus, depending on how the dancer arrived in sous-sus (pas de bourrée ending in sous-sus, temps lié to pointe, or plié relevé) and on how the step was set. The first way called for rolling down through the back foot and adjusting the front foot while maintaining stretched legs. The second called for rolling down through the back foot into plié and adjusting the front foot as that leg pliéd. In either case, after lowering herself through both feet, she finishes in a tight fifth.

The technique for descending from sous-sus that we worked on most often in class called for *both* feet to spring out simultaneously from their tightly held position on pointe. The dancer catches herself at the base of her toes and continues to lower into a controlled demi-plié. Mr. B watched to make sure that both feet participated in the action and moved about the same distance and that they came down together at the same time. The dancer takes herself down through her feet from sous-sus with resistance in the feet and thighs; she does not fall onto the whole foot. This requires the most fully developed legs and feet. It is also especially important for the kind of "on top of the music" attack Mr. B wanted in allegro.

If the dancer executes a series of sous-sus properly, there need be no traveling; she rises and descends on the same spot on the floor. However, sous-sus can also travel front, side, and back. The technique is the same as for sous-sus in place, in that the feet must arrive on pointe together, making one sound. "I want to hear TAH, not ta-ta," Balanchine would say, referring to the single sound made by the pointes as they hit the floor. In the traveling variants, however, a definite jumping action is required. The dancer must take care to keep her weight over her legs—that is, she must bring her hips and upper body with her as she scoots her feet front, side, or back into the next sous-sus. Again, this is very important for staying "on top of the music."

Although men do not usually practice consecutive sous-sus (or bourrée or échappé relevé or certain other steps) in class, they can be called on to do it in some ballets. For example, in the third movement of *Symphony in C,* the male and female principals simultaneously do four sous-sus in place. When men do these "women's steps," the technique is basically the same. So here is an advantage to giving one class that the entire company attends, rather than having a separate one for women that is devoted to pointework. The men may pick up some information useful for present performance, and they will also be better prepared to be ballet masters, choreographers, and teachers when the time comes.

I think a good company class schedule in most cases will give about half the classes combined and half separated, with one class for men and one for women. This will allow more sustained attention at least three times a week to the specific needs of each group, yet bring them together as well. In his combined company classes, Peter Martins, ballet master-in-chief of the New York City Ballet, often finishes with partnering work, which, of course, requires men and women together in class. What is needed and what is feasible will also change based on the repertory being danced, whether the company is performing or only rehearsing, whether the company is at home or on tour, and so on. However, the most important idea is to make decisions about the kinds of steps and corrections in class based on what one sees, rather than settling into a standardized, automatic routine.

RELEVÉ: RISING TO POINTE
OR DEMI-POINTE

In the interest of clarity, I have so far discussed rising to pointe, relevé, as if there were two distinct ways (see page 44, this material must be understood). In fact, it is a little more complicated, because there are four ways and they have some shared characteristics, so they are not fully distinct. The first way is the most traditional; this relevé is the spring to pointe in which the dancer does a

small but sharp jump and pulls her toes under the center of her foot. The second way is almost the same—a small but sharp jump, with the dancer leaving her toes approximately where they are. As I have said, Mr. Balanchine worked on a third way, a roll-up through the entire foot to pointe. This is the technique he most often emphasized at the barre, and it is the ideal the dancer aims for in roll-up relevé in the center and in performance. However, due to varying factors of timing, of placement of the dancer's weight, of the dancer's strength, etc., the complete roll-up on one foot cannot be consistently achieved without the support of the barre. So in the center and onstage, there is a fourth way: The dancer often rises to pointe by starting to roll up, finishing with a minimum spring, only what she needs to get her to pointe. This will be much less than is required when she springs up from flat and often will be so smooth and unobtrusive that it is barely perceptible.

When I first learned to pirouette on pointe as a student in San Francisco, I was taught to do a spring relevé, pulling the toes under my working leg so as not to have to readjust my balance. By the time I came to New York, Balanchine had long since rethought this traditional method for rising to pointe for turns. With a well-controlled relevé through the foot, the toes did not have to adjust at all, as they did in the spring relevé. The dancer simply presses the foot into the floor, executing the relevé where the toes are. She arrives on pointe with a straight supporting knee as she pulls up off her legs and out of her hips. Because the dancer starts with her weight over the ball of the supporting foot, she is already where she needs to be for the turn or at most needs only a very slight adjustment (usually forward) to be over the supporting pointe; there is no need to think about any transfer of weight. My colleague Stanley Williams used to tell both men and women to relevé "into the big toe." This method not only makes the relevé stronger and smoother, it also helps the dancer maintain her balance and turnout and arrive on pointe with her supporting knee straight, rather than finish straightening it when she is already on pointe. This not infrequently happens when she springs up. When the weight is settled back in the heel, it is impossible to roll up without a shift of weight, and consequently the dancer will often spring or jump up as she heaves herself to pointe. When the dancer begins the turn, she must keep her weight forward, not letting it fall backward, as is the tendency in nearly all turns. Whereas the spring action jarred the body and required some adjustment of the foot, the roll-up method offers greater stability, since it involves a smaller change of position.

I have already discussed the importance of rolling through the foot for the strength it develops for jumping and the control it develops for landings. It must be clear at this point that rolling through the foot is one of the keys to much of Mr. Balanchine's technique. Unlike some of the qualities he wanted, which are matters mainly of awareness and habit, rolling through the foot requires a lot of strength as well as awareness and good habits. That is why Balanchine emphasized it in class and insisted on it for many exercises at the barre. Since a complete roll-up is, as I have noted, often not possible in the center, Balanchine wanted the dancer to begin the relevé with a roll-up and finish it as smoothly as possible.

The technique for the roll-up relevé is covered on page 44, because it is common to all dancers and used at the barre. However, Mr. B gave extensive relevé exercises facing the barre that were part of his exploration of the tiniest details of pointework. Even though he generally preferred a short barre, when time permitted and when he felt it necessary, Balanchine made the time for relevé exercises in class. Sometimes he would concentrate on relevé from demi-pointe to pointe on two feet (as in first position) and on one foot alone, often rolling up relatively slowly. At first, if necessary, we actively pushed against the barre to help us to roll up to pointe and to slowly descend. Eventually, our feet became so strong that we no longer needed much support from the barre. In addition to rolling down at normal speeds, he would also ask us sometimes to practice coming down from full pointe to demi-pointe very, very slowly. This exercise could also be done lowering to the full foot with or without demi-plié. The dancer also concentrates when lowering on bringing the heel (or heels) forward. In each exercise the aims were to strengthen the first joint of the toes and the metatarsals and, of course, to develop the habit (reinforce muscle memory) and cultivate awareness of the entire relevé action.

For the men also doing these exercises, adapting Mr. B's steps to working in ballet slippers, the goal was to roll up from flat to a high demi-pointe, then roll down with resistance and control so the heel

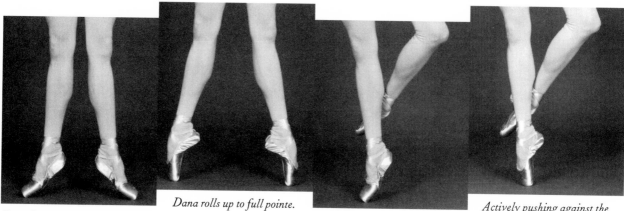

From first position on pointe, Dana lowers with resistance toward demi-pointe.

Dana rolls up to full pointe.

Actively holding the barre, Dana lowers with resistance toward demi-pointe.

Actively pushing against the barre, Dana rolls up to full pointe.

just grazed the floor. This will strengthen the foot and calf, although it does not work the toes in the way that rolling to and from pointe does. It led Mr. B to suggest from time to time that the boys try pointe shoes for some exercises, but almost none ever did.

Such simple relevé exercises facing the barre might be done eight times in a variety of positions such as first or standing on one foot, with the working foot held in coupé back, low arabesque, or in a low à la seconde. We might practice eight roll-up relevés in first with demi-plié, followed by eight without plié, concluding with eight from demi-pointe to pointe. This whole series might then be repeated on each foot. Such exercises worked the whole foot and ankle and the calf, the knee, thigh, and hip, but in particular, they strengthened the top and the underside of the foot. Balanchine often stressed the need for the heel to be brought forward during the descent from relevé. When we were facing the barre, working on one foot to build strength, Balanchine did not pay much attention to the other leg and foot. It was to remain out of the way (e.g., in sur le cou-de-pied back) so we could focus on the active supporting foot. Since this was company class, not a designated pointe class, Balanchine did not give the usual series of barre exercises with the dancers continually executing relevés and/or remaining on pointe. That kind of class is necessary in early training in school, but it was less important for his female company dancers. They not only took class in pointe shoes, they also rehearsed and performed a repertory that was nearly all on pointe, so they worked in the technique all the time anyway.

The women did quite a few exercises at the barre that did involve pointework, holding it sometimes with one hand, sometimes with both hands. These exercises included fondu relevé, sissonne to pointe, hops on pointe, adagios on pointe, and so forth. On occasion we also practiced brief excerpts from Balanchine's ballets: Holding the barre with one hand, we might do a plié; sous-sus; développé à la seconde with the arm in fifth high; balance as we move

the other arm to fifth high; turn to arabesque facing the barre; and take the barre "as if it were the man," as Balanchine liked to say. In essence, what we had done was a snippet from the second movement of *Symphony in C.*

Most of the men did the same steps, but on demi-pointe. If the step was totally inappropriate for men and not really adaptable, the men would skip it.

Besides helping us to gain strength and precision, these relevé exercises also helped develop the instep and the arch, which gave the foot a better shape on pointe. In addition to the curve of the arch, which enhances the shapeliness of the foot when the foot is seen in profile by the audience, Balanchine was interested in the look of the pointe when it is seen from the dancer's front. What he liked was a pointe that tapers from the big toe's first joint down to the base, where the shoe and toes make contact with the floor. Since the placement of the dancer's weight, and therefore the center of the pointe, are determined by the first and second toes, Balanchine wanted to see the inside of the pointe taper to that central area.

The presence of a small bunion alongside the big toe's first joint contributes to such a tapered look, since the additional width of the first joint makes the toes appear to taper more dramatically to the tip of the pointe. Without this augmented first joint the toes in the pointe shoe can sometimes seem almost to sickle inward. So Balanchine liked the way a small bunion made the pointe look. In my own case, my big toe was set in so straight a line with the joint that the tip of my pointe looked square and my foot a little sickled. With a twinkle in his eye as he said it, Balanchine suggested I go home and work on developing a slight bunion. So I went home and walked around on pointe, slightly rolling in toward my big toe. In several years I produced the tapered look that he wanted and that is so beautiful.

In the mid-'60s, when Balanchine's classes concentrated most heavily on relevé and relevé-related movements, the level of pointe technique of all the women in the company rose markedly. At about that time the younger "girls" in the corps began to perform steps on pointe that had previously been the exclusive province of ballerinas. "My corps dancers are like soloists in any other company," Balanchine liked to say. I remember his visiting my advanced variations class at the School of American Ballet in the early '70s. How pleased he was to see all the girls perform a difficult variation from the 1951 version of his *Minkus Pas de Trois*. He said, "In those days, only one dancer could do those turns, and now, in a class at the School, everyone can do."

COMING OFF POINTE

The descent from pointe is as important as getting onto pointe. Traditionally, there were four ways of coming off pointe: 1) coupé front or back; 2) tombé; 3) a little spring down, usually followed by a fall to the full foot; and 4) on occasion, a roll-down

that finished with the weight distributed over the whole foot, with some most likely settled back in the heel. Typically, Balanchine reconsidered all four methods and refined the technique of each. We practiced all of them in class, but the one we worked on most, and especially at the barre, was the roll-down. The descent from pointe going through the foot that he taught helped to maintain the weight over the balls of the feet, which was essential to dancing his ballets. It required the most skill, strength, and control.

In going from pointe on one foot to coupé, Balanchine asked us to place the tips of the toes of the working foot on the floor and then roll down through the foot bringing the heel forward, rather than placing the entire ball of the foot on the floor and then lowering down or, worse, placing the full foot flat on the floor. The toes were placed either under the dancer's center or into an overcrossed

Peter and Dana in coupé

Peter and Dana placing the toes to the floor

Peter and Dana "coupéing"—cutting—the supporting foot away as they roll through the foot

Peter and Dana lowering into plié with the weight over the ball of the foot

Peter and Dana in demi-plié with the knee extended over the toes and the weight maintained over the ball of the foot

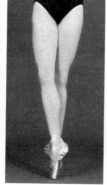
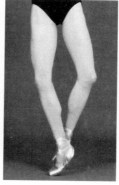

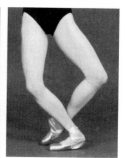

position. This method looked beautiful and delicate and built strength and control in the foot because it emphasized going through the foot, the presentation of the heel forward, and the turnout of the leg.

When we descended in tombé, we first extended the working leg in the traditional way, but as it reached its full height we took our hips in the direction of travel, leaving the body slightly behind and showing the "off-balance" look. We landed on the tips of our toes and went through the working foot, still keeping the weight on the ball of the foot, not falling onto the full foot, and not necessarily putting the heel down. The original supporting foot was still on pointe as we tombéd and remained pointed as we landed. Our step was longer because of the use of the hip, and this gave the movement energy and force. Balanchine used this dynamic tombé often in his choreography—for example, in the first movement of *Concerto Barocco*

Deanna working on tombé side

(when the second soloist makes her first entrance), in the fourth variation of *Divertimento No. 15*, in the "Shylock" variation in the "Emeralds" section of *Jewels*, and in *Valse Fantaisie*.

Ballet dancers are supposed to be pulled up. It's a correction they hear constantly, and being pulled up gives them part of their characteristic look. But when the dancer comes off pointe or demi-pointe with tombé, by springing down or by rolling through the foot, Mr. B wanted a little something extra, a little something more. He wanted the dancer to grow up before going down with resistance. He wanted her to lift her weight up, almost seeming to make space for the legs and feet to move into plié, or, in the case of tombé, to lift her weight up as her hips and legs continued out and over. The result is an enhanced look of lightness and ease, even though the dancer is descending. You might think of it as another "going away to return." Or you might see him once again asking for a little more.

Peter tombés off his supporting leg and foot.

As Peter continues to fall off demi-pointe, he catches his weight with the tips of his toes.

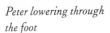

Peter lowering through the foot

Peter has transferred his weight as the back foot finishes pointing.

Peter showing the "off-balance" look while executing tombé in écarté back

The spring down was the same almost imperceptible jump dancers traditionally used, but the landing was different. Balanchine asked us to catch ourselves at the base of the toes and let ourselves down through the foot. As usual, we had to avoid letting the weight settle back in the heel. If we were landing on both feet, we caught ourselves simultaneously at the bases of the toes of both feet and then continued to roll down at the same time.

To roll down, the dancer releases the ankle and starts down through the foot as the knee bends out over the toes. Her toes are actually pressing into or holding the floor. They certainly do not relax and spread out. Meanwhile, as the dancer lowers into demi-plié with resistance, she brings her heel forward and her knee to the side, thus maintaining and controlling the turnout. The calf and thigh muscles control the plié in the ankle and at the knee. The weight remains over the ball of the foot. Mr. B sometimes said that we should be able to slide a piece of paper under the heel; if we could, we were

controlling the process. If the heel finally touched the floor, it was only to begin the reverse action of the plié. The touch lasted just a fraction of a second, thus keeping the weight over the ball of the foot, the plié continuous, and the dancer in total control. In descending into plié from pointe, Mr. B emphasized that the plié occurs simultaneously in the knee and the ankle. "You do together," he would say, "not foot, then knee, or knee, then foot, but together."

Balanchine explored another method of getting off pointe and used it much more frequently than the normal "tombé" described above, both in our exercises and in the ballets. It combines pliéing on the supporting leg (simultaneously rolling down through the foot) with placing the working foot to the floor and then transferring the weight onto it. Mr. B was a little vague about the name, preferring just to show what he wanted, but sometimes he called the step "tombé," although it really is not. I call it "tombé," too, but I usually have to show it. The dancer starts the plié and the rolldown through her supporting foot while bringing the extended working foot to the floor. She places the toes of the working foot to the floor and then goes through that foot as she transfers her weight onto it in plié. For example, she can do fondu relevé in effacé front, plié

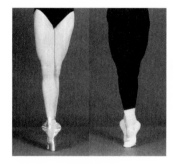

Dana and Peter in sous-sus

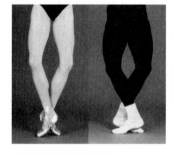

When springing down, Dana and Peter adjust the feet slightly as the knees bend and they go through their feet.

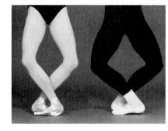

Dana and Peter arriving in fifth position plié with the weight over the balls of the feet

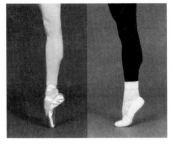

Dana on pointe, Peter on demi-pointe on one foot

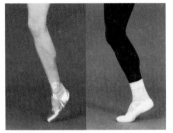

Dana and Peter starting to go through the foot as they release the ankle and bend the knee

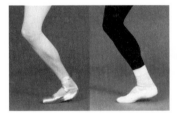

Dana and Peter continue to plié, maintaining the turnout.

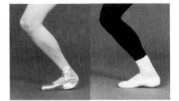

Dana and Peter arriving in full demi-plié; the knee extends over the toes, the weight is over the ball of the foot, heel forward.

on the supporting leg as she rolls down through the foot and brings the working leg down to place the toes on the floor in fourth front. She transfers the weight through plié to the front foot as she pushes off the back foot to relevé in first arabesque. The entire movement is, of course, continuous. A somewhat more common (and not at all desirable) way to get off pointe is to drop down to demi-pointe or to full foot with very little plié or none at all and fall onto the working foot. This looks ungraceful, haphazard; it is happening *to* the dancer, she is not making it happen. Mr. B wanted the dancer to go (if possible, roll) through her foot and move into plié on her supporting leg, controlling

1. Dana on pointe in effacé front 2. Dana coming off pointe, going through her foot as she starts to plié 3. Dana continues to plié as she places her toes to the floor. 4. Dana transferring her weight to the front foot 5. Dana continues transferring her weight and is about to relevé. 6. Dana relevés in first arabesque.

her weight over the ball of the supporting foot as she placed the toes of the working foot to the floor. In this way, she is actively transferring her weight.

Balanchine would say, "Look at the soles of your shoes. Clean heels." Not literally true, of course, but true comparatively. I think of Vladimiroff telling Jacques about the dancer even backstage in the theater, weight forward over the balls of the feet. As always, it's the idea, in this case of clean heels. The idea leads to awareness and effort. Our dancing was then changed, energized in both kinds of tombé, when other dancers relaxed.

RELEVÉ PASSÉ

Balanchine's relevé passé taught us to move from fifth position to pointe on one foot, with the working foot at the knee or passing over the knee.

Traditionally, dancers could choose between the spring relevé and the roll-up relevé in going to passé. Balanchine's relevé passé exercises in class emphasized the latter. Even so, we practiced spring relevé to passé in class, and he used it in choreography when it fit the music better. For relevé passé, the spring relevé did not usually include pulling the pointe under the center of the foot; the toes remained approximately where they had been. In Dewdrop's solo near the end of "The Waltz of the Flowers" in *The Nutcracker*, the ballerina does sissonne (see page 251) to pointe in first arabesque, pliés in fifth, then springs to relevé passé, repeating this several times. Usually, when Balanchine wanted the dancer to go "BANG!" from fifth to relevé passé, he asked for a spring or a jump.

There are two ways to do the roll-up relevé to passé. In the traditional method the dancer pushes off from both feet and rolls up through the supporting foot as the working foot moves up to passé. The more difficult relevé passé that we also worked on quite frequently was not off two feet, but off one foot, a refinement Balanchine made in the step. This relevé passé, which is naturally not as quick, needs to be done at a moderate to slow tempo to

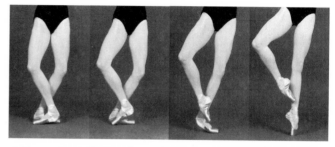

1. Dana releases the front foot as she pliés. 2. Continuing to plié and to release the front foot (no demi-pointe) 3. Coming up out of plié, she lifts her knee to the side and starts to roll up. 4. On a straight supporting leg, on pointe, she continues lifting the knee to the side.

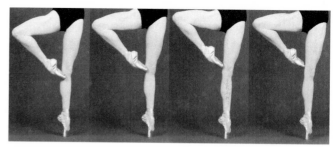

5. Dana on pointe, arriving in passé 6. In passé 7. Her knee carrying her pointe up and around the supporting leg 8. Her pointe moves just behind the supporting leg.

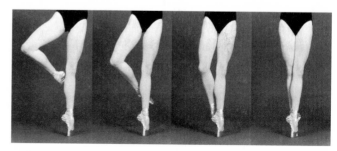

9. Dana lowers her working foot down the center line of her supporting leg. 10. Continuing to lower her foot 11. Aiming the pointe of the working foot right behind the pointe of the supporting foot 12. In sous-sus

concentrate the dancer's attention on the relevé of the supporting foot. He wanted the working foot to release from the floor with a gentle caress just before we reached the bottom of the demi-plié. It should not push against the floor, to help to initiate the relevé action of the supporting foot and leg. He wanted us to develop enough strength to be capable of the single-foot relevé at a relatively slow tempo.

As the supporting leg and foot do the relevé, the tip of the pointe of the working leg is drawn up the center of the supporting leg, along the shinbone, until it can go no farther. It is the action of the working knee moving up and out to the side that brings the foot up the leg. Mr. B asked us to think of a marionette with a string attached at the knee, not the foot. Traditionally, the working pointe is then moved to the back of the leg, but Balanchine asked us to lift the knee a bit higher to the side at this moment and then pull it around to the back in a kind of "rond de knee" action; this was his second change in the step. Thus the working foot reaches its highest position while at the side of the supporting leg. The hips remained as square as possible as the knee passed, bringing the foot around. The pointe, with the heel forward, then goes diagonally down to just below the back of the knee. Then the inside of the heel and the inside anklebone continue on the center line down the back of the supporting leg until the working pointe reaches the floor. Then both feet come off pointe together.

Balanchine also modified the way the dancer brings her foot from the back of the supporting leg to the front when doing relevé passé starting from fifth back. Traditionally, the knee and the foot passed to the front together, but he asked us to try to hold the knee back while we brought the working foot up and then forward, over the supporting knee to the front. To the dancer, this feels like she is bringing the working foot up and under the working knee in order to come front. Again, the tip of the pointe reaches its highest position while on the side of the supporting leg.

The strength and control that we built in our feet through practice of this relevé passé are used in many ballets that call for slow adagio relevés into passé, développé, fondu, or any kind of turn. This roll-up off one foot into relevé passé is usually a continuous movement from fifth front to fifth back and in reverse. We also practiced it from fifth front or back to sous-sus on pointe. And Mr. B's change in the way the pointe passed from front to back and vice versa helped us sustain a fuller turnout.

In choreography and in class Balanchine used relevé passé to pointe in two ways: as a held pose, or as a continuous move into another position. The pose was usually done from two feet, but the move into another position was done from one foot or two feet. In a pose the dancer "stays" or "makes a picture" with the working pointe in passé. In contrast, when he wanted to see passé work as a continuous movement, we might descend into fifth or we might go from relevé passé to a lunging fourth position with the front leg in a low plié and the back leg extended long and straight. The weight is concentrated over the ball of the front foot as the dancer goes through it into plié and continues by placing the back foot to the floor in a long fourth. This relevé passé to fourth, which often precedes a pirouette, is typical in demanding a strong relevé in

---

DETAILS I OFTEN INSIST ON IN RELEVÉ PASSÉ:

1) in passé relevé off one foot, be sure that the working foot does not overcross as it leaves the floor or at any other time
2) the little toe goes along the shinbone in front; the inside of the heel goes along the center line of the calf in back
3) take the knee side, up, and back
4) when time allows, use a deep demi-plié before and after the passé
5) the pliés before and after the relevé passé are usually equal in depth
6) the supporting knee must be straight by the time the dancer arrives on pointe
7) take the hips and torso up—change levels

Dana on pointe, moving through passé front

Dana on pointe, lifting her knee to the side

Dana goes through her supporting foot as she starts to plié while extending and lowering her working leg.

Dana arriving in tendu side in plié, with the knee extended over the toes

the supporting foot and leg, while the working leg and foot, moving continuously, go up and around the supporting leg in a rond de jambe action in the knee and thigh that extends the turnout. As she pliés on the supporting leg, meanwhile keeping her weight forward and over the ball of the supporting foot, the working foot aims directly for fourth back.

Another exercise for relevé passé off one foot calling for continuous movement is a presentation of the working foot to the floor. It is done to a moderately slow tempo (at faster tempos, the dancer will probably push off the floor from both feet, then continue to roll up through the supporting foot). After arriving on pointe with the working foot at the supporting knee, the dancer lifts the working knee slightly to unfold the leg toward the floor in a gentle circular action as she rolls down through the supporting foot into plié. The working leg then turns out as it straightens and as the foot is presented to the floor to the side or in effacé front or back. The working leg moves continuously from the faster start to the slower unfolding as the dancer controls the timing of the roll-down and the plié so that she arrives in plié just as the working foot is presented to the floor. It is important that she maintain the weight over the ball of the supporting foot. When the working foot is presented to the side, the dancer usually ends with her body bent to that side, looking toward the working foot. The bending and

the direction of her gaze are coordinated with her arms and the unfolding of the working leg and the presentation of the foot.

In class we worked on the roll-up method more than on the spring relevé, because the former is harder to do and it builds strength and control in the feet very effectively. But even when using the spring relevé, we picked up the knee to draw the working pointe up the center of the supporting leg, and we used Mr. B's methods for extending the turnout. "Take the knee back," he would say to us.

As noted, Balanchine used both the roll-up and spring versions in choreography and in class. Since the roll-up gives a smooth effect at a range of speeds, the choice depended generally on the music and the look required. When the tempo was fast but the line legato, Balanchine often used the roll-up relevé off two feet, which did not necessarily require much plié and which was more stable than the spring relevé, since the whole action is controlled in the foot. The relevé passés for the Swan Queen in his version of *Swan Lake* are an example of this. At the tempo that Tchaikovsky dictated and that Balanchine insisted we keep, there is no time for a big plié. The dancer simply moves through her foot aiming for the next fifth, not stopping or really establishing the relevé on full pointe—"and down, and down, and down," he would say—and moving through passé with very little or no plié. The dancer stays on the music by putting her feet to the floor on the beat. Very fast relevés passés are also seen in *Square Dance*. If he wanted us in passé on pointe immediately, because the music was fast and sharp or because he wanted to show the position, we again pushed off two feet and we might use a slight spring at the end of the roll-up while lifting the working knee immediately. This approach is seen often in *Concerto Barocco*.

Men usually did not practice the spring relevé passé or any relevé passés at very fast tempos. However, Balanchine expected the men to practice roll-up relevé passé at moderate to slow tempos, because it helps develop the stability and strength in the calf, ankle, and foot they need to dance, particularly when executing pirouettes.

OTHER ROLL-UP RELEVÉS

Balanchine also gave some other slow, controlled roll-up relevé exercises on one foot at the barre and in the center. It is very difficult to roll up and down slowly and smoothly on one foot, and we often did not have the technical skill or the strength to achieve this goal in the center. However, the real purpose of these exercises was the concentrated effort to achieve the result, even if most of us would not be able to accomplish this in the center. "Impossible" exercises such as the following ones, sprinkled all through the class, changed the way we looked when we danced. As we reached for the im-

possible, Balanchine often encouraged us by saying, "It's the effort that makes you better. The results come later."

Slow, controlled roll-up relevés in attitude and arabesque were given at the barre and in the center. The dancer could hold an attitude effacée derrière or an arabesque, keeping her back and working leg up, maintaining the turnout, showing soft arms and a proper line for the head. She tries to roll up through the supporting foot to pointe, establishes that position on pointe, and then rolls down through the supporting foot into plié while keeping the weight over the ball. With the support of the barre, this is possible; in the center, it is almost impossible. She moves continuously, smoothly through the entire plié, maintaining the turnout in both legs. If she could not roll completely up, she started through her foot and then finished with a very small spring. If she couldn't begin her descent by rolling down, she made the smallest possible spring, catching herself at the base of her toes, and then completed the descent by rolling or going through her foot, keeping the weight over the ball of the foot, and maintaining the turnout in both her legs and her feet. When Mr. B gave these relevés in the center, we could do them in place or we could slowly turn. When we turned we did not spot, and three or four relevés usually gave about one turn.

As in all descents from pointe (or demi-pointe), the dancer maintains the turnout and brings the heel forward (but see page 202). This is especially important when doing consecutive relevés that turn

---

DETAILS I OFTEN INSIST ON IN OTHER ROLL-UP RELEVÉS:
1) start by rolling up; a small spring is acceptable to reach pointe; try to leave the toes in place
2) if you are unable to roll down from pointe, catch yourself at the base of the toes and, resisting the plié, descend through the foot under control; do not fall back onto the heel
3) do not heave the body back when making relevé or collapse forward in the plié
4) the head, torso, arms, and hands participate in and complement the movement; they are not a "handicap"

en dedans. The dancer brings the heel forward as she pliés.

Slow roll-up relevés with the working leg in a low à la seconde or extended to the front could be done at the barre and repeated in the center. Mr. B might make a little combination in the center, such as fondu relevé to a low à la seconde (about forty-five degrees), two controlled relevés with the working leg remaining in a low à la seconde, and then pas de bourrée front, side, back (see page 283), ending in sous-sus. The combination was repeated to the other side and then in effacé front. Again, we moved smoothly through the foot and continuously through the plié while establishing and briefly holding the relevé position.

Whenever the dancer relevés, she tries to create the illusion that the movement requires little or no effort. Achieving this look of lightness naturally requires more strength and skill in relevés from one foot. The dancer works to develop the power and coordination to lift her hips and torso up off her supporting leg as she starts up and out of plié, pushing into and away from the floor. The impression of lightness is clearest when she pulls up as she lowers down into plié and lifts up just before she starts to relevé.

Balanchine compared exercises like the previous one (or relevés facing the barre, see page 237) to "taking a one-a-day vitamin pill." It didn't taste good, but in the long run it would make you feel better. Such exercises were not fun to do, they did not seem like dancing, they were difficult and tedious. However, in the end they gave us the strength and the control to move freely and easily when we did steps that did feel like dancing, when we really danced.

FONDU RELEVÉ WITH DÉVELOPPÉ

This exercise is essentially the same as fondu at the barre, which must be understood before addressing fondu with relevé to pointe. In the barre exercise the dancer practices the technique and the coordination of the straightening of the supporting leg and the lifting of the knee and the unfolding and final presentation of the working leg and foot. This coordination takes on an additional dimension when the exercise is done with relevé, especially relevé to pointe (see page 98).

When I first joined the New York City Ballet we practiced fondu with développé so the supporting knee and the working leg straightened at the same time. This worked fairly well when the fondu relevé was low and fast. But if the fondu relevé was slow and/or high, we would be on pointe with a bent knee that straightened only when the développé reached its fully extended line. Consequently Balanchine rethought fondu and fondu relevé, especially at slow tempos.

His solution for slow fondus with high extensions had us on pointe on a straight supporting knee as the working leg continued to unfold. From plié with the working foot in coupé front, the supporting leg starts straightening as the pointe of the working foot is drawn up the center line of the supporting leg. The dancer arrives on full pointe with a straight supporting leg as she would in relevé passé off one foot. Through this change in timing for the fondu, the roll-up relevé to pointe is usually completed a little more than midway through the développé, when the working leg has moved through passé. Of course, Balanchine never wanted the working leg to stop, or "take a coffee break in passé," as I tell the students. From passé the knee lifted higher and then the working leg unfolded, stretched, and reached out to its final, climactic position. This was used for high extensions in fondu adagio exercises at the barre or with a partner and in slow fondu relevés in the center.

Whatever the direction of the fondu développé in a high extension, the dancer lifts her knee as high and as close to her body as possible before unfolding the lower part of her leg. In fondu développé front the heel seems to take charge, presenting the inside of the leg and the foot. To the back the thigh is in charge, lifting up and out as the hip releases and then moving the leg into arabesque. When we went to the side, Mr. B would say, "Lift your knee out of your décolleté evening dress." In each direction, the lower part of the leg unfolds until the pointe is about two inches short of full extension. Then, as we stretched our working knee, he would say, "Turn out even more!" This additional turnout works as a brake to slow down the movement so the leg does not kick up or jerk to a stop. Consequently, even on fast fondu relevés with low développé the dancer is up on a straight supporting leg an instant before the final presentation of the working leg. With this final turn-out braking action, the leg almost seems to lower slightly. Whether the leg stretches front, side, or back, the same technique applies to those last two inches. The purpose is to reveal the end of the movement and the beautifully turned-out leg in a clear and dramatic way. On high extensions, it was as if we were placing our foot on top of a high table or shelf.

When Balanchine wanted us to establish the final "picture" or line quickly, both legs seemed to arrive in the final position simultaneously. The relevé is quick, requiring a fast roll-up and most likely a little spring to finish getting to pointe; the développé leg moves rapidly, but the final turning out brakes it. In the fifth variation of *Raymonda Variations*, after the dancer enters, she begins her solo with a plié fondu relevé to a high à la seconde with the arms in fifth high, establishing a brilliant picture before she turns to first arabesque pliée, making a dramatic pose. Here we have a contrast not only in direction (between the extension in second and the arabesque) but also in height (between pointe and plié). The contrasts can be seen only if the fondu "picture" is fully established. The "picture" includes the entire body—arms, head, torso, legs. The arms arrive in fifth high at the same time or even an instant before the dancer arrives on pointe and the working leg is extended à la seconde. The tendency is for the arms to arrive late, so it is helpful to many dancers to aim to have them arrive a little early. When the dancer lifts to turn to arabesque, the arms lift up and over to first arabesque before

she descends through her foot as she moves into a deep plié (see page 214).

In the fourth variation of *Divertimento No. 15*, which I danced, there is a fondu combination that is nicknamed the "yes step," because the dancer nods her head up and down seven times en face in coordination with the plié and unfolding of her working leg. The dancer pliés on the right foot, bringing the left foot to coupé back and the arms to fifth low as she lowers her head as if to say, "Look at my foot in coupé." She does fondu relevé arriving on pointe as her working leg establishes à la seconde at about ninety degrees. Her arms open to second through an overlapped first, and she lifts her head as she presents herself—face, arms, torso, and working leg—to the audience: "Here I am." Then she pliés again on her right foot, bringing her left foot to the front near the supporting knee, and her arms move out and up from second to fifth high as she lowers her head and gaze again, announcing, "My foot is in passé front now." Next she does fondu relevé to pointe to the side to about shoulder height as she raises her head and opens her arms out to second, palms up. The working leg must move rapidly because she has to arrive in the pose and on pointe simultaneously, as if she is saying, "YES! Here I am again." This sequence is repeated to the other side, and then the whole set is repeated. She begins her relevés going through her foot, usually finishing with a slight spring; she descends from pointe as usual by going through her foot.

When the dancer lowers her leg from any fondu line, the movement has to be done with control. Moving the working leg into coupé from ninety degrees or higher, the dancer starts the leg down straight, and then the working knee begins to bend at about forty-five degrees as the supporting leg begins to plié. The working and the supporting knee start bending at approximately the same time. However, the working leg follows a different path, coming down from the one going up. The plié for fondu relevé at slow tempos was slow and always continuous, while the beginning of the développé was usually quick; the final unfolding of the développé was again somewhat slower. The descent of the working leg begins quickly and then slows to fit the music. This contrast in tempos clarifies the movement and makes it more interesting; dancing with that much inflection requires another aspect of control the dancer must develop.

In typical class exercises for fondu relevé, set to moderate to slow music, we worked on going through the feet, if possible, rolling up; at faster tempos, either a slight spring or roll-up was acceptable.

In the "Pas de Neuf" of Balanchine's *Swan Lake*, the soloist does several moderately slow fondu combinations. The first one is plié in coupé front, relevé développé side, plié in coupé back, relevé to attitude croisée derrière, and repeat on the other side. The second one is fondu relevé croisé front, plié in coupé front, fondu relevé écarté devant, plié in coupé back, fondu relevé in first arabesque, plié in coupé back, fondu relevé in effacé front, then repeat on the other leg. All four fondus are with the same leg, and the body faces the same direction for the first three before switching to the other diagonal for fondu relevé effacé front. In all these fondu relevés the relevé should be smooth and the descent controlled; the working leg lifts, unfolds, and pauses briefly in the extended line to show the position. I often give these two combinations in class because they are excellent for building stamina and control and they let the students feel as if they are dancing. And they are!

Mr. Balanchine was often telling us to show ourselves. Sometimes he would remind us with a pun that dancers are performers: "You know, dear, this is *show* business. Our business is to *show*."

Mr. Balanchine emphasized rolling up to pointe and rolling down from pointe because that technique gives the best control and the smoothest look. When the dancer is in the center, especially when on one foot, she will often need to complete the roll-up or start the roll-down with a small spring. However, by going through her foot under control rather than jumping up or clunking down, she will have the same smooth, strong, and beautiful look.

DETAILS I OFTEN INSIST ON IN FONDU RELEVÉ:
1) lift the working knee up and side, then unfold the leg; do not kick the foot out
2) coordinate the timing and the movement to establish the final line with the whole body—head, arms, torso, legs, feet—and show the pose
3) make the relevé smooth
4) control the descent—go through the supporting foot, do not fall down with the weight settled back on the heel

---

SPRINGING AND JUMPING TO POINTE (STRAIGHT-KNEE LANDING)

Balanchine worked on a variety of springs and jumps to pointe. In such movements he often emphasized the change of levels, accentuating the contrast between plié and pointe. Sometimes he emphasized the element of contrast and surprise: The soft, low, catlike plié explodes into a startling pose.

The men usually did not practice jumps onto demi-pointe. A few men might act on Mr. B's suggestion to practice this or other such steps and learn what they feel like, since one day they might teach women or direct a company. Mr. Balanchine often made a combination for the men that had something in common with what the women were doing in these exercises, but sometimes he left them alone: to watch, to stretch, to chat, or, perhaps, to indulge their love of multiple pirouettes.

The dancer can land on pointe from a spring or a jump with a straight knee or with plié. The straight-knee landing was used mainly for jumps to two pointes, such as échappés, assemblés in place and traveling, or for certain steps onto a single pointe, such as a jump or spring to passé, traveling ballonné relevé and sissonne. This group will be considered first.

ÉCHAPPÉ

A spring from fifth position plié to second or fourth position on pointe, échappé is a basic step. Balanchine paid close attention to the timing of our pointes striking the floor and of the straightening of our knees. Our pointes had to strike the floor together, making the sound "ta," not "ta-ta," and our knees had to be straight upon arriving on pointe.

In general, there are two kinds of échappé. One involves a slight spring up from fifth position; the other is more like a sharp sliding out on the floor. In both kinds, the dancer lifts her hips and torso off her legs as she pulls up, helping them to shoot out to échappé. Balanchine often preferred and concentrated on the former. On occasion he went even farther and asked us to jump high enough off the floor that we could just show (or at least attempt to show) second (or fourth) position in the air before we landed on pointe. You can see still further development of the step in *Ballo della Regina*, when the ballerina executes a jumped échappé followed by a second jump from straight legs to an even wider second position.

If the échappé was taken at a moderate tempo, the wide position on pointe was extremely important (see page 232). In the ballerina's solo in the first movement of *Symphony in C* or in the first pas de trois from *Agon*, for example, Balanchine wanted to see the movement in its full dimension. Preceded by a big plié and a big opening movement and finishing with a correct stance in second or fourth, this échappé reveals the contrasting elements of the step most dramatically: the changing levels and the "escape" (which is what the French word means).

In general, Balanchine acknowledged that when a movement is faster, its size will have to be smaller. Performing fast échappés, for example, meant shortening the distance between the pointes and using less plié, sometimes barely bending the knees. Yet even when the tempo was fast, as it often was in class to prepare us for certain choreographic se-

quences (e.g., those for the ballerina and corps in *Square Dance*), Balanchine still wanted to see the simultaneous landing of the two pointes with straight knees. He insisted on that precise timing. Fast échappés necessarily open to and close from a second or a fourth position that is smaller than usual, but they still should reveal the distinctive qualities of the step through exact timing and through the effort of the dancers to open the legs out to second (or fourth) and to bring them into a correctly crossed fifth.

Balanchine also wanted both feet, upon shooting out of fifth, to travel equally from the center. When échappés were followed by a plié in second (or fourth) and a pas de bourrée or some other step traveling in any direction, he was especially watchful that we land on pointe together and that we start the plié equally in both legs. This limited the tendency to anticipate and transfer the weight too soon to the future supporting foot. To guard against this, Balanchine watched to see that our pointes landed simultaneously (the "ta") and at equal distance from the échappé's starting point. Then we usually went through both feet together as our knees bent together, making plié on our arrival in second (or fourth) position. A good exercise of this kind is échappé side, plié in second, and a fast pas de bourrée ending in sous-sus, and repeat on the other side. Then three échappés en croix ending in sous-sus.

You can see the sequence échappé to second, plié in second, pull the feet into sous-sus in the fourth variation of *Divertimento No. 15*. It is also done by the female principal in the first movement of *Symphony in C*. Now both feet shoot out and pull in an equal distance, landing on pointe simultaneously in second and in sous-sus.

The échappé to fourth on pointe is similar to that to second on pointe. In general, however, the length of the fourth on pointe is not greatly exaggerated, although the feet move equally away from each other—that is, they "escape" from fifth. What is important is to see that the thighs are crossed and both pointes are on the center line (see page 233).

When closing to fifth position plié at a moderate

to slow tempo from second or fourth on pointe, the dancer can lift her hips and torso off her legs an instant before she uses the inner thigh muscles to pull the legs in toward fifth position before releasing the knees. In other words, Mr. B did not want the dancer to be on pointe on bent knees. She lowers as usual in control through her feet into a smoothly continuous plié. Of course, Balanchine didn't talk of inner thighs, and we didn't think "Use inner thighs." He talked about being in control ("Don't fall down. Take yourself down!") and energy ("Use your legs") and awareness ("How wide is second position?" or "Be on time!"). He made clear the look required for his aesthetic.

At any tempo the dancer goes through her feet into fifth position plié, bringing her heels forward and keeping her weight over the balls of her feet.

DETAILS I OFTEN INSIST ON IN ÉCHAPPÉ:
1) make second and fourth position as wide as they are supposed to be
2) cross the legs in fourth position
3) both feet arrive on pointe together with straight legs; both legs move equally out and in
4) go through the feet into plié, making a precise, tightly crossed fifth position

---

ASSEMBLÉ TO POINTE

Assemblé to pointe is a quick allegro jump to sous-sus that can be done in place or traveling. It is done in the same way as regular assemblé (see page 322), except that assemblé to pointe (or, for men, to demi-pointe, although this step is rarely done by men) is done with a straight knee landing. It is also done, on occasion, landing on pointe in demi-plié (see page 285).

An example of assemblé to pointe in place is in the coda of *Raymonda Variations*. The dancer steps

side onto pointe on the right foot, with the left leg making passé. Next, she steps into an overcrossed fourth in plié on her left foot, immediately brushing her right foot side and pushing off her left to assemblé, landing on pointe in sous-sus with her right foot front. She steps into an overcrossed fourth in plié on her right foot and repeats the combination to the other side.

For a traveling assemblé to pointe, the dancer can start in tendu left foot croisé front and step diagonally forward into plié on her left foot on count one. She pushes off and brushes the back (right) foot side on "and" so she is in the air with her feet together. She lands on pointe in fifth (sous-sus) right foot front on count two, does plié in fifth on count three, relevé passé on her left foot on count four (arms to fifth high), steps back on her right foot through fourth plié on count five (as arms open out to second position), and on count six stretches her left leg in tendu croisé front (the arms move into an extended second). The step repeats traveling diagonally across the room.

DETAILS I OFTEN INSIST ON IN ASSEMBLÉ TO POINTE:
1) both pointes land simultaneously
2) if the tempo allows, really jump
3) if traveling, jump and travel

SISSONNE

Balanchine paid very close attention to one particular jump to pointe, sissonne to arabesque. This move from fifth position to an arabesque on pointe is another step that Balanchine virtually redefined to clarify the picture seen by the audience. He wanted the dancer to move the supporting leg sharply forward as she moves the back leg up to arabesque: "Both legs go away from each other." The two actions occur simultaneously. This sissonne explodes from fifth to the pose, because both

*Dana in sissonne
to pointe*

lands on pointe at the same time that her leg arrives in arabesque, without any kick-up or bounce, thus creating a clear, sharp picture. At the end of the first movement of *Symphony in C* the two demi-soloists do sissonne to arabesque toward the center of the stage from opposite sides and then away from the center while the ballerina performs a sissonne step to pointe that travels both forward and back while facing the audience. The intended effect is not achieved unless all three perform the step with as much "pop and pow" as Mr. B wanted.

In closing the sissonne Balanchine wanted to see both legs move simultaneously into demi-plié. To do this it is necessary to lower the arabesque leg rapidly to join the supporting leg; this allows the two legs to move together into an immediate fifth position demi-plié. But the dancer does not land with a "thud"; she catches herself at the base of her toes and, continuing through her feet, descends into a controlled plié.

In class we practiced many combinations with sissonne on pointe. Whatever the sissonne pose (attitude or leg extended front or arabesque), the emphasis was the same. The dancer really had to travel, and the working leg had to reach the desired position at the same time the supporting foot arrived on pointe. This was true even when the working leg had to reach a high arabesque or attitude line. It was also true when we practiced the kind of sissonne in which the foot in fifth back comes forward to pointe while the front foot moves to assume a line in the back. The aim is always to create a clear, sudden picture through simultaneous arrival at the finish, including the head, arms, and torso. Every part of the body must participate and arrive together to give the look that made Mr. B exclaim, "That's right, dear!" when he saw it.

In the female's variation in *Tchaikovsky Pas de Deux*, there are sissonnes onto pointe in third

legs move very quickly into position and stop at exactly the same moment. The sissonne should surprise, even startle the audience, "like the pop of a champagne cork," said Mr. B.

As visualized by Balanchine, the step is a move forward equal in distance to the height of the arabesque leg to the rear. In practice the supporting leg and foot rarely move so far, but Balanchine stressed it as the ideal. "You need to send the leg forward in front of you and go there. If you move the body and don't send the leg, you have nothing under you." When the dancer shoots her supporting foot and leg forward, she must take her hips and back with her so she lands with her torso on top of her supporting leg, not behind it. Her chest, face, and front arm seem to lead the way. The jump is out and forward, not so much up and down. The dancer arabesque, attitude effacée derrière, and first arabesque. In the coda she does sissonne from fifth position to attitude derrière croisée, bringing the back leg forward to pointe and lifting the front leg up to a back attitude.

The timing principle governing sissonnes also applies to allegro ballonné relevé or spring relevé to positions such as passé, attitude, arabesque, or dégagé. Always in this kind of allegro, both legs arrive in position simultaneously and freeze, allowing the audience to see the position clearly for an instant before the dancer moves on.

Deanna travels forward as she does ballonné relevé to effacé front.

DETAILS I OFTEN INSIST ON IN
SISSONNE TO POINTE:

1) really move the supporting leg and foot— don't land where you started
2) don't let the working leg kick up, bounce, or shake as it arrives
3) establish the line with a correct upper body as well as the correct legs and feet
4) arms and head arrive an instant before the legs
5) in descending, go through the feet, don't fall onto the full foot when moving into plié

Deanna travels forward as she lowers to coupé front.

BALLONNÉ RELEVÉ

Ballonné relevé in Mr. B's exercises usually traveled and was often done in effacé front. The dancer springs to pointe traveling forward, arriving on pointe at the same time the working leg reaches its position at forty-five or ninety degrees or even higher. The step travels on the descent as well, when the working foot returns directly to coupé, with the knee and thigh held back to sustain maximum turnout. Ballonné relevé is usually done in a series, keeping the same working leg. There is only a slight développé action, with the working knee lifting a bit as the lower leg unfolds and the foot is

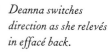

Deanna switches direction as she relevés in effacé back.

presented. If the working leg is extended at about ninety degrees or higher and the tempo is moderate to slow, the dancer brings it down straight and then bends it at about forty-five degrees to return to a low coupé position. This is the same action used in lowering the working leg from a high extension in fondu relevé.

We also did ballonné relevé exercises traveling side (usually in écarté) and back (usually in effacé). The principles for traveling front apply. A combination combining traveling front and back could go: four ballonnés relevés in effacé front, traveling forward on the diagonal; and, staying on the same supporting leg but switching diagonals, four ballonnés relevés in effacé back, traveling back; then coupé; and repeat in the same pattern to the other side. This was done with the working leg extending to about forty-five degrees.

After he set a ballonné exercise on pointe for the women, Balanchine might then give the men a jumping ballonné step. We "girls" did it too.

DETAILS I OFTEN INSIST ON IN BALLONNÉ RELEVÉ:

1) be sure to travel on both the relevé and the descent from pointe
2) arrive on pointe with a straight supporting knee
3) control the plié on the descent, maintaining the weight over the ball of the supporting foot
4) the working leg moves as fast as possible and is presented; it does not kick up
5) the working leg must extend precisely front, side, or back
6) maintain the torso upright over the ball of the supporting foot and take it with you; no leaning back on the relevé, no collapsing forward on the descent into plié (don't heave)

OTHER JUMPING (SPRINGING) STEPS

We also practiced other allegro springs and jumps to pointe that traveled; Mr. B liked to use them in the ballets. We had to spring or jump to pointe in any direction with the working leg in a variety of positions. For example, in the fourth movement of *Western Symphony,* the ballerina does two traveling ballonnés in a high écarté followed by two in arabesque, the sequence being performed three times. She travels during the jumps to pointe and also as she springs down to plié. As the lead Butterfly in the scherzo of *A Midsummer Night's Dream,* I had six consecutive relevés in arabesque that traveled backward. On each relevé and plié I traveled as far as I could: I pulled strongly back on the foot as I sprang up to pointe and also when I descended into plié.

In a rare exception to his usual practice, Mr. B had me ignore the counts in the music during these six traveling arabesques relevés. I was to do them as fast as I could. He sometimes used the same approach to maximizing movement and dynamism in consecutive turns. He would say, "Don't listen to the music! Turn as fast as you can." At other times, when the tempo of the music was fast, he might tell us, "Don't pay attention to the music! Turn at a comfortable speed." An example of the latter is the series of relevé turns in attitude to the front and back in *Tarantella.* It all depended on the effect he wanted the dancer to make at a particular moment.

PIQUÉ: STEPPING ONTO POINTE

"Stepping onto pointe, the leg is extremely straight, not a bit of bend. Then you roll onto pointe."

Stepping to pointe is known as piqué. Although

also executed by men onto demi-pointe, piqué achieves its most dramatic effect when it is done onto full pointe by women.

Balanchine was very specific about the way we were to place our pointe on the floor in piqué. Until he refined the technique, the dancer might put her pointe on the floor in any of several ways, and the movement was accepted as long as she was stable on pointe and ready for what came next. His approach helped ensure that the dancer maintained a beautifully shaped pointe and fully turned-out working leg and that she stepped onto pointe with a stretched working leg.

Stepping forward, the dancer first places the outside edge of the box (where the little toe is) on the floor, making sure the heel is well forward and the foot is not sickled, and then rolls up onto pointe until her weight is centered over the big toe and the toe next to it. For stepping back, the process is reversed—that is, when the dancer reaches back with her leg and foot, she places the big toe side of the box on the floor and then rolls up to the proper stance. When stepping to the side, the dancer places the bottom edge of the box on the floor and then rolls up and over onto pointe. In no case does the dancer place the whole box on the floor at once. Stepping with the whole box on the floor at once has a clunky, ungraceful look and also can prompt the dancer to sickle the foot when stepping to the back and, when stepping in any direction, to release or bend the working knee. As we stepped to pointe, the working leg and foot were turned out and the knee was stretched. Executed in this way, the movement was precise, delicate, and refined.

The traditional piqué traveled very little; it was a comfortable and easy step in which the working leg was extended front, side, or back, with a slight plié in the supporting leg. The working pointe was placed on or dropped to the floor at a comfortable distance from the supporting foot, and the dancer transferred her weight to it. The original supporting leg then followed to the designated pose or position, often "kicking up" if its destination was in the air. Balanchine re-thought that approach and

Stepping front: Dana places the little toe edge of the box to the floor.

Stepping front: Dana begins to roll up onto pointe.

Stepping back: Dana places the big toe edge of the box to the floor.

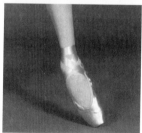

Stepping back: Dana begins to roll up onto pointe

Stepping side: Dana places the bottom edge of the box to the floor.

Stepping side: Dana begins to roll up onto pointe.

concentrated on making the piqué more dynamic and the finishing pose clear. As the dancer prepares to step, she pliés more fully and pushes energetically off the supporting leg in the direction of the step so the working leg (with fully stretched knee) reaches farther. Mr. B's "juicier" plié thus gives the dancer the impetus that allows her to place her pointe beyond the range it could reach in the traditional piqué. His "juicier" plié transformed the piqué into a genuine traveling step.

In allegro the working leg must arrive in its designated line (e.g., arabesque, attitude, or passé) as the dancer arrives on full pointe. The whole movement is completed simultaneously. This establishes the position before the dancer moves on to the next step. In adagio the working leg can follow just a bit, but it then "grows" in its position, just as the standing leg does as the dancer pulls up. A momentary pause allows the pose to register. We see the adagio piqué in the second movement of *Concerto Barocco* when the ballerina does two piqué arabesques, supported by her partner as she circles him. She piqués to arabesque, allowing the movement to grow a moment until it reaches full height and reveals the pose; she then brings the arabesque leg down and places the toes on the floor as she rolls through the foot into plié. Only then does she begin the next développé piqué.

To perfect the step Balanchine had us constantly practice a variety of piqués. One exercise was piqué walks forward and back. The dancer begins with a small développé to the front, holding the knee back and presenting the heel forward. Although both legs were important to the action, Balanchine reminded us that it is the moving leg that commands the attention of the audience. This is the leg that développés and to which the dancer piqués. So, regardless of the direction in which we were moving, we had to pay very close attention to the way we executed the développé and how we stepped onto pointe. We needed to be aware of presenting our legs and feet to the audience in the développé. The

Darci and Nikolaj show piqué arabesque (Concerto Barocco).

dancer turns out even more as she stretches the straightening knee, showing a fully turned-out and energized foot and leg from the hip to the pointe.

As the dancer développés, she rolls down through the supporting foot into plié, maintaining the turnout of the entire supporting leg and presenting the heel forward. Using the plié of the supporting leg to project herself forward, she then, with a straight knee, puts the outside edge of her pointe shoe to the floor directly on the center line as she steps (rolls) up to pointe, taking her torso and arms with her. Simultaneously, the back leg, with the knee held back, slightly lifting and drawing to the side, passes through to start to développé front. She continues the développé as she rolls through the supporting foot into the next plié. In the plié the weight remains over the ball of the foot. So we thought as we did the combination: piqué left, développé right; piqué right, développé left, each time with an accent on the end of the développé to show the foot by turning out as we arrived at the bottom of the plié.

Going back, the entire process is reversed. The dancer lifts her thigh and reaches back through a slight circular motion out and then down toward the floor as she pliés. She steps directly behind the center line of her body, onto the big toe side of the box (again, with a straight knee), and arrives on (rolls onto) pointe as the other leg lifts slightly and the knee pulls back and side. The dancer again lifts her thigh to the back, presenting her foot and opening her leg as she rolls down through her supporting foot, maintaining the turnout and bringing her supporting heel forward.

During these walking exercises the torso is over the legs and the arms generally remain in a low à la seconde, a little in front of the dancer's body, but they are not rigid, like sticks. The backs of the wrists lift gently, leading the arms to rise a bit as the dancer steps to pointe, and the insides of the wrists and the elbows soften and bring the arms

down a little as she descends into the plié. The hands trail slightly and the fingers extend, reacting to the air.

Balanchine insisted that every piqué forward or back be on the dancer's center line. Whether going forward or back, we had to make a single line with our pointes, as if we were walking on that tightrope. In class Balanchine might take one of us over to a seam in the linoleum and say, "Now walk this line." The rest then watched to see how long it would take for the dancer to miss and fall off the "wire."

We did these walks at fast and at slow tempos. At slow tempos the développé could be almost as high as hip level, and we might travel a little more. When the tempo was faster, the leg passed at mid-calf and we projected ourselves out somewhat less. Usually the musical accent was down in the plié on the beat and up in the piqué on the "and," but it could be reversed.

Fast piqué walks forward can be seen in *Tchaikovsky Piano Concerto No. 2*. Slow piqué walks backward and then forward in a circle can be seen in the principal variation in *La Source*.

Dana has piquéd, bringing her working heel forward as she holds her knee back.

Dana continues to plié, keeping her weight over the ball of her foot as she presents her working foot front.

Dana pliés to step strongly forward on her center line, presenting her foot to the floor, straight leg, heel up, and toes pointed.

Dana rolling down through her supporting foot and pliéing as she développés the working leg front

Although continuous piqué walks are really a step for the women, men can benefit from practicing them because the piqué walk helps reinforce the awareness of front and back for all dancers. Also, men should practice presenting the turned-out working leg and foot in the little développé and stepping onto a straight leg, because they often step to demi-pointe—for example, to make sous-sus preceding a turn or jump or to do piqué arabesque.

Temps lié on pointe is basically the same as the exercise described in Temps Lié, page 200. The dancer makes a small développé with the working leg and pushes off her supporting leg to project herself forward, stepping onto the outside edge of the box (when going front), rolling up onto pointe and immediately bringing the former supporting leg into an exact sous-sus. Even though she pushes off to be able to travel, she does not jump or fall onto her pointe. The same principle applies when she piqués back and side, the only difference being that she steps onto the inside edge of the box (big toe side) when stepping back and onto the bottom edge of the box when stepping side. She then moves into plié in fifth position or into plié as she releases the foot into coupé, maintaining her weight over the balls (or ball) of her feet (or foot).

The dancer can also do temps lié to attitude or à la seconde. After the développé she pushes off the supporting leg to step out to pointe as she lifts the working leg to the extended line very quickly. She tries to have the working leg in position as soon as she arrives on pointe and then holds the pose for a moment to show it. This kind of temps lié should never look like the dancer steps onto pointe and

then slowly lifts or rapidly kicks her working leg. After showing the pose she can close, going through her feet into demi-plié in fifth.

In addition to temps lié to pointe and piqué walks, we practiced piqués in a series and alone, moving into many poses: piqué arabesque, piqué attitude, piqué passé, etc. A piqué arabesque in effacé that Mr. Balanchine liked and often used travels diagonally forward or side, with the downstage arm in fifth high and the upstage arm in second. In the finale of *Raymonda Variations*, the corps does three piqués in this arabesque traveling side, dégagé to a low à la seconde in plié, sous-sus (assemblé to pointe), and then three piqué arabesques, dégagé, and sous-sus to the other side. The dancer shows a small développé before stepping strongly forward onto a straight leg (outside edge of the box) as she immediately establishes arabesque. She then brings the working leg down and places the foot, toes first, to the floor in plié in front of the supporting foot, which has come off pointe.

A piqué step seen in many Balanchine ballets is a piqué traveling side with the working leg moving to passé. This is followed by a step crossing in front of the supporting leg and then a second step crossing in front to the opposite direction. Then the dancer steps side again in piqué and can continue the zigzag pattern. She usually bends her body and looks toward the knee in passé. This sequence is seen en masse in *Scotch Symphony*. Often Balanchine combined a piqué in one pose—for example, arabesque effacée—with two crossing steps followed by a piqué to that same pose or to another—for example, passé. He liked com-

---

DETAILS I OFTEN INSIST ON PIQUÉ WALKS AND TEMPS LIÉ TO POINTE:
1) step directly front or back, the toes right on the center line
2) do a small but beautiful développé, presenting the working foot and a fully turned-out leg
3) step onto pointe correctly—straight knee, beautifully pointed foot, correct edge of the box
4) control the descent from pointe, going through the feet and bringing the heels forward

1. Dana has piquéd to arabesque effacée.

2. The arabesque leg brought down and across

3. A step across to the other side

4. Développé side to piqué

5. Dana in piqué passé

6. A step across with the passé leg

binations with quick, sharp reversals of direction.

Stepping to pointe is really much easier than relevé. Because stepping to pointe is easier, it can be taken for granted, not practiced with enough care and attention in class and, perhaps, not carefully corrected. In a combination based on piqué to a pose, the attention can very often be directed at the pose—the arabesque or attitude. For Mr. B the quality of every moment in the movement from start to finish was important, not just the big pose. He paid careful attention to how we stepped onto pointe and to how we came off.

He looked for a beautiful little développé that presented the leg and foot to the floor and to the audience, or else, depending on the step, a fully stretched and turned-out leg with a well-pointed foot. He noticed which edge of the box of the toe shoe was placed on the floor and how, and whether we had traveled. Almost any teacher will see if the working leg is in the desired line, but Mr. B was equally interested in the way we brought, for example, the working leg in arabesque effacée down to cross in front of the supporting leg, in how we placed the toes to the floor going through the foot, and whether we had brought the heel forward as we lowered into plié. How the leg came down and how the foot touched the floor needed constant awareness. The leg did not just fall by gravity, and the foot did not just whack down and slap the floor. We had to remember, "It is the moving leg and foot that the audience sees."

In the piqué combination with the zigzag pattern it is how the dancer places her feet on the floor in the two crossing steps that adds nuance and beauty to the combination. On each step the toes are placed first and then the heel is brought forward into plié. But the pliés are not alike. On the second plié the dancer needs to plié lower to be able to

> DETAILS I OFTEN INSIST ON
> IN ANY PIQUÉ:
> 1) present the working leg and foot in the développé
> 2) use the plié to push off the floor and to reach far out
> 3) step onto a very straight leg
> 4) step to pointe with care on the appropriate edge of the box; do not plunk down on the whole tip of the pointe shoe
> 5) place the feet to the floor
> 6) in allegro combinations the working leg arrives in position as the supporting foot arrives on pointe; the entire body establishes the pose at once, although the torso, arms, and head may sometimes just precede the legs and feet

travel out on the piqué to follow. We had to remember the lesson of the centipede, "Place all two of your feet."

The Balanchine aesthetic requires just as much attention to those quick, simple steps before or after the piqué as to the pose itself. And each step in the combination has to be on time.

PIQUÉ WITH DÉGAGÉ (PIQUÉ BALLONNÉ)

There are two kinds of piqué ballonné: an allegro that shows a small, sharp opening of the working leg; and a slower version, with a more expansive opening. We worked on both in class, although in his ballets Balanchine used the allegro kind more often. It is seen in the last movement of *Concerto Barocco*, in *Tchaikovsky Piano Concerto No. 2*, in *Ballo della Regina*, and in many others.

In doing both kinds the dancer steps energetically from a low coupé to pointe onto a straight knee, directly under her center. In the allegro piqué ballonné the step from coupé can almost be a small jump, as she pushes up out of plié, putting her on pointe—BANG! At the same moment the pointe strikes the floor, the working leg arrives at its position. Usually this position is à la seconde at about forty-five degrees. In the slower, bigger piqué with dégagé, the attack is less sharp, and the working leg, since it has to go higher, reaches its position just after the dancer arrives on pointe. The dancer completes the step by bringing the working foot energetically into coupé. As she does this, she comes off pointe by rolling through the foot, keeping her weight over the ball of the foot, and presenting the heel forward.

The feeling of the allegro piqué ballonné is dynamic, while the feeling of the slower ballonné was stretched and expansive. Balanchine wanted to see the characteristic "picture" of each step so it could register with the audience. The simultaneous arrival in position of the working and supporting legs and feet created the "picture" in the allegro step, while a tiny pause at the moment of maximum extension revealed the "picture" in the slower step. Attention to this kind of distinction was a key element of Balanchine's aesthetic and was asked of us at all times.

Piqué with dégagé can also be a traveling step. In this case the dancer usually steps to the side, and using the plié of the supporting leg, transfers her weight to the other leg, meanwhile lifting the new working leg to à la seconde. The step can also travel forward or back. When we traveled forward, we piquéd forward and often lifted the working leg to attitude back. Balanchine liked to explore and extend the classical technique. This led him to make many variations on a step, and he often amused himself by coming up with new solutions. In *Donizetti Variations* he amused himself and surprised the audience by choreographing a solo for the ballerina that used piqués ballonnés that first stayed in place, then traveled, then turned while staying in place, and, later, traveled while turning.

By endlessly practicing the many forms of piqué we developed muscle memory. Also the men, who mostly did piqué forward to sous-sus, piqué arabesque, and piqué attitude. Whichever variant was called for in the choreography—piqué ballonné, piqué arabesque, piqué turn, piqué attitude, piqué passé—our legs and feet knew what to do.

DETAILS I OFTEN INSIST ON IN
PIQUÉ BALLONNÉ:

1) in piqué ballonné in place, step directly front or back
2) do not step onto a bent knee
3) in allegro, a fast, sharp, working leg is required
4) in coming off pointe, bring the heel forward and go through the foot, keeping the weight over the ball of the foot

---

PIROUETTES AND OTHER TURNS ON POINTE

Before considering the details of any particular turns on pointe, I will cover certain aspects of the technique that are common to all the turns. I have not generally addressed any comments specifically to the men in the section on turns, because the principles in turning are the same for them. As they relevé they can think relevé toward the big toe or relevé to pointe, even though they actually go only to demi-pointe.

POSITION OF THE WORKING FOOT WHILE TURNING

While turning, the pointe of the working foot is usually placed in front and on the midline of the supporting leg at the knee or just below it. The toe should not "overcross"—that is, go beyond the supporting leg. Also, the toe should not be pressed against the supporting leg. Balanchine liked to say that we should be able to slip that piece of paper between the little toe and the supporting leg. Only if this is possible can the dancer be sure she is maintaining the turnout with the muscles of the working leg and hips, rather than forcing the knee back by actively pushing the working foot against the supporting leg. Maintaining the turnout in the correct way strengthens the pirouette and gives life to the position.

Sometimes Mr. B liked to have us place the pointe of the working foot behind the supporting knee. This helped the dancer to hold her knee back, keeping the turnout in passé. He liked to add variety. He sometimes had us place the working foot at lower levels along the center line of the supporting leg. Occasionally he asked us to wrap the foot in sur le cou-de-pied, another position that helps the dancer hold the knee back. He was always trying different ways to help us maintain the turnout.

These variations on the standard position gave us an adaptability that was also useful in choreography and, on occasion, in supported turns, when a more compact position was sometimes necessary to avoid hitting our partner with our knee. We could achieve this compactness by placing the working pointe slightly below the supporting knee while turning, although at the finish we might raise it to the knee. Even in slow, unsupported turns we often raised our working pointe at the end of the turn to give it added energy and life, sustaining it before ending in fifth or fourth, or lifting the working leg to an extended line for a pose such as arabesque in plié.

Deanna's extended fourth . . .

ARMS IN TURNING

The arms and hands should help the turn, but they should not be exaggerated. Remember Mr. B's pun, "Hands shouldn't be a handicap." On pointe there is very little friction with the floor, so women need only a minimum of force to turn. The last thing Balanchine wanted was arms that looked as if they were flailing at unseen opponents. "Too much force!" he would say if one of the women used her arms too aggressively, "enough for a hundred turns. We need two beautiful turns, right and left."

Men definitely need more than two turns, and their turns also require more force because there is more friction on demi-pointe. Therefore they need to learn to get much of the impetus from their legs through the power in the plié and the push off from the floor of the working leg and foot, as well as from the coordination of the arms and the torso. They also cannot become dependent on throwing their arms around.

Balanchine was very particular about the look of our arms before the turns. In our big fourth position lunge, he usually wanted beautifully stretched third arabesque arms. Sometimes, to get us to really

Peter in a lunging fourth

extend our arms, Balanchine would say, "What do you like? Ice cream, diamonds, or money?" To a dancer who chose money, he would say, "Here's a million dollars!" as he held the imaginary bait in front of her leading hand, "Take it! Take it!" He used this ploy not only to lengthen the line but also to remind us to bring the face forward and lengthen the neck, to give life to our fingers and focus to our eyes, thus imparting dynamic energy to the whole pose.

Balanchine was very specific about the way we

. . . is long enough!

Peter before the plié for a turn from fifth or for an en dedans turn from fourth

The front arm opens forward and toward the side as he pliés for the turn.

The second arm starts to close as he starts to relevé.

His arms closing to an overlapped first as he turns

Peter's arms closed in a compact over-lapped first, nothing hanging out

used our arms during various turns. Just before the plié starting a turn en dehors from fifth or en dedans from fourth or fifth, we usually had one arm rounded in first position and the other to the side in second—standard pirouette arms. During the plié the front arm opened forward and toward the side. This helps the dancer keep her weight forward as well as giving her some impetus for the turn. Then, as we turned, both arms closed to a rounded, slightly overcrossed and somewhat lower than usual first position, a relatively tight first position that is similar to a gentle squeeze—a little like hugging yourself. "Leave nothing hanging out, nothing extra," Violette Verdy likes to say, refer-ring to elbows jutting out as well as to hips hanging back. The arms should stay roughly on the same plane; they don't lift higher than second or lower down to waist level to close. This is especially im-portant in consecutive turns from fifth. The posi-tion is relatively compact, but there is still space and air between the arms and the body.

In turns en dehors from the extended fourth po-sition he wanted the front arm to come directly in toward the dancer's chest. Unlike the arms in pirouettes from fifth or en dedans from fourth, the front arm in pirouette en dehors from fourth gives

Deanna demonstrates the overlapped first for a woman.

Deanna in a lunging fourth, arms in third arabesque

The front arm comes straight in; the side arm comes around and in.

Her arms are nearly in position for the turn, but she leaves her head where it was in the lunging fourth.

With her arms in turning position, Deanna spots front for one or more turns.

little or no impetus to the turn. The arm simply comes in by lowering the elbow and bringing in the hand, with the palm facing in, toward the chest (right arm to the left side of the chest when turning right). If Balanchine saw the front arm start out to the side when we were doing pirouettes from an extended fourth, he would stop us and say, "You're going to hit your partner! Don't you like him?" Of course, this was only a joke, because we did not have a partner behind us in class. Mr. B's real concern was the way the dancer looked as she started the turn. The arm swinging out or swinging back to either side was unnecessary and could make her look like a ballplayer winding up, and therefore less like a dancer. It also gave away the fact that a turn was coming. The impetus of the turn comes mostly from the legs and back foot and somewhat from the back arm, which starts slightly behind à la seconde and then moves around through second and then toward the chest, and closes over the other arm. From the third arabesque line, the upper arms pull

Peter ready to turn en dehors from a lunging fourth

Lifting his hands past his face, slightly exaggerating the bend in the elbows

in and down from the sides of the back (under the armpits). The two arms are coordinated, which also gives some impetus, moving at the same time to the final position, which is elbows down, forearms crossed, and palms facing in. They are presented gracefully and supported; there is air and space between them and also between the arms and the chest; they are not held tight and flat against the chest. The dancer can feel that she brings her chest

Deanna ready to turn en dehors from fifth position

Opening her arm forward and toward the side

Lifting her hands past her face . . .

. . . and to fifth high

Deanna arrives facing front with her arms in fifth high.

up and forward to meet her crossing arms instead of feeling that her arms coming in almost push her backward. She also needs to feel her torso, neck, and head lengthen up as her shoulders pull down.

Men turn with more rounded arms—for example, rounded arms in an overlapped first position.

When the arms were to be held overhead in fifth high, Mr. B's technique for getting them there was different. Traditionally, dancers had opened their arms to second during the plié before the spring relevé and then moved them to the outside over-

Peter lifting his arms toward fifth high . . .

. . . and lifting his arms higher as he spots front

He finishes his turn looking front, arms in fifth high and happy about it.

head to fifth high. This can look stiff and can throw the dancer off-balance because of the greater centrifugal force. Balanchine wanted the arms to rise compactly over the dancer's center. So, starting from fifth position (of the feet) with one arm rounded in front and the other in second position, we moved the front arm forward and toward the side, but not all the way to second. Then, as we started the turn, the elbow of the front arm bent and lifted while the arm at the side came diagonally around and up to meet it a bit higher than head level. Both elbows were bent enough to have the arms almost over the center. Then they extend to fifth high together. All this took place during the first turn. The same arm technique was used for en dedans turns from fourth with arms in fifth high.

In en dehors turns from the extended fourth, the front elbow lifts and bends, bringing the wrist with the palm facing down close to the head. In this case the front arm does not start by moving toward the

side. At the same time, the back arm comes around, and diagonally in and up, meeting the other arm at about head level. Both extend overhead by the end of the first turn. Again, the idea is to keep the vertical line of the body as compact as possible.

The key for the dancer in turning is that she brings everything in toward her center line and over her pointe. Her arms are in, but not so close to her torso that there is no air, her hips are up, the supporting hip over the supporting leg, her chest is lifted, her neck and head are erect and centered.

SPOTTING

In general we used the technique for spotting used by dancers trained elsewhere: We focused our eyes on one fixed point and remained focused on it as we began to turn. When we could no longer see it, we instantly whipped our head around so the same point came into view again. Mr. B did not want to see a "slow spot," momentarily leaving the back of the head to the audience. I tell the class, "I don't want to see your bun, I want to see your eyes!"

He differed from other teachers and choreographers in that he wanted us to spot front in en dehors and in en dedans turns, no matter where we were facing at the start of the turn. This was true not only of pirouettes but also of traveling turns such as piqués, step-ups, assemblés en tournant, and chaînés, whether performed on the diagonal or straight to the side. He did not want the side of the head left facing the audience. Balanchine would joke, "Don't look sideways! Look front. Your mother wants to see your pretty face." It is more than likely that Balanchine wanted to see the dancer's pretty face himself. He once told a photographer not to bother with profile shots of his dancers' faces. "What's half a face?" he asked. Spotting front reveals the dancer's entire front: her face, her turnout, and her open chest.

In spotting, teachers and dancers generally focus awareness on the very fast turn to the spot of the head. My colleague Stanley Williams used to say,

"Stay front!" meaning the dancer should not concentrate her energy on spinning or twisting around. When Sean Lavery teaches the boys, he tells them to bring the chest front, indicating that the chest, as well as the face, should be presented to the audience.

When a dancer's focus is not front, she will often make the mistake of changing her focus to the front before starting the turn. If, for example, she is in fourth position croisé in a third arabesque line for an en dehors pirouette, the tendency is to turn the head to look front as she starts the turn. Mr. B wanted, in contrast, a dynamic lunging fourth with a clear focus over and beyond the leading hand. As the dancer starts the en dehors turn, she leaves her head there and then spots front for the first and each succeeding revolution. Mr. B also gave en dehors turns from fourth position effacé, which are rarely given. In this case, the dancer comes front as she starts the turn and spots front on each succeeding revolution. When the dancer turns en dedans from fourth croisé or effacé, she usually has her neck bent and her head slanted so that her focus is already front, and no change is needed to spot front.

Spotting helps the dancer control the speed of the turn and the number of rotations as well as preventing dizziness. If we were spotting slowly on faster turns or rushing the spot in slower turns, Balanchine would often stop the class and have us count out loud in a *steady* tempo. For a double turn we would count "one-two-land." The "one" was the first spot, the "two" was the second spot, and "land" was our finish. Counting out loud had two effects: It released the tension in the neck, allowing us to spot easily, and it gave us the tempo of the turn. The counting works best, however, if you say the words out loud and with real conviction. I tell my classes to use the tone they would to command a playful dog to sit, "SIT."

Whatever the speed of the turn or the number of rotations, the counts had to be of equal duration. To help us to spot in time, Balanchine sometimes gave a combination that included a turn to a triple rhythm, such as a polonaise. We might do plié on count one, échappé to pointe on count two, hold count three, close and plié on count one, sous-sus on count two, hold count three, plié in fifth on count one, spot on count two, spot on count three, land in fifth back plié on count one, sous-sus on count two, hold count three. We would then repeat the short combination to the other side. Coordinating the rhythm and the spot requires knowing in advance the number of rotations the dancer wants to do (in this case, two). Only then will counting them out during the turn ensure that she finishes as she intends.

A good exercise in triple rhythm for men and women combines changements (see page 295) and a double pirouette. The dancer pliés on count one; does two changements, landing on counts two and three; jumps to a fairly big fourth on count one (weight over the front foot, usually landing on that foot first); turns spotting on counts two and three; and lands in fifth back in plié on count one. The dancer repeats as required, perhaps doing a half turn for each changement after the first set.

When Balanchine choreographed a turning combination with counts that differed from the musical counts, the steps had to be, as usual, exactly in time. For example, in *Tarantella*, in the ballerina's first solo, she has a combination that is in five, although the music is written in four. The combination goes like this: Tombé onto the right leg into plié with the working leg dégagé to the side on count one; soutenu turn to the right on count two; plié on the left leg with the working leg making a fouetté on count three; relevé into passé and fouetté turn to the right on count four; then plié on the supporting left leg, keeping the right leg in passé, on count five. The sequence is repeated three times, and each step has to be exactly in time as well as cleanly articulated—true pliés and pulled-up relevés, showing the working leg side or whipping through front to the side. With these musical and movement qualities the step is legible to the audience and draws their interest.

The one turn we did not spot was the arabesque turn. Mr. B wanted us to assume the pose and simply turn it. Attitude turns, in contrast, were treated as a kind of pirouette and were done with spotting.

PIROUETTES EN DEHORS FROM FIFTH POSITION

When talking about pirouettes en dehors, Balanchine liked to say, "The knee makes the turn." He meant that the knee of the working leg had to pull back against the hip and lead the turn. This not only gives the desired aesthetic quality, it also provides some impetus for the turn. This is not to say that Balanchine neglected the action of the supporting leg; like every aspect of the pirouette, it also received careful attention. The key was turnout; no matter which way we turned, we turned out in relevé just as we did in the basic passé exercises at the barre. Thus, when the dancer turns en dehors, the supporting leg should feel almost as if it turns in the other direction as she pulls up out of it and her hips. Simultaneously, she presses into the floor toward the big toe to relevé, bringing her weight on top of the pointe (hips, back, chest). The tendency in most turns is to lean back, but it is important to keep the weight forward over the pointe or demi-pointe.

In pirouettes as in most other steps, Balanchine preferred that the dancer go through the foot, attempting the roll-up relevé to arrive on pointe. Even a partial roll-up is smoother and helps maintain a stable position. Another factor in getting a smooth turn is to use only as much force in pushing off the floor as is required for the number of turns to be done and their speed. In fact, Balanchine sometimes gave a series of exercises designed to help us find the absolute minimum force we needed for one or two slow pirouettes.

In these slow turns, the pose was not static. Within the passé, we worked on extending the turnout in both legs and on lifting and opening the knee by pulling it up and back against the working hip, not by pushing the foot against the supporting

leg. At the same time, we opened the chest and shoulders. When we came off pointe from a slow turn ending in a fourth position lunge, our working knee maintained the turnout as we lifted it and, in a mini "rond de jambe" action, opened the thigh as the foot reached directly back to fourth position. We pliéd on the supporting leg as the supporting ankle released; our weight remained forward, the working foot being placed to the floor just after we came through the supporting foot. This same action is often used with a partner. In the second movement of *Concerto Barocco*, the ballerina, gently supported by her partner, does a slow pirouette starting from fifth and ending in an extended fourth.

Balanchine worked on a variety of pirouettes. He called one of them passé en tournant. This was a slow relevé passé that turned once as the pointe of the working leg moved up the front of the supporting leg, over, and then down the back of the supporting leg, both feet coming off pointe together into fifth position, all in a continuous action. To get the quality he wanted, Balanchine told us to think of this turn as a continuously moving passé that turns, rather than as "pirouette and land." He really wanted to see the working pointe going up along the center line of the supporting leg, the knee lifting high to the side and the foot coming down the back of the supporting leg to fifth position.

In faster consecutive turns from fifth in which we established a position—for example, those seen *en masse* in the finale of *Western Symphony*—the relevé often acquires a slight spring, because it is very difficult to roll up to pointe so quickly when pirouettes occur in such rapid succession. Balanchine recognized that some spring was necessary. At this fast tempo the working foot reaches only to midshin. If the tempo is a bit slower, the dancer lifts her foot to passé so the pointe of the working foot comes to, or just under, the center of the supporting knee.

The landing was as important as everything that preceded it. When the dancer was landing in fifth, Balanchine wanted both pointes to reach the floor

DETAILS I OFTEN INSIST ON IN FASTER TURNS FROM FIFTH:

1) try to relevé where your pointe is—minimum travel, minimum spring or jump
2) bring the working foot into position immediately
3) spot
4) keep the weight forward
5) take yourself off pointe and aim the working foot for the position (usually fifth or fourth), going through the feet; don't fall onto the full foot
6) when landing in fifth, feet to the floor simultaneously; when landing in fourth, the supporting (front) foot first, then the other
7) all pliés are smooth and continuous

DETAILS I OFTEN INSIST ON IN SLOW (PASSÉ EN TOURNANT) TURNS:

1) use minimum force
2) show the pointe going up the center of the supporting leg
3) the passé action is continuous; keep the knee lifting up, out, and back
4) control the relevé and descent and keep the body forward over the pointe; do not lean back
5) come off pointe into fifth position simultaneously
6) when landing in fourth, come off the supporting foot first

at the same time; then we had to go through the feet together. The roll-down required more skill and control than we could always muster, especially at faster tempos. To land simultaneously in fifth we often used a slight springing action, catching ourselves at the base of the toes and then going through the feet. We did not bang down into plié. Balanchine did not want to see one foot land after the other; he wanted us to turn and land, both feet together, as we moved smoothly into plié. "Put the foot down," Mr. B would say to us. The tendency is to hold the working foot in passé too long; then the dancer cannot land with both feet in fifth at the same time. In the slow passé en tournant turns we also needed to land both feet simultaneously in fifth, but now, as we started off pointe and into plié, we tried to roll down through both feet together to maintain the controlled softness of the turn. In all consecutive turns the ending of one turn was also the initiating action of the next turn. In consecutive turns it is important that the dancer get completely front on each plié as she aims her working foot to fifth so the weight is forward over the balls of the feet and the hips, back, and arms do not trail behind.

PIROUETTES EN DEDANS FROM FIFTH POSITION

We practiced en dedans pirouettes less often than en dehors pirouettes. But like en dehors, en dedans pirouettes from fifth had the same two forms: a slow passé en tournant, and, more often, turns that maintained the passé front position while revolving. On occasion, we also practiced en dedans turns from fifth, leaving the back foot in coupé back and ending in fifth back. In en dedans turns the supporting leg was of even greater importance, because it was the leg that, in coordination with the gentle push off the floor of the working foot and the action of the arms, torso, and hips, started the turn. In the case of passé en tournant turns (which we

DETAILS I OFTEN INSIST ON IN EN
DEDANS TURNS FROM FIFTH:

1) try to avoid jumping to pointe; relevé
   into the big toe and turn out the
   supporting leg to relevé

2) relevé onto a straight and pulled-up
   supporting leg as the working foot
   immediately establishes the position

3) take the hips and back on top of the
   supporting pointe; don't leave the
   working hip out and back, and don't
   lean back

4) take the whole body around on the turn

5) coordinate the arms

6) hold the working knee side and back

7) control the descent to fifth position

8) the plié is continuous before and after
   the turn

that create the impetus of the turn. As in the descent from passé en tournant, the pointes reach the floor simultaneously as the dancer goes through her feet into plié.

Not everyone could descend from this pirouette exactly as Mr. B suggested we do it. In fact, it often happened that only a few of us would initially master a technical detail that interested him. That did not matter, because the awareness of his goal and the attempt to achieve it gave our dancing an extra dynamism that was in itself pleasing and interesting. And, gradually, as time went on, we moved closer and closer to his goal. Mr. B usually asked us for "more," but he also knew how to use what we were capable of doing at each level of our development.

PIROUETTES EN DEHORS FROM FOURTH POSITION

rarely did en dedans), we pliéd on both feet, and then the supporting leg turned out during the relevé, as the working foot gave a gentle push from the floor, and went up the back of the supporting leg, over the top, and then came down its front, joining the other foot to come off pointe into plié simultaneously. As in plain passé from fifth back to fifth front, it is essential to keep the knee back to maintain maximum turnout and to keep the hips and back on top of the supporting leg and pointe. In addition, the coordination of the movement of the arms with the plié, relevé, and push from the floor is vital to the mechanics of the turn as well as to its aesthetic quality.

In plain en dedans pirouettes from fifth we pliéd on both feet. Then we pushed off the back foot as we relevéd into the big toe and immediately brought this foot to the front of the supporting knee while maintaining the turnout by holding the knee back. The working foot arrives in front of the supporting knee just as the dancer arrives on pointe. Again, it is the supporting leg, with the coordination of the push off the floor and the arms,

For these turns Balanchine insisted on a fourth position that was similar in many ways to a lunge: The front leg was in a large plié, the back leg straight and extended. He wanted the big, lunging fourth position to be beautiful, as big as time and muscle allowed, and he wanted maximum contrast in levels between the long, low fourth and the turn that followed. As much weight as possible was over the front foot and leg. The torso was forward with the chest lifted, and the arms and hands were stretched long, in a third arabesque with the fingers of both the front and back hands fully energized. The back arm could be almost in second position or extended a little farther back. The leading arm was directly in front of the center line, the hand at shoulder height or a little above, with the shoulder on that side slightly extended. The head was lifted forward, and the face and eyes were focused a few inches above the leading hand. The impression of a continuous line extending from the fingertips of the front hand through the shoulders to the fingertips of the back hand depended on all these elements.

An exception to the long line of the straight back leg would be a jump into fourth before turning: In this case the distance between front and back foot can be a little smaller, and the back knee can slightly bend (see page 266 for a combination). When the dancer jumps from fifth to fourth, she can on occasion land on both feet simultaneously or, more usually, on the front foot first. If she does a grand jeté en tournant, she naturally lands on the front foot first and places the second one into a large lunging fourth with a straight back leg. If, however, she does a pas de chat to fourth, she lands on her back foot first, but then places the second foot into fourth front, transferring most of her weight to the front. This fourth is naturally a smaller one. In each case most of her weight is over the front foot.

Pirouettes on pointe from this wide, lunging fourth followed the basic technique of turns from fifth. Once again, Balanchine stressed going through the foot for getting to pointe, instead of a jump up or a spring under, not only for its look but also because of its stability: "When turning, you need to have the feeling of turning, of going around, not the feeling of jumping up." Balanchine knew that a slight spring might supplement the relevé in fast turns and also in these turns. Nevertheless, he encouraged us to think of using the floor instead of springing away from it. I tell the students when doing this movement to think of "going into the floor" as they pull up out of their hips, legs, and feet. With a relevé into the floor the pirouette is smooth and extended, a beautiful movement in itself, not just a jarring, snappy trick.

In the lunging fourth position almost all of our weight was over the ball of the front foot and held with a very active supporting thigh; as little weight as possible was on the back foot, and the back knee was straight. Because the supporting hip is over the ball of the supporting foot and because the supporting knee is extended over the foot, the dancer need only keep her weight forward when she relevés. She does not have to transfer her weight forward or adjust the supporting foot as she would if she were in a plié in fourth with both knees bent and the weight divided between her feet. To turn from this extended fourth, we immediately pointed the back foot into the floor (using the muscles under the toes for the final push-off and *not* pliéing on the back leg). As we relevéd for the turn, we brought our hips up and over the supporting pointe and the working heel and hip forward. We pressed the knee back against the working hip to make passé. This all happens instantly, simultaneously.

As the dancer pushes the floor away with the back foot and turns out to passé she relevés. The push and the turnout give most of the force to the turn. At every moment in the pirouette, Balanchine wanted "the knee to lead the way," i.e., the full

---

DETAILS I OFTEN INSIST ON IN EN DEHORS PIROUETTES FROM FOURTH:
1) make a big fourth position with a straight back leg
2) in the big fourth, keep the hips front, with the weight forward over the front foot, controlled by active thigh muscles
3) do *not* plié on the back leg just before the turn
4) the arms are in a good third arabesque line; the leading hand is on the center line of the body; the back arm is just a bit behind second position
5) maintain the turnout in the supporting leg as you begin to relevé
6) try to relevé where the pointe is; arrive on pointe and in position immediately
7) bring the back forward and the hips up over the pointe; do not lean back during the turn
8) spot front
9) bring the front arm directly in, not out and around, establishing a relatively compact position

turnout. It is important for the dancer to pull up her hips and bring all of her body weight forward over her pointe, because the tendency in this turn is to leave her weight back, causing her to lean back and consequently fall. The open feeling of the turnout extends through the whole upper body; the dancer lifts her chest, giving the position and the turn life. This pirouette is usually done from croisé or en face, but it can also be done from effacé, as it is in the cadenza in *Allegro Brillante*.

This pirouette ends most often in an extended fourth, the same position from which it begins. From the turn with the working foot just in front of the supporting knee, the working knee lifts up and around as the working foot then takes the shortest path to fourth back. As the dancer starts off pointe bending the supporting knee and releasing the ankle to plié, she keeps her weight forward. The working foot goes immediately and directly to fourth back, landing an instant after the dancer comes through the supporting foot into plié. This is a case when the two feet do not land at the same time. If this pirouette finishes in fifth position, the feet land simultaneously.

PIROUETTES EN DEDANS FROM FOURTH POSITION

Traditionally, in almost all en dedans pirouettes from fourth, the supporting leg was in plié as the working leg passed through à la seconde, a little lower than ninety degrees, before it came into passé as the dancer relevéd. The rond de jambe of the working leg to à la seconde gave a strong impetus to the turn as the dancer established both hipbones and the shoulders facing front. Although Mr. B used this pirouette in his choreography, he also taught and used one that extended the technique. I, at least, had never seen it before.

In Mr. B's version the impetus for the turn comes mostly from the strongly maintained turnout of the supporting leg and partially from the push off the

floor of the working foot. Thus, from fourth position with a straight back leg, the working foot, after pushing the floor away, moved directly in front of the supporting knee as the dancer brought her hips and torso on top of the straight and pulled-up supporting leg and pointe while leaving her working knee back. Of course, we supplemented the action of our feet and legs with the coordinated movement of our arms, just as dancers did in the traditional version. It was imperative to maintain the turnout in both legs throughout the turn.

Sometimes Balanchine would give combinations with a variety of en dedans and en dehors turns. An

---

DETAILS I OFTEN INSIST ON IN PIROUETTES EN DEDANS FROM FOURTH POSITION:

1) large fourth position with a straight back leg
2) maintain the weight over the ball of the supporting foot
3) at the start, both legs work simultaneously; don't bring the working leg into passé before the supporting leg has begun to make the relevé; relevé immediately to a straight leg
4) starting the pirouette, turn out the supporting leg to make relevé as the working foot is brought immediately into position; relevé toward the big toe
5) bring the hips and the heel of the working leg on top of the supporting leg and pointe—collect yourself and take yourself up and around, including your back
6) at the start of the pirouette, the arm in first moves forward and toward the side as the chest and hips come forward over the supporting leg and foot
7) the whole body needs to feel related to or over the pulled-up supporting hip, leg, and foot

example from his choreography is in the coda of the pas de deux from *Stars and Stripes*. The ballerina does one en dedans soutenu turn, one pirouette en dedans (leg through à la seconde to passé front), ending with coupé back, one fouetté turn ending in fifth front, one en dedans turn picking up the back foot and holding it in coupé back during the turn, plié on the supporting (right) leg as the working leg moves out to a low à la seconde. It is in eight counts (two measures of four counts): plié on count one, soutenu turn on count two, plié on count three, en dedans pirouette on count four, plié on count five, fouetté turn on count six, plié on count seven, en dedans pirouette in coupé back on count eight. The sequence repeats three times and turns to the right.

PIQUÉ TURNS

For Balanchine, piqué turns were almost always a pointe step. In performing them we had to obey the general rule for piqué—that is, we had to step onto pointe with a straight knee. The step begins with a plié on the supporting leg as the turned-out working leg makes a rond de jambe movement from front toward à la seconde. "That is the leg that guides you." This often gives the step the feeling of turning before the dancer even arrives on pointe. As the working leg arrives à la seconde, the dancer, pushing off the supporting leg and foot, steps on the outside edge of the box and rolls up and over toward the big toe as the pointe, leg, and body begin to turn. To arrive on pointe the dancer uses the plié and pushes into and therefore away from the floor so as to step far away, rather than near herself, which would lessen the dynamism of the step. As soon as she pushes off the floor, that leg is brought immediately into position, with the hip and heel forward and the knee held back. The accent is almost always "up"—that is, on the "one" and on the one, the working leg and foot have arrived in position.

In the traditional piqué turn the working foot goes behind the supporting leg a little below the knee. Mr. B did not want the working foot so high that it looked like we were kicking ourselves; he asked us to bring the inside of the heel about to the top of the calf. Balanchine sometimes gave piqué turns with the foot in front of the supporting knee.

Dana in tendu croisé front

Dana pliés as she rond de jambes to the side to piqué for her turn.

Dana turning, delaying the arms, and looking front as she brings her hip and heel forward

Dana sailing around in a slow turn

If the tempo was slow, the working pointe went to or just below the supporting knee. However, when the tempo is very fast, as it is in the second variation of *Raymonda Variations,* when five piqué turns with the foot in front of the supporting leg are done before the final "step-up" turn, the foot is held at midshin. In *Tarantella* Balanchine broke his usual rules: After the man leaves the ballerina, she does piqué turns, stepping on a turned-in, slightly bent supporting knee and then straightens it as she turns. To make the sequence even more unusual and therefore interesting, Balanchine had her turn to the right while traveling on a diagonal to the left with her back to the audience.

Sometimes, instead of stepping or doing a slight jump onto pointe, Balanchine would ask for a traveling jump or a real jeté to pointe. To do this we had to push sharply and strongly off the plié leg and jump out and onto pointe. An example of this jeté piqué turn is found in the coda of *Donizetti Variations,* when the ballerina performs the step in a circle, then on a line as she exits into the wings.

Balanchine wanted almost all piqué turns to spot front, whether they were traveling front to the audience, on a diagonal, side to the wings, or even to the back. In *La Source* he had me do piqué turns going upstage while spotting front. It was very hard to do and, thank God, there were only three!

In class Mr. Balanchine would sometimes ask one of the speedier turners to show him how fast she could turn. Then, using her speed to set the tempo, he would have the whole class do piqué turns on the diagonal spotting front, at lightning speed. For piqué turns at fast tempos some of us opened our arms to the side and then brought them toward first (not necessarily getting them all the way in). But when maximum speed was the point of a turning exercise, each dancer could use the port de bras that was most effective for her, as long as it was aesthetically pleasing. We spotted very fast, almost whipping our heads and ourselves around in the turns.

In direct contrast to fast, whipping turns, Balanchine would sometimes give a series of slower,

---

DETAILS I OFTEN INSIST ON IN PIQUÉ TURNS:

1) step out side (not front) as far as music and time allow, and onto a straight leg
2) bring the hip and back up on top of the supporting leg and pull up
3) maintain the turnout of the working leg by bringing the working hip and heel forward on the piqué
4) keep the inside of the heel of the working foot a little below the knee when it is behind the supporting leg
5) bring the working leg immediately into position; when the turns are slow, make the plié big and juicy
6) do not collapse the body forward in the plié; do not heave it back on the piqué
7) spot front or where directed

"sailing" piqué turns, also going across the room on a diagonal or straight to the side. For this turn he stressed the need to make a deep plié and then a big rond de jambe in order to step far to the side into à la seconde. On the turn the dancer opened her arms in an extended second position (palms down) or flexed her wrists up and left her head tilted to the front, sustaining the beginning of the turn. "Your mother wants to see your face," he would tell us again. This made the dancer feel very open, very turned out, and very beautiful. Then we could gently close our arms and spot as we sailed around.

On certain occasions we did not spot front. For example, when we were doing piqué turns in a circle, we might spot the next point around the circle or, as the fifteen women do in *Serenade,* the dancer ahead of us in the circle. Also in *Serenade,* when the soloist in the waltz traces a figure eight around two of the women, she spots the next point on the path of the figure. Then, for her exit out the back wing, she spots that wing until she stops turning and runs offstage. In fact, Balanchine often choreographed a large circle of piqué turns ending with the dancer exiting into the wing. In these cases the dancer usually spots successive points on the circle and then often spots the wing, not the audience, as she exits. In the coda of the *Nutcracker* pas de deux, the Sugar Plum Fairy circles and then usually exits this way. When turning in a circle, some dancers find it easier to spot out, which is a look he preferred. It is as if dancing in a theater in the round, where the dancer would be spotting to her own front at each succeeding turn.

Piqué turns were not practiced by the men, although when Mr. B forgot about the men for a while in order to explore some aspect of the step with the women, one or two might join in with a few piqué turns, partially as a joke but also learning what the turns are like. He might respond by giving them a turning combination they could do at the same time, such as coupé jeté on the diagonal or emboîté turns with saut de basque or with chaînés. Some women joined in, of course. But, most likely, his main attention would still have been on the women and their piqué turns.

CHAÎNÉ TURNS

"You must turn because the legs don't present anything. It is a person turning around himself."

Chaîné turns started traditionally with a step into plié; he wanted us to start with a piqué. They can be done in two ways: in a very tight first position, or in a correctly crossed fifth position. Either version was acceptable to Balanchine, although most of us executed chaîné turns in first. When we were practicing chaînés he told us to imagine that we had a string tied around our thighs, his way of making us understand how tightly we had to hold our upper legs together and how close our feet had to be.

Chaîné turns are initially taught with an equal rotation on each foot and usually in a first position with the feet slightly apart. In his choreography Balanchine only used this wider turn for character-

ization, as at the end of Columbine's solo in Act II of *Harlequinade*. It was not the turn we practiced in class and danced in most of his ballets. "Conceal your feet. Don't try to travel," he said in class.

When we practiced chaîné turns in first, we tended to turn a little more on the second foot. Our knees stayed straight and pulled up (not locked back), and any adjustment that had to be made to release the foot from the floor was made in the ankle. Both the adjustment in the amount we turned on each foot and the adjustment in the ankle were accomplished more or less automatically. Balanchine never talked about them; they were simply the most efficient way of executing these turns, which are usually very fast.

When doing fast chaîné turns in first position, the dancer is pulled up but does not necessarily maintain maximum turnout. In fact, the men (and the women if on demi-pointe) should not be totally turned out when doing these turns in first position, because it gives a strange, penguinlike look. The men did not regularly do this step, but when Balanchine gave it for them, the chaîné turns could be done on the diagonal but often were done in a relatively tight circle. He had never forgotten that Lew Christensen, who danced for him in the 1930s, could do chaîné turns very fast in a circle. Only a few of us in the 1960s could compare to Lew, according to Mr. B. The man who did was Jacques d'Amboise.

Balanchine did not talk a lot about our arms, which needed to look attractive and to complement the chaîné turn. The arms opened in the traditional way, and with the push off the supporting leg gave the turn its initial impetus. They were then brought into a small, crossed, relatively low first position and held there slightly above the waist. If we had to turn a long time, we brought the arms in more slowly; if we had to turn very fast and only briefly, we could bring them in immediately. We also practiced variants of this port de bras. Sometimes he would have us slowly raise our arms from an overlapped first position to fifth high. In doing this, the elbows bent to "lead" the move-

DETAILS I OFTEN INSIST ON IN
CHAÎNÉ TURNS:
1) maintain the feet close together
2) pull up out of feet, legs, and hips
3) bring the hips and back on top of the legs;
   do not lean back
4) do not open and close the arms for each
   turn; keep the shoulders down and feel
   the arms connected to the back
5) spot front, quickly and lightly

ment, thus keeping our forearms close to the center line of the body. This port de bras is used in the chaîné turn exit in the scherzo of the "Diamonds" section of *Jewels*. Another port de bras that he occasionally used in his choreography had the arms extended to the side, with flexed wrists. He sometimes used this arm position in piqué turns as well.

He also talked about spotting in chaîné turns. Besides spotting in the direction we were going—on the diagonal, straight side to the wings, or moving in a circle, as in a manège—we often practiced spotting straight front as we traveled in various directions. This is what he most often preferred. On occasion he even asked us to chaîné back while spotting front. This is quite hard to do, but it creates an unusual and distinctive look. As with pirouettes, spotting front in chaîné turns presents the shoulders, chest, hips, thighs, and the face, indeed, the entire front to the audience.

Typically, Balanchine choreographed many variations on the chaîné turn. For example, in *Divertimento No. 15*, *Walpurgisnacht*, and *Swan Lake*, some of the chaîné turns for the women are on demi-pointe. In the pas de deux Mauresque in *Don Quixote*, I did chaîné turns on my heels with straight knees and on pointe with bent knees. Onstage, Balanchine broke his own rules, so despite the fact that some things were "always" danced a certain way, Mr. B liked to surprise us and the audience: "Never been done before!"

PAS DE BOURRÉE EN TOURNANT

Balanchine usually followed the traditional step—that is, toe-toe-plié. Going en dedans we usually began with a dégagé side as we pliéd on the supporting leg. Then, with a slight rond de jambe action, we brought the working leg across in front of the supporting leg. We stepped to pointe as we came up from plié, making sure to maintain the turnout as the leg passed into an overcrossed sous-sus. We took another step as we turned, and then with the third step we pliéd, going through the foot and bringing the heel forward as we came off pointe. For en dehors the working leg was again usually to the side; we brought it with a very slight rond de jambe action, crossing behind the supporting leg to an overcrossed sous-sus as we rose to pointe on the supporting leg. We then took one step while turning, bringing our back and hips around with our legs. This was followed by a step going through the foot into plié, again presenting the heel forward.

The arms open to second as the dancer pliés and as the working leg dégagés side; the arms close to

DETAILS I OFTEN INSIST ON IN PAS
DE BOURRÉE EN TOURNANT:
1) maintain straight legs on the pas de
   bourrée
2) place the toes to the floor and bring the
   heel forward (do not let the foot hit the
   floor and the heel fall down) when
   moving into plié
3) take the body around on top of the legs;
   don't lean back
4) coordinate the arms with the legs
5) spot front
6) take two steps on pointe (straight legs);
   third step goes into plié

an overlapped first in coordination with the working leg as it closes into an overcrossed sous-sus.

Balanchine paid very close attention to the toes and the foot moving into plié: We had to place the toes on the floor first and then go through the foot and bring the heel forward into plié. The reason he was so vigilant is that it is very tempting at that moment to turn in and slam the foot down in any old position and to do a "stingy" plié. He also wanted us to keep our knees straight on the two steps and actually take them. He used this step in the pas de bourrée–fouetté combination danced by the four ballerinas in the finale of *Symphony in C*. Balanchine wanted the last step of the pas de bourrée to be turned out and the foot carefully placed to the floor with the weight over the ball. We began the fouetté action of the leg through the front toward second as we started the plié. After each fouetté turn we placed the working foot to the floor toes first, with the heel forward, again with the weight over the ball of the foot, trying not to hit the floor with the heel, before we started the next pas de bourrée.

SOUTENU TURN

Soutenu turn is similar to assemblé en tournant on pointe and should look different from pas de bourrée en tournant. In soutenu turn, the feet land on pointe together with an overcrossed sous-sus in croisé. These turns usually begin with dégagé side with a plié on the supporting leg. However, from fifth back a spring relevé is used when beginning back soutenu turn. In this case the dancer springs gently off the floor, changing feet and landing on pointe in sous-sus, again with the thighs turned out and well crossed.

Balanchine sometimes made combinations showing the contrast between pas de bourrée en tournant and soutenu turn. They made us very aware of the differences between the two turns and helped us to articulate each of them clearly. The turns look alike as they begin: In this case, the dancer does a dégagé side and closes in an overcrossed sous-sus.

The difference is that pas de bourrée is a walking step with a relevé into the sous-sus, while soutenu, especially at very fast tempos, often requires a slight springing action to pointe that is almost a small assemblé followed by a turn. A combination that Balanchine liked to give was dégagé side with the left foot, pas de bourrée en tournant en dedans, plié, dégagé side with the right foot, pas de bourrée en tournant en dehors, then plié, dégagé with the left foot, soutenu turn en dedans, dégagé left, soutenu turn en dedans. This combination was in four and turned to the right. Balanchine wanted us to show clearly the two steps on pointe with straight knees in the pas de bourrée and the single landing on pointe with a turn in the soutenu. Again, we had to go through the supporting foot as we placed it, toes first, heel forward, to the floor and pliéd with the weight remaining over the ball of the foot.

The men did not generally practice pas de bourrée en tournant or soutenu turn, but when they did, it made them aware of the proper placement of the feet to the floor as well as showing two steps for the pas de bourrée en tournant and a single landing for the soutenu turn.

DETAILS I OFTEN INSIST ON IN SOUTENU TURNS:
1) land on both pointes simultaneously
2) maintain the turnout
3) take the body around on top of the legs
4) spot front
5) roll down with the heel forward

ASSEMBLÉ EN TOURNANT ON POINTE

This traveling turn was usually practiced on the diagonal or going straight across to the side of the studio.

Like the piqué turn, the step begins with a rond

de jambe toward second. The dancer pliés and pushes off the supporting leg to make a low, small jump that travels. She lands on both pointes almost simultaneously in an overcrossed sous-sus and turns. She pliés on the supporting leg as she does another low rond de jambe, jumping again into an overcrossed sous-sus. The dancer generally spots front, unless the step is done in a circle.

The action of the arms is similar to that in piqué turns. They open to second on the plié and close to an overlapped first as she jumps to pointe, and they remain that way for the turn. At moderate to slow tempos the arms can be slightly delayed, along with the turn and the spot.

DETAILS I OFTEN INSIST ON IN ASSEMBLÉ EN TOURNANT:
1) travel
2) land on straight, stretched legs
3) second leg in instantly
4) spot front

FOUETTÉ TURNS

"One dancer did ninety-two fouettés, but she fell, ripped her tendon, and her career was over. Too many is not good."

Probably because of Odile's thirty-two fouetté turns in *Swan Lake*, the usual focus in teaching fouetté turns was on mastering the trick of many consecutive turns; less attention was given to the way in which they were done. For Mr. B, mere repetition was not enough.

Many teachers taught the traditional fouetté turn with the working leg opening directly à la seconde during the plié. Then, as the dancer sprang to pointe, the working leg moved to passé back, with the toe touching the back of the supporting knee and then moved to passé front before opening again to the side. The action was similar to that of double frappé to the side—that is, back, front, out, but done at the knee, not at the ankle.

Balanchine realized that in closing back and then front the dancer tended to let her leg turn in and her thigh come forward. Perhaps for this reason, after an initial pirouette, he had his dancers start the fouetté with a rond de jambe action of the working leg through croisé front; he then had them whip the leg to second and relevé with a slight rond de jambe en l'air action, the working pointe then passing the side of the supporting leg and coming in front of the supporting knee. The dancer lowers into plié as she moves the working foot through croisé front and around to à la seconde for the next fouetté.

The turnout of the working leg is maintained by careful attention to a few important details. In doing the rond de jambe through croisé front, the dancer keeps the working foot and thigh at the same level, on a line almost parallel to the floor, not allowing the foot to drop down toward the floor. As the working leg moves toward croisé, the knee is held back and the heel is presented forward. As the dancer whips the working leg to à la seconde, she maintains the turnout, and as she relevés, she holds the working knee back and out while she makes the first half of a rond de jambe en dehors, and then she brings the heel forward and the toe to pass the side of and come to the front of the supporting knee. She does not let the toe go behind the supporting knee and hit it.

Mr. B also wanted us to do the plié and relevé as smoothly as possible and with control. The dancer tries to reach pointe without a jarring jump. Even if she cannot roll all the way up through the supporting foot, she maintains maximum control. Most importantly, the dancer does not fall back down to flat. The heel does not "bang" into the floor, which gives the turn a jarring effect. If the dancer cannot roll down, she "catches" herself at the base of the toes and goes through the foot from there, keeping the weight over the ball. The turnout of the supporting leg and foot is also more easily maintained because of the awareness and effort this kind of control demands.

By insisting on the demi-rond de jambe Balanchine made the fouetté turn a fuller, bigger movement. "A juicier step," he would say. And because the turnout is maintained throughout and the relevés and landings are controlled, the dancer looks more refined. Finally, in his choreography, the step is rarely done many times consecutively— and certainly never thirty-two times—so it is not simply a trick intended to dazzle the audience. When the consecutive fouetté does appear, integrated into the flow of movement with high energy, it does, of course, dazzle. It is danced this way in the fourth movement of *Western Symphony*, in a variation in *Who Cares?*, and by Hyppolyta in *A Midsummer Night's Dream*.

Mr. B sometimes gave fouetté turns set to a triple rhythm to help us learn to do consecutive doubles. The dancer pliés on count one, relevés and turns once on count two, spots again and turns on count three. This step helped him find a cover for Marnee Morris's turning variation in *Who Cares?* A couple of other dancers and I had hopes, but Sara Leland did the step, was more suited to the role, and got it.

Fouetté turns were sometimes done first to a very slow tempo to make us aware of controlling the plié and to give us time to cultivate the necessary control. Then Mr. B might ask for a more moderate tempo and then for fast tempos. This gave us the chance to see how much control we really had and to let us practice maintaining it (e.g., no banging down) as the tempo picked up. Coordinating the arms, the working leg, the spot, and the relevé is essential to make fouetté turns work. On

occasion we also practiced fouetté turns en dedans.

Men did not usually practice fouetté turns in class. Balanchine might give the men relevé turns à la seconde, fast turning hops à la seconde, or perhaps a combination combining tours en l'air and other jumps. Each of these requires control of the plié to avoid banging the heel down.

EMBOÎTÉ TURNS

Mr. Balanchine used emboîté on pointe fairly often in his choreography, and we practiced it in class. At moderate tempos the dancer piqués, bringing her working foot to the front or back of the knee, making a little more than a quarter of a turn. She then piqués on that foot, bringing the other foot to the knee, making a little less than three quarters of a turn. At faster tempos the pointe of the working foot does not come all the way up to the knee. If the tempo is moderately fast, it might come about halfway; if the tempo is very fast, it might go only a little above the ankle. Whatever the tempo, the supporting hip is pulled up, and the turnout is maintained: The knee of the working leg is held back, and the heel of the working foot is brought forward.

We did emboîtés in a variety of ways. We traveled front, side, or in a circle, brought the working foot front or back, and placed it at different heights, depending on the music, the speed, and the look required. One of Mr. B's favorite emboîté exercises was two emboîté turns (four piqués), with the working foot to the front followed by two turns (four piqués), with the working foot to the back, traveling straight to the side or on the diagonal, and spotting front. He might ask us to continue with the same step, but jumping (see page 343). So the combination would be: a set to the front on pointe, a set to the back on pointe, a set to the front jumping, a set to the back jumping.

In the first movement of *Symphony in C* the ballerina does two emboîté turns, bringing the working foot to the front of the supporting knee as she

---

DETAILS I OFTEN INSIST ON IN
FOUETTÉ TURNS:

1) maintain the turnout of the working leg
2) maintain the working leg at the same level; do not lower and lift
3) pull up out of the supporting hip
4) control the plié; do not collapse forward
5) do not heave back on the relevé
6) lengthen neck and spot at eye level
7) coordinate the arms with the turn

travels forward down the center of the stage. She then does a plié in fifth and a double pirouette, ending in fifth position front in demi-plié. She does this sequence twice more. In *Tchaikovsky Piano Concerto No. 2* the second soloist does emboîté turns on pointe, traveling straight forward with the working foot to the back. These start at a medium tempo with a fairly high working foot (inside of the heel at the top of the calf) and then, as the tempo accelerates, the working foot gets lower (almost to the ankle). And in the coda of *Tchaikovsky Pas de Deux* the ballerina has a choice: either fouetté turns or two emboîté turns followed by two fouetté turns.

> DETAILS I OFTEN INSIST ON IN EMBOÎTÉ TURNS:
> 1) keep the hips up; do not sit behind the legs
> 2) keep the working knee back and legs turned out; bring the working foot into position quickly, heel forward
> 3) spot front
> 4) keep the head up and the shoulders down

WALKING ON POINTE

Balanchine made walking on pointe an art. In fact, in the "Emeralds" section of *Jewels* he choreographed an extraordinary "walking" pas de deux in which the ballerina rarely comes off pointe. In class Balanchine gave the women many exercises to practice walking on pointe in the three basic directions: front, side, and back. He wanted to see the working foot come across the supporting foot, he wanted straight knees, and he wanted our thighs crossed. Sometimes he would have us walk forward, going from fifth with the right foot front to fifth with the left foot front. We would do sets of eight or sometimes sixteen in even tempo. Then, when we had mastered the basic technique, he would make a little dance of three or five steps and a briefly held sous-sus, varying the head, arms, and

épaulement. The corps does this combination in the third movement of *Concerto Barocco:* five walking steps and a coupé followed by three piqué ballonnés side alternating legs, ending in coupé back. When we traveled to the side we had to open our legs directly side, not a little to the front or a little to the back, but side, exactly opposite the supporting heel. We could move the leg into a small first or true first. We had to move the foot precisely to the position specified; it could not be placed just anywhere. The leg had to move quickly, then slow and hold its final position to make the movement legible to the audience. Then the other leg was brought to sous-sus front or back or even crossed over, depending on the exercise or choreography. For example, in the very fast variation in *Divertimento No. 15* the ballerina walks backward, right foot sous-sus back, left foot sous-sus back, then steps to the side with the right, to second position with the left and then again with the right, which is brought under her center and then into sous-sus back with the left. This combination is done twice to the back and then is done once in reverse, to the front.

When we practiced walking, Balanchine would have us accent a specific part of the movement. Usually it was the closing to sous-sus, the movement "in." Saying "and IN, and IN, and IN," Mr. B wanted to see the accent exactly as we closed. At other times the movement out or both in and out would be accented. Whatever the emphasis, he wanted to see the difference between accented and unaccented movements clearly.

Sometimes Mr. B wanted us to travel more. In such cases we did not close to sous-sus; instead we stepped front or back to a small fourth. Dewdrop does this in her solo in *The Nutcracker*, as does the second soloist in *La Source*.

The aesthetic effect that Balanchine was after depended not only on the look of the feet but also on the look of the legs. We had to use the full length of the leg, turned out and with the knee straight. Balanchine's walks underscored once again his view of pointe as a means of extending the look, the line, and the function of the leg. The time he devoted to perfecting these seemingly simple movements was reminiscent of the extensive drilling he gave to battements tendus. His demand was the same: The step should look like itself every time it is performed. In fifth position he wanted a tight, crossed sous-sus; in open stances he wanted precise spacing of the feet. When the leg crossed he wanted the cross to be clearly defined from the tops of the thighs to the tips of the toes. And always he wanted maximum turnout and stretched knees.

The walk on pointe with bent knee (in a plié) was not practiced in class, but Balanchine used it in choreography. It offers an interesting contrast, not only because of the bend in the knee, which changes the level, but also because the working leg can do a swooping rond de jambe movement as it passes the supporting foot to come front. This kind of walk is seen in the ballerina's variation in the "Emeralds" section of *Jewels*. In this variation the dancer takes one step in plié on pointe and then straightens the knee as she makes a low rond de jambe (it's almost par terre) and then steps with a stretched leg on pointe with that foot. She pliés then straightens, while making the rond de jambe, and continues with two steps on pointe with straight knees ending in sous-sus front.

When Balanchine gave us exercises for walking on pointe he stressed that the whole body had to participate in the action, not just the legs and the feet. He did not want to see our faces straining in concentration; he wanted to see the energy and vitality of the movement revealed in every part of the body. Because it is very tempting to stare straight front while dancing en face, he often added arm and head movements or some changes in épaulement to walking steps. If we were walking forward, he might have us look down at our feet and then, at a certain point, look up. "Now look beautiful," he would say. Or he might give a port de bras that kept changing the look: for example, from second position to fifth low to fifth high and ending with the dancer in croisé. If we were walking to the side he might have us look out over our hand and change the épaulement to "announce" which leg

---

> DETAILS I OFTEN INSIST ON FOR
> WALKING ON POINTE WITH
> STRAIGHT KNEES:
> 1) keep the knees straight
> 2) step directly front (or directly back) on the center line
> 3) the whole body participates—maintain life and energy

---

had moved. This variety made our movements interesting and beautiful.

Another walk on pointe went through passé. These walks were practiced coming straight forward and going straight back. The shape of the movement was unvarying: Starting in sous-sus, the working leg went up the center of the supporting leg to passé, with the accent up in the lift of the knee, then moved from front to back or vice versa, with the working pointe passing above and to the side of the supporting knee. In the closing or downward movement of the step the toes had to go across the supporting foot as the knee straightened to show the rearranged sous-sus. The accent was up, but the pointe was often down to the floor on the count. In this walk Balanchine stressed the action of the knee in lifting the foot from the floor. If a dancer forgot to lift her knee and lifted the foot instead, the foot often hit the supporting leg.

Although in class we never practiced anything turned in, Balanchine often used turned-in movements, including passé walks on pointe, in his

---

> DETAILS I OFTEN INSIST ON IN
> PASSÉ WALKS:
> 1) step directly front (or directly back) on the center line
> 2) lift the working knee to the side; the pointe is at maximum height on the side
> 3) place the pointe to the floor in a correctly crossed sous-sus

choreography. Near the end of the finale of *Stars and Stripes* the entire corps does four passé walks and two kicks, all in parallel. Even in classical ballets such as *Walpurgisnacht* and *Divertimento No. 15* Balanchine used this turned-in passé position. "Like a cheerleader," he would say when rehearsing the third variation in *Divertimento No. 15*, when the dancer walks back on pointe with turned-in passés, a little like a prance.

OTHER TRAVELING STEPS ON POINTE

Pas Courru

Running forward on pointe is often done in first position, usually with the turnout somewhat diminished, but running backward is usually done in parallel. The dancer moves forward or backward by passing her feet, one at a time, in a tiny step through first position, with the heels and knees almost touching. She has to move her legs as quickly as possible, keeping them stretched but not stiff. This gives the movement a light, skimming effect. Balanchine used pas courru forward in some of his ballets—for example, for the lead Marzipan shepardess in *The Nutcracker*, for the lead bird in the second act of *Harlequinade*, and twice in *Raymonda Variations:* in the second variation before the hops on pointe, and in the ballerina's first entrance in the waltz. By far the most notable use of pas courru is in *La Sonnambula* (originally *Night Shadow*); the Sleepwalker runs on pointe in every direction and uses it in her pas de deux with the Poet to deepen her mystery.

DETAILS I OFTEN INSIST ON FOR PAS COURRU ON POINTE:
1) make fast, tiny steps
2) try to keep the knees close together

When the choreography meant to portray a specific image, e.g., a doll, the forward run could be done less turned out or even in parallel with straight legs. In the ballerina roles of *The Steadfast Tin Soldier*, *Coppélia*, and in Pierrette's dance in the second act of *Harlequinade*, Balanchine used these more parallel runs to enhance the puppetlike stiffness that adds flavor to the characterization.

We rarely practiced pas courru in class. In the Petipa variations, such as those taught at the school for many years by Madame Danilova, pas courru is often used. However, a pas courru that we did practice was made up of two running steps on demi-pointe and a third step through the foot into plié; it often preceded a grand jeté. The running steps are very quick, with the legs thrown forward, but the step moving into plié is slower to allow time to collect energy for the jump to follow.

Bourrée Suivie

A traveling step that we worked on extensively in class was the bourrée. We practiced bourrées to the front, side, back, and in small circles. To achieve the fluid, shimmering effect that Balanchine wanted, the knees had to be very slightly bent, with the ankles very slightly releasing and stretching for each step. We had to keep our thighs as close together as possible, and they had to be crossed. To emphasize how tightly crossed they should be, Balanchine again would say, "Pretend you have a string tied around your thighs."

Aside from wanting our thighs crossed, Balanchine wanted the steps to be equal in size and performed at a constant tempo. "*Travaillez, travaillez!*" he would sometimes tell us, indulging in a little onomatopoeia. He meant that we had to keep our legs and feet working right through the last count, neither slowing down like a wind-up toy or a car braking to stop, nor taking bigger steps to reach our destination with less effort. Because the size and tempo of the steps were constant, the sound of the pointe shoes on the floor was an even, quiet tapping. I tell the students that the tapping should sound like Woody Woodpecker with a subtle touch at work.

Whether moving front, back, or side, the thighs always remained crossed. Usually we traveled side in the direction of the front leg. Traveling this way, there is a tendency to step first with the front leg, while keeping the back knee straight, and then drag the back leg in to meet the front leg. The impression is that the dancer has a peg leg. But Mr. B wanted us to keep the knees very slightly bent and the legs crossed, continually leading with the back leg. Both knees must flex the same amount, and the tempo of all the steps is even. Sometimes, however, we traveled side in the direction of the back leg, leading with the front. Balanchine used this alternative bourrée in the ballerina's solo in the "Diamonds" section of *Jewels*. When traveling front or back, we opened to a tiny fourth position and closed to an overcrossed fifth. Whatever the direction of travel, it was better to be slightly overcrossed than to allow our legs to separate. Nonetheless, when we had to cover a large distance in a very short time, the steps necessarily became bigger, and the thighs might open a bit.

Unlike most of Balanchine's walking steps on pointe, which we did with the body held relatively straight, bourrée suivie to the side was often practiced by leading with the hip and with a bend in the upper body away from the direction of travel. We might reach overhead as we bent, while the hip led in the direction of the step. Balanchine wanted us to bend and reach while pushing our hips strongly in the direction of travel, which was in the opposite direction. He wanted us to feel that we could almost lose our balance if our feet did not

keep up. Sometimes Balanchine emphasized his point by taking our hands and pulling them toward him while he pushed our hips away. The image of a pull on the body so strong that it left the legs struggling to keep up gave dynamic energy to the bourrée.

Peter holds Deanna's hand as she pulls strongly away. This is the feeling the dancer has when she bourrées side, leading with the hip.

We practiced many variations of the basic bourrée that used the head, upper body, and arms in lovely and expressive ways. For example, Balanchine might have us bend our upper bodies to the left and bourrée to the right, straightening and bringing the arms overhead to fifth high. Then we would come off pointe and plié while doing tendu croisé front, meanwhile bending to the side and lowering our arms and hands toward the working (tendu) foot.

Some exercises were set at moderate tempos—for example, bourrée side for eight counts traveling

*Dana bourrées,
leading with
the hip and
back foot.*

across the studio and then return, or bourrée forward and back, or bourrée clockwise and counterclockwise. Other exercises were set to fast tempos, such as bourrée front for one count, plié on count two, two échappés to pointe changing feet and landing on counts three and four, bourrée back for one count, two échappés to pointe changing feet and landing on counts three and four. The dancer develops the ability to bourrée any distance in any direction with fast, smooth steps skimming over the floor. At moderate and fast tempos it is very important to *"travailler!"*: to work the legs and feet continuously, with the thighs crossed and the feet crossing. Meanwhile, the upper body shows the quality appropriate to the exercise and the music (for example, the "push" exercise on page 167).

DETAILS I OFTEN INSIST ON FOR
BOURRÉE SUIVIE:
1) cross the feet and thighs; no gap between the thighs
2) make small, fast, even steps
3) the knees have a slight flex; they are not locked

Pas de Bourrée Dessous-Dessus

This basic classroom step was explored by Balanchine in numerous forms. Although pas de bourrée can be executed on demi-pointe, the pointe versions were the ones that interested him more and probably inspired his reworking of the traditional step. Most notably, instead of asking only for the standard toe-toe-plié version, he had us also practice toe-toe-toe, ending in sous-sus and then plié. "I want to see the RAY," he would tell us, accenting the last syllable; he referred to the third step on pointe ending in sous-sus.

The pas de bourrée seen most often travels side. We could begin the step in a variety of ways: with a piqué under the center of the body; a small développé or dégagé followed by "tombé" (see page 241); or by doing développé or dégagé followed by a true tombé into plié or a dégagé side and then bringing the foot into an overcrossed sous-sus. After this we stepped into a small first and closed in sous-sus on pointe. Finally we did a plié in coupé, with a dégagé side, front, or back during the plié, or we came off pointe into fifth position, either in plié or with straight knees. As usual, when we came off pointe, we descended through our feet, maintaining the turnout by bringing our heels forward and holding our knees out. We usually did pas de bourrée on pointe with straight legs, but we could also practice it with small and large passés.

A typical Balanchine exercise for pas de bourrée on pointe, starting from fifth position flat, went dégagé side right on count one, tombé into plié lifting the left pointe about three inches from the floor on count two, step back on "and," side ("a"), and front (left/right/left), ending in sous-sus on count three, roll down through the feet with or without plié on count four. We did this sequence starting right and then going left and in all directions. Balanchine might start it slowly for control and to establish the form, then repeatedly increase the tempo until it did not seem possible to go any faster. This was typical of Balanchine: Establish the form, push us to the limit, and then ask for "more."

We often practiced pas de bourrée going straight forward or straight back, staying on the same imaginary tightrope as for our piqué walks on pointe. Going front or back, we usually started the step in one of three ways: coupé; développé or dégagé, true tombé into plié; or, a small développé or dégagé with a piqué or with a "tombé" (see page 241) into plié. Then we did a piqué on our center line, stepped into a small fourth, and brought the other foot around the heel of the supporting foot with a very small rond de jambe, ending in sous-sus. Again, three steps on pointe.

There were two usual tempos for pas de bourrée on pointe. In one, each step received equal time and accent; in the other, all three steps were quick, allowing time to reveal the sous-sus. In the first tempo the movement was staccato, the dancer moving each leg and purposefully putting each pointe onto the floor, with each position held a split second so it registered in our bodies and in the eyes of the audience. In the second we moved as quickly as possible through all three steps and held the accented sous-sus for a moment.

Balanchine would vary the pas de bourrée itself in addition to varying the timing of the steps. For example, we did piqué passé pas de bourrée, a step that should usually look as if the floor is too hot to stand on. Balanchine wanted the accent sharply up as the knee lifted the foot off the floor to midshin or higher, depending on the desired look or the tempo. The tip of the working pointe was on the center line of the supporting leg but not overcrossed. Another variant added one or more extra steps to the basic form, giving this a different look. We might do a dégagé front on "and" tombé on count one, pas de bourrée straight front on "and-a-two" and then two walks on pointe on "and-three" into sous-sus, all with straight knees, and descend from pointe into plié on count four. Or we might do pas de bourrée to the side and add side or front walks on pointe to sous-sus.

Other forms of the step not only contributed to a distinctive look but also, and more important, helped us gather energy for a big step to follow. We could do the three steps on pointe as quickly as possible and step across into a plié in a kind of fourth, or we could do only the first two steps quickly on pointe and then step across into plié. Both forms gave us an extra moment for a deeper plié to gather energy for the next step. Their timing has the same basic effect as glissade. When he wanted a different look, Mr. B might put these combinations on demi-pointe.

In the second movement of *Western Symphony*, the ballerina, while staying in place, very rapidly repeats a front-back-side pas de bourrée on pointe several times. The look is up although the timing is down because of the speed and the need to stay in tempo. When rehearsing me in this role, Balanchine would ask for energy and speed in this pas de bourrée sequence, which preceded a series of technically difficult en dedans fouetté turns to attitude. "Don't save yourself! Put all your eggs in one basket," he would say. He knew that dancers have a tendency to let up a little before a difficult step in a variation. And the finish is generally the most taxing part and asks the most when the dancer is tired. So dancers worry about what is coming up and forget what they are doing now. As usual, Balanchine focused only on the now, not on what had come before or on what lay ahead.

DETAILS I OFTEN INSIST ON IN PAS DE BOURRÉE DESSOUS-DESSUS:
1) when doing the step on straight legs, be sure they are really straight
2) the second step is usually small and quick; the third step is usually fast and crosses into sous-sus
3) go through the foot into plié, bringing the heel forward each time

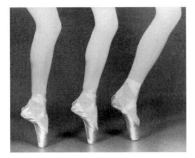

The arch pulls back and the toes curl.

Hopping on Pointe and Jumping to Pointe (Bent-Knee Landings)

When we performed a series of jumps or hops on pointe—consecutive changements or ronds de jambe sautés, for example, or the temps levés in arabesque that Balanchine used in the first variation of *Raymonda Variations*—the landing on pointe

Deanna hopping on pointe

would naturally be with a bent knee.

When a dancer lands on pointe in plié, the arch of the supporting foot must pull back, and the toes must curl a lot, almost "knuckling." To do this, the dancer has her weight fully on the big toe and the toe next to it. Jumps on pointe are controlled by the thigh, knee, and ankle. The foot is held firmly so it does not wobble, as the jump is "caught" in the foot and thigh and adjusted in the knee and the ankle with the plié. At the same time there has to be some "give" in the ankle so the instep can be pulled

Deanna in plié on pointe

back in relationship to the depth of the plié. The deeper the plié, the more the dancer has to pull back. Hence, while hopping on one foot, it is easier to do a bit less plié and almost lock the ankle, thus minimizing the pullback adjustment and maximizing the dancer's stability.

Consecutive jumps on one foot are called hops on pointe. When hopping on pointe, the supporting leg straightens ever so slightly on each takeoff and bends slightly on each landing. Consecutive hops often traveled. In such cases Balanchine wanted to see us really move, whether we were hopping downstage in arabesque on a diagonal, as in *Raymonda Variations*, or upstage on a diagonal in coupé back, as in Pierrette's Act II variation in *Harlequinade*. Another traveling step Balanchine choreographed for Pierrette was the polka on pointe in her first variation in Act I. In the "Alouette" section of *Harlequinade* the dancers move across the stage in chassé on pointe, stretching their legs and pointing their feet between landings, as the back leg chases the front leg. These chassés are fast, there is

very little plié, and, again, the hips are lifted up. In all these sequences he emphasized distance and lightness.

We also did consecutive jumps on pointe on two feet. An example is grand changement on pointe, during which the legs actually straighten and the feet point in the air. In the second variation in *Raymonda Variations* he had me execute a large assemblé that switched directions in the air (from facing diagonally upstage to facing diagonally downstage) and landed on pointe in plié.

When we performed the standard steps his way, Balanchine asked us to jump higher, arrive in the air sooner, turn faster, travel farther, and so on. Then as we got stronger, he asked us for even more. "It's easy to do less," he would say. "I'd rather have more." So, in the first variation of *Raymonda*, the dancer does twenty-eight hops across the stage, each one traveling as much as possible. Dancing for him was often a challenge to do more: fast, then faster; high, then higher; slow, then slower; low, then lower.

1. Deanna pliés on pointe before grand changement.

2. Deanna doing grand changement

3. Deanna landing on pointe from a grand changement

In any step involving elevation, Balanchine wanted to see the dancer rise clearly into the air. When giving big jumps on pointe in class, such as grand changement, or traveling jumps such as chassé, he did not scale the step down just because we were on pointe. On the contrary, he watched us to see that we did not cut back in any way. The drama of the change of levels in jumps and of the change of location in traveling steps was extremely important to him: Each step should be done with maximum clarity. He wanted us to fill as much space as possible. So although the technique of landing on pointe in plié was basically the same as for dancers with different training, the movement was nearly always bigger in scale and more dynamic.

We practiced a variety of hops on pointe in class, usually a series on one leg. For example, the dancer, starting in sous-sus, moves into plié on pointe on the left foot as the right makes a dégagé side to about forty-five degrees on count one. She then does seven hops traveling diagonally forward on the left leg, while the right leg does a rond de jambe en l'air for each hop. Then she piqués onto the right foot as she bends the right knee on count one and hops back on the diagonal with the left foot in coupé back for five counts, a quick pas de bourrée to sous-sus on count seven, plié on pointe on the left leg with the right foot to coupé back on count eight, and repeat to the other side. Another exercise we did combined three or four counts of bourrée suivie with three or four counts of hops in attitude front or back. A particular Balanchine favorite was eight standard jumping emboîtés to the back followed by eight more "sur les pointes," as he would say. He typically started us at a fairly bright tempo and then might even set the tempo faster.

Fast, small changements and grand changements (see page 295) are also excellent for practicing jumps on pointe. Mr. B would give these with a continuous circling port de bras lasting four or eight counts; we usually did at least two sets. He also liked to combine them: three quick small changements, one-and-two, followed by two slower grand changements, three-four. We might open our arms to second on the three fast changements, then leave them there for a change of épaulement for each grand changement.

DETAILS I OFTEN INSIST ON FOR ONE-LEGGED HOPS ON POINTE:
1) maintain the correct hopping stance, with the weight toward the big toe
2) hold the supporting foot and ankle firmly on landing—no wobble!
3) use the thigh muscles
4) if traveling, travel!
5) change levels, do a real hop, as big as the step and tempo allow

DETAILS I INSIST ON FOR TWO-LEGGED JUMPS ON POINTE:
1) change levels; get as far off the floor as the tempo allows
2) if traveling, move!

QUALITY

Pointework is always special because it is unique. Other dancers jump, turn, move fast, move slow, work solo, work in pairs, work in groups. Only the women of the ballet do all this on pointe. They might be tempted to let their pointework become ordinary, because they know that for nearly everyone in the audience it is *extra*ordinary. Mr. B said, "Mediocrity is always at its best and mediocrity [the ordinary] is not good enough." He made a general statement and it applies to everything we ballet dancers and ballet teachers do. But for me it is especially applicable to pointework. Precisely because pointework is uniquely ours, very nearly defining us for the general public, ballet dancers and ballet teachers must be at their most persistent in working to achieve the highest quality in it. Teachers must have the patience and persistence to insist and insist and insist . . .

Jumps

When I visited New York in 1959, I took class at SAB, which was available then, as it is now, to professional dancers. Among the teachers with whom I studied was Pierre Vladimiroff, a famous dancer of Balanchine's time who was, until his death, for many years a teacher at the school. At the end of class one day, a distinguished middle-aged man walked in and sat down to watch just as class was ending. The last exercise was a fast entrechat quatre combination, and that's a step I did very well. I could do little allegro jumps, and I had quick feet. I was energetic and enthusiastic and positive. Plus, at twenty I looked about fifteen; I had a bright, perky manner; and I was quite blond, none of which was a disadvantage with Balanchine, who, I later learned, was the man sitting on the bench.

I stayed in a hotel across the street from City Center with four other girls from the San Francisco Ballet Company. This was my first trip to New York, and as far as I knew it might be my last. More than anything else, I wanted to experience as many of the famous ballet schools and teachers as possible. So every day I took class at SAB and two or three other places around town. Every night we went across to City Center to see the New York City Ballet dance. I had never seen anyone dance the way they danced. I had never seen a repertory like theirs. I wanted to be part of what was happening there. So I inquired about an audition and got an appointment with Mr. B. Arriving on the stage a couple of days later, I found him busy rehearsing. I asked about my audition and he said, "I saw you in class the other day. Your contract is in the office. Go see Betty Cage."

Entrechat quatre! The turning point of my life. I was very lucky, because I didn't have entrechat six, I didn't have high extension, I was still more of a "polite" dancer than he wanted. And yet Mr. Balanchine took me. He saw so completely and so quickly, he never needed more than a minute or two to size up a dancer and decide what she could become and what he could do with her. Despite all that I lacked, he saw that I had something. He gave me time, training, and the performances that let me remake myself as a dancer. He invited me to teach and gave me students to work with and his example and guidance as a teacher. Forty years later, I still live through what he gave me. Because I did one good jump, entrechat quatre, at the end of Vladimiroff's class. Mr. B often urged us to do every step as if it were the last and we would be remembered by it. How easy it was for me to believe him!

It was said that when Vladimiroff was a dancer, he did a magnificent plié to collect energy and then pushed off the floor, soared into the air, and hovered under the ceiling while he wrote his name there, simultaneously forward with the right hand

and backward with the left hand, and then looked down to choose a place to land, and descended noiselessly to the floor into a deep plié, in a beautiful fifth position. There may be some exaggeration in the details of that story, but it is very representative of Balanchine's key idea about jumps: The dancer is in control from the plié before the push-off through the plié at the landing.

Jumping is the opposite of bouncing. Bouncing is out of control. Bouncing is often what is seen when the dancer is not aware of what she is doing or when she lacks adequate control or strength. In jumping, the dancer collects the energy to take herself off the floor and into the air, often assuming a position or pose in the air, and then descends in full control to the floor. Dancers don't just drop down.

The dancer gathers energy for the jump in the plié, similar in its effect to compressing a spring (the exception is very small jumps at very fast tempos). Jumping begins with the dancer using her hips, thighs, calves, and feet, pushing the floor away to take herself into the air. As she moves into the air, she takes her hips up, lifting her torso, chest, and head. The energy she gathered in the plié is released as she straightens her legs. The push from the floor is completed by the feet, which actively push off and immediately point. This pointing is part of the push off the floor, not a separate action that comes later. The tendency is for dancers to plié less deeply and more briefly than is desirable for the jump they are doing. In general they have to be reminded to do as full a plié as the tempo allows. "Don't let the heels get glued to the floor. There is more plié with weight toward the ball of the foot and just a breath between the floor and heel." A very full plié has the same energizing effect on ballet movement as a very deep breath has in life.

Once the dancer is in the air, there are many possibilities, depending on the jump being executed. However, each jump has its own specific look. So in jumps that call for assuming a position in the air (e.g., feet together or legs in second), that is what the dancer must show. If the legs are to move continuously (e.g., standard changement, pas de chat),

Deanna catching herself on the tips of her toes "like a mother bird"

they must do so. Each jump must look like itself.

Mr. Balanchine said that a dancer should descend from a jump like a mother bird landing on her eggs. Like many of his sayings, this one includes a couple of essential ideas. First, she knows where she will alight. And she controls her weight as she lands, softly. The dancer catches herself on the tips of her toes; since the feet are fully pointed in the air, the toes touch the floor first. She does not drop to the ball of the foot, and/or fall down to the full foot; rather, she goes through the foot as the ankle releases and the knee bends over the toes. "It is not keeping the heel off the floor. It is avoiding landing at once on your heel. You control your descent and maybe you touch your heel afterward, not first. You delay the heel, develop the strength to hold yourself. Dancers immediately put the whole foot down because of a very weak ankle."

The plié should be continuous, without pauses, stops, or jerks, and the plié after the jump is usually as deep as the plié before. On landing, the plié serves as the dancer's shock absorber. If the force in the landing from the jump is properly absorbed, there should be only a muffled "taaah" on contact with the floor, certainly no percussive knock or bang. The weight is controlled over the ball of the foot by the placement of the hips and torso as well as by the muscles of the foot, calf, and especially the thigh; turnout is maintained, and the heel does not slip back. The plié can be thought of as a recovery from the jump, especially if it is the last jump in the combination. "Plié is not a stretch," Mr. B said, "it is a recovery."

It is a commonplace idea that, in classical ballet, the women dance on their toes and the men do not. Or, that the men dance on the demi-pointe. And, in a way, the idea is true, but in another way it is not. Both men and women are "toe dancers," because dancers of both sexes need to catch themselves on the tips of the toes when landing from jumps. And both need to go through their feet without dropping to a full demi-pointe or settling on the full foot.

How the heel will touch the floor in landing depends on the exercise and on how the dancer is built—in particular, on the length of her Achilles tendon. At the end of a combination, the heels generally do go down and touch the floor lightly as the dancer straightens her legs, but they will not hit the floor. "The heel is like a brake; it stops the movement," Mr. B liked to say. In a series of jumps, the completion of one landing flows seamlessly, without even a pause, into the beginning of the next ascent. The plié is itself continuous, and the heel can, or can seem to, press into the floor. However, this is a smooth, controlled action, not at all the same as banging down, letting the weight settle back in landing, or stopping the movement. "The heel is toward the floor, but it cannot rest on the floor. When you rest, you are finished. It is the end of the action." If the exercise is very fast, there is no time and no need to put the heel down. If the exercise is very slow and the dancer lands on two feet, she sometimes goes into a plié that is lower than a demi-plié, more like a three-quarter plié, and consequently doesn't put her heels down (see page 295).

Mr. B spent a lot of time teaching us to plié. He emphasized the correct execution of the plié all through the class so we would have it onstage. His ideas were clearly focused on the quality we needed in order to dance as he wanted: plié as a continuous movement with the weight controlled over the ball of the foot, thigh muscles fully engaged, knees going out over the toes. The skill in plié cultivated at the barre is critical to all jumping, so he gave plié special attention. Plié at the barre (see page 58) should be thoroughly understood.

One kind of special exercise that Mr. B liked to give was any relatively simple jump that lands on two feet at a slow tempo. The plié was deep and long to help us develop greater strength and control. The strength and the energy we gathered in the plié made possible a more powerful launch into the next step. In class he sometimes summed up the kind of plié that emphasizes gathering or collecting power by saying, "Collect your dirty laundry off the floor!" Landings onto one foot from big jumps followed by slow, deep pliés are very difficult to control and require a great deal of strength; extra practice of this kind made us better prepared for them.

These especially slow jumping exercises often began with the men, because they need the extra power more often than the women. When they had done the exercise, Mr. B might say, "Gloria, let me

Peter picking up the laundry . . .

. . . and Dana gathering power

see you do." He would have been talking to Gloria Govrin, who had a better jump than many of the men, and soon Pat Neary, who wasn't going to be second to anybody, might join in without waiting to be asked. By the time the men were finished with the exercise, many of the women were jumping with them. I know that I never wanted Mr. B to think there was any step I wouldn't try to do, even those I couldn't really do or couldn't do very well, so I would try. And it was fun to try. I think most of those in class felt the same way. Those who came to his class were hungry, liked the challenge, and put out the effort. This pleased Mr. B.

Épaulement and port de bras are covered in detail on pages 146–179. In this chapter I will cover them in jumping steps only to the extent that there are specific details that are important for making the step work and giving it the look required in the Balanchine aesthetic. However, to achieve the overall look he wanted a jump to have, it is necessary to understand the material covered in that chapter and to incorporate it in teaching jumps. In his daily class Mr. B often included exercises specifically for the head, arms, and upper body, but we were expected to apply the finesse we developed in them to all the rest of the class, including jumps, and, of course, when dancing his ballets.

Sometimes, dancers trying to increase the height

of the jump unintentionally throw the arms out stiffly and heave the torso backward. When he saw this, Mr. B would say, "No! We need just the reverse," and set a jumping exercise calling for the dancer to maintain the arms in fifth low while jumping. This eliminates the boost that some mistakenly think comes from flailing arms, it helps to stabilize the torso forward, and it focuses the dancer's attention on the feet, legs, and hips, on doing a good plié. Once he saw us actively using the power of the plié and keeping the weight forward in the jump, Mr. B might repeat the exercise, asking us for coordinated, active, and attractive arms, and it felt suddenly much easier. "We use the arms for beauty and for help. It can be *twice* as easy with *two* arms."

In many schools, arms are "put out to the side," more or less in second position, for an entire jump combination. They're hung out like the laundry and forgotten. This can make for bad habits, such as lack of épaulement and stiff, jerky, or uncoordinated arms. For this reason Mr. B often said, "If you don't know what to do with the arms, put them down." It can be enough to have the dancers use only the appropriate changes in épaulement, rather than practice incorrectly with the arms stuck stiffly out "like a scarecrow" (see page 294).

In batterie he wanted to see and hear crisp, clear beats from men and women: both legs beating, thighs active, calves striking, feet crossing. In addition to the combinations in the center, he gave us jumping exercises with the support of the barre (e.g., entrechat six, cabriole) to help us develop the necessary skill and finesse.

Many of the Balanchine ballets include passages requiring unusual speed. Mr. B helped us prepare for that kind of dancing by giving jumping exercises at very fast tempos. In this kind of exercise (e.g., changements, échappés sautés) the plié becomes shallower and at extreme speeds may even disappear completely. Even though dancers generally think of controlling their landings with generous pliés using the thighs and going through the feet, in these fast tempo exercises it is the toes, feet, and calves that work the most. The heels rarely touch the floor, and when they do, it is barely, the lightest touch possible. The knees still go out over the toes, but not as far, because the plié is not nearly as deep. Dancers work to develop the skill of pointing instantly when pushing sharply off the floor.

Mr. B had a special liking for jumps in which the dancer "makes a picture"—that is, jumps that called for the dancer to establish a line instantly in the air and hold it. Nothing moving until the last possible moment before landing. One result was that the audience saw the designated shape much more clearly, because it was held longer. Her dancing is once again more articulate. The power, skill, and control, mainly with the feet, legs, and arms, necessary to make and hold any picture is developed at the barre and in other center work but finds some of its most important use in doing jumps. The ballet dancer is partly a creature of the air.

Of all the aspects of control Mr. B wanted the dancer to have, maybe the most ambitious was the ability to defy gravity. Mr. B wanted us to try to *stay* in the air. He would say to us, "Force gravity!" That's not literally possible, but the dancer can work to achieve the illusion. That illusion is the other result of being able to freeze a position in the air. She looks like she is suspended in the air a long time. And then Balanchine wanted us to take ourselves down to the floor. We, not the force of gravity, were to decide when we would land. Again, this was not literally possible, but we worked to create the illusion. To further improve our ability to show him a clear, long-lasting "picture" that stayed in the air, we practiced simple jumps such as échappé sauté, assemblé, soubresaut, and Cecchetti changements with this goal clearly in mind.

Creating that illusion wasn't quite enough. When the tempo slowed, he had one measure for staying in the air that was quite definite. He wanted us to stay in the air for the same length of time we were in plié. This soon becomes impossible, but as usual, seeing maximum energy expended in trying was his immediate goal. Remember, "The effort comes first, the result comes later." He wanted us to really jump, to get well off the floor, to soar, and he

knew that uncommonly good pliés were necessary. So he set lots of slow jumping combinations that let us cultivate slow landings on two feet and on one foot, starting with the tips of our toes, almost grasping the floor with them, going through the feet, lowering into deep, long pliés with full use of the thighs, weight controlled over the balls of the feet without the heels falling to the floor or the weight settling back, the dancer ready to push off again. Mr. B observed that often, even when the music allows them to plié fully, dancers tend to cut the plié short. "Don't be stingy with plié," Mr. B. said, "make it big, make it juicy." His dancing was full of generosity of spirit that starts to show itself in this big, "juicy" plié. As our pliés improved, they provided the power for the long-lasting jumps he wanted to see.

As the dancer's plié gets more powerful and she grows stronger, she has more time in the air. When she also feels more in control of the picture her body makes in the air, her confidence in her ability to create and sustain the illusion of indefinite suspension in the air grows. She can dance as if she is quite at home in the air, deciding how long to stay up and when to land. That adds to the illusion. Sometimes Mr. B made us believe that we could do the impossible. Sometimes we danced and made the audience believe they had seen the impossible.

Mr. Balanchine classified all jumping steps in one of five categories, although he never bothered to state the category in setting an exercise, because systems of categories and definitions did not really interest him. He knew how every step should look and how to get that result, which is what really mattered. I am discussing some representative jumps from each category as they are done using his technique: from two feet to two feet, from two feet to one foot, from one foot to two feet, from one foot to the other, and jumping and landing on the same foot. I think this grouping will be helpful in keeping a clear idea of how each jump actually works. Some people think of assemblé, for example, as a jump from two feet, but we always thought of it as a jump from one foot. The actual jump comes from

---

DETAILS I OFTEN INSIST ON IN ANY JUMP:

1) do not bounce out of plié; instead, plié and push off the floor, taking your body into the air (change levels); the plié never stops
2) point the feet rapidly, including the tips of the toes
3) on landing, the tips of the toes touch the floor first; go through the feet under control; don't fall onto the full foot
4) bring or place the second foot to the floor in steps such as glissade and sissonne faillie, toes first and heel somewhat forward but not necessarily down
5) coordinate the movement of the arms with the jump
6) control the torso throughout the jump; no heaving

---

one foot only; the supporting foot pushes off from the floor, just an instant after the brushing foot has left it. For landing examples, consider sissonne fermée and cabriole fermée; many people think of them as a landing on two feet, but the dancer actually lands on one foot and closes the second foot to fifth an instant or more later. As indicated in this introduction, there are certain qualities that are common to all jumps. It is important to keep these first corrections in mind, because they could be repeated for all the jumps that follow.

FIRST CATEGORY: JUMPS FROM TWO FEET TO TWO FEET

The placement of the torso and the control of the weight are consistent for all these jumps. The weight remains in essentially the same place when the dancer is in plié on the floor and when the dancer is in the air. Mr. B liked to suggest that we think of a boxer in the ring, because the weight should be forward, over the balls of the feet, not back on the heels. In the air, the open chest is lifted up and forward and the legs extend straight down or are a little forward of the hips.

In combinations composed of a series of jumps from this category (but only those starting and finishing in fifth position, thus excluding échappé

sauté), the arms often remain down or in second position, but in second they are not stuck out there like sticks. Instead, they have movement that is coordinated with the jump. As the dancer pliés, the arms in second lower slightly, leading with the inside of the wrists, slightly flexing the elbows, fingers trailing, and, as she begins to jump, the arms can almost seem to lead the way, lifting slightly, leading with the backs of the wrists. As she descends, the arms can be delayed. In each case this is the kind of articulation of the elbows, wrists, hands, and fingers described on pages 145–151. When the arms are to remain in fifth low in jumps starting and finishing in fifth, the "hands open as legs separate" as she pliés, so that her hands are not inside her thighs. As she jumps, she can lift the arms gently, leading with the backs of the wrists. In fifth low, as in second, the arms are not held rigidly in a firm position; instead they show energy and life.

In fast tempo exercises for jumps starting and finishing in fifth position, the arms are often in fifth

---

DETAILS I OFTEN INSIST ON IN JUMPS FROM TWO FEET TO TWO FEET:

1) don't heave the torso back or allow the feet and legs to go behind the hips
2) stretch the knees on leaving the floor (except Cecchetti jumps)

---

low, but Mr. B also liked to give a port de bras in which the arms moved. Using the "small arms" ports de bras (see page 165), we could do four changements for one "small arms" port de bras, or three quick changements and a slow plié for a "small arms" opening and three quick changements and a slow plié for a "small arms" closing. Or he could give eight changements (or seven and a slow plié) to make a continuous port de bras from fifth low, through overlapped first, fifth high, second, and back to fifth low. This port de bras could be reversed and he could add a slow turn: eight (or seven and a slow plié) fast changements to make one rotation.

Changement de Pieds

In changement Mr. B wanted the dancer's feet to pass very close together, separated just enough to make the change possible. From fifth position plié the legs straighten as the dancer pushes off the floor, the toes pull immediately under to point as the feet start to change simultaneously. The feet do not open to where the toes were when on flat,

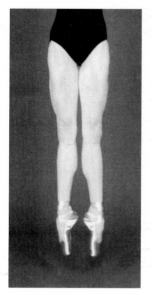

Dana's feet barely passing in changement

and the legs and feet do not flick out to the sides. Also, he wanted to see continuous movement while the dancer is in the air, rather than a quick change preceded or followed by a hold.

Changement was practiced at the widest possible range of tempos. At most tempos and in most combinations the dancer usually does plié on count four of the previous measure or on count one, is in the air on the "and," and lands on the count, going through the feet. At moderate tempos the heels might lightly touch the floor when she pushes off at the start of the next changement. The arms could be in second, but if Mr. B saw the dancers throwing the arms up and heaving the torso back, forgetting that jumps are powered by the plié, he might give changements with the arms held in fifth low. This makes the dancer concentrate on using the legs and feet and plié as well as on controlling the upper body.

At moderately slow tempos Mr. B gave consecutive grands changements to a three-quarters plié, usually with the arms in second position. The heels did not touch the floor because we did not lower to the full foot as we went through demi-plié. We controlled the descent, rather than dropping down to demi-plié and hitting the heels on the floor, stopping the movement, and then continuing to lower into a deeper plié. As we pushed off the floor from the three-quarters plié, the heels rarely, if ever, touched the floor as the dancer passed demi-plié.

The arms and hands in second were not a "handicap," but instead moved in coordination to help with the jumps and landings. They lower gently with resistance, holding the air during the plié. They lift slightly, led by the backs of the wrists, as the dancer jumps, holding this lift while the dancer is in the air. They again lower gently with resistance, slightly delayed, holding the air as the dancer lands and during the plié that follows.

At very slow tempos Mr. B gave changements to a long, deep, almost grand plié: for example, plié on count one, jump on "and," land on count two, straighten on count three, hold on count four. Also in these slowest changements, the heels generally do not make contact with the floor, although they may lower toward it as the dancer passes through demi-plié. The heels do not touch the floor until the dancer returns through demi-plié as she straightens her legs to hold on the fourth count. The main purpose of these slow grand changements (deep pliés and high jumps) is to build power, strength, and control in the hips, thighs, calves, and feet. As usual, the dancer lands on the tips of her toes and goes through the feet, with the weight over the

Peter in a lower than normal (three quarters) plié, heels off the ground, collecting energy for a big jump

Success! Peter landed from his grand changement, deep plié, no heels.

Peter in the air in grand changement

balls. The heels don't even touch the floor, so the weight can't settle on them.

Mr. B also gave petits changements at moderately fast to very fast tempos. Because there is very little time, the toes and feet do most of the work. The jump is small, the plié is shallow and brief, and the heels do not touch at all. At the fastest tempos there really is no time to plié (but the knees might slightly flex), and therefore the dancer pushes off primarily using her toes, feet, and calves; she rapidly points her feet and toes, stretches her knees, and immediately catches herself on her toes to control her landing. These exercises were especially important for cultivating the skill to point the feet, and especially the tips of the toes, instantly. She also learns to control her movement so she lands precisely on the count, no matter how fast the tempo. The timing is maintained because the

dancer learns to put herself down to the floor on the beat, instead of bouncing off the floor and getting stuck in the air, thereby being late. She jumps *to* the floor, so to speak. She jumps *down* and she thinks, "down, and down, and down." As I wrote this, I realized it's a strange way to think! The floor to which she is jumping "down" is the one on which

DETAILS I OFTEN INSIST ON IN CHANGEMENT:
1) the feet open just enough to change
2) the change is continuous; do not change right away and then hold the feet together
3) even at the fastest tempos, the tips of the toes must still point

she is standing. As strange as it is, I know it is what works best for most of my students, just as it worked for me.

Practicing jumps at extreme tempos makes exercises and choreography with jumps at normal tempos seem much easier, almost second nature. Mr. B applied to jumps the same approach he used in other parts of the class: Take the dancer to the limit of what she can do and then ask for a little more. The dancer cannot hold back. She must give 100 percent and even more.

Cecchetti Changement

This step is not commonly given and it is unlike most jumps in that the legs do not straighten in the usual way in the air, although the feet are fully pointed. Mr. B liked it because it gives the dancer practice in getting off the floor and holding a position in the air for as long as possible, and it develops ballon. He also used it in his ballets, for example, *Tombeau de Couperin*, the first pas de trois in *Agon*, and *Donizetti Variations*.

In Cecchetti changement the dancer takes a really good plié to push herself off the floor and in to the air. She definitely changes levels, despite the fact that she does not fully straighten the legs. She instantly brings the tips of her toes and her heels to touch in a sort of first position in the air. This requires the knees to remain bent just enough to bring the feet into position with the tips of the toes in contact, and a firm holding of the inside of the thighs to freeze the legs in this position. She holds until the last possible moment, changes, and then catches herself on the tips of her toes to start the landing in fifth. This sequence—getting herself cleanly off the floor, instantly assuming a position, and holding it as long as possible—is excellent preparation for all the "make a picture" steps. When she is in the air, the whole position should freeze, the chest and head lifted, and the arms usually in second, with the wrists slightly lifted.

Mr. B usually gave Cecchetti changements at

Peter holding Dana in the air as she assumes the correct position of her feet for Cecchetti changement

Peter in the air in Cecchetti changement

moderate to slow tempos. To a slow tempo he might give plié on count one, Cecchetti change-ment in the air on "and," land on count two, stretch on count three, and hold on count four. In this sim-ple exercise the dancer can concentrate on exactly what she needs to do to execute the Cecchetti changement. Then, still to a slow tempo, we could do three quick standard changements on counts "one and two," Cecchetti changement on "and," landing on count three, straightening on "and," and plié on count four to repeat. To a very fast tempo we could do three quick standard change-ments, the first landing on count one, the second landing on "and," and the third landing in a deep plié on count two, followed by a Cecchetti change-ment in the air on count three, landing into plié on count four to repeat. Balanchine liked combina-tions such as this because it requires the dancer to be aware of what her feet are doing to show each type of changement clearly, while asking her to stay in the air while she holds one count there. This requires her to be musically aware to be on time.

The following excerpt from *Donizetti Variations* is from the second pas de trois, which Balan-chine choreographed on me. It includes Cecchetti changement, and it can be done in class to practice freezing and showing the position in the air. Start-ing in fifth position, left foot front, the dancer pliés on count four of the introduction and is in the air in Cecchetti changement on count one, landing in fifth position right foot front on count two, then échappé to pointe in second (see page 301) on count three and close fifth left foot front on count four, then entrechat quatre (see page 305) on "and," landing on count five, Cecchetti changement in the air on the "and," land in fifth position right foot front on count six, échappé to pointe in second position on count seven, and plié left foot front on eight. In the ballet the dance goes on, but for class, the teacher could continue, using three passé relevés changing feet, and one sous-sus, so the dancer can repeat on the other side, starting with the correct musical accent, plié on count eight. Although the arms remain in second position

---

DETAILS I OFTEN INSIST ON IN CECCHETTI CHANGEMENT:
1) freeze the legs in the air and assume a pretty picture of the whole body
2) knees bend only as much as necessary to let the toes touch
3) take the body into the air; change levels

---

during the first part of this combination, they still show some life. As the dancer lowers in plié, the in-sides of her wrists lead the arms gently lower, her elbows gently bending, and when she comes up to relevé or jumps, the backs of her wrists lead the arms gently higher, again with soft elbows. Her épaulement also changes to the side of the foot that is in front. In the passé relevé part of the combina-tion the dancer might do a continuous port de bras from fifth low, passing through an overlapped first to fifth high, then open to à la seconde, plié sous-sus as the backs of the wrists slightly lift up, and plié as the arms gently lower. In the sous-sus, she would use épaulement.

Soubresaut

Soubresaut may seem easier than changement but is actually harder to do, because of the control and skill required to keep the feet together in a tight, precise fifth position in the air.

Soubresaut is the same position as sous-sus on pointe, but now it is in the air. Standing in fifth po-sition flat, the dancer's feet are "glued together," and as the dancer pliés in fifth position, the feet are still "glued together." As the dancer pushes off the floor, she must avoid the tendency to let the feet separate. Instead, her feet remain together and her toes instantly point down and under as she brings her thighs, knees, and calves together. She can think of a vacuum cleaner, sucking everything to-gether and in as she goes up. The toes are in line

Dana in sous-sus

and touching, the heels are crossed, and the anklebones almost seem to lock onto each other. For many dancers this requires the same slight release of the front knee that is required in other kinds of fifth position (on flat, sous-sus). The resulting position is made the same way when dancers do tours en l'air from fifth and is the one the dancer establishes by bringing the legs together in the return to fifth (from second or fourth) of échappé sauté, assemblé, and chassé. Mr. B gave soubresaut for the practice in assuming a position instantly in the air and holding it until the last possible moment before landing. Soubresaut can travel in any direction, but the dancer must be careful to bring her entire body with her as she moves her legs in the required direction.

There is nothing particularly new or novel in that description of soubresaut; I learned the step that way as a child. However, teachers often do not insist that the most fundamental details be done as they should be. When a dancer's feet are not together in soubresaut, the teacher may mention it but let it go. Instead, her students need for her to stop the class and say, "No, I didn't see it. Try again alone." And stay with that dancer until she does it or shows that she knows what to do to improve or at least recognizes that what she is doing is not acceptable as the final result. This is the same with many, many moments in class. Most teachers give the right corrections but then do not demand improvement. Weight over the balls of the feet. Feet barely passing in changement. Feet together immediately in assemblé. Foot tracing an ellipse in rond de jambe en l'air. And so on. Even when teaching advanced or professional dancers, the teacher must insist that they practice or at least attempt to practice everything correctly, not just the "advanced" flashy step. Balanchine taught us that way every

Dana in soubresaut with épaulement

day. The way he taught ballet class also taught us how to learn and how to teach.

Soubresaut was generally given as part of combinations including other steps, so the arms were set to fit the overall flow. An example is soubresaut with échappé sauté on page 302. Another example is soubresaut with assemblé on page 324. Each combination cultivates a particular awareness of bringing the feet together in the air. Usually we did

---

DETAILS I OFTEN INSIST ON IN
SOUBRESAUT:
1) the feet and ankles are locked together
2) the front foot covers the back foot, except for the heel of the back foot; the audience sees one point with two heels

not practice soubresaut at the extremely slow tempos that were used for changement, but Mr. B did like to make combinations in which the dancer must stay in the air for a full count.

Cecchetti Soubresaut

Cecchetti soubresaut, in which the feet make a kind of fifth position in the air, is the companion to the Cecchetti changement in which the feet make a kind of first position in the air. To accomplish this, the knees are again slightly bent and the toes are aligned with each other as in sous-sus on pointe. Even though he did not give it as often as Cecchetti changement, Mr. Balanchine liked to give Cecchetti soubresaut for the same reasons: It builds ballon and awareness of exactly where the feet are; it allows the dancer to practice assuming a position in the air instantly and holding it until the last possible moment.

From fifth position, the dancer takes a good plié and pushes off the floor, taking her torso and hips into the air. She immediately assumes the

Peter in the air,
Cecchetti soubresaut

slightly "bent-kneed" sous-sus position in the air. As in Cecchetti changement, she freezes the position in the air by using the inside thigh muscles. On landing she catches herself on the tips of her toes, lowering herself through the feet into plié.

Mr. B gave sets of Cecchetti soubresaut to help

Peter holding Dana in the air as she assumes the correct position of her feet for Cecchetti soubresaut

DETAILS I OFTEN INSIST ON IN CECCHETTI SOUBRESAUT:
1) the toes of the front foot cover the toes of the back foot, the heel of the front foot covers the arch of the back foot—that is, somewhat similar to sous-sus on pointe, but with slightly bent knees
2) the bend in the knees is minimal and must *not* be exaggerated; the dancer should not look like a puppet or a clown
3) the dancer must really jump, changing levels

us master the technique; the typical timing was plié on count one, jump on "and," land on count two, straighten the legs on count three, hold on count four. He also gave the step in a series traveling forward or sideways and in combinations. The arms were usually in a low or normal second, or, perhaps, the two arms extended to the front.

Échappé Sauté

The traditional approach to échappé sauté (or at least the one I learned at the San Francisco Ballet School) had been to freeze the legs in soubresaut (fifth in the air) when jumping from fifth and only open the legs to second (or fourth) just before landing. In contrast, Mr. Balanchine wanted the dancer to open the legs instantly and hold them in place. This makes the jump seem more brilliant, more energized. This shift in accent is very clearly seen and relatively easy for the dancer to feel when practicing correctly. Échappé sauté is a step (others are soubresaut, assemblé, and sissonne ouverte) in which Mr. B wanted the dancer to put the legs immediately into the position in which she lands.

Achieving the sharp, clear "picture" he wanted to see in the air is again a matter of the teacher's careful work to build awareness in the dancers. They need to demand of themselves that the legs move very rapidly and then truly freeze instantly in precise second (or fourth) position in the air on the jump from fifth. If she sees the legs open past second (or fourth) and pull back in or stop and momentarily freeze in place, only to open out wider to land, she needs to ask to see the jump again with just the right opening. When Mr. B needed to correct the tendency to let the legs move slowly and continuously without ever freezing or to open too wide, he suggested that we mimic the correct action of the legs with our arms. So, starting with an imitation of fifth position made by extending the arms forward, one on top of the other, touching and crossing at the middle of the forearms with the palms facing away from each other,

we opened our arms sharply and stopped them suddenly, almost pulling them slightly in to make the stop abrupt. The dancer feels the muscles on the inside of her upper arms pull in to stop the movement and thus understands better the required quickness and speed in opening her legs and how strongly she must use her inside thigh muscles to stop her legs instantly. Through this little demonstration with the arms Balanchine made it unnecessary to talk about which muscles do what. Instead, we felt the sensation in our bodies. He al-

Dana making second position in the air in échappé sauté

Dana making fourth position in the air in échappé sauté

most never spoke to us about muscles and anatomy.

A similar precision is required when the dancer jumps from second (or fourth) to immediately make fifth (soubresaut) in the air. In this case she must close the legs rapidly, but stop them instantly as they reach fifth in the air so they don't beat. When the dancer achieves the required speed and precision, she creates the illusion that she is suspended longer in the air (see photo, page 299).

It is equally important to the "picture" that the torso, arms, and hands arrive immediately in their positions and freeze. When the dancer jumps from fifth position croisé to second, she turns en face and the arms open through an overlapped first to second. With the simultaneous and immediate opening of the legs, this establishes second position en face in the air, and she lands this way. When she jumps from second, she immediately establishes fifth position croisé in the air, the elbows and wrists leading the arms slightly up, with the hands trailing; when she lands in fifth position croisé, her arms close to fifth low. When the dancer jumps from fifth position croisé to fourth croisé the arms rise through an overlapped first to fifth high or to the standard croisé arm position, which the dancer holds, landing in this croisé. When the dancer jumps to fifth, the arms open to second and pause as the legs freeze in fifth in the air. As she lands, still in croisé, the arms can close to fifth low.

Échappé sauté to second and back to fifth can travel forward and backward and the step can turn,

Peter making second position in the air in échappé sauté; his legs and torso are slightly forward.

but it is still necessary to stop or freeze the legs in precise positions in the air. When the step travels forward, the dancer should bring her legs and chest forward in the air (no heaving back).

In échappé sauté the dancer typically is in the air on "and" and is down on the beat. Mr. B gave échappé sauté at very slow tempos to help us build strength and at very fast tempos to help us build speed, as well as in various combinations at moderate tempos. At the very fast tempos the movements, as usual, became somewhat smaller and the "small arms" port de bras was often used to complement the lower, quicker jump. Balanchine used this in *Square Dance*.

A good combination for making the dancer aware of the action of the legs in soubresaut and échappé sauté was in three counts: Soubresaut land on count one, échappé sauté land in second on count two, return to fifth land on count three. The dancer "rehearses" fifth in the air in the soubresaut, then jumps to second in the air, and then must find that same "rehearsed" fifth in the air from second.

DETAILS I OFTEN INSIST ON IN ÉCHAPPÉ SAUTÉ:

1) jumping from fifth, show second (or fourth) in the air; do not let the legs split open past the position and then pull in

2) jumping from second (or fourth), make fifth in the air, but do not allow the legs to beat

Batterie in Two-Legged Jumps

The basic beating technique for any jump from the first category is the same. The legs start beating immediately. They open directly toward the side and are kept under or slightly in front of the hips (not in back of them). Both legs open equally from the center line, and when they close, both legs return to the center to cross and beat. The knees are stretched (but, especially if hyperextended, they are not locked). Beats are not just a scratching of the heels: A deep crossing of the legs up to the tops of the thighs is needed to enable the calves to beat and the feet to cross. The result is clean, visible beats. If the dancer beats with the idea that beats should be audible, this will help her make them crisp and distinct, and in some cases they will be heard. The depth of the crossing and beating depends to some degree on the tempo. In larger, slower jumps the entire leg is used to make the beat. The thighs cross, as well as the calves and feet. In much smaller, faster allegro jumps the beat is accomplished mainly with the calves but the feet must still cross.

Échappé Sauté with Single Beats

Échappé sauté with single beats is one of the first batterie steps taught to children. In its basic form the legs beat and open side to land in second, then close from second, crossing to beat before changing to land in fifth. This step is one of the easiest and surest to use when any dancer is learning to feel and trying to achieve the scissoring motion necessary for correct execution of all beats.

Starting in fifth with the right foot in front, the dancer pliés, pushes off the floor, slightly opens her legs to the side, beats both legs, opens her legs directly side, and lands through her feet in second. Depending on the way the exercise is set, she may change before beating (good preparation for entrechat quatre) or beat as she is (which leads toward royale). From second position plié she pushes off the floor, immediately bringing both legs under or slightly in front of her to beat, opens to change, and lands through her feet in fifth. As the combination is repeated, the dancer can alternate her legs, beating from second, first with one leg in front and the next time with the other. This basic exercise includes all the elements that must be refined and perfected in order to do the advanced batterie in this group of jumps, so it is important for the teacher to insist that it be learned completely as the foundation. The skill that must be developed is the same for all dancers, although, when the tempo allows, the men will usually jump a little higher and perhaps cross a bit deeper.

In any advanced class there are going to be dancers for whom doing multiple beats presents a special challenge. In some cases the obstacle is elevation, and for them the answer is extra practice of the slow jumps (e.g., changement and échappé sauté) to improve the ballon. Those exercises are designed to enhance the dancer's awareness of pushing away from the floor; as her jump improves, she will be better able to take her hips and torso up in the air. Some dancers will need to develop faster legs and feet; they may make time for extra daily practice of fast battements tendus and battements tendus jetés at the barre to supplement what they do in class. Or they may like the substitute for petit battement (see page 108). The faster the dancer beats, the less time she needs in the air. In other cases the skill and awareness required for good

---

DETAILS I OFTEN INSIST ON IN
FIRST CATEGORY BEATING STEPS:
1) the legs start beating immediately
2) the legs must cross fully—the entire leg in slower jumps, mainly the calves in allegro jumps
3) the feet cross

beating are missing, and the legs and feet beat forward and back instead of to the side. For them, additional barre exercises as well as extra practice beating from second position and landing back in second position are very important, because it is one of the best ways to learn the scissoring action of both legs necessary for almost all beats. Starting in second position, the dancer pliés, pushes the floor away as her legs straighten and feet point, beats her legs *at once*, crossing as deeply as she can, and returns to second to land, going through her feet. In this exercise also, she can alternate her legs, beating first with one in front and then with the other. Beats from second in series are good practice alone, because they ensure the crucial scissoring action and they may be used with the basic échappé battu.

Peter's legs and torso are slightly forward as he beats.

Multiple Beats in Jumps from Second Landing in Second

Practice in doing two beats from second and returning to second is very useful in developing the facility for multiple beats and cultivates good habits. I learned this skill by playing hopscotch in my youth. My specialty was "double clicksy over sixy," a little "frog jump" over the sixth box that included a double heel click. From second position, the dancer pliés and pushes off, straightens her legs, points her feet, and immediately beats front and back, then returns to second, landing through the feet. She needs to sense the sideways motion of the legs. It is very important to keep the legs and back forward, avoiding heaving the torso back and throwing the legs behind the hips. As she repeats the jump, the dancer can alternate her feet. The opening to second is easier than the double beat closing into fifth, the second part of échappé sauté, and really gives her the feeling of what is needed to make entrechat six. This can be given as part of an échappé sauté combination with beats and in a variety of other combinations, but is very useful at moderate to slow tempos by itself: Plié on one, beat

twice on "and," land on two, straighten on three, hold on four. This gives the dancer time to collect her wits and summon her strength.

Échappé Sauté with Two Beats

Double beats in échappé sauté are harder, but, at least for some, are not as hard as entrechat six or grande royale, so they are a good way to practice to acquire more strength and skill.

From fifth position with the right foot front, the dancer pliés and pushes away from the floor, straightening her legs. As she beats from her hips, crossing as deeply as the tempo and her elevation allow, with the right foot going back and then front, she lands in second, going through her feet. This is like entrechat six, but then opening to the side instead of changing to land in fifth. If she beats without first changing, it is like a grande royale, but then opening to the side instead of closing to fifth. From second position the dancer pliés and pushes off, beating from her hips, again as deeply as possible, right foot back, then front and changes, landing through her feet in fifth right foot back. This is again like entrechat six but starts in second.

When developing multiple beats it is often useful for the dancer to think that the leg that is in fifth back is coming to the front to beat, rather than thinking of the leg that is in front going back to beat. This helps to ensure that the legs stay under or slightly in front of the dancer's hips, rather than getting thrown behind them. Consequently there is a better chance that the legs will scissor in and out of fifth through second, rather than struggling to beat forward and backward through a minifourth (a sort of paddling) or else trying to accomplish beats by doing a twisting hip motion. Whatever the dancer thinks to help her visualize and feel the action, it is *both* legs opening and crossing equally and the action of the entire legs that make the beats. It is also essential to start beating immediately after the push off the floor, rather than arriving in the air and then thinking "beat"—most dancers will not have enough elevation to wait, and the few who do will probably not beat deeply enough.

The arms open to second and close to fifth low as described in simple échappé sauté at moderate to slow tempos.

DETAILS I OFTEN INSIST ON IN ÉCHAPPÉ SAUTÉ WITH BEATS, AND IN BEATS FROM SECOND TO SECOND:
1) take the body up off the floor; really jump
2) both legs make the beat and therefore open and close the same amount
3) show the beats: the feet cross; the entire leg makes the beat
4) the legs stay front, forward of the hips, to beat; from fifth, think of the back leg coming front
5) keep the body forward over the hips in the air; don't lean back
6) land in a good second, not too wide, both heels forward, opposite each other

---

Royale

Royale is a jump that we practiced in its traditional form. From fifth position the dancer pliés and pushes off the floor, opening each leg slightly to its side, as she straightens her legs and points her feet. She beats both legs from the hips, crossing as deeply as time allows without changing, opens to change, and lands in fifth position, going through her feet to plié.

The dancer generally pliés on the count and is in the air on the "and." We usually practiced royale at a fairly brisk, bright tempo, our calves doing most of the beating. If the tempo was slow, we could open our legs just a little more to the side before and after the beat and as well as beat more deeply, crossing the thighs as well as the calves and feet. In royales the dancer is usually in croisé and the arms are in fifth low, in second, or doing a continuous port de bras.

Royale is included in the entrechat quatre exercises in the next section.

DETAILS I OFTEN INSIST ON IN ROYALE:
1) open both legs slightly and equally
2) show the beat
3) clean fifth positions

Entrechat Quatre

Entrechat quatre has four movements of the legs: open, beat, open, land. One, two, three, four. Even though I could do the step when I got to New York, I didn't know what its name was about until I had been there for a while. It is another jump we practiced in its traditional form. However, Balanchine did give it at tempos ranging from very slow to very fast. Whatever the tempo, it was essential that the legs cross to the maximum and that the opening for the change not be exaggerated.

From fifth position the dancer pliés and pushes off the floor, straightening her legs, and pointing her feet, as she slightly opens both legs to the side to change and beat. She opens again to change back as she lands in fifth position plié, going through her feet with the original foot ending front. It is important to remember to beat the entire leg, thighs, and calves, that both legs beat, and that both feet cross. To ensure that the legs scissor to the side and not forward and back, the dancer may think of the back leg coming front to beat. She must also remember that both ("all two") legs must beat.

The dancer is usually in plié on the count and in the air on the "and." A series of entrechats quatre was usually done in croisé with the arms in fifth low or second or with a continuous port de bras through fifth high. A simple and useful combination is entrechat quatre, royale done twice, followed by three entrechats quatre and one royale. Mr. B gave it at a range of tempos, usually with the arms down, but with distinct and precise changes of épaulement.

One combination Mr. B liked to give at a very brisk tempo was in the shape of a baseball diamond, that all-American playing field. Starting at "home plate" in fifth position croisé right foot front, the dancer does seven entrechats quatre traveling diagonally back and a royale on count eight at "third base," turning a quarter turn to the right to land in croisé, left leg front. She continues with seven more entrechats quatre, traveling (backing) to "second base," where she does royale, turning a quarter turn left, to end in croisé with the right foot front. Now she is ready to continue diagonally forward, traveling downstage to "first base," with seven more entrechats quatre and a royale turning a quarter right. She completes the reverse circuit with seven entrechats quatre and a royale to "home plate." For each series of entrechats quatre and royale, the dancer does a port de bras from fifth low through an overlapped first to fifth high, opening to second.

> DETAILS I OFTEN INSIST ON
> IN ENTRECHAT QUATRE:
> 1) cross the legs
> 2) show the beat
> 3) clean fifth positions
> 4) if traveling, really travel!

Grande Royale

For most dancers, grande royale is easier than entrechat six, even though it also uses two beats and has six movements of the legs, as does the "six." Grande royale is useful to practice because the dancer has the sensation of, and indeed makes, two beats beginning and ending in fifth position. Even though it can be helpful in learning to do entrechat six, grande royale is a step I have seen only when I took Mr. B's class and in classes given by teachers who studied with him.

In grande royale the dancer finishes with the same foot front as at the start. Grande royale is easier than "six" because the first beat does not change and therefore the legs do not have to move so far or open so wide. The dancer can think of beating in front and then making an entrechat quatre. It looks like entrechat six because the legs beat twice.

Mr. B used grande royale at the end of the first movement of *Symphony in C* when the principal does grande royale followed by one échappé relevé to second, close fifth, sissonne to pointe traveling for-

> DETAILS I OFTEN INSIST ON
> IN GRANDE ROYALE:
> 1) show the beats, particularly the first one
> 2) both legs beat
> 3) don't bounce off the floor—take a good plié

ward, sissonne to pointe traveling back, repeat with grande royale, échappé side, sissonne to pointe traveling back and then forward, plié, grande royale, sissonne traveling forward, plié, grande royale, sissonne traveling back, step pas de chat.

Entrechat Six

Entrechat six has six movements of the legs: open, beat, open, beat, open, land. It used to be a man's step, in fact, a step done mostly by male soloists and principals. In the repertory that Balanchine made, it became a step the entire company must be able to do. Examples include the corps in the finales of *Stars and Stripes, The Nutcracker,* and *Tchaikovsky Piano Concerto No. 2* (formerly known as *Ballet Imperial*).

Mr. B used the traditional form of the step, but, typically for him, he wanted some refinement of the details. Luckily for the dancer, they are the same details that apply to jumps in general or to other beating steps. He wanted to see the dancer take herself down in the plié before the entrechat six and push smoothly off under control. He did not want to see us hitting the floor and bouncing off like the basketball in that other American ball game. In the air, the legs should be straight down, or just slightly in front of the hips; the torso is also just slightly forward.

From fifth position the dancer pliés and pushes off the floor, straightening her legs, and pointing her feet, as she immediately changes her legs to beat, starting the scissoring motion. She changes both legs and beats from the hips, opens again, changes back and beats again, opens a third time, and changes to land in fifth position plié, going through her feet. It is important to remember to beat the entire leg, including the thighs and calves, each time, to beat both legs, and to cross the feet. To make entrechat six especially dazzling, the dancer can open her legs a little more to the side after the last beat, before landing in fifth. This has a similar effect on entrechat quatre and royale.

For some dancers with minor problems with entrechat six, the grande royale provides just the bridge needed. There are a couple of tendencies that make entrechat six more difficult, and some dancers can correct them by thinking about the step in a different way. Dancers can be concentrating so hard, they throw the torso and the legs to the back of the hips, increasing the chance that they will be paddling back/front, rather than scissoring to the side. They can be so focused on getting a good jump that they bounce off the floor in the mistaken belief this will help. It doesn't. Also, they may not start to beat until they are way up in the air. I tell the students to take a very good plié and very actively push off the floor, to start beating immediately, as soon as they leave the floor, so that they are beating on the way up, and to really show the first beat. It is especially important to use all the time available for the plié, rather than getting anxious over the beats and bouncing off the floor. Entrechat six is another step for which the dancer can often help herself by thinking of bringing the back foot forward to start the beat, rather than throwing the front foot back. Finally, for some dancers it can also be useful to think of entrechat six as entrechat quatre with a change of the feet to land.

To help us learn to do entrechat six, Balanchine had some very useful exercises that built the necessary strength and skill. These exercises let the dancer who was having a very difficult time with her "six" work in stages toward the goal. And I was certainly one who did a lot of work to achieve my "six"! To me and to the others with the most problems, he suggested going to a corner of the studio or anywhere that two sturdy barres meet at right angles. The dancer faces the right angle and, putting one hand on each barre, lifts herself off the floor. Holding herself up and her torso and legs forward and pulling her abdominal muscles strongly in, she beats her legs for 20 to 30 seconds in the required scissoring motion. She starts at a moderate to brisk tempo and works to increase her speed. This builds muscle memory of the path the legs need to know. Then, using the barre to slightly prolong her time in the air, she can try double beats from second position, landing again in second position. She pliés and jumps, pushing the floor away as she also pushes on the barre, beats immediately, changes to beat again, and lands in second, all the while keeping both her legs and her torso *forward*. Mr. B suggested the dancer use an exact second position or even one a bit smaller—certainly not a larger second. This narrower position permits a more powerful push from the floor and shortens the distance the legs have to travel to beat. Once she senses that she can do the beats from second with little assistance from the barre, she should try it in the center (see page 304).

Finally, again working at the barre in the corner, she can repeat the process with entrechat six itself. Always first establishing that basic position and action in the air (legs and torso forward, stomach in, legs scissoring), she can develop bit by bit the skill and speed required. In my case the process took almost daily work for what seemed a very long time—almost a year. One incentive I had to learn to do entrechat six was being regularly cast in the Danse Mauresque in *La Sonnambula*. The pas de deux has the combination sous-sus, entrechat six with a quarter turn repeated four times. When I first attempted this role, without an adequate entrechat six, my legs didn't beat; instead they paddled forward and back, and my tutu seemed to do the "twist" due to the wiggling of my hips.

A valuable feature of this stepwise approach is that any dancer can resume work when necessary at a less demanding level at any time—for example, when coming back from injury or layoff. Working

in this way she can clean up basic aspects of her technique and move on to more difficult aspects a little later. Success in entrechat six represents a coming together of the speed and scissoring the dancer starts to cultivate in fast battements tendus jetés and petits battements at the barre, of the elevation cultivated in slow changements, and of the beating action of both legs practiced in multiple beats from second position and in échappé battu. The stepwise approach is a good solution to any problem that does not resolve itself fairly well with regular (maximum) effort. Any method that gets the desired result—in this case the entrechat six—is a good method for that dancer. One mark of the intelligent professional dancer is that she knows how to find what will work for her.

We usually were down on the count and in the air on the "and." But Balanchine also gave entrechat six at a brisker tempo, emphasizing staying a count in the air: Plié on count one, entrechat six and stay in the air on count two, land on count three; this is how the second variation in *Divertimento No. 15* begins.

When he gave eight or sixteen entrechats six, Balanchine usually let us leave the arms in second. But despite the effort required for the jumping and beating, he wanted to see that the arms complemented the movement and still had life. I described this briefly on page 294, and the subject is treated fully on pages 145–151. The look Mr. Balanchine wanted will not be achieved unless the torso and head and arms are also used properly. When he saw us throwing our arms back or trying too hard in some other way, he might stop the music and tell

---

DETAILS I OFTEN INSIST ON IN ENTRECHAT SIX:
1) don't bounce off the floor; plié and push away from the floor, taking the hips and upper body into the air
2) keep the legs and the upper body a bit forward of the hips
3) make the first beat immediately upon leaving the floor and really show it
4) scissor the legs sideways; both legs participate in making beats

us to repeat the exercise with the arms remaining in fifth low. This is actually very beneficial when dancers are working to develop maximum power in the legs. But that is only a temporary solution to problems with the port de bras. The real answer is knowing how to move the arms correctly. And then doing it that way.

A combination that Balanchine gave that was based on the first category jumps covered so far went like this: Starting with a plié on the last beat of the preparation, soubresaut land on count one, changement land on count two, royale land on count three, entrechat quatre land on count four, grande royale land on count five, entrechat six land on count six, straighten on count seven, plié on count eight, and repeat to the other side. It was given at a moderately slow tempo to emphasize the deep plié, the push off the floor, the moment of suspension in the air, and the clear articulation and differentiation of each jump. When I give this combination I often add a count in between jumps in which the dancer can straighten her legs and plié. That gives her more time to collect her thoughts and energy. Then I repeat without the extra count.

A combination I give that focuses exclusively on the multiple beats goes like this: Plié on count one, grande royale landing on count two, straighten on count three, hold on count four, plié on count one, entrechat six landing on count two, straighten on count three, hold on count four. A moderately slow tempo is again useful so the dancer can be fully focused on a good plié, the push off the floor and the step in the air.

Another very simple, but hard, combination I give to help students work on multiple beats is also done to a moderately slow tempo. The dancer starts in second position and pliés on count one and beats front/back on the "and," landing in second on count two; does tendu side with the right leg on count three; and closes fifth front on count four. She pliés on count one, does entrechat six on the "and," landing on count two in fifth, left foot front. She does tendu left foot side on count three and lowers to second position with straight legs on

count four. She is ready to repeat to the other side. I tell them to focus on getting good pliés and making a real push (no bouncing); keeping the legs under or *slightly* in front, beating immediately and deeply, and scissoring to the side; and controlling the torso over the hips (*no heaving back*). The arms will, of course, also help if their movement is properly coordinated with the jump. Remember, "Two arms, twice as easy. Beautiful too!"

Entrechat huit has eight movements of the legs, one more beat than is required for entrechat six: open, beat, open, beat, open, beat, open, land. It's most definitely a man's step, done mainly by virtuoso soloists and principals. If a man wants to achieve it, he needs first to have acquired a good entrechat six, meaning he has perfected the scissoring action of the legs. He needs higher elevation to give him additional time in the air and faster legs to make the beats happen very quickly. I've known several women and many men who had an entrechat huit and a few men who had entrechat dix, so the stories we all know of Nijinsky and his "dix" seem impressive but not incredible.

Tour en l'Air

Double tour en l'air is generally a step for men. When Balanchine made *Stars and Stripes* in 1957, he choreographed four counts marching in place, plié, double tour en l'air for the entire male regiment, made up of twelve corps dancers and a soloist. This was repeated three times. At the time, that was not only exciting but also very ambitious, because male professionals didn't all have a secure double tour. Perhaps that dance helped set the standard that prevails today, when double tour en l'air is now expected of any advanced or professional male dancer. When Mr. B gave it in class there were many women who attempted the step and a few who could do it. He certainly encouraged the women to try this and other "men's" steps—and got a result we know he liked. In several of the ballets we see the proof. He made dances for a solo woman or a woman and one or more men (all doing generally the same steps) that were a lot like men's dances. Examples for a solo woman include the role of Hippolyta in *A Midsummer Night's Dream* and the "I'll Build a Stairway to Paradise" variation in *Who Cares?* Examples of a woman and a man or men include the third movements of *Symphony in C* and *Western Symphony*, the pas de trois in *Tchaikovsky Piano Concerto No. 2* (formerly known as *Ballet Imperial*), the dance for a demi-soloist woman and four men in the first movement of *Brahms-Schoenberg*, and the "Discord and War" dance in Act III of *Coppélia*.

There are three types of tour en l'air that land in fifth position. The dancer can turn toward the front foot without changing his feet, he can turn toward the front foot changing his feet, and he can turn toward the back foot changing his feet. Whichever tour en l'air we were doing, Mr. B emphasized the importance of feeling the turn as we pushed off the floor. He did not want to see the dancer rise into the air and try then to start the turn. "When you turn, you must have the feeling of turning." That feeling starts in the way the dancer uses the legs and feet in the plié and in pushing the floor away, not in some "windup" of the upper body.

A very common tour en l'air combination for men is sous-sus, plié, tour en l'air. Balanchine did not want to see or hear the heels slam down in the plié before the jump or the dancer bounce off the floor. Instead, he pliés with control in a real fifth, the heels barely touching the floor, and then, with the weight still forward over the balls of the feet, pushes the floor away. The initial impetus for the turn comes from the tight fifth position of the feet and the force of the legs and feet pushing the floor supplemented with the coordination of the arms and the spot; the control is lost if the dancer hits the floor or bounces off it. If the feet are to change, this is accomplished immediately as he pushes off the floor; otherwise the dancer makes fifth in the air immediately, as in soubresaut (see page 298). He lands as softly as possible by catching himself at the tips of his toes, going through his feet, and using his

thigh muscles as he pliés. The turnout is maintained as the knees are held to the side and the weight is controlled forward over the balls of the feet.

Only the force needed is applied with the upper body; the dancer does not throw his torso and arms around into the turn. Instead he coordinates the movement of his arms, opening the front arm slightly forward and toward the side and then bringing the second arm around and in. Both arms close to a rounded, fairly tight overlapped first in the air, concentrating the turning energy they generate. The dancer feels he is centering the energy of the turn underneath, in the arms, rather than distributing it around the circumference of the circle. He "looks for" his spot, almost leading with his eyes and head, especially in double tours. He as usual keeps the head level rather than tucking the chin, the gaze focused at eye level, and really sees the front as he whips his head around twice. Again, it is useful to think of the chest coming front twice. As Stanley Williams would say, "Come front! Don't turn."

When Balanchine gave an exercise with consecutive single tours, the tempo was usually quite fast. He used this for the male lead in *Donizetti Variations*. He often gave a jump before double tour. That makes the landing and plié of the first jump the takeoff of the double tour—for example, two changements, double tour, plié, straighten, and plié; or two entrechats six, double tour, straighten, and plié. Some of the women would do the combination but substitute another step for the double tour—for example, they might do two changements and a pirouette or an entrechat six. Other women would try the double tour. I did with limited success, but Pat Neary and Gloria Govrin showed again that they could jump with the men.

Another combination given generally for men is two moderate to slow emboîtés back (legs to a low attitude) in place (see page 343)—bigger than coupé but not necessarily lifting the thigh to forty-five degrees), coupé assemblé front (see page 323), double tour. A more typical Balanchine combination (it uses only two steps) is pirouette from fifth,

*Peter coming around, looking
for his spot, arms closed in a
rounded compact first; he
immediately changed his feet.*

*Peter in plié just before he takes off,
weight over the balls of his feet*

*Peter landed in fifth position plié,
heels just off the floor.*

closing fifth front and double tour landing fifth front and repeat; this is seen in *Theme and Variations*. In these combinations the dancer tries to ensure that he controls the pliés before and after the double tour, making them continuous and smooth, avoiding hitting the floor, "WHAM," and then bouncing back into the air or else stopping in the plié. Again, the dancer is always trying to make a clean and clear fifth position. The keys, aside from staying on time and holding the torso in one piece, are: aiming the toes to fifth after the pirouette and immediately closing fifth for the tour; and, on landing, catching the weight at the base of the toes, and going through the feet smoothly into plié while maintaining the weight forward over the balls of the feet. This intense control is very demanding and will not always be complete, but, as with rolling up and down for the women on pointe, the

DETAILS I OFTEN INSIST ON IN TOUR EN L'AIR:

1) take a good plié with the weight forward over the balls of the feet, followed by a push into the air with a feeling of turning to the front; do not throw the torso back
2) look for your spot
3) doing singles or doubles, bring the feet to the final position immediately upon leaving the floor
4) establish and maintain a compact, fully energized position in the air: hips up, chest lifted and front, arms rounded and relatively close to the body

effort and energy he expends will make his tours en l'air look more refined.

In single and double tours en l'air the dancer usually pliés on the count, turns on the "and," and lands again on the count.

SECOND CATEGORY: JUMPS FROM TWO FEET TO ONE FOOT

In these jumps the dancer uses both legs and feet at once to push off and to power herself into the air, but it takes extra effort and strength to control the landing on one foot.

Sissonne

Mr. Balanchine used many kinds of sissonne, but the ones we practiced most often in class were sissonne fermée in all directions, sissonne ouverte in arabesque and attitude croisée back, sissonne with développé à la seconde, sissonne faillie, and sissonne battue fermée in arabesque effacée. Each kind of sissonne has its own particular look, but two characteristics were common to all. In any kind of sissonne, the dancer needs to ensure that she

---

DETAILS I OFTEN INSIST ON IN ANY SISSONNE:

1) jump sharply up and away from fifth, moving the legs apart, even when the jump is not large
2) take hips and torso up with you and travel, maintaining the alignment of the entire torso and the head
3) establish the designated line immediately in the entire body, showing life and energy

---

takes her supporting leg, hips, torso, and chest up and in the direction of travel. Remember, "If you don't move your supporting leg, you have nothing to land on." Her entire body moves as a unit in one piece, rather than the torso heaving back and then collapsing forward. Also, sissonne for Mr. B was a very dynamic step. As in sissonne to pointe, the dancer should explode out of fifth, like a champagne cork from a bottle. The cork is popped by the energy of the pressurized gas; the dancer is propelled by the energy stored in the plié. The "explosion" propels her into the air, as she immediately assumes the designated line, and she lands some distance from where she started.

Sissonne Fermée

Sissonne fermée can travel in any of the three directions and, depending on the tempo and the exercise, it can be big or small.

As soon as she has left the floor, the dancer makes a picture in the air. Balanchine wanted to see both legs move away from each other immediately and extend to the designated line. The lifted leg moves very rapidly, like a flash of lightning, as the other leg moves as quickly toward its destination. The dancer rises into the air, taking her hips and torso up, and travels, showing both legs, not just the leg being lifted (almost thrown) up to the extended line. When she is traveling forward, the leading leg moves sharply forward and out; when she is traveling side, it moves side and out; and when she is traveling back, it stretches down, out, and back. However, neither leg kicks up. The dancer freezes the action of the legs as quickly as possible in the air, even if only momentarily.

As the dancer pushes away from the floor traveling forward, her leading leg extends rapidly front as she takes her hips up and forward and lifts her chest, torso, and head in the direction she's traveling. The front leg does not split up, but moves out in front of the hips. Meanwhile, the back leg lifts instantly to arabesque and the arms shoot into their designated line, such as first or third arabesque, completing the "picture." "If you don't move the hands fast enough, they will stop you, stop the jump. Something must be there first: the hands."

As the dancer descends, the front leg remains extended forward. Since it did not split up, it does not need to pull back, and it should not pull back. This helps to maximize the distance of the jump. The dancer's hips and torso move even more forward over the supporting foot as she begins to land on the front leg. As usual, the dancer catches herself at the tips of the toes and goes through her foot into plié. Meanwhile, the back leg is brought rapidly to the floor. If the tempo is slow, the tips of the toes touch lightly, gently caressing the floor as the foot is brought in and placed into fifth position plié. If the tempo is very bright, the leg is brought down speedily, and toes touching first, the foot is placed quickly into fifth position plié. The foot does not drag into fifth, "polishing the floor" as it goes. In fifth position plié both thighs are active and the toes hold on to the floor. When the dancer does sissonne fermée to the side or back, the basic principles for going to the front also apply.

There is a variety of ports de bras that may be done, always in coordination with the movement of the legs; the arms usually arrive in position an instant before the legs. The dancer may also, for example, hold the arms down in a demi-second or slightly opened fifth low. However, the arms should not become stiff or rigid, even though the dancer establishes them very quickly in the designated line.

It is important to observe precise directions with both legs, whether the sissonne fermée is traveling forward, to the side, or to the back. Traveling forward and to the back, the thighs are crossed, bring-ing both pointes onto the center line of the body. In sissonne fermée to the side, the extended leg should not be allowed to go back of à la seconde or turn in; in fact, it may be a little in front of the working hip and it stays turned out. The dancer also does not heave the upper torso to the back, but keeps it forward, over or just in front of her hips.

Peter does sissonne in third arabesque.

Peter in the air in sissonne to the side

Mr. B gave an exercise for sissonne fermée forward, side, and back that makes a box. Starting in fifth position en face with the right foot front, the dancer does one sissonne fermée forward, one to the side to the right with a change of feet in landing, one to the back, and one to the side to the left with a change of feet in landing. Once again, working en face helps the dancer to maintain the fullest awareness of precise directions and positions. She

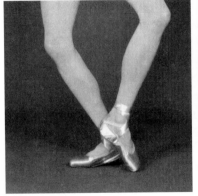

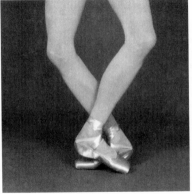

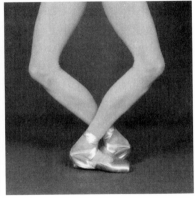

Dana placing her toes to the floor after a fast sissonne to the side

Dana lowering into fifth position

Dana in fifth position plié, weight over the balls of the feet

can see clearly that her feet are on the center line of her body in sissonne fermée forward and back and can sense more easily that they are directly side in sissonne fermée to the side. The combination could continue with a glissade (see page 331) and three assemblés (see page 322), or three sissonnes to the side changing feet (right, left, right) and sous-sus, or some other combination of steps to end with the left foot front so the dancer is ready to repeat it to the other side. A shorter solution, also typical of Mr. B's way of working, is to follow the four sissonnes in a box with a changement or a sissonne to the other side, changing feet. Since the combination is now in five, he would usually ask for music in five. Or else, with the music still in eight, we might do the same combination in five counts, then straighten our legs on count six, hold count seven, and plié on count eight, then begin on the other side.

This sissonne combination is more usually done with épaulement, which is more comfortable for the dancers because they are not nearly so exposed. Starting in fifth position croisé, right foot front, the dancer does one sissonne fermée in third arabesque traveling forward. She then does one sissonne fermée in écarté derrière moving to the right, closing with a change of legs (the left foot finishes front) as she inclines her body and head away; her arms pass through second to close to fifth low. Next, she does one sissonne fermée traveling back, in croisé, then

one sissonne fermée side moving to the left in écarté derrière, changing her legs and facing the original corner (the right foot is again front), inclining her body and head away, passing her arms through second to close in fifth low. She can continue with three sissonnes fermées in first arabesque traveling diagonally forward to the right. She finishes with a changement landing in croisé, left foot front, as her arms close through second to fifth low, and repeats to the other side.

Another typical, but slightly easier, exercise with changes of épaulement for sissonne fermée also starts in fifth position croisé, right foot front. The dancer does one sissonne fermée forward in third arabesque and then one sissonne fermée traveling to the right in écarté derrière, changing feet and turning to the other diagonal. She repeats the combination to the other side, doing one sissonne fermée forward in third arabesque and then one sissonne fermée traveling to the left in écarté derrière, changing feet and turning to the original diagonal. She can continue with three sissonnes in first arabesque and a changement, as in the foregoing exercise. This exercise can be and should be done in reverse—that is, starting to the back.

Another good exercise starts with the dancer in fifth position croisé with her right foot front and moves on the diagonal. She does two sissonnes fermées in first arabesque, traveling forward to the right, and then two sissonnes, traveling diagonally back to the left in effacé front. All of these sissonnes are on the same diagonal. The exercise can continue in a variety of ways—for example, sissonne faillie (see page 320), two simple assemblés (see page 323), and a soubresaut and repeat on the other side.

Sissonne Fermée Changing Legs

Sissonne fermée changing legs has the same qualities as sissonne fermée but includes a change of legs, which makes it more difficult when moving front and back.

Starting in fifth position en face with the right foot front, the dancer pushes off the floor as described for sissonne fermée. If she is doing sissonne traveling forward, she immediately brings her left (back) leg directly to the front, as she pushes off the floor. Her right leg lifts directly up to the back, to the designated line, as the left stretches forward and down. She lands with her left foot front. Because she is really traveling forward, the leg that goes to the back just lifts up; it does not kick back. If she is doing sissonne traveling back, the action is re-

versed. In either direction, the idea is to immediately establish the designated line in the air with both pointes on the center line of the body. Practicing sissonne fermée changing legs en face makes the dancer very aware of her center line.

Mr. B gave an exercise of alternating sissonne fermée no change with sissonne fermée changing legs, going forward in a series. This can be done at a relatively slow tempo, which requires strength and control. At a brisk tempo it is shown by the male principal in *Mozartiana*. The arms may be in a demi-second. He gave it going back also.

Sissonne Ouverte

Sissonne ouverte was usually practiced assuming arabesque or attitude croisée back in the air. The same basic principles apply as for sissonne fermée. The dancer explodes out of fifth position. She immediately and clearly assumes the designated pose with her entire body and travels in that pose. Because she maintains the designated pose as she lands instead of closing to fifth, there are some additional considerations.

Because the dancer lands on one foot, it is even more important than for sissonne fermée that the hips and upper body move forward over the supporting leg as she descends through her foot into plié. This will help to ensure that she maintains her weight over the ball of her supporting foot as she controls and cushions the landing. She also holds her back up and her chest lifted and forward.

The extended leg should not kick up or bounce as the dancer lands. It holds and may even slightly extend the line it assumed in the air. The arms usually hold their line as the dancer lands, but she does not let them become rigid or stiff.

Sissonne ouverte is always followed by another step. A common and useful exercise that we often did includes sissonne ouverte landing in first arabesque in profile. The dancer starts in tendu croisé front and transfers her weight to the tendu foot, then glissade faillie (see page 335 for Mr. B's

---

DETAILS I OFTEN INSIST ON IN
SISSONNE FERMÉE:
1) take yourself—hips and chest—up off the floor, change levels; do not simply split the legs with a minimal jump; travel
2) travel in the designated pose in the air
3) controlled plié using the feet, ankles, and thighs before and after the jump
4) show both legs, freezing them in the air
5) doing sissonne forward and back, keep both pointes on the center line
6) the arms are coordinated with and should help the jump, assuming the designated line rapidly and showing the pose while maintaining life

approach to this step), traveling assemblé (see page 325; she is in écarté in the air), sissonne ouverte in first arabesque, pas de bourrée. The dancer lands from the assemblé in a low plié with the torso inclined away from the front leg; she bends over with her arms extended down in fifth low "to collect her laundry." As she pushes off the floor and takes herself into the air for the sissonne ouverte in first arabesque, she lifts her torso up and turns to profile. She also lifts her arms rapidly up through fifth high and over to first arabesque (putting the laundry on the table, one might say). As she travels, she assumes first arabesque in the air. She lands in profile in first arabesque (weight over the ball of the foot) and then turns toward the front on the pas de bourrée as she lifts the backs of her wrists slightly and moves her arms to second. A second common exercise is sissonne ouverte in attitude croisée back, step on the back leg to coupé, and brush the front leg forward for an assemblé traveling front in croisé. Again, she makes and shows the pose in the air: attitude croisée with the arms, head, torso, and legs. Again, she controls the landing in the foot and thigh, keeping her weight forward with her hips up. And again, she holds her arms in croisé as she lands. This exercise travels diagonally forward, landing from the sissonne on count one, making the step behind (coupé) on "and," and landing from the assemblé on count two. It does not change sides, but the teacher can add sous-sus and entrechat six so the dancers can repeat on the other side.

DETAILS I OFTEN INSIST ON IN SISSONNE OUVERTE:
1) details cited for sissonne fermée, plus:
2) maintain the line of the entire body in landing
3) in sissonne to arabesque or attitude back, take the body forward in the air and keep it forward on landing, weight over the ball of the foot

Sissonne Ouverte Changing Legs

Sissonne ouverte changing legs was often done to arabesque or attitude croisée back. The key result of the explosive jump out of fifth in this type of sissonne is to propel the dancer so far forward as well as up that the leg that starts in front is just lifted into the designated line.

Starting in fifth position croisé, right foot front, the dancer pliés, pushing sharply off the floor as the back (left) leg is brought immediately diagonally forward and front, across into croisé. As the left leg moves diagonally forward, the hips and torso move up and forward, immediately assuming croisé, with the right arm in fifth high, the left arm in second, and the head slanted. The dancer bends her right elbow enough so that the hand moves across the center line of the body through an overlapped first to fifth high to remain over the center of the head. The right leg lifts immediately to arabesque or attitude croisée.

In most schools, sissonne ouverte changing legs is done in attitude croisée, and when it is followed by assemblé, it is usually with a step behind the supporting leg (or coupé back) into assemblé traveling forward (see page 323). However, Mr. Balanchine usually gave sissonne ouverte changing legs, traveling and ending in croisé arabesque, followed by a large step forward on the diagonal staying down in plié, then assemblé going up and traveling forward. In either case the assemblé finishes in croisé left foot front, so the dancer is ready to repeat on the other side. He liked this combination, because it travels more and is more dynamic. The traveling assemblé in each case is followed by a plié that is deep, low, and usually slow to collect energy for the sissonne, which is, of course, also a traveling step. When possible, the plié before the jump is as deep as the plié after. In this case the dancer tries to plié deeply on the step forward before the assemblé to match the plié after the assemblé and again to plié after the sissonne to match the plié before. In between these

Peter does sissonne, changing legs to arabesque croisée.

Peter lands from the sissonne in croisé.

Peter in demi-plié in fifth position, collecting energy; note the heels are just releasing.

Staying in plié, Peter brings his back leg forward and places his toes to the floor to plié and collect energy for assemblé front.

DETAILS I OFTEN INSIST ON IN SISSONNE OUVERTE CHANGING LEGS:
1) details cited for sissonne fermée and sissonne ouverte, plus:
2) move the back leg strongly forward on the diagonal as the torso and hips come forward and go up
3) don't kick up and split the leg that moves to the back

pliés are high, soaring jumps. These pliés, when done slowly and low, feel uncomfortable. However, it is the effort that produces the result. When the dancer has learned how to use and control them, they supply a lot of force and power.

Sissonne with Développé à la Seconde

The dancer jumps from fifth position, taking herself into the air and traveling to the side in one piece. The working knee lifts the foot toward or to passé, and then the leg développés while the dancer continues to travel in the air. The height of the jump and of the développé line established depends on the tempo.

When this jump is done to a fast tempo, the sissonne is relatively small, the working knee does not fully lift, and the développé is low, to about forty-five degrees. This is often called "petite." At moderate tempos the dancer needs to lift the working knee as high as time allows, bringing the toe at least to passé, before extending the lower leg to the side and establishing the line at about ninety degrees. At the slowest tempos she jumps very high and really travels to the side. She should have the knee of her working leg lifting as high as possible. "Aim for the armpit," I say. The extended leg should finish in a high line, at or somewhat above ninety degrees. This is often called "grande" and it should all happen in the air.

The dancer lands on count one with the working leg extended and after a slight pause usually brings the working foot quickly down in back of the supporting foot to do coupé for assemblé traveling side on "and" (see page 325), landing fifth back on count two. In the male variation in *Tchaikovsky Pas de Deux*, Balanchine set this combination four times and the dancer travels across the entire stage. An alternative that Mr. B often used includes ballonné. After the dancer lands on count one from the sissonne with développé, the working foot is brought quickly down behind the supporting foot to do coupé ballonné side on "and" (see page 372), end-

Peter lifts his knee high and close to his body, as he makes sissonne with développé side.

Peter flying sideways, completing the développé

ing in the coupé back position on count two. She next coupés on "and" in order to assemblé front, landing on count three, followed by a big changement or entrechat six landing on count four. She can now repeat on the other side.

The port de bras that we typically used for sissonne with développé starts with the arms in fifth low. As the working foot is drawn up the supporting leg, the arms are raised to a slightly overlapped first. As the leg extends side, the dancer rapidly moves (it almost feels like a throw) the same arm as the working leg to fifth high and opens the other one to second. She usually inclines her head in the

DETAILS I OFTEN INSIST ON IN
SISSONNE WITH DÉVELOPPÉ À LA
SECONDE:
1) make a good plié to push off with force
2) lift the knee close to the body before
   rapidly extending the leg to the side
3) when the tempo allows, show the
   extended line in the air
4) control the plié as you land

direction of the arm in second. As the working foot is lowered toward fifth back, the arm in fifth high opens to join the other one in second. Both arms lower a bit as the dancer coupés, lift slightly as she jumps in assemblé and changes her head direction toward the front foot, and close to fifth low as she lands in croisé in fifth position plié. This step usually travels directly side or diagonally back. If the dancer does coupé ballonné she could open her arms to second on the ballonné coupé assemblé, moving them to fifth low on the plié and through an overcrossed first to fifth high for the changement or entrechat six, landing in fifth with the arms to the side. Or, when the tempo is fast and the développé is low (forty-five degrees), the dancer can use the "small arms" port de bras.

Sissonne Fermée in Arabesque with Battu

Sissonne fermée with battu adds a beat that the dancer does before establishing the line in the air. She pliés, pushing sharply off the floor in the direction of travel as she immediately changes her legs to beat. The beating action is essentially that described for entrechat quatre, but instead of landing again in fifth position after the beat, she establishes the designated pose in the air when time allows. This is usually arabesque effacée although she could travel side in à la seconde or back in effacé front.

Immediately following the beat, the leg finishing the beat in back moves strongly forward, while the front leg moves rapidly back and extends to arabesque. Neither leg kicks up. As she opens her leg to the front, the dancer's torso and hips continue to move forward to enhance her travel. The energy of her forward movement enables her to extend the arabesque leg to the back. As she lands on the front leg, the back leg is brought to fifth as speedily as possible. The dancer lands, going through her feet and maintaining her weight over the balls of the feet, bringing her hips over her feet and holding her back up, not allowing it to collapse forward or heave back.

We usually practiced this jump traveling on the diagonal in arabesque effacée with the arms drawn gently back of a low à la seconde, sloping from the shoulders. The chest is opened and lifted; the head slants in the effacé line. This is a "winged victory" or streamlined look, similar to the hood ornament on a Rolls-Royce. A typical exercise would start in fifth position effacé with the arms in a low second. We would do three sissonnes fermées with battu and a royale or an entrechat six to change direction and repeat on the other side.

In *A Midsummer Night's Dream*, Oberon does six sissonnes fermées with battu in arabesque effacée and an entrechat six and then repeats the sequence to the other side. We sometimes did this combination in class.

Sissonne fermée in arabesque with battu was

DETAILS I OFTEN INSIST ON IN
SISSONNE FERMÉE IN ARABESQUE
WITH BATTU:
1) show the beat
2) take the hips and torso forward as well
   as up
3) move both legs rapidly into position
4) bring the arabesque leg down quickly to
   make fifth position plié

generally done at a fairly brisk tempo, and as usual the plié is on the count and the dancer is in the air on the "and." Naturally, the faster the tempo the smaller the jump and the less time to show or freeze the picture in the air.

Sissonne Faillie

"Sissonne faillie presents a next step, to be ready for something else," was the way Mr. B stated the difference in this sissonne.

To Balanchine, the key to sissonne faillie to the front was to bring the back leg down quickly, transferring the weight to that leg as it bends and as the chest is brought forward. The back (working) leg crosses in front of the supporting leg quickly to have time to make a good plié to collect energy for the step to follow. However, bringing the extended foot rapidly to the floor did not mean that it could bang down haphazardly. It was important that the dancer place the pointed toes deliberately to the floor, bringing the heel somewhat forward but not necessarily down.

At faster tempos this is a quick, small jump. The back leg lifts only to about forty-five degrees, and the dancer does not rise very high nor travel very far. The emphasis is on instantly pointing the feet and bringing the back leg very quickly down and across into the plié with weight on it to move on to the next step, so she does not even try to freeze in the air, as is the case for most other sissonnes.

At more moderate tempos the dancer jumps relatively high, really travels, and the back leg lifts to forty-five degrees or a bit higher, making a momentary picture in the air. The back leg then moves rapidly down and across as the dancer transfers her weight on to it.

Even at more moderate tempos, sissonne faillie usually has the same kind of phrasing as glissade (see page 331), because the second leg closes very soon after the landing of the first foot. It is the second leg in sissonne faillie, as well as in glissades to fifth and glissade faillie, that collects the energy and

provides the power for the next step the audience really notices. However, for Balanchine, such steps merited the same attention and consideration from the dancer as the step that follows and that the audience remembers, such as flying assemblé or grand jeté. No movement could be taken for granted just because it was a link or a preparation.

In doing sissonne faillie to moderate and slower tempos, the arms are often in effacé, one arm in fifth high, one arm in second. In small, quick sissonnes faillies to faster tempos, the small arms port de bras is often more suitable, more efficient.

In this slower sissonne faillie exercise, the dancer changes direction and does assemblé in effacé front. Starting in fifth position croisé, right foot front, she does sissonne faillie in effacé back, immediately bringing her left foot across into croisé. She rapidly transfers her weight onto her left foot and, staying in a low plié, does a kind of rond de jambe par terre en dedans (more like a demi-rond side and front) with her right leg, switching her di-

Deanna landing from a small, fast sissonne faillie; she rapidly brought her second leg down, placed her toes to the floor, and is transferring her weight forward onto that leg.

rection to the other diagonal and ending in croisé. She steps forward onto the right foot, placing her toes to the floor and bringing the heel forward while staying down in plié, then brushes her left foot in front of her and does a tremendous, flying assemblé forward (see page 325) in effacé. She lands in effacé with her left foot front in fifth position, going through her feet into a low plié. The timing is sissonne faillie on "and"; land with the weight on the left foot on count one; step across with the right foot into plié on "and"; and assemblé in the air and land, making a big, slow plié on count two. She starts from fifth effacé to repeat to the other side. She needs to show clearly the directions and the full changes in épaulement.

DETAILS I OFTEN INSIST ON IN SISSONNE FAILLIE:
1) show both legs in the air
2) bring the second (back) leg down and across immediately, rapidly transferring the weight forward and onto it
3) place the toes to the floor, go through the foot, the heel somewhat forward
4) take a good plié on the front leg, as deep as the tempo allows

---

Sauté with Rond de Jambe

Mr. Balanchine seldom gave this in class, but he used it in some ballets, e.g. *Divertimento No. 15*. In this particular rond de jambe step the dancer pushes off the floor with both feet, similar to sissonne but now staying in place as the working leg shoots up. In the other, more usual, version of sauté with rond de jambe, the working leg starts by brushing out and up to à la seconde at about ninety degrees, making it a jump from one foot that has some similarity to the beginning of assemblé. I find it useful

to give both versions in the same class because it makes the dancer very aware of exactly how she leaves the floor. To do the "sissonne" version she must resist the tendency to brush.

The dancer starts in fifth position, pliés, and jumps, using both feet and both legs to push off the floor together. As she rises in the air, the working leg, which is usually in front, opens immediately à la seconde in the air, to forty-five degrees or a bit higher. It does not brush before the jump, but as in sissonne, it opens in the air with a dynamic "pop." The supporting leg remains stretched straight down. The dancer holds this position as she shows it momentarily before starting the rond de jambe. She starts the rond de jambe en dehors at the height of the jump and completes it during the descent. A single rond de jambe is large and full, a double rond de jambe is smaller and quicker, and the dancer usually begins it sooner (see page 119).

After landing, the dancer may step out into piqué, being sure to reach out onto a straight leg—for example, into attitude effacée. A common alternative is to follow the sauté with a simple assemblé (see page 323). In this case the continuous plié of the landing gathers energy for the jump of the assemblé, and the straightening of the working leg from the rond de jambe becomes the beginning of the assemblé, which usually closes back.

DETAILS I OFTEN INSIST ON IN SAUTÉ WITH ROND DE JAMBE:
1) push off both feet together; do not brush
2) take the hips and torso up
3) arms assume position needed in the air as working leg immediately opens to designated height
4) show a full single or double; don't just shake the working leg
5) control the descent into plié
6) hold the body up when landing

THIRD CATEGORY: JUMPS FROM ONE FOOT TO TWO FEET

Jumps off one foot obviously require more strength than jumps off two feet. The dancer must push herself off the floor and into the air using only one foot, and once in the air she often must be able to assume and show a designated position. To help us develop the necessary strength, Balanchine gave exercises such as this one. It combines jumps from two feet to one and from one foot to two and was generally done at moderate and slower tempos.

Starting in fifth right foot front, the dancer echappé sautés (see page 301) to land in second. From second she jumps and makes coupé (see page 80) with the right foot back in the air, and lands on her left foot, going through the foot into plié with some resistance. Using a slow, controlled, continuous plié with the weight over the ball of the foot, she pushes off the floor from her left foot and immediately makes second position in the air, then lands in second, going through her feet into plié. Again keeping the action of the plié continuous, she jumps and makes coupé with the left foot back in the air, landing on her right foot and going through it into plié. This sequence would be repeated several, perhaps many, times, usually starting with moderate tempos and repeating with slower ones.

This combination stays in place; the dancer does not move to one side and then the other. Each leg must open equally to the side, to second position, and each must return to the center line of the dancer's body in coupé. The opening to second from coupé is a particular challenge, because the dancer must achieve sufficient elevation jumping from one leg and foot to establish and show second position in the air before landing.

The dancer usually remains en face for the entire combination, but with a change of head and arms.

> DETAILS I OFTEN INSIST ON IN THE ÉCHAPPÉ SAUTÉ/COUPÉ EXERCISE:
> 1) push strongly off the floor; change levels and show both positions in the air
> 2) stay in place
> 3) control the plié in the thigh, foot, and ankle, especially when landing on one foot

The arms open through first to second while she is in the air in échappé sauté. When she jumps from second to coupé, the arm on the side of the foot in coupé moves in front of her body to first position and the head turns and inclines to the same side, with the gaze directed over and past the forearm. When she jumps from coupé to second, her arm returns to second and her head straightens and faces front as she shows this position in the air.

Assemblé

The word *assemblé* in French means assembled; the dancer has assembled her feet in the air. This usually means that the thighs are crossed, the legs stretched, the ankles and feet together in soubresaut position. The one exception is for Cecchetti assemblé, for which the feet are pointed in a kind of fifth position (the toes just crossed and the heels slightly overlapped), which requires a slight bending of the knees (see page 300).

Assemblé can travel or remain in place and, depending on the tempo, can be small or large. However, Mr. B did not give the "grand" assemblé for which the working leg is thrown up as high as ninety degrees. This higher extension in assemblé tends to separate the plié from the jump and to make impossible or at least delay assembling the feet in the air, which for him was the real point of the step. He preferred a dynamic jump that propelled the dancer through space with the feet together.

As the dancer begins to bend her knees in plié, the working foot starts to brush out of fifth position. There is no pause in the action of the plié. The precise coordination will depend on the tempo, but the dancer does not stop the movement and "sit" in the plié with the leg extended out.

The dancer brushes the working foot lightly, pointing the foot as the knee stretches and the foot brushes off the floor. Balanchine did not want the heavy push against the floor in brushing that is preferred by some teachers. The legs and feet come together as quickly as possible. Assemblé happens in the air. Once in contact, they do not shake or bounce off one another (the beating in assemblé battu is, of course, deliberate). Some say, "Pretend you have Velcro on your ankles," because the legs and feet are so stuck together.

Several kinds of assemblé starting in fifth position are discussed in the sections that follow. However, assemblé is often preceded by sissonne faillie, coupé, glissade, chassé, pas de basque, or just a simple step. Whatever precedes the assemblé is done with full attention to the presentation of the foot to the floor, to the alignment of the knee over the foot in plié, and to the plié itself. There is no change in the action of the assemblé.

When the dancer does sissonne faillie before as-semblé, she brings her working leg across, places the toes to the floor, and brings the heel somewhat forward (see page 202) as she transfers her weight and goes through her foot into plié; she uses this plié to push off the floor. When the dancer coupés into assemblé, she brings the working leg directly in back or in front of the supporting leg, the toes are placed to the floor as the heel is brought forward, and she goes through her foot into the plié she uses to push off the floor. When the dancer does glissade before assemblé, the second leg is brought rapidly to the floor either to place the toes in fifth position plié or, as in glissade faillie (see page 335), is brought rapidly down and across the body, placing the toes to the floor as she transfers her weight and goes into plié. When the dancer does pas de basque before assemblé, the second leg passes through first and rapidly extends to the front as the knee stretches and the foot points. The toes are placed to the floor and she transfers her weight going through the foot as the knee bends into plié to collect energy for the assemblé. When the dancer chassés or steps out, she places the toes to the floor and goes through the foot into plié, as she transfers her weight forward and onto that foot and leg. It is the plié she steps into that provides the energy for her jump. In no case does she slam or slap the full foot onto the floor. In all cases she immediately transfers her weight and controls the plié, making it as deep as she can in the time available to collect maximum energy for the jump to follow.

DETAILS I OFTEN INSIST ON IN ANY ASSEMBLÉ:

1) the plié does not stop, it is part of the jump; don't sit
2) brush exactly in the designated direction—foot on the center line front and back, or side (no drift to the back)
3) show the feet together in the air
4) change levels; take the hips and torso off the floor
5) coordinate the arms and épaulement with the step

Simple Assemblé

Simple assemblé, the basic form of assemblé, does not travel. It is done in all three directions, but in each case it is done in place.

As the dancer pliés, the working foot brushes from fifth. The working leg is thrown with the knee stretched and the foot pointed to about forty-five degrees as the dancer pushes off the floor with the supporting foot virtually simultaneously. Already when the dancer is just off the floor, the working leg is instantly brought in under her center, where the working foot joins the supporting foot in soubresaut position. The feeling is that the legs and feet are immediately pulled together, perhaps by strong magnets. When she closes to the front, she can think that the working leg and foot come in to "cover" the supporting leg and foot. Both legs are fully stretched and the feet are "glued" together. This is the "picture" the dancer makes, and it is held as long as possible before the dancer lands in fifth position plié, going through her feet.

Depending on the exercise, the arms may be held in fifth low, may be opened through first to second, may "swing" open to second after a long glissade faillie, or in the case of three or four consecutive simple assemblés may do a small arms port de bras (one or two assemblés to open the arms and one or two to close them). In combinations this step would normally be done with épaulement and often with at least one other step.

The dancer pliés and lands on the count and is in the air on the "and." Mr. B gave simple assemblé at a wide range of tempos. At very fast tempos the brush and the push off the floor are nearly or actually simultaneous, and the working leg may not reach forty-five degrees. At slower tempos the dancer leaves the floor a little after the brush, but the dancer will still not "sit" in the plié. At all tempos, she brushes with the idea that the leg will be brought back under the center; it is not being thrown out.

A good combination to build awareness of and the skill to make the "glued together" position of the feet and legs in assemblé is to put it with soubresaut. The dancer tries to achieve the same precise, secure fifth position in the air in assemblé and in soubresaut; each presents its own challenge. The combination is in two and is done with épaulement. The dancer starts in croisé left foot front and does assemblé side with the right foot, landing in croisé right foot front, then soubresaut, assemblé side with the left foot landing in croisé with the left foot front and soubresaut. The arms could open from fifth low with a small arms port de bras to a low sec-

ond in the assemblé and rise, led by the backs of the wrists, in the soubresaut, before closing again to fifth low, opening again as the dancer starts the next assemblé; the arms lead the way, arriving first. Remember, "Two arms, twice as easy."

The awareness and skill to do the simplest movements were qualities Mr. B worked on regularly with us, even though we were professional dancers. What he started with the last exercise, he might continue by putting glissade (see page 331) before the assemblé and soubresaut to make a combination in three. The dancer must show second in the air in glissade and fifth in the air in assemblé and soubresaut; glissade travels, but the other two remain in place. Mr. B's insistence that each step look like itself meant that the dancer had to be aware of the differences and show clearly the contrasting looks.

A characteristic combination to practice this basic assemblé side is: glissade, assemblé, glissade, assemblé, glissade, and then three more assemblés side (closing front-back-front), all three using the same leg. The dancer must again clearly show the difference between glissade and assemblé. Using the same leg for three assemblés in a row now requires extra strength and effort to jump off the floor and to bring the feet together in the air *all three* times.

Both of these combinations are done with épaulement, the head inclined toward the foot in front. They can and should be reversed.

DETAILS I OFTEN INSIST ON IN SIMPLE ASSEMBLÉ:
1) the working leg is brought back toward the supporting leg; don't travel
2) change levels; take the hips and torso up with you and bring the legs together underneath you
3) in assemblé side don't brush behind à la seconde, either directly side or very slightly in front; don't heave

Traveling Assemblé

In each of the four kinds of assemblé (simple, traveling, Cecchetti, battu), the feet are brought together, but in four diferent ways. In traveling assemblé the feet are brought together in a way that maximizes the travel in whichever of the three directions has been designated (usually front or side), as well as the height of the jump. Mr. B generally had us traveling to the side in écarté, forward in croisé or effacé, or, on occasion, back in croisé or effacé.

After the dancer brushes the working leg out and pushes off the floor, her tendency is to bring each leg in toward the other. However, the traveling assemblé is most effective when the supporting leg moves rapidly to the working leg and the working leg does not drop down or lower to join the supporting leg. In simple assemblé her awareness helps her to bring the working leg in to the supporting leg, which she holds under her center; in traveling assemblé her awareness helps her maintain the extended line of the working leg as she brings the supporting leg up to it. In either case, she needs to take herself *off* the floor and into the air.

The action of traveling assemblé is the same as that for simple assemblé as it starts (plié, brush, push off the floor). Because the working leg is being maintained in the extended line, the dancer must resist the tendency to lean back in traveling assemblé to the front and side. Instead, she maintains her torso forward with the chest lifted. The dancer must also ensure that she rises into the air, bringing her hips up. The real source of the power to change levels comes from the push off the floor of the supporting foot, leg, and hip, not the throw of the working leg. But it is both legs working together with coordinated timing, and with coordinated movement of the torso and arms, that makes the most effective and dynamic assemblé; the dancer seems to hang in the air.

Balanchine gave traveling assemblé at tempos

from very fast to quite slow. When the music is very fast, the dancer's attack must be even faster, the jump is not large, the brush is not high, but the dancer must still use her plié, rather than bouncing off the floor, to rise into the air and show her feet together. When the music is slower, the dancer makes a deeper, lower plié on the supporting leg to collect the energy to push off the floor to fly through the air with the feet together.

In a big, slow traveling assemblé to the side, the working leg could be thrown a bit higher than forty-five degrees but not up to ninety degrees, and slightly in front of à la seconde. The body is inclined slightly forward toward the legs; the dancer looks over her arm in an écarté line, with the palms facing down, suspended momentarily in the air. In large slow traveling assemblés to the front, the dancer should have a slight feeling of "sitting in the air" with her legs thrown to her front and the feet together, her torso up and forward, with her abdominal muscles actively working. "Take stomach in!" we might have heard.

A combination that Mr. B gave at either fast or slow tempos for traveling assemblé goes sauté in first arabesque, step across, glissade ("mini" failli, see page 333), traveling assemblé on the diagonal. It is done at a fast tempo by the second set of corps girls entering in the finale of *Divertimento No. 15*. Their toes point instantly (no heels down) and they use the "mini" failli to help them to really cover space, as they must in this case. Closing and crossing only as far as fifth, they will lose a few inches on each glissade as well as some of the impetus for the traveling assemblé. At slower tempos a real glissade faillie can be used (see page 335).

A favorite combination Balanchine usually gave at slower tempos starts in fifth position croisé right foot front (see page 316). It is a counterpart to the sissonne faillie exercise on page 321. He liked to give exercises that showed the same step from different angles and other contrasts. The sissonne faillie exercise shows assemblé in effacé front; this exercise uses sissonne ouverte changing legs and shows assemblé in croisé front. Both assemblés

Peter in traveling assemblé in écarté, torso and legs slightly front

Peter in traveling assemblé forward, seeming to "sit" in the air

have a "sit in the chair" feeling. After the dancer does sissonne ouverte changing legs traveling forward, landing in croisé arabesque on her left foot, she steps forward on her right foot while staying in plié, opening her arms side to à la seconde. She brushes the left foot through first to the front as she pushes strongly off the floor with her right foot, bringing her right leg quickly up to join her left leg for assemblé forward in croisé: "sitting in a chair." Her arms are stretched out to the side, palms down with the right arm slightly higher than second and the left in second; her head is in croisé. As the dancer lands in a good, deep plié, her arms close to fifth low as she bends her torso slightly forward; her head remains in croisé but her gaze is lowered. This is a deep plié to "collect the laundry." This combination repeats. We usually did it four or more times, until we ran out of space in the studio. The dancer should really explode out of fifth in the sissonne and sail through the air in the assemblé.

Cecchetti Assemblé

Another assemblé we practiced was Cecchetti assemblé. This step helps achieve ballon as the dancer develops the feeling and the technique to make and freeze a position in the air. Mr. B usually gave it in fifth, as in Cecchetti soubresaut (see page 300).

Cecchetti assemblé can remain in place, or it can

DETAILS I OFTEN INSIST ON IN
TRAVELING ASSEMBLÉ:
1) get a good plié; really push off the floor
2) take the hips and torso with you as you jump up and travel
3) bring the supporting leg to the working leg on the assemblé
4) make clear pictures in the air, the whole body participating

travel. In each case the action of the step is the same as for the simple and traveling assemblé, except that immediately after brushing, the working leg starts to bend. For Cecchetti assemblé both knees are bent just enough to bring the feet into the required position, and the thighs are held. The dancer jumps as she makes the position as rapidly as possible and shows it by holding it as long as possible. She must change levels.

The dancer is usually in plié on the count and up on the "and," the arms are usually in an extended second position with the wrists slightly lifted when she is in the air.

DETAILS I OFTEN INSIST ON IN CECCHETTI ASSEMBLÉ:
1) don't just bend the knees; get off the floor, change levels, take your hips up
2) bend the knees just enough to make the correct fifth position in the air

---

Assemblé Battu

Assemblé battu is another step that can remain in place or can travel, depending on the way the exercise is set. The dancer needs to be sure to observe the differences in the way she does the jump.

For the simple assemblé battu to the side, the dancer needs to stay in place and therefore should jump high enough so her working leg can come back in toward her center to beat. The action of the step is the same as for simple assemblé side until the beats. It is necessary to show both legs beating with a deep crossing. The scissoring action is the same as is used in royale.

Assemblé with a single beat can also be done traveling. Now the supporting leg comes up to meet the working leg, and then both beat once and open slightly to change.

In doing traveling assemblé, with or without beats, the dancer does not actively think about traveling. If, for example, she is doing glissade faillie side ending in fourth (see page 335) and a traveling assemblé, she ensures correct timing of the glissade and a good plié on and a good push off the front foot. She thinks up, pushing the floor away and lifting her hips and torso. The impetus of the jump is also supplemented by the throw of the working leg in assemblé by bringing the supporting leg up to meet it in the air and by bringing the upper body forward—all this makes her travel.

DETAILS I OFTEN INSIST ON IN ASSEMBLÉ BATTU:
1) take the hips up; don't brush behind second
2) show the beats
3) avoid traveling to the side unless called for in the way the exercise is set

---

Entrechat Cinq (Entrechat Six de Volée)

We called traveling assemblé with two beats entrechat cinq; it is also known as entrechat six de volée. It is usually done on the diagonal in écarté, but can be done directly front while traveling forward. The action is the same as for traveling assemblé until the beats. As usual, the working leg does not lower; instead the supporting leg comes up to meet it, and then both legs beat in the usual scissoring action. The supporting leg beats to the back, to the front, and then changes to the back to land in plié in fifth position back.

When doing entrechat cinq traveling to the side, the dancer actually brushes the working leg a little in front of à la seconde, pushing off the floor, taking her hips up, and bringing her torso (back and chest) slightly forward. She coordinates her arms, often gently swinging them down as she pliés, and out and up as she brushes and pushes off the floor,

DETAILS I OFTEN INSIST ON IN
ENTRECHAT CINQ:

1) get off the floor, taking your hips with
   you
2) bring the supporting leg up to the
   working leg
3) don't lean back; use the abdominal
   muscles
4) doing the beats to the front, be sure the
   feet are on the center line; doing the beats
   to the side, bring the legs a little front of à
   la seconde
5) show the beats; cross deeply

finishing in the air in an extended second with the palms down (see page 340). The position of the legs, which facilitates the beating, can feel slightly reminiscent of effacé front. The dancer uses her abdominal muscles to help her maintain her torso and her weight forward. Her head is up, and she looks out over the front hand. In the air the dancer still looks like she is in écarté (see photo, page 326).

When doing entrechat cinq to the front traveling forward, often preceded by a glissade faillie in fourth or a step forward, the dancer brushes the working leg through first and throws it up to about forty-five degrees, with her pointe on the center line of her body. The dancer as usual coordinates the brush and throw of the working leg off the floor with the push off the floor of the supporting leg and brings the supporting leg up to meet it. The arms are coordinated with the jump and normally swing down and out and up, ending a little in front of second, with the palms facing down. Both legs then scissor sideways to make the beat. She does not lean back; instead she uses her abdominal muscles to bring her back forward and keeps it there. It should give her the "sitting in the air" feeling and look.

If a dancer was having trouble mastering the scissoring action of entrechat cinq, Balanchine sug-gested that she try an assemblé front or side with double beats but without changing the legs. The supporting leg comes up and beats behind the working leg, and both legs beat again in the same place before landing together in fifth with the same foot front. In this way she at least has the feeling of two beats. And this approach prevents her from paddling front and back.

Entrechat cinq can also be done with a three quarter tour (one and three quarters by men). It usually begins with a chassé moving diagonally up-stage. The dancer brushes the working leg through first, throwing it up and around and pushing off the floor, taking her body up, but now both legs come together to beat. She beats more under her center than off to her side. The arms are coordinated with the brush and with the push off the floor and usually lift to fifth high.

Brisé

Brisé is a beating step that is usually done on the diagonal, in effacé front or effacé back, traveling forward or backward. "You don't have to travel far away. You travel because you bring the bottom leg up and because you are healthy." The principles for the action of the legs and feet are the same for brisé forward as they are for brisé back, but the upper body and port de bras may vary.

Defining front and back precisely on the center line of the body makes a real difference in the look of brisé. Instead of allowing dancers to brush somewhere generally in front or in back or even side, which is accepted in many schools, Mr. B carefully concentrated on our brushing the working leg exactly front or back. Brushing in either direction, the dancer made maximum effort to bring the working foot to the center line, which is not easy to do. However, beating with the legs directly front or back makes her three-dimensional rather than flat; it gives depth to the step. As usual, the effort she makes gives the step a different look as well as adding life and vitality to her dancing.

He also concentrated on our getting into the air and on our bringing the supporting leg up to meet the working leg so we traveled, rather than allowing us to lower the working leg to beat, which tends to leave the dancer more or less in place. He wanted to see both legs beating and changing, rather than only the supporting leg beating and the working leg changing; and, finally, he wanted to see the feet landing simultaneously in a clean fifth, rather than one after the other.

For brisé forward the dancer starts in fifth position croisé, left leg in front, and begins to plié. Her back (right) leg moves around the supporting leg, her working foot (leading with the heel) brushing lightly, but quickly, forward through first position and in to her center line. She throws her stretched leg and pointed foot briskly to about forty-five degrees as her supporting leg and foot push off the floor. She coordinates the throw of the working leg and the push off the floor so her jump is supplemented by the energy of the throw of the working leg. As soon as her supporting foot leaves the floor, that foot is brought very rapidly and energetically up to the back of the working leg to beat; she does not let the working leg come down to beat. Since the supporting leg comes up to beat with the work-

ing leg, the step will *travel* diagonally front. The torso is brought forward and the hips are up, not hanging back; again, the dancer can feel as if she is briefly sitting in the air with her legs extended front. Both legs beat as she scissors her legs in the usual way, beating her thighs and calves, her feet crossing, both legs opening to change. The dancer's pointes touch the floor simultaneously as she descends into fifth position plié, left foot front. All of these actions, from the beginning of the plié before the brisé through the plié after, flow together in one continuous, rapid movement.

In many schools, brisé front is taught with the arm on the side of the working leg (the upstage arm) held in first position and the other arm in second or with both arms extended outward from these positions. Balanchine used these arms but also often reversed them so the arm opposite the working foot (the downstage arm) was in first—for example, the left arm in low first when the right leg is extended front. The effect of this opposition is to help the dancer brush the working leg and foot directly front, or at least to make her more aware of where her foot and front actually are. In effacé front the head and the gaze are directed out over the arm in low first position.

For brisé back, the dancer starts in fifth position croisé, right leg in front, and begins to plié. Her front (right) leg moves around the supporting leg to effacé back, her foot brushing lightly through first

Peter begins to plié for brisé forward; he is using opposite arm as leg.

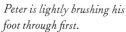

Peter is lightly brushing his foot through first.

Peter brings his working foot in front of his center line.

Peter throws his working foot in front of his center line.

as she continues to plié. She brings her foot to the center line as her toes point behind her spine, throwing the working leg briskly back to about forty-five degrees as her supporting (left) leg and foot push off the floor. She again coordinates the throw of the working leg and the push off the floor to ensure a good jump. As soon as she is in the air, her supporting leg is brought immediately to the working (right) leg to beat; she does not let the working leg come down to beat. Since the supporting leg comes up to beat with the working leg, the step will *travel* diagonally back. Both legs beat, scissoring and opening to change in the usual way. She lands both feet simultaneously in fifth position croisé, right foot front, going through her feet, descending in plié.

At the height of the jump the dancer is in effacé back with the legs thrown back, the torso lifted, and the chest open and up. We usually had the arm on the side of the working leg rounded in a low first when we did brisé back; in this case the right arm in front in a low first and the left arm in second. In effacé back the head is in a standard effacé line, with the gaze directed out.

A combination designed to help the dancer work on perfecting her brisé gives her some extra time to focus on a good brisé in both directions and then a chance to reproduce what she did on the single brisé in a series of brisés. Like many teachers, Mr. B could give brisé diagonally front landing on count one, straighten the legs on "and"; plié on count two; brisé diagonally back, landing on count three; straighten on "and"; plié on count four; three brisés diagonally front, landing on counts one, two, and three; and a royale or entrechat six, landing on count four, with a change of épaulement and repeat on the other side. This combination can and should be reversed. Starting in fifth position croisé the dancer pliés in fifth, avoiding a step out of fifth, and brushes directly front, bringing her supporting leg up to beat, then lands with her feet together in fifth position plié and straightens. It could be practiced first at a moderate tempo to give the dancer the time she needs to collect her wits and

energy, and then the tempo could be increased.

Balanchine also liked to give brisé with assemblé battu to contrast these two beating steps: Assemblé brushes side and can stay in place, but brisé brushes forward or back and travels. For example, he might give glissade (next exercise), assemblé battu, and two brisés traveling diagonally forward in effacé front and then continue to the other side. A harder but simpler alternative is brisé traveling forward in effacé and assemblé battu side staying in place. The point of such combinations is to enhance the dancer's awareness of the differences between assemblé and brisé by requiring that she clearly enunciate them. "It is very difficult to make a great difference between similar movements." The combinations also can and should be reversed.

Mr. B liked to remind us that the classical vocabulary has a relatively limited number of movements. Compared to English, it has only a few "words." The dancer must therefore show very clearly what makes each movement different. As Mr. B liked to say, "Show me this and then show me that." His classes often featured combinations like these to make us aware of the specific qualities each step should have so it will look like itself.

In the ballets, Balanchine occasionally used a brisé that really covered space. It is done in a series traveling in effacé front diagonally across the floor. The dancer places the second foot to fourth front, which helps her really travel.

DETAILS I OFTEN INSIST ON IN BRISÉ:
1) don't step before brisé; instead plié, brush and throw the working leg, and jump to it, traveling
2) the pointe of the working leg is on the center line front or back
3) bottom leg comes up to beat
4) the pointes land simultaneously on the floor, finishing in a clean fifth position

FOURTH CATEGORY: JUMPS FROM ONE FOOT TO THE OTHER

These jumps are like the jumps from one foot that land on two feet in that they can require maximum energy and power in the supporting foot and leg to take the dancer off the floor. Once in the air, the dancer often must establish a position and hold it, rather than move through it to the landing. Then the dancer needs the strength and awareness to control the landing on one foot rather than on both feet. For most dancers, exercises requiring the power and control for slow consecutive jumps from one foot to the other are very hard.

Glissade

The word "glissade" tells us some important characteristics of the step, but in this case the information comes partly from the meaning of the word and, for me, partly from its sound, including the accent on the second syllable. Glissade comes from a French word that means slide, and all glissades begin with the first foot sliding out (although we usually say "brush" in English) and end with the toes of the second foot lightly sliding into their designated position (skimming the floor, really). The "gli" sound makes me think of brushing out and making second or fourth position in the air, and the sound of "ssade," the accented second syllable, makes me think of the second leg coming very rapidly to the floor. Simple glissade (glissade to fifth) is a relatively small, quick jump in which the legs momentarily stop or freeze in second or fourth position in the air. It is a linking step that often is done to a bright allegro tempo and it can set the dancer up for another allegro movement. It is done in all three directions. Whatever the direction, the dancer must rise high enough into the air in the

jump to establish the position, even if only for an instant. She is in second or fourth in the air with straight legs and pointed feet and with her torso up over the lifted hips and centered between the legs. Simple glissades in all directions, in series and in combinations, were very important to Mr. Balanchine, and we worked hard to perfect them.

Glissade faillie is my term for a glissade Mr. B wanted done very specifically in which the second foot is placed in an overcrossed fifth or in a kind of overcrossed fourth. It is usually a slightly larger jump that travels more than simple glissade and is often not so quick, being done usually to a slower tempo, often to a much slower tempo. In glissade faillie to the side, the legs momentarily show second position before moving on; in glissade faillie to the front, the back leg stretches and is then brought immediately to the front, so the dancer does not freeze in fourth in the air. Glissade faillie is also a linking step, and if the movement that follows is a jump, it, too, nearly always travels and is larger than the glissade faillie.

In both simple glissade and glissade faillie, the second foot follows to the floor very quickly after the landing of the first foot. The landing is "ta-ta," not "ta . . . ta." This timing is critical to the function of the step. Quick—as nearly immediate as possible—placement of the second foot to the floor is required so that the dancer has as much time as possible to plié to collect energy for the next step.

There is another kind of glissade that Mr. B gave that I did not know when I came to him. He called it glissade lente. It is a glissade, but it is an exception to most of the rules for doing the standard glissade and glissade faillie, so I will describe it last.

Simple Glissade to Fifth Position

The most important aspects of glissade to fifth for Mr. B were to jump off the floor, show second or fourth position in the air, bring the second leg down to the floor very quickly, and place the second foot cleanly into fifth position. By getting it there immediately with weight on the ball of that foot, the dancer has enough time to collect the needed energy in the plié for the right attack and dynamic for the next movement.

Glissade to the side closing fifth also starts in fifth position. The dancer begins to plié and then brushes directly side. She pushes off the floor and establishes second position in the air with both legs straight and both feet pointed, making sure the second leg remains turned out and does not move back behind her hips. The dancer avoids the tendency to let the legs open too wide or split up and then pull in to land, but instead should freeze the legs momentarily in the air in second. The freeze fosters the illusion that the dancer has stopped in midair, and it will help her to execute the jump with the correct look if she thinks of it that way. At a moderate to fast tempo the second position in glissade is only as wide as the feet are in the échappé relevé to second. Both pointes are level with each other a couple of inches or so off the floor, the hips are up on top of the legs, the shoulders are over the hips with the torso lifted and forward, and the weight is centered between the legs. The first foot lands toes first where the pointe is; the second leg is brought rapidly to the floor. The second foot makes fifth position by bringing the toes to the floor, aiming for and closing immediately to fifth. If necessary the toes slide lightly on the floor (nothing like a drag, no pressure; not a long slide into fifth); the heel is maintained forward and the knee side. The weight does not settle back on the heels but remains centered over the balls of both feet. If the next movement after glissade is a jump from both feet (e.g., soubresaut) or a pointe step off both feet (e.g., sous-sus), the dancer will keep her weight equally on the balls of both feet. However, in many combinations, the dancer will need to immediately transfer most of her weight to the second leg as she arrives in plié. The first leg in the glissade will again be the first leg in the next movement, leaving the floor first; the second leg will again push off the floor. For example, starting in fifth position croisé

left foot front, the dancer does glissade side to the right without changing her feet and assemblé brushing her right foot side, landing in fifth position croisé with her right foot front.

On occasion Mr. Balanchine took extra care to be sure that we knew the look we were trying to achieve in the air in glissade. When he was giving combinations with glissade side, for example, he might ask us to do échappé to pointe (or demi-pointe for the men) in second position. We were all reminded of the stretched legs at the correct distance from each other, pointed feet opposite each other and directly side, hips up over the legs, torso lifted with the shoulders over the hips and weight centered between the legs, which are important elements of this position. Lifting one of his female dancers a few inches off the floor, he would say, "This is the position we need."

Glissade forward is essentially the same, except that the dancer brushes directly front, usually with the front foot, bringing the pointe to the center line instead of directly side. In glissade back she brushes directly back, again bringing her working pointe to the center line. In both glissade forward and glissade back, the foot that pushes off the floor must also come in toward the center line so both pointes are on the center line, just as they are when she is standing on pointe in fourth. Again, the position is very similar to échappé to fourth on pointe: both knees straight; both feet pointed; and the distance between the feet about the same. However, she is a couple of inches off the floor, pointes equally off the floor. Her hips are lifted in the air; the dancer has made a real jump. The foot that brushes out lands toes first where the pointe is, neither kicking out nor pulling in. The second foot is brought immediately to the floor, toes first, and makes a clean, precise fifth plié with heels forward and the weight on the balls of the feet.

A simple and good combination to help the dancer work on perfecting the action of glissade closing fifth, including establishing second or fourth in the air, is glissade in a box followed by glissades side to side. Starting in fifth position with the right foot front, the dancer pliés on the last beat of the introduction and does glissade forward, landing in plié on count one, then glissade side to the right, changing feet to land in plié on count two with the left foot front. Now she does glissade back, landing in plié on count three, and glissade side to the left, changing feet, landing in plié on count four, right foot again front. Next she does three glissades to the side (moving right-left-right), changing feet each time and a soubresaut, finishing in fifth position plié with the left foot front, ready to repeat to the other side. We practiced this combination freezing the legs in fourth and second in the air and with such an accent in the landings in fifth that the plié would almost stop. By separating one glissade from the next and holding on to the plié in this exercise, rather than blending them together in the more usual way, the dancer further develops quickness. She shoots the first leg out, freezes both legs in position and rapidly brings the second leg down, and pauses in fifth position plié before starting

again. This is equally important in the glissades side to side, when the second foot of one glissade becomes the first foot of the next glissade. The dancer needs to show each and every fifth before moving on. Stopping sharply (abruptly), then starting quickly (suddenly), make each movement more articulate and clear.

This combination can be done with one "small arms" port de bras for the glissades in a box and another "small arms" port de bras for the three glissades to the side, arms lifting toward second as she jumps in the soubresaut, closing to fifth low in the plié. When Balanchine saw that we were flailing our arms or having some other problem, he might ask us to repeat the combination with the arms held in fifth low. When he saw that the glissades without port de bras looked acceptable, we might repeat the combination with the original small and controlled port de bras to see that we had it all together.

When the dancer remains en face, this exercise helps her build awareness of precise directions; when she does it with épaulement, the exercise incorporates practice in the changes of head, neck, and torso. The dancer meanwhile practices a small, quick glissade, establishing second and fourth in the air followed by soubresaut with the feet together in fifth. Needless to say, each "picture" had to display all the required characteristics. Remember, "Show me this and show me that."

Following glissade with jumps that push equally and simultaneously off both feet (such as soubresaut in the previous exercise or sous-sus in the following exercise) helps ensure that the dancer brings the second foot down to fifth, with the weight distributed equally over both feet. However, when glissade side is followed by a jump off one foot, such as assemblé in this exercise, or jeté, Mr. B, like other teachers, accepted a kind of "mini" glissade faillie. The dancer could bring the second foot down crossing a little over the first foot, but not passing it completely, not making a kind of "fourth." This is especially useful when the jump following the glissade travels side in the same direction as the glissade. The dancer starts in croisé,

Peter holding Deanna a couple of inches off the floor as she shows the position of the legs and feet in glissade side

right foot front, and does glissade front with a "small arms" port de bras opening and sous-sus, slightly lifting her arms and leading with the backs of the wrists on the relevé, then lowering her arms to fifth low on the plié; and then glissade back and sous-sus, repeating the "small arms" port de bras. Next she does glissade side, toward the front foot, or to the right, changing feet, and two assemblés side, brushing the right foot and then brushing the left foot. She does one "small arms" port de bras for the glissade and two assemblés. She finishes the phrase with sous-sus, again lifting her arms to a low second position leading with the backs of the wrists and, since she has ended in fifth position plié croisé, left foot front, her arms lowered to fifth low, she is ready to repeat the combination to the other side.

The "mini" glissade faillie could come after the glissade side before the assemblé. I have emphasized the general importance of fifth position to Mr. B, and I have been describing glissade closing to fifth. And yet, in a combination such as this one, Mr. B accepted the second leg going a little past fifth to an overcrossed position. If the timing was correct, if the weight was transferred quickly onto the second leg, if the plié was used, if both feet (but especially the second, which is often a problem) were placed toes first to the floor with the heel forward, if the second position in the air was clear—in short, if good form was otherwise adhered to—he would accept it. But if either foot slapped the floor, if the second foot and leg turned in, if the timing was off, if he couldn't see second—in short, if it looked like the dancer was simply sloppy and unaware—Mr. B most assuredly would stop the class or at least that dancer, describe what he had seen, and ask for better execution.

In some cases, crossing over to a kind of "mini" fourth adds something dynamic to the movement, makes it a little larger, and if good form is not lost in the process, he was happy to use those advantages to enhance the flow of movement. Dancers sometimes changed some details to advantage, and sometimes he wanted everyone to use an idea that came to him because of what one dancer did. Ballet

for him was a living art, something that was still in development, not only in new choreography but also in teaching. Gloria Govrin remembers him referring occasionally to company class as his laboratory. He was less interested in our reproducing a codified "perfect" step defined in the past than in what looked good and worked well at the moment.

Following glissade with assemblé contrasts the glissade, with the feet held in second or fourth in the air, with a jump in which they must be brought together to fifth as quickly as possible. Starting in fifth position croisé right foot front, the dancer can do glissade forward and assemblé front, then glissade back and assemblé back. She opens her arms from fifth low with a "small arms" port de bras in glissade and raises them gently, leading with the backs of the wrists in assemblé, lowering toward fifth low as she lands in plié. Notice that in both glissade front and assemblé front the dancer must be aware of brushing directly front; this applies equally to glissade back and assemblé back. Next she does glissade side to the right, changing feet, and an assemblé right followed by an assemblé left and soubresaut (or sous-sus). She opens her arms with a "small arms" port de bras in glissade, raises them gently, leading with the backs of the wrists in the two assemblés, lowering them to fifth low before the soubresaut, lifting them, backs of the wrists leading to a low second, and bringing them down to fifth low as she lands in plié. Again, she is ready to repeat to the other side. The dancer stays in the same croisé for the first half of the exercise and then uses changes of épaulement in the second half to end each jump in croisé.

When glissade closing fifth is followed by another glissade using the same leg to brush out or a brushing step such as assemblé, there is a tendency for it to blur into something like grand jeté traveling and a step or a long leap and a coupé. This is true of glissade to the front, side, or back. The timing and the fifth position plié tend to lose their clarity. In describing the glissade in a box exercise I noted that the landings in fifth were done with

---

DETAILS I OFTEN INSIST ON IN GLISSADE TO FIFTH POSITION:

1) open the legs precisely to second or fourth (as in échappé); do not let them split
2) show second or fourth in the air, knees straight, toes pointed and level, hips up
3) bring the second leg very rapidly to the floor to plié on it and gather energy for the next movement
4) place the toes of the second foot to the floor and into fifth position
5) show the plié, show the jump, show the contrast of levels

---

such emphasis that the plié seemed to pause for an instant. Similarly, when glissade front is followed by assemblé front or when glissade back is followed by assemblé back, it is important that the dancer really bring her second leg down to a clean fifth position plié and show it before the assemblé. Again, the plié can almost seem to pause for an instant. This clear articulation of bringing the leg, placing the foot in fifth plié, and then the brushing out is comparable in function and importance to the way Balanchine wanted battement tendu practiced (see page 62).

In fact, when Mr. B felt that our glissades needed a thorough clean-up, he divided the class into several groups and gave glissade side changing feet straight across the floor. It took about sixteen glissades and when we had all crossed the studio, he sent us back the other way. Each glissade was done with a change of feet and épaulement. We could do a "small arms" port de bras to open on the first glissade, another to close on the next, and so on. And we paused for a moment in each fifth position as we pliéd with resistance to help us practice full articulation of each movement.

Clear, precise enunciation of every step (word) in our ballet language was a critical part of the look Mr. Balanchine wanted us to have. He worked very consistently in class to help us develop quickness and lightness of the feet and legs, partly with exercises of this kind. When dancers have reached the level of skill required to display the clarity and articulation of movement he wanted in class, the steps will remain fully legible in performance.

Glissade Faillie

There is a very common tendency for glissade faillie to become in practice a simple step-step or run-run, which is not even ballet. Or the dancer leaps, kicking the second leg up and out, and then brings the second foot down crossing the first foot, a step across, to some, a kind of failli. This is especially true in performance, but it can also happen in class. None of these is glissade, none look like it, and none of them allow the dancer the time for the full plié needed to collect the energy that she will use in the next step. Consequently, Mr. B almost always gave glissade faillie or another ballet step (e.g., chassé), but not step-step or run-run, before a big jump. He gave glissade faillie in class, both to the front and to the side (and on rare occasions to the back) and corrected them carefully to make sure that they remained true glissades. The dancer must know exactly what is set and then make each movement, position, and gesture look like itself: When glissade is set, then glissade should be done.

To help us to understand how quickly the second leg should be brought to the floor in most glissades faillies (and glissades précipitées) and where our weight needed to be, Balanchine said, "Pretend the big toe on the first foot is very sore and you don't want to put any weight on it when landing." The second foot comes right in to relieve the first before *any* weight settles on it. The dancer centers her weight over the ball of the second foot, the foot and leg that collect the energy to push off the floor.

It may be useful in most ways to think of glissade faillie as a slower, more generously scaled version of the standard glissade or, more specifically, of the "mini" glissade faillie. Glissade faillie travels more, the plié is deeper, and the movement that follows is generally much larger. Glissade closing fifth is most often a small, quick jump that usually sets the dancer up for a movement that is similar in size and feeling, probably another allegro step; glissade faillie often precedes a really big jump or larger other step, such as développé relevé. However, as is usual with Balanchine, this is also not a "throw-away" preparation; it has a correct form that must be observed. Combinations with glissade faillie are generally done to slower tempos than those with the standard glissade closing to fifth or the "mini" glissade faillie.

Glissade faillie to the side is done by briskly brushing the first foot out, pushing off, and establishing second position in the air. However, the emphasis now being somewhat more on traveling, the dancer establishes the position in the air and moves sideways in it. After the first foot lands toes first, the second foot is brought immediately to the floor across and in front of the first foot and placed in an overcrossed fourth position with a deep plié and almost all of the weight on it. Glissade faillie through fourth does not freeze and hold fourth position in the air, because the second leg starts to come forward as soon as it has stretched and the foot has pointed. As the dancer lands, she does bring the second leg quickly down to the floor in fourth front, so the jump retains the flavor of glissade traveling forward. The second leg has most of the weight and is in a deep demi-plié.

Glissade Faillie Through Fourth, Traveling Diagonally Forward (Two Kinds)

Glissade faillie forward to fourth usually starts with the dancer in tendu croisé, left foot front, but on occasion might start in fifth. Traveling diagonally forward through fourth, she will plié on the front (left) leg and foot, so she starts by centering her weight over the ball of the front foot; this requires a full transfer of her weight as she moves her hips and torso forward over her supporting leg. As she pliés on the front leg, she brushes and throws her back (right) leg through first to fourth front, with her toes reaching the center line of her body. Her supporting leg pushes off the floor, stretches as she travels forward, and, as she lands toes first on the right foot, the second (left) leg is brought rapidly through first, toes skimming the floor, to the front, with her toes again reaching the center line of her body. She places her toes to the floor in fourth with resistance and brings her heel slightly forward and her knee side as she transfers almost all her weight onto this (left) leg, taking a good plié and using her thigh muscles. Depending on the tempo and the following step, the fourth may be slightly smaller or larger than a standard fourth, and, if the tempo is slow, the plié is deeper. This deeper plié is similar in effect to a shallow "kneeling" with the back knee bent and the back foot on demi-pointe with very little weight on it. The chest is forward and the hips are up and over the front leg and foot, where almost all the weight is centered. Glissade faillie traveling diagonally forward often precedes a large jump, such as grand jeté (see page 355) or cabriole effacée front (see page 374).

Mr. B gave another type of glissade faillie traveling diagonally forward through fourth that we often practiced with a développé relevé. This glissade has some resemblance to a hitch kick. It begins in the same way as the glissade faillie I have just described. After the dancer throws the first (right) leg front and immediately after pushing off the floor with the second leg, she brings the second (left) leg forward, in front of the first (right) leg. She makes a "small" fourth position in the air, the pointes of both feet on her center line but only eight to twelve inches apart; her hips and torso are lifted. She lands in fourth position plié, ta-ta, (right-left) again with the weight moving right away over the front (left) leg. After this kind of glissade Balanchine often gave a relevé with a développé with the right leg

Dana . . .

> *. . . and Peter in the air in glissade faillie through fourth, having stretched the back leg, are already bringing it forward.*

Dana . . .

> *. . . and Peter bringing the back (second) leg across and into an overcrossed fourth with the weight on it*

Dana landing from a glissade faillie that resembles a "hitch kick"

dancer moving through the air in second position; and it collects more power for a bigger next movement, because the plié can be deeper. Meanwhile, by holding to the correct timing and showing second in the air, the traditional vocabulary is enhanced, not abandoned, in the interest of energy and movement.

Glissade faillie traveling to the side can start in fifth croisé but more often starts in tendu croisé front. Having transferred her weight so it is centered over the ball of the front foot, the dancer rapidly brushes the back leg side, pushing off the supporting leg very strongly to pro-

Deanna's landing from a glissade faillie to the side; her weight is coming over the front foot as she collects power for the next jump. This is like a shallow "kneel."

into effacé front. As the dancer pliéd on the supporting leg, she placed the développé foot to the floor for another forward glissade faillie with the other foot front, landing left-right, and then a développé front with the left leg in croisé and so on.

Glissade Faillie Through Second, Traveling Side

When a dancer is asked to "move big," to really travel, in a combination that includes glissade to the side, she often brings her second foot well past fifth position in a true glissade faillie side, a larger step generally done to slower tempos than the "mini" glissade faillie (see page 333). Mr. B wanted a true glissade (second position in the air, second leg very rapidly down). The result was a more open, dynamic glissade done to the side that added to the dancer's ability to fill space in two ways: It does not close to fifth, so it travels more, the

vide the impetus for the glissade itself to travel, and establishes second in the air, but usually one that is slightly wider than in the standard glissade to fifth. She does this by throwing the first leg out a bit farther, and avoids the tendency to allow the second leg (the leg that pushes off the floor) to flick back or kick up. Since she is traveling to the side, she points the second foot where it comes off the floor and brings the entire shape, two pointes level in the air (the same shape she makes in échappé sauté to second but now a bit wider), with her. The second position travels in the air. She lands going through the first foot and starts into plié, bringing her second foot rapidly (remember the sore toe) and energetically down in front of her and across her center line while placing her toes to the floor and very lightly sliding her second foot to an overcrossed position (a kind of fourth). The dancer brings her heel somewhat forward, avoiding the tendency to let the second foot and leg turn way in, but the turnout should not be so fully maintained that she has little power for the following movement. She transfers her weight onto this leg and foot, meanwhile deepening her plié. Typical jumps to follow this glissade for which the dancer can often use extra power or more impetus are a huge traveling assemblé (with or without beats), a grand jeté à la seconde (see page 355), a large pas de chat (see page 348), a cabriole side (see page 374), a rond de jambe sauté or a relevé beginning with a brush, or a développé à la seconde. However, if she lets herself do step-step or a leap to the side and step (failli), the movement is not glissade and she will not have the time to plié deeply enough to collect the energy for such big jumps. Remember, "No bouncing!"

A typical combination with large jumps traveling continuously across the floor in the same direction is sauté in arabesque, step across, glissade faillie to the side, assemblé. Mr. Balanchine wanted to see all its energy going without interruption in the direction of travel. The dancer moves out in a traveling sauté in arabesque and brings the arabesque leg down, placing it well across the supporting leg into plié before pushing off for the glis-sade faillie. She moves through the air with the second leg brought along, showing second in the air. On landing from the glissade, the failli across is relatively large and the plié is fairly deep. Although this plié is low, it does not stop; the dancer does not look like "she hit a brick wall." It is a continuous plié down and up as she pushes off energetically and flies up and out, with the second leg immediately joining the first leg to make assemblé with the feet together.

Arms in Glissade Faillie and the Jumps That Follow

Since glissade faillie usually precedes a larger movement, the arms generally are used differently than they are for glissade closing to fifth, for which the dancer can use "small arms." In combinations including large, traveling glissade faillie Mr. B wanted the arms to really help the dancer get off the floor and travel in a way that makes the whole phrase, including the movement that follows, more dynamic. This comes from having the arms complement the thrust of the jump and coordinate their timing with the push off the floor. Often the arms slightly precede the jump, arriving in their extended line slightly ahead of the top of the jump, thus enhancing the illusion that the dancer stays in the air as well as adding to the boost they give as the dancer rises in the air. If the glissade faillie is in fourth front and is followed by a jump like cabriole effacée front (see page 374) or grand jeté with effacé arms (see page 355), or if the glissade faillie is side and the feet are picked up off the floor (as in pas de chat with the arms in fifth high, see page 349), the arms are often held in second on the glissade, close down through an overlapped fifth low on the failli, and are lifted up through an overlapped first and continue on to the designated position on the push-off of the jump. The arms are sometimes lifted so rapidly, they might have a slight feeling of being thrown to effacé or to fifth high respectively.

*Deanna starting her arms down toward fifth low
as her foot moves to an overcrossed fourth*

*Deanna crosses her wrists in fifth low so her arms
can move closer to her body to fifth high.*

If the glissade faillie is to the side and if the jump after the glissade starts with a brushing motion by the working foot to the side as in assemblé, the arms often have a slight feeling of swinging. The dancer starts in croisé in fifth position or tendu croisé front with the arms in second. She shifts her weight to the front foot on two of the preparation and pliés as she lowers her arms toward fifth low. As she brushes and pushes off for the glissade on the "and," she brings (with a little swing) her arms up to an overcrossed first, but not too high, with the elbows a little lower than the wrists. As she lands on the sec- ond foot, the arms lengthen and swing down, coor- dinating with the plié, and, as the working leg brushes up to the side, the arms continue by lifting up, still with a swinging feeling, to second. In mak- ing assemblé side, the arms can move to an ex- tended second position with the palms facing down in écarté. When the dancer does glissade faillie with cabriole side, she is usually en face rather than in écarté. In the brush of the cabriole, the arms swing down, up and out to the side to an extended second with the elbows stretched and the fingers extended, palms down. The dancer bends toward the leg after

*Deanna lifting her hands to fifth high as she
jumps in pas de chat*

*Deanna freezes her arms in fifth high at the
height of the jump.*

the beat. There is a swinging feeling as the arms move in on the glissade and down and out on the failli, and up to the side on the brush of the cabriole. When doing glissade faillie followed by a grand jeté to second or third arabesque, the arms may have a similar swinging feeling although they move on a different path. In such cases also, the port de bras helps the jump. The ports de bras for this kind of jump make use of the overcrossed and more extended movements and positions Balanchine taught that I describe on pages 146–160. They are not in the least stiff; they should be tension-free and very light in feeling. The elbows and wrists bend and stretch and extend, and the dancer does not lock herself into careful, little rounded shapes.

Many students have been systematically taught to work with very controlled arms that are almost stiff or tense and that contribute in only a limited way to the energy and flow of movement of their jumps (and of the rest of their dancing). Doing glissades, for example, they tend to want to leave their arms in second or hold them rigidly in a large rounded first; in glissade and assemblé in écarté they will tend to show stiff, rigidly held and tightly contained arms, or stiff arms wildly thrown up. The wide range of arm movement used by Balanchine in glissades and glissade combinations will be especially new to them. Just to close the arms to traditional first or fifth low in basic glissade might require some relearning. Then they are unfamiliar with the "small arms" used for many glissades closing to fifth, especially fast ones, and they have not practiced the overlapped positions; these are each a kind of smallness or compactness he used. At the beginning they are equally unfamiliar with Mr. B's bigness of movement, such as I have just described. Words like "swing" and "throw" are sometimes used by me to evoke energy, and expansiveness or weightlessness; the dancer should look like she is moving with abandon, but she does not therefore have to abandon her sense of form.

Before I came to the New York City Ballet I had been taught to try my best to be "little Miss Perfect" as a dancer. I had a certain perkiness and spontane-

1. *Dana's arms start down toward fifth low as she pliés for the glissade.*
2. *Dana's arms have swung in at the height of the glissade.*
3. *Dana's arms swing down and then up to écarté for a traveling assemblé.*
4. *Dana's arms swing down and out for a cabriole side.*

ity in manner, but everything about my actual dancing, my actual movement, was just so, small and contained. Learning to move big, learning to use what I might call "big arms," was totally new to me and therefore a challenge. Maybe that is why I am willing to risk the use of words like "swing" and "throw" to characterize the movement of the arms at certain times. Of course, I do not mean for any dancer to use her arms in a way that will make her look like a ball player or a circus performer. It is really only by being in total control that the dancer can appear to be totally free. If I say "throw" in class I actually mean for the dancers to move the arms very rapidly, without stiffness and tension, toward the designated line, but then smoothly slow somewhat into it. I do not intend that any dancer throw away the movement, the position, the line. If I get too much exuberance from my students, if I see any wild hands or arms, I am there to remind the dancers of good classical form. I can't be present when those who read this book try out ideas in it that are new to them—and I hope teachers and advanced and professional dancers do try. In general, I am willing to see such people try, and do, too much, rather than see them try nothing new at all. Remember, "No polite dancing!" Or, "More, I want to see more."

DETAILS I OFTEN INSIST ON IN
GLISSADE FAILLIE:

1) going side, show second position momentarily in the air; the entire shape travels; going front, bring second leg immediately front

2) bring the second foot to the floor with the correct timing, placing the foot to the floor—toes first and somewhat turned out—with weight immediately on it

3) land with a good plié but keep the movement flowing; don't lose the momentum

4) coordinate the arms with the jump

Glissade Lente

Glissade lente can be viewed as an extension of glissade faillie to the side, which is itself an extension of the simple glissade to fifth. Glissade lente is a grand, sweeping variant of glissade faillie that stays low to the floor and that includes very little jump or no jump at all. But this step travels a lot! That is, there's lots of distance, but no elevation. It also differs from traditional glissades in that it is a slow, legato movement often used in adagio, instead of a brisk one better adapted to allegro work.

On pages 216–218, I describe and provide illustrations of a valse lente that incorporates glissade lente and provides an example of the kind of sweeping port de bras that goes with it. These combinations show how Mr. B worked to extend the traditional vocabulary and stretch the traditional limits in the interest of a greater amplitude of beautiful movement, without losing the sense of good form that they provide.

The dancer starts in croisé left foot tendu front, left arm in an extended second, right arm extended side, with the hand at about head level. She starts by transferring her weight onto the tendu foot and pliéing on the left leg as she lowers her arms a little below second. She brushes the back (right) leg out to the side, her toes skimming the floor, remaining down in a low plié as she does so, which enables her to reach with her leg and foot and pointe far to the right, very far. Remaining down in plié, she pushes off her left foot onto and through her right foot; this push is much more lateral than vertical, and the dancer does not really jump off the floor. As she begins to transfer her weight to her right foot she stretches her left knee and points her left foot before bringing it across. Her hips come over her right leg, and her right arm sweeps out and up toward fifth high in a circular motion as she starts to bend her torso to the left. With her weight centered over the ball of the right foot, she brings the left foot, with her knee bending and her toes lightly sliding on the floor, past the right foot into plié in an overcrossed or extended "fourth." As she reaches and arrives in this extended fourth, her arms continuing their circular motion and her torso now bending back to her left, making them trail behind her hips, she reaches back with both arms (right arm through fifth high, left arm in an extended second). She transfers all her weight onto the ball of her left foot while staying down in a low plié. This is the glissade lente, but Balanchine generally continued the step by having the dancer extend her right leg as her pointed toes stretch out along the floor. Turning into profile, sweeping her right arm down and through to her front, and shifting her weight forward as her right leg and foot reach out in front of her, she pushes off her left leg. She transfers her weight to the right leg in plié, supporting hip over the ball of the right foot, torso erect over the hips, arms in first arabesque line as she lifts her left leg into arabesque. After establishing and showing the arabesque in plié, she straightens her supporting leg. To make an exercise, the teacher could give glissade lente to arabesque, followed by a step across and pas de basque to tendu croisé right foot front and repeat on the other side or follow the glissade lente to arabesque with a promenade in first arabesque and some additional adagio movements.

The low pliés used in glissade lente, with the weight transferring some distance from one foot to the other, both develop and require power and control to give the step the look it should have.

Emboîté

Mr. B made extensive use of emboîté in his ballets, and he gave the step regularly in class. His combinations included many kinds: to the front, to the back, small and quick, large and slower, staying in place, traveling, and turning. His choreography for children often included emboîté, because it is a simple ballet step they learn to do fairly early in their training. It makes good use of their high energy and their enthusiasm and excitement in performance. Larger emboîtés can have a festive, can-can flavor, and his choreography, especially to French composers, has a lot of them, for example in *La Source* (Delibes) and *Walpurgisnacht Ballet* and *Gounod Symphony* (Gounod), as well as in *Stars and Stripes*.

Perhaps because emboîté seems relatively easy to do, it often loses some of its qualities. Balanchine insisted on seeing the jump looking like itself at all times. "Emboîté is a jump, not a walk." In emboîté in place and in emboîté traveling without turning, the foot had to land on the floor on the center line of the dancer's body so she did not move from side to side. In all emboîtés the lifted foot crossed the center line of the dancer's body. Also, on the jump the feet passed very close together, and the dancer needed to keep her hips up and her legs turned out. When doing emboîté to the back, maintaining the turnout includes preventing the working knee from falling in; when doing emboîté to the front, it includes lifting the working heel.

Emboîté really is a jump, so the head changes level, although when emboîté is done fast, the jump is naturally smaller. However, emboîté cannot just

DETAILS I OFTEN INSIST ON IN GLISSADE LENTE:
1) stay low in plié, no rise and fall; the head does not change levels
2) use the plié and the push off the floor to travel
3) place the tips of the toes to the floor
4) although slow, the movement does not stop
5) the second leg is brought across right away; as in glissade faillie to the side, there is no delay, although the leg moves more slowly; do not let the step become lunge side, and then step across to fourth

DETAILS I OFTEN INSIST ON IN ALL
EMBOÎTÉS:
1) really jump—take the hips and torso with
   you into the air
2) be aware of where the feet should land,
   and get them there
3) catch the weight on the tips of the toes,
   and go through the foot
4) the working foot crosses the center line of
   the body

be a changing of the feet without changing levels. It should not look as if someone is sitting on the dancer's head or as if she fears her head is about to bump a low ceiling. The way the dancer's feet touch the floor on each landing is of utmost importance. The dancer controls the landing by catching her weight on the tips of her toes and going through the feet into a continuous plié; she makes sure that the heels do not fall to the floor.

Emboîté in Place

The dancer might tend to use less energy for emboîté in place because it does not travel. However, she should not do this, because she needs to get off the floor and replace the supporting foot on each jump. Also, she must be aware of bringing the working foot back under her center when landing on it and across her center line when lifting it.

Small, quick emboîtés in place need to make an instantaneous, clear picture with the working leg and foot even though they do not rise very high into the air. As she pushes off the floor in emboîté front, the dancer thinks of instantly pointing her feet and toes and of lifting her heel as she raises the working thigh sharply to about forty-five degrees. She bends her lower leg to bring her foot across the center line, showing the crossing of the working leg and foot. As she pushes off the floor in emboîté back, the dancer thinks of taking her knee and thigh back. If the tempo allows, she needs to freeze the position. If the tempo is very fast, she may lift her working foot only to coupé front or back, or a little higher, and show it there, even if only for an instant. In landing, the dancer brings her working foot down to the floor on the center line of her body under her hips so she stays in place, not moving side to side nor forward or back. She catches herself on the tips of her toes and goes through her foot into plié, but keeps her weight forward over the ball of her foot so her heel generally remains just off the floor in these fast, quick emboîtés.

In larger, slower emboîtés in place, the dancer jumps higher into the air and does a fuller, slower plié. She needs a good push off the floor from the plié as she lifts her hips up, taking herself into the air. Balanchine wanted the pointed feet to pass each other in the air to ensure a high jump, rather than just a change of feet on or near the floor. Practicing large emboîtés helps develop power in the legs and feet, just as practicing small emboîtés develops quickness in the feet. In large emboîtés to the front, the working leg is lifted to attitude, with the thigh at about ninety degrees. The dancer thinks of lifting her knee and, most importantly, of lifting her heel up because it helps maintain the turnout. The thigh stays in front of the working hip; the working foot crosses over the center line of the body. In large emboîté to the back, the dancer lifts the working knee and thigh up to about forty-five degrees, while keeping the heel down to help maintain the turnout. Again, because the dancer really jumps, the feet pass each other in the air. The working foot crosses over the supporting leg, with the heel lower than the knee. Both to the front and to the back, there is time to show the jump and to show the position with the foot crossed over and the leg lifted. The landing is the same as for small emboîtés, except that now she goes through her foot more slowly. In slow emboîtés the feet and thighs resist the plié, helping to control the landing. The plié must be

DETAILS I OFTEN INSIST ON IN
EMBOÎTÉ IN PLACE:

1) jump! and pass the feet in the air, especially in slow emboîtés

2) present the working leg and foot in a clear, articulate coupé front or back, or a low attitude that is really front or in back, with the working foot across the center line

3) when there is time, freeze the working foot in small emboîtés

4) the pliés are controlled; the heels don't hit the floor

5) in emboîté in low attitude lift the working thigh up in back, working heel up in front

---

fairly deep, controlled, and continuous. The heel may in some cases lightly touch the floor, depending on the tempo and the dancer's body, but the weight should still be kept over the ball of the foot. As she lands, she keeps the hips up and the chest lifted up. When doing emboîtés to the back it is also important that the chest be slightly forward. Remember the boxer in the ring.

Mr. B typically gave exercises for practicing emboîté in place with the dancers en face and at very fast or very slow tempos. He also gave them at a moderate 4/4 tempo and combined small and large jumps to help us cultivate musicality and control. For example, he could give two sets of three small emboîtés landing on counts one, "and," two, pause; counts three, "and," four, pause; then four large emboîtés in place, landing on each count. Such exercises for emboîté in place could be done en face with emboîtés front and back. We might use one "small arms" port de bras for the two sets of faster emboîtés, ending in a low second. The backs of the wrists led the arms slightly up on the large jumps, and the softened elbows and insides of the wrists led them back down on the descents and landings.

Emboîté Traveling

Emboîté traveling (but not turning) is generally done forward or back on the diagonal. The basic technique for the step is the same as for emboîté in place. The working foot is across the center line in the air, the thigh is lifted in front or in back of the working hip, the working foot and leg are shown in the air, and so on. The key difference is that the working foot lands in front of or in back of the dancer so that she travels as well as rising into the air. The working foot is brought down on the center line, not underneath the dancer, but at a distance. The dancer can think of it as jumping along a tightrope. However, the jump is usually more up than out; the dancer pushes strongly off the floor to take her hips and torso into the air as she moves forward or back. Although Mr. B used emboîtés at medium tempos that had only slight elevation, but traveled and covered large spaces in some ballets (e.g., in the "Snow" scene in *The Nutcracker*, and in the *Walpurgisnacht Ballet*), we did not regularly practice them in this form in class. The more challenging emboîté exercises are the ones at the extreme tempos: those that are very fast that demand quick toes and feet, or those at slow tempos that demand good elevation and controlled landings.

Mr. B's exercises for emboîté traveling on the diagonal often included going forward and back in a combination like this one, which would be done at a slow to moderate tempo. Starting, for example, in fifth position croisé, left foot front, the dancer does two sets of three faster emboîtés in attitude front, traveling diagonally forward, followed by one set of three and two slower emboîtés in attitude back, traveling back on the other diagonal, and then repeats on the other side. In other words, the dancer does emboîté traveling forward, landing in effacé (left arm in fifth high, right arm in second), with her right leg lifted in front on count one, then emboîté traveling landing in croisé with her left leg lifted in front on "and," then emboîté traveling landing in effacé with her right leg lifted in front on count two, and pause. She repeats, keeping the same arm positions on counts three, "and," four, left leg, right leg, left leg. Next, she does emboîté traveling diagonally back, changing her direction so her body is effacé back. She lands on her left foot; her right foot is in a low back attitude, and she could open her arms to second position with the wrists flexed and the palms facing out. She does two more quicker emboîtés traveling back to finish the set, left foot up on "and," right foot up on count six, then two large, slower emboîtés traveling back, landing on counts seven, eight (left foot up, right foot up). She coupés to jump, landing on count one with her left foot up in effacé attitude front, passing her arms through first to raise her right arm to fifth high and open her left arm to second. She has traveled an inverted "V" and is now ready to repeat the sequence to the other side. As in any emboîté she must get off the floor, and in this case she must travel to make the "V" visible.

Another exercise that Mr. B liked to give combined emboîté front, traveling diagonally forward, with jeté (see page 351). Starting left foot front in fifth position croisé, the dancer does three quick emboîtés (lifting her left leg, right leg, and left leg to forty-five degrees), with her arms coming from second into an overcrossed first. She steps diagonally forward toward fourth croisé into plié on count three with her arms lengthening down past fifth low; then, as she throws her leg out to the side for the jeté, her arms swing out to an extended à la seconde, stretched with the palms turned down (an example of Mr. B using a freer, jazzier port de bras within classical limits). She lands on four on her right foot with a change of épaulement. She then does the other side. This exercise can be done to a brisk 4/4 with the three emboîtés on counts one-and-two followed by a pause after the third emboîté, step on count three, jeté on "and," land on count four. It can also be done to two measures of a waltz with the emboîtés on counts one-two-three, step four, jeté in the air on count five, and land on count six. The emphasis in these emboîtés is more

on a sharp attack than on covering space, although they do travel.

Another exercise he gave combined emboîté with fondu relevé and jeté and was done to two measures of a 4/4. The dancer starts in fifth position croisé left foot front and does three quick emboîtés, traveling diagonally forward, lifting the left leg, the right leg, and the left leg on counts one, "and," two (arms from fifth low through an overcrossed first to croisé, right arm up), and steps onto the left leg on count three (upraised arm opens out to second, both arms to fifth low). On count four she does fondu relevé développé the right leg in effacé front (arms through an overcrossed first to effacé), step moving into plié on the right on count five (upraised arm opens out to second), fondu relevé développé left on count six in croisé front (right arm lifts to fifth high, arms now in croisé), step moving into plié on the left on count seven (upraised arm lowers through first), and jeté right with change of épaulement on count eight (the arms swing down and out to an extended second). She then does the other side. These emboîtés are a traveling jump with a can-can flavor.

DETAILS I OFTEN INSIST ON IN EMBOÎTÉ TRAVELING:
1) change levels, get off the floor
2) travel
3) the step should look light and lively, fun to do

Emboîté Turning

In emboîté turning, the dancer often travels on the diagonal, but also travels directly to the side as well as in a circle. When traveling on the diagonal or to the side, the dancer traditionally spotted the corner or the wings. With Balanchine, she usually spots front. Mr. B liked to joke that when the dancer looks side to spot, the audience will think there is something fascinating in the wings and focus their eyes there. Better, therefore, to spot front and keep the attention of the public focused on what they actually can see—the dancer in particular, the dancer's face and her beautiful dancing. When doing emboîté in a circle the dancer generally spots the next point on the circle.

The working foot is presented each time in coupé front or coupé back as the dancer lands. She needs to be aware of maintaining the turnout and keeping her hips up and the working knee drawn to the side, as well as landing through her foot (toes touching first, no banging down by the heel). And she needs to remember while traveling and turning that emboîté is a jump and that she must really get off the floor each time. Traditionally, dancers had done a series of emboîtés with the working foot usually in coupé front, but Mr. B liked to make combinations using both coupé front and back as the dancer turned. He also tried a variety of ports de bras, notably including one with the arms extended à la seconde with flexed wrists, which he liked to use when the dancer was turning in coupé back.

Mr. B often gave emboîté turning that traveled straight to the side as well as the more traditional emboîté turning on the diagonal. Spotting front, we often did four in coupé front (two turns) and then four in coupé back (two turns). He watched to make sure we jumped and landed lightly as we traveled directly side, maintained the turnout, presented the foot in coupé, and spotted front. In the "Rubies" section of *Jewels*, the male principal exits alternating one coupé back and one coupé front doing emboîté turns faster and faster (in this choreography keeping the knees together and really overcrossing each coupé position) and traveling into the wing. In class Mr. B could have given the same combination (with normal coupé positions) traveling directly side. The dancer jumps up and onto the right foot and raises the left foot to coupé back, doing a half turn. Then she jumps up and onto her left foot and raises her right foot to coupé front, doing another half turn. She continues across the floor spotting front, usually with the arms held in second with the wrists flexed.

An exercise I learned from my SAB colleague Madame Tumkovsky combines emboîté turning and emboîté traveling forward and back on the diagonal with assemblé and ballonné (see page 372). The dancer starts in fifth position croisé, right foot front. She does four turning emboîtés all in coupé front, traveling directly side to the right, raising her left foot, right foot, left foot, and right foot. Next, she does three ballonnés in effacé front landing on her left foot, traveling diagonally forward (downstage right), then assemblé brushing to effacé front, but with the working foot then closing to fifth back in croisé left foot front. Continuing on the same diagonal, she does four emboîtés in attitude front traveling forward, raising her right leg, left leg, right leg, left leg. Her arms are in fifth high, and her head remains in the croisé line. Then she does three emboîtés in low attitude to the back, traveling back on the same diagonal, raising her right leg, left leg, right leg, ending with assemblé to the back closing back, landing in fifth position croisé left foot front, arms closing to fifth low. She is now ready to do the other side. On the first emboîté back, the arms open and extend out; the left arm is extended diagonally up, with the palm facing out and down, and the right arm is extended à la seconde with the palm down. The head is slanted right and tilted up, with the gaze directed up and out past the left hand. She is in a kind of effacé line.

As I marked Tumi's exercise for myself in order to write it for you, I noticed that for the three emboîtés back, I swept my arms gently back—they were no longer side, in line with my shoulders—and I adjusted the line of my head slightly to harmonize with my arms. I was reminded that in class some dancers might have done the very same thing or altered the shape in some other subtle way. Mr. B looked at these individual contributions to his exercises and very often accepted them. Sometimes he adopted them for certain others or for the women or for the men or for everyone. Side did have a precise definition, and a leg or an arm to the side had to fit the definition, but if a dancer subtly altered a port de bras with an awareness that made the result as interesting, as harmonious as, or even more pleasing than, what he had set, Mr. B was very often willing to accept what she showed. This was most unlikely if the dancer had simply let an arm drift off the designated line without her being aware of it. Don't forget, "You must remember all two arms, dear."

DETAILS I OFTEN INSIST ON IN EMBOÎTÉ TURNING:
1) jump into the first emboîté, keeping the working knee back
2) show a clear coupé position
3) spot front

Pas de Chat and Gargouillade

Mr. B said, "Pas de chat must be suspended. It must be a jump, not a walk." Like emboîté, pas de chat can lose its dynamism.

There are many kinds of pas de chat, and in Mr. B's classes we did a variety of them. Since they are all acceptable, the dancer must know which one she is doing and then do it so it looks like itself. For any pas de chat to look like itself, it is important to remember that *chat* is French for cat. The action of the legs and especially of the feet in landing must recall the delicacy and quiet with which a stalking cat places its feet to the floor as it walks or even runs. Mr. B never accepted sloppy feet in class in any movement, but his attention to proper placement of the feet to the floor (tips of toes first, heel forward, no hitting or banging) was perhaps even sharper in pas de chat.

Gargouillade is an unusual jump in that it is rarely if ever done by men. Although he used gargouillade in his ballets, Mr. B did not give it very often in class. When he did give gargouillade or pas

de chat, the men usually were given another step, such as brisé or sissonne battue.

The kind of pas de chat that is very commonly seen has the dancer freeze her legs in the air and then land, with the feet coming to the floor almost or actually simultaneously. We practiced this version, and it is used in some of the ballets. However, Balanchine usually gave pas de chat with the feet landing one after the other. The legs could instantly freeze in the air or move continuously. When Violette Verdy, a dancer trained at the Paris Opéra, joined NYCB, she often did a pas de chat with the first leg doing a sharp développé side and the second leg immediately making passé. The picture she made in the air must have intrigued Mr. B because he gave it to her in several roles he made for her, and then the rest of us learned how to do it.

I was also less familiar with doing pas de chat with the legs moving continuously. The dancer starts to push off the floor with both feet, but picks up the first knee and continues by pushing off the floor strongly with the second foot and picking up that knee. When the tempo allows, the jump can be large, with the knees lifting almost to ninety degrees and the feet tucking quite high under the hips, but it can also be small, with the knees lifting only to about forty-five degrees. In both cases it is important to really jump; even in small, quick pas de chat, the head changes levels, the hips are lifted off the floor. Once the dancer is in the air, the legs continue moving. The first leg lifts to the designated height, quickly followed by the second leg. When the second leg reaches its height, the first leg is already part of the way down. The first foot, which had a much smaller part in pushing off the floor, lands first, and then the second foot is placed *toes first* into fifth (or an overcrossed kind of fourth) position. The dancer, of course, maintains the turnout in both legs, but she needs to be especially careful with the second leg, avoiding the tendency to let the knee fall in while she is in the air and/or the heel slip back when landing.

In describing the way in which pas de chat should be done, and also how the dancer visualizes the energy in the step, I have again indicated that since it is a jump, the hips should be lifted off the floor. One of my teachers at SAB was Madame Felia Dubrovska, a very grand lady, and quite proper. She could not bring herself to say "behind" or "bottom" or "derrière" and not even the somewhat euphemistic "hips," which I have been using. I remember her correcting pas de chat and saying to us, "Lift this heavy place," as she gestured somewhere toward the back of her skirt. She sure got the message across . . . and remained her very dignified self.

When Balanchine gave pas de chat with the legs freezing to make a picture in the air, the jump started the same way. The knees picked up and the legs moved as quickly as possible to the point when the second leg is at its highest and the first leg has started down. At this point both legs freeze in place, making a picture in the air. The first foot generally lands a bit ahead of the second foot, but at fast tempos the feet might land together.

In pas de chat with développé, the dancer also makes a picture in the air, but a different one. The jump is usually done going straight side or on the diagonal, with the dancer lifting the foot in fifth (or fourth) back first. It again starts in the same way, but as soon as the first foot leaves the floor, the knee instantly and as rapidly as possible lifts and the lower leg unfolds in a développé out to the side, to a bit less than ninety degrees. This is how Violette did the step, but some dancers now show the leg parallel to the floor, at ninety degrees. The second foot arrives in passé as the first leg stretches out in the développé and the dancer freezes the legs in this position. As she descends, the first leg extends diagonally toward the floor and she lands in fifth position or a kind of overcrossed fourth with no change in the feet, often landing with the feet reaching the floor simultaneously.

Gargouillade begins with the dancer lightly brushing the first (front) foot to the side, and she immediately starts a fast double rond de jambe en dehors. As the first leg is starting its double rond, the second leg, continuing its push off the floor, im-

mediately does a fast double rond de jambe en dedans. The knees are raised only to about forty-five degrees. The step happens in the air; the dancer must get off the floor so she finishes the ronds with both legs, especially the first, before she lands. The dancer slightly extends the first leg before landing, and the second leg immediately follows into fifth position or is placed across the first leg into a kind of overcrossed fourth.

An exercise combining simple pas de chat on the diagonal and in a circle could be done with music to a moderate to brisk tempo and was usually set with the legs continuously moving in the air. The dancer starts in tendu, left foot front in croisé. She begins by transferring her weight to the tendu leg and does four pas de chat, traveling diagonally to the right, lifting her right (back) foot first and closing her left (second) foot to fifth front, keeping her right arm in first and her left arm in second. Next, she does four pas de chat to the right in a small circle, continuing to lift her right foot and close her left in fifth front and also continuing with the same arms. The combination is done twice or more, until the dancer has crossed the studio on the diagonal.

To a slower tempo, Mr. B often combined a simple pas de chat using continuous movement of the legs and some other jumps. The dancer starts in fifth position croisé with her left foot front. She does glissade faillie side to the right, ending overcrossed, and pas de chat to the side to the right, with her legs continuously moving and her arms in fifth high, landing one-two in a kind of fourth. The dancer must take particular care that she really gets off the floor, maintains the turnout in the second leg, and places the second foot, toes first, carefully and beautifully to the floor as she lowers into a good plié. She brushes her right foot side for a traveling assemblé to the right in écarté, landing in a big plié, bringing her arms to fifth low, and inclining her body to the left ("picking up the laundry"). She does sissonne ouverte to the right, opening her arms through fifth high, to land in first arabesque in profile (in effect "delivering the laundry" she picked up). She brings her working leg to the back for pas de bourrée, ending in sous-sus with the left foot front in croisé, and finishes with three entrechats six. He might also give one entrechat six and have the dancer step back through plié and tendu her right foot to croisé front. With either finish she is now prepared for the other side.

Here is an exercise that combines simple pas de chat to the side with entrechat quatre. It could be done with the legs freezing momentarily in the air (typically to a slightly slower tempo) or with the legs constantly moving (typically to a very fast tempo). In both cases it incorporates a change of épaulement with each pas de chat. Each pas de chat begins with the front foot instead of the commonly used back foot. The dancer lands from each pas de chat one-two, going through the first foot and placing the second foot, toes first, into fifth position an instant later. Starting in fifth position croisé, right foot front, she does pas de chat to the right, changing her feet (and épaulement) so she lands in croisé with her left foot front. This is followed by an entrechat quatre. She repeats the first two steps to the other side. Now she does four pas de chat (each time changing feet, always moving toward the front foot), one to the right, then to the left, another to the right and to the left, changing her feet and épaulement on each. The exercise can now be repeated. For this kind of brisk combination Mr. B might have us leave the arms in a low second but maintain life through a gentle lift of the wrists on the jumps and a lowering on the landings.

I do not recall any exercises with Mr. B that included pas de chat in reverse. But I have often seen Madame Tumkovsky give pas de chat combinations to the back, so on occasion I do, too. It's good for students' minds and good for their technique. In the standard pas de chat to the front, the back foot is picked up first; the front foot is picked up second and closes front. In the standard pas de chat to the back the front foot is picked up first and moves diagonally back; the back foot is picked up second and closes behind in fifth back.

One of her exercises starts with the dancer in fifth position croisé left foot front, right arm in first,

left arm in second. The combination is pas de chat front, pas de chat back, three pas de chat front, royale. Picking up her right (back) foot first, she does pas de chat to the front, moving diagonally forward, closing her left foot in fifth front in plié on count one. She straightens her legs on "and" and pliés on count two. Picking up her left foot first, she does pas de chat to the back, traveling diagonally back, placing her right foot in fifth back in plié on count three. She switches her arms to the back—that is, the right arm is opened to second, and her left arm closes to first. Again, she straightens her legs on "and" and pliés on count four. Next, she does three pas de chat to the front, traveling diagonally forward, each time picking up her right foot first and closing her left foot to fifth front, and, again, her arms switch as she moves forward to right arm in first, left arm in second. She does a royale, opening her right arm to the side, and is now ready for the other side. The entire combination is then done in reverse.

Mr. B made a combination with gargouillade for the "Marzipan" dance in *The Nutcracker* that I sometimes give in class. In the ballet the dancer starts left foot front in fifth croisé. She does sissonne faillie to the left, her right foot coming across in front of her left foot with her weight on it. Her right arm moves to first and her left arm to second. She steps (coupé) onto her left foot, lightly brushing her right foot side, immediately starting her fast double rond de jambe as she pushes off the left foot and does a fast double rond de jambe with the left leg. Her right arm opens out to the side. She lands right-left with her left foot front in fifth position croisé, her arms remaining in a low second. She repeats the combination three times; I usually give it three times and switch to the other side with sous-sus entrechat six. The sissonne faillie is smaller, presenting the next step, the larger gargouillade.

The first variation in *Divertimento No. 15* also includes a combination with gargouillade. The dancer can start right foot front in fifth position croisé. She does four emboîtés in place, jumping and landing on her left foot, right foot in coupé front, then jumping and landing on her right foot, left foot in coupé back, and repeating. She coupés onto her left foot and turns her body as her right foot brushes out to make grand jeté in first arabesque, going directly side to the right. She coupés behind the right foot onto her left foot as she faces front, brushing her right foot out to immediately do gargouillade, ending in fifth position left foot front. This combination alternates side to side.

One of Balanchine's most distinctive ballets is *Square Dance*. The choreography is based on classical steps, but with an overlay of American square dance manners, gestures, etc. In the original production and for a number of years it used Italian baroque music played on the stage and a square dance caller using calls he wrote for the ballet. As the dancers performed, his voice rang out:

> Lonesome gent, hurry up quick
> All right, Pat, here comes Nick.

The caller was talking to the original leads, Patricia Wilde and Nicholas Magallanes. The ballet was built on Pat's exceptional technique, which featured unsurpassed speed and clarity in beats, jumps, and turns. The caller noticed:

> Make your feet go wickety-wack
> All the ladies do the same.

DETAILS I OFTEN INSIST ON IN PAS DE CHAT AND GARGOUILLADE:

1) get the hips up into the air
2) maintain the turnout of the second leg
3) place the toes first to the floor in landing; do not hit the floor with a full, flat foot, especially the second foot
4) in gargouillade make fast, small double ronds de jambe en l'air with both legs, really showing the ronds of the first leg

---

Pat made her feet go "wickety-wack" all through the ballet, and one of her steps was gargouillade. She probably did more gargouillades than any dancer ever had in one ballet, but as the caller saw, Mr. B sometimes had *all* the ladies do the same.

Jeté

Although jeté can be done in all three directions, in class Mr. B usually gave it to the side, moving both forward and back. Simple jeté is a very familiar step; everyone starts to learn it early in training. But for me it became almost a new step in Mr. B's class.

Most of my teachers had taught me to brush side, jump a little, and land in coupé. Some had suggested holding the legs in second for an instant in the air before landing in coupé. I generally landed a short distance to the side and a little forward of where I started. I had been allowed to settle for something that worked and that basically looked like a jeté, but it had lost some of its specific jeté character. In contrast, Mr. B kept after us until we showed him the correct form. He wanted to see a jump in which the dancer landed on her center line, on the same line from which she took off. She should not travel to the side at all. Therefore, as in simple assemblé, the working leg brushes side and is brought back under the dancer's center, to the supporting leg, but in jeté the supporting leg often makes coupé *in the air*.

Balanchine's other new idea for me about jeté was a jump I call "jeté cambré." He didn't really have a name for it, but we never had any trouble recognizing what he wanted, from his description and gestures. It actually reverses the impetus from the throw of the leg as the dancer changes the direction of the movement as she goes up in the air. His insistence on a true, simple jeté that did not move to the side was an improvement over the informal step I had been doing when I came to him, and his jeté cambré was even better.

Simple Jeté (Including Battu)

As the dancer pliés, the working foot brushes side from fifth or from coupé back or front. The working leg is thrown, with the knee stretched and the foot pointed, a little lower than forty-five degrees (or much lower if the tempo was very fast) as the dancer pushes off the floor with the supporting foot virtually simultaneously. The plié, the throw of the working leg, and the push off the floor all need to be coordinated. When the dancer is just off the floor, she starts to bring the working leg in to her center line, where it joins the supporting leg. In assemblé the feet become "glued" together in fifth position in the air, soubresaut position. In jeté the supporting leg stretches, and it immediately makes coupé back as the working leg comes in front of the dancer's center (coupé front when the working leg goes in back). At slow to moderate tempos the dancer will be able to make coupé in the air before landing; at very fast tempos the dancer may not even be able to completely stretch her supporting leg and will only be able to make coupé on the landing. Thus the tempo and the look desired determine if the "picture" of the dancer in coupé is made. The coupé position is held as the dancer lands and as she goes through her supporting foot (the foot that was brushed).

When she is doing one jeté or a series of jetés, the dancer brushes out as she starts to come up out of plié; as usual she generally does not stop the plié in coupé and never does so when the leg is extended to the side. The plié, the brush, and the push off the floor are parts of a coordinated, continuous movement. She brushes directly side or a little in front of à la seconde, but certainly not toward the back. As soon as her working leg is extended in the brush (she is now

in the air), she generally brings it rapidly back in to the supporting leg. When it is a jeté that really travels in any direction, it can be set so she holds the legs opened and stretched in a kind of minisplit in second or fourth in the air, showing that picture, and making coupé only as she lands. In all landings the dancer lands on the tips of her toes and goes through her foot. Her weight is maintained forward, both on the floor and in the air, by keeping her torso over her hips (which are pulled up) and her chest lifted and forward; it's the boxer-in-the-ring feeling.

Mr. B gave jeté at a range of tempos. Even when doing a series of fast jetés, the dancer must remember that it is a jump; she must change levels,

Peter does a large simple jeté, showing the coupé position in the air.

get off the floor at least a little. Jetés were sometimes given in slow combinations with temps levé (see page 367), cabriole back (see page 374), or assemblé side, front or back. The step was the same, but as the tempo slowed, the challenge shifted from quickness and clear articulation to power and control while maintaining clarity of movement.

Balanchine gave an exercise to a rapid 4/4 that combined slow and fast jetés: glissade, jeté, glissade, jeté, jeté. The dancer lands from the first glissade on count one and from the first jeté on count two. She lands from the second glissade on count three, and follows with two quick jetés, landing on the "and" before count four and on count four. It was essential in this exercise to practice the most important thing: to be on time. In fact, the first three landings and the last were each followed by a very brief "pause" to separate the landing from the next jump: glissade, "pause," jeté, "pause," glissade, "pause." The "almost pauses" are a little like the fifths in some tendu exercises at the barre in which the dancer must show the fifth as clearly as she shows the pointe. This is an example when the plié could seem to stop with the working foot in coupé. The next two jetés were very quick and were done without separation. To keep the timing in the two quick jetés the dancer needs to think she is jumping down to land on "and" and count four, rather than thinking she is jumping up to hang in the air. And, again, there is a brief pause on count four.

This exercise is designed around the matter of timing. Mr. B also watched for the second most important thing: how we looked on time. After the dancer lands in coupé from the jeté and pauses, she does glissade. It is much easier to do a quick glissade from fifth than from coupé. No matter: He wanted to see a true glissade with second (knees stretched, feet pointed and level, correct spacing) established and shown in the air, a little travel to the side, and a quick second leg. Then he wanted the jetés to stay in place: no movement side to side. And all through, feet to the floor toes first, good turnout, etc. There was one "small arms" port de

bras for the entire combination, but the changes in épaulement were more detailed. The dancer started in croisé and changed épaulement on the landing from the first jeté and kept it for the following glissade. On the next jeté she started to change, but there is really no time, so it's more of a feint or a hint in the head and upper torso than a real change. On the last jeté she returns to the line she established on the first jeté. This is a very simple exercise, with very simple steps. Mr. B made it a challenge, and interesting, in a company class. A beautiful little dance. "We are entertainers."

Jeté battu was important to Mr. Balanchine, shown in part by its appearance in the finales of so many ballets. The dancer begins and ends the step in the same way as the jeté simple. She gets off the floor and usually beats as close to her center as possible, both legs beating and both feet crossing, not just scratching the heels, before landing in coupé. When doing jeté battu the dancer must be especially aware of making the coupé as she lands and showing it before moving on to the next step.

The universally known combination glissade, jeté battu, brisé volé front, brisé volé back (see page 365) is based on two steps with something in common; Mr. B used it to enhance our awareness of their differences. Jeté battu and brisé volé both include batterie and both end in coupé, but they should not look at all alike. Jeté brushes side; brisé volé brushes front and back. In jeté the beats are done almost under the hips; in brisé volé the beats are done in front and in back of the dancer. Jeté stays virtually in place; brisé volé can travel. This is a case where clear enunciation is required to make the steps legible. An exercise useful in the same way combines assemblé battu and brisé (see page 330).

There is a Balanchine "staple" I often give; it's in *Serenade* and in the finale of *Symphony in C.* The combination is sauté in arabesque, step, jeté battu. The dancer can start in fifth croisé right foot front and does a small développé with the right leg stepping to the side as she pliés on her supporting leg, turning her body to move into second arabesque in profile—Mr. B liked to see a deep plié and a long, reaching step out. She does sauté in second arabesque really traveling side, brings her arabesque leg down across in front of her supporting foot—he watched to see that we placed our toes and foot to the floor—and does jeté battu changing épaulement; he always let us know if it traveled too much on the jeté to the side rather than remaining on or very near the same line. He really wanted us to show the ending in coupé back, which we did by overcrossing the coupé (almost making a low attitude back, overcrossed). As she steps after the sauté, she needs to absorb the impetus to the side so her jeté battu does not travel. It might even feel to her that the jeté moves back in the other direction. From the landing of the jeté she stays down in plié and extends the left leg out as she begins the other side. This combination zigzags side to side, and the sauté can be more of a "chug" than a flying jump off the floor (see page 369).

DETAILS I OFTEN INSIST ON IN JETÉ:
1) always show coupé in landing and when requested in the air
2) don't travel to the side
3) brush side, not behind à la seconde

Jeté Cambré (Including Battu)

The aspect of the last combination that most clearly marks it for me as Balanchine's is the implicit reversal of direction when the dancer does jeté after she steps across. There is an energy in those reversals that intrigued him. Also, it is missing the usual linking step, glissade; the combination is *not* sauté in arabesque, step, glissade, jeté. When I guest-teach I often find that such combinations, even when the steps are simple, are unexpectedly hard for students not used to Mr. B's ideas. His special jeté that I call "jeté cambré" is a bit of a challenge because it really reverses direction, as well as requiring the dancer to throw her legs to effacé back and establish an effacé line in the upper body as she rises into the air.

Mr. B usually gave us jeté cambré in combinations, although it could be given from tendu croisé front, with the dancer transferring her weight to the tendu foot as she pliés. As the dancer pliés she starts to turn her hips and upper body to the other diagonal in order to make effacé, simultaneously brushing the working leg toward her back. As she continues to turn to effacé she throws the working leg back in effacé, to about forty-five degrees, pushes off the supporting leg, and throws it back to meet the working leg, meanwhile arching up and over. Already as she turns to effacé and pushes off the floor she knows the spot on which she is aiming to land. Although the step can be done without a beat, we nearly always included one in this effacé back line. On landing, the working leg is brought across her center line. As she goes through her foot into plié, she makes an overcrossed low attitude back with the original supporting leg.

As the dancer turns to effacé she opens her arms to an extended line to the side. It is the same port de bras that is typically seen in brisé volé to

---

DETAILS I OFTEN INSIST ON IN JETÉ CAMBRÉ:
1) make sure you place your toes to the floor as you take a good plié before the push off the floor
2) switch the body to effacé as the first leg is thrown to effacé back
3) don't travel sideways
4) show the beat
5) land through the foot and really cross the foot in coupé back (almost a low attitude)

Grand Jeté

In grand jeté Balanchine wanted to see the dancer suspended in the air making a high-flying picture: legs extended, both feet at the same level, upper body lifted up over the hips, arms and head in the designated line. "Stay and then land." This is very hard to achieve and requires strength and power as well as coordination and practice. The dancer must make a good plié (not a bounce) and push herself off the floor, taking her whole body into space in one connected movement. "Throw your front leg only as high as you can push yourself with your back leg. The battement leg can help you a little, but it can't pull you up." In many schools dancers learn to do grand jeté starting with a *huge* grand battement, followed by a slight push with the back leg and then a large kick up with the back leg. Consequently their bodies arc up into the air with a bucking bronco or rocking horse motion as if jumping over a hurdle, and a clear picture is not established. In contrast, Balanchine wanted a grand jeté with everything happening at once, in a flash, and then that picture moving through space.

Peter in effacé back in jeté cambré just before the beat. His legs are thrown to effacé back and his body is arching up and over.

the back: both arms swept slightly back, with the upstage arm higher and the downstage arm lower. If she starts with the arms in an overlapped first (e.g., when jeté cambré is preceded by fast emboîtés), the swing down, out, and up of her arms gives her additional impetus for the jump. Jeté cambré can be done instead of simple jeté in the exercise on page 346. It also is good with balancé front and step jeté and with sauté step jeté, Mr. B's finale step for *Symphony in C,* in which the jeté battu is jeté cambré and the sauté in arabesque is similar to a "chug."

The correct coordination of the battement—the push off the floor, and the movement of the arms—is essential for making the picture and certainly helps the dancer get off the floor and high in the air. However, the primary source of the power is the push off the floor. It is therefore very important that the step before the grand jeté be executed very well so she can collect the energy for the soaring jump; she will not succeed with this if she hits the floor and bounces or pops off or if she stops the plié. If the preceding step is glissade faillie, she brings her second foot rapidly and cleanly toes first to the floor so she has the time and a secure base to take a good, strong plié; if the preceding step is pas courru (see page 281) or chassé (see

Peter straddling a chair in effacé and pulling his legs in   *Peter in grand jeté in effacé*

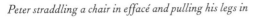

page 359) and step, she stretches her leg in the last step, puts the toes with resistance to the floor, and bends the knee, with the thigh muscles very active. In discussing pliés at the barre I suggested that the dancer think of the descent as compressing a spring and the ascent as the release of the energy gathered. That idea is especially applicable to grand jeté and other big jumps. The dancer jumps—"Whoooshhh"—propelled by the force, the energy, of the "spring." Or, better yet, "springs," because the resistance in the muscles of the foot as it comes to the floor adds to the energy stored by the dancer in the leg, especially the thigh, as she pliés.

Once the dancer has pushed the floor away, taking her hips and body up, and is moving into the air, she lifts the back leg quickly to the designated line, fully extended for grand jeté in "arabesque" (referring to grand jeté with both legs stretched, rather than grand jeté with the back knee bent for attitude). The torso, slightly arched, is up over the hips with the chest lifted, open, and forward. If "arabesque" line is designated, both legs extend equally, the toes being in the same plane parallel to the floor. She does not allow her legs to kick out or

fly up; it is more important to get off the floor and to make and show the picture than to achieve a sort of seesaw split. She uses the inside thigh muscles to control the extension, freezing her legs in the air. Mr. B never talked anatomy, never mentioned inside thigh muscles. To help us understand the feeling, he brought out a chair and asked one of the women to place herself across it in a fourth position or "minisplit." If a chair was not readily available he might assume a kind of turned-in second position demi-plié and hold the dancer up by the waist while she straddled his thighs. He then asked her to pull her legs toward each other. The feeling needed in her legs was immediately clear to her.

Mr. B gave a supplemental exercise with a modified landing to reinforce his point about the control needed to achieve the look he wanted in the air when both legs are stretched and extended in grand jeté with the pointes on the same level. We did glissade faillie and then grand jeté, with special attention to getting up off the floor and to having both feet equidistant from the center line of the body and from the floor. We worked on freezing the line by pulling our legs in, as if we were still sitting on the chair. The legs don't actually move in, but the extra energy controls and stops the splitting and kicking action and the seesawing. We also worked on keeping the front leg extended, rather than letting it drop when landing, and on keeping most of our weight over it. We landed almost simultaneously on both feet in a lunging fourth (back knee straight!), but with the front foot reaching the floor first and with most of the weight over it. He believed this would also help us acquire the skill to stop the legs with the pointes level and hold them in the extended line we needed as we flew forward in the air.

If grand jeté in attitude is called for, the dancer brushes, throws, and extends the first leg as she did for plain grand jeté, but immediately after pushing off the floor and taking herself into the air, the back leg lifts and the knee bends in to about ninety degrees. Again, the dancer travels in the pose in the air, her entire body (especially the back leg) in the designated line; she does not kick the back leg up to attitude on landing. She has lifted the back leg into attitude in the ascent, and it remains there in the air and as she descends. Mr. B very frequently gave grand jeté in attitude croisée and occasionally in attitude effacée. It is more difficult for many dancers to achieve the picture of attitude flying through the air with the entire body contributing to the look. There is a particular tendency to leave the head straight and to let the upper arm fall back instead of slanting the head and framing it with the arm in fifth high (including bringing the fingertips over the center line of the slanted head).

The dancer keeps her weight moving forward as she stretches and extends her front leg out to the ground. As she lands, she goes through the foot of the front leg into plié. Although the front leg is fully turned out as it is thrown up, on landing it is only slightly turned out. Landing on one foot fully turned out from a big traveling jump (also cabriole) is dangerous and risks injury; landing slightly turned out is very secure, very solid, and safe. She keeps her weight forward over the ball of her foot, which helps her to avoid hitting the floor with her entire foot or letting the heel slam down. She main-

tains the line of her upper body and can slightly lift her back leg as she pliés. In class exercises we usually continued into the next step; we controlled but seldom "sat" in the landing position.

There was one Balanchine exercise, which my colleague Gloria Govrin recalls, in which we did hold the landing in arabesque. The dancer starts in fifth position croisé with the left foot front or in "B-plus," standing on her left foot. (B-plus is an unofficial but universally used position that was probably named after Mr. B and may by now be widely known by that name, or it may have other names in other places. In B-plus the dancer stands with her weight on the front leg. The back knee is bent and the foot gently crossed behind, with the toes pointed and the top of the tip on the big toe side on the floor. Her thighs are touching, and her knees are together.) The music is a waltz. The dancer steps back on her right foot into plié on one (count one of the first measure) and does fondu relevé with her left leg to croisé front; steps forward with the left leg on the diagonal into plié on two (count one of the second measure); does glissade faillie to the side, landing on three (count one of the third measure); pushes off the left into a long but high jeté à la seconde, almost splitting and holding the legs in second, landing on her right foot with her left in coupé back on four (count one of the fourth measure); does pas de bourrée en tournant ending in plié on the left foot for the fifth measure; and pushes off into grand jeté in first arabesque in profile, landing on her right foot on six (count one of the sixth measure). The dancer holds through the seventh measure, then on eight (count one of the eighth measure) lowers her left leg to B-plus as she pivots to the other diagonal, still standing on her right foot. She continues on the other side. The idea was to really move across the room from side to side, jumping and traveling continuously, but controlling the way the feet went to the floor and holding the last plié for a measure without double hops.

He often gave a combination (sauté, step across to fourth, glissade, grand jeté, all on the diagonal) to show the difference between glissade and grand jeté. The dancer starts in B-plus, standing on her left foot in croisé, pliés, and does a little développé (leg straightened, knee stretched) with her right leg to the front. She steps forward (toes presented to the floor) and transfers her weight through fourth position plié, to sauté on the right leg in first arabesque on the diagonal, and on the landing brings the left foot across to fourth. Next she does glissade faillie ending in fourth and grand jeté in first arabesque traveling on the diagonal and landing on her right foot. After landing in first arabesque she continues on by stepping across with her left foot and repeating. She may start with a small sauté in coupé back and continue with the little développé as she steps into plié for the sauté. Mr. B watched to see that the glissade looked like a traveling glissade faillie and that we did not let it look like run-run or leap-step; that we placed the second foot to the floor; that we had learned to hold the legs in the air in the grand jeté; that, as we descended from the grand jeté, we extended the leg out to land going through the right foot; and that we placed the left foot across, toes first heel forward, also going through that foot. Again, each part of this combination travels, moving across the floor.

A very common exercise Mr. B often gave us uses a simple glissade faillie and grand jeté in second arabesque, zigzagging diagonally across the studio. The dancer starts in croisé tendu left foot front and steps on the left to glissade faillie and grand jeté in second arabesque, landing on the right, then glissade with the left foot brushing out and grand jeté landing on the left. As usual, Mr. B insisted that glissade be glissade, not a leap and step, and that grand jeté be grand jeté.

Mr. Balanchine also gave an interesting grand jeté combination in five that traveled back and forth, straight across the floor. The dancer starts in B-plus, standing on her left foot on the left side of the studio. On count one she steps across in front of her left foot, pliéing on her right foot to do contretemps on "and." She sautés in first arabesque on

her right foot on count two and brings her left foot across in front of her right, transferring her weight to it on count three. She lands on count four from glissade faillie, then grand jeté in first arabesque, landing on her right foot on count five. She continues to the other side by stepping across in front of her right foot on count one. Mr. B would ask for music in five; this cultivated our musicality while we practiced the jumps.

An excerpt from the coda of *Minkus Pas de Trois* (coupé ballonné, step saut de basque, step grand jeté, step grand jeté) includes two grand jetés in attitude. The dancer starts in B-plus in croisé standing on her right foot, left foot back, arms in a low second. She coupés on her left foot on count one, throwing her right foot side for one ballonné (see page 372), ending coupé front on count two; her right arm is in first and her left arm is in second. She reaches way out to the side, staying in plié, coordinating the opening of her right arm to second as she extends her right leg to step through her foot into plié on count three. She does saut de basque (see page 364), closing her arms to first position and spotting front, and lands on the left foot with her right foot in coupé front below the knee on count four. She stretches and extends her leg way out, again staying in the plié, inclining her body toward the right on count one. She does grand jeté in attitude croisée moving diagonally forward (downstage right), with her arms moving through fifth low to first and opening à la seconde palms up (as if throwing flowers to the public) and lands on her left foot on count two; her head is in croisé. Again, she stretches her right leg front as, staying in plié, she steps forward on the diagonal in effacé with her body inclined on count three and then does grand jeté in attitude croisée, moving forward on the same diagonal, bringing her arms rapidly through fifth low past an overlapped first, her right arm then up to fifth high and her left arm à la seconde. To supplement the energy of the jump the arms are coordinated with the push off the floor and may even slightly precede it. After landing in attitude croisée on count four (good croisé arms!), she brings her working leg down to coupé back as she repeats to the other side.

There is a kind of turning grand jeté in attitude that we all did in class, although in the ballets it is generally a male jump. The dancer starts on her left foot with her right foot in B-plus and arms in second or she can do it following a jeté ending in coupé back. It begins with a hop or chug back, moving upstage, on the left leg with the right leg extending to arabesque croisée; her right arm usually moves from second through fifth high and extends front, her left arm remaining in second. The dancer puts her right leg to the floor in back of her and steps behind it and across with the left foot. She coupés onto the left foot (right foot is in front) as her arms move through an overlapped first and does battement with the right leg as she pushes off the left foot into grand jeté in attitude as her arms move to the standard croisé line. This grand jeté turns three quarters, traveling around and forward, landing in attitude croisée on the right foot and facing front. The effect of Balanchine's asking for the coupé behind with the left foot, rather than a perhaps more traditional step in front, is to make the turn a very tight "U," similar in feeling to a "barrel turn." Again, it is primarily the push off the floor, helped by the coordinated throw of the battement leg, the lift of the torso, and the thrust of the arms, that gets the dancer into the air. The tight "U" turn, the flying jump, and the croisé attitude line make this jump surprising and exciting. He gave it to Jacques d'Amboise in *Stars and Stripes*. It is also in the first male variation in *Theme and Variations* and in the man's solo in *Raymonda Variations*.

One kind of grand jeté we rarely practiced was "stag leap." In stag leap the first leg shoots front in a développé coordinated with the active push off the floor, both legs establishing the usual line of grand jeté in the air, although the legs are opened a little more (almost to a split), and the back leg is usually thrown a little higher than the front leg. Balanchine used the jump in his ballets—in fact, he even gives a series of stag leaps in a circle to the female principal in *Valse Fantaisie*, and the corps in

the "Snow" scene of *The Nutcracker* does many of them. For class, however, he felt it was less useful as an exercise, because it is much less demanding than grand jeté.

Often in stag leaps and in grand jeté the dancer tries to get off the floor by heaving her torso forward with a straight back and hunched shoulders. This does not help the jump and tends to make the dancer look like her back is made from a stiff, hard sheet of cardboard or plywood. In stag leap (and in standard grand jeté) it is important that the chest is lifted and comes forward and that the upper back is arched, with the shoulders back and down.

DETAILS I OFTEN INSIST ON IN GRAND JETÉ:
1) take a good plié before grand jeté, placing the toes to the floor with the heel somewhat forward, and push off the floor
2) take the body into the air; do not just split the legs
3) do not make three separate movements (battement, jump, kick); establish the designated line in the air immediately and travel in it
4) keep the weight traveling forward on landing

Chassé

The French word *chassé* aptly describes the action of this jump. The second leg and foot seem to be "chasing" the first as the second leg rapidly closes to the first leg, coming in behind it to make a soubresaut position when the dancer is going forward (it comes in front when the dancer reverses the step). Chassé can be done in all three directions and with épaulement. It can also be done turning or in a circle.

The chassé that is discussed in this section is

truly a jump, a traveling jump. The dancer must get off the floor and establish the soubresaut position in the air. The jump can be very light and quick and travel less, and it can be slower and be higher and travel more. The choice depends on the tempo and the other steps in the combination. (Chassé is also the name of a step used in adagio; the dancer slides the working foot out of fifth position, maintaining contact with the floor, and transfers her weight onto it.)

Chassé and glissade are used in similar ways but look very different. They can both be petit allegro steps done in a series or set in a combination with other steps. They both can also be used in grand allegro to slower tempos, finishing with a deeper plié to gather energy for larger jumps or any other step. In chassé the second leg is brought rapidly to the first leg to make soubresaut position in the air; the dancer freezes the legs for a moment to reveal the position. This is, of course, the opposite of glissade, in which the dancer makes and shows second (or fourth) position in the air.

In Mr. B's classes chassé forward in petit allegro includes a presentation of the toes to the floor in a small fourth, followed by a short slide just a little bit forward, with the toes just grazing the floor and with the heel forward. It is a light traveling step, with the hips and torso maintained on top of the legs as the dancer pushes off the floor from the back leg. She brings the pointed feet together in the air, with the second leg chasing the first and reaching it as quickly as possible. She lands on the back foot first and begins to plié as the leading foot touches the floor lightly. It can slide a bit forward with minimal contact before she transfers her weight onto it to again push off the back leg for the next chassé. The look of this allegro chassé is up and light. The plié is not low, and the look is not down. The same principles apply going back and to the side.

As a child I was taught that chassé lands in fifth from the soubresaut and then the dancer energetically slides the foot forward from fifth to fourth. After a few years in New York I still did chassé close to that way. I no longer landed with the feet in fifth, touching down simultaneously, but I still had a lot of slide. At a Ford seminar in the 1960s somebody noticed the difference in my chassé and said to Mr. B, "Some dancers barely slide the foot at all, they mostly present the toes to the floor in fourth, but Suki really slides the foot along the floor." He said, "Oh, you know, a little more of this, a little less of that . . . it's all fine as long as it looks good." This little anecdote shows once again that Balanchine was less concerned with complete uniformity in technique than with the way his dancers looked doing the steps. My chassé was acceptable because it had a lot of energy, it was precise in execution, I made a tight fifth in the air with pointed feet, I presented the toes to the floor, and the slide was light in feeling (the floor was not being scrubbed).

Chassé often starts in fifth and can begin in two ways. For a series forward I usually give it following a traveling soubresaut, because the dancer gets a subtle reminder about bringing the feet together in the air in chassé. A good alternative is a small sauté with a quick développé; the dancer lands and then presents the toes of the working foot to the floor in fourth or almost in fourth with no, or very little, slide.

Here is a light, quick combination with three chassés and an assemblé that demands instantly pointed feet. It was an old standby of Pierre Vladimiroff. The dancer starts in fifth position croisé, left foot front, arms in fifth low. She begins with a traveling soubresaut, landing through the back foot and going in to plié, presenting the front foot to the floor and gently sliding it out. The arms are raised from fifth low through an overlapped first to croisé (looking under), the left arm to fifth high, the right arm to second. The head is inclined toward the right, and gaze is directed up and under the left arm (to "see the moon"). As the dancer pushes off her back leg, the weight is transferred to the front leg for a moment before it pushes off to move her forward. Her back leg "chases" the front leg and joins it as soon as possible, making fifth in the air and traveling forward. Her hips and torso remain up, over the feet; they are not left behind. She does two

*Dana landing from chassé,
the toes of her working foot
skimming the floor*

*Dana in chassé in the air,
feet together, back foot
chasing the front foot*

forward. She avoids the tendency to slap her foot to the floor, and there is very little or no slide. When chassé moves from the downstage corner diagonally back before a grand jeté en tournant or cabriole back (see page 374), it is important that the second leg close behind the first leg on the chassé. Also, the dancer leaves her head and shoulder line front. See page 363 for a discussion of chassé before grand jeté en tournant (or assemblé en tournant) and page 364 for a discussion of chassé before saut de basque.

Pierre Vladimiroff's exercise is an example with conventional arms for chassé in petit allegro when the jump is done in a series. "Small arms" are pretty and convenient and efficient to use with allegro chassé as they are for allegro glissade. In combinations with other steps, the arms must coordinate with the step that follows.

A ballet in which chassé is very

more chassés, with the arms and head remaining. The dancer lands from the third chassé and completes it by transferring her weight onto her front leg. From this approximate fourth position she immediately brushes her back (right) leg side to make assemblé while the arm in fifth high (left) opens out to second position. She lands from the assemblé in croisé, her right foot front. She is now ready to repeat the combination to the other side and then can reverse it to the back. Going back, it is even more important to remember to keep the hips lifted up; the dancer does not lead back with them, letting the torso trail by leaning forward.

Chassé in grand allegro is basically the same as chassé in petit allegro. However, she travels more, jumps higher, and pliés more deeply, staying down in plié longer as she reaches farther out with the working leg to place her toes to the floor, going through that foot and bringing the heel somewhat

---

DETAILS I OFTEN INSIST ON IN CHASSÉ:

1) jump—really take yourself off the floor
2) bring second leg in immediately to join the first (pointed toes, stretched legs)
3) in petit allegro, place the toes to the floor and, if sliding the toes out, do so with a very light touch—just grazing the floor
4) in grand allegro, place the toes to the floor as you go through the foot to take a good plié before the next jump, which is normally large
5) bring the hips and torso on top of the legs and feet

prominent is *Tombeau de Couperin*. Many combinations with one or a series of chassés, a very old step of Couperin's time, and jumps such as Cecchetti assemblé and fouetté to supported arabesque are seen throughout.

Grand Jeté en Tournant (Entrelacé)

"You don't only turn, but while you are jumping you are going from one place to another."

Grand jeté en tournant can be done traveling in any direction and with various arm positions. When the tempo allowed, Mr. B wanted to present the dancer up in the air in arabesque. To slower tempos the dancer should actually fly backward, showing that picture moving through the air.

Achieving this result requires first that the dancer plié and push herself up into the air and that she do the required movements quickly to establish and show the picture. She must also maintain full awareness of her center line and directions so she articulates each position. The first leg brushes through first position directly front, with the toes aiming for the center line of the body. On the jump, the body does a half turn as the second leg swings sharply back to arabesque, passing very close to the first leg, almost on the same track. The second leg meets the torso as it draws up to arabesque. This dynamic is maintained as the dancer lands, the torso lifted, the back held and the leg raising against it; there is no "nosedive." The weight is maintained forward over the ball of the supporting foot so the dancer does not fall back on her heel or onto the other foot.

Grand jeté en tournant is always given with a preceding movement such as chassé, balancé and step, or a simple step. It can be practiced on the diagonal with chassé with the dancer starting in the right front corner (equivalent to the downstage right corner), left foot in tendu back in effacé, with first arabesque arms, right arm front. Her gaze is directed out over her front hand. To begin the chassé she pliés on her right (supporting) leg and, just releasing the tendu foot from the floor, reaches directly back on the diagonal with a little lift in the left leg as she starts to turn her hips toward the opposite corner. As her hips begin to turn she extends her arms à la seconde and delays the turn of her upper body. Her chest and shoulders remain open on the diagonal with a feeling of écarté and her head remains facing toward the right front corner as long as possible. Continuing to plié on her right leg, she places the tips of the toes of her left foot to the floor and goes through that foot, transferring her weight, and pushes off in chassé. Making fifth in the air, she avoids the tendency to allow the right leg to close in front of the left; the right leg closes behind. As her hips turn to the back corner, she lands on her back (right) foot going into plié, and, extending her left leg toward fourth front, staying down in plié, she takes a *long* step, again placing her toes first to the floor and going through the left foot. She transfers her weight and pliés fully with resistance on the left leg ("coil the spring") as she brings her arms through fifth low. She brushes her right leg through first to her front with a strong battement almost to ninety degrees, aiming for the opposite (upstage left) corner as her toes aim for the center line of her body. In coordination with the battement she pushes off the floor with her left foot, raising her arms rapidly (they are almost thrown) through a slightly overlapped first, with the elbows bending and leading up to fifth high. The arms should add energy and thrust to the jump; to ensure that they do, they can slightly anticipate the battement and the push off the floor. The body turns in the air to face the original corner as she throws the left leg back against her strongly held back. Her arms may remain in fifth high or open to the designated line, e.g., first arabesque. She holds the line in the air (left leg raised, right leg aiming down or a little forward, arms as directed) and may, if time allows, really travel back showing the pose. As she lands, holding her working leg up against her back, she goes through the supporting foot into plié, keeping the weight forward over the ball of the foot.

Dana . . .

. . . and Peter plié and reach out, presenting the toes to the floor, as they delay the turn of the body.

Peter transfers his weight to his left leg as he leaves his head back.

Peter in chassé, his second leg closing behind his first; his arms have swung into an overcrossed first and when they open they will add to the thrust of the cabriole back.

Dana, having landed from the chassé, stays in plié as she reaches and steps out for a grand jeté en tournant.

Mr. B rarely asked us to hold and freeze the arabesque line after the jump, but he sometimes asked us to hold the arabesque in order to relevé, which, of course, also requires the weight forward over the ball of the foot plus continuous control to ensure a smooth, soft, secure plié and a strong relevé. Even landing in a wide or lunging fourth, the weight is maintained forward over the front foot. When descending from the jump into a large fourth, the dancer lands initially on her front foot and keeps almost all of her weight there, even when the second leg has been placed to the floor. In class Balanchine sometimes gave grand jeté en tournant to a large fourth, followed by a pirouette en dehors. This combination is seen in the *Nutcracker* pas de deux. To do this pirouette without a transfer of weight, the dancer's weight must remain over the front foot when landing in the lunging fourth position.

Balanchine liked to give an exercise with grand jeté en tournant in which every step moves directly side. The combination is step fouetté, chassé, jeté en tournant two times, glissade faillie, piqué arabesque, close fifth front. It travels straight across the floor in waltz time. The dancer starts in fifth position croisé, right foot front, arms in fifth low. She does a small développé right to effacé front, turning her body almost in profile, and steps directly side into fourth as she bends to the right and opens the right arm through first to a low second with the palm up. She coupés her left foot back and fouettés her right leg to arabesque as she brings her right arm up and over through fifth high to second arabesque. The dancer is now in profile. She steps back (moving sideways across the room) and does chassé (left leg closes behind right in fifth in the air), turning a little past the front, leaving her head inclined to her left, and opening

DETAILS I OFTEN INSIST ON IN
GRAND JETÉ EN TOURNANT:
1) place the tips of the toes on the floor
   and take a good plié before the
   jump
2) make a real jump that travels; do not just
   switch legs
3) the legs stay close together as they pass,
   one leg directly to the front, the other leg
   directly to the back
4) in landing, keep back up and aligned
5) control the landing, keeping the weight
   over the ball of the foot

her right arm down and out to an extended second. She lands from the chassé in a kind of effacé on her left leg, head inclined left and arms still in an extended second, and rotates her hips to the right while delaying the turn in her upper torso and head. The dancer steps out with her right leg (a low, long step), again sideways, into fourth position plié and does grand jeté en tournant, landing in profile with her right leg up, moving her arms through fifth low and fifth high to open in first arabesque. She continues with another chassé and grand jeté en tournant. Although the exercise is designed so each step really travels as it moves straight across the room, the dancer needs to ensure that she takes herself into the air in the jumps. She then steps back (to the side) with her right leg as she starts to turn en face, then steps with her left leg across in front of herself and brings her arms together to an overcrossed first as her body continues to turn (the step with the left leg has the same effect as a glissade faillie to the side). She completes her turn to profile as she piqués to first arabesque (demi-pointe for men) on her right foot. She closes her left foot to fifth front demi-plié as she brings her arms to fifth low. The exercise is now repeated to the other side.

Saut de Basque

Saut de basque is usually practiced traveling side across the studio or on the diagonal. When he gave saut de basque, Balanchine often asked that we spot the front instead of spotting the side or the corner. He also wanted the dancer to stay down in plié before each saut de basque, whether it is being done in a series (step saut de basque, step saut de basque) or following another jump.

Mr. B generally gave saut de basque in a combination following chassé or emboîté turning and step. As an alternative, the dancer can start in croisé standing on the left leg, with the right foot in tendu front; her right arm is in first, and her left arm is in second. Pliéing on the left, the dancer does a demi-rond de jambe, extending her right leg toward à la seconde, beginning to turn and opening her right arm to second in coordination with the movement of her leg. She places her toes to the floor and transfers her weight as she goes through her foot and into plié. This is not a true second and also not quite fourth, because her torso and hips are coming around. She continues to turn and to plié on her right leg to collect energy. The dancer brushes her turned-out left foot through first to fourth as she pushes off the floor, taking the hips into the air (remember Dubrovska: "Lift this heavy place") and rises, turning, into the air. As she leaves the floor,

DETAILS I OFTEN INSIST ON IN SAUT
DE BASQUE:
1) step way out as you stay down in plié
2) place the toes to the floor and go through
   the foot before the saut de basque
3) really jump; take your hips up in the air
4) lift the leg quickly to its position in the air
   and hold the knee back
5) control the landing

Dana in tendu croisé front

Dana steps out on a straight leg as she presents her toes to the floor.

to remain in plié to step *way out*, whether the next step was another saut de basque or a step before another jump—for example, step and grand jeté in croisé. Another example is the way he set the very common exercise, four emboîtés turning followed by two sauts de basque. The dancer remains in plié after the fourth emboîté as she steps way out, straightening her working leg to reach out, placing her foot toes first to the floor, transferring her weight into the plié for the first saut de basque; after the first saut de basque she again stays in plié to reach way out and collect energy for the second saut de basque. In this combination the emboîtés turning and the sauts de basque all spot front.

In the grand jeté en tournant combination that travels sideways (see page 363) Mr. B often substituted saut de basque for the first grand jeté en tournant.

she can close her arms to first or raise them to fifth high. She rapidly assumes the position in the air: The pointe of the right foot is just at or slightly below the knee (or, at fast tempos and if needed when doing doubles, even as low as midshin). Her hips are taken up over the extended leg, her working knee is held back to maintain the turnout. By spotting front and brushing through to fourth, the dancer's body and turned-out working leg are revealed to the audience, not her side or that "heavy place." The dancer tries to land quietly through the tips of her toes, with no noise, maintaining her weight over the ball of the left foot and keeping her hips up over the supporting leg. She does not fall down into the plié, and she keeps the right knee lifted to the side, maintaining the position, presenting herself to the front with both arms opened to second or with the right arm in first and the left arm in second. Staying in the plié (which is slow and continuous) on the left leg, she extends the right leg out again, stretching the knee. This is when the dancer tends to come up out of plié, but Mr. B wanted her

Brisé Volé

Part of the importance of brisé volé is probably due to Nijinsky's brilliant use of it as the Bluebird in the pas de deux of that name from Petipa's *Sleeping Beauty*. Some dancers still do the step his way, with a little rond de jambe action to pass the leg from front to back and back to front and keeping the working leg straight, with the working foot several inches off the floor. According to Mr. B, this method was suited to Nijinsky's proportions, but the standard method and the one Balanchine taught had us pass the working foot through first, throw the working leg forward or back, beat, and land in coupé. The beats were done on the center line of the body, both in front and in back.

Brisé volé is practiced in a combination and almost always starts to the front. As an example, I'll use the combination I mentioned in connection with jeté battu (see page 353): glissade, jeté battu, brisé volé front, brisé volé back. The dancer starts in fifth position croisé, left foot front, and does glissade right no change (her arms come together in an overlapped first) and jeté, which brings her to plié on the right leg, left foot in coupé back, arms in second. She brushes her left foot from coupé back through first and throws her left leg forward on the diagonal, but aiming out and toward the center line of her body, to about forty-five degrees as she pushes off the floor. Her supporting (right) leg comes up to beat, making her seem almost to "sit" in the air. Her torso is lifted up and inclined forward and her arms are open to an extended line, with palms down. After the beat, both legs open slightly to change as the dancer lands on her left foot in demi-plié, with her right foot ending in coupé front. As she lands, with her torso still inclined forward and to the left, her left arm can come in front to first, and her right arm can usually stay out in an extended second position. She ends with her head slanted to the left and her gaze directed over her left arm. Next, the dancer brushes her right foot from coupé front through first to the back and throws her right leg back to about forty-five degrees as she pushes off the floor, aiming her right foot out and back toward the center line. The (left) arm, if in first, opens with a slight lowering as the foot brushes to be almost swung up to an extended line, with the palms down as the leg is thrown. Her left leg comes up to meet and beat the right leg in effacé back as she lifts her torso up and arches her back slightly and her body seems to hang in the air. She lands

Peter showing his working (brushing) leg in front of his center line as the supporting leg comes up to beat

Peter showing his working (brushing) leg in back of his center line as the supporting leg comes up to beat

on her right leg in plié in croisé with her left foot in coupé back, her head inclined to the right complementing the line of her arms. Mr. B wanted us to show him the brushing working leg directly front or back in the air and the supporting leg coming up to beat.

Brisé volé can travel forward on the diagonal, as in the "Bluebird" pas de deux. It can also stay in place by coming a bit forward on brisé front and going a bit back on brisé back.

DETAILS I OFTEN INSIST ON IN BRISÉ VOLÉ:

1) jump; the bottom leg comes up to beat
2) beat on the center line of the body, both front and back
3) show the coupé position on landing
4) bend the torso

FIFTH CATEGORY: JUMPING AND LANDING ON THE SAME FOOT

The jumps in this group are often practiced to slower tempos to help the dancer develop strength, power, and control in the thighs, calves, ankles, and feet. These qualities lead to improved elevation and soft landings. When the jumps in this group are practiced to brisker tempos they help the dancer build the skill and the responsiveness required to point the feet instantaneously. However, Balanchine rarely gave these jumps to exceedingly fast tempos because a real plié is required to get off the floor from one foot. (See page 296 for a discussion of very fast changements done with little or no plié.) He often gave exercises at slow tempos with three or four or more consecutive jumps on one foot because the focused, repetitive effort on the same leg and foot builds not only the strength but also somehow a determination, a willingness in the dancer to put out the extra effort needed. Exercises of this kind are the hardest from all the five groups.

Temps Levé on One Foot

Temps levé is a prime example of a jump Balanchine gave in a series or in very simple combinations to help us build staying power. The exercises were done at tempos ranging from bright to moderate to very slow. Often we started with moderate tempos, and then Mr. B asked for slower tempos and sometimes even slower tempos on the repeats.

Some people refer to the position of the working foot in temps levé as sur le cou-de-pied. For Mr. B this was not possible, because the working foot in sur le cou-de-pied is wrapped in front and maintains the same shape in back (see page 76). In his standard temps levé the working foot remains fully pointed at the ankle; this is the same position used for fondu plié (see page 98).

Temps levé can be a traveling jump but it is often done in place. In both cases the dancer ensures that as she pushes the floor away, she takes her hips up and gets herself into the air. As she leaves the floor, her supporting leg stretches straight down from the top of the hip to the tips of the toes, and she points her toes rapidly and directly under; there is no kick or flick out to the side. When she travels in temps levé the dancer brings her supporting leg with her hips and torso on top as a unit in the designated direction. When she lands she works on catching herself on the tips of her toes, going through the foot and controlling her descent, maintaining her weight over the ball of the foot. The working foot and leg maintain their position throughout the jump, usually in a low coupé front or back, although a low attitude or the leg extended at about forty-five degrees (a low arabesque, if to the back) are also used. In temps levé in coupé one arm is usually rounded in first (or in fifth high) and the other is in second, but the dancer ensures that the arm in second does not lose its life and become rigid.

Mr. B might give the simple combination glissade, jeté, two temps levés starting at a moderate tempo and slowing as we repeated it. The dancer starts in fifth position croisé, left foot front, arms in fifth low. She does glissade to the right (no change of feet), opening her arms to the side with a small arms port de bras and jeté onto the right, landing in croisé on the right foot, left foot in coupé back, and closing her right arm to a rounded first. She now does two temps levés on her right foot. She travels side on the glissade, but takes care to come back to her center line for the jeté and to remain on the same line for the two temps levés. She continues glissade left, opening her right arm side, and repeats the rest of the combination as requested. He might, for variety, ask for glissade jeté and six temps levés in place or traveling diagonally back, with a continuous port de bras with the right arm from fifth low to fifth high, and have us repeat to the other side.

On occasion, to make us really push ourselves, to see us expend maximum energy and put out maximum effort, Mr. B called for battu at a relatively slow tempo, so the jeté and all six temps levés were done in place with beats. This is a particular challenge in temps levé because the supporting leg should remain under the dancer during the beats. She really has to get off the floor and control the supporting leg so it does not fly off to the side to beat.

I sometimes give two or three temps levés traveling forward on the diagonal when the preceding movement provides some impetus. For example, starting fifth position croisé, left foot front, glissade to the right ending with the left foot front on count one, jeté landing on the right foot on count two (left foot in coupé back); remaining in plié, coupé on the left foot on count three to ballonné side with the right (see page 372), landing on the left foot on count four, and piqué pas de bourrée with straight legs back, side, front (traveling left). The "front" is done stepping out diagonally forward into plié on the right foot, through fourth on count five. Then, traveling diagonally front, temps levé on the right foot, left foot in coupé back, with the right arm in fifth high on counts six, seven, and eight. The dancer now repeats to the other side. This exercise can be done briskly or more moderately with beats.

Mr. B also liked to give a simple combination of emboîtés and temps levés to slow tempos. The dancer starts in fifth position en face, right foot front, arms in fifth low. She does emboîté to a low, overcrossed attitude back, landing on her left foot, opening her arms to a low second, and does temps levé in the same low attitude. Then she does emboîté onto the other leg, ending in a low attitude back, landing on her right foot, and temps levé. And then emboîté again to a low attitude back, landing on her left foot and three temps levés. Again, she repeats the combination as requested, being careful not to move from side to side. The dancer tries to point instantly and catch herself on the tips of her toes and lower herself into a smooth, continuous plié on each landing. She extends her

supporting knee well out over her toes, keeping her weight over the ball of the foot and allowing herself to plié deeply. She pushes strongly off the floor and takes herself (hips and torso) up as she tries to make a really good jump. As the tempo slows, this is more and more challenging. This combination was also done in reverse, with the working leg in attitude front. The arms usually remained in a low second, but with life, as described in the emboîté exercise. If we were falling quickly down onto the full foot with a "BANG," Balanchine would smile and say, "No heels down, and make the plié continuous." This usually set us straight; at least we put out the effort in the right direction.

Balanchine did not often set combinations that left us en face for an entire exercise, but in this case he did. The effect is to make the dancer much more aware of bringing the supporting foot down on the center line. To make us even more aware of crossing our legs to the center line and avoiding any gap between the thighs, he might set the combination with the working leg straight and extended at forty-five degrees or a little lower.

A basic and simple combination en face was given by Stanley Williams. It is done in eight counts. The dancer starts in fifth, left foot front, arms in fifth low. She does three jetés, changing feet, then five temps levés and repeats the combination to the other side; it is also reversed. Stanley usually gave this combination at a very brisk

---

DETAILS I OFTEN INSIST ON IN
TEMPS LEVÉ:
1) point the toes quickly
2) take the body (hips) up into the air
3) keep the working foot in position; don't let it wander off or wobble back and forth
4) don't collapse the body on landing
5) land on the tips of the toes and go through the foot, keeping the weight over the balls; do not fall on the heel

tempo. However, it is a good exercise to repeat at both slower and faster tempos. The whole combination remains on the center line; no traveling to the side. "Over point! And in, and in, and in!" Stanley said to the class, meaning that the dancer's weight is caught on the tips of the toes when landing and is centered over the ball of the supporting foot in the plié and that the toes of the landing foot come in to one point on the center line.

Sauté in Arabesque

Although it is a jump off one foot that lands on that foot, both legs participate together to make sauté in arabesque.

The dancer can begin sauté in first arabesque from fifth position croisé, right foot front or B-plus standing on her left foot. Starting with the right leg and moving into effacé, she reaches out with a small développé, beginning to plié on her supporting leg and extending her working leg forward as she stretches her knee, meanwhile bringing her hands to a traditional or to an overlapped first. She places her toes to the floor and goes through her foot into plié, bringing her hands down toward fifth low. As she transfers her weight forward into plié she picks up the back leg, lifts it up to arabesque, and immediately pushes off the floor, almost lightly swinging her arms up to first arabesque, leading with the backs of the wrists. At the same time, she brings the supporting leg forward, using the impetus of the plié, the step, and the transfer of weight to travel forward as she rises into the air. It is important that all of these actions are integrated in a single, continuous flow. The dancer must not separate the movements by stepping out, kicking up the back leg, jumping, and throwing the torso backward. Also, the legs do not split apart; instead, the dancer establishes arabesque line in the air. She flies forward with the supporting leg stretched, extended slightly front, hips and torso up over it, head and chest lifted, arms in first arabesque, and back leg extended in arabesque. She comes down where the

impetus of the step carries her; she does not let the leading leg and foot pull back and under. In landing, she catches herself on the tips of her toes. As she descends through her supporting foot into plié, she briskly brings the working foot, toes first, to the floor, usually stepping into fourth front.

This sauté in first arabesque has a look of freedom that is an aspect of the result Mr. B worked for. Certainly it is energetic, dynamic, and more sweeping in movement. But the freedom is an illusion for the audience, because for the dancer the traditional discipline has been replaced (wrists may be crossed in first, arms moving down and out as if swung, etc.), not merely discarded. Mr. B was not satisfied with us in a step like this when the ports de bras looked small, careful, calculated, prim, and "polite," when the step and transfer of weight did not supply energy to help the dancer to fly forward, and so on. Some movements should be done with a look of such abandon that one feels like telling the girls to take their hair down. However, he was also not satisfied when a dancer lost her awareness of good form (center line of the body, shoulders down, showing arabesque in the air, placement of the foot to the floor, etc.).

A widely used standard sauté arabesque exercise starts in fifth position croisé, right foot front. The dancer, turning her body into effacé, does sauté in first arabesque on her right leg, step to fourth on her left foot, glissade forward to fourth, left foot front, then grand jeté in effacé with the arms in effacé (left arm fifth high, right arm in second). She lands on her right foot and repeats on the same diagonal, using a "catch step" (contretemps) to start again. There is a strong and consistent forward impetus to this combination: The sauté arabesque travels forward, the dancer's weight comes forward onto the left leg and foot in both the step and the glissade faillie, and the grand jeté soars and moves forward. The exercise also works well with traveling assemblé (with or without beats), pas de chat, cabriole, and rond de jambe sauté, among others.

A combination Balanchine must have liked is sauté in second arabesque, step, jeté battu. He

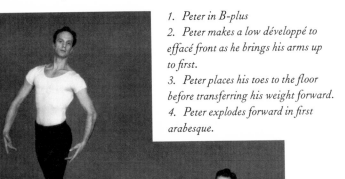

1. Peter in B-plus
2. Peter makes a low développé to effacé front as he brings his arms up to first.
3. Peter places his toes to the floor before transferring his weight forward.
4. Peter explodes forward in first arabesque.

brings the working leg of the jeté down, landing where she took off. As she brushes her right foot side for the jeté, she opens her arms to an extended second. The jeté is followed immediately with the beginning of the next sauté, the dancer stepping way out to the left side with a small développé from the coupé back position and repeating the combination three or more times as requested.

I often give this combination in two different ways. The first time I will have the dancers emphasize a quick, sharp sauté that travels a little, really stretching their knees, strongly pointing their feet, and stressing the upward swing of the arms to second arabesque; this is the look used in the exit of the four "Russian" girls in *Serenade*. The next time I will tell them to stay in plié on the supporting leg longer as they développé, enabling them to reach way out on the step. This sauté travels more to the side than up in the air (similar in feeling to a "chug"), and the port de bras reaches lower, with a "sweep the

used it in ballets (*Serenade*, *Symphony in C* finale) and he gave it in class. A typical class exercise would start with the dancer in B-plus in croisé on her left foot (or in fifth position croisé, right foot front), arms in a low second. Moving directly side, she does a small développé with her right leg and steps way out on it, moving into plié in the usual manner. She immediately continues with a sauté in second arabesque. It is important that her left arm sweep down with her torso rotating and then up to second arabesque line as she sautés. Her face and gaze are directed over her arm, toward the audience. She lands and immediately brings her working foot down to step across in front of her supporting leg, takes a good plié on the left leg, and then does jeté battu or jeté cambré, landing in croisé on her right foot, left foot overcrossed in low attitude back. Switching the direction of travel after the step, she floor" feeling, and then out in a nearly horizontal motion, with the back participating strongly in the movement; this has the look Balanchine wanted in the finale of *Symphony in C*. Balanchine also gave sauté in this combination with the arms in effacé, rather than with the arms in second arabesque. Now, instead of feeling a rotation in the torso to reveal part of the back, the dancer feels her chest lifted and forward, her face tilted, her cheek and chest almost leading along with the supporting leg in the sauté. It is a high traveling jump. It is important that the dancer step across to an extended kind of fourth after the sauté, placing her toes to the floor first and bringing her heel somewhat forward as she goes through the foot.

This combination lends itself to another modification that shows the dancers how the same sequence of steps can present a variety of looks. It can travel sideways or diagonally forward or back, depending on the direction of the step into the sauté arabesque. In the descriptions to this point, the sauté has been set to the side. If the dancer rotates her hips toward the upstage corner when starting her développé, the combination will travel diagonally back—that is, upstage. This is how it appears in *Symphony in C*. If the dancer steps diagonally forward—that is, downstage—it will travel forward. I sometimes give four of each—four moving back, four moving front.

At the end of the pas de trois in *Piano Concerto No. 2* the principal woman and the two men do four consecutive sautés in arabesque, going diagonally toward the right downstage wing, starting with the small développé front with the right leg and stepping out onto the foot, toes first, to sauté in arabesque effacée with effacé arms and head. After landing on the right foot they rapidly bring the arabesque (left) leg down and forward, across in front of the right and step, placing the tips of the toes of the left foot to the floor in order to sauté off that leg in arabesque croisée, the right arm moving from second position through fifth low to fifth high as the left arm moves from fifth high to second. They are in croisé arabesque in the air: legs and

arms and head. They repeat this sequence with another sauté arabesque in effacé and one more in croisé arabesque. The feet are placed each time to the floor toes first, and then the dancer goes through the foot bringing the heel somewhat forward. Meanwhile, with coordination, the arm and head move down as the dancer steps into plié. Then, as she starts to push off the floor to sauté, the arm lifts up, the elbows bend, and the backs of the wrists lift the hands up over the center line to arrive in effacé or croisé, with the head and gaze complementing the movement of the arms. The tempo accelerates, and the passage ends with the lady doing a few chaîné turns and plié relevé arabesque. The two men watch her as she chaînés and then catch her arms at the wrists to hold her for a moment as she relevés in arabesque. These same arabesque sautés apear in *Serenade* as the Waltz Principal exits the first time; they should also have a look of abandon, a "let the hair fly" feeling.

Peter Martins on occasion has given a similar combination in company class as well as to an advanced class at SAB. It also has four sautés in arabesque alternating legs and orientation (effacé, croisé), but it has a change in direction of travel. Its look is also different because the dancer's arms stop and show the picture, rather than moving more continuously, which gives a look of greater abandon. The first two sautés go to the right downstage corner; the next two go to the left downstage corner. The sauté arabesques are in effacé, croisé, croisé, and effacé, because the legs keep alternating but the direction changes. The last sauté in effacé ends in fifth position (in other words, with an assemblé in effacé back). The combination starts in fifth position croisé right foot front. The dancer turns her body to effacé as she développés and steps onto her right foot to sauté in effacé arabesque. After the sauté, she brings the left leg down and steps, through, placing her foot to sauté off it in croisé. As the dancer lands on her left foot, she begins to turn toward the left corner, and she brings her right foot down and across and steps to the left corner to sauté in croisé arabesque. She then lands on her right foot and steps through with her left foot to sauté in effacé arabesque. She lands in fifth right foot back and with her body in effacé. She repeats the combination to the other side. Here the dancer moves her arms quickly and softly (by bending the elbows) to position, complementing the energy in her legs, and showing the arms in effacé or croisé in the air, staying for a moment while holding the leg in arabesque behind her center line. As she lands, she places her feet properly to the floor each time. Remember, "We have two feet. Place all two of them."

In all of these combinations with sauté in arabesque, it is important that the dancer travel forward while taking herself into the air, guarding against staying in place, heaving the torso back, and kicking up the arabesque leg.

Balanchine's choreography for *Raymonda Variations* includes several entrances for the corps doing sauté in arabesque from the wings at a fast tempo. I led Victoria Simon on doing sauté in arabesque in the coda. We were the first of several pairs of women who came out doing the step. The crossing pattern done by all the women progressed zigzagging downstage, and, as the leader of the first two out, it was my job to be sure the dancers traveled all the way from one side of the stage to the other. "Come onto the stage like shot from cannon. Make the man in the back row with his nose in the program in the dark look up to see what happened," Mr. B said. As if I needed to be told! I knew what Mr. B wanted from the first girl out, and I wasn't about to lose my place. So I danced as big as I could, determined to show him that even though I was as small as a BB, I could fill space as well as those who were, in comparison, like artillery shells (just in length, that is).

Ballonné

Ballonné is a jump that can be done in place, or it can travel in the direction in which the working leg is extended. When the dancer does ballonné from fourth (as in step forward) or fifth (as in coupé ballonné), she brushes the working foot lightly on the floor and throws her leg in the designated direction as she pushes off the floor. When she does ballonné from coupé she throws and extends her leg directly out and up to about forty-five degrees without brushing the floor.

Ballonné can be another "make a picture" jump. In this case the dancer throws the working leg front, side, or back to about forty-five degrees immediately as she rises into the air. The supporting leg is stretched straight down, with the foot fully pointed as soon as it leaves the floor. Then, as the dancer lands, going through the supporting foot with control, she brings the working foot cleanly down to coupé front or back. As with temps levé, the position on landing is sometimes referred to as sur le cou-de-pied, but Balanchine wanted the dancer's foot fully pointed in coupé.

When the dancer does coupé ballonné alternating legs, she usually stays in place; at moderate tempos she can usually show the working leg ex-

---

DETAILS I OFTEN INSIST ON IN
SAUTÉ IN ARABESQUE:

1) travel, move, energy
2) point the supporting foot instantly as you push off the floor, and bring the supporting leg forward as you leave the floor
3) the back leg does not kick up to arabesque; it lifts rapidly and holds its line
4) maintain awareness of the way the feet come to the floor in each part of the step
5) do not throw the upper body back; travel forward with the head lifted and the chest lifted and forward
6) arms and head arrive in position first, so the entire pose is seen in the air, moving through space

tended in the air and freeze it, showing the coupé position when she lands. When the dancer does a series of consecutive ballonnés off the same leg, she descends by catching herself on the tips of her toes, maintaining her weight over the ball of the foot and making each plié continuous. Consecutive ballonnés usually travel. The dancer pushes strongly off the floor, instantly pointing the supporting foot and bringing the supporting leg in the direction in which the working leg is extended (i.e., the direction of travel), with the hips and back on top of the leg. She travels on each jump as time allows, making sure she immediately stretches her supporting leg and rapidly and fully points her supporting foot.

A combination that shows the contrast between a ballonné that stays in place and one that travels starts with the dancer in fifth position croisé, left foot front. The dancer does glissade to the right no change of feet as her arms open through first to second landing on count one; jeté ending on the right foot, right arm to first, left foot in coupé back landing on count two; steps on the left on count three; to ballonné, throwing the right leg to the side, right arm joining the left arm à la seconde to make a picture, landing in place on the left foot with the right in coupé back as the left arm closes to first on count four; slight pause, pas de bourrée moving to the left piquéing back, side (as the left arm joins the right in second position), and stepping forward into plié in fourth on the right foot on count five; ballonné in effacé front traveling forward on the diagonal with the right arm moving through fifth low and up toward first on count five, landing on count six, but immediately continuing with grand jeté in first arabesque landing on count seven; and pas de bourrée with the arms opening to second, stepping down on the right foot on count eight. The dancer is now ready to repeat on the other side. This combination is also good because the second ballonné, the one before the grand jeté, requires the dancer to push strongly, quickly, and forcefully off the floor to travel forward and land from the ballonné with a similar continuous plié in the supporting leg, and

again the same kind of strong, fast, and forceful push off the floor to travel for the grand jeté. Meanwhile, the working (front) leg makes similar actions for the traveling ballonné and for the grand jeté.

I sometimes give five ballonnés traveling in effacé front, grand jeté, pas de bourrée, jeté, other side. The dancer starts in fifth position croisé, left foot front. She pliés on the last count of the introduction as she throws her right leg forward for ballonné in effacé front landing on counts one, two, three, four, and five; grand jeté in first arabesque landing on count six; pas de bourrée to the side finishing in plié on the left foot on count seven; and simple jeté landing on count eight on her right foot, left foot in coupé back. The dancer repeats the combination to the other side by throwing the left leg forward in effacé, traveling diagonally forward to the left. I give this at a relatively slow tempo, which calls on the dancer's strength, energy, control, and determination. The ending of each ballonné is the beginning of the next. The plié is moderately slow and also is continuous, done without a pause. When given at a much brisker tempo, this exercise is excellent for building speed in pointing the feet. Also, see Madame Tumkovsky's exercise including ballonné on page 347.

Ballonné battu usually follows coupé and usually stays in place. For example, after a jeté, the dancer does coupé back onto the left leg, brushes the front (right) foot out to the side, and throws the leg up to about forty-five degrees as the back leg pushes off the floor. The supporting (left) leg moves to the right side just enough that the two legs can come together sharply and beat with the right foot front. The top leg opens slightly, and the dancer lands in plié on the left foot, with the right foot in coupé back. Ballonné battu is also done in reverse.

A favorite combination of Balanchine's is often done with beats but is also good without them. It is done to two measures of a fairly brisk 4/4. It starts with the dancer in fifth position croisé, left foot front. She does glissade to the right, ending left foot in front on count one; jeté battu landing on the right on count two; coupé stepping on to the left on count three; ballonné battu side brushing out the right ending in coupé back on count four; coupé stepping onto the right on count five; assemblé to the front ending left foot fifth front on count six; entrechat six landing on count seven; and sustain the plié through count eight. The dancer is now ready for the other side. We might do this combination without beats first and then repeat it with battu; similar combinations with battu appear in several ballets.

DETAILS I OFTEN INSIST ON IN BALLONNÉ:

1) really jump, using the hip, thigh, and foot; change levels
2) stretch the supporting leg and point the supporting foot
3) show the picture in the air when required
4) control the landing, keeping the hips up and over the supporting foot; don't fall back on the heel when landing

---

Cabriole

Cabriole, when done slowly and especially when done in series, is a difficult jump requiring tremendous power for the push off the floor and great strength and control in showing the desired look in the air and landing smoothly. It is done in all three directions and can end ouverte (with the working leg extended in the air) or fermée (with the working leg quickly brought to the floor). When it is done to slower tempos, the working leg is thrown front to about ninety degrees (almost parallel to the floor) and back almost as high, but when it is done to faster tempos, and often to the side, the working leg is thrown only to about forty-five degrees. Balanchine was definitely not interested in having the working leg thrown above ninety degrees. Good elevation and a clear, energetic strike were more important to him than high extension in cabriole.

An exaggerated extension often seen on the landings is sometimes used to try to camouflage poor elevation and generally causes the dancer to lose the line of the upper body he wanted to see.

Balanchine emphasized certain qualities of the traditional cabriole that are sometimes lost in execution. He wanted an even timing in each of the three stages of the cabriole—plié, jump and strike, land. He did not want the dancer to land very rapidly after the strike, almost falling to the floor. The dancer is more likely to achieve even timing when using a good plié followed by a strong push and when the bottom leg comes rapidly up to strike the top leg. The top leg should not lower to strike the bottom leg. It is a striking or hitting action by the supporting (bottom) leg, not at all a beat with the two legs coming together and scissoring. Balanchine would say that the sound of the impact should be heard: "I want to hear the beat!" This reference to the sound helps the dancer understand the amount of energy needed in the leg that is striking. And the leg that is hit, the working (top) leg, lifts up a bit, reacting in part to the energetic strike.

Cabriole is practiced following another jump (very often glissade faillie) or a step into plié. For cabriole front the working leg often brushes front through first position; for cabriole back it brushes and lifts (or only lifts) directly back; and for cabriole side it brushes directly side. As the dancer throws (or lifts) the working leg to forty-five or ninety degrees, depending on the tempo, she pushes off the floor. To the back, the dancer does not want to heave her torso back into the leg. When she steps forward or chassés forward preceding a cabriole back, the working leg does not brush, does not really feel like a throw; instead it feels like a quick lift. In all directions, the action of the working leg is very energetic. As the dancer moves into the air, the push off the floor, the battement by the working leg, and the coordination of her arms with the jump help her to take her hips and body off the floor. However, the dancer avoids letting her torso fall away from the working leg. In cabriole to the front she does not lean back but remains erect, opening her chest and shoulder line, with a slight arch in her upper back. In cabriole to the back she avoids heaving back or hunching forward; in cabriole to the side she inclines her torso toward the working leg rather than leaning away. In striking, the entire leg participates; just as in all other beating, the dancer works for a deep crossing. The thighs and calves strike, and the feet are crossed. The sound of the legs hitting is clearly heard. The working (top) leg lifts slightly upward, helped by the force of the strike. As the dancer lands in plié, she needs to go through the supporting foot and keep her weight over the ball of the foot, maintaining her upper body pulled up. In cabriole front the dancer avoids letting the torso go back and does not do a cambré or a back bend unless called for. In cabriole back she holds her back up, lifting her chest forward, and avoids letting the torso heave back or collapse forward. In cabriole side, after the beat, she inclines her torso toward the working leg. In cabriole ouverte the top (working) leg remains extended to show the pose before moving on; it does not shake in place or bounce up and down out of control. In cabriole fermée the working leg is brought to the floor rapidly, but only after the lift from the strike.

The tendency is for the dancer to shorten the time between the strike and the landing. The cabriole must not become a slow plié, a slow beat, and a quick fall to the floor. The dancer needs to really get off the floor and works to ensure that there is an equal amount of time for each action. An example of even timing would be: Plié on count one, strike on "and," land on count two.

Achieving the "sit in the air" look of cabriole front is often helped by asking the dancer to mimic the pose on an actual chair. Mr. B sometimes sat on a chair and extended his legs directly in front of himself, almost at a ninety-degree angle—that is, parallel to floor. His feet were together, similar to soubresaut position. At the same time, he held his back up, opening his lifted chest, taking the stomach in, and put his arms and head in effacé. With his impish look he would say, "Cabriole like this. This is the position." Even when sitting with some sup-

port from the back of the chair, it takes strength in the back, abdomen, and thighs. But this is the look and feeling needed when cabriole is done both at forty-five and at ninety degrees in effacé front.

Another version of cabriole front, more commonly done by men than by women, is done without the legs striking. Instead, the dancer brings the supporting leg immediately to the working leg at about forty-five degrees or slightly higher and holds the line with the feet and legs together, hovering in the air, again as if sitting on the chair in the air. When Jacques d'Amboise did this jump it made me think of a large pussycat, the mountain lion, bounding across the stage in slow motion and with freeze frame.

The action and timing of cabriole back is particularly difficult to perfect, so Mr. B often had us go back to the barre for a supplemental exercise, just as he did for entrechat six. Facing the barre and using it for support, we lifted one leg to arabesque and then pliéd on count one, pushed off the floor with a strike on count two and landed on count three, straightened on count four. We repeated the exercise, four or eight at a time, to a relatively slow tempo, pushing down on the barre with both hands to help us really get off the floor and keep the correct timing as well as the proper form. Until we were strong enough to manage without assistance, this exercise helped enable us to bring the bottom leg up to strike and to delay and control the landing. Using the support from the barre, the dancer can feel what she is trying to achieve in the center. Also, allowing one count for each movement at the deliberate tempo helps make the dancer aware of the amount of effort needed to keep the correct timing.

In cabriole side the dancer brushes her working foot directly side from fifth in the usual way and throws the leg to about forty-five degrees. It is important that the working leg not be thrown behind second position; if anything, it might be thrown a little in front of second. She gently inclines her torso toward the working leg, again, a little in front of second, certainly not in back of it, as the sup-

Peter demonstrating "cabriole in a chair" as Mr. B did for us

Peter holding his legs together in the air at 45 degrees

porting leg pushes off the floor and lifts to strike behind the working leg. Her arms are in an extended second with the palms down, a little in front of her. With the torso still inclining toward the legs, the working leg is propelled or lifted slightly up. Cabriole side is usually done fermé. After the strike and lift of the top leg and as soon as the dancer lands on the supporting leg, she closes the working leg to fifth front or to an overcrossed fifth. In either case she is careful to place the toes first to the floor.

Coordination of the arms with the battement and the push off the floor is valuable for all jumps but is especially helpful in doing a difficult jump such as a cabriole.

A typical combination for cabriole ouverte in effacé front is glissade, cabriole, plié, relevé in first arabesque. It starts in the upstage left corner and travels across the studio on the diagonal to the downstage right corner. The dancer begins in tendu left foot croisé front. She steps onto her left foot and does glissade faillie to fourth front, ending with her weight forward over the ball of her left

foot in a good plié. By maintaining the correct timing of glissade (the fast second leg) and having her weight over the left foot, the dancer ensures that she can get a good push off the floor for the cabriole. The brisk but not stiff (bend the elbows) swing of the arms through fifth low passing through an overlapped first to effacé as she does battement and pushes off and moves into the air is critical to the success of the jump. She lands on her left foot; however, it is important to avoid landing on a fully turned out foot (as with grand jeté, see page 357, too much turnout in this case can also be dangerous). After showing the cabriole ouverte in effacé, she brings her right foot down toward fourth front, placing her toes to the floor and pliéing as she transfers her weight to the right foot to relevé in first arabesque. She establishes first arabesque and then brings the arabesque leg down to the floor, passing through first to fourth front and transferring her weight forward. Her weight is over the ball of the left foot, and she is ready to take off in glissade and repeat the combination.

Another typical exercise for cabriole ouverte in effacé front starts in the same corner and in the same pose, and travels the same diagonal, but it combines cabriole in effacé front and emboîté. The dancer steps onto her left foot and does glissade faillie to fourth front, ending with her weight forward over her left foot. The fast second leg in the glissade, the weight forward in a good plié, and the brisk arms are all again important for the cabriole in effacé front that follows. She lands in cabriole ouverte and jumps on her extended right leg, lifting her left leg in a low, overcrossed attitude back and follows with a second emboîté back, lifting her right leg in a low overcrossed attitude. She repeats the combination on the same side, now starting the glissade from a low attitude back.

A cabriole exercise that is an excellent example

of Mr. B using the simplest possible combination to focus our attention on a few details is glissade side ("mini" failli), closing to an overcrossed fifth, cabriole side fermé bringing the working foot down to a slightly overcrossed fifth. We began at the back of the room and came gradually forward until there was no more space, doing the combination to the right, then the left, again and again. The dancer starts in fifth position croisé, left foot front. She does glissade right with no change of feet and cabriole right. The arms come together in an overcrossed first as the dancer does glissade and open down and out to an extended second as the working leg is brushed out to the side for the cabriole (see page 339). The dancer inclines her torso, turning her head toward the working leg in the cabriole. Mr. B concentrated on the timing of the glissade, on our placing the second foot to the floor with proper transfer of weight, and on even timing in the cabriole with a definite lift of the working leg after the beat, before it is brought down in an overcrossed fifth.

Peter Martins has given sets of four consecutive cabrioles at forty-five degrees—two to the front,

one to the back, and then one to the front. This exercise is excellent practice in clear changes of épaulement, exact directions of the working leg in the air, and presenting the working foot to the floor. The dancer can start tendu croisé front, left foot in tendu. She steps on her left foot and brushes her right foot through first to effacé front for cabriole ouverte in effacé front. She steps forward on her right foot and brushes her left foot through for cabriole ouverte in croisé front. She steps forward on her left foot and lifts her right leg to the back for cabriole ouverte in croisé back, with her arms in third arabesque. Staying on the same (left) leg, she brushes her right leg through first to effacé front for cabriole ouverte in effacé front. Then this combination repeats on the same diagonal, but starting on the right foot. When she does cabriole front, she extends the opposite arm to the working leg in a low line complementary to that of the leg and directs her gaze out past her hand; for the cabriole back, her arms are in arabesque, with the same arm extended front as the working leg to the back. She starts the repeat by stepping forward on her right foot and brushing her left foot front, making

Peter pliés before the jump.

Peter pushing down while his bottom leg comes up to strike

Peter's bottom leg has come up to the top leg.

1. Peter showing the second half of the combination, starting in fourth arabesque pliée

2. Peter deepens his plié and reaches back, placing his toes to the floor.

3. Peter in the air in chassé, feet together, back foot chasing front, arms in an overcrossed first, head left back

4. Peter lands and again reaches out as his arms swing down and out.

5. Peter transferred his weight; his arms continued swinging up to this line as he did cabriole to the back.

the sequence cabriole in croisé front, effacé front, effacé back (arms in second arabesque), croisé front.

I sometimes give a combination with glissade and cabriole fermée front, back, and side that finishes in sous-sus. The dancer starts in croisé with the left foot in tendu front, arms in a low second. She steps forward on her left foot, and moving on the diagonal, does glissade faillie forward, ending in fourth, pliéing on her left leg, with her arms moving toward fifth low on count one and then does cabriole in effacé front, ending in fifth position, right foot front (arms to effacé) on count two. Next, she does glissade back on the same diagonal, ending right foot fifth front (arms to a slightly overlapped first) on count three and, brushing the left leg back, cabriole back in first arabesque, ending by bringing the left foot through first to step into an overcrossed fourth, pliéing on the left leg with her arms in a low second on count four. The dancer now does glissade traveling side to the right (arms in overcrossed first), ending with left foot front on count five and cabriole side brushing her right leg out (arms in an extended second, palms down), ending by bringing her right leg down in

front to an overcrossed fifth, with her arms in a low second, moving toward fifth low, on count six. She continues to plié on the right foot as she makes a small développé to the side with the left leg and steps out onto pointe, bringing her right foot to sous-sus front with her arms in an extended second. Having arrived in sous-sus on count seven, she steps forward to fourth in croisé with the right foot in plié on count eight and is ready to repeat on the other side.

So often, Mr. Balanchine came up with a simple but challenging exercise that stripped away everything except the bare essentials. He made a classic combination of this kind, alternating chassé and cabriole back (similar to the use of chassé with grand jeté en tournant, see page 363). The dancer starts in the downstage right corner, standing on her right foot with the left foot in tendu back and with first arabesque arms. She chassés diagonally upstage and steps out on her left foot, continuing to turn to her left, then does cabriole back aligned on the diagonal. On the chassé her arms swing in, crossing into an overlapped first; then they go down and out, lifting to fourth arabesque on the cabriole. This step alternates sides (going from

fourth arabesque to first arabesque on the cabriole) as the dancer repeats the combination, traveling on the same diagonal to the upstage left corner. I watch to see that the dancer places her feet correctly to the floor before and after the chassé and especially on the step before the cabriole, and that she really swings her arms in coordination with the cabriole. She, of course, needs to bring her feet rapidly together for the chassé and really jump for the cabriole.

DETAILS I OFTEN INSIST ON IN CABRIOLE:

1) maintain even timing, really push off the floor
2) the bottom (supporting) leg comes up rapidly to strike the working leg
3) the working leg must react to being struck; lift it up
4) land softly through the foot and hold the back up
5) coordinate the arms with the battement and the push off the floor

---

THE USE OF THE TOES

The toes of the ballet dancer are always active, always fully alive. In this sense, too, they are all—men and women alike—"toe dancers."

Even when the dancer is on flat, the toes are not passive, relaxed, spread out. They have a very active life. While the dancer stands, the toes sense the floor, actively controlling the weight, which is toward the front, over the ball of the foot. They have a *positive* contact with the surface; they know what kind of surface it is. Sometimes the toes actively press into the floor, sometimes they almost hold onto the floor. The toes initiate many movements, so they are always ready for instant action: to strike like the cobra, to pounce like the cat. There is a variety of actions, from lightly skimming to forcibly striking and every kind in between.

The instant the foot starts to leave the floor, the instep stretches and the toes point, immediately. Training in and practice of this skill starts with the most basic exercises at the very start of a child's lessons. It continues until the ballet dancing life is over. This skill is cultivated in many barre and center exercises and is not used only for pointework and the related relevé. It is also essential for ballet dancers' jumps, for how they look—for the beautiful line of the turned-out leg, completed by the beautifully pointed foot—and for the ability to do them at all—for the extra energy in getting off the floor from the actively pointing foot, pushing the floor away.

Placement of the foot to the floor also starts with the toes and is of equal concern with the pointing of the toes when the foot leaves the floor and with the work of the toes when the dancer rolls up through the foot. The dancer presents the toes to the floor and the heel forward when moving terre à terre. In landing, she catches her weight on the tips of her toes and controls it as she goes through her foot, again presenting the heel forward.

The regular use of very simple, very basic exercises in Balanchine's company class is a theme of this book and one reason for writing it. No jump is really simpler than changement and dancers start learning it by the end of the first year of training. Mr. B regularly gave grand changement to grand plié, saying, "It forces you to realize how to use the pointes." Precisely because it is so simple, grand changement lets the dancer refine and refine and refine the way she catches her weight on the tips of the toes. He continued, "First, in descending, we have to force ourselves not to touch the floor with the heels," which brings us to . . .

The Use of the Heel

"In plié before you jump off two feet, you have to take the heels off the floor. Don't tell! It's a secret. If you keep the heels down, you have only your poor knees to lift the body off the floor. It may look like heels are down, but you feel two points, not four. With the heels just off, you push with the thighs and feet. You have a lot more force."

I touched on the subject of the heel in jumps at the beginning of this chapter. In describing the individual jumps I have made it clear that the dancer is working from the tips of the toes through the ball of the foot. Because Balanchine's teaching about the heel is so noteworthy, it is important to try to convey what he was trying to accomplish.

"Don't put your heels down" is probably the least understood of Mr. B's "rules." When he made the remark it created an uproar, because it clashed with what dancers were used to doing because of how they had been trained. He certainly did not mean that our heels were never to touch the floor. In fact, in almost all his teaching and choreography, nothing was ever "always" and nothing was ever "never." A part of what made him special was his ability to focus all his energy on getting the result he wanted as quickly and efficiently as possible, rather than limiting himself with rules and systems.

However, if anything could qualify as an "always" rule, placement of the foot to the floor is the likeliest candidate. Balanchine wanted us to be fully aware of how we placed each foot to the floor at all times, every time. We needed to place them down and treat them like the valuables they are. We didn't place them the same way every time; this changed with the step, the tempo, and so on. But we maintained the full awareness at all times.

In training us to move with the quick, sharp attack he liked, Balanchine taught us to bring our weight forward over the balls of the feet and maintain it there. He wanted the weight placed securely over the ball of the foot, not settled back in the heel or distributed over the whole foot. Even when the dancer was standing on two feet, the weight had to be concentrated over the balls of the feet. I have described this as having the weight over two points, not four. Placing it otherwise requires a shift forward before the dancer can move, which delays the initial attack. He wanted us to be like cats ready to pounce instantly or like boxers "dancing" around in the ring, weight forward, ready to go "POW!" or dart away from a punch. So he could tell us both as an explanation and as a correction not to put the heels down. In neither case did he intend this to be understood as a general rule to be followed at all times. He simply meant that the heel should not touch the floor in the step we were practicing at the moment. In the same way, he could give that as a correction to a particular dancer with a tendency to let the weight settle back on the heel, without meaning that her heels could never touch.

He often said that he should be able to slip a piece of paper under the heel of a dancer in plié, but this was also not a hard-and-fast rule. When a dancer was working at the barre with the full foot on the floor, the heel would be touching the floor, but the weight was still placed over the ball. In center combinations, too, the heel often had contact with the floor, even though the weight remained concentrated over the ball. Each dancer was allowed a certain latitude in applying the "rule" to her own body and the step so that her position was stable, secure, yet allowed instant movement. Sometimes, at the barre, during a demi-plié, the heel could release, especially if he wanted a very deep ("lawyer") plié or if the dancer's Achilles tendon was short. In this case it was better to let the heel release to make a large, "juicy" demi-plié rather than locking the heel to the floor, because the important actions were the use of the thigh and the bending of the knee and ankle. Here again, Balanchine looked at each dancer individually, considering her body and what would work for her.

The degree of heel contact with the floor also depended on the step and the tempo. Moving at fast tempos requires the weight to be brought so far forward that the heels almost automatically leave the floor. Balanchine joked, "We don't need the heel; we could cut it off." When the tempo is slow, the heel is more likely to have contact with the floor. However, we were not allowed to land or "fall down" on the heel. We had to control the descent, keeping the weight securely concentrated over the ball of the foot. At times the whole foot might be used to push off from the floor. This was the case for some jumps and relevés. Still, the weight was maintained over the balls of the feet and the plié remained a continuous action, providing the impetus

for the next movement. If the weight is allowed to settle back in the heels and if the heels are locked into the floor, the movement will stop.

When we came off pointe or landed from a jump, Balanchine did not want the heels to hit the floor and then release as the plié deepened. Rather, he wanted the knees to extend over the toes with the weight over the ball of the foot as we went through our toes and feet to land. The heels might possibly make contact with the floor, but only as we began the next jump or other movement. If the tempo was very slow, our heels might not touch the floor at all. For example, he gave us grand changement to a near-grand plié, an exercise that built strength in the feet, ankles, calves, and thighs. Descending this way made the plié a continuous action that went down to come up, collecting energy and force for the movement to follow. He definitely did not want us to hit the floor and bounce off again like a ball.

Balanchine did acknowledge that the heel is very important in stopping and for this reason compared it to a brake. Putting the heel down was the finish, the full stop or period at the end of a dance sentence. For example, in simple battement tendu the foot, including the heel, had to be placed to the floor and held momentarily in fifth, thus separating each tendu insofar as the tempo allowed. This starting and stopping built speed. But the descent had to be controlled, whether landing from jumps, coming off pointe, or closing to fifth position from a battement. The heel had to be placed purposefully on the floor at the right time and in the right position. Without this control the heel simply banged to the floor, landing unpredictably. The controlled descent Balanchine wanted required a great deal of strength in the thighs, calves, and especially in the ankles and feet.

Mr. B could have talked to us about the use of the muscles of the feet, ankles, calves, or thighs. Instead, he chose to take a verbal shortcut, telling us not to put our heels down. "Dance on your chicken tops! Chicken doesn't walk on heels," he would say. The result was the same!

Partnering

In the simplest possible terms, the male partners the female in Balanchine's choreography to enhance her movement. He presents the woman, he shows the woman, he *dances* the woman. Since, for Mr. B, dance is movement in time, the last way of saying what the man does is the most apt. The emphasis is on the woman moving to music, and her movement can be more when partnered by a man. She may dance higher or lower, she may do more beats or more turns, she may dance faster or slower, she can go farther off her balance, and she can combine with her partner to flow in and out of more shapes. This contrasts directly with the choreography of many others in whose work the effect of the static poses made by a man and a woman together is very important, perhaps most important. When Mr. B does want to show a held supported pose, the woman can even be partnered by the female corps. They can support the solo dancer by the hand or wrist, enabling her to remain on one pointe to show a pose or execute a series of développés, for example. Or the women of the corps support each other. However, these groupings generally form and dissolve quickly and do not have the look or feel of static poses.

Balanchine said, "Put a man and a girl on the stage and there is already a story; a man and two girls, there's already a plot." That chemistry between male and female is surely the source of many of his ballets. There is an intrinsic interest in the images they make. In the music he chose he sensed a quality of relationship and made a dance. How the man partners, how the woman responds, how they relate to each other onstage show what Mr. B found in the music. In his case, the plot was very rarely a story told in full. There is almost never a narrative to be conveyed in literal detail, requiring mime and acting. By plot, Balanchine usually meant an emotional climate indicated by the music. It exists because of what has gone before the curtain rises and will condition what comes after it falls. But we don't see the before or the after; we just see the people living (and dancing to the music) in the moment. In "the now."

Balanchine also said, in reference to the man in ballet, "Man is an attendant to a queen. He is consort, he is noble, brilliant, but finally merely good enough to be her partner." That says poetically what everyone who casts pairs of dancers always has to determine practically. Can I find a man who will be good enough to partner the woman I have in mind? It's assumed that almost any woman who can dance a solo or principal role can *be partnered* (leaving aside obvious mismatches in size). Ballet masters, ballet teachers, and ballet dancers always think and talk about who the good male partners are, because it's known that some men, who are good or even excellent dancers, do not partner very well, even when they are big enough for the woman in question. Balanchine's saying also conveys subtly another message. As a consort, he is there to serve, he himself is not the main person of consequence. In the case of the ballet partner, the service he renders is to make the woman look better and to draw attention to her by the way he supports her and presents her.

In my opinion the critical issues in partnering are really from the man's side, so it is probably true that an authoritative and comprehensive discussion of Balanchine's partnering should be done by a man. I hope that at least one of the men who did a lot of roles for Mr. B comes forward one day with his report. Until then, I can try to help by offering what I know from my own dancing and from staging his ballets, mostly for students at SAB.

When I stage a Balanchine work that includes partnering for our students, I always try to invite a man who performed or performs the role to help for some of the rehearsals. Sometimes the dancer on whom a role was made is available at the right time. In either case, his contribution is partly what one would think on aspects such as how to coordinate the dancers' timing, where and how to place the hands, when to apply power from the arms, the back, the legs, how to absorb force and carry weight, etc. Every dancer is different, every performance is different. It is the man who has to adjust to give the woman what she needs at the right time. When an experienced male partner watches the students rehearse, he usually can better see and feel the changes needed to make it possible for each couple to do the choreography more effectively. But the men I invite also pick up details on the look that add purely to the visual quality of the result, such as how to give more space to the woman, how to take and hold the hands, or how to achieve a harmonious line.

In my years in New York, Balanchine did not give partnering classes himself. He provided no systematic analysis and practice of partnering technique purely as technique, unrelated to any specific music, any specific ballet, any specific cast. I there-

fore approached this chapter *without* memories comparable to those I have of him in company class (and at the school, in Ford Foundation seminars, etc.), teaching technique for the individual dancer. I started by thinking through the ballets and began to ask myself what Mr. B might have given in a pas de deux class. There is an immense variety of choreographic detail and precise repetition is very limited, although there are basic elements that can be traced from the earliest to the latest works. I also found that there are some generally applicable ideas and some technical details I can offer for turns, lifts, balance, and so on. And I will offer examples of corrections that come up in staging his works that may help make the application of the general ideas clear.

Every dancer hoped most of all, of course, that Mr. B would make a new ballet on her or him; the partnering was then really for them. As he made a new ballet, Mr. B set the partnered movement, and the dancers tried it out. Conrad Ludlow recalls that when he and his partner seemed not to get it to work right away, Mr. B often came up quickly with another idea. This could happen almost immediately; Mr. B always seemed able to devise a new movement suited to the music and with the same gestural quality. As the man *danced* the woman in the new choreography, they often showed new looks or employed new techniques that other dancers would soon learn.

Dancers in my time in the New York City Ballet (and in the years until Balanchine died) acquired Balanchine's approach to partnering as we were cast in the ballets. We learned the choreography of existing ballets, and when Mr. B took rehearsals, we got his insightful suggestions. The final rehearsals for principals he almost always took himself, as he did the rehearsals of the complete ballet onstage. Perhaps to help people doing solo and principal roles for the first time, he often cast the newcomer, man or woman, with a partner who had long experience in the role. I know that I learned a lot from the men I danced with, such as Nicholas Magallanes, Edward Villella, Arthur Mitchell, and Con-

Darci on pointe in passé, held on balance by Nikolaj

Nikolaj moves Darci off balance.

rad Ludlow. When I began to coach students from the school for lecture demonstrations and for the annual year-end performances, Mr. B supervised some of my rehearsals, and I got pointers from his corrections for the dancers. What I heard most often was, "He shouldn't pose," "He's planted," "He's too close to her," and "He needs to take her nicely." In fact, I heard those comments quite often. Those words, which I'll try to explain, are about as basic to his view of partnering as front, side, and back are to his view of classical ballet technique.

There is, of course, a basic classical ballet partnering technique (also referred to as adagio or pas de deux) that is essential to learn and to practice: promenades, pirouettes, lifts, etc. I first studied adagio in San Francisco in classes given by Lew Christensen and by Nancy Johnson (with Conrad

Ludlow as her partner for demonstrations). In New York I went to SAB for adagio classes with Anatol Oboukhov and Nicholas Magallanes, and many others from NYCB did the same. In the 1960s Jacques d'Amboise and Conrad Ludlow also gave adagio classes at the school, as did Stanley Williams when he came from Denmark. Most important is that boys and girls learn to work with each other and how to synchronize and coordinate their movements. Everyone has to get a little confidence, learn how to judge distance and height, and so on. It's important that girls learn how to hold themselves in a variety of movements, positions, and poses, and that they discover where they have to be stronger. Usually they need to work on the abdominal and back muscles and cultivate a firm connection of the arms to the back. The girls need to learn how to hold themselves firmly and how to let the man take them on and off balance without trying to adjust or accommodate. They must also learn that they usually have to

Jock supports Wendy with one hand in an off-balance arabesque.

let the man do it all, meanwhile getting over their fears and shyness. Boys learn a sense of timing; how to find a girl's balance, put her on it, take her off as required, and put her back on, and keep her on it; how to present the girl; how to do traditional lifts, turns, and promenades; and where they have to be stronger.

Balanchine used basic classical ballet partnering technique in some of his ballets. It is often done by the corps, and it is the basis for much of the solo and principal partnering in ballets that derive more directly from Petipa or that were made to older music. That technique is the foundation on which Balanchine built as he went on to develop partnering for the later ballets and for ballets to modern music. The level of skill and finesse of the corps in partnered dancing in the New York City Ballet in the late 1950s was not very high. For example, a woman being placed to the floor from a grand jeté carry lift could be set down with her weight so far back that she had to put both feet on the floor, rather than being placed down with her weight over the front leg and foot. Over the years, partnering technique developed and the skills of the dancers improved dramatically. In the ballets being made nowadays, corps dancers have a number of places that demand as much in partnering skill as is required of the soloists and principals.

Since Peter Martins took over the company and the school he has introduced changes that will help today's young dancers become as proficient as they now need to be. Principal men from the company regularly teach adagio class and use exercises derived from its repertory as well as more traditional combinations. Because Adam Lüders, Sean Lavery, and Jock Soto dance (or recently danced) this repertory, what they say is current and very credible. Peter has also brought in three specialty teachers who know the requirements of the theater. Pierre Dulaine and Yvonne Marceau performed on Broadway as a ballroom and adagio team, and founded a performing company of their own; they teach the basics of ballroom dancing. Peter Frame, a former NYCB principal dancer, works with the boys in weight training. When Peter Martins teaches company class he sometimes includes partnered exercises at the end.

Balanchine made many traditional pas de deux (adagio, variations, and coda) as well as many less structured dances for a man and a woman. In some cases these dances are in ballets in which the man partners more than one woman, sometimes dancing with more than one woman at a time (*Apollo, Serenade, Divertimento No. 15*, "Emeralds" from *Jewels, Who Cares?*). The numbers of men and women are not always equal, also resulting in a variety of combinations. In some cases the man briefly dances with members of the corps (*Serenade, Piano Concerto No. 2, Allegro Brillante, Agon, Stravinsky Violin Concerto*). As was his way, Balanchine used the dancers he had available to him. He developed his dances on their abilities and attributes, but at the same time he developed them and extended them by seeing what could work. When I look back over the range of dances he made for pairs of principal dancers and even soloists, I see him at times giving freer rein to his imagination than in dances for individuals. With the man to support her weight or restore her balance, the woman can be manipulated into shapes no one can make alone; with four arms and four legs to work with, Balanchine can involve them in intricate tangles. He is reacting to what he has found in a particular piece of music and setting a movement that will be done in this particular way only in this ballet. Sometimes what the public sees is the result of trial and error to discover what will work, what is possible for the two (or three or more) who will dance it the first time.

When I joined the New York City Ballet there were three leading partners. Nicholas Magallanes was the oldest; he had first created a role for Mr. B eighteen years before, in 1941, when I was two years old. Nicky was a man of great dignity and a complete professional onstage. He was the most conservative in approach, but he knew the repertory and had by far the most experience. Because of the skill he had developed over the years in supporting the woman, he was said to have "magic hands." Conrad Ludlow and I had been in the San Francisco Ballet together, but when I was a young corps dancer in New York he was already much in demand as a partner by all the leading women. He had wonderful timing, an excellent sense of the woman's balance, making her feel very secure and very well taken care of, and he also knew how to make her look good. Jacques d'Amboise had already created roles for Balanchine, who continued to make ballets on him until 1980, for more than twenty-five years (that's about half of Mr. B's life

as a choreographer). His partners in created roles include Tanaquil LeClercq, Patricia Wilde, Diana Adams, Maria Tallchief, Melissa Hayden, Suzanne Farrell, Patricia McBride, and Karin von Aroldingen. Jacques, a very handsome man, was an extraordinary dancer who also had size and strength and the adaptability to take on every kind of Balanchine role. He had unmistakable magnetism and charm, and, certainly as important, he was daring, and thus temperamentally well suited as Mr. B continued to experiment with asking the man to take the risk of leaving more space between him and the woman or of coming in later to give support.

In my later dancing years there were shorter dancers, such as Helgi Tomasson, John Clifford, and Paul Mejia, who were much admired as partners. But the arrival of Peter Martins from the Royal Danish Ballet gave Mr. B a ballet prince in every way. He was blessed with Nordic handsomeness; had a royal or even godly bearing; a beautiful, tall body; an exemplary technique; and innate musicality. He also had strength and daring, which Mr. B used to continue to extend his exploration of difficult movements—for example, when the woman is off-balance or is partnered with a fingertip touch.

Since being taller is no guarantee that a man will be a good partner and being shorter is not a barrier to becoming one, it is important to offer some observations on the characteristics that men who are good partners in Balanchine ballets share. They are always in short supply, even harder to find than men who have a presentable technique. Casting the boys who will have to partner is one of the most critical steps SAB faculty faces each year when we plan our year-end performance.

Another Balanchine saying is, "The ballet is a purely female thing; it is a woman, a garden of beautiful flowers, and man is the gardener." That makes the man even more subordinate to the woman than he is as consort to a queen, which was Mr. B's idea of the specific place of the male partner in ballet. However, in each saying there is a valuable clue for men who want to be good partners in Balanchine ballets. A measured quality of self-effacement is necessary. It is measured self-effacement, because the man cannot (with a couple of exceptions allowed) seem to disappear onstage. He must remain part of the artistic whole. However, he is less the focus of partnered dances than the woman (or women). Since he is there more to enhance the woman's movement than for any other reason, the willingness and ability of the man always to adjust as needed are of paramount importance.

Some men are fascinated with all the mechanics of partnering. They are truly interested in learning what works and in understanding how and why it works. They look for opportunities to practice partnering, finding a spare woman to dance with whenever there is an opportunity to get in a little extra work. But it probably doesn't feel like work to them or to their partners; it's more like a challenging kind of fun. They even take extra adagio classes or practice with a woman in the back in rehearsals. This was an attribute shared by Jacques d'Amboise, Conrad Ludlow, and Paul Mejia. When I was a young corps dancer, Conrad asked if we could work together, even though he was far more established at NYCB. Jacques often worked with one of the many younger dancers still in the corps. Among his favorites were Merrill Ashley, Suzanne Farrell, Kay Mazzo, Marnee Morris, and Christine Redpath. It must have been a wonderful experience and Jacques had a good eye; they all danced a lot of important roles and had roles made by Balanchine for them. When Suzanne Farrell was busy, Paul Mejia often asked me to take adagio class with him.

Other men are not as fascinated by partnering. They might spend the same time practicing jumps or that old male standby, endless turns. This difference in attitude may be apparent very early. Often, when I am staging a ballet or when I look at SAB adagio classes, I notice that some boys use the time when they are not dancing to do another big pirouette or another big jump. Other boys are attentively watching the other couples dance or are marking the combination with a girl or are trying different ways to make a movement with a girl work. Later,

as professional dancers, it may be harder for men who always gave a very strong priority to their own dancing and their own look to shift their attention to how their partner looks.

There is another potential drawback to maintaining a one-sided focus on being able to do a lot of the traditional show-off steps: The Balanchine repertory offers fewer opportunities to use them. There is a lot of partnered dancing, but there are fewer traditionally structured pas de deux with a male and female variation and coda in which dazzling, show-stopping tricks can be done. Regardless, I might note, of whether it was there originally or fits the music. This is true in part because Balanchine used a lot of music that was not composed for dancing. And even if it was composed for dancing, he did not choreograph in keeping with the performance practices of the nineteenth-century opera house in which set pieces performed by the stars who were leading dancers (and singers) were generally the big attraction.

Balanchine always resisted the idea of the star partnership, along with all the rest of the star system. He wanted people to come to see the dancing and hear the music, no matter who was dancing. No one had star billing, he did not publish the casting long in advance, he didn't name the company after himself, he listed the composer ahead of the choreographer, and he cast the partnered roles in the ballets with as much variety as possible. As I noted, this included casting dancers just moving into roles with partners who had been doing them a long time. These practices endure today in the New York City Ballet.

And yet certain combinations were especially memorable. Before I came to New York, I had heard about Maria Tallchief and André Eglevsky. Jacques d'Amboise and Melissa Hayden struck sparks when performing that echoed the way they egged each other on in rehearsal and backstage. Edward Villella and Patricia McBride were a good match in size and worked well together. He was so exciting, dancing full-out with a cheeky grin, a sparkle in the eye, and an infectious charm; she was unflappable, moving in a most natural way and responding quietly to that charm. Peter Martins and Suzanne Farrell shared a cool, remote stage manner. His presence had Olympian (even Apollonian) serenity, while hers seemed inward and spiritual, and yet her spontaneity in movement tested the outer limits of his daring and of his ability to cope. I think that each of these pairs became at least a partial exception to Mr. B's "no stars" rule for many in the public. Even he, on occasion, admitted it. In any case, what makes such partnerships work in an exceptional way is really outside the scope of what the teacher can offer.

Schools can stress the importance of musical training and awareness. If dancers share a common foundation in musical understanding, they should find it easier to establish musical rapport, to develop a complementary musical response. Dancers—male and female—must take on the responsibility to sense each other and communicate. I recall so clearly how good Arthur Mitchell was in communicating with me. Taking my hand before a balance in the pas de deux from *Stars and Stripes,* and immediately sensing how nervous I was, Arthur looked at me with his infectious smile and purred, "Relax, baby!" I almost laughed, but I had to relax. But the most important message from the man comes through total competence and delivers the assurance that whatever the girl does, he will be there. However, women also need to be good communicators, responding straightforwardly to their partners, displaying confidence in the partner's ability and trust that the partner will come through when needed. The male has primary responsibility to adjust in the actual mechanics of dancing, but in the larger sense, each should look for ways to supply something needed to make the dance happen.

When Conrad Ludlow retired from performing there was a considerable sense of loss among the women because he was highly valued as one of the most reliable partners. He probably set the all-time standard one night when he and Patricia Wilde were dancing the pas de deux from *The Nutcracker.*

As he ran forward to catch Pat in the flying shoulder sit, he lost his footing and slipped to the floor. Pat saw him go down, but she must have had total confidence he would manage anyway. She jumped as the woman is supposed to do, and somehow Conrad got up in time to catch her on his shoulder. Even he didn't know how he managed it.

OFFERING AND TAKING THE HAND

The technique for shaping the hand and fingers that is first practiced at the barre and used throughout class is fully applicable to partnering work, starting with offering and taking the hand and continuing all the way through. The material on pages 145–151, on the hand and fingers, reacting to the air, phrasing, articulation of the wrist and elbow, going away to arrive, and directing the attention of the audience by use of the dancer's head and eyes must also be thoroughly understood to achieve the look Balanchine wanted in dancing with a partner. This is, of course, also true of his ideas on the orientation of the body (en face, croisé, effacé, écarté) and on the standard poses (arabesque and attitude), which are also discussed in that chapter.

When he didn't see the look he desired in the way the man offered his hand and the woman took it, Balanchine could spend what seemed like a lot of rehearsal time working to refine just these two gestures. That might seem surprising until one recalls that many dances start this way and that offering and taking the hand can be repeated frequently in the course of a dance, often when a new combination or phrase begins and even when a dance ends. Therefore, this offering and taking regularly set the tone for the dancing that follows, or they complete the mood of a dance just finished. One sign of the importance Mr. B gave to having the right tone at the start is the number of occasions on which very proficient partners had to spend time working on a single arm movement and

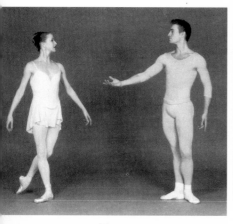
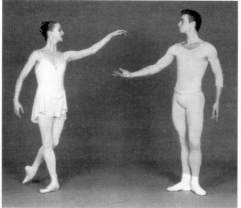
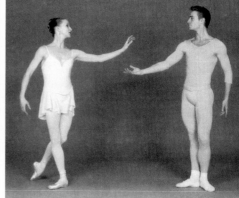

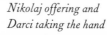

*Nikolaj offering and
Darci taking the hand*

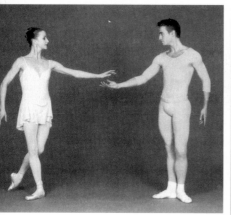

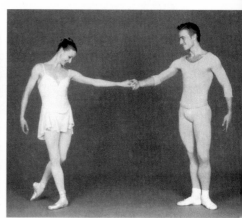

related action of the hand until he was satisfied.

In general, the man offers his hand, inviting the woman to join (or rejoin) him in the dance. If the tempo allows, she usually considers, taking a moment to react, and then accepts. There is in all this an aristocratic graciousness and reserve that are part of any classical ballet, but Balanchine carried the formality into even the most "American" classical adagios, although he changed the look in keeping with the style of the ballet and the generally lighter tone of the relationship between the man and the woman. The difference in tone is evident in the music for ballets such as *Stars and Stripes, Western Symphony,* and *Who Cares?*

He also carried the formality into some of his modern pieces. In one of his early works, *Apollo,*

the young god stands behind Terpsichore and offers his left hand at waist level on the left side a little in front of her. She looks for a moment at his hand before placing her right hand on it. They repeat the process on the other side. The resulting pose was certainly new for ballet, but the old formality has been retained.

In some very modern works there can be a feeling of abstraction, of gesture for its own sake, and there is less explicit offering and taking. However, the dancers still take hands with a certain restraint. For the woman I think of it without reservation as delicacy; for the man I tell the students that they have to show consideration, care, and concern while remaining manly. For both sexes the aim is to avoid anything that looks like clutching or grab-

Nikolaj offers and Darci takes a hand in a sequence used in Who Cares?

bing, holding on in the way an acrobat or a gymnast might. This quality is also necessary when the man and the woman take hands (often very quickly) just to make a dance work—for example, when she needs his support to remain on pointe. She must also keep this in mind when she takes support from him on his shoulder, upper arm, or some other part of his body. The woman needs to place her hand with care; she should not grab, or look like she is grabbing, her partner.

When she takes the man's hand or places her hand on the man's body, the woman generally needs to maintain a light hold. She doesn't clamp down with an iron grip, because the man is then unable to adjust instantaneously when a movement develops in an unexpected way or actually

Nikolaj offering and Darci taking both hands in Apollo

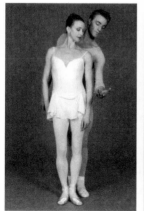

Jock offers his hand with care,
concern, and consideration;
Wendy accepts it with delicacy.

while presenting her as an independent person. The man offers a lead; the woman accepts and allows herself to be led. Balanchine once said it is like a groom leading a horse: The man leads, to be sure, but the horse shows that it is allowing itself to be led. The groom pulls on the reins, and the horse, with some resistance, accepts the lead by allowing its head and neck to respond, and then the legs. Dancers are not horses, but he often wanted the effect of the goes wrong. The exceptions arise when the woman requires the man's support in order to do the choreography, but she still must maintain a very refined look.

LEADING THE WOMAN

Sometimes a dance or a section of a dance begins with the man leading the woman while she walks or bourrées or even runs. Balanchine was generally concerned that this be done in a way that leaves as much space around the woman as can be managed, so she can be seen as clearly as possible.

In leading the woman by one hand, the man works to maintain some distance from her. He shows that there is a connection between them man's lead to flow through the dancer's body. She avoids anticipating, she often gives some resistance, and she uses her phrasing to help clarify her start. Her torso often initiates the response to the lead, the reaction flowing into the neck, head, and other arm and the legs and feet.

In the adagio section of *Scotch Symphony* and in the third movement of *Brahms-Schoenberg* there is a sweeping, curving feeling to the path on which the woman is led. Both the man and the woman need to be sure that the figure she traces as she moves around the stage is not flattened or shortened. The same preference for big, generously proportioned, round movement that Mr. B had for grand port de bras applies here as well.

In some cases the man will remain on or near the same spot after leading or gently guiding the woman, who will go on, perhaps by passing him. Balanchine wanted the man to continue to participate actively in ways that contribute to an illusion that she is covering more ground than she is. In some choreography the man moves a short distance

ple comes near the end of the opening of the "Emeralds" section of *Jewels* in which the man leads the woman diagonally downstage and then steps diagonally upstage to show the lady passing by him; meanwhile, the corps weaves in and out between them. The man offers the woman his other hand and again moves in front of her to change hands again and lead her on past him as he moves back. This is repeated several times. Whatever movement is set for the man must be done with energy, grace, and clarity for the desired effect to be achieved.

Nikolaj leads Darci in sweeping curves as she bourrées . . .

. . . and as she runs.

in the opposite direction, making a kind of zigzag pattern; in other cases the effect is achieved through gesture—for example, a fingertip touch or touches suggesting a pull-by. Balanchine uses this approach in the pas de deux of *Raymonda Variations*. When the woman bourrées almost straight back and the man zigzags behind her, it creates the illusion that she, too, is really moving side to side when in fact she is hardly doing so. Another exam-

The man may also lead the woman by taking one of her hands in one of his and placing his other hand at or near her waist on the side of her back. He maintains distance by extending both arms. The woman does not initiate or anticipate, but again offers some resistance. However, she is probably less able to delay and sequence her response than she is when led by her hand alone. But she can create the same effect by opening her chest and putting herself

*Nikolaj sends Darci away,
yet remains connected.*

*Darci, with
her working leg
à la seconde,
supported by
Nikolaj, who
is ready to
walk around
her*

clearly back into the man's hand that is on her waist and by the reaction in her neck, head, and free arm.

Remember Mr. B's four most frequent corrections for the boys when he came to my SAB rehearsals! If you forgot them, they are: The boy should not pose (himself); the boy should not plant himself (losing mobility and flexibility); the boy should not stand too close (hover); and, the boy should take the girl nicely. Any or all of them might apply to leading the woman, depending on what a man is doing or not doing. For the woman, the most important ideas are to wait to be led and to remain somewhat supple through the body so its reactions help show she is being led.

When the man and woman separate, the man often "leads" her away. As she steps or bourrées or runs away from him, the man removes his hands so it looks like a gentle push, as if he is sending her out knowing they remain connected and that they will come together again. It gives her space and separateness yet conveys relatedness. It's so simple, but it takes time to refine.

SPACE BETWEEN THE MAN AND HIS PARTNER

Maintaining space between the man and his partner remains necessary most of the time in Balanchine partnering. It was very important to him that the hovering male presence be eliminated. Indeed, Balanchine partners do come together, lean on each other, become intertwined, and get tangled up in many ways, some of them quite suggestive. When they are close, they are often very close. But in gen-

eral his point was to allow the woman to be seen alone. His women could be delicate and vulnerable and yet they were not frail and weak beings who needed the constant assistance of an attending man.

The man's support is needed for sustained poses, for continuous pirouettes, and he must be there to lift. However, when he is not actually needed, Mr. Balanchine often wanted the man to step clearly away, taking his hands off the woman's waist or other point of support, usually opening them to the side. This shows the woman alone, without a hovering man.

In many ballets (e.g., *Raymonda Variations*, the "Diamonds" section of *Jewels*) the woman is on pointe on one foot, being supported by one hand. While walking around the woman or turning her, the man may offer his other hand. These sequences require space between the dancers, refined ports de bras, and correct offering and taking of the hand to achieve the desired effect.

In promenades he wanted the man to keep as much distance as possible from his partner and yet remain consistent with the look of the ballet. Usually, the farther away the man was from her, the better, as long as he could keep the woman securely on-balance. This applied to the many promenades done facing each other with one hand, as at the end of the adagio of the pas de deux from *The Nut-*

Nikolaj walks around Darci, raising his arm to pass over her extended leg and foot.

right next to the woman, the man remains at some distance, lets the woman move away or steps away himself, and then comes in at the last moment to give support for a pose or turn or for a lift. The woman can start a conventional pirouette from fourth and the man can step in from behind to offer support at the waist after the turn has begun; this is Balanchine's normal approach to supported pirouettes from fourth at moderate to slow tempos and is seen in many of his ballets. In the third adagio of *Divertimento No. 15* the woman runs to cen-

Nikolaj continues around, bringing Darci's arm to fifth high.

Darci lowers her arm to the side, perhaps for a promenade.

cracker; to promenades with the woman's working leg à la seconde and the man at her side holding one hand, both facing front as in *Stars and Stripes;* or to promenades with the woman in passé facing front and the man at her side facing back holding one hand as in the "Diamonds" section of *Jewels;* and so on. In *Concerto Barocco,* at the end of the second movement there is a promenade in attitude in which the man holds both hands of the woman, but he still gives her as much space as he can, and he shapes his body to maximize her visibility and complement her line as he promenades and walks around her.

Sometimes, rather than standing or walking

ter stage, leaving the man several yards away. She starts to pirouette from an extended fourth; the start of the pirouette is the cue for the man to run to her, supporting her at the waist as she continues turning for a double pirouette, which finishes in arabesque penchée. Another version of this idea is seen in *Donizetti Variations* and in *Scotch Symphony.* In *Scotch Symphony,* it is seen when the woman does one turn finishing in attitude back as the man comes quickly in to take her hand while she takes his shoulder. He continues with a promenade as she extends her leg to arabesque and he supports her in

Jock presenting Wendy from all angles, promenading her and himself around her

a penché. Or the woman can piqué to pointe in arabesque or attitude at some distance from the man, briefly sustaining the pose or turning it, with the man coming and taking her by her waist or wrists. This is seen near the end of the pas de deux from *The Nutcracker* and in Balanchine's *Swan Lake*, when Odette runs past the man and does plié piqué arabesque, bringing her arms to fifth high. The man follows and takes her by the wrists. In some cases there is movement over a longer distance by the man. In several ballets (for example, the fifth pas de deux of *Divertimento No. 15*, the opening section of *Donizetti Variations*, and the Act II pas de deux from *Harlequinade*), the woman starts a piqué turn in attitude and then the man comes in to take her and to partner her for the rest of the turn. In *Who Cares?* the man is doing a curving run toward her as the woman does a relevé turn in arabesque, and after one turn he steps in and takes her hand as she takes his shoulder. In *Liebeslieder*, the woman often starts an arabesque or attitude turn with the man several steps away; at the last moment he runs in so she can take support on his shoulder and hand to finish the turn.

In the pas de deux from *Stars and Stripes*, Balanchine asks the man to come in to support turns in contrasting moods. In the adagio he starts slightly behind the woman and walks nonchalantly away,

tracing a circle as she starts to carve her own circle by bourréeing in the opposite direction and doing a step-up turn ending in arabesque. He arrives back at her side just in time to take her by the waist just before she makes first arabesque. This sequence is repeated twice as she completes her large circle. In the coda the man flies off into the wings, the woman comes on, and she chaînés diagonally downstage, very fast. He runs back on, arriving just in time to take her by the waist to stop her in arabesque after her fast step-up turn. He then sends her out, almost seeming to throw her, to repeat the chaîné and step-up turn to arabesque. This sequence is done a total of three times.

There is almost no wing space at City Center, where *Stars and Stripes* was first performed. So Jacques d'Amboise, who created the role, "choreographed" a little offstage routine that added excitement and that ensured he reached his partner, Melissa Hayden, on time. He told the corps to keep the wall on the left side clear. He then exited into the wing with such velocity from the preceding manège that the audience would believe he was continuing offstage for half a block. However, because of his ploy, he could quite literally bounce off the wall and ricochet right back onto the stage to reach Melissa to catch her in arabesque after her first step-up turn.

In various movements that the woman can initiate by herself, Balanchine's advice for the women was always, "Do as if alone, the man will come, the man will be there." I think that is probably easier for most girls to get used to than it is for the boys. The boys must develop the skill, the timing, and the confidence in both their skill and their timing to leave as much space as Mr. B wanted, counting on arriving in time to provide the support needed. He sometimes gave us practice by setting a class exercise in which, from an extended fourth, we did a double pirouette en dehors, finishing in attitude and remaining on pointe (demi-pointe for men). This leaves the dancer turning on pointe (or demi-pointe) in attitude without support. "Don't worry about the ending. The man will be there and take you," he would say to the women. So we did the double pirouette and then sailed around in attitude until we came off pointe, either falling or in control; in this case, it did not really matter. Another such exercise he gave was an en dedans turn with the working leg à la seconde, stay on pointe, and turn to arabesque. The men, of course, need to be able to sustain their balance in such turns and show a controlled ending for their own variations.

Near the end of the coda of the pas de deux from *The Nutcracker* the man walks to the side and the woman chaînés rapidly toward him. At the last moment the man steps in and places his left hand on her waist as she continues to turn, then pulls her off-balance and into his right arm. She, turning once or twice more, falls into his right arm; he stops her and holds her with both arms and hands. This is the finishing pose of the coda. This shows the woman turning on her own, apart from the man, who comes in only when he is needed for the final turn, flip, and fall. In the adagio of the pas de deux from *The Nutcracker* there is a shoulder sit for which the woman runs and does a forward glissade toward the man and jumps for his shoulder

with a half turn. She ensures that she gets a good plié on the second leg of the glissade in order to jump high as she turns immediately and pulls her right leg up so she is *up* in the air traveling backward toward the man in a sitting position. The man adjusts his spacing and times her jump so he catches her on his shoulder. With correct timing and spacing this jump and catch are not problems. The audience sees the woman up in the air, flying back, being caught at the center of the stage, and presented. Once I had a new partner and we could not make it work. Probably the man's timing was a little off and, after missing a couple of times, I probably lacked confidence and cheated by not really jumping. I could only get to his chest, so he never caught me on his shoulder. After Mr. B had rehearsed us several times, he could see that there was no hope of our working out the shoulder sit. He calmly substituted the Bluebird lift from *Sleeping Beauty*, saying, "Don't tell anyone. Surprise them!" His little ploy removed the negative feelings, gave us something positive to look forward to, and, in fact, the performances with that partner went fine.

Mr. B's original choreography for the shoulder sit is certainly exciting, yet so typical of his approach. It happens quickly in the flow of the dance without any extra flourishes and is not used for a prolonged pose, it is done once on each diagonal, and the audience sees the woman facing them while flying backward in the air before she is caught. His ready substitution of another combination when a new partner and I had trouble making the original one work is also very typical. We were not the only ones who found that moment difficult, however. Conrad Ludlow knew an alternative approach in which the woman jumped without the half turn in the air. The man takes her left knee and she stretches her leg, pushing down as she turns. He pushes her up and gets his shoulder under her hips. This method works quite smoothly, and the woman can jump from a greater distance. Conrad had worked out the mechanics of many difficult moves when partnering Nancy Johnson in San Francisco and still credits their work together for much of what he knows. Good communication from the woman will pay off in helping the man understand what is needed.

In *Raymonda Variations* the woman chassés forward on the diagonal and does a double pirouette en dedans. The man steps toward her while she is still turning and takes her by the waist, bringing her forward into a fall with her arms extended front. They do this three times. Again, the man is not next to the woman when she starts the turn, but comes in and partners her just at the moment he is needed. At the end of the ballet the woman runs directly downstage on the center and jumps, diving straight toward the audience. The man, who has been downstage, somewhat off-center, steps in to catch her in a fish as the ballet ends.

In the ending of *Tchaikovsky Pas de Deux* the man and woman start next to each other and do this combination going straight across the floor: tombé, pas de bourrée, glissade, assemblé. But the man travels farther, creating quite a bit of space between them. After the assemblé the woman jumps up and out, continuing in the same direction. The man steps up to catch her as she starts to drop down, taking a couple more steps in her direction of travel to maintain the dynamics of the jump, meanwhile lowering her into fish. The combination is done once to each side.

I could give other examples of the woman jumping into the arms of the man from the Balanchine ballets (*Brahms-Schoenberg*, *Coppélia*, *Walpurgisnacht Ballet*). Mr. B didn't build his ballets on razzle-dazzle tricks, but he was not rigidly opposed to virtuoso display either. The key to the visual impact of these moments for the audience is the timing of both dancers in relation to the music and their timing and spacing in relation to each other, so the woman is seen alone in the air as long as possible. Dancing many kinds of combination with space between partners when possible helps dancers to manage these jumps with aplomb. The other key to success is good pliés that help produce good jumps.

FINGERTIP PARTNERING

Mr. B carried his interest in a restrained use of the hands to the point that in some of his ballets there is fingertip partnering. The dancers go well beyond simply avoiding the kind of encompassing grip that is necessary for circus aerialists fifty feet in the air. He wanted us to learn to partner whenever possible with no more than fingertip contact, and the contact was often very brief. That makes the hand and fingers much more fully visible than they are when engaged in a deep, locking hold. See pages 55–57 and 145–146 on the importance to him of seeing the whole hand and all its features.

In some cases the contact is fleeting, no more than a touch in passing. I have mentioned this in connection with leading the woman. It is an illusion of support even when no support is needed. It communicates connectedness, lightness, fleetness. This is often seen when the woman piqués to arabesque or fouettés into arabesque and then moves on to the next step. For that brief instant when the woman is on pointe and in arabesque, there is no need for strong support, and his fingertip partnering is enough. Balanchine also used this idea in some allegro jumps. The woman does a pas de chat or a tour jeté, and the man touches her for a moment at the waist or on her hand. He doesn't actually do much of anything for her jump, but he does become part of the dance.

WRISTHOLDS, FOREARM SUPPORT, ARMPIT SUPPORT

If the partners do not take hands at all, the hands and fingers of at least one of them (nearly always the woman) will be fully visible, even when substantial support is being provided. Balanchine explored the ways the rest of the arm (as well as the rest of the body) can be used to partner the woman in a variety of poses and movements.

In many ballets the man takes the woman's wrist with the last couple of joints of the thumb and the index and/or middle fingers; this more fully reveals the man's hand and fingers, and the woman's hand and fingers are completely shown. Balanchine generally used this technique whenever it provided sufficient support for the woman in the combination and was consistent with the overall look of the ballet. In the pas de deux from *The Nutcracker*, Mr. B uses the man's forearm as support: The man steps

Jock takes Wendy by her wrists in arabesque.

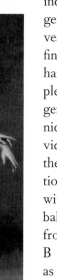

Darci leaning back on Nikolaj; their hands are free.

Jock lightly holds Wendy's wrists with thumb and index finger.

Wendy leaning on Jock's arm; she does not need to clutch his hand for support.

Jock supports Wendy with a delicate fingertip hold.

Delicate fingertip holds

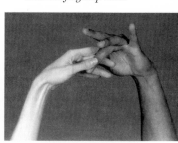

forward into a lunge, extending his arm. The woman's arm is on top and she gently leans on his arm as he supports her in arabesque penchée on pointe. This extends the line of the woman's arms from fingertip to fingertip.

In some ballets the man leads by making contact

Nikolaj offers his arm.   *Darci accepts it.*   *Nikolaj catches Darci's arm.*

*Nikolaj leads a
turn using
forearm contact.*

with the woman's forearm with his forearm; typically, a turning movement follows. With the dancers' forearms crossing, the hands of both are fully visible. Balanchine uses this in some of the more modern ballets, such as the "Rubies" section of *Jewels, Stravinsky Violin Concerto,* and *Symphony in Three Movements,* and in very romantic settings like the second movement of *Brahms-Schoenberg* and the first pas de deux of *Who Cares?* pictured above.

Mr. Balanchine's aim was to use just the support needed. As he made new ballets and as different combinations of dancers came into rehearsals for existing ballets, he worked to see how each couple could manage the choreography with the lightest possible touches and holds from the man. What the audience saw could be a little different for each cast.

In the years since Mr. B died, I have noticed that the trend has continued; in many cases, the men often use less of a hold than they did before. In some ballets, holds and even catches that were done with two hands are now done with one. It shows the woman off even more, as well as adding excitement to the performance, so I am sure he would approve.

Near the end of *Apollo,* the three Muses loop their forearms, forming rings around Apollo's linked arms, and stand up, then shuttle back and around during which the dancers lead one by one and are led one by one by the forearms and crooks of the elbows. It sounds confusing and it's too complicated to describe in further detail. What is noteworthy is that it is not confusing to see, because the dancers maintain as much space as possible. Also in *Apollo,* Terpsichore leads Apollo up from a seated

Jock catches Wendy at the crook of the elbow as it is done in Symphony in Three Movements.

Jock promenades Wendy linked at the elbow as it is done in the "Rubies" section of Jewels.

Nikolaj lifting Darci under the armpits with his forearms. This can be seen in the Divertissement of A Midsummer Night's Dream.

Jock has caught Wendy under the armpits as the man does in the "Rubies" section of Jewels.

Jock centers her.

Jock twists her to the other side.

Jock restores her to her own balance.

pose on the floor by linking elbows. So we see that Mr. B began working with these ideas very early.

Balanchine also had the man catch, lift, and lower at the armpits, which leaves the woman's entire arm fully visible. In the first theme of *The Four Temperaments* the man does a series of bouyant lifts at the woman's armpits. In the "Rubies" section of *Jewels* the woman falls backward and is caught by the armpits quite close to the floor; the dancers call this "the collapse." While in this position she does a series of leg movements similar to passés going back.

FOR THE MAN: LOOKING GOOD AND PARTNERING WELL

There can be a tendency for some men to forget that looking good when partnering is mostly a matter of how the man makes the woman look. So the man will often need to do something a little different from what he would do if he were alone. He maintains his own classical form but makes the subtle modifications necessary to provide the support required. Above all, he recognizes that he cannot just stand and pose his handsome self; he must remain alert and aware of his partner and her needs as he makes himself an active part of the dance. This is true at all times, but it is especially important when the man must step in from a distance to give support or do a lift at the culmination of a combination that the woman starts on her own.

The man should usually look noble and elegant, even when using a slightly turned-in supporting leg, which can give more stability, or while maintaining a slight flex in the knees, which enhances his ability to move quickly or adjust in order to provide the support the woman needs. This was an attribute shared by Jacques d'Amboise, Nicholas Magallanes, and Conrad Ludlow, and, more recently, by Sean Lavery, Peter Martins, Nikolaj Hübbe, and Jock Soto. For some men such a subtle adjustment

Nikolaj, looking elegant, supports Darci while standing with a bent knee in a slightly turned-in line.

may come intuitively; for others it may require specific time, attention, and correction to see what will work. All men will benefit as partners by practicing with a variety of women with a range of sizes and proficiency; they learn what works for them in many steps, at a range of tempos, and with partners of different sizes and capability. Then they can draw on this in performance, particularly when something a little unexpected develops.

One source of ideas for men in how to model and present themselves while partnering is classical sculpture. They can see how harmonious compositions can be achieved. A couple of superficially balletic looks are generally best avoided. It is usually not a good idea to stand behind the woman to partner her in a turned-out first position with straight legs. The man can add very little stability, and it looks odd. Almost any straight-legged, turned-out position, whether standing on one leg or two, can look stagy and artificial and is often a bit precarious.

When a woman is supported in an arabesque penchée on pointe, Balanchine wanted her to go well forward, to the degree that her weight is centered over her pointe. If the man is beautifully posed, pulled up, on a turned-out, straight supporting leg, working leg in tendu back, looking regal,

he is planted. In fact, his pose has no real strength and is quite insecure; he can absorb no force, especially unexpected force when the woman is moving. The woman will sense this, feel limited in her freedom to move, and consequently will move timidly. The man cannot easily adjust to give her the changing support she needs to have her weight where she wants it. Mr. B's priority was generally the flow of movement from arabesque into arabesque penchée, establish the position in penché, and come back up or move on, rather than any pose along the way. When the man has more flexibility in his stance, he will be able to adjust to his partner, in this case putting her forward over her pointe in the penché, when needed. She will look better, and the overall effect of the movement will be enhanced.

In all movements and poses, at all times, the man needs to be able to adjust his stance subtly, smoothly, and usually without it being noticed, to give the woman the support she needs and help her look beautiful. As the woman takes her position, the man remains able to adjust until she is in place. The man does not pose himself for his own good looks; rather, he is attentive to his partner and her needs. Waiting until the woman is in place also ensures that the man can establish his line to comple-

Nikolaj has his weight forward on a turned-in leg so that he can securely bring Darci far forward in arabesque penchée.

Nikolaj lifting Darci from arabesque penchée onto his shoulder and placing her again on the floor in an off-balance lean in arabesque

ment hers. For example, the steadiest, strongest stance is often a small lunging fourth with the front leg parallel or, at least, not fully turned out. Alone, the man might go for a bigger, longer lunging fourth with more plié and with the front leg beautifully turned out, but with a partner he will see what works best for her and for them together.

OFF-BALANCE PARTNERING AND PARTNERED LEANS

Balance on pointe was a look that was very much admired in traditional classical ballet. Being able to hold a balance alone was an important skill that was developed in exercises at the barre and in the center. Being able to find the girl's balance and keep her on it a long time was a critical partnering skill for the man. It's a partnering skill that remains important for boys to master. However, Mr. Balanchine was less interested in extended static balances, with or without a partner, but added a new dimension by asking the man and woman to learn to partner off-balance as well. Many of the movements he asked for, especially when done with one hand on her waist, for example, actually work better when the woman is a little off-balance. The reason is that when she is on-balance she can as eas-

ily fall in any direction. When she is just slightly off-balance the man knows where her weight is at all times and can support her appropriately.

In the previous section I described Mr. B's approach to arabesque penchée. Rather than making a statuesque pose, the man and woman are both more forward, their movement often constant. In the dance for Apollo and Terpsichore from *Apollo*, the man supports the woman as she penchés and then lifts her in the penché, taking her up, back, and onto his shoulder as he straightens. He then comes forward to place her on pointe again, but this time he puts her way forward, off her balance, in ara-

Nikolaj supporting Darci in a very extended lean from the "Rubies" section of Jewels.

Wendy in an off-balance lean back supported by Jock

besque, momentarily showing that pose, and the dance continues. About forty years later Balanchine put the same kind of off-balance arabesque in the second movement of the "Rubies" section of *Jewels*. I find it useful to think of these movements as partnered leans, a term I am borrowing from Conrad Ludlow.

Another example of a fairly traditional supported movement being extended into a partnered lean is attitude back with the woman then taken off balance to lean against the man. In the adagio of *Tchaikovsky Pas de Deux* the woman does a double step-up turn and the man comes in to partner her as she continues to turn, ending in attitude croisée back. The man steps back in a shallow lung-

1. Wendy in an off-balance lean in arabesque, supported by Jock (note his secure, turned-in stance, which gives him great flexibility) 2. Jock has brought Wendy forward and she is slowly starting to fall into his other arm. 3. Jock catches Wendy as she falls forward. 4. Jock switching hands as he lowers Wendy forward 5. Jock continues to lower Wendy. 6. Jock and Wendy in the finishing pose of the pas de deux from the Divertissement of A Midsummer Night's Dream

Jock holds Wendy in an off-balance lean like the one seen in Firebird, *counterbalancing her thrust with his weight.*

Jock holds Wendy in an off-balance lean used in the "Rubies" section of Jewels.

Jock holds Wendy in an off-balance lean used in the "Sanguinic" section of The Four Temperaments.

ing fourth and brings her back to lean on him briefly before putting her back on-balance in arabesque. The same partnered lean (woman's back to man's chest) can often be seen with the woman's working leg extended in effacé front and the man supporting her with his chest and their arms extended à la seconde (see photo, page 399).

In *Brahms-Schoenberg* and in the pas de deux from the Divertissement of *A Midsummer Night's Dream*, (see page 405), the man catches and turns and in various ways manipulates the woman when her body is way off-balance, closer to horizontal than vertical. In *Firebird* the man pulls away to counterbalance the woman, who is in a pull-away développé à la seconde. In the more modern ballets the woman is sometimes in an off-balance lean, with her weight on her heel. The man uses his weight in a similar way all through Balanchine's choreography, meanwhile harmonizing his line with that of the woman (photos on left).

TURNS

Balanchine developed an approach to supported turns that shows he was left unsatisfied by many aspects of the traditional technique. Traditionally in en dehors pirouettes from fourth, the woman began in demi-plié, not exactly in fourth and not exactly in second, with her front arm rounded in first. From this undefined, rather unattractive squat, a turn always followed. Since she usually held this pose for a couple of seconds to take full advantage of the "windup," she gave away any element of surprise. The man, meanwhile more or less planted right behind her, had rather active hands. He started her turning with a "push-pull" motion at her waist, often "paddled" her once or twice to keep her going, and could continue to paddle her around if the choreography called for many turns, and then stopped the turn in an unsubtle, obvious way with both hands when it was time to end or go on with another movement. One could almost forget that

Wendy en face in an extended fourth; Jock, leaving space, stands behind her.

Jock keeps Wendy's balance in his left hand during the turns.

Jock uses his right hand to keep Wendy's balance in his left; his right hand can also add a little impetus to the turn. He applies pressure with the palm of his right hand to stop her.

and *very* briefly before she starts the turn so she knows he is there. If she is turning en dehors to her right, she brings her front arm straight in so there is no "windup" look and she avoids the possibility of hitting him. This is, of course, how she should turn when turning alone (see page 269). The man steps in to support her with one or both hands; his left hand is the support and his right guides her and also gives her more force if and when necessary. He partners her minimally.

the woman should be able to do at least two turns by herself.

Mr. Balanchine believed in contrast that it should generally look as if the woman is turning with her own force, even when she turns a long time, and that she is on her own balance, almost completely by herself, even though the man is partnering. The woman begins in a beautiful large extended fourth; one arm is extended front, and the other is slightly behind second in an extended line. From this fourth, a dancer can do any kind of movement, so a turn, if a turn is the next step, can be a surprise. The man is usually not close behind her, but even if he is, his hands do not necessarily touch her. Sometimes he is a step or more away from her as she starts the turn. Sometimes it is reassuring for the man to touch the woman lightly

Jock turns Wendy in the "strumming" turns used in The Four Temperaments.

He doesn't paddle her around to turn her and he does not squeeze in on her waist with both hands to stop her. Instead, he stops her by pushing with the palms against her back and slightly up on the right side of it, braking her mostly with the palm of his right hand. Peter Martins often talks about how to use different parts of the hand at different times in partnering. In this case, for example, the thumb can help stop the turn.

Sometimes Mr. B uses a traditional turn, but gives it his own look by what follows. In *Apollo*, Terpsichore does a standard finger turn. But after the double pirouette, Apollo lifts her up and makes a lunging fourth, putting her onto his thigh in a kind of attitude-front-attitude-back pose. Pivoting to one side and then the other, he presents her from various angles as she does a port de bras.

In *The Four Temperaments* Mr. B briefly makes a passive object of the woman and has her turned without her active participation. In the third theme she is on pointe in plié on one foot, with her working pointe resting on her bent knee, and one arm in first. The man holds the other arm over her head by the wrist for balance and turns her by "strumming" her, gently pulling (as if strumming a guitar) her forearm once for each rotation (see page 407).

LIFTS

The underlying factors for success in lifts are the same for Balanchine dancers, but because many of the lifts in his ballets are more difficult than the traditional ones, they bear repeating. Coordination of the timing and movement are essential elements; it is very important that dancers practice together with a variety of partners to develop proficiency. Men need to develop more strength in the arms and upper torso, abdominals and lower back, and thighs, so calisthenics and weight training under the supervision of a teacher who understands the needs of dancers is very beneficial. In his adagio classes at SAB, Jock Soto often begins and ends with push-ups and sit-ups for the boys. The plié is

Jock takes Wendy on his right.

once again critical. For example, in grand jeté lifts with the arms fully stretched overhead, the man needs to plié to get under the woman's weight on the take-off. Much of the power to lift comes from applying the strength of the man's thighs, as well as that of his torso and arms.

Women need strong upper bodies so they can hold themselves together to sustain supported positions on pointe as well as in the air; doing appropriate calisthenics, such as the various sit-ups, is very beneficial. Women need to learn how to hold themselves using abdominal and back muscles, depending on the look and the movement desired.

There are three basic timing patterns that men need to learn to use in different kinds of lifts. The patterns are quickly up and quickly down, slowly up and slowly down, quickly up and slowly down. The pattern that requires cultivation of a special skill is quickly down. The man needs to convey the sense that the woman is being brought down by him, rather than simply responding to gravity. He must learn to sense the moment of suspension at the top of the lift, before she begins to fall, and to take her down quickly to the floor. This skill is needed for allegro partnering and is roughly analo-

Jock moving Wendy to his left

Jock traveling with Wendy as she extends her left leg

gous to jumping down to the floor (see page 296). Remember, "The most important thing is to be on time."

Another special timing skill is waiting until the last possible moment to place the hands on the woman. When a woman was to be lifted at the waist, in a carry lift, Balanchine did not want the man to hover with both hands on the woman before he was needed. Instead, he wanted as usual for the man to give her space and often to place the first hand on her back on the glissade or step and the second hand just before or just as she starts to push off. The first hand to be placed is the higher one and is placed on the back or trailing side; the second hand is the lower and goes near the hip on the leading side. Coordinating the hands and the

Jock and Wendy in a full-arm grand jeté lift

Jock and Wendy in the midchest lift skimming the floor used in the "Sanguinic" section of The Four Temperaments *and in* Symphony in C.

rest of the movement in traveling combinations requires practice.

In traveling lifts, the man often works to enhance the illusion that the woman has traveled farther than she has. For example, in a grand jeté or pas de chat carry lift, the man needs to learn to pick her up from one side of his body, carry her across the front of his body, and set her down on his other side. However many steps he takes, this adds several more feet to the length of the lift and adds to the impression of dynamism and energy. The energy is no illusion; this technique takes more strength and skill (see photos, pages 408–409).

In the Balanchine ballets, some of the lifts have special features that make it necessary for the man to have more strength or more skill (or a combination of the two) than is required in lifts that are more traditional. In some cases the man slowly lifts the woman (almost pushes her up) to midchest level and carries her, giving the gesture a skimming quality (e.g., "Sanguinic" in *The Four Temperaments*) rather than the look of a high arc, like the seven grand jeté carry lifts in *Concerto Barocco*. In some higher lifts the woman changes the line of her legs in the air (*Serenade*). In *Tchaikovsky Pas de Deux* the man lifts the woman in one line, lowers to about midchest as she changes her legs and torso to a different line, then lifts her again as he walks on the other diagonal. In these high lifts, as the woman begins to change her line, the man often adjusts his

hand position on the woman's back while he is holding her up. In the second movement of *Symphony in C* the man must smoothly reverse the woman's direction of travel and carry her in a midchest lift to the other side of the stage. Conrad Ludlow, who partnered just about all the principal dancers of his time, tells about making this carry look right with different women. The music for this passage has a certain gravity, and Mr. B wanted the carry lift to have the same sense of weight, no matter who was dancing. In this case the woman was not to suggest a weightless sylph. When Balanchine cast a very light dancer, he had her start the jump by herself and then asked Conrad to take her in the air, but when he cast a heavier dancer, Balanchine had Conrad and the dancer coordinate the lift from the floor in the usual way. Catching and lifting a light woman in the air and lifting a heavier woman from plié each require a comparable effort from the man, so in both cases the lift gave the impression of weight that Balanchine wanted.

All lifts need to be timed and coordinated by the man and woman working together. When the woman is lifted, she has to help the man by holding her body so she is easy to lift. For almost all kinds of lifts, she needs to learn to arch the upper back so he is pushing up from below, rather than trying to lift from her sides. In grand jeté lifts it is a little

Jock's hands at the start of a lift: The trailing (left) hand is higher, under the "shelf"; the leading (right) hand is lower, just above the hip.

Close-up of Jock's hands as he places Wendy's weight forward in arabesque

down with the hand near her hip to ensure that her weight comes down over the supporting leg and foot. It is both arms and hands, working together, that ensure a successful descent. It is as if he is lifting her up and over, in the direction of travel.

FISH

The combined pose for a man and a woman called a "fish" is often seen in nineteenth-century ballets and, as traditionally performed, is usually fairly static. If there was more than minimal movement it tended to come from the man lifting or throwing the woman straight up, a little higher than neces-

Nikolaj holding Darci in a fish, with his weight on his front foot

Nikolaj holding Darci in a fish, with his weight on his back foot

more complicated. She needs to learn to arch her upper back even more, giving the man a little "shelf" under her shoulder blade on the side of her back leg. The man's trailing arm and hand do most of the lifting. His other hand steadies her and helps to lift from just above her hipbone on the side of the leading leg. His hands are thus not on the same level; the one in back, pushing up under the "shelf," is a little higher.

When the woman is placed again on the floor, the man uses his plié to help cushion her landing. There is an adjustment of the force and pressure of the arms and hands that is also required at this point. For example, on the landing from a grand jeté lift the man pushes forward and a little up and over on the woman's back, applying additional pressure with the thumb to bring her weight over the ball of her foot. As he does this, he also leads forward and

sary, and taking her straight down, or down and back, into a fish. Often the man took a step back as he brought the woman into the pose.

Mr. B used the basic idea of the "fish" in a number of ballets but made it much more dynamic. At least the woman, and sometimes the man as well, are in motion. The woman sometimes jumps to the man from some distance away and is caught. Sometimes the woman is thrown by the man as she jumps up and out, increasing the height and length of her jump, and then is caught. After catching the woman, the man often takes a step or so forward in her direction of flight, adding to the impression of energy and daring as he puts her into a "fish" and presents her.

The details vary, but this basic idea is used in the pas de deux from *Coppélia, The Nutcracker, Raymonda Variations,* and in *Tchaikovsky Pas de Deux.*

BALANCHINE'S
TCHAIKOVSKY PAS DE DEUX
OBSERVED

I have seen *Tchaikovsky Pas de Deux* since the premiere in 1962, when it was danced by Violette Verdy and Conrad Ludlow, and I have also seen various later casts that were rehearsed by Balanchine himself. At Mr. B's request I learned and performed it with Conrad Ludlow for lecture demonstrations. I have staged it several times for SAB students and for several principal dancers of the American Ballet Theater. So I know it in its evolution while under his care and I have continued to work with it since he died. Even when rehearsed by him, it was not always performed with exactly the same steps, but there is a choreographic base that must be preserved if it is to be representative of his aesthetic. I will use it as a source for examples of how his ideas on partnering are visible in a pas de deux. It is widely performed and it is on tape, so there is a good chance you have seen or can see it.

The music, like most of the music Balanchine choreographed, was not part of the standard ballet music when his pas de deux was first performed. It had been composed for the Black Swan and Prince Siegfried in *Swan Lake,* but it had been "lost" for many years, then turned up in the archives of the Bolshoi in 1953. In the 1950s and 1960s there was great public excitement over the many spectacular pas de deux performed by visiting Soviet companies, some of them in complete ballets and some of them only on "highlights" programs. Balanchine's response to the music of the most important Russian composer showed how wide the divergence had become between those of his generation who had stayed in Russia and himself.

The woman flies on from the upstage left wing in a sauté, runs straight across the stage past the center, and pauses; she looks out and around, a little uncertain; perhaps she expected that someone would be there. The man soars on in a jump from the first downstage right wing with his back to the audience, bounds across past center stage, stops, and turns to look toward the woman. They see each other, take a few quick steps toward each other, and veer away, just missing touching hands. They stop at a short distance from each other and pause, facing opposite corners but still looking toward one another.

Observations: The music is quiet throughout, there is no buildup, yet they each burst onto the stage with great energy, *making* the audience look at them; the man enters and looks upstage, toward the woman, rather than presenting himself to the audience.

The man turns to the woman to offer his hand, and she accepts. With a fingertip touch, they walk diagonally upstage, the woman backing, the man walking her upstage on the diagonal at arm's length, with his back to the audience. He steps away and she does a reverence using crossed-arms technique as he bows very slightly to her, turning to gesture to indicate the open space, inviting her to dance with him, and then turns and steps forward to offer his hand. Leading her forward, again with just fingertip contact, he leaves space around her as she does a windswept bourrée. As she starts a step-up finger turn, he steps forward enough to bring her hand over her head; finishing the turn, she sustains herself, lifting her knee up in passé as she gives life to the free arm, wrist, and hand, then she kneels in croisé. Still holding her hand, showing their connectedness, the man echoes the line of her kneel by making an attitude in croisé back in plié. She steps forward and then piqués out, making sous-sus, almost pulling away from the man. He brings her back, leading her with fingertip contact, as she bourrées in the same windswept manner and circles forward in front of him. She repeats the turn and kneel as the man again makes the attitude pose.

Observations: The man uses the minimum possible contact with his hands and maintains maximum possible space, stepping in only as necessary; the man adjusts his stance, bending, reaching, and turning his torso, doing ports de bras that complement her line and movement, remaining part of the dance as he leads the woman; they flow, they dance, quickly in and out of the pose so it does not look static, planted.

She does a glissade, the man coming in at the last moment to lift her in écarté, traveling forward on one diagonal. He lowers her to chest height as she starts to change the line of her legs and he changes directions, carrying her forward on the other diagonal as she battements her right leg front and he lifts her again. He sets her down with her weight forward over the ball of her foot in third arabesque. As she steps back and bourrées, he backs away directly upstage, opening his arms to the side. She bourrées back and does two different kinds of turns that he partners, the first with very little contact and the second with more contact to give the necessary force. He stops her turns and supports her in attitude croisée front, which is followed by a quick loop-dee-loop port de bras as she moves into arabesque penchée.

Observations: The man takes the woman already in motion and lifts her and they work together to change her line during the lift; the music remains quiet, and the gentle swooping of the lifts matches its subdued but lyrical feeling; as soon as possible, he reestablishes the space between them before stepping in to support her again when needed; the penché happens very quickly, in keeping with a musical accent, and after showing the position, they go on.

The man steps away upstage as the woman does développé in écarté with her left leg, failli and piqués toward the downstage corner. She steps diagonally toward him and does two and a half turns, with the man stepping forward at the last instant to support her on the turns, then taking her back off-balance and placing her to lean back on his chest as he steps back in fourth. She is on her left pointe, right leg raised in attitude back croisé. He brings her up on-balance and turns her to face him in arabesque in one direction and then to pirouette in passé back in the other.

Observation: The man again reestablishes space, coming in at the last moment to gently support her on her turns and to take her in an off-balance lean; he restores her balance and steps away to give her as much space as possible as he turns her one way and then the other, ending in développé écarté front.

The woman takes two steps away, the man lifting her, carrying her diagonally forward in a pas de chat with développé lift and placing her to the floor; then he moves quickly away diagonally upstage as she does piqué arabesque toward the corner. She turns and runs toward the man. He takes her at the waist and presents her in a high tour jeté lift. Immediately bringing her to the floor to keep her on the music, he steps away as she chaînés straight downstage. He comes in at the last moment to support her in a step up turn. After doing a soutenu turn, she brushes his hands off her waist and runs diagonally forward to do sissonne to arabesque on pointe. He follows to support her an instant after she has arrived in that arabesque.

Observations: The woman is again taken off the floor at the last moment and carried briefly at midchest; the big tour jeté lift is also a movement, not a held position, and it is not fitted to

1. Wendy in arabesque 2. Wendy goes into penché. 3. Jock tips Wendy forward. 4. Wendy's bottom leg stays straight as it moves closer to the extended leg. 5. Jock lowers Wendy into fish. 6. Jock and Wendy in the final pose

a musical climax; instead, it just flows to the music.

The dance continues in much the same way, but I want to note that Balanchine's ending to the adagio is interesting for what it shows of his approach. The music has again become quiet and lyrical after louder passages he used for big carry lifts and sup-

ported turns. The man steps in to gently support the woman in some bourrée turns in which he "strums" her around in a gesture suggesting the lightest possible touch and then in a promenade and a swooping grand rond de jambe that he controls with fingertip partnering. Finally they are together, and he leads a series of ports de bras switching hands, then lifts her with her hands in his in a variant of the "fish" that leaves the line of her body and legs more fully presented to the public than in the traditional version.

The music for the variations certainly offers opportunities for showing one or more tricks comparable to the famous fouetté turns in the traditional Black Swan. Balanchine passes on all that and gives the dancers challenging and varied choreography at a brisk and steady tempo.

The pas de deux ends with the man dancing behind the woman as they travel across the stage. He begins a foot or so behind her and finishes a couple of steps ahead of her, opening a space of several feet, across which she jumps up and out. Her body arcs up like a dart and dives forward and down into the pool. He catches her in his arms and continues traveling forward as he takes her into a fish. As he lifts her upright to set her into arabesque, he steps behind her and a bit to the side. They then repeat the combination traveling in the opposite direction. He starts outside and behind her, passes her, and finishes on the other side of her, each time maximizing the movement before the jump and dive. They end with a carry lift offstage with the woman in attitude and with the man's arms fully extended. Again, this is to a brisk tempo and happens so quickly it comes as a surprise rather than being announced.

Afterword

I wrote this book to pass along what I learned from George Balanchine. I wanted to help teachers of advanced dancers, and the dancers themselves, to learn and understand the way he worked and the result he worked for. With that knowledge, I hope teachers and advanced dancers are more able to work to achieve those results. I believe this will be possible even for those who never knew Mr. B and never knew any of us who danced and taught for him.

In writing this book, I am also showing that I learned something from Balanchine quite apart from ballet technique. He and his devoted patron, Lincoln Kirstein, set an example of working for an ideal that goes beyond a person's immediate self-interest. Their shared commitment was to do what was needed for the work, work that served the art of classical ballet. As a teacher, Mr. Balanchine developed dancers and became their "dance supplier." He dismissed the word "choreographer" as too grand for him as a maker of dances. And then he shared his company with other "suppliers," most importantly Jerome Robbins. And he shared the dances with other companies, offering them quite readily, and often free of charge.

Balanchine showed us a way of life. Without ever saying a word about it, he gave us a philosophy. We could choose to live it or not. It was our choice. I learned everything I could from him, so

that I could dance and teach in keeping with his aesthetic. The way he taught gives me the opportunity as a teacher to continue to serve classical ballet by passing on what I have learned to future generations. It is a privilege. And an obligation!

Mr. B observed that people often want to jump ahead to do the big things. In fact, it is necessary to start modestly. Even to do an "easy" Balanchine ballet in keeping with his aesthetic, it is necessary to start by cultivating a refined musicality and learning to work consistently with maximum energy, effort, and awareness. One does that as one works in class with the little things—the carriage of the torso and of the head, how to move the arms, how to hold the hands, how to take the foot off the floor, how to place the foot to the floor, and so on. "You must be patient," he would say to me, when I wanted to see a result right away. "A dancer must really study, eight years of [intermediate and advanced] study every day for one and a half hours. Then I might say she is a dancer. After that I have to help her develop a beautiful style and more and more velocity. That takes many years, until she retires."

Simply learning and performing the choreography of Mr. B's ballets will not generally teach what he thought was most important: to know how to do, to know what is right, to know the right approach. And also to know what is not usually right, as well as when and how and why a "rule" might be broken. At the end of his life, he was saying that dancers will remember the steps of the ballets, but forget the idea. The ideas I can convey are those he talked about in detail and consistently with his dancers. They are his ideas about all the little things and his overall approach to the dance phrase (musicality, energy, movement). He did not talk to us about stories or big ideas in his ballets. Nor do I.

Energy. Movement. Even in a pose. He said, "No matter how long you stay, you must feel like you are moving a little. This is a little like the octopus." Not that he had many places in which the dancer imitated an octopus, undulating her arms and waving her fingers like tentacles. He just wanted her to feel her arms to be that alive and her hands to be that sensitive to the air and everything around them. Not looking heavy and lifeless and dead like the marble of a statue.

Vitality. Music. Movement. Even from the corps. He said, "Even the ensemble I don't want identical. Better a little personality and then you have a corps that is alive. When you beat them into just one shape, it becomes dead." Not that he cared nothing for a certain unity of movement. He just wanted each dancer to be as alive and responsive to the music as she could be in performing the steps and gestures of the choreography. He did not want a corps that looked like perfect little porcelain figurines, precious, pretty and too perfect for life.

Mr. B asked me to start to teach when I was very young and didn't know much. I think he knew that I could see, really see, all the little things, but without losing sight of the entire movement, its thrust, its music and its precise timing and phrasing, the general approach, the underlying ideas. He saw that I could communicate and get a positive result and he saw that correct execution mattered as much to me as it did to him. He could therefore count on me to teach "how to do."

In each exercise, some will do better than others. No one will be best all the way through the class. That is true at every level and no one can change it. But the teacher of advanced dancers can ensure that every dancer learns what is right and where

to put the effort. That is what Mr. B taught. His classes were a challenge for everyone who came, but in different ways. Many exercises emphasized pointework, so the men could say they were better suited to women. Many combinations included slow jumps and men's steps, so some women might feel that this part of the class was for the men. I had relatively short, tight muscles, and the emphasis on many fast battements tendus and battements tendus jetés might have tightened me up even more. Instead, I stretched a lot on my own, swam, and did Pilates exercises. Very limber, long-muscled women might wish for more lush adagios instead of yet another combination emphasizing quick tendus or quick jumps and beats. And so on. But we each learned the right approach for dancing in his aesthetic, because he insisted on, and got, maximum effort—and a result—all the while enjoying in each dancer her individual qualities, including her little quirks. That is what I have tried to convey to teachers and dancers about his technique.

Balanchine used to say that a dancer is the one person who can have her cake and eat it too. As a dancer, I was certainly having my cake and eating it too. I enjoyed the daily work of perfecting the movements of classical ballet. I worked in a wonderful musical environment and the music was very much a part of what I did. Balanchine said that the composers create the dancers' time and that the dancers swim in the music. There is no better environment or time for work. And then I got to go onstage and use classical ballet in performance and I enjoyed that even more. And I was paid for it, too! I thought that to be a dancer was to be the best kind of performer, because a dancer is many performers combined in one. A dancer develops physical ability surpassing what is required of most athletes. A dancer must show herself as effectively as any model, but does it moving beautifully to music.

Mr. B said, "I am a teacher. That is my contribution." No one doubts it. He taught me to dance and to teach. I hope that in some small way I too can say that teaching is my contribution.

Technical Cross-reference

A Note About the Author

SUKI SCHORER danced with George Balanchine's New York City Ballet from 1959 to 1972, achieving the rank of principal dancer. Since then, she has taught full-time at the School of American Ballet, which is NYCB's affiliated school. She lives in New York.

A Note on the Type

This book was set in Fournier, a typeface named for Pierre Simon Fournier *fils* (1712–1768), a celebrated French type designer. Coming from a family of type-founders, Fournier was an extraordinarily prolific designer of typefaces and of typographic ornaments. He was also the author of the important *Manuel typographique* (1764–1766), in which he attempted to work out a system standardizing type measurement in points, a system that is still in use internationally. Fournier's type is considered transitional in that it drew its inspiration from the old style, yet was ingeniously innovational, providing for an elegant, legible appearance. In 1925 his type was revived by the Monotype Corporation of London.

Composed by North Market Street Graphics, Lancaster, Pennsylvania
Printed and bound by Quebecor Printing, Leominster, Massachusetts
Photographs by Carol Rosegg
Designed by Anthea Lingeman